CRISIS/MEDIA

sarai READER

The Sarai Programme
CSDS, Delhi

February 2004

[csds]

SARAI READER 04: CRISIS/MEDIA
Produced and Designed at the Sarai Media Lab, Delhi

Editorial Collective: Monica Narula, Shuddhabrata Sengupta, Ravi Sundaram,
Ravi S Vasudevan, Awadhanedra Sharan & Jeebesh Bagchi (Sarai)
+ Geert Lovink
Editorial Assistance: Annie Gell
Translations: Shveta Sarda, Debjani Sengupta

Design: Renu Iyer
Design Coordinator: Monica Narula
Cover Photos: Monica Narula
Cover Design: Renu Iyer

Published by
The Sarai Programme
Centre for the Study of Developing Societies
29, Rajpur Road, Delhi 110054, India
Tel: (+91) 11 2396 0040 Fax: (+91) 11 2392 8391
E-mail: dak@sarai.net, www.sarai.net

Delhi 2004

Any part of this book may be reproduced in any form without the prior written permission of the
publishers for educational and non-commercial use. The contributors and publishers, however,
would like to be informed.

The contents of this book are available for free online browsing and download at
http://www.sarai.net/reader/reader_04.html

ISBN 81-901429-4-1

Published by the Director, Centre for the Study of Developing Societies
and printed at Excellent Printing House, Okhla Industrial Area, New Delhi
Price: Rs. 295, US$ 15, Euro 15

CONTENTS

INTRODUCTION

"The darkest, hottest place in hell waits for that repulsive angel choir
Which, at the hour when crisis strikes, sings equivocal, neutral songs".
Dante, *Inferno, Canto III.*

From the very beginning of this century, we have hurtled on as if from crisis to crisis. The images of entire cities being bombed into submission from the air, of planes crashing into skyscrapers, of neighbourhoods aflame, of occupying armies and fleeing civilians, of suicide bombers, ethnic cleansing, and riot police assaulting unarmed demonstrators have branded themselves onto our consciousness with mounting frequency. These are the substance of the meditations of all our mornings, as we pick up the day's newspaper, switch on the radio in the kitchen, or the television in the living room, or log on to the internet. These are times for sober reflection, and that, precisely, is what we often find missing, as newscasters, editors and experts – contemporary versions of Dante's "repulsive angel choir" – sing their 'equivocal, neutral songs', every day, every night.

Such times demand an urgent renewal, rather than the abdication, of critical sensibilities in media practice. Ranjit Hoskote, in the essay that opens the arguments of this collection, reminds us that the two words – 'crisis' and 'critique' – "derive from the same Greek root: *krinein*, to decide. But where 'crisis' denotes the forcing of an individual decision by structural compulsions, 'critique' connotes an autonomy of decision, a power of reflexive agency on the part of an individual".

A commitment to critique is based on the assumption that, when it comes to the things that are most important to us, dissent, difference and disagreement are of far greater value than bland consensus. But passionate commitments need not detract from sobriety. Muzamil Jaleel writes, in concluding his reflection on being a reporter in Kashmir, "We have to have a sense of the boiling point and keep our writing always a few degrees below that threshold ... Flow like a river and follow events as they happen".

Jaleel is not arguing for reticence, but for an act of bearing witness that remains partisan to what it sees, while ensuring that its narratological credibility can survive to bear the burden of the story that it seeks to tell. This is the difference between 'safe' and 'engaged, but responsible' practice. The crucial difference between self-censorship and self-reflexivity.

This accumulation of situations of crisis and their rapid, almost real-time, dissemination in the media, has no doubt precipitated new opportunities for communicative action and global reflection, just as they have signalled an onset of a severe crisis within the media – a crisis of over-stimulation and under-statement, of exaggeration and exhaustion, of censorship and spin-doctoring, of fear and favour. The overproduction of crises perhaps leads to a deeper malaise, a persistent and growing lack of attention to what we, in this book, call the 'Deep Instabilities' of our times.

Arundhati Roy, while talking of the need to be cautious about the media's notion of crisis, the media's obsession with war, television-friendly images of disaster and conflict, and a 'critical mass' of the dead and the dying, says, "For most people in the world, peace is war – a daily battle against hunger, thirst and the violation of their dignity. Wars are often the end result of a flawed peace, a putative peace. And it is the flaws, the systemic flaws in what is normally considered to be 'peace', that we ought to be writing about. We have to, at least some of us have to, become peace correspondents instead of war correspondents. We have to lose our terror of the mundane". In variation, we could add: crisis is a state of normality, with stability and prosperity the exception.

Having lost our terror of the mundane, is it possible for us to begin to debate and problematize the whole notion of 'representation' itself? The routines of the 'expert', the 'victim', the 'star campaigner', the 'primary witness' and even the 'special correspondent' are often deemed necessary to give reality the burnish of crisis in order to make it newsworthy. Can we wrest the desire for attention to reality back from the grip of the need for constant crisis?

This is true not only in situations where, peace, clearly is war, but also in situations that are perhaps best described as 'lapsed crises'. Lapsed in the sense that they have gone under the radar, and hence, for all intents and purposes, do not exist. This is what Meena Nanji has to say about Afghanistan today. "Afghanistan doesn't really make the headlines anymore, unless one of the hundreds of international aid workers or American troops is attacked, or more than thirty Taliban are killed ... We hear nothing of the struggles of everyday life, the small, mundane things that are made almost insurmountable by the destruction wrought during the last twenty five years of war. We hear little about how people manage without running water, without electricity, little of the 'reconstruction effort' its successes and failures. We hear little of the Afghan women who were so recently asked to galvanize the US call to war".

These are open questions, with no satisfactory and coherent answers, but *Sarai Reader 04* would like to take them on, so as to map new territories of thought about media practice. Running through this book is a concern to develop agile, responsive ways of doing media that are not captive to 'events and issues' but that actually expand communicative potential in society. Ricardo Rosas, in his essay on Tactical Media in Brazil, spells out an exemplary vision of what these practices might be. While discussing the Autolabs project in São Paulo, he says that tactical media means "...opening up new spaces for cultural, artistic and media interaction, creating forms of access to knowledge resources for individuals or groups excluded from the new paradigm raised by the technological revolution ... developing visual, sonic and textual sensitivities, and making social actions of collective utility possible".

We see this book as hoping to embody what Rosas would consider to be an ensemble of tactical media practices. Both the text and the design of the book are thought of in terms of a series of arguments with the visuality of the ordered, the spectacular and the dull. Our visual credo in this book was to find a viewer's antidote to what Tarun Bhartiya has called the "belching of excited news anchors".

The book itself has its genesis in the Crisis/Media Workshop that was jointly organized in Delhi by Sarai-CSDS, Delhi and the Waag Society, Amsterdam, a year ago in March 2003. The concept, outlined in the workshop publication by Shuddhabrata Sengupta and Geert Lovink, was a response to 9/11, the invasion of Afghanistan, the violence in Gujarat and the Kargil war. Over 3 days, participants from many different parts of South Asia and the world gathered to debate and dissect the relationship between the notion of crisis and the media, exactly one year after Gujarat had gone up in flames, and just as the 'Coalition of the Willing' was gearing up to bomb Baghdad. The process of editing the Reader only confirmed what we felt that the workshop had already set in motion – an unruly but very necessary set of forays into the realm of 'the unspeakable'. Our contributors were opening out new spaces for dialogue, not only by inaugurating discussion on things that had hitherto been left unsaid, but also in the way that different elements were speaking to each other. Our task was to enable this conversation to interrupt itself, to make all sorts of unruly connections, to foster linkages between disparate truths and conflicting claims to attention.

As the emails bearing texts from all over the world thickened our inboxes in response to the call for proposals, it became apparent that apart from the magisterial register that had raised the bar of discourse at the Crisis/Media Workshop, we were going to have to listen to a new set of unruly voices. Often, these voices belonged to unauthorized inter-locutors. They came from within the vortices of crises. They were voices of witnesses; voices that were young, voices that were trying themselves out and that were often excluded from communicative entitlement. In times of crisis, the temptation to go for the ordered, predictable voice of authority is often paramount. In this collection, we have tried to resist this temptation, and let the crisis in the contents be.

This book brings together media professionals, activists, critics, writers and scholars in order to create a dialogue between different kinds of approaches to the question of com-munication itself. It examines how popular culture and cinema 'memorialize' crisis situa-tions, or create the conditions for selective amnesia. Most of all, this book recognizes that there is a crisis in and of the media, and this cannot be addressed simply by calling for less reportage and more analysis. Instead, we argue for analysis in the reportage, and a dis-ruption of the apparatus of centralized and centralizing information networks. We need to break down the same images that everyone sees, worldwide, in many different ways. And we need to find new ways to tell stories, and to distribute the untold story. The problem of critical media analysis of global crises so far has been to deconstruct the ownership of media and its ideological agenda, attempting to uncover a 'truth' of state and corporate control behind the news. The book, by and large, takes this for granted, and hopes that its readers will ask how we may go beyond it, and how alternative media too can stop looking and feeling like cheaply produced versions of mainstream media production.

As this book goes into print we find ourselves having to reflect on a situation here in India where communication, the very fact of saying things, is increasingly becoming fraught with difficult consequences. A festival of documentary filmmaking suddenly finds itself paralyzed by the spectre of censorship, books are banned, journalists and writers are imprisoned, overheard phone conversations lead to death sentences being pronounced, libraries get vandalized and paintings destroyed. Ideas and information, words and images, are beginning to be treated as if they were the vectors of an epidemic, which could unleash uncontrollable disasters on a vulnerable social body. While it flatters writers, media practitioners, journalists, filmmakers, artists and anyone who deals with ideas to be treated with such importance, only a paranoid society demands such fealty to the writ of the censor. Perhaps it is time for us to ask whether we are beginning to live in such societies, and whether we are willing to continue doing so. The exiled Bangladeshi writer, Taslima Nasrin, whose essay "Homeless Everywhere", written in response to the ban on her recent volume of memoirs, *Dwikhandito* (*Broken*) in West Bengal, says, "Riots don't break out because of what I write. Whatever happens, happens in my life. I am the one who is punished for what I write. Fires rage in my home. I am the one who has to suffer exile. I am the one who is homeless everywhere".

The moderate, safe, domesticated voice can never be the only register in which an illiberal, immoderate, chaotic, insane world can stumble towards its provisional truths. Those who speak with passion often do so with the sober awareness of its consequences on their lives. By seeking to suppress these voices, the mandarins of the moment only seek to take detours away from the fact that utterance is the ground where every crisis seeks its first consciousness of itself. It is perhaps with this in mind that Lawrence Liang says, "Very often the assumption of desirable forms of speech presumes a pre-tailored relationship between media and the properly constituted public sphere (much like the imagination of the seamless web), and a plea to the state to rule out undesirable forms of speech abandons the site of politics and converts it into a site of regulation that will merely heighten the crisis rather than resolve it".

But the contemporary moment is also marked by a festive excess of what the mandarins consider 'undesirable forms of speech'. And so, we have filmmakers deciding to challenge the sterility of an official festival with their own alternative festival. We have writers putting their banned writings on the web, for anyone to download. We have independent media coalitions come together when necessary and disappear into anonymity when their visibility becomes a handicap. The world has changed, but ways of talking about it have changed as well.

This book welcomes and celebrates this change. It carries with it the unreasonable expectation that the myriad realities that seek to make themselves known in a world that usually silences them, will find voice, and that we will all find the wherewithal, and the patience, to listen very carefully.

Editorial Collective
Delhi/Amsterdam
February 2004

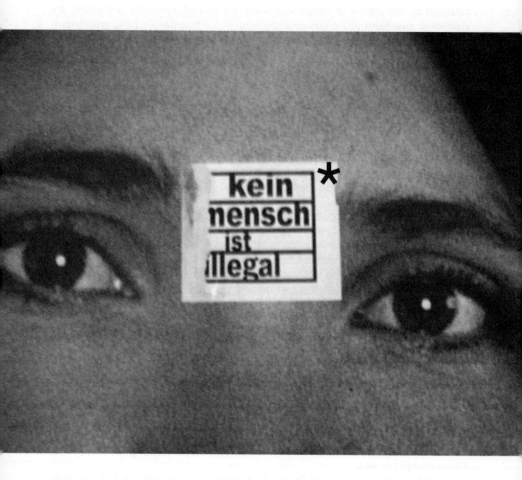

* No One Is Illegal

Approaching
CRISIS

Bearing Inconvenient Witness
Notes in Pro/Confessional Mode

RANJIT HOSKOTE

The Changing Textures of Crisis

I recall the excitement that I felt as a child when faraway but dramatic events unfolded in the course of a day: the quiet morning, with no presentiment of momentous happenings; the first buzz of rumour at school; then long-distance telephone calls from relatives (a most unusual occurrence twenty or twenty-five years ago, and imbued with the rarest significance, and if the calls came from relatives in the armed forces, you knew the crisis was of national importance). Then Father coming home from the office, with the confirmation printed in the evening papers. Finally, State-run television reluctantly announcing the death of the President or the assassination of the Prime Minister, that a cyclone had swept through coastal Andhra Pradesh, or that a border skirmish had intensified into a war. *The slowness of media technologies meant that there was time to assimilate the shock, to savour the drama in its nuances of fear, trepidation and anxiety, to absorb the textures of the crisis and prepare for its denouement.*

Today, all is immediacy: the denouement is staggered across a fluctuating pattern of sub-shocks. There are no buffers, no modes of gradual effect by which the faraway becomes proximate and immediate, no degrees of internalization. By a butterfly effect, reportage intensifies the import of events and reproduces their repercussions at an accelerated rate of amplification. The twin towers are hit and collapse before our eyes, over and over again, as we sit at the breakfast table. We follow troops into war in the deserts of West Asia as we eat lunch. Teatime finds us accompanying the ever-watchful eye of the TV camera into the backwoods of former Soviet Central Asia. By dinner, we are prepared for a vicarious night-vision penetration of hostile strongholds in Afghanistan. Satellite television, running twenty-four hours all week, has robbed horizons and time differentials of meaning. And yet this ubiquity of sight conceals motive, context, backdrop and detail – the myth of instantaneity and on-site coverage conceals the fact that these self-repeating, self-sustaining phenomena do not add up to produce either information or insight.

The old-style ethical question that confronted news coverage had to do with fundamentals: What is the *raison d'etre* of the news operation? That is: Was Hearst justified, if we are to believe the apocryphal tale, in bankrolling a war so as to justify his correspondent's trip to an uncharacteristically quiescent Central America? The new ethical questions for news coverage address the same question, somewhat differently. Whose interests is this proliferation of information meant to serve? What are the limits that a news operation ought to set before it launches itself on a wave of information that unsettles, defames, disturbs and misinforms people with breaking news that is unchecked? Does rumour become more respectable simply because it is purveyed by smart young newscasters, rather than making the rounds of the marketplace?

In the celebration of crisis as the chief justification for endless news coverage, do we not perpetuate specific modes of presenting, and even packaging, crisis – modes that are, in turn, determined by our investments and compulsions in the arenas of power and influence? And is not the faculty of critique, the critical consciousness, a casualty of such pre-programming? When the script is already in place, testimony laid out in prescribed formats, where can the act of bearing inconvenient witness be accommodated?

Crisis and Critique

I have already counter-posed crisis to critique in this discussion. Significantly, the two words derive from the same Greek root: *krinein*, to decide. A crisis, in its original Greek sense, meant simply a point of decision: an aberration in the fabric of normality, when society and the cosmos waited upon the epic hero to commit himself one way or the other; and on that decision depended the path of the hero's individual destiny, as well as the history of those connected to him. A critique also marks a decisive moment: it is the culmination of a process of weighing, reflecting and arriving at judgement, a commitment that places the individual in a certain position to his society and its axioms, its debates. But where crisis denotes the forcing of an individual decision by structural compulsions, critique connotes an autonomy of decision, a power of reflexive agency on the part of an individual.

Since we live in the aftermath of epos, and in the absence of heroes, I would hazard the suggestion that critique is the current and secular translation of the old, sacred sense of crisis: it connotes an interrogative mode of addressing reality, an *ethical* understanding of decision-making that embraces the value of means and ends and the imperative of justice. Critique, thus read, incarnates *responsibility*. Correspondingly, I would read crisis, today, as *the ongoing and foundational text of our epoch*, determined as it is by the erratic interplay of hegemony and resistance, by the workings of emergency states and improvisational guerrilla groups, randomized societies and transitional economies. Crisis, thus read, denotes a stimulus summoning forth a *pragmatics* that embodies decision-making in the form of *resolution*, however arbitrary.

The identification of critique with the ethical imperative, and crisis with the pragmatic, bears a specific polarizing implication in the context of mainstream media practice in contemporary India, for the *writing of crisis* – whether that crisis is international or local in nature, whether it arises out of military or ecological causes, whether it is precipitated by the actions of groups towards whom the media practitioner has a definite antipathy or sympathy.

By writing I mean here all forms of mediatic representation and reflection, whether textual, televisual or auditory: whatever the medium, the individual media practitioner must confront the dilemmatic nature of the act of writing crisis. As we have seen, crisis calls for explanation and defusing; it invites *resolution* as a singular closure. By the very gesture of defining a given situation as a crisis, one may be tempted into idioms of writing that do not complicate themselves by engaging fully with the issues under review – idioms that serve only to perpetuate crisis as a condition of mind by *disassociating* specific crises from their specific environments of causality.

Critique, by contrast, demands a sustained investigation premised on the disclosure of *truth* in its multi-faceted fullness, so that the practitioners of critique cannot hope to make friends, although they may well influence people through the depth and range they bring to their examination by *confronting* specific crises in their specific environments of causality. I propose to consider, necessarily somewhat schematically within the brief compass of this essay, the landscape of social, political and cultural determinations in which media practice in India negotiates between these etymologically twinned but actively opposed phenomena.

Organizing the Delivery of Crisis

Media practice, almost more than any other form of cultural production, must take into account the public contexts in which it articulates itself. These public contexts, making particular conceptual and material demands as they do, form the pretext for the manner in which the media organize crisis for presentation. The media claim that they must work within the implicit and explicit parameters of say-ability and show-ability laid down by the State; they cite public culture – the hazy spectre of 'popular feeling' in its religious, regional, linguistic or ethnic biases – as a marker of limitation. More often than not, media corporations tend to manipulate directly, or acquiesce in the manipulation of, the public contexts of their operation. Media corporations are being somewhat disingenuous when they identify their interests with those of the people. As evidenced in their patterns of reportage, analysis and comment, their interests are more often contiguous with those of the nation-state, or of influential actors in the polity and the economy; or then, they align their interests with those of globally dominant institutions – a fact that demonstrates the compromised nature of their pragmatics.

Media corporations deploy various strategies of representation in organizing the delivery of crisis as they deal with a scale of situations ranging from the mere disturbance to the cataclysm. Typically, they *cast the catastrophic as the spectacular*, playing the occasion for theatre. The newsroom has its Procrustean formats, to which the rawness and complexity of crisis situations may be reduced. Guided by the commandment of speed, obsessed with projecting the illusion of confident authority, caught up in the succession of variations that pass for updates, the news operation tends to ignore the weave – the knitting together of the local and the global, the mediaeval and the contemporary, the religious and the secular. Conflicts over the allocation of resources and authority in Sri Lanka or Bihar may be glossed through the default narratives of inter-ethnic strife or inter-caste rivalry; material desires and constructed identities, entering into complex transactions and belligerences in Iraq or East Timor, can be accounted for under the readymade rubric of religious antagonism.

At a time when identity has become a fluid bargaining position, the news operation assumes entrenched, even primordial identities of self and community: the intricacies of otherness pose difficulties of interpretation and hold up the speed with which news must now be disseminated. The other, even when it has penetrated the self, is sought to be captured in alienating definitions; tradition is reified into an immutable formula, even though the news derives a considerable proportion of its events and its substance from the recensionary acts of revanchism, irredentism, revivalism and neo-tribalism, which illustrate how tradition has become a special form of modernity. A nineteenth century colonialist mentality continues to determine the media view of its subjects: ethnicities and nations, languages and regions are routinely essentialized, with dangerous results, as we have seen in Rwanda and in the countries that were formerly provinces of the Ottoman Empire.

Another basic feature of contemporary media treatment, especially in its televisual dimension, is what I would term *repeatage*, which has comprehensively supplanted reportage. By repeatage, I mean the impoverishment of discourse, both visual and explicative, that results when the media reinforce key images to the point of banality, or replay unexamined clichés to package a difficult situation in a semantics of simplification. From repeatage, there follows naturally the phenomenon of the shallow present: a present that floats without reference to the deep archive of the past, dangerously buoyant in the programmatic absence of contexts and frameworks in which to assess the information offered by the media on any given situation. The shallow present is a particular malaise of the electronic media, although the print media in India are struggling to catch up. It is to be hoped that in a utopian but not-too-distant future, the news operation will extend itself through intermedia options, linking TV with the internet in ways that would achieve a currently unobtainable relay between instantaneity and the archival.

The emphasis on the shallow present serves a crucial ideological function: it focuses the attention of readers or viewers on the narratives that are sanctioned by the media apparatus, and such steady focus confers upon them a dominance and widespread acceptance. As a corollary, the mainstream media render various 'unsuitable' narratives inaudible. Entire histories of struggle, suffering or resistance thereby become invisible, *unspeakable*. Among these, in the Indian media context, are phantoms of lost solidarities (between India and the Arab world), tokens of a discarded compassion (in relation to project-displaced people), awareness of provinces governed in quasi-military fashion (Jammu & Kashmir, and the North-eastern regions, which are, for all practical purposes, under martial law). These unsuitable narratives have either become yesterday's, or the last decade's, news; or they are perceived to be irrelevant by the manipulators of public opinion – under which rubric I place the owners and editorial mandarins of many print and electronic conglomerates, as well as their political respondents and interlocutors. It is still possible, with courage, tact and ingenuity, for individual media practitioners and individual media corporations to secure 'liberated zones', even within a mediascape sustained largely by such manipulation, but this tends to be the exception, not the rule.

In practice, through the 1990s – as the two terms around the hyphen in 'nation-state' have come apart, and the idea of the consensual nation has collapsed to reveal a hegemonic and even paranoid state apparatus – it is through the mainstream mediascape that various conceptions of the public, the people, and even the nation have been constructed and floated. To no one's surprise, these are instrumental fictions of collectivity, constituted around entertainment events such as cricket matches, around sports icons, quizzes, game shows and talk shows; they reflect a subscribership to high-consumption culture and resurgent nationalism. This offers us a clue to the influence of powerful interests on the domain of the media.

While I do not wish to reify or essentialize the mainstream media as a monolithic entity, it must be said that large sectors of the Indian mass media apparatus (with a few honourable and courageous exceptions) are complicit with, or neutralized by association with, the *fixities* of State hegemony, resurgent majoritarian nationalism, and globally fluid capital. Such compromising involvements weaken the Indian media's claim to independence, objectivity and critical mobility. What we see in the mainstream media – despite occasional campaigns against corruption or nepotism, which cannot mask the fact that their columns have no place for long-running droughts or famines, the dilapidation of infrastructure and the immiseration of the rural artisanate – is a *surrender of critique.*

The Paradoxes of Complicity
The complicity of the media with the formations of the State, majoritarianism and global capital has translated as a conflation of its attitudes with theirs, an identification of its material and symbolic interests with theirs. The outcome of such conflation and identification is manifested in three specific paradoxes.

First: while claiming to act in, and speak for, the public interest, the media deliver their readers or viewers to their advertisers and protectors, as so many minds, bodies and sensory imaginations to be subjected to State and corporate agendas. The media, on examination, will be seen to be replicating the pathologies of the State and exponentiating the market-lust of the corporations – a tendency that is greatly dramatized during the reportage of periodic catastrophes that threaten State or corporate agendas. In these instances, crisis is packaged within definite parameters. When India tests a nuclear device or Pakistan is caught shipping nuclear technology or materials to regimes intent on manufacturing nuclear weapons, the Indian media follow an official line, as though the State's foreign policy were also the foreign perspective of the media. In dealing with the war mythology of Kargil, too, the media follow the State in its triumphalism. So too, in reporting and analyzing the attack on Parliament in 2001, most of the media have gone along with the official account.

I would contend that this unquestioning adoption of the official line on terrorism, militancy and foreign affairs – doubtless in the national interest – has only served to further restrict a public sphere already constricted by draconian measures concerning the expression of dissent, the articulation of contrary viewpoints, and the advocacy of the cause of individuals, groups or entire regions officially classified as inimical to the State.

Second: as the Indian media lose their autonomy – reflecting a nation-state hemmed in by its commitments to a world economy dominated by the industrially advanced nations – they have begun to take their cue from the global (i.e.: American) media, in matters that range from the number of column-inches or air-minutes devoted to soft news designed around Page 3 people, the beauty industry and entertainment, to the mapping of international perspectives, as on Iraq, the House of Islam, South-east Asia, environmental issues and the patterns of world trade.

This reliance on American media directives – a loss of *swaraj*, if there was one – takes its place in a culture of defeatism, animated (if that is the right word) by a general belief that India has been chasing shadows for five decades, that the Non-Aligned Movement, India's tilt towards the Soviet Union during the Cold War, and Nehru's insistence on economic autonomy, were grievous errors. Conventional wisdom suggests that it is far better to follow the State Department, the *LA Times*, CNN and Fox TV, in the management of our public life; signals from the mass media, both subliminal and overt, encourage us in this delusion.

Third: (and this is the paradox in chief so far as media practice is concerned): while claiming to mediate and reflect the desires of their subscribers by mounting a sometimes farcical *populism* – the spirit behind numerous call-in polls, email surveys and random interviews – the Indian mainstream media often display a remarkable *solipsism* towards their subscribers, treating them as pawns, addicts or creatures *produced by the mediatic process*, recorded as numbers in the periodic warfare over popularity ratings and circulation figures, to be toyed with at will, their passive and un-empowered reception mitigated by token efforts towards interactivity.

The renunciation of autonomy, the marginalization of the dissident critical function as too adversarial to be countenanced, the proposal of a symbolic order of dependency for the nation – all these speak of that particular tragedy which overtakes the media when its practitioners forget that theirs is, *or must be*, a discourse of communicative action, *not* a discourse of hegemony. What I have sought to trace here are the outlines of a *crisis of representation* that faces Indian media productions. It is also, at once, a *crisis of self-understanding* for its practitioners: What are we meant to represent, and how? And who, precisely, are we meant to function as, and from what platform of credibility? In these circumstances, as media practitioners, how exactly shall we render our self-avowed function as *bearers of truth?*

Redemption by Critique

Nothing can be easier than to transfer the blame for individual compromises on the parameters of the institution, the systemic constraints. But media practitioners must face themselves squarely: their selves, as compromised observers. On such inquiry, the media-practising self unravels. We must be prepared, after unpeeling the institutional skin, to place our personal conditioning under the interrogative scanner of critique. At which point it becomes inescapably clear that the crisis is not external – comfortably out there and elsewhere, a feature of the institution and the system – but that it is inside you; that you *embody* the crisis in your anxieties, as you find your *truth-bearing claim* breaking down.

There are no holidays for the media practitioner. You cannot set aside your media-practitioner self, with its guarantees of neutrality and its actualities of compromise, silence and evasion, ready with the answers. You cannot sidestep this role and slip into the role of concerned citizen, full of questions. This brings us to a consideration of the paramount question of the ethics of media practice.

In times of crisis (and which times, now, are not?), are you a media practitioner first, or a citizen first? How meaningful is this dichotomy, this Plotinian model of two natures in one body? Whatever one self wishes to leave unsaid, in times of crises, the other will wish to articulate. The option of *self-censorship* is an agonizing one: to strip the self to its commitments and convictions in order to meet the criterion of neutrality, only to find that neutrality is a vexed and contested state. You find that you have sometimes internalized the defence mechanisms of the system. Often, too, you will have played mouthpiece to a populism that phrases itself in blithe talk of 'national interest' and 'popular feeling', justifying elisions and omissions in the name of avoiding offence to patriotic sentiments or religious sensibilities. This is the voice of a media practice that has become so embedded in civil society, polity, economy and their emotional investments, that it cannot stand apart and play the role of agonist and questioner – a media practice that has failed in the function of critique.

Consider a redemption from this fallen state, achieved through the resumption of critique. Consider, in other words, the media practitioner who acknowledges his or her occupancy of the skin of the citizen: here is a self that must avow its doubts, its hesitations, even its *alterities*. And not by writing in a self-indulgent, autobiographical vein, but rather by pursuing allusion, oblique provocation, inserting uncertainty in place of dogma, even in the conventional formats of the mainstream media paradigm, playing subtly through the proto-cols of report, feature, analysis, and comment. Critique is all too often thought of as a cor-rosive move; but it can accomplish its redemptive moves by being playful and riddling, by affirming the excluded through festive rather than solemn resistance.

Eventually, in the inter-media future to which I have alluded briefly above, critical media practice would move towards tactical, transitive, inter-genre modes as alternatives to the mainstream paradigm. As necessarily partisan modes interrupting the circulation of domi-nant discourses, these would cast the media practitioner as a combatant, an ally of other agents of resistance, such as activists, artists and literary producers. Media practitioners would evolve, through such alignments, a new subjectivity; they would explore the mate-riality of their media in refreshingly novel ways, developing new communities in spaces of convergence that are also spaces of emancipation.

Concluding Caveats

The festivity with which I have delineated the future of critical media must be balanced by the discipline of ethical vigilance. Practitioners of resistance in the media ought not to lapse into an irresponsibility of their own, to match that of the dominant discourses and their pur-veyors, which they oppose. *If the crisis is embodied by the practitioner, so too must the critique be embodied by him or her.*

This caveat acquires urgency in the light of the repeated instances when resistance in the media has been guilty of its own errors of omission. The complacency of the high moral ground assumed by exponents of the Left-liberal position can cause a blindness towards crises that do not fit into their prescribed paradigm of grievance and horror. No sadder instance of this can be found than the prolonged Left-liberal refusal to recognize the predica-ment of the Kashmiri Pandits, whose travails were not only *not* accorded recognition, but were even dismissed as State-sponsored hallucinations, through the 1990s. In this account, the Kashmiri Pandits were viewed as members of the 'majority community', and therefore, by definition, immune from suffering. In truth, the impartial criterion of minority status, and the mandate of protecting minority rights, ought to have been applied to the Pandits, who were a minority in Kashmir; their membership of India's Hindu majority did not help them while they faced militant persecution and exile. Predictably, Left-Liberal commentators blamed the government for this tragedy, rather than the increasingly far-right Wahabbist forces of militancy, which also destroyed the Sufi openness of Islam in Kashmir, virtually unchallenged by resistance media practitioners and human rights activists.

When the Pandit predicament became too visible to be denied, the script changed: Left-liberal observers were discouraged from commenting on it because 'this was not the right time' (it never is) and we ought not to 'weaken the cause' (perish the thought). Robust honesty was regarded as a strategic disadvantage, while the desire to project a favourite victim ('the Kashmiri people', presumably excluding the Pandits) over other candidates (the Pandits), and the immediate and automatic privileging of a carefully rehearsed under-dog narrative (that of the militants), conspired to destroy Left-liberal credibility on the Kashmir issue.

Among the victims of this victimology-gone-wrong were, in addition to the Pandits, the Muslims of the Valley, who suffered the violent attentions both of the State and the militants, as well as the Ladakhis and the denizens of Jammu. Across religious lines, political free-doms were snatched away by the State (reported by resistance media practitioners) while cultural freedoms were robbed by the militants (silence from the above, some of whom would, in other contexts, have upheld the rights of women, of dissenters, of variations in belief). In the end, the cause was weakened – and large numbers of potentially liberal Hindus tipped over the fence into the arms of aggressive *Hindutva* – because of the foolish hypocrisy of the Left-liberal intellectual formation.

The moral of the parable is a simple one: that, while celebrating the festivity of resist-ance and overturning the ideological restrictions of the establishment mass media, we ought not to replace one dogma with another. Partisan as we are, we must submit ourselves to our own professional structures and mechanisms of review, cognisant of the realization that, in many conflicts and other crisis situations, neither conventional even-handedness nor defiant partisanship are relevant – since there are more than two sides to the truth. These are issues that will become ever more urgent, it seems to me, in a media environment where the newspaper aspires to the televisual, the electronic media rejects depth, and the internet, in its very freedom and relative absence of refereeing, becomes vulnerable to regressive agendas.

This text was presented at the "Crisis/Media" workshop, organized by Sarai-CSDS and the Waag Society in Delhi, March 2003.

Peace is War
The Collateral Damage of Breaking News

ARUNDHATI ROY

There's been a delicious debate in the Indian press of late. A prominent English daily announced that it would sell space on Page Three (its gossip section) to anyone who was willing to pay to be featured. (The inference is that the rest of the news in the paper is in some way unsponsored, unsullied, 'pure news'.) The announcement provoked a series of responses – most of them outraged – that the proud tradition of impartial journalism could sink to such depths. Personally, I was delighted. For a major mainstream newspaper to introduce the notion of 'paid for' news (Noam Chomsky, Ed Herman and a few others have been going on about it for some years now) is a giant step forward in the project of educating a largely credulous public about how the mass media operates. Once the idea of 'paid for' news has been mooted, once it's been ushered through the portals of popular imagination, it won't be hard for people to work out that if gossip columns in newspapers can be auctioned, why not the rest of the column space? After all, in this age of the 'Market', when everything's up for sale – rivers, forests, freedom, democracy and justice – what's special about news? Sponsored News – what a delectable idea! "This report is brought to you by". There could be a State regulated sliding scale for rates (headlines, pg. 1, pg. 2, sports section etc.) Or on second thought we could leave that to be regulated by the 'Free Market' – as it is now. Why change a winning formula?

The debate about whether mass circulation newspapers and commercial TV channels are finely plotted ideological conspiracies or apolitical, benign anarchies that bumble along as best they can, is an old one and needs no elaboration. After the September 11th attack on the World Trade Centre, the US mainstream media's blatant performance as the government's mouthpiece was the butt of some pretty black humour in the rest of the world. It brought the myth of the 'Free Press' in America crashing down. But before we gloat – the Indian mass media behaved no differently during the Pokhran nuclear tests and the Kargil war. There was no bumbling and very little that was benign in the shameful coverage of the December 13th attack on the Indian Parliament and the trial of S.A.R. Geelani who has been sentenced to death by a sessions court – after having been the subject of a media trial fuelled by a campaign of nationalist hysteria and outright lies. On a more everyday basis, would anybody who depends on the Indian mass media for information know that 80,000 people have been killed in Kashmir since 1989, most of them Muslim, most of them by Indian security forces? Most Indians would be outraged if it were suggested to them that the killings and 'disappearances' in the Kashmir Valley put India on par with any Banana Republic.

Modern democracies have been around for long enough for neo-liberal capitalists to learn how to subvert them. They have mastered the technique of infiltrating the instruments of democracy – the 'independent' judiciary, the 'free' press, the parliament – and moulding them to their purpose. The project of corporate globalization has cracked the code. Free elections, a free press and an independent judiciary mean little when the free market has reduced them to commodities available on sale to the highest bidder.

To control a democracy, it is becoming more and more vital to control the media. Few know this better than the prime minister of Italy, Silvio Berlusconi. He controls ninety percent of Italy's TV viewership. The principal media in America is owned by six companies. Four conglomerates are on the verge of controlling ninety percent of America's terrestrial and cable audience. Even internet websites are being colonized by giant media corporations.

It's a mistake to think that the corporate media supports the neo-liberal project. It is the neo-liberal project. It is the nexus, the confluence, the convergence, the union, the chosen medium of those who have power and money. As the project of Corporate Globalization increases the disparity between the rich and the poor, as the world grows more and more restive, corporations on the prowl for sweetheart deals need repressive governments to quell the mutinies in the servants' quarters. And governments, of course, need corporations. This mutual dependency spawns a sort of Corporate Nationalism, or, more accurately, a Corporate/Nationalism – if you can imagine such a thing. Corporate/Nationalism has become the unwavering anthem of the mass media.

One of our main tasks is to expose the complex mess of cables that connect Power to Money to the supposedly 'neutral' Free Press.

In the last couple of years, New Media has embarked on just such an enterprise. It has descended on Old Media like an annoying swarm of bees buzzing around an old buffalo, going where it goes, stopping where it stops, commenting on and critiquing its every move. New Media has managed to not transform but to create the possibility of transforming conventional mass media from the sophisticated propaganda machine, that Chomsky and Herman wrote about, into a vast CD Rom. Picture it: the old buffalo is the text, the bees are the hyperlinks that deconstruct it. Click a bee, get the inside story.

Basically, for the lucky few who have access to the internet, the mass media has been contextualized, and shown up for what it really is – an elaborate boardroom bulletin that reports and analyses the concerns of powerful people. For the bees it's a phenomenal achievement. For the buffalo, obviously, it's not much fun.

For the bees (the nice, lefty ones) it's a significant victory, but by no means a conquest. Because it's still the annoyed buffalo stumbling across the plains, lurching from crisis to crisis, from war to war, who sets the pace. It's still the buffalo that decides which particular crisis will be the main course on the menu and what's for dessert. So here we are today, the buffalo and the bees – on the verge of a war that could redraw the political map of the world and alter the course of history. As the US gears up to attack Iraq, the US government's lies are being amplified, its re-heated doctrine of pre-emptive strike talked up, its war machine deployed. There is still no sign of Iraq's so-called arsenal of Weapons of Mass Destruction.

Even before the next phase of the war – the American occupation of Iraq – has begun (the war itself is thirteen years old), thanks to the busy bees the extent and scale, the speed and strength of the mobilization against the war has been unprecedented in history. On the 15th of February, in an extraordinary display of public morality, millions of people took to the streets in 750 cities across the world to protest against the invasion of Iraq. If the US government and its Allies choose to ignore this and continue with their plans to invade and occupy Iraq, it could bring about a serious predicament in the modern world's understanding of democracy.

But then again, maybe we'll get used to it. Governments have learned to wait out crises – because they know that crises by definition must be short-lived. They know that a crises-driven media simply cannot afford to hang about in the same place for too long. It must be off for its next appointment with the next crisis. Like business houses need a cash-turnover, the media needs a crisis turnover. The US Government hopes that Iraq can be occupied, as Afghanistan has been. As Tibet has been. As Palestine has been. All the US government needs to do (or so it believes), is hunker down and wait. Once the crisis has been consumed by the media, picked to the bone, its carcass will gradually slip off the best-seller charts. And once the media's attention shifts, it shifts decisively. Whole countries become old news. They cease to exist. And the darkness becomes deeper than it was before the light was shone on them. We saw that in Afghanistan when the Soviets withdrew. We are being given a repeat performance now. Eventually when the buffalo stumbles away, the bees go too.

Crises Reportage in the twenty-first century has evolved into an independent discipline – almost a science. The money, the technology and the orchestrated mass hysteria that goes into crisis reporting have a curious effect. Crisis reporting isolates the crisis, unmoors it from the particularities of the history, the geography, and the culture that produced it. Eventually it floats free, like a hot-air balloon carrying its cargo of international gladflies – specialists, analysts, foreign correspondents and crises photographers with their enormous telephoto lenses.

Somewhere mid-journey and without prior notice, the gladflies auto-eject, and parachute down to the site of the next crisis, leaving the crestfallen, abandoned balloon drifting aimlessly in the sky, pathetically masquerading as a current event, hoping it will at least make history… There are few things sadder than a consumed, spent crisis. (For field research, look up Afghanistan 2002, Gujarat, India, 2003 A.D.)

Crisis reportage has left us with a double-edged legacy. While governments hone the art of crises management (the art of waiting out a crisis), resistance movements are increasingly being ensnared in a sort of vortex of crisis production. They have to find ways of precipitating crises, of manufacturing them in easily consumable, spectator friendly, formats. We have entered the era of crises as a consumer item, crisis as spectacle, as theatre. It's not new, but it's evolving, morphing, taking on new aspects. Flying planes into buildings is its most modern, most extreme form.

Crises as Spectacle, as political theatre, has a history. Gandhi's salt march to Dandi is among the most exhilarating examples. But the salt march was not theatre alone. It was the symbolic part of an act of real civil disobedience. As a result of the Dandi March, thousands of Indians across the country began to make their own salt, thereby openly defying Imperial

Britain's salt tax laws. It was a direct strike at the economic underpinning of the British Empire.

The disturbing thing nowadays is that Crisis as Spectacle has cut loose from its origins in genuine, long-term civil disobedience and is gradually becoming an instrument of resistance that is more symbolic than real. Also, it has begun to stray into other territory. Right now, it's blurring the lines that separate resistance movements from campaigns by political parties. I'm thinking here of L.K. Advani's *Rath Yatra*, which eventually led to the demolition of the Babri Masjid, and of the '*kar seva*' campaign for the construction of the Ram Temple at Ayodhya which is brought to a boil by the *Sangh Parivar* each time elections come around.

Both resistance movements and political election campaigns are in search of Spectacle – though, of course, the kind of spectacle they choose differs vastly.

On the occasions when symbolic political theatre shades into action that actually breaks the law – then it is the response of the State which usually provides the clarity to differentiate between a campaign by a political party and an action by a peoples' resistance movement. For instance, the police never opened fire on the rampaging mob that demolished the Babri Masjid, or those who participated in the genocidal campaign by the Congress Party against Sikhs in Delhi in 1984, or the Shiv Sena's massacre of Muslims in Bombay in 1993, or the BJP/VHP/Bajrang Dal's genocide against Muslims in Gujarat in 2002. Neither the police, nor the courts, nor the government has taken action against anybody who participated in this violence.

Yet recently the police has repeatedly opened fire on unarmed people, including women and children, who have protested against the violation of their rights to life and livelihood by the government's 'development projects'.

In this era of crises reportage, if you don't have a crisis to call your own, you're not in the news. And if you're not in the news, you don't exist. It's as though the virtual world constructed in the media has become more real than the real world.

Every self-respecting peoples' movement, every 'issue' needs to have its own hot-air balloon in the sky advertising its brand and purpose. For this reason, starvation deaths are more effective advertisements for drought and skewed Food Distribution than cases of severe malnutrition – which don't quite make the cut. Standing in the rising water of a reservoir for days on end, watching your home and belongings float away to protest against a big dam, used to be an effective strategy, but isn't any more. People resisting dams are expected to either conjure new tricks, or give up the struggle. In the despair created by the Supreme Court's appalling judgement on the Sardar Sarovar Dam, senior activists of the *Narmada Bachao Andolan* began once again to talk of *Jal Samarpan* – drowning themselves in the rising waters. They were mocked for not really meaning what they said.

Crisis as a Blood Sport.

The Indian State and the mass media have shown themselves to be benignly tolerant of the phenomenon of Resistance as a Symbolic Spectacle. (It actually helps them to hold down the country's reputation as the World's Biggest Democracy). But whenever civil resistance has shown the slightest signs of metamorphosing from symbolic acts (*dharnas*, demonstrations, hunger strikes) into anything remotely resembling genuine civil disobedience (blockading villages, occupying forestland) the State has cracked down mercilessly.

In April 2001 the police opened fire on a peaceful meeting of the *Adivasi Mukti Sangathan* in Mehndi Kheda, Madhya Pradesh; on the 2nd of February 2001 police fired on a peaceful protest of Munda Adivasis in Jharkhand, who were part of the protest against the *Koel Karo* hydroelectric, killing eight people and wounding thirty-six; on the 7th of April 2001, the State Reserve Police *lathi*-charged a peaceful demonstration by the *Kinara Bachao Andolan* against the consortium of NATELCO and UNOCAL who were trying to do a survey for a proposed private port. Lt Col Pratap Salve, one of the main activists, was beaten to death. On the 31st of October 2001, in Rayagada, Orissa, three *adivasis* were killed for protesting a bauxite mining project. On the 11th of November, at a peaceful protest against these killings, two more *adivasis* were killed. In Chilika, police fired on fisherfolk demanding the restoration of their fishing rights. Five people were killed.

The instances of repression go on and on – Jambudweep, Kashipur, Maikanj; the most recent of course is the incident in the Muthanga in Wyanad, Kerala. In February 2003 four thousand displaced *adivasis*, including women and children, occupied a small part of a wildlife sanctuary demanding that they be given the land the government had promised them the previous year. The deadline had come and gone and there had been no sign that the government had any intention of keeping its word. As the tension built up over the days, the Kerala Police surrounded the protestors and opened fire, killing one person and severely injuring several.

Interestingly, when it comes to the poor, and in particular *Dalit* and *Adivasi* communities, they get killed for encroaching on forest land (Muthanga), as well as when they're trying to protect forest land from dams, mining operations, steel plants (Koel Karo, Nagarnar).

In almost every instance of police firing, the State's strategy is to say that the firing was provoked by an act of violence. Those who have been fired upon are immediately called militants (PWG, MCC, ISI, LTTE). In Muthanga, the police and the government claimed that the *adivasis* had staged an armed insurrection and attempted to set up a parallel government. The speaker of the Kerala Assembly said that they should have either have been "suppressed or shot".

At the scene of the firing, the police had put together an 'ammunition display'. It consisted of some stones, a couple of sickles and axes, bows and arrows and a few kitchen knives. One of the major weapons used in the uprising was a polythene bag full of bees. (Imagine the young man collecting bees in the forest to protect himself and his little family against the Kerala Police. What a delightful parallel government his would be!)

According to the State, when victims refuse to be victims, they become terrorists and are dealt with as such. They're either killed or arrested under POTA (Prevention of Terrorism Act). In states like Orissa, Bihar and Jharkhand which are rich in mineral resources and therefore vulnerable to ruthless corporations on the hunt, hundreds of villagers, including minors, have been arrested under POTA and are being held in jail without trial. Some states have special police battalions for 'anti-development' activity. This is quite apart from the other use that POTA is being put to – terrorizing Muslims – particularly in states like Jammu & Kashmir and Gujarat. The space for genuine non-violent civil disobedience is atrophying. In the era of Corporate Globalization, poverty is a crime, and protesting against further impoverishment is terrorism. In the era of the War on Terror, poverty is being slyly conflated with terrorism.

Anyone who protests against the violation of their human and constitutional rights is labelled a terrorist, and this can end up becoming a self-fulfilling accusation. When every avenue of non-violent dissent is closed down, should we really be surprised that the forests are filling up with extremists, insurgents and militants? Vast parts of the country are already more or less beyond the control of the State – Kashmir, the North-east, large parts of Madhya Pradesh, Chattisgarh and Jharkhand.

It is utterly urgent for resistance movements, and those of us who support them, to reclaim the space for civil disobedience. To do this we will have to liberate ourselves from being manipulated, perverted and headed off in the wrong direction by the desire to feed the media's endless appetite for theatre because that saps energy and imagination.

There are signs that the battle has been joined. At a massive rally on the 27th of February the *Nimad Malwa Kisan Mazdoor Sangathan* (Nimad Malwa Farmers and Workers' Organization) in its protest against the privatization of power, declared that farmers and agricultural workers would not pay their electricity bills. The MP government has not yet responded. It will be interesting to see what happens.

We have to find a way of forcing the real issues back into the news. For example, the real issue in the Narmada Valley is not whether people will drown themselves or not. The NBA's strategies, its successes and failures are an issue, but a separate issue from the problem of Big Dams.

The real issue is that the privatization of essential infrastructure is essentially undemocratic. The real issue is the towering mass of incriminating evidence against Big Dams. The real issue is the fact that over the last fifty years in India alone Big Dams have displaced more than 33 million people. The real issue is the fact that Big Dams are obsolete. They're ecologically destructive, economically unviable and politically undemocratic. The real issue is the fact that the Supreme Court of India ordered the construction of the Sardar Sarovar dam to proceed even though it is aware that it violates the fundamental rights to life and livelihood of the citizens of India.

Unfortunately, the mass media, through a combination of ignorance and design, has framed the whole argument as one between those who are pro-development and those who are anti-development. It slyly suggests that the NBA is anti-electricity and anti-irrigation. And of course, anti-Gujarat. This is complete nonsense. The NBA believes that Big Dams are obsolete. They're not just bad for displaced people; they're bad for Gujarat too. They're too expensive, the water will not go where it's supposed to, and eventually, the area that is supposed to 'benefit' will pay a heavy price, like what is happening in the command area of India's favourite dam – the Bhakra Nangal. The NBA believes that there are more local, more democratic, ecologically sustainable, economically viable ways of generating electricity and managing water systems. It is demanding more modernity, not less. More democracy, not less.

After the Supreme Court delivered what is generally considered to be a knockout blow to the most spectacular resistance movement in India, the vultures are back, circling over the kill. The World Bank's new Water Resources Section strategy has announced that it will return to its policy of funding Big Dams. Meanwhile the Indian Government, directed by the venerable Supreme Court, has trundled out an ancient, hair-brained, Stalinist scheme of linking India's rivers. The order was given based on no real information or research – just on the whim of an ageing judge. The river linking project makes Big Dams look like enlightenment itself. It will become to the Development debate what the *Ram Mandir* (Ram Temple) in Ayodhya is to the communal debate – a venal campaign gimmick that can be rolled out just before every election. It is destructive even if it is never realized. It will be used to block every other more local, more effective, more democratic irrigation project. It will be used to siphon off enormous sums of public money.

Linking India's rivers would lead to massive social upheavals and ecological devastation. Any modern ecologist who hears about this plan bursts out laughing. Yet leading papers and journals like *India Today* and *Indian Express* carry laudatory pieces full of absurd information.

Coming back to the tyranny of crisis reportage – one way to cut loose is to understand that for most people in the world, peace is war: a daily battle against hunger, thirst and the violation of their dignity. Wars are often the end result of a flawed peace, a putative peace. And it is the flaws, the systemic flaws in what is normally considered to be 'peace', that we ought to be writing about. We have to – at least some of us – have to become peace correspondents instead of war correspondents. We have to lose our terror of the mundane. We have to use our skills and imagination and our art to recreate the rhythms of the endless crisis of normality, and in doing so, expose the policies and processes that make ordinary things – food, water, shelter and dignity – such a distant dream for ordinary people.

Most important of all, we have to turn our skills towards understanding and exposing the instruments of the State. In India, for instance, the institution that is least scrutinized and least accountable makes every major political, cultural and executive decision today. The Indian Supreme Court is one of the most powerful courts in the world. It decides whether dams should be built or not, whether slums should be cleared, whether industry should be removed form urban areas. It makes decisions on issues like privatization and disinvestments, on the content of school textbooks. It micro-manages our lives. Its orders affect the lives of millions of people. Whether you agree with the Supreme Court's decisions – all of them, some of them, none of them – or not, as an institution the Supreme Court has to be accountable. In a democracy you have checks and balances, not hierarchies. And yet, because of the Contempt of Court law, we cannot criticize the Supreme Court or call it to account. How can you have an undemocratic institution in a democratic society? It will automatically become a floor trap that accumulates authority, that confers supreme powers on itself. And that's exactly what has happened. We live in a judicial dictatorship. And we don't seem to have even begun to realize it.

The only way to make democracy real is to begin a process of constant questioning, permanent provocation and continuous public conversation between citizens and the State. That conversation is quite different from the conversation between political parties. (Representing the views of rival political parties is what the mass media thinks of as 'balanced' reporting). Patrolling the borders of our liberty is the only way we can guard against the snatching away of our freedoms. All over the world today, freedoms are being curbed in the name of protecting freedom. Once freedoms are surrendered by civil society, they cannot be retrieved without a struggle. It is so much easier to relinquish them than to recover them.

It is important to remember that our freedoms, such as they are, were never given to us by any government; they have been wrested by us. If we do not use them, if we do not test them from time to time, they atrophy. If we do not guard them constantly, they will be taken away from us. If we do not demand more and more, we will be left with less and less.

Understanding these things and then using them as tools to interrogate what we consider 'normalcy' is a way of subverting the tyranny of crises reportage.

Finally, there's another worrying kind of collateral damage caused by crisis reportage. Crisis reportage flips history over, turns it belly up. It tells stories back to front. So, we begin with the news of a crisis and end (if we're lucky) with an account of the events that led to it. For example, we enter the history of Afghanistan through the debris of the World Trade Centre in New York, the history of Iraq through 'Operation Desert Storm'. We enter the story of the *adivasi* struggle for justice in Kerala through the news of police firing on those who dared to encroach onto a wildlife sanctuary. Crises reportage forces us to view a complex evolving historical process through the distorting prism of a single current event.

Crises polarize people. They hustle us into making uninformed choices: You're either with us with the terrorists. You're either pro-privatization or pro-State. If you're not pro-Bush, you're pro-Saddam Hussein. If you're not good, you're evil.

These are spurious choices. They are not the only ones available to us. But in a crisis, we become like goalkeepers in a penalty shoot-out of a soccer match. We imagine that we have to commit ourselves to one side or another. We have nothing to go on but instinct and social conditioning. And once we're committed, it's hard to re-align oneself. In this process, those who ought to be natural allies become enemies.

For example, when the police fired on the *adivasis* who 'encroached' on the wildlife sanctuary in Muthanga, environmentalists did not come to their defence because they were outraged that the *adivasis* had dared to encroach on a wildlife sanctuary. It was not reported that in actual fact, the 'sanctuary' was actually a eucalyptus plantation. Years ago, old-growth forest had been clear-felled by the government to plant eucalyptus for the Birla's Grasim Rayon Factory set up in 1959. A huge mass of incriminating data accuses the factory of devastating the bamboo forests in the region, polluting the Chaliyar river, emitting toxins into the air and causing a great deal of suffering to a great number of people. In the name of employing 3,000 people, it destroyed the livelihood of what has been estimated to be about 300,000 bamboo-workers, sand-miners and fishermen. The state government did nothing to control the pollution or the destruction of forests and rivers. There was no police firing at the owners or managers of Grasim. But then, they had not committed the crime of being poor, being *adivasi*, or being on the brink of starvation. When the natural resources (bamboo, eucalyptus pulp) ran out, the factory closed down. The workers were never compensated.

Crises reportage elides these facts and forces people to make uniformed choices.

The real crises, the dispossession, the disempowerment, the daily violation of the democratic rights and the dignity of not thousands, but millions of people that has been set into motion not by accident but by deliberate design, does not fit into the pre-determined format of crisis reporting.

Fifteen years ago, the corrupt, centralized Indian State was too grand, too top-heavy and too far away for its poor to have access to it – to its institutions of education, of health, of water supply and electricity. Even its sewage system was inaccessible, too good for most. Today, the project of Corporate Globalization has increased the distance between those who make the decisions and those who must suffer them even more. For the poor, the uneducated, the displaced and dispossessed, that distance puts justice out of reach.

The unrelenting daily grind of injustice goes unreported and the silent, un-formatted battle spreads subcutaneously through our society, ushering us towards a future that doesn't bear thinking about.

But we continue sailing on our Titanic as it tilts slowly into the darkened sea. The deck-hands panic. Those with cheaper tickets have begun to be washed away. But in the banquet halls, the music plays on. The only signs of trouble are slightly slanting waiters, the kebabs and canapés sliding to one side of their silver trays, the somewhat exaggerated sloshing of the wine in the crystal wine glasses. The rich are comforted by the knowledge that the lifeboats on the deck are reserved for club class passengers. The tragedy is that they are probably right.

This text was presented at the "Crisis/Media" workshop, organized by Sarai-CSDS and the Waag Society in Delhi, March 2003.

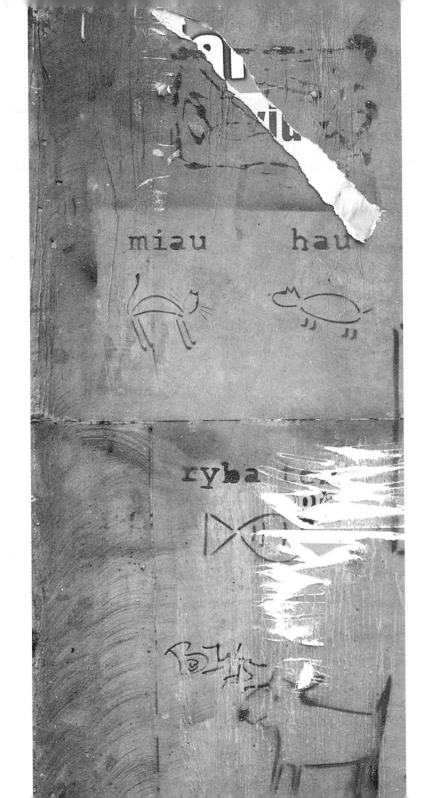

Financialization, Emotionalization, and Other Ugly Concepts

TOBY MILLER

In the last ten years, the US media have gone from being controlled by fifty competing companies to five (Schechter 2003). Many of these institutions are corporate conglo-merates for whom the traditions of journalism are almost incidental to profit making. News divisions have been fetishized as individual profit centres rather than their previous function as loss-leaders that helped to give television networks a character that 'endorsed' other genres (Smith, 2003). In search of 'efficiencies', owners have closed investigative sections and foreign bureaux (Chester, 2002: 106), other than in Israel (Project for Excellence in Journalism, 2002). ABC News once maintained seventeen offices overseas; now it has seven (Higham, 2001). In 2001, CBS had one journalist covering all of Asia, and seven others for the rest of the world. The BBC boasts over fifty foreign bureaux.

Numerous academic studies have found that principal US networks do not pay attention to other countries other than as dysfunctional or as threatening to the United States (Golan and Wanta, 2003). TV coverage of governmental, military, and international affairs dropped from 70% of network news in 1977 to 60% in 1987 and 40% in 1997 (Project for Excellence in Journalism, 2002). The 'big three' (CBS, NBC, and ABC) devoted 45% of their newscasts to foreign news in the 1970s ("Did 9/11?", 2002). In 1988, each network dedicated about 2000 minutes to international news. A decade later, the figure had halved, with about 9% of the aver-age newscast covering anything 'foreign' ("Battle Stations", 2001). In 2000, just three stories from beyond the US (apart from the Olympics) made it into the networks' twenty most-covered items, and all were directly concerned with domestic issues: the Miami-Cuba custody dispute over Elian Gonzales, the second Intifada, and the bombing of the USS Cole off Yemen. *Médecins sans Frontières* (Doctors Without Borders) issued a list of ten humanitarian disasters, such as the famine in Angola, civil wars in Somalia, Liberia, and Sudan, and expansion of the conflict in Colombia, that barely rated a mention on these programs (Lobe, 2003). Nicolas de Torrente, director of the US branch of MSF, put it this way: "Silence is the best ally of violence, impunity and contempt ... these enormous catastrophes don't seem to exist for most Americans" (quoted in Rotzer, 2003).

Did this change with the shocks of 2001? Fox News executive Roger Ailes describes its new method of covering global stories in this helpful way: "We basically sent hit teams overseas from out of here", while Leslie Moonves of CBS explains that entertainment now dominates news: "As you get further away from September 11th, that will revert back to normal" (quoted in "Battle Stations", 2001). And sure enough, the Project for Excellence in Journalism (2002) revealed that TV news coverage of national and international issues fell by 33% from October

2001 to March 2002, as celebrity and lifestyle issues took over from discussion of the various parts of the world that the United States directly and indirectly rules and controls. And a third of local TV news directors surveyed in 2000 indicated that they were under pressure not to portray key station advertisers negatively, or to do so positively.

How did this extraordinary state of affairs come to pass in a media environment of hugely wealthy and massively differentiated media audiences, and equally gigantic and diverse niche programming? The answer is available to us in the seemingly arid, almost archaeological world of political economy. For at times of crisis most of all, one must return to structures for explanations – return to conditions of possibility. Enough culturalist reductionism; time for some grubby talk. This deracination derives from ownership and content deregulation and the subsequently dominant influences on US current-affairs TV: financialization and emotionalization. These tendencies typify the consumer-culture, genre-driven nature of television in a deregulated era.

Finance, Feelings, and Entertainment
The neo-liberal agenda was the only point of the Clinton administration's policies that was uncritically accepted and even applauded by the mainstream media. Contemporary coverage of the market is beloved of the conglomerates. Its specialized vocabulary is accepted; a community of interest and commitment to fictive capital are assumed; and the deep affiliation and regular participation of viewers in stock prices are watchwords of a neo-liberal discourse. So in 2000, finance was the principal topic on ABC, NBC, and CBS nightly news programs, and it was second only to terrorism in 2002 (Lobe, 2003). News stories are evaluated in terms of their monetary significance to viewers. Neoclassical economic theory is deemed palatable in a way that theory usually isn't, other than the weather. Business advisors dominate discussion on dedicated finance cable stations like CNBC and Bloomberg, and are granted something akin to the status of seers when they appear on cable news channels like MSNBC and CNN or the networks. The focus is on stock markets in Asia, Europe, and New York; reports on company earnings, profits, and stocks; and portfolio management. Economic and labour news has become corporate news, and politics is measured in terms of its reception by business (Alterman, 2003: 118-38). The heroization of business executives by fawning journalists was part of a doubling of time dedicated by TV news to the market across the 1990s. Along the way, labour fell into irrelevancy, other than as so-called 'X-Factor inefficiency', while promoting stocks where one had a personal financial interest became *de rigueur* for anchors and pundits (Alterman, 2003: 123-24, 127, 133). There is a sense of markets stalking everyday security and politics, ready to punish all anxieties, uncertainties, or collective political action to restrain capital. The veneration, surveillance, and reportage of the markets is ever-ready to point to infractions of this anthropomorphized, yet oddly subject-free, sphere as a means of constructing moral panic around the conduct of whoever raises its ire. That's the financialization side – knowing and furthering the discourse of money and its methods of representing everyday life, substituting for politics and history.

Then there is emotionalization. Valourized by some as an expansion of the public sphere to include issues hitherto excluded from view, such as sexual politics revealed on television talk shows, I'd rather see emotionalization as the tendency to substitute analysis of US politics and economics with stress-on feelings – in the case of Iraq, the feelings of serving military and their families, viewers, media mavens, politicians, and state-of-the-nation pundits. The latter in particular produced a shortage of knowledge and a surfeit of opinion, a surplus of bluster filling in for an absence of skill. It can be no accident that Fox News Channel, which employs few journalists and staffs just four foreign bureaus, has the most pundits on its payroll of any US network – over fifty in 2003 (Tugend 2003). Margaret Carlson, a correspondent for *Time* and one of CNN's pundits, explained the key qualifications for her television work in these damning words: "The less you know about something, the better off you are … sound learned without confusing the matter with too much knowledge" (quoted in Alterman, 2003: 32).

Of course, powerful emotions are engaged by war, and there is value in addressing them and letting out the pain. But as per financialization, this exclusivity helped to shore up a mendacious administration and a teetering economy in the name of raw, apolitical, emotional truth. The point is to work through inchoate feelings to generate an apparatus that makes sense of them – especially given that so many in the audience will simply not share particular forms of identification, knowledge, or ignorance.

The search for positive stories by *Yanqui* journalists once their heroes were not greeted with universal acclaim upon invading Iraq reached its regrettable, Pollyanna-ish acme with the case of Jessica Lynch, an enlisted woman who was injured and captured during the war. While she was in an unguarded Iraqi hospital receiving treatment, US forces violently entered this site of healing, modestly videotaping their heroic mission for instant release. Numerous stories were immediately concocted to make emotions run still higher – she had fought off her attackers in the desert; she had been knifed; the US military had conquered serious opposition to lift her out – all fabrications, none subject to first-hand knowledge or back-up sources, all reported unproblematically by CNN, Fox, NBC, ABC, *The Washington Post*, and *The New York Times*, and all just as instantaneously regarded as dubious, if not spurious, by media from other countries, including the BBC. US journalists who questioned the story were derided as unpatriotic on Fox (Eviatar, 2003) even though the soldier herself subsequently testified that her story had been propagandized by the Pentagon. Of course, how people felt mattered most, not military reality. After all, the mission of the US media is to provide therapy at times of national risk, and not maintain too many foreign bureaux. In the next section, we shall see the result of this ad hoc emotionalism.

US Television and the Iraq Invasion
Seventy percent of the US public obtained 'information' about the 2003 invasion of Iraq from television rather than newspapers (Fitzgerald, 2003; Sharkey, 2003) and whilst all media increased their audiences during the crisis, the largest growth was achieved by cable (Lavine and Readership Institute, 2003). Studies of the two major cable news channels, Fox and CNN, reveal that despite the former's claim that it is less liberal, each delivers a pro-Bush position on foreign policy as if they were organs of the Pentagon (Pew Charitable, 2002). During the invasion of Iraq, both MSNBC and Fox adopted the Pentagon's cliché 'Operation Iraqi Freedom' as the title of their coverage. MSNBC used as its slogan to

accompany stories of US troops: "God bless America. Our hearts go with you" (quoted in Sharkey, 2003). Its president, Erik Sorenson, said that "[t]his may be one time where the sequel is more compelling than the original" (quoted in Lowry, 2003). The US flag was a constant backdrop in coverage, correspondents identified with the killer units they travelled with, and jingoistic self-membershipping was universal (Sharkey, 2003; Folkenflik, 2003). The proliferation of US flag pins on reporters, and the repeated, embarrassingly crass, use of such othering membership categorization devices as 'we', is simply not permitted by major global newsgatherers, whether they are regionally or nationally based or funded. British viewers were so taken aback by the partisanship of Fox, which was rebroadcast in the UK via satellite, that they protested against it through the local regulator, the Independent Television Commission, which calls for impartiality (Wells, 2003).

As the invasion of Iraq loomed, Rupert Murdoch said, "there is going to be collateral damage ... if you really want to be brutal about it, better we get it done now" (quoted in Pilger, 2003). The Project for Excellence in Journalism's analysis of ABC, CBS, NBC, CNN, and Fox found that in the opening stanza of the Iraq invasion, 50% of reports from journalists embedded with the invaders depicted combat but zero percent depicted injuries. As the war progressed, there were deeply sanitized images of the wounded from afar (Sharkey, 2003). Coverage of the impact of the invaders on the Iraqi people was dismissed by PBS *News Hour* Executive Producer Lester Crystal as not "central at the moment" (quoted in Sharkey, 2003). NBC correspondent David Bloom astonishingly offered that the media were so keen to become adjuncts of the military that they were "doing anything and everything that ... [the armed forces] can ask of us" (quoted in Carr, 2003). Marcy McGinnis, Senior Vice-President of news at CBS, claimed that the networks brought "this war into the living rooms of Americans ... the first time you can actually see what's happening" (quoted in Sharkey, 2003), and Paul Steiger, Managing Editor of the *Wall Street Journal*, divined that US media coverage of the invasion of Iraq "was pretty darned good" (quoted in Friedman, 2003). What counted as "happening" and "darned good" was extraordinarily misshaped, unbalanced – in fact systematically distorted – by Yanqui media. This contrasted drastically with what other nations received. Military manoeuvres took second place to civilian suffering in the rest of the world's media coverage of the Afghan and Iraqi crises, invasions, and occupations (della Cava, 2003; Greenberg, 2003).

No wonder Defence Secretary Donald Rumsfeld's thought-disordered remark about Baghdad – "It looks like it's a bombing of a city, but it isn't" – received much uncritical US coverage. Statements by the International Red Cross and many other notable non-Pentagon sources detailing Iraqi civilian casualties from the bombing-of-a-city-that-wasn't received virtually none (Wilkinson, 2003; FAIR, 2003b), just like the memorable Congressional speeches against this bloodthirsty militarism by Senators Robert Byrd and Ted Kennedy (Schlesinger, 2003). First-hand accounts of an unarmed family in a car being shot by Yanqui soldiers were overridden by the desire to promote the Pentagon's strenuous insistence that the protocols for shooting an unarmed family in a car were followed (FAIR, 2003c). There was no mention on any network of the US military's use of depleted uranium, and virtually no consideration of the impact of cluster bombs – both major stories everywhere else and subject to serious complaints by Amnesty International and Human Rights Watch. The US claim to have dropped just twenty-six cluster bombs was belied by the thousands and thousands that had to be 'cleaned up', but this information was not available through domestic media outlets (FAIR, 2003d). Even wounded US soldiers were left unnoticed by the mainstream media, with no bedside interviews from hospitals. Fallen men and women had become the 'disappeared' (Berkowitz, 2003). After the invasion, 82% of US residents believed that serious efforts had been made to spare civilians – infinitely higher numbers than in any other country, including those whose forces were present (Pew Research Centre for the People & the Press, 2003).

When it was decided to co-opt journalists for the Iraq invasion through the embarrassing quasi-homonym of 'embedding' them with the military, reporters were required to sign a contract agreeing with Pentagon instructions on coverage, including no off-the-record interviews, which had been crucial in Vietnam (Taiara, 2003; Thussu and Freedman, 2003: 6). This cosy arrangement was widely condemned in the international media as a deathblow to independent war reporting (Jones, 2003), and it had a chilling impact on gender balance amongst the media (Huff, 2003). When added to the speeded-up routines of twenty-four hour news channels, it also led to disgraces like the day when nine separate announcements were made that Umm Qasr had fallen to the invaders, none of which was accurate (Tryhorn, 2003), and a Fox news producer saying: "Even if we never get a story out of an embed, you need someone there to watch the missiles fly and the planes taking off. It's great television". No wonder that Bernard Shaw, former CNN anchor, saw these journalists as "hostages of the military" (quoted in Bushell and Cunningham, 2003). But on the dominant side of the debate were hacks like Marvin Kalb, for whom the events of September 11, 2001, meant "the rules have now changed", and anxieties over patriotism misplaced.

Domestically, more than half of TV studio guests talking about the impending action in Iraq in 2003 were US military or governmental personnel (FAIR, 2003a). TV news effectively diminished the available discourse on the impending struggle to one of technical efficiency or state propaganda. A study conducted through the life of the Iraq invasion reveals that US broadcast and cable news virtually excluded anti-war or internationalist points of view: 64% of all pundits were pro-war, while 71% of US 'experts' favoured the war. Anti-war voices were 10% of all sources, but just 6% of non-Iraqi sources and 3% of US speakers. Viewers were more than six times as likely to see a pro-war than an anti-war source, and amongst US guests the ratio increased to 25:1 (Rendall and Broughel, 2003). When the vast majority of outside experts represent official opinion, how is this different from a state-controlled media (Johnson, 2003)? *The New York Times* refers to these has-been and never-were pundits like this: "[p]art experts and part reporters, they're marketing tools, as well" – and, of course, retired killing-machine hacks were paid for their services, something quite shocking given the traditions of independent critique (Jensen, 2003). CNN's gleeful coverage of the invasion of Iraq was typified by one superannuated military officer who rejoiced with, "Slam, bam, bye-bye Saddam" as missiles struck Baghdad (quoted in Goldstein, 2003). Their virtually universal links to arms-trading are rarely divulged, and never discussed as relevant. Retired Lieutenant General Barry McCaffrey, employed in this capacity by NBC News, points to the cadre's "lifetime of experience and objectivity". In his case, this involves membership of the Committee for the Liberation of Iraq, a lobby group dedicated to influencing the media, and the boards of three munitions companies that make ordnance he proceeded to praise on MSNBC. Could these ties constitute conflicts of interest (Benaim at al. 2003)? Perhaps not when NBC itself is owned by one of the world's biggest arms suppliers, General Electric.

This says something about US journalistic practice more generally. Emad Adeeb, the chair of *Al Alam Al Youm* and host of *On the Air!* in Egypt, summed up Yanqui foreign-correspondent techniques like this: "You come and visit us in what I call the American Express Tour – 72 hours. ... You stay at the same hotel where the 150,000 colleagues before you have stayed. You eat at the same restaurant because you've been given its name. You have the same short list of people who have been interviewed ... you buy the same presents for your wives or girlfriends or mistresses, because you have the same address from your friends before you. You don't do anything out of the norm, and you come writing the same story with the same slogan – a minute-and-a-half bite, or a 500-word story – and you think that you know the Middle East. ... And then when a crisis happens, you are interviewed as an expert" (Pew Fellowships in International Journalism, 2002).

In editor Fuad Nahdi's (2003) words, dumping "young, inexperienced and excitable" journalists in the Middle East who are functionally illiterate and historically ignorant means that the US media depends on "clippings and weekend visits" of dubious professional integrity. No wonder that CNN's Jerusalem Bureau chief, Walter Rodgers, insensitively proclaims that "[f]or a journalist, Israel is the best country in the world to work in ... On the Palestinian side, as is the case in the rest of the Arab world, there is always that deep divide between Islam and the West" (quoted in Ibrahim, 2003: 96). He seems to think there are no Israeli Arabs and no Christian Palestinians. Or perhaps he does not think. CNN, of course, reached its Middle Eastern nadir, and lost viewers to Al-Jazeera and others, when one of its 'reporters' stated that some nomads would be thunderstruck by seeing "camels of steel" (cars) for the first time (MacFarquhar, 2003). This makes CNN's rejection of Ted Turner as a war correspondent because of his inexperience entirely laughable (Auletta and Turner, 2003).

Attempts to provide a different story met swift rebukes. The noted CNN foreign correspondent Christiane Amanpour told CNBC after the war: "I think the press was muzzled, and I think the press self-muzzled ... I'm sorry to say, but certainly television and, perhaps, to a certain extent, my station was intimidated by the administration and its foot soldiers at Fox News. And it did, in fact, put a climate of fear and self-censorship, in my view, in terms of the kind of broadcast work we did".

She was immediately derided by Fox as "a spokeswoman for *Al Qaeda*" (quoted in Zerbisias, 2003). And because MSNBC's Ashleigh Banfield occasionally reported Arab perspectives during the 2003 conflict, Michael Savage, then a talk show host on her network, called her a "slut", a "porn star", and an "accessory to the murder of Jewish children" on air, for which he was rewarded by NBC's executives by being named as their "showman" (quoted in Lieberman, 2003). Banfield told a Kansas State University audience during the Iraq invasion that "horrors were completely left out of this war. So was this journalism? ... I was ostracized just for going on television and saying, 'Here's what the leaders of *Hezbollah*, a radical Moslem group, are telling me about what is needed to bring peace to

Israel'" (quoted in Schechter, 2003). She was immediately demoted and disciplined by NBC for criticizing journalistic standards.

Conclusion

Domestic ignorance is not the only cost associated with these tendencies. A study by the International Federation of Journalists in October 2001 found blanket global coverage of the September 11th attacks, with very favourable discussion of the United States and its travails – even in nations that had suffered terribly from US aggression. But the advertising firm McCann-Erickson's evaluation of thirty-seven states saw a huge increase in cynicism about the US media's manipulation of the events (Cozens, 2001), and the Pew Research Centre for the People & the Press' (2002) study of forty-two countries in found a dramatic fall from favour for the US since that time, while a 2003 follow-up (Pew Research Centre for the People & the Press, 2003) encountered even lower opinions of the US nation, population, and policies worldwide than the year before, with specifically diminished support for anti-terrorism, and faith in the UN essentially demolished by US unilateralism and distrust of Bush Minor. "Which country poses the greatest danger to world peace in 2003?", asked *Time* magazine of 250,000 people across Europe, offering them a choice between Iraq, North Korea, and the United States. Eight percent selected Iraq, 9% chose North Korea, and … but you have already done the calculation about the most feared country of all (Pilger, 2003). A BBC poll in eleven countries in mid-2003 confirmed this and found sizeable majorities everywhere disapproving of Bush Minor and the invasion of Iraq, especially over civilian casualties ("Poll", 2003).

The challenge is to right the ignorance of the US public – to ensure that the quality of coverage and comment from *The Washington Post*, CBS, ABC, NBC, CNN and *The New York Times* can begin to approximate what is available via *La Jornada*, *The Independent*, *Al-Jazeera*, CBC, *Le Monde Diplomatique*, All-India Radio, or *El País*. For now, those of us who live in the US must rely on such outside truth-telling and political pressure. The places that provide the US with bases, material, personnel and ideological support, must change their tune. There must be pressure within the UN, NATO, OAS, the African Union, ASEAN, the Arab League and the EU against the US and specifically contra Israel's position on territory claimed since 1967 and its anti-Arabism. There must be pressure on totalitarian US allies, such as Egypt, Jordan, Saudi Arabia, Morocco and Pakistan, to become genuinely democratic. There must be pressure to open up the US media system to retrain journalists in keeping with best democratic practice and to require internationalist content on the air. We need fewer ugly concepts and more cosmopolitan words: less finance, less emotion, more knowledge.

REFERENCES

"Battle Stations", *New Yorker* (10 December, 2001).

"Did 9/11 Change Foreign News?", *On the Media*, National Public Radio (9 March, 2002).

"Poll Suggests World Hostile to US", *BBC News Online* (16 June, 2003).

Alterman, Eric. *What Liberal Media? The Truth about Bias and the News* (Basic Books, 2003, New York).

Auletta, Ken and Ted Turner. "Journalists and Generals", *New Yorker.com* (24 March, 2003).

Benaim, Daniel, Visesh Kumar and Priyanka Motaparthy. "TV's Conflicted Experts", *The Nation* (21 April, 2003) pp. 6-7.

Berkowitz, Bill. "Wounded, Weary and Disappeared", *TomPaine.com* (28 August, 2003).

Bushell, Andrew and Brent Cunningham. "Being There", *Columbia Journalism Review* (March/April, 2003).

Carr, David. "Reporting Reflects Anxiety", *The New York Times* (25 March, 2003).

Chester, Jeff. "Strict Scrutiny: Why Journalists should be Concerned about new Federal Industry Media Deregulation Proposals", *Harvard International Journal of Press/Politics* 7, No. 2 (2002) pp. 105-15.

Cozens, Claire. "Viewers Greet September 11 Coverage with Cynicism", *The Guardian* (26 October, 2001).

della Carva, Marco R. "Iraq gets Sympathetic Press around the World", *USA Today* (2 April, 2003) p. 1D.

Eviatar, Daphne. "The Press and Private Lynch", *The Nation* (7 July, 2003) pp. 18-20.

FAIR(a). "In Iraq Crisis, Networks are Megaphones for Official Views" (18 March, 2003).

FAIR(b). "Media Should follow up on Civilian Deaths" (4 April, 2003).

FAIR(c). "Official Story vs. Eyewitness Accounts" (4 April, 2003).

FAIR(d). "TV Not Concerned by Cluster Bombs, DU: 'That's Just the Way Life is in Iraq'" (6 May, 2003).

Fitzgerald, Mark. "Study Shows Readership at Crossroads", *Editor & Publisher* (6 May, 2003).

Folkenflik, David. "Fox News Defends its 'Patriotic' Coverage", *Baltimore Sun* (2 April, 2003).

Friedman, Jon. "Editors See Success in Iraq Coverage", *CBS Market Watch* (8 May, 2003).

Golan, Guy and Wayne Wanta. "International Elections on US Network News", *Gazette: The International Journal for Communication Studies* 65, No. 1 (2003) pp. 25-39.

Goldstein, Richard. "The Shock and Awe Show", *Village Voice* (26 March-1 April, 2003).

Greenberg, David. "We Don't Even Agree on What's Newsworthy", *The Washington Post* (16 March, 2003) p. B1.

Higham, Nick. "Media Confronts a New World", *BBC Online* (25 September, 2001).

Huff, Richard. "The Nets' Gender Gulf", *Daily News* (24 March, 2003).

Ibrahim, Dina. "Individual Perceptions of International Correspondents in the Middle East", *Gazette: The International Journal for Communication Studies* 65, No. 1 (2003) pp. 87-101.

International Federation of Journalists. "Les Journalists du Monde entier Produisent un Rapport sur lesMédias, la Guerre et le Terrorisme" (23 October, 2001).

Jensen, Elizabeth. "Network's War Strategy: Enlist Armies of Experts", *Los Angeles Times* (18 March, 2003).

Johnson, Peter. "Media Question Authority Over War Protests", *USA Today* (24 February, 2003).

Jones, Chris. "Peter Arnett: under Fire", *BBC News Online* (4 April, 2003).

Kalb, Marvin. "Journalists torn between Purism and Patriotism", *Editor & Publisher* (24 March, 2003).

Lavine, John and Readership Institute. *Beyond Impact: Engaging Younger, Lighter Readers: A Joint Venture of NAA, ASNE, & Media Management Center* (2003).

Lieberman, David. "NBC Hopes Big Investment in News Coverage Pays Off", *USA Today* (24 March, 2003).

Lobe, Jim. "All the World's a TV Screen", *Asia Times* (4 January, 2003).

Lowry, Brian. "Will the TV Factory Shape a New War?" *Calendar Live* (26 February, 2003).

MacFarquhar. "Arabic Stations Compete for Attention", *The New York Times* (25 March, 2003).

Nahdi, Fuad. "Doublespeak: Islam and the Media", *openDemocracy.net* (3 April, 2003).

Pew Charitable Trust. *Return to Normalcy? How the Media Have Covered the War on Terrorism* (January, 2002).

Pew Fellowships in International Journalism. *International News and the Media: The Impact of September 11* (11 September, 2002).

Pew Research Center for the People & the Press. *What the World Thinks in 2002: How Global Publics View Their Lives, Their Countries, America* (2002).

Pew Research Center for the People & the Press. *Views of a Changing World* (June 2003).

Pilger, John. "We see too much. We Know too much. That's our Best Defense", (6 April, 2003).

Project for Excellence in Journalism. *The War on Terrorism: The Not-So-New Television News Landscape* (2002).

Rendall, Steve and Tara Broughel. "Amplifying Officials, Squelching Dissent", *EXTRA!* (May/June, 2003).

Rotzer, Florian. "The World is what the Media Reports", *Telepolis* (7 January, 2003).

Schechter, Danny. "The Media, the War and our Right to Know", *AlterNet.org* (1 May, 2003).

Schlesinger, Arthur, Jr. "Today, it is we Americans who Live in Infamy", *Los Angeles Times* (23 March, 2003).

Sharkey, Jacqueline E. "The Television War", *American Journalism Review* (May, 2003).

Smith, Dow. "TV News Networks better Cure their Myopia", *Newsday* (6 May, 2003).

Taiara, Camille T. "Spoon-Feeding the Press", *San Francisco Bay Guardian* (12 March, 2003).

Thussu, Daya Kishan and Des Freedman. "Introduction", in Daya Kishan Thussu and Des Freedman eds. *War and the Media: Reporting Conflict 24/7* (Sage Publications, 2003) pp. 1-12.

Tryhorn, Chris. "When are Facts Facts? Not in a War", *The Guardian* (25 March, 2003).

Tugend, Alina. "Pundits for Hire", *American Journalism Review* (May, 2003).

Wells, Matt. "ITC Tackles Fox News Bias Claims", *The Guardian* (8 May, 2003).

Wilkinson, Marian. "POWs Vanish Amid War on Nasty Images", *Sydney Morning Herald* (25 March, 2003).

Zerbisias, Antonia. "The Press Self-Muzzled its Coverage of Iraq War", *Toronto Star* (16 September, 2003).

Interventionist Media in Times of Crisis

SOENKE ZEHLE

O n December 3rd, 2003, the International Criminal Tribunal for Rwanda (ICTR) announced that "Ferdinand Nahimana, founder and ideologist of the *Radio Télévision Libre des Mille Collines* (RTLM), Jean-Bosco Barayagwiza, high ranking board member of the *Comité d'initiative* of the RTLM and founding member of the Coalition for the Defence of Republic (CDR), and Hassan Ngeze, chief editor of *Kangura* newspaper, were convicted today for genocide, incitement to genocide, conspiracy, and crimes against humanity, extermination and persecution."[1] In what was dubbed 'the media trial', the ICTR examined the role of the radio station RTLM and the newspaper *Kangura* in the 1994 genocide in Rwanda to address, for the first time since the Nuremberg Trials, the role of the media in the context of international criminal justice. The ICTR judgment echoes the 1946 judgment of the International Military Tribunal against the NS journalist Julius Streicher, and will continue to inspire commentary on media accountability and the status of the long-dormant 1948 UN Genocide Convention as a core element of contemporary international criminal justice.[2,3]

But rather than approaching the controversial case as a new benchmark in the politics of human rights, I want to explore some of its implications for the idea of an 'interventionist' media: What happens to the idea of a media 'intervention' in the context of media incited and sustained mass violence, when 'intervention' is no longer conceptualized in the subversive terms of an autonomous counter-imperial multitude, over and against corporate mediaspheres and over-powering states, but may have to be rearticulated in the imperial terms of an interventionist 'peace media' in response to violent conflict in weak or failing states? Aware of the scope of such an effort, I offer no more than an initial research report that identifies possible vectors of inquiry. What follows are comments on the rise of media as a new direction in humanitarian intervention, the emergence of state failure as permanent feature of the post-colonial era and as conflict-analytical concern, and the increasing attention to media as autonomous actor in conflict-analytical work, concluding with the suggestion to explore in greater detail, with more attention to nuance than such a short essay allows, the implications of an imperial humanitarian media interventionism for 'alternative' theories of autonomous, interventionist, and tactical media.

New Directions in Humanitarian Intervention

Following the end of one-party rule and the establishment of a transitional coalition govern-ment in 1992, the Hutu-dominated Movement for Democracy and Development (MRND) lost its control over Radio Rwanda. The quasi-governmental Radio Rwanda had been the only national radio station and had already been used to broadcast a violently pro-Hutu message, but moved toward a non-partisan agenda when moderates took over the Ministry of Information. Radio Muhabura, a new station established by the Rwanda Patriotic Front (RPF), a Uganda-based rebel army composed of mostly Tutsi exiles, also followed a nationalist – rather than ethnic – emphasis consistent with the RPF commitment to minimizing the diffe-rences between Hutu and Tutsi. In response, Rwandan Hutu hardliners incorporated their own radio station as RTLM and began broadcasting in 1993, circumventing the ban imposed on 'harmful radio propaganda' to which the new Rwandan government had formally committed itself. Nominally independent of Radio Rwanda, RTLM was linked in a number of ways with the national radio, with other state agencies, and with the MRND: RTLM was allowed to broadcast on the same frequencies as the national radio when Radio Rwanda was not transmitting; it included well-known MRND and Radio Rwanda personnel, it used equipment owned by various government agencies, and it had access to an emergency source of energy. While this structural support helped to quickly extend the reach of RTLM, its popularity had its roots in the informal, spontaneous and witty style it pioneered, includ-ing the use of interactive broadcasting. Prior to the genocide, RTLM became popular even among the Tutsi soldiers of the RPF. Following the death of President Juvenal Habyarimana in a plane crash on April 6, 1994, and the subsequent seizure of power by a self-proclaimed interim government, a systematic genocide commenced, intensifying a process of informal repression that had already begun in 1992, orchestrated primarily by centrally-organized militias linked to the MRND and its extremist offshoot, the CDR. Once the genocide began, targeting minority Tutsis as well as moderate Hutus opposed to the MRND, RTLM took up themes of the extremist press, never losing its spontaneous style that gave voice to both government officials and listeners, and soon displaced the paper *Kangura* as the most influential voice of extremism. Eventually, Radio Rwanda came under extremist influence as well. Taking advantage of their reach and popularity, the two 'sister' stations broadcast incitation to slaughter and directions on how to carry it out. Throughout the genocide, the two stations collaborated to deliver a single message about the need to extirpate the 'enemy', articulated in the terms of an essentialized Hutu-Tutsi difference, of lavish praise for everyone who took matters into his or her own hands, and of disdain for political action that fell short of such radical extremism.[4,5]

The centrality of hate radio to both informal repression and the actual genocide campaign did not escape international attention and, with the likelihood of an armed intervention absent, raised calls for a media intervention. Early suggestions to jam RTLM by General Roméo Dallaire, the Canadian commander of UN forces in Rwanda, were quickly taken up by human rights activists. But as is well known, no such media intervention occurred, in part because of technical difficulties: after RPF forces had captured the capital, RTLM switched to the use of mobile transmitters, whose jamming would have required precisely the kind of immediate involvement unpopular at home – not least because of the traumatic experience in Somalia, which major UN members were eager to avoid.[6,7] The official rationale for the decision not to jam provided by the US was, however, that radio jamming constitutes an act of interference and thus a violation of international law, and the question of whether or not such a 'humanitarian' media intervention could indeed have prevented massive violence continues to be a matter of controversy.

In his account of the role of RTLM in the genocide, Jamie F. Metzl, a former UN Human Rights Officer, traces the insistence on a position of non-interference to the Cold War and wonders "whether the US Cold War interpretation of the international law of radio jamming remains an appropriate standard in the post-Cold War world".[8] Metzl worries that "there is a danger that, in a post-Somalia world less willing to respond forcefully to international crises, the baby of information intervention will be thrown out with the bath water of armed humanitarian intervention", and makes the case for the creation of an independent information intervention unit under the auspices of the UN that could monitor local media in regions of conflict, offer 'peace broadcasts' to de-escalate a conflict, and intervene if need be, authorized on a case-by-case basis by the Security Council.[9] While the communications-rights NGO Article 19 also supports the use of radio jamming in individual cases and leaves no doubt that RTLM broadcasts should have been stopped once the genocide began, it also cautions that such media interventions can never prevent 'another Rwanda', since the genocide cannot be attributed exclusively to the influence of inflammatory media and would have continued with or without the support of RTLM.[10] In her case study for another Article 19 report on state-sponsored violence, the political theorist Linda Kirsche notes that many accounts and analyses of the genocide tend to foreground the role of inflammatory radio broadcasts in inciting the killing, even though "there is abundant evidence that the genocide was a carefully planned operation, directed by informal state networks against both Tutsi and moderate Hutu", and cautions that exclusive emphasis on the role of hate radio will "serve as an attempt to cover the lamentable failure of the international community to heed the abundant warnings of impending disaster" and thus re-localize a conflict that needs to be understood in translocal terms.[11]

While there has been almost unanimous agreement on the need to jam RTLM, it is less obvious what should happen in other cases once the question of intervention becomes unhinged from the extremism associated with the Rwandan genocide. The idea of 'interventionist' media is inextricably intertwined with the ongoing controversy over the criteria used to identify the threshold for a 'humanitarian' intervention in general.[12] Approached in this context, interventionist media is always already on an imperial terrain, part of an imperial project of governance not (only) because of the geopolitical ambition of the powers that be, but because the complex contradictions of decolonization and the post-colonial order it helped create, including the inability of weak and failing states to protect the human rights of its own subjects, call for a conflict-analytical as well as media-theoretical response.

State Failure at the Edge of Empire

David Rieff, journalist and a sober observer of the practice of human rights, notes that most 'humanitarian' crises are not, in fact, humanitarian crises, but the by-product of civil wars and massive state failure, and cautions that humanitarian intervention should never be understood in terms of a selfless engagement: "So if we are going to intervene, let us understand the project that we must engage in, which is not just humanitarian intervention, nor even nation-building, but the de facto recolonization of some of the most unfortunate parts of the world".[13] Rieff suggests that, "[I]t may not be politically correct to say so, but there is a strong argument to be made that humanitarian interventions are positive for the people of a Liberia or a Bosnia and negative for the US since, whatever the conspiracy theorists of the anti-globalizing left and the isolationist right imagine, such wars almost never serve any geo-strategic or economic interest of the US or Western European powers". Michael Ignatieff has commented on the contemporary moment of empire in similar, if even stronger, terms. For him, the acknowledgment that decolonization has failed must be the point of departure for any politics of human rights: "The age of empire ought to have been succeeded by an age of independent, equal and self-governing nation-states. But that has not come to pass. America has inherited a world scarred not just by the failures of empires past but also by the failure of nationalist movements to create and secure free states – and now, suddenly, by the desire of Islamists to build theocratic tyrannies on the ruins of failed nationalist dreams. ... The case for empire is that it has become, in a place like Iraq, the last hope for democracy and stability alike".[14] In *Empire Lite*, a collection of essays on Bosnia, Kosovo, and Afghanistan originally published in *The New York Times Magazine*, Ignatieff has been even more direct: "Empire used to be the White Man's Burden. But just because empire has become politically incorrect does not mean it has become dispensable".[15] Such voices have often been dismissed as 'hawkish', offering a narrative of humanitarian legitimation whose claim to universality has become tainted by association with a geopolitical project of imperial expansion.[16] What emerges, however, is not so much (or not only) a naive view of empire often attributed to human rights activists by an older anti-imperialist left, but a sense of the inescapability, even inevitability of a transformation of the terrain on which the power of de-territorialized sovereignties is deployed.

A 2003 NGO report on state failure suggests, "What is central to a failed state is that the state apparatus is unable to uphold an effective monopoly of violence over its whole territory, lacks an effective judicial system to guard the rule of law and promulgate judgements that are internationally regarded as legitimate and sound (especially in commercial matters), is unable or unwilling to fulfil international obligations (such as in debt repayment) and cannot prevent various forms of transnational economic crime or the use of its territory for the perpetration of violence (politically motivated or otherwise) against other states in the international system".[17] The report examines the respective roles played by the colonial legacy and post-colonial state building, the end of Cold War, and processes of socio-economic globalization, and concludes that "it would be misleading to address failed or collapsed states merely as a temporary dysfunction of the Westphalia inter-state order. State inability to supply basic public services like justice, health and educational systems is not anymore an anomaly in the 'normal' inter-state system (something to be solved through technical institutional and capacity-building strategies), rather, it has become a structural trait of the contemporary international system" (ibid.). Few have been willing to acknowledge that state failure is here to stay. Some "have begun to take war into account in terms of development, but it is still considered a crisis and not as part of the economic and political make-up of collapsed states' societies, let alone as a manifestation of the changing international system. ... It should be realized by policymakers that failed states, and particularly the ones that have collapsed, never return to how they were prior to breaking down, even in the event that they do succeed in regaining coherence after a period of failure (e.g. Uganda). What a post-state or other new entity will eventually become is one of the most important challenges facing the international system. ... Failed states, then, do not exist in isolation: they are an integral part of the world system of governance" (ibid.). Consequently, "[S]tate failure is the pivotal issue for explaining intra-state conflicts, the vulnerability of crisis countries to external destabilization and continued obstacles to development",[18] and it offers a possible point of departure for reflections on interventionist media.[19]

The 'intractability' of conflicts invoked to substantiate the claim that state failure is really a failure of decolonization is, of course, itself in need of explanation. One of the ironies of statist theories of international relations is that they cannot – or do not want to – offer much analyses of either the stealth interventionism associated with 'good governance' and 'trade liberalization' or the complex dynamic of ethnicization that exposes the common attribution of conflict to 'ancient ethnic hatreds' to analytical ridicule. Because the various brands of realist orthodoxy treat the state more or less as a 'black box', unable to give an account of its often violent constitution as actor and geopolitical subject, they also have little to say on the topic of weak and failing states, let alone their functionality in and indeed indispensability to various imperial projects. Instead, they envision a world with few stable states engulfed and threatened by a rising tide of non-state actors, whose chaotic activity amounts to nothing less than a tribalist counter-modernity. And while the attention to 'ethnic conflict' in the immediate post-Cold War era was widely believed to call into question the neo-liberal triumphalism of the end of history that coincided the arrival of Francis Fukayama on the stage of geopolitical commentary, Fukayama's controversial suggestion that all thought on the political will from now on be contained in the idea of a free-market-cum-liberal-democracy seems to be confirmed by the specter of a statist modernity coming apart at its ex-colonial seams, calling into existence an imperial sovereignty based on these very principles.[20]

Conflict Analysis meets Interventionist Media

Statist and non-statist approaches do not, then, differ so much in their diagnosis of state failure than in the account they offer of its emergence: an often presentist analytical internalism, even pathologization on the one hand, and translocal, historical, process-oriented approaches on the other. While peace and conflict researchers have long been attentive to the limits of an analytical statism,[21] the field of conflict analysis itself has only recently begun to address the way issues of media and representation in general complicate its task. When the US-Carnegie Commission on Preventing Deadly Conflict (CCPDC) "moved to recognize this issue of the media and the information edge in conflict" in the 1990s, this was applauded as exceptional yet long-overdue by the BBC journalist Nik Gowing.

Gowing has written extensively on the complex relationship between media and conflict since the early 1990s.[22] Following an early study that examined the common assumption of a 'CNN effect', i.e. a direct link between increased conflict coverage and foreign policy action, one of his primary concerns has been the way the emergence of new media actors complicate the task of conflict analysis.[23] In an influential report on the African Great Lakes crisis in 1996-7, Gowing concludes that "there has been an important paradigm shift in the principles of handling and managing information in conflict. Even modest sub-regional forces from small, supposedly badly-resourced nations and factions have learned and assimilated much of the latest thinking of information warfare, information control and information manipulation".[24] The easy availability and proliferation of communications technology has transformed the notion of media itself, no longer exclusively associated with the institutions of official journalism but an ever-expanding network of media makers. It is less obvious what 'independence' means when the state against which it could be defined no longer, or not yet, exists, and as the role of hate radio in aggravating the genocide in Rwanda suggests, the mix between state failure and (nominally) independent media can be quite volatile.

Gowing's work stands out because he worries about the mismatch between the "tyranny of real-time news" and the speed of political processes that articulate and authorize possible responses, far from celebrating such a shift to an access-for-all information regime in terms of a 'tactical' subversion of mainstream media. Instead, he carefully assesses the troubling implications of circumventing official information management. As international media coverage becomes a symbolic resource for local actors, their clout and leverage vis-à-vis a government concerned about its image abroad increase. Some events take place only to generate their own representation, upsetting the traditional logic of conflict reporting as mere 'witnessing of the truth'. And as Gowing notes in his contribution to a forum on war and accountability organized by the International Committee of the Red Cross, "[M]ost significantly, the bearing of witness in crises can now often be done not just by journalists but by a whole new cadre of impromptu information 'do-ers', amateurs with little or no training in the principles of good journalism – namely, balance, impartiality and accuracy. A growing number are motivated advocates or partial campaigners who have found low-cost, low-tech but highly effective ways firstly to record and then to distribute their information and views in near real time".[25] Since news saturation and sheer overload might cause stock images and interpretations to prevail, the proliferation of media 'agents' Gowing outlines complicates enormously the task of conflict analysis. So for better or worse, it seems that 'interventionist' media theory will have to take at least some of its cues from conflict analysis, preferably those approaches whose non-statist conceptual idiom is capable of articulating the complex interdependencies Gowing outlines.[26]

In the late 1990s, the issue of media as an active force in the process of conflict management has received increasing attention, and various journalistic think tanks and human rights organizations have created manuals on conflict and human rights reporting.[27] While many of these manuals continue to embrace the concept of objectivity, others share the interventionist approach outlined by Robert Manoff of the US Centre for War, Peace and the News Media: they turn the traditional approach to the media-conflict nexus around to ask what it is conflict prevention and management require of the media. Among the various approaches that already exist, *Reporting the World* (RTW) is most explicitly based on the analytical apparatus of peace and conflict studies. Published by a UK journalism think-tank, RTW incorporates a set of analytical principles from *Conflict Transformation by Peaceful Means*, a manual published by the peace research centre *Transcend*, and prepared originally for the Crisis Environments Training Initiative and the Disaster Management Training Programme of the United Nations.[28] As Manoff notes, such propositions continue to be controversial: "[I]n a number of countries, no single issue has so bedevilled the discussion of Media & Conflict as the deeply held belief on the part of many journalists that the very idea of media-based preventive action violates the norm of objectivity – whose corollary, disinterestedness with respect to the events being reported, is an essential element of the professional creed. ... But whenever in recent years events such as the war in Bosnia or the genocidal violence in Rwanda have provoked discussions concerning the role of the media, the conversation-stopper has been the passionate assertion by senior correspondents that such concerns lie beyond the pale of legitimate journalism".[29] And even though it is far from promoting a simplistic sense of partisanship over and against the cherished journalistic principle of impartiality, RTW's 'peace journalism' approach, too, continues to generate controversy.[30]

One of the consequences of such analyses might be the acknowledgment that the separation between imperial and counter-imperial forms of interventionist media is not, or no longer, easily made. David Rieff insists that to intervene is to take sides. But even more so, to witness is to intervene; and the gaze of such interventionist media is inextricably intertwined with the ambiguities of empire. This is apparent, for example, in a 2003 report on 'Media in Vulnerable Societies' by Mark Frohardt, Africa Regional Director of the US communications NGO Internews, and a former official with the United Nations Human Rights Field Operation in Rwanda, and co-researcher Jonathan Temin that was published by the United States Institute of Peace. Introducing an entire spectrum of possible media interventions that include radio jamming, but also the training of journalists, support for independent media, and the monitoring of local media content, the report offers a revealing definition of intervention: "The term 'intervention', as it is used here, does not denote any sort of military or armed initiative (with one exception in the segment on 'aggressive interventions'). Rather, the term refers to support for the development of diverse, pluralistic independent media outlets giving voice to a variety of views and opinions. Such interventions are not carried out by soldiers or peacekeepers, but by journalists, professional media trainers, and non-governmental organization (NGO) workers".[31] Possible media interventions are then divided into three categories: structural interventions (support for independent media and diversity in media ownership, journalism training, legislative interventions to protect private media outlets and address hateful and antagonistic content, cooperation with international media networks as well as NGOs to complement and monitor local media), content-specific interventions (directly addressing the content produced by media outlets), and aggressive interventions (using force or prohibiting media outlets from operating).

The assumption about what media constellation and content escalates or de-escalates conflict must also – and necessarily – imagine a rather specific form of communicative sociality, for example, and the comprehensive manual of such a media interventionism is also a script of multicultural co-existence that is based, more or less, on the pluralistic public sphere, sandwiched between state and market but never subsumed by them, that is supposed to characterize liberal democracies. And without exception, the US serves as the point of reference and paragon of a 'really existing' media pluralism. This is, of course, the report's main assumption: a society that does not have a pluralistic media is, by definition, more vulnerable to conflict. One could also draw the conclusion, however, that the absence of major social contestation in the US is in no small part related to the particular structure of its mediascape, and that the unquestioned invocation of these structures as point of reference for other non-conflictual public spheres raises a host of questions regarding, for example, the future structures of ownership in vulnerable societies: the privatization of state media is no longer legitimized in economic but in conflict-analytical terms. And yet, the interventionist gaze of humanitarian surveillance the report envisions appears to remain neutral, untroubled by the need to explore its own locatedness vis-à-vis the space in which it aims to intervene.

I am not suggesting that the report does, in any way, support specific foreign or trade policy objectives. On the contrary, its focus on media interventions is a most welcome contribution to the de-militarization of the logic of humanitarian intervention. But its logic resonates with other projects of global governance that are, in turn, related to the issue of state failure. It is here that theoretical approaches to 'interventionist' media need to link up with conflict-analytical work. The report seems to approach intervention as neutral in the sense that the emergence of conflict is what authorizes the intervention on behalf of a general humanitarian concern that is itself left unexplored: conflict is just not a good thing. Ultimately, the report, it seems to me, reproduces the Hobbesian assumptions of mainstream conflict analysis. But what constitutes conflict, and who is to judge the desirability of any one conflict over another, cannot be answered by a just-say-no-to-conflict approach, and the question of which kind of conflict analysis is to ground the broad array of media interventions is indeed crucial. Coverage cannot solve the question of what comes after information, and one of the fallacies of an interventionist journalism might be that it sub-sumes the necessarily contentious politics under 'better' coverage and 'better' protocols of conflict analysis. This is where 'best practice' expertism creeps in even in the case of 'counter-imperial' human rights journalism, reflecting in an odd way the techno-determinist faith that open media will necessarily give voice to those who suffer and deserve our sup-port the most. Human rights journalism that follows 'best practice' anticipates a post-conflict 'public sphere' where actors follow certain scripts of civic co-existence, and as long as both local and trans-local reporting followed 'best practice' in its coverage of human rights issues, how could the emergence of the corresponding multiethnic civil society implied in these protocols possibly be jeopardized? But what if they do not? What role does genuine incommensurability play in these scripts that all-too-often follow a logic of diversity and a tolerant mutuality? Local journalism, an important element of the much celebrated re-emergence of 'civil society', is centrally linked to the work of transnational non-state actors like Internews, and such 'subaltern' views are likely to be affected by the protocols of an international human rights journalism. Internews claims, for example, that it "uses the media to reduce conflict within and between countries". This is a rather sweeping claim, and if conflict journalism and conflict analysis are as closely intertwined as I am suggesting, it matters which conceptual and historical assumptions regarding the genesis of conflict feed back into local and trans-local human rights reporting.

One might also object that one of the countries where the media is likely to aggravate conflict along pre-meditated vectors of escalation is the US itself, as became evident in the belligerence of mainstream coverage of the Iraq crisis and a corresponding meekness in relationship to what critics have called the Official Sources Industry. Commenting on the militarized expertism that characterized much network coverage, for example, the inde-pendent journalist Amy Goodman contends that CNN et al were already giving the concept of 'general news' an entirely new meaning.[32] But rather than focusing on the contradictions of such a media pluralism, what is important to me in this context is that the implied focus (and site of deployment) of any and all media interventions appears to be an imaginary abroad, understood in terms of a social volatility that renders it open to outside interven-tion. Such an approach might, as Kirsche suggest in the case of the RTLM, encourage a re-localization of conflict that obscures the role played by non-local actors. While I share the assumption of the Internews/USIP report that "robust independent media can play a critical watchdog role in societies vulnerable to civil conflict, but that the capacity of underdeve-loped media to resist insidious abuse and manipulation is often limited", the interventionist localism of its approach to the question of 'vulnerability' says very little about the need to challenge mainstream references to 'ancient tribal hatreds', for example, that contribute their own share to the stabilization of a conflict in local terms and the reluctance to organize a humanitarian intervention.

The Internews report is, I think, a good example of the irreducible imperial ambiguity of any kind of 'interventionist' media. A key player in the 'official' US politics of media intervention, Internews receives almost four-fifths of its funding from USAID and the US State Department and might be an all-too-easy target of criticism.[33] Similarly, the faith of its director that US-sponsored media initiatives might "bring the light of free speech to places that breed terrorism"

can be dismissed as the arrogant voice of a new imperial mission.[34] But while Internews celebrates its cold-war origins, such networks do not constitute a post-Cold War Congress for
Cultural Freedom, and the open-society idiom it employs is already shifting from an older anti-
totalitarian statism that used to serve as foil for the concept of independent media in an open
society, not least in response to the question of media in 'vulnerable' societies'.[35] And yet,
if state failure is taken seriously, the project of a NGO-sponsored media pluralism rooted in
local 'civil society organizations', shared even by 'peace media' organizations like the
Hirondelle Foundation,[36] might still fail if the (teleological) assumption of statist normalcy serves
to stabilize the construction of a pluralist mediasphere.

Interventionist Media on New Terrain

For better or worse, interventionist media will operate on imperial terrain, and in this context, media theory can no longer ignore the imperial implications of weak, collapsing, or
failed states. Empire is not, of course, merely a consequence of the 'failure' of the conceptual and geopolitical agenda of third worldism, of its project of tri-continental liberation,
and of a new world economic order. On the contrary, Empire is itself the ambiguous
consequence of a multitude of social struggles whose logic of self-organization is
markedly different from the logic of sovereignty imagined in Bandung, and it still remains
necessary to articulate alternative genealogies of Empire, and indeed reclaim the concept
of Empire itself.[37] But this is also where the question of an interventionist media arises, challenging the re-localization of conflict encouraged by the conceptual idiom of statist orthodoxy by drawing on trans-local approaches to conflict analysis.

It is in this context, sketched all-too-briefly, that I have come to wonder – a question I
have, not an assumption I am making – whether the various 'subversive' concepts of
autonomous, interventionist and tactical media also depend on the assumption of a strong
state, and whether there is a need to examine the (constitutive) assumption that such interventions are part of a counter-imperial dynamic of multitudinal self-organization. I am not
suggesting that the post-colonial in general is somehow absent from media-theoretical
reflection. Quite the contrary, the 'info warriors' and 'communication guerrillas' in the idiom
of contemporary (metropolitan) media activism continue to refer to the anti-colonial struggles of an earlier era and serve as – often unexplored – markers of post-coloniality. Even
the "ABC of Tactical Media" by David Garcia and Geert Lovink, an attempt to offer an alternative media aesthetics that is ambiguous enough to approach analytically even the kind of
media usage characteristic of the RTLM, acknowledges the centrality of such martial
metaphorics by both mobilizing and mocking it: "Tactical media do not just report events,
as they are never impartial, they always participate and it is this that more than anything
separates them from mainstream media. ... But once the enemy has been named and van-
quished it is the tactical practitioner whose turn it is to fall into crisis".[38] Having lost its subversive innocence in the gruesome, unexpected literality that characterized the media-
orchestrated genocide in Rwanda, it seems to me now that it is the idea of interventionist
media itself that is called into question. And one way to approach something like a rethink-
ing of this idea is to acknowledge that state failure, and the deterritorialization of violence
that this implies, is indeed a permanent feature of the post-colonial era.

NOTES

1. ICTR, "Three Media Leaders convicted for Genocide", ICTR/INFO-9-2-372.EN (3 December, 2003). <http://www.ictr.org/ENGLISH/PRESSREL/2003/372.htm>
2. International Military Tribunal. The Trial of German Major War Criminals. Judgment: 30th September, 1946 – 1st October, 1946 <http://www.nizkor.org/hweb/imt/tgmwc/judgment/j-defendants-streicher.html>
3. Dworkin, Anthony. "Rwanda Tribunal Finds Media Executives Guilty of Genocide", *Crimes of War* (9 December, 2003). <http://www.crimesofwar.org/onnews/news-rwanda.html>
4. For an account of the role radio, especially RTLM, played in inciting and sustaining the mass killings, see Human Rights Watch, *Leave None to Tell the Story: Genocide in Rwanda* (March, 1999, New York). <http://www.hrw.org/reports/1999/rwanda>
5. "Hate Radio: Rwanda". Dossier on "Counteracting Hate Radio" maintained by Radio Netherlands <http://www.rnw.nl/realradio/dossiers/html/rwanda-h.html>
6. Power, Samantha. "Bystanders to Genocide: Why the United States Let the Rwandan Genocide Happen", *Atlantic Monthly* 288.2 (September, 2001). <http://www.theatlantic.com/issues/2001/09/power.htm>
7. Adelman, Howard, Astri Suhrke, and Bruce Jones. "Early Warning and Conflict Management", *Synthesis Report: The International Response to Conflict and Genocide: Lessons from the Rwanda Experience.* Steering Committee for Joint Evaluation of Emergency Assistance to Rwanda (Danish Foreign Ministry, 1997). <http://www.um.dk/danida/evalueringsrapporter/1997_rwanda/book2.asp>
8. Metzl, Jamie F. "Rwandan Genocide and the International Law of Radio Jamming", *American Journal of International Law* 91.4 (October, 1997). <http://www.asil.org/ajil/radio.htm>
9. Metzl, Jamie F. "Information Intervention: When Switching Channels Isn't Enough", *Foreign Affairs* (November/December, 1997).
10. Article 19. *Broadcasting Genocide: Censorship, Propaganda & State-Sponsored Violence in Rwanda 1990-1994* (1996, London).
11. Kirsche, Linda. "Case Study: Rwanda", *State-Sponsored Violence in Africa*, Ed. Article 19 (October, 1997). <http://www.article19.org/docimages/477.htm>
12. ICISS, *The Responsibility to Protect: Report of the International Commission on Intervention and State Sovereignty* (2001, Ottawa). <http://www.dfait-maeci.gc.ca/iciss-ciise/report-en.asp>
13. Rieff, David. "Beware Wars of Altruism", *Wall Street Journal* (10 July, 2003).
14. Ignatieff, Michael. "America's Empire is an Empire Lite", *The New York Times* (10 January, 2003). <http://www.globalpolicy.org/empire/analysis/2003/0110empirelite.htm>
15. Ignatieff, Michael. *Empire Lite: Nation Building in Bosnia, Kosovo, Afghanistan, Minerva* (2003).
16. See especially the work of David Chandler, one of the most vocal critics of the new politics of humanitarian intervention: "New Rights for Old? Cosmopolitan Citizenship and the Critique of State Sovereignty", *Political Studies* 51 (2003) pp. 332-49; "International Justice", *New Left Review* 6 (November-December, 2002). <http://www.newleftreview.net/NLR24003.shtml>; "Kosovo and the Remaking of International Relations", *Review of Global Ethno-Politics* 1.4 (2002) pp.110-118. <http://www.ethnopolitics.org/archive/volume_I/issue_4/chandler.pdf>; and "The Road to Military Humanitarianism: How the Human Rights NGOs Shaped a New Humanitarian Agenda", *Human Rights Quarterly* 23.3 (2001) pp. 678-700.
17. TNI et al. "Failed and Collapsed States in the International System". A report prepared by the Transnational Institute, Amsterdam, the African Studies Centre, Leiden, the Center of Social Studies, Coimbra University,

Portugal and the Peace Research Center- CIP-FUHEM, Madrid (December, 2003). <http://www.tni.org/reports/failedstates.pdf>

18. Debiel, Tobias. "Do Crisis Regions Have a Chance of Lasting Peace? The Difficult Transformation from Structures of Violence", in Tobias Debiel and Axel Klein, eds., *Fragile Peace: State Failure, Violence and Development in Crisis Regions* (Zed Books, 2002) pp. 1-30.

19. The US-American research project *State Failure* defines state failure in terms of "internal wars and failures of governance". For concepts and case studies, see <http://www.cidcm.umd.edu/inscr/stfail/index.htm>.

20. Kaplan's "Coming Anarchy" is still one of the best examples of this dystopian vision. See Robert D. Kaplan, "The Coming Anarchy: How scarcity, crime, overpopulation, tribalism, and disease are rapidly destroying the social fabric of our planet", *Atlantic Monthly* 273.2 (February, 1994) pp. 44-76. <http://www.theatlantic.com/politics/foreign/anarchy.htm>. For an approach that near pathologizes state failure, see Daniel Thuerer, "The 'Failed State' and International Law", *International Review of the Red Cross* 81. 836 (31 December, 1999). <http://www.icrc.org/also<http://www.globalpolicy.org/nations/sovereign/failed/2003/0725law.htm>. Even the ambitious 'Economics of Civil War, Crime and Violence' research project at the World Bank (<http://econ.worldbank.org/programs/conflict/>) remains committed to an analytical internalism. For a critique of the WB approach, see Arvind Ganesan and Alex Vines, "Engine of War: Resources, Greed, and the Predatory State", *Human Rights and Armed Conflict: Human Rights Watch World Report 2004* (January, 2004). <http://hrw.org/wr2k4/14.htm>.

21. Ryan, Stephan. "Peace and Conflict Studies Today", *Global Review of Ethnopolitics* 2.2 (January, 2003) pp. 75-82. <http://www.ethnopolitics.org/archive/volume_II/issue_2/ryan.pdf>

22. Gowing, Nik. "Real Time Television Coverage of Armed Conflicts and Diplomatic Crises: Does it Pressure or Distort Foreign Policy Decisions?" *Working Paper Series #1994-1* (The Joan Shorenstein Center on the Press, Politics and Public Policy, 1994, Cambridge). <http://www.ksg.harvard.edu/presspol/Research_Publications/Papers/Working_Papers/94_1.pdf>

23. Gowing, Nik. "Media Coverage: Help or Hinderance In Conflict Prevention?" (Carnegie Commission on Preventing Deadly Conflict, 1997, New York). <http://wwics.si.edu/subsites/ccpdc/pubs/media/medfr.htm>

24. Gowing, Nik. "New Challenges and Problems for Information Management in Complex Emergencies: Ominous lessons from the Great Lakes and Eastern Zaire in late 1996 and early 1997", Conference Paper, 'Dispatches from Disaster Zones: The Reporting of Humanitarian Emergencies' (27 and 28 May, 1998, London). Available online via the US Institute of Peace <http://www.usip.org/events/pre2002/gowing.pdf>. The paper is still marked 'Not for Citation' but is used here by permission of the author. Also see Nik Gowing, "Information in Conflict: Who Really Commands the High Ground?" *Annual Liddell Hart Centre for Military Archives Lecture* (King's College, Liddell Hart Centre for Military Archives, 2 March, 2000). <http://www.kcl.ac.uk/lhcma/info/lec00.htm>

25. Gowing, Nik. "'Noisy emergencies and the Media", Humanitarian Practice Network (2002). <http://www.odihpn.org/report.asp?ReportID=2450>

26. Scherrer, Christian P. "Peace research for the 21st century: a call for reorientation and new priorities", [Institute for Research on Ethnicity and Conflict Resolution (IFEK-IRECOR)], Moers (2001). <http://www.copri.dk/publications/workingpapers.htm>

27. See, for example, Michael Bromley and Urte Sonnenberg. "Reporting Ethnic Minorities and Ethnic Conflict

beyond Good or Evil" (European Journalism Centre, 1998, Maastricht).
<http://www.ejc.nl/hp/rem/cotents.html>; Karen Howze, "Reporting Ethnicity and Other Diversity Issues: A Manual for Discussion Leaders and Journalism Trainers", European Centre for War, Peace and the News Media and International Federation of Journalists (1999). <http://www.ifj.org/pdfs/repdiv.pdf> (a project initiated by Robert Manoff, Director of the Center for War, Peace and the News Media at NYU); Ross Howard, *An Operational Framework for Media and Peacebuilding*, Vancouver: Institute for Media, Policy and Civil Society (IMPACS), (2002). <http://www.impacs.org/pdfs/framework_apr5.pdf>; David Tuller, "Reporting Diversity Manual," London: Media Diversity Institute & Samizdat B92, 2002. Access PDF via <http://www.media-diversity.org>; and Ross Howard, Francis Rolt, Hans van de Veen and Juliette Verhoeven, *The Power of the Media: A Handbook for Peacebuilders*, European Centre for Conflict Prevention, European Centre for Common Ground and the Institute for Media, Policy and Civil Society (IMPACS), (2003). <http://www.conflict-prevention.net/>. Also see *Crimes of War* (<http://www.crimesofwar.org/>), a project organized by a group of reporters and legal scholars to raise awareness of international humanitarian law among journalists.

28. Lynch, Jake. *Reporting the World: The Findings. A practical checklist for the ethical reporting of conflicts in the 21st Century*, produced by journalists, for journalists (Taplow Court, Berkshire, UK: Conflict and Peace Forums, 2002). <http://www.reportingtheworld.org/>

29. Manoff, Robert. "Telling the Truth to Peoples at Risk: Some Introductory Thoughts on Media & Conflict", *The Legitimacy of Intervention for Peace by Foreign Media in a Country in Conflict* (2-4 July, 1998). <http://www.nyu.edu/globalbeat/pubs/manoff0798.html>

30. See, for example, a 2003 debate on 'journalism in times of war' archived at Open Democracy <http://www.opendemocracy.net/debates/issue-8-92.jsp>. RTW also maintains a list of peace journalism-related publications (<http://www.reportingtheworld.org/clients/rtwhome.nsf/h/3pbx>).

31. Frohardt, Mark, and Jonathan Temin, "Use and Abuse of Media in Vulnerable Societies", *USIP Special Report 110* (October, 2003). <http://www.usip.org/pubs/specialreports/sr110.html>

32. Goodman, Amy. "Independent Media in a Time of War" (2003). Access video and transcript at <http://www.democracynow.org/static/IMIATOW.shtml>. Also see Alexander Cockburn, "The Military & CNN," *San Jose Mercury News* (23 March, 2000). <http://www.commondreams.org/views/032300-107.htm>

33. <http://www.internews.org/>

34. Hoffmann, David. "US can bring light of free speech to places that breed terrorism", *Christian Science Monitor* (20 September, 2003). <http://www.internews.org/articles/2003/20030930_csmonitor_oped.htm>

35. Also see the definition of 'open society' now used by the Soros-sponsored Open Society Institute: "OSI and the network implement a range of initiatives that aim to promote open societies by shaping government policy and supporting education, media, public health, and human and women's rights, as well as social, legal, and economic reform. To diminish and prevent the negative consequences of globalization, OSI seeks to foster global open society by increasing collaboration with other nongovernmental organizations, governments, and international institutions" (<http://www.soros.org/about/overview>).

36. <http://www.hirondelle.org/>

37. Hardt, Michael. "Porto Allegre: Today's Bandung?" *New Left Review* 14 (March-April, 2002). <http://www.newleftreview.net/NLR24806.shtml>

38. Garcia, David and Geert Lovink. "ABC of Tactical Media" (1997) <http://www.waag.org/tmn/frabc.html>

Western Wars and Peace Activism
Social Movements in Global Mass-Mediated Politics

MARTIN SHAW

In February 2003, some of the largest ever globally coordinated street protests took place against the proposed attack on Iraq by the United States and the United Kingdom. In London, between one and two million people took part. Whatever the correct figure for the number of participants, even the police agreed that this was the largest demonstration on record. By April 2003, however, US and UK forces had launched their attack, deposed the Saddam Hussein regime, and 'won' their war. In the same interval, the peace movement shrank from massive mobilizations to a largely irrelevant rump of small political organizations. The movement's criticisms of American power reverberated through post-war politics, not least in Britain where Prime Minister Tony Blair suffered seemingly irreversible political damage. But it had disappeared as a mass political force. Although, by general consent, the USA had not prepared its rule in Iraq as successfully as its war, so that the post-war situation was marked by chronic failures in physical and social security, the peace movement offered no coherent voice in this crisis. Politicians, journalists and non-governmental organizations (NGOs) made damaging criticisms of US-UK policy, but no significant mass activist voice was heard.

How can we explain the paradox of the meteoric rise and fall of street protest? What does this example tell us about the nature and causes of the successes and failures of peace movements? How distinctive was this case, and how far does it fit into a pattern that can be discerned in earlier movements? What is the relationship between the character of current Western wars and the dilemmas of peace movements? How far do the politics of the movements and their modes of operation explain their limitations? In what ways does the fact that both wars and movements exist in a globally mass-mediated political environment explain the experiences? How far are the lessons of peace movements applicable more generally to contemporary social movements? These are some of the questions raised by this case, which this essay will try to explore in a general historical perspective. I write as a sociologist whose work has combined an interest in media and social movements with research on contemporary war and genocide (as well as personal experience as a peace movement activist in an earlier period).

The context of Iraq

Sociologists have often sought to explain social movements in terms of general social characteristics, such as the nature of the social groups that support them (for example, Parkin's 1968 idea of 'middle-class radicalism') and the general values of their supporters (e.g. Inglehart, 1977). However, as Mattausch (1989) argued in a study of the 1980s nuclear disarmament movements, these kinds of accounts 'explain away' the professed causes around which movements campaign, treating them as epiphenomena of more general social causes. Social science will give a more convincing account of people's actions, he argued, if it takes seriously their manifest, conscious as well as supposed, latent reasons for engaging in them. In the case of the movement against war in Iraq, our first port of call should be to examine the threat by the USA and UK to attack Iraq, the rationale and history of the conflict that led to this threat, and the reasons why millions of people responded to this threat by taking to the streets and other forms of protest. Clearly the numbers of protestors were of a historically significant order– something very specific must have been going on to make so many people protest. Thus we need to examine both the immediate political context of the threat of war, and behind that the larger contexts of contemporary world politics and war to which this specific crisis referred.

The outbreak of large protest movements is not easily predictable. Big movements, like the disarmament movements of the early 1980s, often arise as if from nowhere and their rapid success takes even their organizers by surprise. Few who had observed the rather small-scale, muted protests against the 2001-02 war in Afghanistan – or indeed the 1991 Gulf War (for an account of the British case, see Shaw 1996) – would have expected the massive actions against the 2003 Iraq War. Explanations must generally be post hoc: it is mainly in retrospect that opposition to the recent war appears to be over-determined, in contrast to these other cases. However, with the benefit of hindsight, it is quite clear that the war on Iraq was crucially different from other wars in which Western states have been involved in recent decades. This Western campaign was not a more or less direct response to provocative military action by an enemy state or movement, as were the British campaign in the Falklands, the Gulf War, NATO's campaign over Kosovo and the Afghanistan campaign. Uniquely, this was a 'pre-emptive' strike, according to a radical new US strategic doctrine that had little legitimacy outside the USA. Partly because of this different context, unlike any of the other cases, the USA's proposed war had virtually no active support from major states either within or outside the West. Britain's support, resulting from Blair going out on a limb against the weight of opinion in his party and even his government, gave the USA a fig leaf of international credibility – but it was not enough, and indeed it provoked intense hostility within the UK. The many months of build-up to war, the failed Blair-led attempts to secure international legitimacy, and President Bush's clear determination to go to war despite the opposition of the UN majority and despite the ongoing weapons inspections, all created an atmosphere of intense crisis.

In this context, the anti-war movements on the streets of the world's cities were able to build up a massive base of support over a series of demonstrations, with an unprecedented breadth of political legitimacy. Protestors were cutting with the grain of public opinion (even in the countries where governments gave some kind of support to the war, polls often showed large-scale opposition: of over 90% in Spain, 80% in Italy, 60% in the UK and 40-50% in the USA). In all cases they could claim to be speaking alongside the UN majority, and in many cases, such as France, Germany and Russia, they were on the same side as their governments. Because of these various kinds of international and national legitimacy, movements also received unusually favourable media coverage. Indeed many national and regional newspapers echoed their opposition to the war. In Britain, for example, not only the traditionally anti-war *Guardian* but also the tabloid *Daily Mirror* saw the possibility of audience gains through speaking for the opposition to military action.

From 'Stop Cruise Missiles' to 'Stop the War'

In many senses, then, the context for the recent anti-war movement was uniquely favourable, and this was the largest 'peace' movement since the campaigns against nuclear weapons twenty years earlier. However, unlike those earlier movements in which mass protests (demonstrations, sit-downs, peace camps, etc. involving hundreds of thousands) built up over about two years from their origins in late 1979 to their 1982 peak, and only gradually subsided after about 1984, the recent movement was, as we have noted, very short-lived. Although it built up over about six months, its decline was extremely rapid.

The reasons for this difference are obviously connected to the nature of the realities against which the movements were protesting. The nuclear disarmament movements of the 1980s took their cue from NATO's November 1979 decision to introduce new intermediate-range Pershing II and cruise missiles into six Western European countries. The decisions required several years of preparations, and in some cases parliamentary approvals, to be implemented. Until missiles were actually installed, it remained possible to block their installation on a country-by-country basis. National elections provided focal points for opposition: it was not until after conservative victories in German and British elections in the first half of 1983 that the decisions taken by NATO were clearly secure, and in the Netherlands it was 1986 before there was a national basis to go ahead.

In the case of actual wars, rather than weapons decisions, clearly the dynamics are different. In none of the Western wars of the last two decades, to which I referred above, was the build-up period to conflict longer than six months. In all cases, the main phase of armed conflict was even shorter, no more than three months, and military success more or less complete and (apparently) relatively low-cost in terms of life. Despite (or because of) huge and intensive bombardments, only around one hundred fifty Americans and forty Britons died in the main phase of combat in Iraq, and many of these were casualties of accidents and from 'friendly fire'. Civilian deaths have been estimated in a range of 6,100-7,800 (Iraq Body Count, 2003). Iraqi military deaths are unnumbered.

In contrast, the Vietnam War had been prolonged, costly and unsuccessful: the main phase of US involvement lasted a decade, from 1965 to 1975, there were several peaks of fighting, and tens of thousands of US military personnel died together with hundreds of thousands of Vietnamese fighters and civilians. A huge anti-war movement arose, the most important political movement in the USA since the Second World War and one with worldwide ramifications, linked in the minds of many establishment figures to adverse media coverage in the first 'television war'. In fact, academic studies (e.g. Hallin, 1986; Mandelbaum, 1987) showed that adverse coverage mostly followed rather than caused military difficulties and political opposition to the war.

However, it was from the understanding of the 'Vietnam syndrome' as a product of television coverage that the US and other Western governments concluded that it was necessary to avoid long wars and large-scale casualties, and to manage media coverage to avoid damaging political effects. Hence the (so far mostly successful) preference of the USA, UK and NATO for quick military fixes, through intense, mostly aerial bombardment (although in Iraq artillery was also important), risking relatively few military lives. And hence the evolution, through the Falklands, Gulf and Kosovo campaigns, of a model of media management that attempted to direct journalistic attention and (in the latter two cases) massage the effects of Western military action on local civilians.

It was these models of combined war fighting and media control that were deployed in Iraq to limit the war. Although the Iraqi resistance in the second week of the war encouraged critics to believe that they would not be so successful this time, in the event the USA was able to prevail (to the extent of overthrowing Saddam and gaining overall control of Iraq) even more quickly than in 1991. It seems improbable that any anti-war movement could have made great headway in these conditions: focused on preventing the war, the movements were largely irrelevant once the war was begun; and calling for 'stopping the war', they had little to contribute once Bush's forces sped towards their 'victory'. Thus the difficulties of any anti-war movement in contemporary conditions are starkly underlined. Despite the largest mobilization in recent history (and huge international political opposition), the USA was undeterred. Only if this mobilization had gained overwhelming ground where it mattered to Bush politically (i.e. in US public opinion) would it have been likely to make a difference to the outcome. Alternatively, only if the war had (like Vietnam) lasted years rather than months, had gone badly for the USA and had led to very substantial (and apparently pointless) deaths, would the movement have been likely to impact on the actual outcome of the war.

Dynamics of demonstration movements and global mass media

I have suggested that mainstream media (television, newspaper and radio) coverage of the 2003 anti-war movement was probably uniquely favourable. It has long been an article of faith in all protest movements that 'the media' are a homogenous, hostile force, which misrepresents and distorts their aims. While studies have shown that there is truth in these beliefs (most stations and papers usually take their cues more from governments and corporations than from protestors), they nonetheless obscure the fundamental dependence of many late modern social movements on mainstream mass media. Without media coverage, would movements – especially protest movements – be able to develop with the rapidity that we saw in the recent Iraqi conflict?

To appreciate the significance of media to late-modern movements, let us consider the very different situation a century ago. Early modern social movements, especially labour movements, parties and unions, developed in the nineteenth century at a time when the press was much more restricted and electronic media had not been invented. They developed extensive face-to-face organization, based on elaborate hierarchical structures of local, regional, national and international organization. Alongside and through these structures, they also developed their own media of communication – labour and socialist newspapers that were widely read in the working class. The German workers' movement, in many ways the prime model, was famously analysed by Roberto Michels (1915) as a state within a state. Later analyses of the Western working class in its formative and classical periods before the Second World War emphasised its 'hermetic', closed world (Anderson and Nairn, 1965).

Media, as well as political developments, in the twentieth century transformed this situation. Many historic labour movements, like Germany's, were in any case destroyed or weakened by totalitarianism and war. Electronic media (radio, cinema and television) developed either as state monopolies or as commercial enterprises, largely bypassing traditional workers' movements. Labour papers tended to pass out of movement hands – Britain's *Daily Herald*, metamorphosing into the *Sun* and eventually becoming the tabloid flagship of Rupert Murdoch's media empire, is the most notorious case. Where workers' organizations survived or revived, they did so utilizing their traditional organizational and cultural structures. The functions of labour movements, institutionalised in wage-negotiation, electioneering, etc., enabled such resilience despite often hostile mass media.

The 'new' social movements that developed from the mid-1950s onwards were of a different type. Although they tended, as Parkin and others noted, to be strongly based on the 'middle class' (more specifically, the educated, professional and state-employed middle class, including students), their aims were not to represent that class as such. They had no 'natural' social functions embedded in the ongoing self-organization of a social group, comparable to those of unions, or in institutionalised politics, like parties. Instead, these movements were often organized around specific goals – opposition to nuclear weapons, apartheid and racial discrimination, wars, environmental pollution, etc. – that were in principle of concern to people of any group. Only some 'new' movements sought to organize groups, like women and gays, who were previously largely unorganized, and to represent their specific values and interests.

Because these movements were organized around specific issues, or sought to organize very broad unorganized groups that did not always have 'natural' foci for organization, they nearly always relied significantly on mass media to gain public attention. The British Campaign for Nuclear Disarmament (CND) for example, the first major anti-nuclear weapons organization at the centre of the 1958-64 'Ban the Bomb' movement, was launched through letters in the press (Taylor, 1988). Although CND later evolved a local group structure, its leaders saw it from the start as a public actor establishing its presence through established institutions – parties, churches, unions, etc., as well as the media. However, as CND became the centre of a social movement, mobilizing people into action on the streets, it also became more rather than less dependent on mass media. Press and, increasingly, television coverage of demonstrations were a powerful mobilizer of new people onto future demonstrations, alongside the sort of direct propaganda (leaflets, local meetings, etc.) that CND itself produced. Interestingly, the more direct forms of action favoured by the more radical wing of the movement (sit-downs, blockades, etc.) were ones which were more likely to have visual impact in the new medium of television (which took off in Britain after 1955) than the more traditional, law-abiding actions initiated by the CND establishment. Although radicals were more suspicious of the media, their mobilizations depended considerably on the notoriety that civil disobedience brought them in the newspapers and television news. Although mainstream media may have largely represented these events in negative, censorious terms, sympathisers (especially young people) would often deconstruct these accounts, so that notoriety only increased their attraction.

Since demonstration-based movements often launched actions at short notice in response to events that were reported in the media, they were often equally dependent – before the internet – on media to publicise what they were planning. As a local and regional organizer of European Nuclear Disarmament and CND in the early 1980s, I would send out written notices of events and activate 'telephone trees' that would spread urgent information quickly to activists. However I always knew that a mention in the local newspaper or on the radio would be a more effective mobilizer, reaching a larger number of people and giving the action more credibility than something publicised only via movement channels. Television and the press were vital for building the dynamics of demonstration movements. The success of one march, reported in the media, often leads to significantly increased turnouts for future demonstrations. Even negative coverage can draw in wider circles of sympathisers: they learn that they are not alone, that others are already acting, and that action is publicly significant.

There is therefore a cycle of demonstration-coverage, larger demonstration-even greater coverage, even larger demonstration, and so on, up to the point where the maximum marching constituency has been mobilized, or it is clear that goals are not going to be met, or activists become exhausted, or some combination of these factors. It is noteworthy that Mandelbaum (1987), in generally dismissing the idea that television coverage 'caused' the US failure in Vietnam, nevertheless credited it with one major effect: to fan the cycle of anti-war protests. This demonstration-media cycle also operates internationally, as stories and pictures of demonstrations in one country encourage people in others to follow suit. Thus in the 1960s, the first television decade across the Western world, anti-Vietnam War and student protests spread rapidly from the USA to Europe, Japan and beyond. These effects can be seen in the very rapid build-up of protests against the Iraq war: however the cycle was cut off by the launching of the war and the rapid success of the US and UK forces.

Changing Politics, Organization and Media of Peace Protest

Although we can trace major similarities between peace movements in the 1960s and today, it is clear that much has changed. Important changes in the media of communication certainly facilitate protest. The internet enables activist groups and movement organizations to make their ideas available directly to potential sympathisers via websites, and to communicate instantly with large numbers of supporters via email (the telephone tree seems like a technique from another age). Of course, it is very obvious that globalisation of communications has facilitated global protest. (The paradox of 'anti-globalisation' activists 'using' globalisation has become a well-worn cliché of journalists writing about the movement). Movements' web presences may also strengthen their visibility in the mainstream media, since it becomes much easier for journalists to obtain authoritative statements of movement goals, contact activists, etc. Moreover, in the worlds of television and newspapers that are ever more niche-oriented, any sizeable activist cause is likely to find outlets that will cater for its views and activities.

Nevertheless, the virtual disappearance of the anti-war movement, with which I began this essay, underlines the fact that technical fixes are not enough, and cannot offset funda-mental political difficulties. Peace politics has become more complicated in the last decade, and not only due to the USA's invention of the 'quick fix war'. During the Cold War, the over-riding threat of nuclear destruction appeared to simplify much of the politics of peace. The slogan 'Better Red than Dead' was maliciously attributed to pacifists, but it did sum up (in a distorted way) the simple fact that the threat of the total destruction of human society seemed to negate any possible political goal for which it might be carried out. Of course, nuclear pacifism still allowed other wars to be fought, and peace politics itself was divided between pacifists who supported no wars and revolutionaries who supported wars of national liberation and other struggles against Western and colonial power. However the Cold War meant that peace politics tended to be the province of those who opposed the West's world role as well as its nuclear strategy.

Even during the Cold War, peace movements struggled with the paradoxes of this posi-tion. In the 1980s, the emergence of opposition within the Soviet bloc highlighted the con-tradictions in the Western nuclear disarmament movement's tendency to reduce the Cold War to an 'equal' conflict over weapons. Eastern European oppositionists often demanded that Western activists support their demands for human rights and what would now be called 'regime change' (Kaldor, 1990). The Western movements were increasingly divided between those who emphasised the linkage of human rights and democracy in the Soviet bloc with nuclear disarmament in dismantling the Cold War (see e.g. Edward Thompson's 1982 polemic), and those who felt that linkage diluted the core issue of nuclear disarma-ment. The irony of the decade was that the Western movement was largely defeated, and declined, after 1984; the Cold War unwound afterwards as a result of elite détente between Mikhail Gorbachev and Ronald Reagan, beginning around 1986; and it was the seeds sown by the small groups of dissidents that sprouted into the massive democracy movements in countries like East Germany and Czechoslovakia, definitively ending the Cold War in 1989. The decade began with mass protest movements against nuclear weapons in Western European capitals; it ended with mass democracy movements in Eastern European capitals. The links between the two were essential to ending the Cold War.

This dilemma has been magnified in the 'new wars' (as Kaldor, 1999, has called wars that combine international and civil conflict based on identity politics) of the 1990s and 2000s. Anti-war movements have tended to respond to specific Western campaigns as dis-crete events (for example, the small protest movements against the Gulf, Kosovo and Afghan wars; the huge movement over Iraq). However these campaigns have often been responses to crises that lie within state and society in the zone of conflict. And the effect of Western military intervention is often to transform those crises.

Anti-war movements focused exclusively on 'stopping the war' often appear naïve in their attitudes to underlying conditions. Thus my study of the peace movement in 1990 showed that the movement had no answers to the new problems posed by the Iraqi rebel-lions and Saddam Hussein's repression immediately after the Gulf War (Shaw, 1996). The recent movement against the USA's Iraqi war was effective in highlighting the lack of legiti-macy in the manifest case for war, based on 'weapons of mass destruction'. It did not, how-ever, offer a credible answer to the underlying issue of the war, namely the totalitarian regime of Saddam, and the latent case (often stressed by Bush and Blair) for removing this regime. Thus the curious divergence between the demands of Western-left and Islamist anti-war activists and the ambivalence felt by many Iraqi exiles (not to mention activists within Iraq), who willed the USA to remove their torturer. The anti-war movement was effective, but it would have been more so if it had actually advocated a credible alternative method of removing Saddam. But that would have taken the movement into the complex politics of the United Nations, sovereignty and international justice, which was probably impossible for a very loose and broad coalition to achieve.

Likewise, as I pointed out above, a simple demand to 'stop the war' left the movement with little to say when the USA predictably did the stop the war, having claimed 'victory' over Saddam, after barely four weeks. This was, of course, the point at which the contradictions of US policy were most sharply revealed. The administration that had spent tens of billions of dollars preparing for war had spent only a tiny fraction of this preparing for post-war administration. The USA had not put planning and resources into restoring basic services, so that electricity and clean water continued to be cut off from millions of Iraqis – not for days, but for weeks and months after the 'victory'. Trigger-happy US troops were quick to shoot Iraqi civilians and ask questions after. Despite the obvious contradictions between different Iraqi factions, the USA had little idea of how to go about constructing a new Iraqi government. Law and order proved fragile, and killings both of US soldiers and of Iraqis continued at a serious rate not just in the immediate aftermath of the war, but for a long time afterwards. (This is written in September 2003, five months after the USA's success, and there appears no early end to any of these problems). Thus the continuing crisis of Iraqi society and politics posed many issues that a movement that had opposed war should have contributed to. Once again, however, the seeming necessity of simple focus in 'movement' politics made such a contribution difficult, if not impossible, to achieve.

One conclusion that we could draw is that a mass demonstration movement is a blunt instrument. In an intense crisis, which poses one seemingly simple question above all others, such movements offer ways in which large numbers of people can offer an answer, and influence more conventional political processes in parliaments, governments etc. But when issues become more complex, and the single question is replaced by many questions, this kind of movement could be less relevant. Indeed we could posit a functional specialisation, since clearly while movements as such often don't offer more complex answers, organizations that are related to and overlap with them – NGOs – do develop more sophisticated and complex analyses and recommendations, and offer alternative, more consistent modes of ongoing pressure. The history of activism, like that of media, in the last two decades could be seen as a movement towards more sophisticated, diverse and specialised forms of action and organization.

However an alternative answer to the limitations of protest movements is that, even within these constraints, they often suffer from over-simplified politics. As in the 1980s, it actually weakens the cause of peace if movements don't offer alternatives to war rather than a simple 'no'. In the twenty-first century, the protagonists in local conflicts, like Saddam's regime, are often perpetrators of gross human rights abuses or even genocidists. It is not enough to say that the West should not wage war against them, and to say this is an issue for their own people: they need to be removed from power and the world community has a duty of solidarity with the oppressed. Simple anti-Western politics, such as fuelled much of the organizing of anti-war protests, are not enough.

Anti-War and Other Social Movements
This essay started by arguing that we need to take the specific characters of social movements seriously: a 'one size fits all' analysis will not work. However, it is obvious that anti-war movements do not exist in a vacuum, unrelated to other kinds of contemporary social movement. The movement against the Iraq War clearly mobilized networks and constituencies that had already been mobilized, not only by earlier campaigns against the US war in Afghanistan, but also by the 'anti-globalization' movement which had organized a new generation of young activists since the late 1990s. Indeed, this relationship repeated a general pattern throughout the history of 'new' social movements in the second half of the twentieth century. There has been constant cross-fertilization of ideas, tactics and activists, so that one movement often leads to another.

However, the specific form of each movement depends on its aims and the structural conditions to which it responds. As I have argued elsewhere (Shaw, 1994), some movements, like the movement against the Iraq War, respond to very specific crises. This means that they tend to be narrowly focussed and find it difficult, as movements, to go beyond their initial objects. Other movements (historically women's movements are good examples) are more diversely based in a range of issues. Clearly the 'anti-globalization' movement is closer to the latter model, which may be why it has lasted longer than the anti-war movement. However the 'anti-globalisation' movement was also, arguably, very incoherently focused, so much that 'anti-globalization' was an inherently implausible idea – not just because activists needed the technology and infrastructure of globalization, but also because global change also offers possibilities for progressive development (as some activists with the new preference for 'global justice movement' use as a way of describing it).

Conclusions
This essay has used a discussion arising from the anti-war movement over Iraq to advance arguments about the changing relations of social movements, media and global politics. Historically, modern social movements (in the nineteenth and early twentieth centuries) were strongly rooted in subordinate classes in national societies. Their aims centred on class interests and international issues in relation to these; they were closely linked to class-based parties; and their modes of action integrated their social bases through face-to-face organization and printed media. Late modern ('new') movements (in the second half of the twentieth century), in contrast, were based primarily among educated middle class youth. Their aims centred on universal, chiefly global issues; they integrated their bases both through more flexible modes of organization and via mass media dominated by television; and they were often successful to the extent that they pursued single issues free from party agendas.

I have suggested that in the post-1989 global era, simultaneous changes in the political and media contexts have created a crisis of movement activism, with major new challenges and opportunities. The argument of this paper is that so far movements have responded better to new media than to the transformed political and ideological conditions of the global era. While some herald a new era of movement activism in the twenty-first century, I shall contend that movement politics remains in crisis: the changed political environment has created political and organizational dilemmas that movements have not and may not overcome.

This article was first published in Wilma de Jong, Neil Stammers and Martin Shaw, eds., *Global Activism: Global Media* (Pluto Press, 2004, London). Published with the permission of Pluto Press.

REFERENCES

Anderson, P. and Nairn, T. *Towards Socialism* (Fontana, 1965).

Hallin, D. *The "Uncensored War": the Media and Vietnam* (Oxford University Press, 1983, New York).

Inglehart, R. *The Silent Revolution: changing values and political styles among Western Publics* (Princeton University Press, 1977).

Iraq Body Count. *www.iraqbody.count.net* (accessed 2 September, 2003).

Kaldor, M. *Europe from Below: an East-West Dialogue* (Verso, 1990).

Kaldor, M. *New and Old Wars: Organized Warfare in the Global Era* (Polity, 1999).

Mandelbaum, M. "Vietnam: the television war", *Daedalus*, III (1987) pp. 4, 157-69.

Mattausch, J. *A Commitment to Campaign: a sociological study of CND* (Manchester University Press, 1989).

Michels, R. *Political Parties: a Sociological Study of the Oligarchical Tendencies of Modern Democracy* (Dover, 1959 [1915], New York).

Parkin, F. *Middle Class Radicalism: the Social Bases of the British campaign for Nuclear Disarmament* (Manchester University Press, 1968).

Shaw, M. "Civil Society and Global Politics: Beyond a Social Movements Approach", *Millenium: Journal of International Studies* 23, 3 (1994) pp. 647-68.

Shaw, M. *Civil Society, Media and Global Crises: Representing Distant Violence* (Pinter, 1996, London).

Taylor, R. *Against the Bomb: the British peace movement, 1958-1965* (Clarendon Press, 1988).

Thompson, E.P. *Beyond the Cold War* (European Nuclear Disarmament, 1982, London).

IMAGE
Disturbance

Let us Become Children!
Training, Simulations and Kids

KRISTIAN LUKIC

There are lots of theories and analyses around the current 'War against Terrorism', and discussions about war against sovereign countries, reduction of human rights, insecurity and many other different questions. During warfare, it's 'normal' that State Securities practice censorship, and that media and press freedom is more or less reduced. Also, public media receives information from army press conferences and spokesmen, completely non-objective and tendentious. War propaganda is nothing new. From ancient wars till now, propaganda served the need to strengthen combat lines, to encourage warriors and the people, and to demoralize enemy forces. And with the rise of nation states, the ideological element becomes most important in the times of big national mobilizations.

It's interesting to see how certain war propaganda materializes itself today, and through which medium targets whom. In today's globalized networked capitalism, when tautology – 'everything is connected with everything' – tries to relativize any kind of deep research and traceability, it is important to focus more and to read between the lines.

Story

Hari Kunzru has written in an essay, "Beyond Good and Evil",[1] about the connection between the boom of fantasy literature and the 'War against Terrorism' (referring to JK Rowling's *Harry Potter* series, Tolkien's revival of *Lord of the Rings* and the lesser-known *Dark Materials* trilogy by Philip Pullman). For instance, Tolkien's *Lord of the Rings* revival is coming thirty years after it was popular in counterculture in the sixties, with its simple ethico-political categories. Sauron's nihilism, Saruman's polluting heavy industry, feverish productivity, and alienated Asiatic hordes are an analogy for evil dehumanized industry; on the other side, it is quite easy to recognize the Shire as an organic pastoral community under threat. Kunzru emphasizes "full-scale breakout from speculative fantasies, home in the airbrush/metal-head underground". He explains that the boom of fantasy literature, alternate worlds, and visionary romance draws its energy from a contemporary desire for moral clarity in situations of clearly drawn conflict.

Bush's phrase 'Axis of evil' is similar to slogans during WWII, or young, campus readings of Tolkien. Blair claims that there is no moral ambiguity in today's 'War against Terrorism', that is to say we can't dwell on whether or not our decision is righteous if we are resolutely determined to defeat the enemy. Terrorist, Bin Laden, Saddam Hussein, Orcs, Voldemort, Azkaban...it's all the same. In *Harry Potter*, the evil magician Voldemort, obsessed by the purity of blood, wants to destroy 'mixed' ones. On the side of the Good is Dumbledore, a wizard who is for democratic principles, for intercultural dialogue, against death as punishment and against repressive methods. Consequently, the fanaticism that characterizes Voldemort and his followers corresponds with common prejudices about Islam as a religion of exclusions and of radical religious fanaticism.

The movie industry has been, for a century now, a strong psycho-ideological weapon of the state, often using sophisticated methods to shape certain ideological frameworks. *Lord of the Rings* and *Harry Potter* are breaking sales records with hundreds of millions of dollars only from cinema distribution; there are also the DVD distribution and brand-image marketing sections. Extremely long (for example *Lord of the Rings*, part three is of 3h 40 min duration), in a way these are contemporary Great stories, sagas like Wagner's operas whose durations too were sometimes more than several hours.

Content wise, it is interesting that in these movies Evil is presented with great energy and obsession extremely powerful and brutal.

Connected with post 9/11 trauma, a fantasy literature and movies avalanche brought about deep existential worries in their audiences: us or them? In the *Lord of the Rings* trilogy, the Evil enemy is purified; and one can say that evil in these visualizations is so described, and total in such a deep sense, that we cannot even communicate with it. The logic of narration doesn't allow us to approach the forces of Evil. Evil is without doubt, and in this way, transcendent; it is beyond our experience and reasonable perception and understanding. This evil is so powerful and omnipresent that is impossible to stop it and destroy it. It is impossible to perceive it with rational logic.

Similar things happened in the beginning of the war in Yugoslavia in the nineties. When official Yugoslav socialist ideology started to decline in the eighties, there were more and more publications that sought to explain the evil past and future destiny of the Balkan peoples. Suddenly, people realized that Serbs have been victims from the longest time, from the famous Kosovo defeat in 1389 by evil Turks, until genocide committed by Croats and others during WWII. The year 1389 was like 9/11 in USA, a shifting point in history when the linearity of space-time continuum was broken. After that, everything was different, and as everything had been allowed as revenge for those horrors and sufferings. When Slobodan Milosevic came to power, an increasing range of occult, pseudo-religious groups and individuals started to show up on state TV to explain the universal position of Serbian people in the past, present and future without clearly differentiating between all these times. This was a mixture between real global and local socio-political facts and persons, military traditions, saints, heroes and kings from national history, and mythical creatures like dragons and vampires. There was the astrologist Milja Vujanovic who explained that the Pentagon is a symbol for the pentagram, G7 is the seven-headed dragon from Saint John's Gospel, and so on. The painter Milic od Macve proclaimed himself the Baron Lepenski, leader of world vampires. He accused America of wanting to destroy the Serbs, and threatened that if America would not help Serbia, Serbia would make a deal with Japan to build the New Byzantium. He also sent a squad of vampires to destroy America.

Milja Vujanovic had a weekly evening prime-time slot on national TV. Milic od Macve was the first living artist to have a solo exhibition in the history of the National Museum in Belgrade. His exhibition was opened by the Minister of Culture of the Republic of Serbia and travelled all over Serbia; the estimated number of visitors was more than 350,000 (Serbia has around 10 million inhabitants), so it was approximately 3.5% of the population. Never has one art exhibition in Serbia, before or after, had so many visitors.

Slobodan Milosevic held his first big, successful meeting on Kosovo Field in 1989, where the legendary and symbolic Battle of Kosovo had been fought 600 years ago. This meeting was a gathering of Serbs from every corner of Yugoslavia and the world, bringing almost two million people in one place.

Fantasy literature has always existed in Western civilization, from early medieval King Arthur's and Holy Grail fantasies till the Tolkien worlds. But, from the end of the nineties, suddenly this literature starts to take on an immediate presence. Tolkien's *Lord of the Rings* was known, but not in the way that it is presented now. In the recent few years, the situation is such that an army of readers intensely awaits every new issue of JK Rowling's *Harry Potter*; the whole planet awaits the new episode of *Lord of the Rings* (it seems that this is the first truly globalized movie).

What is so special in this literature, these movies, and other things that connect with stories about a great battle with Evil? These kinds of scenarios where Good and Evil are fighting, in a way, have always been present.

(What connects all these movies together, at least, as well as the *Matrix* and the *Terminator,* is that the producer of all of these films is Warner Brothers, a company that is now a subsidiary of the huge merger of AOL Time Warner.)

Training
We are witnessing the fact that ICT (Information and Communication Technology) is rapidly growing and that tech products are changing very fast. People who are using computers have difficulty in gaining additional technological knowledge required for everyday activities; their skill upgradation is reduced, especially if they have learned different/obsolete applications that are not operable in the new operating environments. The system needs people who will learn faster and act resolutely.

Today's kids (significantly in North America and Europe) are growing up in front of their computers. Most have parents who are just computer-users, if barely that. These children are a population that naturally acquires knowledge fastest; the creativity of kids is a category that is omnipresent and universal. In the realm of cyberspace, kids are in their 'natural' environment, often exploring and challenging the potential of technologies and tools. Hackers and crackers have very often been children or young people.

Today's oft-repeated 'Revolution in warfare' becomes a mantra for contemporary warriors and leads to 'cyberwar', a war with advanced technological devices and tools. Fragile security in the networked world becomes the weak point of national security, when complex systems are connected and when strikes could be fast and almost invisible. For this, kids could be useful in collecting information, deciphering, breaking into the enemy's security systems or the interception of terrorists' communications. For all this information, missions and objectives, there is a special web site, the CIA KIDS Homepage, where you can find lots of useful information about the Agency, its goals, future activities and directions. There are also the nice movies *SpyKids* I, II and III (Twentieth Century Fox), now playing in your cinema, where children are agents working for the Agency, solving problems and saving the planet from fantasy creatures. In *Master and Commander* (Twentieth Century Fox) there is a young officer on a ship (a kid), who in a in moment of crisis in a sea battle takes on responsibility, fires a cannon and shoots the enemy's sail.

Kids, like dolphins, can be useful in protecting national security. Dolphins are used to carry bombs and with free will, like *kamikaze*, destroy enemy ships. Dolphins are smart, innocent and loyal. Like children.

Like with Frodo Baggins or Harry Potter, the time will come when the child will decide to be more active and take more concrete steps in defeating world evil. Then he/she (mostly he) will choose different training simulation applications. The training of children is highly advanced, with complex theory and practice involving numerous different disciplines such as psychology, fight experts, flight experts, strategic combat advisers, geopolitics, geography, history, weapon science, logic, religion, military strength and the constitution of different world armies, position and trade routes of oil, and other energetic resources.

So-called computer games like *Mortal Combat* or *Ultimate Fight* teach kids how to fight hand to hand; *Wolfenstein, Quake, Doom* and *Perfect Assassin* teach how to combat as an individual in real war combat experiences. For more organizational types and potential future managers or soldiers there are games like *Command and Conquer: Generals, Tiberian Sun, Generals, Age of Empires, Civilization, Ceasar*. In these games, children gain the skills of organizing and building citizens, troops, cities. You must defeat all your enemies, capturing their structures, facilities, cities, workers... Before each mission you receive your mission objective. This is, for example, one mission objective: "Hassan communicates to the Brotherhood through a nearby TV station. With the Brotherhood in chaos, the opportunity to divide Hassan from his followers presents itself. Capture the TV station and those ones loyal to Kane. The technology of peace will return to the fold. And as for Hassan's pathetic guards – crush them" (*Tiberian Sun*, © Westwood, Electronic Arts).

A special aspect is navigational training. There are different tutorials and training programs like: *FA-18 Korea, F-22 Air Dominance Fighter, F-16 Fighting Falcon, Euro Fighter 2000, Back To Baghdad* and *Flashpoint Kosovo* for flight combat simulations; *Armored Fist 2, M1A2 Abrams* for tanks; *688 (I) Hunter/Killer* for nuclear submarines. All these useful things can be found in every corner-shop selling games.

Long before movies and literature, in the realm of computer games, fictions and fantasies were in their natural environment. From the first games like *Warcraft, Heroes of Might and Magic*, till now, there have been hundreds of fantasy and mythological games produced. Some of them are: *Lands of Lore: Guardians of destiny, Realms of Arkania, Diablo, Legacy of Kain, Warlords, Lords of Magic, Blood & Magic, Lords of Realm, Warhammer: Dark Omen, Arthur's Knight's – Secrets of Merlin*. Also, we can't forget sport as a substitute for war where companies like Electronic Arts are dominant: *FIFA Soccer Series, NBA, NHL, Formula 1...*

As Isabel Smadja in her text *"Harry Potter* and the Forces of Evil"[2] points out, there have been numerous of examples of the economy of salvation in Judaeo-Christian history. But what is different now is that tasks, commands and missions in these novels and movies are undertaken by kids. In *Lord of the Rings*, there is a young Hobbit who has the task to save the World and defeat the enemy. In *Harry Potter* its the same, so in Philip Pullman's *Dark Materials*. And in lots of interesting new movies like *Terminator 3, Master and Commander, Spy Kids* I, II & III. Why suddenly so much focus on kids, and in such brutal environments?

After 9/11, the US apparently changed a lot. It was the first time after Pearl Harbour that the US was jeopardized to this extent. Today's generation doesn't remember WWII, and many of them not even Vietnam, so they don't have a real experience of war (for American citizens, the theatre wars around the globe in the 1980s and 1990s were legitimate police actions). The real results on the ground of US foreign policy during the nineties were mostly unknown to US citizens. Suddenly, 9/11 happened. People were living ordinary, usual ways, working and shopping, and that horrible thing happened. Evil people attacked a peaceful people, a peaceful and decent people who would never kill an ant. Why? Can this be rationally explained? You behave all your life as good and charitable, and somebody attacks you? All the time you are proclaiming democracy and peaceful solutions all over the planet, and it returns to you in this way. This must to be punished; it needs revenge. In order to revenge, an eye for an eye, a tooth for a tooth, you must abandon your democratic reasonable heritage, you must behave as a child, with heart, with honesty and without scruples. You need to become a child. A child that has the right to revenge, that has the privilege to react with anger. But a child that is able to take responsibility – a responsibility that in the right moment can execute its task in order to protect the community.

NOTES

1. Kunzru, Hari. "Beyond Good and Evil", *Mute Magazine* (May, 2002).
2. Smadja, Isabelle. "Harry Potter and the forces of Evil", *Le Monde Diplomatique* (December, 2002).
   <http://mondediplo.com/2002/12/>

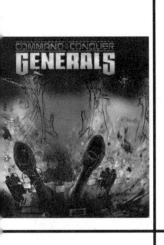

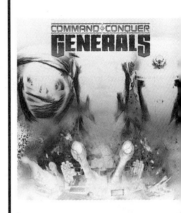

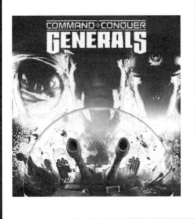

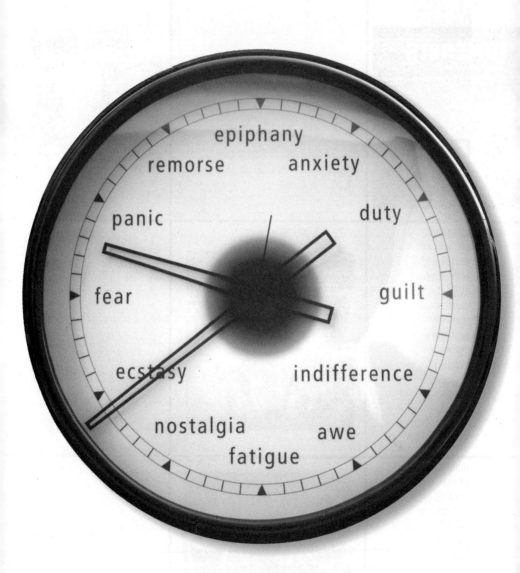

What is to be Done?

BHRIGUPATI SINGH

Everywhere we turn, the intolerable has become a permanent state of daily banality. This turning is our cue to investigate crisis-media, in between and within ourselves. What is to be done? There are those who yearn for the dictates of a set of transcendental principles, or the stricter enforcement of an existing moral law. Nothing could be more detrimental. Remember that the Bush apparatus invaded Afghanistan, attacked Iraq, showered bombs accompanied by the twin war cries: Human Rights! Democracy! There are others who would immediately decry such a move: once you disable transcendence, what are you left with? "You have flattened out the terrain", they would say, "to the point where anything goes". Nothing could be more absurd. To be done with morality is not to be done with ethics. To subvert transcendent judgment is not to end the possibility of immanent evaluation (i.e. to refuse the *a priori* distinctions of 'good' and 'evil' is not to disable the investigation of 'good' and 'bad'). This essay sets up certain concepts of the term 'crisis', primarily what shall be called the 'anxiety of incipience', while simultaneously evaluating the problem of machine-becoming, or the non-human as posed by two films, *The Matrix* (most significantly in the first film of the trilogy), and Quentin Tarantino's recently released *Kill Bill, Vol.1*. This is done keeping in mind an inheritance, however bastardized, of voices and echoes from Western philosophy, in posing one of its oldest questions; namely, the relationship between ethics, aesthetics and politics, the three great books of Aristotle. This, then, is an essay of philosophy, in the most traditional sense of the term.

Virtual, Potential, Possible, Actual, Eventual

There are constantly overlapping distinct levels of being in which we participate. The 'we' is quite open here: it could include a human being, a particular combination of words, a sack of rice, a horse, a bicycle, a gesture, a computer, a police report and so on. Call these intersecting levels: the virtual, the potential, the possible, the actual and the eventual (moving in two divergent and related series: the virtual-potential and the possible-actual-eventual). For our purposes here, it is sufficient to work seriously with only the latter concepts: the potential, the possible, the actual and the eventual (the virtual being the whole composed of infinite singularities). These cannot be 'defined,' but their relations can be mapped: the potential requires conditions of possibility – a concrete assemblage – to be captured and brought into the actual. And so something (a memory, a particular strand of amoebae, a legal document, a particularly virulent form of political association, etc.) can lie dormant, subsisting at the level of potential; particular conditions of possibility might wrench it into the actual.

However, what re-appears is never the 'same'. Difference precedes repetition. This is a theory of becoming, of the evented-ness of the everyday: specific movements and particular combinations produce the singularity of events in conjunction with apparatuses of capture and blockage in relation to a whole that is open. This is an ontology of movement: difference precedes repetition; movement precedes stasis. Change and instability, chaos and complexity, contingency and unpredictability: these do not catch us off guard; rather we learn to work with the fact of their open limits, as scientists have been learning to do for some time now.[1] What accompanies this is less a set of moral principles and more an ethics of becoming, of potentialities. Politics is the relationship between the actual and the eventual, less what we 'are' in our separateness (the source of 'identity' politics, each of us sealed off in our hermetic particularities) and more what we are in the process of becoming, or what we might enable differently, becoming-together, in our relatedness. This is post-finalist, non-dialectical, non-Hegelian, anti-vanguardist. Have I been understood?

'We are in Crisis!'
Let us move closer to the immediate matter at hand. At the level of potential, the mass 'media' does anything but mediate. It directly instills and effectively circulates politically and morally operative affect. Then a 'crisis' of media is not a crisis of 'representations'; rather it is a crisis within and between ourselves. Altogether now: We are in crisis. Of this there is no doubt, regardless of who the 'we' are, or what the 'crisis' is. Right and left, liberal and conservative – almost anyone with an opinion is ready to make such a declaration (this should worry us, too). There are those who seek to put an end to this state of crisis. This is comical. If things take a turn for the worse, it turns tragic, or at its worst, it becomes horrifying (as is the case with 'final' solutions). There are infinite forms of crisis, and since we do not know in advance how things will turn out, the valence of the term need not necessarily be negative. At any given step, it is crucial to be able to sift the good from the bad in attaining the specificity of the problems invoked, the plane of immanence being constructed. And equally, to recognize that there will be no end to this fragility – this, if anything, is the one constant – for person, place, animal, thing. (Can we say that the affective desire to be invulnerable, to be rid of all threats, to be 'safe' whatever the cost, is what convinces ordinary Americans into war, even those who are not interested in oil or money? This would then be the nation's primary social sickness, one that is aging it rapidly, eroding the possibility of freedom, the first premise and promise of its constitution. What cure does this require, and who among us is fit to administer it?).

Three Varieties of the Crisis: Accident, Erosion and the Anxiety of Incipience
Let us put it differently, bringing ourselves more firmly into the realm of the ordinary: at any given point (and a point is always one on a series), between any relation-assemblage (a couple, a group of people working in an office, a political party, a farmer tending crops), at the level of potential there is a set of crises that might happen. The rains might not come, a bomb might wipe out a building, funding for a program might suddenly be withdrawn, an accident might result in a death, etc. These are big contingencies, a 'what if…' unpredictability. Different from these, and more difficult to spot, are the smaller crises that take

place at the level of the ordinary or the everyday in the realm of possibilities and actualities: unmelodramatic, uneventful, those that arrive almost unnoticed. This is the realm of something that 'might...begin to happen' through a process of erosion, entropy or decline. A creative collaboration might gradually wither, the loss of one element might slowly make a larger assemblage less joyful, banal repetition might dull a set of words, a niggling problem might start that will explode at an unnameable future date, an alteration in external conditions might render an older set of excitements redundant. Crises such as these require constant alertness to the level of the possible-actual (towards the eventual): the realm of possibilities within oneself and others, an attentiveness to the unnoticeably shifting contours of the everyday. This is why for Cavell, as for Deleuze, love, or philosophy, or revolution, is an ongoing journey requiring constant work, and not something that ends happily ever after, all at one go. And so we must keep turning the ground on which we walk, since in most cases the ice is thin; our conclusions being findings, rather than permanent foundations, temporary points of rest ('finding as founding'): a junction of interactions (a *sarai?*) rather than a fixed address.

But what we are centrally concerned with here is a crisis of another kind, related and distinct from the first two varieties, albeit equally difficult to spot – subsisting at a different level from either accident or erosion, both of which remain at the level of the possible, as outlined above. This third form of crisis is at the level of potential, which has not yet made it into the realm of the possible: not one but rather a mess of crises – inarticulate, vaguely proto-formed – that subsist below the level of consciousness. Diagnosing these requires intuition or perhaps foresight (*divyadrishti?*) as much as attentiveness, since the realm of potential demands a different mode of engagement than the possible-actual. With *The Matrix* we will attempt to delineate one such not-yet fully formed crisis, taking it to be a source of nervousness: call this the anxiety of incipience. Rather than being about 'uncertainty' per se, this has more to do with the constitutively vague and nervous certainty that things are rapidly changing, moving in ways over which we have very little control. This is the realm of affect, ontologically prior to cognition (thus it is completely beside the point whether any existing persons, or the people who brought these films into actuality ever thought of them in this way). A different but related point: with a crisis or an attempted diagnosis of its form comes a certain horror of the actual – we might even call it revulsion – a dismay with the way we find the world as it presently exists. This is an impulse to be found in philosophers as different as Marx, Nietzsche and Wittgenstein, and we find its presence in different forms, both within *The Matrix* and *Kill Bill*. Let us map the trajectory of these questions, starting with *The Matrix*.

The Anxiety of Incipience

Bodies, organic and inorganic, are involved in productive combinations. Call these combinations machinic phylum. A human body, a horse and a saddle are a particular combination that at a certain point in history created a new form of war. A different combination and a different set of possibilities reside in a man, a spade and a piece of land. Or a hand and a ball point pen; an eye, a camera and a situation; a screen, an interface, fingers and a brain. All of these are machinic phylum, vaguely or sometimes quite specifically dateable events in world history. Every time a new machinic phylum is produced, it alters the world ever so slightly. When it occurs (in nature, in technology, in art, and where else?) we can say that 'newness' has come into the world. In modernity, such alterations are taking place at an exponentially advancing speed (witness the effects produced by the internet and digital technologies in less than a decade). 'The modal conversion of the human has sensibly begun'. This has always been the case in varying degrees. These conversions, often unnoticeable in their ubiquity, occasion anxieties about speed, survival and adaptation that percolate between different points, lines and surfaces.

Keeping this in mind, let us come to *The Matrix* series, among the highest grossing Hollywood films of recent years. These films set off a not-so glamorous set of debates in philosophy departments across Europe and America. It was, after all, the cinematic articulation of the central concern of scepticism, or sceptical doubt regarding reality (How can I be certain of this world's presence to me? Or of its nature, and who controls it?), the advent of which in Descartes inaugurates modern Western philosophy. But let us enter *The Matrix* from a completely different angle, starting not from philosophy's internal emergencies (which are not completely different from those of other domains, say religion or politics – who is in charge of this world? – this is everyone's question and no one's, from Pope John Paul to Noam Chomsky. Whose answer will assuage our suspicion?), but rather let us take cinema's anxiety regarding itself and its own survival, since this is what *The Matrix* is potentially about.

Every mass-produced technological upheaval affords us a form of pleasure specific to its machinic capabilities. Thus, the printing press yields the novel. The machinery of the industrial revolution, in conjunction with other visual technologies, yields the cinema. This sort of a major aesthetic pleasure-form (with its specificity, its own artistes, publics and forms of criticism) is yet to be invented for the internet, which in itself, as a technology, is qualitatively different enough from most of what preceded, or informed it, as ingredients. As yet we don't know what that art form might be. But we can conjecture based on possibilities. We might say, for example, that it will have to combine two different kinds of present experiences, both of which are still at a highly nascent stage. The first is the high-end 'virtual reality' video game in which you plug in and participate. As of now, participation in this form still requires the interface of a screen. This node will develop to the point where you can close your eyes and plug into it directly, without a screen. Doing this will both require and enable a significant shift in the image-brain/matter-neuron interaction around which cinema, or television for that matter, are structured. But there will have to be a second, equally important aspect of this art form-to-be. One might notice that people don't like to be alone in an aesthetic experience; they need either the imagined community of the novel or television, or the physical audience of a cinema hall: some kind of an actual collectivity in either case with whom this experience is shared as it takes place. To negotiate this desire, our future art form will then have to combine the possibilities offered by the high-end virtual reality game with the present actuality of the internet chat room, i.e. the possibility that one could interact with 'others' whom we believe to have some kind of empirical existence, and with whom (once we are outside this game/art form) we could possibly discuss our experiences or the story/events that took place. Perhaps I could log on from

India and enter a story line with a friend in Brazil. Or alternatively, I might enjoy the present anonymity of the internet chat room, mingling with total strangers. We realize immediately that this art form-to-be is not very different from 'the matrix' that we see in these films (with wires attached to your head, you plug in and move into a different world – interestingly, in the films you need a phone connection, an old style land line, to get out of the matrix i.e. to unplug the modem?). In effect, this internet art form-to-be will require a new man-machine relation; a new machinic phylum producing a new set of human capabilities. But it does not yet exist. What kind of collaborations will such an art form require to produce its conditions of possibility? One can only guess but some key participants will have to be computer scientists, mathematicians, neuroscientists, web designers, new media artists, fiction writers and so on.

But why is *The Matrix* so anxious about all this? Perhaps because it is still cinema. Cinema responds nervously to the arrival of the internet. This is a cinema of crisis, anticipating a shift internal to its trajectory of existence. Once this new internet art form, this fictional net-world, is invented, mass-produced and circulated within the circuits of capital (as some kind of an apparatus that we could bring home, from say, a supermarket), using which people from distant parts of the world might connect and experience a story together, cinema will lose its special place as a form of affective experience in modernity; a position already eroded considerably by the advent of television (several films a generation earlier already responded to that arrival) as a globally available, domestic apparatus, as well as accompanying material shifts the world over in the forms in which film is publicly available. This is then the crucial anxiety *The Matrix* virtually senses: the digital world of the internet and the potentially impending 'death' or loss of privilege of cinema as a material-aesthetic-technological-affective-popular form. In this experience of loss (of privilege, of an assured audience), in this crisis-ridden concern with its own survival, cinema comes closer than ever to philosophy. And this in, the first instance, is the cause of the unnatural affinity between *The Matrix* and Euro-American departments of philosophy, a point not unrelated to the threat of scepticism. This, then, is the anxiety of incipience.

Total War

It is time to insert a new variable into the discussion, Quentin Tarantino's *Kill Bill*. Martha Nussbaum's recent book, *Upheavals of Thought,* is a mediocre exploration of the question of compassion. Despite the non-stop carnage in the film, or precisely because of it, Tarantino can be seen to take up the exact same question, beginning from an inverted premise: *Kill Bill* is a universe completely without fellowfeeling and with relations of pure enmity. One of the first spoken sentences in the film is a voiceover while Uma Thurman is driving the stolen jeep. She remembers the teaching of her trainer, the sword-maker from Okinawa: "The first rule of war: you must banish all compassion for the enemy". This is a film about total war, "The state of emergency has become the rule rather than the exception. We are now living in a permanent state of exception" (Agamben's revival of the darker Cabalistic Benjamin seems to have struck a chord in the post 9/11 American academic left). Indeed, we are not asked to mourn even one of the many spectacular and violent deaths in the course of the film.

We might notice two regimes of the image in *Kill Bill*: (a) the documentary real (the facial close-ups of a battered Uma Thurman, her flashbacks, the police investigating the church in Texas where the mass murder took place, the comatose body at the hospital) and, (b) the comic fictional (karate films, Japanese animation art, techno-science special effects). Like many of the real wars around us, the momentum of Kill Bill is structured around an original injustice or wound. In the film, this first wound is the mass murder in the church, the attempted killing of Uma Thurman, compounded by the many humiliations she subsequently undergoes, followed by the slow, determined process by which revenge is exacted. Our preliminary identification with her (she is our narrative hook into the world of this film) is guided by this original wound, as its description is placed in regime (a), of the documentary real. Notice that the character played by Lucy Liu, whom she murders, also has a first wound (the murder of her parents by the head of the Japanese mafia), but this is narrated in regime (b), of the Japanese manga, since she is not our primary character.

The question of culpability, of punishment, haunts this world of war and of politics, democratic or otherwise. Who among us has a theory of forgiveness, whether it can be given, and in what way? In which cases is retaliatory violence justifiable? To right what wrong are you willing to stake your life? These are the central questions of a revenge narrative, as they are of 'humanitarian interventions' or of 'just' and 'unjust' wars, so much back in vogue amidst the stupidity that crowds American international relations theory. At some stage in the film, as Uma Thurman begins her murderous rampage, regime (a) and (b) begin to blur. Kill Bill is a film about war, inasmuch as war is about cycles of violence – as the victims of yesterday become the killers of today – part victims-part perpetrators (Is this also the story of Israel?) – leaving an opening for an equally violent future to come. In Kill Bill this opening is in the beginning of the film with the murder of the first 'enemy' in her own home, the black woman from the 'deadly viper squad' (which Uma Thurman used to be a part of, and which attacked her after she left it). There is an uneasy conversation, followed by a fight, in which each tries to kill the other. The killing takes place as the murdered woman's daughter accidentally bears witness to the act. Uma Thurman turns to the girl (whom we know from the previous scene is four years old, Lucy Liu's character was eight when her parents were murdered): "If you want to settle the score when you grow up, I'll be waiting for you," she tells the girl. Is Tarantino the patient, or is he the doctor of a sick America, and a sick world?

Two Varieties of the Non-Human: Machine-Becoming and the New Human
The second question of philosophy: What is it that distinguishes a human being from, say, an animal or a machine? (Consciousness? Compassion? Thinking? Are these satisfactory answers, or is the question not good enough?) Keeping this in mind, let us bring the two films together. The Matrix, like Kill Bill is about re-inhabiting a space of devastation (in the former, machines have taken over the world; in the latter, an attempted world has ceased to exist). Both re-inhabitations require that a war be waged. In both films, the wars are 'just' inasmuch as our sympathies lie on one side of the combat, the other side being inhuman, or non-human. The war against machines in The Matrix is fought to protect the human form of life. How is this battle waged, and what will lead to its resolution? Precisely by using, and in being used by, machines, and in Neo finding a new form of human life, part human-part machine, with a new set of capabilities. So, in The Matrix the proper defence of the human

form of life involves becoming part machine. There is a parallel to this in *Kill Bill*. Uma Thurman's character used to be part of the deadly viper squad, an elite corps trained to kill without compassion with great skill and technique – a group of machines, we might say. In leaving the squad, and getting married in a small church in Texas, she was attempting in some way to attain a human form of life. At this point, the deadly viper squad arrives to kill the entire marriage party, including her. She survives the attack and must exact her revenge by re-learning all her 'deadly viper' skills, including the forgetting of compassion. In other words, by becoming part-machine again. But this slight shift of emphasis – becoming something 'again' – makes all the difference in the world (and this is what philosophy, like politics, is all about: slight shifts in emphasis. As has been pointed out, in a given situation whether you place greater emphasis on 'liberty' or on 'equality' will determine whether your position is that of a liberal or a socialist. What are you willing to compromise?). In *Kill Bill* there is an exacting set of past skills to return to, but no world to re-inhabit. Not so in *The Matrix*: here there is no 'past' set of skills to return to, no ideal to which a return must be desired. Rather, something new must be 'found' because there is a world to re-inhabit. Neo is 'newness': *The Matrix* cuts a line of flight of becoming. *Kill Bill* has no becoming, no passages, nothing but a series of fights: visual-aesthetic clichés wholly without a soul. One could say that world history, as also its present, is composed of a series of fights. Or that the world has lost its soul. Or that people now speak in clichés. But what then is the value of pouring further clichés into that world? How do you distinguish the world's dehumanizing of its inhabitants from your depersonalizing of them? How do you know whether your asserted impossibility of love (of conversation), or of life, is anything more than an expression of your distaste for the difficulty of its tasks? To say that all these terrible things are common in our world (and commonly deserved, if you are inclined to think so) is not news and to spread its commonness is not art. Or rather, it is not art inasmuch as it is precisely that – 'news' – particularly, if you watch TV in America, a fascinating and vicious beast, unique in the world as far as I have seen. 'We need reasons to believe in this world': *The Matrix* struggles with this question, *Kill Bill* scorns it. None of this could have been said about *Pulp Fiction* or *Reservoir Dogs*, Tarantino's earlier films, in their wonderful intonations of speech and camaraderie, their reinvigoration of the gangster B-film genre, in their respective lines of flight from the aesthetic past they invoked.

The Question Concerning Technology
Re-entering the problem from a different angle, let us return to the question of 'crisis-media'. Central to the whole concept of 'crisis' is what was earlier called the 'horror of the actual': a dismay with the way we find the world as it presently exists. As aesthetic forms, the above films (since that is what they are, films and nothing more; but neither are they anything less) bear a certain relation to their surroundings: previous films, other forms of image circulation, television, video games, comic books, science fiction, technological developments, their own conditions of possibility, the world as an open totality (the world as a whole). In relation to its surroundings, *Kill Bill* faces the question of the image glut – everywhere we look we are surrounded by images of violence till we do not know how to tell the difference between provocation and titillation, how to prioritize the claims of suffering or whether we

actually care that the world exists at all, in its difficulties. In this regard, as a relation to the image, this film fails to sustain any possibility (let alone potentiality) inasmuch as it faces this question not with sorrow, but with derision. In a word, *Kill Bill* faces no crisis. No crisis – no necessity. No serious necessity, then no possibility of freedom (since without gravity there is no walking). *The Matrix*, on the other hand, is a film about 'crisis' at every level. It poses the question of the image glut not as one of effects ('images are proliferating', 'there is a lot of violence'), but rather it moves to causes: the question concerning technology. The battle within *The Matrix* between weaker man and stronger machines can be brought into actuality as such: Human beings are thrown into a world where technology has far outpaced our capacity to think about it, let alone handle it with ethical or pragmatic competence. The fact that one can now watch the news or be instantly aware of events in faraway places does not mean that we have begun to think any better about them. The fact that we are in touch with people in distant places faster than ever before doesn't necessarily mean that very many good conversations are taking place. The fact that the human genome is now open to perusal doesn't mean that thought and life have entered a better relation. How does *The Matrix* address this question? Clearly, it cannot 'answer' it. This was the disappointment many people incipiently felt with the final part of the trilogy, (appropriately called) *Revolutions*. There was no final answer. Should there be one? At the very least, we can witness the enormous suggestion present here at the level of potential. Once again let us ask, how does *The Matrix* approach this question? The suggestion: by putting itself into crisis, in relation to the past of its enterprise and the world as a whole, sensing thus the portent of the new, the arrival of newness and the anxiety of incipience. Will the emergent net-world, the potential (not-yet possible) art form-to-be have its internet version of the documentary film? In both genres of fiction and non-fiction, sitting in India, I could possibly make friends; inhabit a world together with someone in Brazil whom I don't yet know, releasing a truly post-national solidarity. In many ways this is already happening: to begin with, the emergence of something such as the World Social Forum. Is this a call for an alternative form of 'globalization'? Well, partly, but that is not the whole story: no dichotomy is more uninteresting than that of the 'local', as held in opposition to something called the 'global'. Or another relevant question: Is this an unabashed celebration of the internet, of the arrival of new technologies? Not really, because it is equally a mourning – keep in mind that a man, a spade and piece of land is equally a machinic phylum as is a group, a laboratory and a strand of DNA. We were always, and still are, part-machines, parts and wholes, in formation, in expression, in production. It would be more appropriate to say that this is an attempt to calculate the possibility of inhabiting 'proper' machinic phylums, since what inheres in the portent of the new, in the anxiety of incipience, constitutes both a threat and a possibility.

This is also a Marxist essay. To say this would appear as a joke to some but I am wholly serious. The term machinic phylum enters a region already inhabited by its progenitor concept: 'modes of production'. Unfortunately, many of those on the academic left might have a predictable knee-jerk reaction. "Ah!" they will say like automatons, with a profound and conspiratorial air, "but all this merely reflects the logic of late capitalism which demands the constant hyper-production of novelty". And to whip up a moral fervour with this repetition they will invoke the latest newsworthy example of suffering. All right then, what is your relation to newness, to change, to movement? Do you have anything to offer but nega- tions? Is this not your foremost crisis, to have nothing to say but "No", to be reduced to a guilty conscience? But then I say, as I said above, that I am partly you, trying to make a ten- tative step towards ontological positivity. And this is an intricate walk – between the posi- tive and the negative, surplus and lack, affirmation and negation – each needs the other (unfortunately we have too much of the latter and none of the former, having learnt only how to subtract and not to add). And we would walk better if we were not so quick to trip each other at every step.

To spot, connect and create as many points as possible is making ourselves aware of the matrix, as Neo begins to see it, in fragility, under threat. All we are asked to do (and this is anything but simple), is to remain responsive, patient, alert and attentive: to remain in touch with 'crises' to come, those that are already taking place among us, most honest to the specificity of the enterprise in which we actually participate, and those in which we might, potentially, possibly, eventually. To put ourselves into crisis at as many points as pos- sible, to create and sustain new planes of contact, this is already a lot of work. But we are not exhausted. And when we are, we will be joyful, since it is only a temporary point of rest. This is revolutionary-becoming rather than a grand plan for a final redemption. Nothing would be worse than a world completely without crises: a total peace worse than the present state of total war. To rue the possibilities of crisis and the anxiety of incipience is to be disappointed with thinking itself, to negate life in its potentialities. Because it is only in relation to the un-thought that thought can move to find its temporary bearings. Don't forget.

NOTES

1. I see the views regarding *The Matrix*, *Kill Bill* and the 'anxiety of incipience' as new. Everything else in this text is directly plagiarized from a resonating conceptual line that moves through Spinoza, Nietzsche, Bergson, Gilles Deleuze, Stanley Cavell, and the very recent work of Brian Massumi, William Connolly, and Veena Das, amongst others.

Disreputable and Illegal Publics
Cinematic Allegories in Times of Crisis

RAVI VASUDEVAN

C inema has been the central audio-visual medium of our times. Since independence, Indian cinema has provided powerful documentation of key passages in the imaginary world of our society, accessing issues of social justice and transformation, visions of community as well as intimations of social fragmentation, despair and violence. Despite its powerful presence in modern Indian culture, the cinema's institutional history has been a beleaguered one. Mainstream or popular cinema has lacked state recognition as a legitimate cultural form until very recently. As a form of cultural production, governments and cultural elites have regarded it as lacking authenticity and artistic merit, whether measured against the 'traditional' canons of Indian art or international standards of industrial film-making, on the model of the Hollywood cinema. In this sense, even at the peak of its influence, between the 1950s and 1970s, the cinema lacked cultural standing.

Discourses about the cinema are discourses about its publics, their cultural status and cognitive dispositions, and are often governed by anxiety about the unpredictable nature of mass culture. Regulatory frameworks such as censorship, mandatory state documentary screenings, and a regime of financial exactions were used to control and shape the contents of the cinema. Its low status in governmental and elite critical circles persisted until the 1980s, when its identity as a mass audio-visual format was threatened by the falling off of cinema audiences in the wake of video piracy. This threat has persisted in shifting technological formats – VHS, VCD, DVD – and competing delivery circuits – video parlours, media markets, satellite and cable broadcasting – down to present times. However, the new globalized framework of the 1990s has seen the emergence of cinema as an object of cultural investment by the government. Industrial recognition was given for the first time in 1998, and the Information and Broadcasting Ministry and Indian missions abroad have showcased high-end popular products in international markets, festivals and cultural centre screenings. The diaspora market for a cinema with lush production values provides the context for this new engagement, indicating the substantial returns on film exports, and the new cultural confidence of a globalizing nation. Sectors of the industry have made a bid to create corporate structures, financial accounting and transparency to woo legitimate finance. And the cinema as exhibition venue has been reorganised though the development of multi-screen halls often tied to ancillary returns in mall-style ventures. In this development, the cinema has moved from a mass cultural form disreputable in the eyes of the state and the elite, to a burgeoning part of an entertainment industry offering substantial returns in global and local markets.

The downside of this triumphal narrative lies in the persistence of old forms: illicit finance and underworld dealings, even if recent reports suggest that policing has curtailed the influence of extortion gangs in the industry. But even leaving aside the lack of comprehensive industrial transformation, the pitch has been queered by a new configuration of the disreputable public as a non-legal one. If the cinema and its publics earlier lacked cultural standing, moral and critical opprobrium, and state repressive and regulatory frameworks have also shifted onto a monitoring and policing of the illicit media market and media public which consumes pirated video copies of films. From the disreputable public we move into the register of a specifically illegal public. Publics who are not, and never will be, the imagined publics of expensive multiplexes are accessing film through these new technological formats. On the other hand, regulation appears increasingly helpless in the face of the cheap and easily available copying technologies that have entered the media market. How matters will move from now, and whether the current media crisis of cinema will set up new synergies between digital versions and cheaper projection venues is open to speculation. But this dispersed media public, illicit, ungovernable, will remain a key dimension of media futures.[1]

From the disreputable, inauthentic and unsystematic cultural form we have transited to the outlines of a legitimate cultural commodity held ransom by a culture of the copy avidly participated in by a dispersed film public. From a historical sketch of the public for the cinema, I would now like to turn to a more speculative, allegorical register: that of the public imagined by the cinema. This is specifically a public imagined in situations of crisis, brokering a relationship between political and normative protocols, constraints and their corrosion, and transformative energies. This exercise stands separate from the narrative of the marginal and illicit public I have recounted. But I will hold onto an overlapping thematic to help us move registers and think of parallels. Focusing on the popular cinema, this essay tries to highlight certain political and formal resonances which emerge in the cinema's recurrent engagement with the subject of crime. Crime hardly dominates the narrative imagination of the popular, and there are a number of other genres, such as the mythological, the historical, the social, and the family or family social (critical to the recent diaspora film), which have been important to the differentiated output of the popular cinema. Crime films were initially a subset of the social, the genre understood to narrativize modern social issues. However, arguably, the crime film had a distinctive significance, providing an important format to address issues of social indignity and marginality. And, in terms of its characteristic topography, the crime film genre accesses a dimension critical to the shaping of marginal and illicit publics. This is the domain of urban being as a significant experiential and experimental space for the reinvention of selves.[2]

From the 1950s onwards, Bombay cinema has taken crime as a key framework to generate a subaltern image of the city. In films such as *Awara* (Raj Kapoor, 1951), *Baazi* (Guru Dutt, 1951), *Aar Paar* (Guru Dutt, 1954), *Taxi Driver* (Chetan Anand, 1954), *House No. 44* (M.K. Burman, 1955), *CID* (Raj Khosla, 1956), *Howrah Bridge* (Shakti Samanta, 1958) the cinema addressed criminality as a critical index of the hierarchies and prejudices of the urban social order, and to explain how criminals were made by society. However, this was not merely an exercise in social argumentation. Criminality provided a particular access to the city as experience and afforded experimentation with film style. The genre gives the spectator access to the sensorium of the city in novel ways. As Moinak Biswas has argued, these films moved out of the living room and the studio generated street – what he refers to as a studio style governed by static interiors and flat lighting.[3] They moved the spectator into the dynamics of city shooting, and also drew on the complexities of chiaroscuro lighting to render the narrative world in terms of shadow, depth of field and density of *mise-en-scène*. Generically, the chase sequence and the rapid alternation in editing strategies endemic to the form of the thriller simulated the viscerality of everyday speed and distracted attention. And new spaces, gangster hide-outs, warehouses for smuggled goods, and, of course, more familiar spaces figured through novel techniques, such as the gambling den and cabaret bar, surfaced into view. While pegged to a social justice theory of crime, these films also highlight the city in terms of moral ambiguity, the thrill of action and movement, the allure of danger.

This type of generic engagement was to be taken from the sphere of the crime thriller into a definite investment in urban action and spectacle in the 1970s. As many writers have argued, this cycle of films, associated with the screenwriters Salim-Javed and the star Amitabh Bachchan, indicated a basic shift in social and political perspective. Now the state was no longer seen as the arbiter of social justice, and was seen to be riddled with complicity, corruption, or, at best, incompetence. As Madhava Prasad has written, the police always arrive too late, signifying the toppling of the state from a position of symbolic value. Authority lies elsewhere, in the 'traditional authority' of the family, or, more commonly, in the protean figure of a hero at once lonely but also bearing historical ties to subaltern community.[4] At its core, the problematics of crime and violence in the cities of Indian cinema complicated the notion that class could be a coherent model on which to build a strategy of social transformation. Amitabh's characters derive from realist typage and display a representational capacity as the worker who has the moral and physical courage to take on exploiters and represent his class. But, in films such as *Deewar*, (Yash Chopra, 1974) he demonstrates this only to sidestep the representational function. For, in a world which was increasingly to see the demise of trade union forms (*Deewar* captures this in the destiny of Amitabh's father), the film appears to anticipate this and to take its hero into a world of crime and the illicit accumulation of wealth, although, of course, in the name of the mother. This body of work is thus entangled in a particular vision of the de-legitimisation, not only of the state as vehicle of social justice, but of critical representational institutions such as the trade union.

Central to the formal shifts in the treatment of crime is a new sense of the city and subjectivity. In Amitabh's presence and formal articulation, the monumental hero who represented a myriad of the displaced and homeless, is architecturally of apiece with the city, its high-rises and its breadth of field relayed through the cinemascope lens. In films such as *Muqaddar Ka Sikandar* (Prakash Mehra, 1978) Amitabh renders the city experience as a philosophy of present time, living in the moment and in the face of adversity. There is something here which speaks not only of fortitude, but also of the thrill of challenge. But the challenge is also a narrative one, and one of moral economy, where earlier messages urging a striving for social justice through the state were derailed: a more perilous path was embraced, and often, in Amitabh, one with tragedy built into the choice. As a number of writers have argued, these films function as a critique of existing developmental paradigms and the authoritarian modernization of the 1970s[5] which would culminate in the Emergency dictatorship of 1975-1977, where amidst a wider attack on civil liberties, the poor of the cities were uprooted and subject to population control. In the displacement of earlier social justice vistas, and their exchange for the uncertainty of a criminalized subalternity, the period maps a critical frame for our times.

Ankush (N. Chandra, 1985) suggests how the social imagination, and the imagination of the city, has shifted from the time of Amitabh's ascendancy. Here Bombay is clearly on its way to becoming Mumbai, the nomenclature that a regionalist imagination has now given the megalopolis. The film opens with a gang contest over right of way for processions celebrating the *Ganesh Chaturthi* festival, a key, and contested, institution of religious, regional and social identity since the late nineteenth century.[6] The film deploys a documentary evocation, with its semantics of street corner, neighbourhood and bazaar. Contra the 1970s movies, a strong sense of locality emerges here. So too does a new configuration of the protagonist. In the Amitabh cycle, city and hero were architecturally of apiece, instituting a monumental sense of city, protagonist and, indeed, of the cinema as an institution of mass culture. From the mid-1980s, alongside the continued prominence of the singular hero, such as Sunny Deol (e.g. *Arjun*, Rahul Rawail, 1985), we observe a scaled-down, interdependent construction of the protagonist, that of the male group which clusters at the street corner. It is as if monumental hero and city have been exchanged for a more fragmented, localized sense of the urban, and a sense of distended rather than eventful time; as if this could be one day, everyday. The film was made in the backdrop of the decimation of the huge Bombay textile labour strike, and, in turn, the substantial dispersal of the city's textile industry. The four main characters gesture both to this, and posit a more general condition. This is of the educated unemployed who have been unable to adjust to the demands of a corrupt society, again an important distinction from the uneducated orphan who was to be important to the Amitabh cycle.

This group's sense of status is under attack. They are fallen, and this sense of unjust social demotion embitters them. Public assertion is critical, and takes the form of contests with other gangs. All of this supports the thesis that the film is like a propaganda vehicle for the Shiv Sena,[7] a political formation which drew heavily for its influence on local cadres and networks. It also, in its social configuration, anticipates the national conflicts that were to erupt a few years later. In 1989, VP Singh, the Prime Minister of a minority government, decided to implement the recommendations of the Mandal Commission on reservation of jobs for historically backward classes. Public protests followed, an elite public arguing that such policies would cut at meritocracy and brake India's developmental dynamic. More complicatedly, a high caste, lower middle-class, a more complicated and distinctly subaltern population, expressed a frustration and despair in the face of what they saw to be a drying up of the limited avenues they had for securing regular employment. A spate of suicides resulted.

Of course, it is not in the imagination of an *Ankush* to capture this last scenario. Male bravado is its chosen route, as the protagonists undertake the annihilation of a corrupt bevy of businessmen and accept their guilt and public execution in the manner of martyrs to a social cause. That such trajectories were not the only ones possible in the imagination of the city is indicated by two other films of the period, *Nayakan* (Mani Ratnam, 1987),[8] and *Parinda*, (Vidhu Vinod Chopra, 1988).[9] *Deewar* was meant to gesture to the career of Haji Mastaan, a gangster who was also seen as something of a godfather figure in the Bombay of that time. While *Deewar* hardly touches on such issues, the Tamil film *Nayakan* alludes to the paternalist legitimacy of the criminal in its evocation of the important Tamil gangster, Varadarajan Mudaliar, for its protagonist Velu Naicker. The narrative could be read as pitted against the emergent Shiv Sena, sons of the soil, vision for the city, which took as its first target the immigrant from Tamilnadu and Kerala. The film adapted Coppola's *The Godfather* (1972) for its story set in the Tamil slums of the megalopolis, doubly marginalized by poverty and ethnic subordination. Here *Ankush*'s iconography of the violent slum neigh-bourhood is carried on with a different inflection. Kamalahasan essays a bravura conden-sation of Brando and Pacino's performances, and, perhaps, the iconic Tamil star, Sivaji Ganesan.[10] The iconography of the chaste, *dhoti* wearing leader is familiar from Tamil poli-tics, and political resonances are echoed, too, in the way art director Thotta Tharani and cameraman PC Sriram stage Naicker's home. Rather than the sepulchral inner world of Don Vito Corleone, this is a brightly lit space blocked to emphasise frontal registers for those who supplicate the Tamil mobster. There are suggestions here of the architecture of the political realm. The film subtly traverses the field from crime to politics in such a *mise-en-scène*, suggesting not only the links but also the rhetorical structures through which con-stituencies converge around the image of the leader.

Nayakan takes the lexicon of slum/crime/politics into a different direction from that signposted by N. Chandra. But there is also an internal, deconstructive cinematic relay in the re-imagining of the contemporary. Vinod Chopra's *Parinda* takes the figure of the Tamil gangster, strips him of political functions or references, and makes him the ambiguous psy-chotic villain, Anna (Nana Patekar). This is not so much a depoliticization of the ethnic narrative of Bombay subaltern life as a generic, and indeed, realistic description of the cross-ethnic dimensions of the criminal world. As Ira Bhaskar has pointed out, gothic ele-ments now emerge strongly in the genre.[11] Bombay is the night city alternately composed of anonymous crowds, or an empty canvas for the staging of irrupting violence. And it is a city where the subject is never quite remote from the enquiring eyes of a malevolent net-work which may penetrate law courts, sacred religious spaces, and the household itself. The specifically gothic rendering emerges in the revelations about Anna's factory system, the city's underbelly. Apparently organized to produce drugs under the guise of an oil press, perceptually it is only available to us as a dis-assembly line for the production of death. An assembly of steel vises, industrial mixers and chutes mangle the bodies of Anna's opponents and betrayers, and produce them as destroyed end-product. Romantic conventions too are disrupted. As Ranjani Mazumdar has shown, the putative formation of a couple that bids to escape from the criminal nexus is constantly interrupted, as the domestic idyll is threatened by anonymous telephone calls and sudden blackouts. Film noir and gothic elements function to destablize the romance fiction otherwise available in the Bombay cinema of the time.[12]

As we enter the preceding decade, an extraordinary one in terms of political, economic and technological transformations, there is an emblematic set of films produced by the Bombay cinema that in some fashion stand by themselves. Ambivalence towards the certitudes of state justice and moral economy is here compounded by complication of character motivation and narrative explanation. Baazigar (Abbas-Mustan, 1993) stands in contrast to the way crime and violent assertion are located in relationship to community and public forms. Shahrukh Khan plays a protagonist whose motivations for a series of malevolent manoeuvres, including the murder of a number of innocents, remains mysterious until two-thirds of the way through the film. Until this point, it seems the objective is to ensure a ruthless business takeover. Negative flashbacks appear to suggest that there is, indeed, an explanation for his homicidal behaviour. The explanation, when it comes, justifies actions in terms of standard paradigms: revenge on behalf of the family, and, in particular, of the mother. Nevertheless, the wilful suspension of motivation suggests that the narrative invites spectatorial immersion in a world without moral economy, one driven entirely by cutthroat business logic. Mazumdar has suggested how the story of Baazigar highlights the phenomenon of the modern city as one composed of strangers, a perilous space where identity is duplicitous.[13] This persuasive observation dovetails with a sense of how the narrative manipulates generic codes and moral strictures, generating a vision of anomie, where the city is entirely deprived of the resources of community forms or public registers. At the climax of the film, when Khan is viciously attacked by his opponents, there is a moment when he flails around, hitting wildly at the air, the earth, his entire surroundings, suggesting a moment of dread, where the sources of his trauma appear beyond personification. Baazigar was swiftly followed by another essay on the protagonist as isolated entity. In Darr (Yash Chopra, 1994), Khan plays a psychotic; a weak, secretive entity who stalks a young woman, the fiancée of a heroic naval commando. The film splits spectatorial identification between the psychotic and the powerful representative of the state, rendering the concluding victory of the latter – amounting to the execution of the obsessive counter-hero – as distinctly ambivalent in its resonance.

These films signify an important transition, in a sense severing the Bombay popular cinema from its paradigmatic moral economy. While the psychotic cycle ended quickly, it opened up a space from which another dimension of the Amitabh ur-text, that of the criminal underworld, acquired a distinct generic shape. The gangster film appears, alongside the family diaspora film, to be the main film genres to emerge in the last decade. Arguably, the gang can be productively interpreted not so much as pathology, but as morphology of the social organism. In this sense, it has been present since the 1950s cycle of crime films, and carries on through the Amitabh cycle of the 1970s. These films outline certain basic structures, if we leave aside the social causality through which they are framed. These structures include a visceral, instinctual assertion of self; the constitution of a male social world, with distinct hierarchies of leader, protégé, perhaps a competitor, and a more or less colourful set of followers. The gang offered for viewer engagement and empathy is distinguished from other gangs in terms of skills, daring, in a word, its charisma. But it is also distinguished by a morality based on group loyalty. However, the gang is inevitably a vulnerable form defined by a sense of impending doom. It is threatened not only by the law, but also by the possibility of shifting loyalties (competition within the group, realignment with other groups); changes in the leader's perception of group needs in ways which may clash with others in the group; and external questions, such as the way in which other loyalties and pressures, primarily here of the family as moral unit, may act upon the behaviour of individual group members. It is the last which, of course, runs through films from *Awara*, through *Deewar* and down to *Parinda*, where the protégé becomes subject to a moral probity that he cannot finally ignore, and causes him to take on the leader or the gang structure itself, leading to its annihilation.

The individual hero, the leader's protégé, provides the main source of viewer identification in the pre-1990s cinema, although such a paradigm carries on into films such as the Aamir Khan vehicle, *Ghulam* (Vikram Bhatt, 1998). On the other hand, in instances such as *Hathyar* (JP Dutta, 1989), the hyper-viscerality of the hero makes him inherently unstable, a weapon out of control, and one charged with the hubris of an earlier upbringing amongst feuding Rajput clans. What is distinctive to the 1990s is a new sense of horizontality in the constitution of the group. I will take Ram Gopal Varma's *Satya* (1999) as a model of this transformation. Firstly, Satya, a migrant to the city, entirely lacks, or refuses, memory or identity. There is no space or time outside the here-and-now for him, making him properly anonymous. He proceeds through a series of visceral responses to the everyday weave of brute power which surrounds him, both in society and, decisively, in jail. It is this sheer indifference to authority which captures the attention of Bhiku, a gang leader who is part of a larger edifice in which Bhau Thakre, the gangster who would be politician, is the ultimate authority. Satya's disregard for hierarchy leads Bhiku's gang into daring gambits, including the flouting of Bhau Thakre's rulings, and the assassination of the Bombay police chief who has pulled out all stops in dealing with the gangs. While Satya develops a romantic attachment, this finally remains external to the logic of the 'professional' engagement which drives him. There is sentiment built into the gang universe in Satya and Bhiku's friendship, based on a giving of mutual recognition and honour. The generic universe provides a vision of urban positioning where the anonymous migrant without history or moorings can enter the city, prove his credentials and then draw upon a network, a set of resources which will provide him with a 'job', a dwelling, a share of the spoils. In turn, he can work out the logic of such a network by destabilizing the systems of authority which frame it.

The networked nature of the universe is perhaps technologically highlighted in the way mobile phones facilitate command and coordination. Deployed in the staging of an assassination of a film producer in an early sequence, its logic is interrupted when a phone call relays the command of Bhau Thakre to desist from inter-gang rivalry. The gang has to completely break free, constitute its own network and follow its own logic in order to establish itself against its treacherous competitors. (When it goes back on this, accepting Thakre's treacherous offer of renewed ties, the result is disastrous, Thakre killing a naïve Bhiku). There is also a stylized sense in which the social is penetrated by the network. Steadicam hurtles through the narrative world, yoking spectator to the chase sequence and tumultuous movements from street to interior, cutting a swathe through the city and breaking down divisions between inside and outside, home and the world. At the same time, the camera in *Satya*, a highly self-conscious one, often remains at a distance from this swirling action, constituting itself as a super-ordinate intelligence. It facilitates a vision of this cutting, this scything through hierarchies, orchestrating a new level field for initiative that also disestablishes the symbolism of entrenched authority. As I have pointed out elsewhere, a climactic scene has Satya cutting the ground from the deployment of the Ganesh image in contemporary politics. He breaks into Thakre's display of symbolic authority, stabbing the newly anointed politician as he presents himself and his followers before the deity to seal his newfound legitimacy. A top shot places the camera above the deity, now strangely liberated from its entanglements in the effrontery of an exploitative politics, as both look down on the dead gangster politician floating in the surf below.[14]

* * *

From the mass institutional format of the 1970s, which condenses its marginalized public into the monumental hero straddling the architectural expanse of the city, the cinema dwindles. It eerily anticipates the diminishing of state legitimacy, large-scale forms of production, and representational institutions such as the unions, and appears to lurch into decline along with these forms in the 1980s. If the 1980s saw the first substantial technological inroads into the cinematic institution, with the emergence of video piracy and intimations of a more dispersed media space, there also emerges a more fragmentary imagining of the city. A new sense of locality and a downscaled, interdependent protagonist for the marginal public provides the ground for a variety of imaginations, of chauvinist assertion, ethnic contest and even cinematic self-reflexivity. There is a scary other side to this scenario, a subjectivity entirely adrift of community resource or public reference, as in the early appearances of Shahrukh Khan. This alienated figure is the nightmarish other scene of public imagination, inhabiting an isolated, obsessional universe. The stranger city of Mazumdar's formulation here rends the moral economy of cinematic convention and spectatorial coherence. The scalpel like severing ushers in a new logistics of space and subjectivity. The underworld provides a morphology of horizontal, non-hierarchical space. Indifferent to history, the anonymous subject of the contemporary contemplates the city as a space for self-assertion, and discovers the networks and resources that it offers in the perilous hideaways that exist cheek by jowl with the everyday world of middle-class tenements. Dispersed, ungovernable, here is an allegory that refers back to the very conditions of spectatorship and media consumption of our present.

NOTES

1. For ongoing research, see publications of the Sarai project, *Publics and Practices in the History of the Present* (PPHP): *Old and New Media in Contemporary India*. Most recently, Rakesh Singh ed. *Medianagar* (Centre for the Study of Developing Societies, 2004).

2. The following arguments come in part from my "Selves Made Strange: Violent and Performative Bodies in the Cities of Indian Cinema, 1974-2003" in *body.city* (Tulika Books, 2003, Delhi). This draws attention to political transformations, including the identity violence, that precedes and follows on from the *Hindutva* movement, a phenomenon not addressed in the present essay.

3. Biswas, Moinak. *Historical Modes of Realism* (PhD thesis, 2003, Monash University).

4. Prasad, M. Madhava. *The Ideology of the Hindi Film*, (Oxford University Press, 1998, Delhi).

5. Prasad, *The Ideology of the Hindi film*; Ranjani Mazumdar, "From Subjectification to Schizophrenia: The Angry Man and the Psychotic Hero" in Ravi S. Vasudevan edited, *Making Meaning in Indian Cinema* (Oxford University Press, 2000, Delhi).

6. Kaur, Raminder. *Performative Politics and the Cultures of Hinduism: Public Uses of Religion in Western India*, (Permanent Black, 2003, Delhi).

7. This is the argument put forward by Ashish Rajadhyaksha and Paul Willemen in *Encyclopedia of Indian Cinema*, 2nd edition, (Oxford University Press, 1999, Delhi) p.469.

8. For *Nayakan*, see Lalitha Gopalan, *A Cinema of Interruptions* (British Film Institute, 2002, London).

9. Mazumdar, Ranjani. "Ruin and the Uncanny City: Memory, Despair and Death in Parinda", *Sarai Reader 02: The Cities of Everyday Life*.

10. I thank Indira Chandrashekhar for this observation.

11. Bhaskar, Ira. "Melodrama and the Urban Action Film". Paper presented at the workshop, *The Exhilaration of Dread: Genre, Narrative Form and Film Style in the Urban Action Film*, Sarai, Centre for the Study of Developing Societies, Delhi, November 2001.

12. Mazumdar, Ranjani. "Ruin and the Uncanny City".

13. Mazumdar, Ranjani. *Urban Allegories* (PhD dissertation, 2001, New York University).

14. See my "The Exhilaration of Dread: Genre, Narrative Form and Film Style in the Urban Action Film", *Sarai Reader 02*.

Protesting Capitalist Globalization on Video

OLIVER RESSLER

Since the mid-nineties, video has played an important role in my artistic practice. In theme-specific relevant installations realized in art institutions, such as (*Learned Homeland*) *Gelernte Heimat* (1996), *Institutionalelle Racismssismen* (1997), *The Global 500* (1999) and *Nachhaltige Sustainable Propaganda* (2000), video was a central element that was employed in combination with text/image montages or photos in wall and spatial installations. These videos are based on interviews that were conducted for segments of the topic of the exhibitions.[1]

Since 2000 I have been making videos apart from exhibitions, which can also be presented outside the immediate field of art. These videos move between art and political activism, and deal with themes and practices of resistance in a non-institutionalized left.

In this text I would like to formulate some thoughts on two videos finished in 2002, which focus on a partial area of the movement that is usually called the 'anti-globalization movement' in predominant media discourse.

The video *This is what democracy looks like!* (38 min., 2002) deals with events revolving around a demonstration prohibited by the police against the World Economic Forum on July 1st, 2001, in Salzburg, in the course of which 919 demo participants were surrounded for seven hours for no immediate reason by martial police forces. The basic democratic right to free speech in public was suspended, while the non-democratic but legitimate leaders of corporations were able to expedite the neo-liberal reconstruction of society without disruption within the framework of the WEF behind closed doors. As a participant in the demonstration, I ended up inside the encirclement by the police and tried to film the events with a video camera from within the demonstration.

Shortly after July 1st, I decided to take my video material of the encirclement of the demonstrators as the starting point for a video. At the same time, I was confronted with the fact that I was addressing an event, the course and dramaturgy of which were strongly determined by repressive police tactics and the arbitrary actions taken by politicians and police. Through being encircled by the police, the demonstrators were forced into a predicament where the possibilities for reacting to the hourly-changing negotiation positions, and the repressive conduct of the police, were severely limited. This unequal power relation convinced me to address the events exclusively from the perspective of the demonstrators and to leave out the perspective of the police, the mayor, or 'neutral' observers, which already dominate media reports. For this reason, I conducted interviews with six demo participants several weeks later, whose descriptions and assessments would now be marked by the distance of time and a critical reflection.

The decision to realize the video *This is what democracy looks like!* was accompanied by the intention to additionally work on another video about a different segment of the anti-capitalist movement – to focus more on political practices and options for taking action beyond immediate reactions to police tactics. I decided to make a video about one of the groups that I find most interesting, the Italian *Disobbedienti* (The Disobedient Ones). The Disobbedienti emerged from the Tute Bianche during the demonstrations against the G8 summit in Genoa in July 2001. The Tute Bianche were the white-clad Italian activists who used their bodies – protected by foam rubber, tires, helmets, gas masks, and homemade shields – in direct acts and demonstrations as weapons of civil disobedience. They first appeared in Italy in 1994. This was the time when the 'mass labourer', who had played a central role in the 1970s in production and in labour struggles, was gradually being replaced in the transition to precarious post-Fordist means of production. By forcing the closing of detention camps through specially developed acts of dismantling, the Tute Bianche became involved in protests against precarious working conditions, and the immigrants' struggle for the freedom of movement. The Tute Bianche were part of the demonstration against the WTO in Seattle in 1999 and the IMF in Prague in 2000. They sent delegates to the Lakandon rainforest in Chiapas, and accompanied the Zapatist Comandantes three thousand kilometers to Mexico City.

At the G8 summit in Genoa the Tute Bianche decided to take off their trademark white overalls that had given them their name and instead blend in the multitude of 300,000 demonstration participants. The transition from the Tute Bianche to the Disobbedienti, the Disobedients, also marked a development from 'civil disobedience' to 'social disobedience'. The repressive actions, mass beatings, and death by the police force in Genoa brought social disobedience off the streets and into the most diverse social realms. In my video, the Disobbedienti spokesperson Luca Casarini describes the Tute Bianche as a subjective experience and a small army, whereas Disobbedienti is a multitude and a movement.

Disobbedienti maintains the political form of the Tute Bianche, and attempts to create bet-ter legal justice for and from the people – a process initiated by people, which would also bene-fit them. Spectacular actions are still being carried out against detention centres, such as the dismantling of the detention camp in the *Via Mattei* in Bologna on 25 January 2002, as shown in the video. Additionally, attempts are being made to further develop 'social disobedience' as a collective practice of various groups, to block the flows of goods and communication, to make general the strikes of individual groups, and to plan and carry out general strikes.

With the video, I wanted to address the actions and theoretical considerations of the Disobbedienti, who are still too little known outside Italy. For this reason, I conducted a series of interviews with the protagonists of the Disobbedienti for the video in collaboration with the author Dario Azzellini in summer 2002.

In both the video *This is what democracy looks like!* and the video *Disobbedienti* (54 min., 2002), only people involved in the "movement of movements" speak up and assume the role of active speakers in the video. The images in *This is what democracy looks like!* consist of video material shot by myself and other video activists in Salzburg dur-ing the demonstration. The interview partners are not seen, but only speak about the events represented by video images. In *Disobbedienti*, on the other hand, there is an emphasis on the physical presence of the discussion partners. All the interviews were filmed standing in places that are immediately significant for the practice of the Disobbedienti. The ways the interview partners are staged, and sequences shot while walking, underscore the impor-tance of the body for the Tute Bianche.

Both the videos largely dispense with off-camera commentaries. Such commentaries are often used in reports on television to create a distance from the interviewed people when they represent something radical, so that an identification with the radical content is made difficult for the audience. Dario Azzellini and I approach the intellectual position of the interview partners through this formal reduction, and through the strong presence of the protagonists. The conceptual arrangement of the video indicates our fundamental agree-ment with the analyses and practices of the Disobbedienti, and this way the video becomes a further political statement.

The videos are thus fundamentally contrary to the investigative journalism of bourgeois media, which insists on its alleged neutrality. The 'democratically balanced' television news features, for instance, that contribute to the exclusion of left-wing perspectives and per-petuate this exclusion despite asserted objectivity, are a direct point of reference to the extent that this is exactly reversed in this video practice. The motif of the political activist, so popular in television news reports, as a 'violence-prone demonstrator' (the attribution

invariably occurs only in the masculine form) is the starting point in both the videos for debating the discourse on violence, through which attempts are made to divide the anti-capitalist movement into 'violence-prone' and 'peaceful' demonstrators, pitting them against one another and thus weakening the movement.[2]

In discussions, the video *Disobbedienti* is sometimes criticized for the density of its information and the simultaneous complexity of what is said, since the video requires the full attention of viewers throughout its 54 minutes. In the way it is edited, *Disobbedienti* uses the high speed of the speech of the interview partners as a formal element, and makes no attempt to resolve it with breaks. In order to focus the viewers' attention even more on the arguments of the protagonists, the continuous flow of images in the video is interrupted in several places with white surfaces. These white surfaces are directly related to the white overalls of the Tute Bianche, the function of which is explained in more detail in the video, but they are also the expression of a wish to inspire viewers to fill the visual lacuna with their own ideas. In other words, the white gaps represent the attempt to find an open visual correspondence for a development that is to progress questioningly, and without prefabricated models, in keeping with the concept of the Disobbedienti.

Less often there is a criticism that the video tends to heroize the Disobbedienti. Yet when one asks people, who are in part politically active themselves, about the reason for this criticism, one hears that the rejection is based on the spectacular appearance of the actions and an asserted avant-gardist comportment of the Tute Bianche or the Disobbedienti, which they themselves negate. As the representatives of the Disobbedienti eloquently describe in the video, the spectacle is purposely used to attract the attention of the media. It is thus not an end in itself, but rather a calculated strategy. Contrary to the argument of heroization, in the video Francesco Raparelli also states that it is a problem when the Disobbedienti's civil disobedience becomes a logo or verbal representation of practices that have have already been carried out by other subjects of the conflict.

I would counter these objections with the importance of conveying the political practice and assessments of the Disobbedienti, thus providing audiences outside Italy with an opportunity to learn from these experiences, to critically reflect on them, and to perhaps even adapt one facet or another into one's own ideas or practice.

Because of their subject matter, the videos *This is what democracy looks like!* and *Disobbedienti* are also shown and received outside an immediate art context. In addition to presentations in political contexts, there are also presentations in cinemas and at video festivals. For me, though, it is immensely important to continue to show the videos in art institutions because I regard them as central places where there is a certain scope for dealing with marginalized political perspectives and practices.

A former version of this text has been published in the framework of republicart (www.republicart.net).

NOTES

1. For further information: www.ressler.at.
2. Cf. Dario Azzellini & Oliver Ressler, *Die Macht des Gewaltdiskurses*, Kulturrisse 04/02.

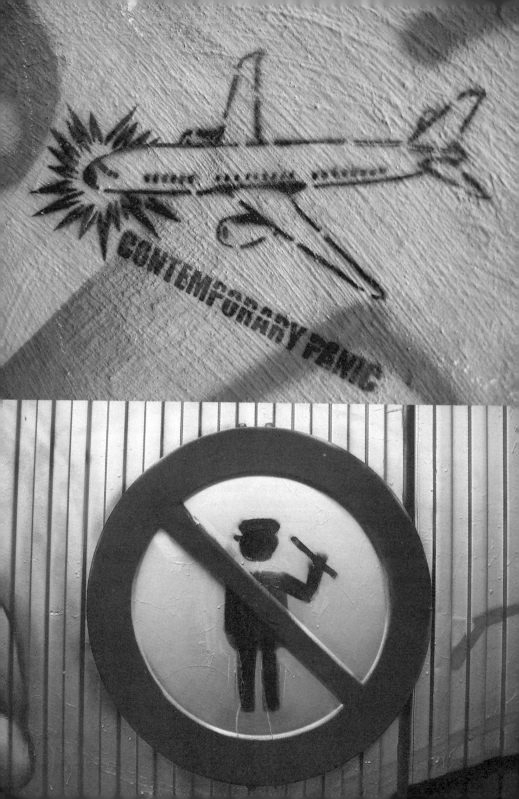

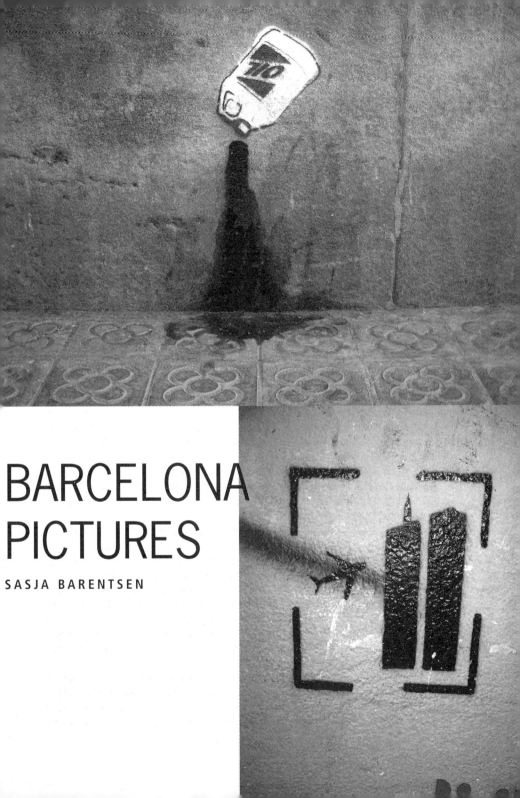

BARCELONA
PICTURES

SASJA BARENTSEN

From One Crisis to the Next
The Fate of Political Art in India

NANCY ADAJANIA

The 1990s will be remembered in India as the decade of liberalization, when Indian society and economy were opened to the world after fifty years of political non-alignment and economic protectionism. For Indian art, this was a period of self-criticism and reassessment, during which many artists, especially the younger and more globally aware among them, realized that their peculiar inheritance of nationalist sentiment and Modernist aspiration had limited their practice in fundamental ways. As images and information poured across the now-opened borders from the global metropolitan centres, the biennales and triennales and from other post-colonial societies, Indian artists, critics and curators began to subject their work to closer scrutiny in the light of these parallel histories and alternative lines of development.

At the same time, these artists had to deal with the threat of *Hindutva* – the militant Hindu-majoritarian movement – which had consolidated itself in reaction to the perceived cultural and political challenge of globalization, in parallel with its long-term aim of securing India as a Hindu nation rather than a multi-religious formation. The political upsurge of *Hindutva* manifested itself through demands for censorship, the violation of artistic freedom by right-wing activists, and a general claim by the Right to monopolistic privileges of articulation in the public sphere.

Indian artists gradually realized that the history of their practice had not prepared them to confront such provocations. The first generation of post-colonial Indian artists, active between the late 1940s and early 1990s, had espoused a Modernist aesthetic, and worked within a gallery system that they perceived as the space of recognition. Who could have guessed – in that first optimistic phase – that the gallery system, which liberated Indian artists from the constraints of individual patronage, would eventually compromise their freedom to interact with the wider public sphere? Especially in the last decade, as the demands of the political have become pressingly urgent, it has become clear that the artists of the white cube and the black box are inadequate to the task of formulating positions that engage the public sphere.

As such, quietism, rather than activism, has been the leitmotif of Indian art; and the activism that some artists in India have displayed relies on outmoded strategies of protest, weak in the face of the ideological and technological challenge of a Hindu Right that is at home in the world of global communication and urban warfare. The greatest challenge for

Indian artists today is to counter the Hindu Right's claim over the symbolic reality of India, a claim that runs counter to the Nehruvian national imaginary, which was based on secular and broadly progressive ideals. At the material level, the *Hindutva* mobilization is sustained through a pervasive network of grassroots political organizations, schools, and volunteer 'self-help' groups, as well as through the dissemination of pamphlets, broadsheets, television serials, cheap audio- and video-cassettes, and now, the internet – in the form of Hindu nationalist websites, chat groups, and mailing lists. As against this, activist-artists have neither inspirational symbols with which to engage the popular imagination, nor updated technology to vehiculate their secular ideas, nor indeed the organizational abilities to mobilize people into audiences and support bases.

Artists across disciplines – whether in painting, theatre, music or dance, and with different political backgrounds – have found themselves in an embattled situation where freedom of expression is threatened by censorship and violence. They have worked with one another, and in collaboration with activists and NGOs, to resist these repressive forces. For instance, SAHMAT (Safdar Hashmi Memorial Trust), an organization of artists, activists and intellectuals that was formed after the murder of the Communist theatre activist Safdar Hashmi in 1989, has emerged as a significant voice against *Hindutva* communalism. It has set up encounters with different kinds of publics by holding outdoor exhibitions, poetry readings, seminars, dance and music programmes, etc. Unfortunately, their programme has tended to be event-based; it has also constantly been phrased in the form of reaction to right-wing outrages, which limits its usefulness as it does not conduce to long-term dialogue, mass outreach and an autonomously evolving project of defining a secular imaginary. SAHMAT has attempted to grapple with several problems: it tries to sensitize artists to political reality and political activists to art; and also to sensitize artists, activists and the general public to the misuse of the sacred by politicized religion. But in its desire to achieve a tactical solidarity (which is a laudable aim), it opts for a reductionist approach, glossing over problems of interpretation and translation between the sacred and the secular.

More recently the artists' initiative, Open Circle (founded in 2000), has replicated the tried-and-tested strategies of confrontation and resistance employed by Left, environmentalist and feminist groups. While Open Circle has served as a forum for the enthusiasm of young artists, adding its energy to the cause of ecological refugees among others, this group of artists must realize that new situations demand new strategies; and that its methods must politicize the aesthetic and aestheticize the political in the same act of transformation. One without the other would be a vain gesture.

Indian artists seem to have reduced their imaginative ability to deal with political situations to a simple reactive attitude, critical but devoid of affirmative content. This is, moreover, a cellular imagination confined to individuals and small groups who are not able to make effective interventions in larger public life. A pertinent question arises: Are artists engaged in showing fashionable solidarity with politically correct causes, or are they seeking genuine ways of connecting with the larger public?

What explains this disjunction between the aesthetic and the political? Why has the pursuit for an artistic style led to a muted response to their ambient life-world on the part of many Indian artists?

The first generation of post-colonial Indian artists – including major figures like F N Souza, M F Husain and S H Raza – showed no interest in the temporary but provocative, perishable but site-and-audience specific, mutable but memorable artwork that was process-oriented rather than market-terminated. These artists also suffered from the romantic legacy of the artist-as-genius: in the early post-independence period, they embraced this self-image because they urgently needed to abdicate the social roles of the artist as portraitist, society painter or national mouthpiece. Most importantly, these Indian Modernists wished to escape the lingering image of the artist as folk artisan. They asserted their autonomy by aspiring to a universal internationalist style (which was not, in fact, internationalist, but West-centric).

In hindsight, we realize that certain key themes and impulses of Indian culture were not expressible in the languages of Modernism that became available to Indian artists from the Western metropolitan centres during this period. The logic of these Modernisms – whether that of the School of Paris, Abstract Expressionism or Soviet-period abstraction – was essentially transcendentalist and universalist. Having adopted Modernist conventions, Indian artists were not able to express aspects of their experiential reality and expressive culture, such as the figure set playfully between the icon and body, the performative and the deco-rative, the heightened body-consciousness experiences of time as duration and time as trance, and the sensorium of the everyday. Significantly, since the Modernist aesthetic privi-leged the individuality of the artistic self, it precluded the formation of communicative rela-tionships between the studio artist and other cultural agents of the public sphere. Therefore (with the exception of the Santiniketan school, which evolved a local modernism precisely from such crossovers between classical and folk, metropolitan and tribal culture, in the 1920s and 1930s), synaesthetic and participatory experiences like the festival had no place in the aesthetic of Indian Modernism.

These exclusions were not redressed until the 1990s, not even by the post-modernist practitioners who emerged during the late 1960s and early 1970s (see Ranjit Hoskote, "In the Public Eye", *Art India*, Vol. 5, No. 4, 2000). The Indian post-modernists emphasised the form of the little narratives, as against the universal iconographies of Modernism, using per-sonal and political realities as material, and engaging with elements of popular culture. Even though artists of this generation displayed close interaction with local subjects so that the content of painting became more dynamic, their artistic form still remained largely stagnant. With significant exceptions such as K G Subramanyan, they made little play with unusual materials and display methods outside gallery spaces.

To borrow a formulation of art historian Ranjit Hoskote, Indian artists in the 1960s and 1970s still produced 'well-behaved' artworks. Also, since they were fighting for a place in the gallery system, they could not rebel against the very art institutions that stifled creativity. It was only in the 1980s that the Radical Group, a set of painters and sculptors, brought sculpture down from the pedestal and began to explore the possibilities of environments and installations. This marks the beginning of the move, in contemporary Indian art, from the isolated individual self to the artistic self expressed through notions of community, sharing and collaboration.

Before I pass on, a clarification. In both of the broad generations of Indian artists that

I have discussed above, there were individuals who sought to negotiate between the aesthetic conception of an avant-garde and the political one (the fact that both phenomena are described as 'progressive' does not mean that they are identical). It was through practice that artists such as F N Souza, Ram Kumar, J Swaminathan and Navjot (among others) – all of whom were associated with Communist formations of various shades in different locales – realized that there was, in fact, an irreconcilable contradiction between the two.

The aesthetic avant-garde demands the individuated, isolated self, adversarial to society, that is committed to the autonomous logic of art practice. The political avant-garde in its Marxist nuance demands the opposite: a self that is socially engaged and instrumentally astute, directing people and resources tactically, making strategic dispositions across the terrain of the social. Obliged to choose, each of the above artists opted for the aesthetic avant-garde; in retrospect, this appears to have saved them from Communist dogma, and even empowered some of them to seek resolutions to the apparent contradiction between the aesthetic and the political in extremely productive explorations. I think particularly of Swaminathan's and Navjot's various intellectual and emotional investments in rural and tribal society and art-making.

Thinking further on these lines it may be noted that over-reliance on an orthodox Communist epistemology led even socially sensitive artists, during the 1960s and 70s, to ignore the urgent categories of gender, caste, ethnicity and sub-national identity: these were seen as dangers which could dilute the revolutionary agenda of urban proletarian solidarity, with class as its primary mode, and the objective, however dream-like, of seizing State power.

* * *

During the 1990s, there developed a variety of forms of performance-based video art and video installations (Rummana Hussain, Sonia Khurana and Subodh Gupta); inter-media installations comprising web and painting interfaces; painting and video interfaces; and composites of text, video, photographs and sound pieces (Nalini Malani, Ranbir Kaleka, Baiju Parthan, Shilpa Gupta, Raqs Media Collective, among others). These forms retrieved many of those aspects of expressive and performative culture that had remained excluded from contemporary Indian art. These new genres allowed for a greater play of subjectivity: they generated an interplay between the illusionism of painting and the immediacy of performance; they problematized the iconic, set avatars and morphs in motion, and generally had the effect of politicizing the private and attempting to create solidarities and environments conducive to redefining the role of art in society.

Unfortunately, when conventionally trained fine artists experiment with new media, they carry their old attitudes with them and are not able to interface well with the new-media domain. These fine-arts-trained artists still tend to see the world as readymade subject matter. Committed to a strict avant-gardism, they would take on technology as a new mode of salvation/redemption from the two-dimensional frame, or other prior formal and institutional constraints. But the mere renewal of the artist's career does not automatically mean a situationally lively response: all it means is that you have a new dogma to play with, a new approaching boundary of exhausted novelty to fear.[1]

Instead of expecting conventionally trained visual artists to reinvent themselves, we need to extend the frame of art, and include in our critical purview new agents and new sites of art-making. We need to look at new media works in hybrid and inter-media art practices. Otherwise, as art critics, we would acquiesce in the self-serving career moves of conventional visual artists who take up new-media instruments to participate in the making of generic 'international' art. It helps that many of them have, also, belatedly discovered the political. (In this context, I have to say that few of the younger, conventionally trained Indian artists have undergone genuine politicization experiences, as through Left or anarchist affiliations, or involvement with street theatre or alternative pedagogy. For at least some younger artists, engagement with the political and collaboration with activists is more a strategy dictated by the expediencies of global art funding than the outcome of real conviction.)

I would like to add that those who are also belatedly discovering net art should remember that it will not automatically deliver a new democratic practice; long-etched differences at the level of caste, class, gender and ethnicities will not disappear with a click of the mouse. That is why it is crucial to generate new online and offline communities of users, viewers and players. Net art will find its artists and audiences not among the traditional community of academy-trained fine artists and art-gallery viewers, but among computer nerds, animators, architects, designers, cultural theorists and political activists.

* * *

Already, in the manner in which the shift to new media practices is being valorized in India, we can see nascency turning into dogma: the new as something to be played with and feared, an engine of redemption, a promise of the charmed status of 'future art', an escape from the curse of being passé. As a remedy to this descent into dogma, we must acknowledge the very specific historical, artistic and technological locality in which new media art practices have been manifested in India during the last decade. Necessarily, I would argue, the history of new media art in any local context is dependent on the technological advances and the politics of communication as they prevail in that locale.[2]

This is why I choose to describe this phenomenon, in a situation such as the Indian, as that of new-context media. Let us recall that the new media began as tactical and situational practices. However, through the inevitable codification and institutionalization enacted by the global art world, these forms have now been subsumed within a certain predictability so that new media is seen as a universal tool kit. Indian experiments in this field need to be explained as local improvisations, not simply custom-made variants of the universal.

Viewing these practices under the rubric of new-context media alerts us to the weak moments when artists take up new media production for the sake of production. In such instances, technology becomes a mere vehiculation of the artist's intent rather than an articulation of its expressive potential. It runs the risk of becoming an art reduced to its medium and suspended in a vacuum (in a curious reworking of the Greenbergian obsession with opticality, the basic mediumistic possibility, the so-to-speak core competency of painting in the 'high modernist' period of the 1950s and 1960s).

Although the rhetoric is one of moving away from the gallery-based commodity, the same gallery reflexes of the past tend to be reiterated. The emphasis on the latest techniques can lead us away from art-making as a cultural act with political resonances. Artists often complain about a lack of infrastructure, but that is only a part of the problem; the real problem is that the old habits of privileging the production of an artwork, rather than making an audience, continue. In such a model, the artist-as-genius is more important than the phenomenon of art – with all its interactive, inter-textual and collegial dimensions – so the context gets killed even before it can be addressed. Our art world has a strong 'insider syndrome' – very quickly, because the institutional controls remain in the hands of the old establishment, it commodifies even alternative approaches to conventional art history, and domesticates them within entrenched patterns of organization, curatorship, exhibition and response.

And lastly, individual artists have tried to push the form, but there is no realization of a critical sociality of art. The question that is never asked is: what is the ontological status of this artwork? Who is it for, what is its immediate environment? What we require most urgently is a paradigm shift in our understanding of the sociology of the new-context media. Let us not remain asleep and awaken only when the next political crisis presents itself.

Some of these ideas were first presented in a paper, "Against the Languages of Withholding: *Ulat Bhasha* as the Art of the Future", that I read at Documenta 11, Kassel, 2002.

NOTES

1. See Nancy Adajania, "Anchored Illusions, Floating Realities: Two Mediatic Claims to the Public Sphere", lecture text (Neuer Berliner Kunstverein, September 2003, Berlin). Publication forthcoming.

2. New media practice in India does not have a local tradition going back to the early 1960s, as is the case with such art in the industrially developed nations – where, of course, advanced communications technologies were powered by the needs of the military, espionage and surveillance concerns of the Cold War military-industrial complex. In India, however, as is well known, there has been a consistent technological lag through the Cold War period: the belated arrival of advanced technologies ensured that video art in India was a phenomenon of the 1990s.

   In the virtual reality context of the late 1990s, we witness a double-edged situation. Even as the technoscape was dominated by big information technology corporations, their monopoly was challenged by the new heroes of the info-tech world: hackers, copyright-defying pirates, exponents of data flows, the brains that have used such phenomena as Linux, Napster and so forth to advantage. The mercurial nature of the technoscape and its social matrix influenced artists who chose to work with new media to ideally replace the gallery object with the project and the market with the community. This marked a turn in contemporary Indian art, so far limited to the acceptable context of the gallery, with the formal artwork privileged as commodity.

On Representing the Musalman

SHAHID AMIN

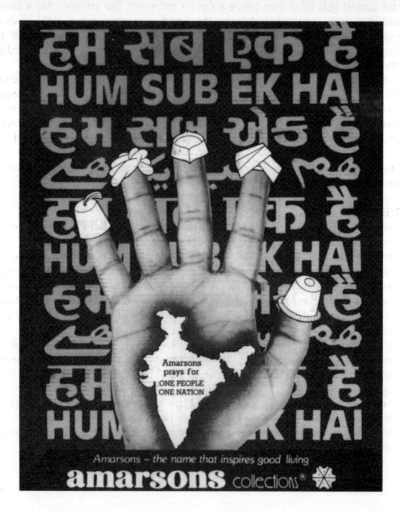

"Our people should be exposed to the reality of history very carefully" (Letter to the Editor on the controversy regarding the screening of Bhishm Sahani-Govind Nihalani's tele-serial Tamas on Doordarshan, *Times of India*, 30 January, 1988.)

There has been a steady rise in majoritarian politics and majoritarian history in India since the mid-1980s. Over the past years, these two desires have moved from the margins of popular discourse to the centre of political deliberations. The descriptive phrase, 'India has a majority of Hindus', has now been fashioned into the battering ram of Hindu nationalism – an aggressive ideological tool aimed at redrawing the basic contours of an avowedly secular nation-state. Its logic is to enforce the majoritarian idea of the singularity of national history, such that the enactment of historical vendetta against Muslim conquest of pre-colonial India becomes simultaneously the condition for the realization of Indian history and for demarcating the natural citizens of India. In this view, Indian citizens have, at the very least, to give assent to the forging of a 'New Hindu History' – the continual journey of a Hindu past, a national history whose positivist base is alloyed crucially with religious belief and nuggets dug out from the seams of a single, collective memory. This paper is an intervention in the debate over nation-building and the contest over India's medieval past.

The sense of belonging – belonging to the present nation – involves a replication of a sense of them and us through icons, stories and narratives. The siring of communities into being, and narratives about long-existent collectivities, very often take place simultaneously. And they have a duplex claim to history and to particularistic remembrances of times past. There has developed in India, especially since the mid-1980s, a powerful undertow that pulls all public discourse into: "That may be your History, but this is my/our past". Extant histories of the Indian landmass, such a view insists, don't answer to our present needs. Rather than simply confront pasts, ingenious or disingenuous with definitive historical records, history-writing, I argue, must have a place for the ways pasts are remembered and retailed, and for the relationship of such pasts to the sense of belonging. As a practicing historian, one must then pose afresh the relationship between memory and history, the oral and the written, the transmitted and the inscribed, stereotypicality and lived history.

A 'true history of communalism', to use a slightly tendentious phrase, would be one that sets out to unravel not just what happened between India's two, or three, or four communities, but also how these communities remember, understand, explain and recount pasts and presents to themselves. We could well replace the term 'nation' for 'community' in the above statement, and the problem would still remain. This, to my mind, is the significance of the periodic struggle over history primers in our country.

I do not wish to analyze the relationship between popularly fabricated pasts and professionally reconstructed histories in any detail. Rather, I take the Musalmans of Hindustan and the way 'they' are remembered as my reference point. My concern in this essay is with the expressive category Musalman. What constitutes the common sense on the North Indian Musalmans? What are the elements of their otherness? What is the relationship between the recognition of everyday difference and attachment to different pasts, such that the antagonists are believed to be carriers of two violently different histories? What is the mixture of

history, memory, innate difference and the changed context of the present in statements about the resident-Indian Muslim as 'the other'? The essay seeks to address a clutch of such questions.

The Indian-Muslim Cap
A major problem confronting the Indian nation today is this: How can difference be represented without stereotyping the group concerned? That this subject is not usually editorialized is an index of the refusal of our op-ed writers to step outside a self-inflicted *lakshman-rekha* of Indian nationhood.[1]

The question of representation of difference also gets elided in scholarly endeavours to 'put secularism in its place'. The main concern of such academics is to shake the 'modernist minority' out of its secularist trance. Political democracy and a secular society, it is pointed out, are incompatible in contemporary India. The westernized *neelkanth* Indian is therefore advised to gulp down this bitter truth for the greater health of the body politic. However, the contrast between the extra-ordinary secularist and the ordinary Hindu/Muslim is painted in such terms that the problem of how the nation represents its people to itself loses its poignancy.[2] The question has, however, a tremendous immediacy in contemporary India. This is so because the issue of difference relates to the basic Nehruvian axiom of "Unity in Diversity".

How is this diversity to be represented on a billboard framed by the unifying rectangle of the nation state? The question is not just rhetorical; it is something that stares us in the face. I am referring to that ubiquitous national integration poster that underlines the slogan "We are One" by painting a beard and a Turkish cap onto the visage in order to make it a Musalman. This is the visual shorthand by which difference is officially advertised.[3]

I do not wish to enter the debate on whether a beard (of whatever sort) is a requirement for representing Muslim fellow-citizens in India. Let us pass the beard over. But what about the Turkish cap, the fez? Who put it there? The answer is that it does not really belong to the representative Musalman. It has been put there by the advertisers of our multi-religious nation-state.

The Turkish cap as a marker of Muslim distinctiveness is of course nonsensical. One hardly encounters a *Turki-topiwalla* outside the publicity posters and handouts. In fact, it would be as difficult to procure a dozen Turkish caps in a standard-sized town as it would be to arrange for period costumes for a Shakespearean play. Yet that miniature waste-paper basket with a tail sits neatly on that abstract head.

The stereotypical image of the billboard is not a real life-image, but it is officially reproduced in the interest of the nation. The result is a paradox: We Indians are not used to a Turkish cap in our midst, yet it is a prominent sign for the Indian Muslim of the national integration poster. In other words, the national advertisement asks us to recognize an image which we do not encounter within the geographical confines of the nation-state.

Let us follow this paradox a bit further. If people with impeccable 'secular Muslim' credentials were to appear in a gathering sporting that particular head-dress, they would be seen to be making a sectarian, fundamentalist, and, who knows, even an anti-nationalist statement! Were that all those who could afford it donned it in public, the effect would be electrifying. A gratuitous and unsavoury gesture, a politics of looking different, would come into being. This in turn would be queried from a national viewpoint. The *Hum-ek-hain* billboard would fall flat on its fez!

But let us put the billboard up once again and peer at it a bit more closely. Don't we find the fez in other representations of twentieth-century Musalmans as well? In a sketch in his recent Raj-Series, M.F. Hussain portrays a "Retired Khan Bahadur" with a veiled lady, an umbrella, and that headgear. The Muslim League functionary in the television serial "Tamas" is distinguished by his beard, chaste Urdu and that *topi* once again. The Turks, of course, did not bring the cap with them in the thirteenth century. In fact, as late as the 1910s it was known as the *Rumi topi*, or Roman cap. Originating in Constantinopole, or the second Rome, the cap came to carry the name of that imperial city![4] It was only with the dismemberment of the Ottoman empire and the rise of the Khilafat movement in the post-World War years that the fez became a sign of anti-colonialism in India. Do our collective memories and history primers aid us in appreciating the value of this sign within its historical context? Does the *topi* tell us anything of the camaraderie between the followers of Gandhi and those of the Ali brothers, a coming together that challenged colonial rule in the early 1920s? I doubt it very much. Rather, it is made to stand for an essential marker of the otherness of things 'Muslim', as witness the following digression on the Turkish cap in a discussion of the influence of Persian on Hindi language:

"Just as Sanskrit, Persian etc. are Aryan languages, so are Arabic, Assyrians...called Semitic. Arabic and (Hebrew) have had a great influence on Persian, and that perhaps is the reason why despite the fact that it (Persian) is an Aryan language from within, it appears to be an un-Aryan or Semitic language. Just as a Hindu wearing a tasselled Yunani fez cap is mistaken by the people for a Musalman, similarly seeing Persian dressed in Arabic garb those with mediocre intelligence think it is a Semitic language".

And then follows this footnote:

"Some years ago seeing Sarojni Naidu's son wearing this kind of a cap, it was published in newspapers that he had converted to Islam. But the Hindus of Hyderabad also wear such a cap and the late Vitthalbhai Patel wore it as well. Vitthalbhai was the chairman of the reception committee at the Special Congress held in Bombay under the chairmanship of Hasan Imam in 1918. Those days he sported a long beard and the fez, and so appeared a full-fledged (*pakke*) Musalman".[5]

The faces of the national integration poster are not burdened with particular histories; they try vainly to capture innate differences. We therefore end up with stereotypical projections. The face on the poster does not match the man in the street. To be sure, the man-in-

the-street is no less an abstraction than the one stuck on the billboard. What we have are real-life men and women with distinct class positions, social backgrounds and individual dispositions. Yet the problem of the stereotypical image refuses to go away in everyday chance encounters. With stereotypes we leave biography and history behind, recognizing those different from us largely through visible signs, as if such human beings belonged to a different species altogether. It is such stereotypical sightings that isolate an Azim Premji, a Rohinton Mistry or a Mahmood Mamdani under the racial profiling regime at post-September 11 American airports.

Let us take a common example from nearer home. Unless a Musalman announces her or his presence by acceptable and well-recognized signs – these could be speech, appearance, or mode of address – the possibility is not normally entertained that one out of the ten percent out there could be in our midst. So that if a person is asked the routine question: "Aap ki caste kya hai?" ("What is your caste?") – with which chance meetings on a train are still rendered meaningful in the Hindi belt – and replies that he/she is a 'Muslim', the polite response is: "Accha! Aap lagte to nahin" ("Oh, I see! But you don't look it"). This is no provincialism. The probing query and the stock reply offer us an insight into a majoritarian view of a minority.

Either a Muslim should be stereotypically so, or be found in a particular locality – in his or her habitat. This special area is normally in and around the major mosque of the town. There, of course, anyone could be a Musalman; no outward signs are required of a specie in its proclaimed habitat! If this is a social fact, as I believe it to be, then we are back to the paradox of the national-integration poster. No diversity is countenanced unless 'they' appear different to 'us' in the way 'we' expect them to.

Stereotypical images by which we recognize the Musalman are elements of a larger process of the 'fabrication' of the past. Groups, large and small, simultaneously "construct, manufacture, invent and forge" (Concise OED) their identities. The urge to define ourselves vis-à-vis the other is no respecter of a systematic narration of things past – of history in short. It picks out past events no doubt, but it is equally a product of belief, memory and imagination. This imagination thrives on 'facts' without contexts, events without history, and it soars unruffled by contradictions.

It is in this light that the strange slogan about taking revenge from the *"santan* (progeny) of *Babur"* – heard during the *masjid-janambhoomi* episode – becomes intelligible. By what stretch of the imagination, one may well ask, can a young citizen of India be conceived of as an offspring of the founder of the Mughal Empire? The point needs to be pressed further. Those who believe in such a historic vendetta also maintain (and rightly so this time) that the majority of Muslims of India are converts to the faith of Islam. Indian Muslims are not a race apart. Raja Todar Mal was surely closer to the scions of the adventurer from Farghana than an Abdullah from Gorakhpur district. The irrational slogan, *"Badla lenge Babur ki santanon se"* ("We will revenge ourselves on the children of Babur") flies in the face

of such facts. But that matters little. It is the belief in the Musalman as someone recognizably different that counts and endures variedly. That many Muslims of the subcontinent fabricate exotic Arab, Central Asian, and Iranian lineages only goes to prove, in this instance, the point about imagined pasts that clutter our segmented minds.

* I dedicate this paper to Arvind Narayan Das (1949-2000) for whom I wrote an earlier draft. I also wish to acknowledge the friendship of Shobhit Mahajan which began at a discussion of this paper.

This is part of a larger argument; forthcoming in *Subaltern Studies* XII, Permanent Black, New Delhi, 2004.

NOTES

1. This section is based on an article that I wrote for *The Times of India*, October 16, 1988 (Special issue on Culture). The context was the Ramjanam movement. I have not tried to cover the journalistic origins of this discussion, nor change its rhetoric.
2. See T.N. Madan, "Secularim in its Place", *Journal of Asian Studies*, February, 1988; Ashis Nandy, "Anti Secularist Manifesto", *Seminar 314* (October, 1985, Delhi).
3. For a perceptive engagement with some of these issues, see Patricia Uberoi, "'Unity in Diversity': Dilemmas of Nationhood in Indian Calendar Art", *Contributions to Indian Sociology* 36:1-2 (2002), pp. 191-232.
4. Very often in ancient times the word *Rom* meant Constantinople and not Rome. See Gopinath Kaviraj, "The *Tantra Vartika* and its Author", in Gangannath Jha ed., *Kumarilla Bhatta, Tantra Vartika*, vol. 1 (1983 [1923],

    Delhi) p. xvi. The confusion persisted right down to the modem times. *Mullas* in some Mymensingh villages asked Muslims to burn 'fez' caps (*Rumi topi*) in protest against the Italian invasion of Tripoli in 1913! See Tajul Hashmi, "Peasants and Politics in East Bengal, 1920-47" (Ph.D. thesis, Univerisity of Western Australia, 1986) p. 67. That in late nineteenth and early twentieth centuries Muslim gentry in the town and the countryside wore the fez does not affect my argument about the incongruity of the *Turki topi* in the national integration posters of today.
5. Vajpayee, Pt. Ambika Prasad. "Hindi par Farsi ka Prabhav", (Hindi Sahitya Sammelan,, 3rd edn., 2100 *sam vat*, Prayag) p. 24.

Andamanese group with measuring rod, c.1876. Photograph by E. H. Man (RAI Collection)

Machines Made to Measure
On the Technologies of Identity and the Manufacture of Difference
RAQS MEDIA COLLECTIVE

"...We may classify human beings and human features but cannot bring about or find a precise agreement between any two; we have white men, red men and yellow men; we have well ascertained and defined types of humanity; we have in each type classifications of hair, eyes, noses, mouths and so on; but we have a large residue of difference between any two individuals and so on; but a large residue of difference between any two individuals remains as it were a recurring decimal which cannot be distinguished; the difference between each human face and every other of its species. Upon which evidence of identity has been always so firmly rested can be easily observed, but it cannot be specifically and completely isolated. We know that it is there, but we cannot in any case completely define the details.

But in the case of finger impressions, there is no question of dealing with those evanescent expressions which so largely contribute towards recognition of the identity of the human face. The exact differences in such impressions may be pointed out with as much certainty as the differences between the maps of two countries..."

[Emp. Vs Sahdeo - cited in K J Aiyer, *Law and Practice of Evidence in Criminal Cases in India and Pakistan* (Allahabad, 1949) p.461].

Bodies and Maps
Images of human beings construct a map of the world. Even the judgement in a criminal case has to rely on the metaphor of the difference between the maps of two countries when talking about the difference between two impressions of the ridges and whorls at the finger-tips of two human beings. As if the body were a territory, and its features possible to render as lines, ridges and whorls on a map. As if the body were a territory, the mapping of which would be the first step in its governance, and in the subjugation of its boundaries, to regulation and control.

Images of human beings, like maps of the world, locate like and unlike, near and far, familiar and strange. These categories, which are premised in the sense of what we see as being similar or different to who we are, or where we stand – on our sense of orientation. It is through these that power creates the binaries needed to inscribe in our minds *its* map of the world.

When this happens, images of the body (or of clusters of bodies) can become weapons of offence, and the instruments of a siege. They can be used to maim or injure, or imprison. No war or skirmish (local or global) is fought without its own arsenal of images. Images are endowed with the ability to create proximities and distances that can impel or sanitize acts of violence. Consider the aerial photograph used to identify targets for bombardment in cities, or the identikit photograph of the 'Wanted' person that often sticks to the walls of cities. Both kinds of images carry with them the charge of an anticipated act of violence, a bombing, an imprisonment, perhaps an execution. Both act as indexes, as maps, as locators of targets, and as the means to zero in on them. They are both navigation aids for missiles in the mind, and the radar that locates the enemy for the eye.

Consider the image of the typical 'other', the one who renders a distance between anyone we say is like 'us' and anyone we are accustomed to thinking of as unlike us. At its barest, it is a measurement of the distance – between us, and those we are mobilized to think of as being different, or exotic, or banal, or inferior, or superior, subhuman, or superhuman in relation to us. At its barest, this is what the issue of identity and difference are about.

Identity and Difference[1]

Identity (following Liebniz) is an assertion that two expressions are equal regardless of the values of any variables. Difference is the residue that remains when any two entities stand in a relation to each other such that all that is identical between them is subtracted out.

Any unambiguous statement of difference in human beings presupposes a certainty about identity. Similarities, such that they are available to the naked human eye, and to experience, are at best evanescent and do not yield certainties. In fact, the problem for those who have sought to mark out differences are that certainties do not exist *sui generis*, but need to be harvested or produced in order that a clear distinction can be ascertained.

The uncertainty about identity is not a reflection of the cognitive impossibility of identity. In a philosophical sense, identity is an enigma, but it is not an impossibility. We can say with a sense of certainty that a person x is indeed x, but we may not be able to completely spell out the reasons for our certainty.

It is possible to recognize that a person x is someone distinct – from ourselves, from another person y and from all other persons – and to give voice to our recognition of x's individuality. However, it is almost impossible to exhaustively list what it is that makes us recognize x's identity. At best, we can make an estimate that x is indeed x and not y out of the constellation of perceptible physical attributes, our memories of x and x's actions and utterances, what we have been told about x, and our affective responses when we encounter or consider x.

This constellation contains many items of information that will overlap with other constellations that we attach to our cognitive and affective map of other human beings. There are things that we could say of x, which could also hold true for y – these could be physical, or affective, or to do with x's and y's place in society, or in our lives. We may even say that it is difficult to tell x and y apart, but our very recognition of their similarity is at the same time a statement about their difference. No two objects may be seen as having attributes that are similar, or even identical, if they are not in the first instance, different. In other words, even if x and y are clones of each other, they still are x and y, or at the most, x and x^-, but it would be meaningless to say that they are x and x. A person cannot be one and another at the same time.

This statement does require a caveat. Person x may not be one and another at the same time, except for circumstances where x pretends to be or is actively engaged in becoming, or is seen to be 'possessed of', or is under the impression that he/she is someone other than what we and he/she understand to be x. This covers a wide range of behaviour – performance, 'self-improvement', masquerade and imposture, ritual possession, trans-gendering of the self. In each of these circumstances our sense of who x is needs to be glossed against what x is in the process of becoming, or what x has become, as distinct from the x that we consider as the ground against which the said, transformation of the self occurs. It may be difficult or even un-necessary to construct a hierarchy of the veracity of x and the other iterations of selfhood in such cases, and the conundrum of which 'person' is 'true' may tell us less about the person, and more about our anxiety to fix an overarching identity in the face of manifest ambiguities. This anxiety describes a desire to see people as if there were 'original' and 'fake' aspects to their being, and to their performance of their self. If we understand that the self is a narrative, and a performance (how else can we know another if they do not narrate and perform themselves to us), then the desire to privilege any one of these narratives and performances as the 'original' leads to an automatic relegation of all other iterations to the status of the counterfeit. This idealization of what is arbitrarily assigned the status of the 'original' is something that is fixed by the observer, and is in turn based on what is processed from the information that the observer harvests from the person encountered in a chosen context.

It is also possible that with time, things may be added or subtracted from the constellation that we have used to describe x. We may recognize x after twenty years even if x loses his hair or a limb, and our feelings about x may change from affection, to indifference, to desire, to hostility over time. Nevertheless, we are still able to satisfy ourselves that x is not y, and that the x we meet after twenty years is still the same x that we knew earlier. Our recognition of x's individuality, in its specificity vis-à-vis others, and its diachronic continuity vis-à-vis the x we knew twenty years ago, is a function of our ability to comprehend the 'inextinguishable recurring decimal' that marks the identity of x to our eyes. Perhaps the only way we can talk of how we access this elusive reality of the person before our eyes is by referring to something of the order of 'insight'.

Faced with these difficulties, we can say that the identity of a person is something that we experience, and intuit, and surmise, more than we know.

Knowing would mean the processing of information from the body and the being of the person into a set of fixed data that can act as a metaphorical barcode of the person in question. Such a barcode is constructed by abstracting a set of pre-defined parameters of what is needed to be 'known' and 'made known' about the person. This process involves a transformation of the experiential and the intuitive in relation to the fluid ambiguities of a person, to a set of insensate certainties that stay frozen. It is in order to achieve this fixity that blue prints are designed for the machines that measure man.

What are these measuring machines that render the differences that can then be computed? What measures do these machines undertake, and which measures do they conform to? What makes these machines, made to measure, work?

The Measure of Man

In a photograph taken in the year 1876, forty-six men, women and children, aboriginal inhabitants of the Andaman Islands (an archipelago off the south-east coast of India), are portrayed arrayed about a single measuring rod. The rod, at the very centre of the image, stands in relation to the people about it as a scale would to features on a map, or a silhouetted, stylized human figure would to an architect's drawing of a building. Perhaps, more crucially, the rod can be read as an indexical allegory, or as a barely concealed code inscribed into the image that ironically points to an imputed and immeasurable distance that separates the photographed from the photographer, or, man from his measure.[2]

The photograph, titled simply and prosaically as "Andamanese Group with Measuring Rod", is one of a series of images taken by Ernest Horace Man as part of his project to study Andamanese aboriginals, then considered to be a 'pure' primitive race in serious danger of extinction. E H Man's copious photographic record paved the way for an intense process of the scrutiny of the bodies of living and dead Andamanese (which lasted through to the early years of the twentieth century and which continues, somewhat erratically, till today). They were photographed against anthropometric grids, clothed as well as naked, their skulls were measured with calipers, and their nostrils, ears, eye sockets, buttocks and hair were measured and tabulated on cross indexed tables. The photographs, which were circulated as ethnographic studies, images in travelogues, items in popular encyclopaedias and museum catalogues, illustrations in missionary literature and as pornographic curiosities, continued to have a career well into the late twentieth century.

The measurements and images harvested from the Andamanese were worked on to compute statistical averages – means and medians that could then express the idea of what an 'average' Andamanese might be.

This in turn could then be taken to express the 'identity' of the Andamanese; a figure that could substitute a mathematical metaphor for the inconvenient tendency of the individual human body to exhibit variation. The figure of the measure of the 'average' Andamanese – expressed through calculations or through photographic composites – was then something that could be compared to other 'averages' to create clusters of information about niches within the social spectrum. Photographic composites of Andamanese skulls, for instance, were mapped on to composites consisting of the images of the skulls of Irish indigents, prostitutes, convicts and the criminal insane. Finally, there were more photographs and measurements than there were people. The Andamanese became more data and less a living community of human beings. It could be said that the technology that indexed their 'identity' and hence their 'difference' to those who did the indexing also measured out the terms of their subtraction from life, until they remained only as the ghostly prisoners of photographic negatives in the collections of anthropological museums and archives. The measure of man in the end became a calculus of cadavers — a detail in the arithmetic of violence of the nineteenth century.

The Smear of Truth

If Anthropometry sought to compute an average that flattened differences in the name of a composite image of an identity, then fingerprinting, another way of reading the body for signs of identity, sought to locate and fix the individual as a unique and unvarying entity.[3] Nineteenth century India, which was one of the greatest anthropometric field laboratories in the world, was also the prime experimental site for the development of technologies for registering and interpreting fingerprints, and the rise of fingerprinting as a precise forensic science. From the pioneering usage of fingerprints as identity markers in land records in the village of Jangipur in the Maldah district of Bengal by James William Herschel in 1858, to Francis Galton's enthusiastic 'anthropometric' endorsements of Herschel's experiments, to the systematization of forensic fingerprinting (along with 'Bertillonage' or anthropometric measurements after the manner of Alphonse Bertillon) by Sir Edward Henry, Azizul Haque and Hem Chandra Bose of the Bengal Police in 1897, the nineteenth century in India saw the creation of a rich body of knowledge about the principles that animated technologies of identification. In a sense, the techniques of ruling through information that were perfected in the colonies were then exported to the metropoles, and thereafter became generalized as the standard technologies for the affixture of identity and the recognition of difference that we have come to know today on a global scale. Had the early experiments with anthropometric image-making not been undertaken in remote parts of the world, or the intense desire to read the smears of fingertips as markers of truth not taken root in the minds of colonial administrators in rural Bengal, the techniques of biometric identification and surveillance that we have become familiar with in recent years all over the world would not have had such a smooth and untrammelled career as the necessary exigencies of power, articulated as knowledge in and about bodies, read as maps, and subjugated as conquered territories.

It is important to understand that this anxiety to produce certainties about identity emerged from a deep cognitive gulf that separated power from its objects in colonial Bengal. To the rulers of the day, the 'natives' they governed were infamously disingenuous. Their 'un-veracity' and the desire to confuse those who ruled them was a matter of great concern to administrators, judges, prison authorities and even to those assigned with the tasks of collecting taxes and revenue. Thomas Babington Macaulay once famously remarked, with some exasperation and considerable rhetorical flourish: "What horns are to the buffalo, what the paw is to the tiger, what the sting is to the bee, what beauty, according to old Greek song, is to woman, deceit is to the Bengalee. Large promises, smooth excuses, elaborate tissues of circumstantial falsehood, chicanery, perjury, forgery, are the weapons, offensive and defensive, of the inhabitants of the lower Ganges..."

It was against these weapons, this modest arsenal (deceit, circumstantial falsehood, chicanery, perjury, forgery) of everyday insurgencies in the offices, courts and corridors of power that the emergent colonial state invested into the development of an armoury for ascertaining identities and recognizing differences. That this project of ascertaining who was 'what' took place at the broadly anthropological level (as in the case of the Andamanese, and many other ethnic groups spread across the South Asian landmass) as well as the microscopically forensic level (as in the case of the Bengali peasant) tells us about the scope and pervasiveness of this anxiety.

The Inextinguishable Recurring Decimal

It is difficult to imagine why or when and under which circumstances one would like to yield a complete transparency about oneself to the scrutinizing apparatus of power. However, the increasingly fraught operation of power in society requires the harnessing of exponentially amplified means of visualizing us as transparent vessels of bodies of data. This means that the slightest shadow, the smallest reticence or hesitation in yielding the substance of ourselves and the iteration of our selves through actions, encounters and interactions with others, is liable in many places today to be read as 'deceit, circumstantial falsehood, chicanery, perjury and forgery'. This is the means by which the true test of citizenship is not a level of commitment to and participation in the polis, but the degree to which the subject is prepared to make him or herself known to the state. This votive offering of knowledge about ourselves to the guardians in power then guarantees us a place in the polis, and a certainty that we are what the state says we are and distinct from those aliens that it seeks to protect us from.

In an early book of the *Mahabharata*, one of the great epics in the Indic tradition, Ekalavya, an aboriginal teenager, is found copying and practicing the education being imparted to the Aryan warrior princes, the Pandavas, the protagonists of the narrative. Their teacher and guardian, who is concerned that Ekalavya has greater mastery over the art of archery than his favourite pupil – the Pandava prince Arjun – demands of Ekalavya his right thumb as *Guru Dakshina* (a gift that every pupil must make to his teacher on the completion of his education).

Ekalavya, bound as he is by the protocols and codes that govern the transmission of knowledge in society, cuts off his thumb (the one with which he grips the bowstring) and offers it to the guardian. The subaltern exchanges his mastery of archery for the knowledge that the warriors will always be different from him, and that it is his identity as a lowborn aboriginal that will underwrite this difference. The difference will locate him, as well as them, in the places assigned to them by the guardians of social order, and his bloodied thumb seals the terms of this inexorable contract.

The subaltern Ekalavya's bloodied thumb (the first demand for a digit as a mark of identity) remains with us as a resonant smear of the truth of power. Ekalavya's thumb, which guided his grip over the bowstring, can be seen as a symbolic place holder for the inextinguishable recurring decimal, which makes the low-born aboriginal teenager similar to the warrior princes by the same logic that makes all human beings similar or different from other human beings – their individuality. It is that complex interplay between their genetic inheritance, their social experiences and environment, and their specific desires. The rounding off of this digit, this inextinguishable recurring decimal to the nearest available whole integer, marks the 'identity' of the subaltern, and the clear 'difference' of the subaltern from the prince. The bloodied smear of the truth produced by the apparatus of identification tells Ekalavya, overriding all ambiguities, who he is, who he is not, and what, he never can hope to be. A technology of location, registration and the production of knowledge does successfully extinguish the obstinate recurring decimal. The digit is cleaved from the body and Ekalavya, like all of us when we give up all our digits to the state, loses the means and the skills acquired with effort to defend himself.

What the technologies of identification do not take into account, however, is the ability of a person to enact different iterations of the self. Crucially, this means that the story of personhood, and the narratives of identity that gather around a person, are material available for constant re-fashioning. It means that the question of identity can also give rise to a hyperlinking of aspects of being – an expanding and cross referencing matrix of acts, attributes and attitudes that constitute the database of a person's 'becoming' over time. Thus, even if Ekalvya's amputated right thumb is an emblem of the way in which a discourse of power wishes to reduce his identity, it cannot guarantee that Ekalavya, in some other narration of his story, may not decide to learn to use his left hand.

The identity of Ekalavya, then, is something that emerges from the relationship of two kinds or enactments of selfhood. It is something that bridges the person whose right thumb got cut off and the person who decided to learn to use his left hand, and cultivate a left-handed knowledge of the world. The inextinguishable recurring decimal by its very nature resists being rounded off to the nearest whole number, and continues its fractal dance on the adding machine. This takes us back to the person x who cannot but continue to transform himself/herself, and whose process of transformation holds in abeyance all attempts to frame his/her identity in a timeless embrace. Let us call x – Ekalavya.

Ekalavya's effort with his left hand may give rise to speculations in some quarters about the distance between the 'original' and the 'counterfeit' Ekalavya – the first, the devoted disciple willing to efface himself out of deference to the knowledgeable guardian, and the second, the one who goes against the 'moral of the story' and rises above or beyond his 'station' to be something or somebody he never should have been. This is not to say that the 'fake' Ekalavya, who keeps the label of his name but changes the content of his person, does not have an identity. However, this identity is something that he fashions, taking something from a story already told about him and something from a story yet to be told in such a way that it is impossible to construct a hierarchy of veracity. What he is, what he is reduced to, what he desires and what he becomes, are impossible to place along a graduated scale of more and less truth. They tell different truths about the different acts of personhood that are possible to imagine on the ground of Ekalavya.

Ekalavya's Left Hand

In these random reflections, we have tried to sketch an itinerary that moves from a set of fading photographs in the basements of archives, to the thumbprints on a ledger of land-holdings, to a strange story about a bloodied thumb. These digressions have been a way for us to think about the present we find ourselves in. A climate of paranoia about national security has made it possible for key factions within the Indian state to argue for the creation of a nationwide citizens identification database tied to a system of smart cards containing biometric data about every 'legal' Indian citizen. This apparatus, which is being touted as the solution to all problems ranging from terrorism to the crisis of identities within contemporary India, is in our eyes the worthy inheritor of the legacy that produced Ekalavya's thumb in mythic antiquity, the measuring rod amidst the Andamanese in 1862, the fingerprints of the peasants of Jangipur in Bengal in 1858, and the system devised by Henry, Haque and Bose of the Bengal Police in 1897. In a single digital move, it is able to forge a solution to the problem of identity that bridges the realities of the twenty-first century, the history of the colonial era, and an ancient fable.

A continuous state of emergency (what Agamben has characterized as the state of 'exception' peculiar to our contemporary reality) produces its own specific sense of fatigue - an exhaustion that comes from remaining alert to yielding oneself up to acts of random or routine scrutiny. This wakefulness and watchfulness, this baleful insomniac rendition of the self into units of meaningful information, is the unexamined personal collateral damage of the rise of a global apparatus of interlocking security and surveillance systems.

For some time now, many parts of the world, particularly those that are governed by the imperatives of the global war against terrorism, have learnt to live with a state of emergency – a moderate intensity level of panic and anxiety that makes the predatory excesses of the scrutinizing eye seem banal by the mere fact of exhausting repetition. And so we succumb. We do so not only at airports and border posts, but also at workplaces and public spaces in large cities the world over, to routine and random searches of our persons, to scans, registrations, surveillance and recordings of the traces of our actions, our encounters with others, our presences and transiences, our itineraries, purchases and decisions, our intimacies and our public acts, our utterances and our secrets, our habits and our desires – the minutiae of all our lives.

We see surveillance, particularly new technologies such as facial recognition, retinal tracing and biometric scanning, as performing a similar set of operations to those undertaken by early anthropometry and fingerprinting. The body as data is also put to analogous uses, especially for 'racial profiling' at airports and other transit points, just as anthropometric photographs were used to substantiate elaborate theories of racial typage. The intensive application of surveillance technologies at public places, work, and even in the home or in the private sphere leads to a monitoring of thought and affect to a degree that suggests that we can now begin to speak tentatively of an 'anthropometry of the soul'.

This essay was first published in *Technology and Difference II*, edited by Irina Aristarkhova, Leonardo Electronic Almanac, Volume 11, number 11, November 2003, ISSN #1071-4391.

NOTES

1. The following discussion on the enigma of identity is indebted to our reading of "'The Identity Puzzle" in *A Princely Imposter* (Permanent Black, 2002, Delhi) by Partha Chatterjee.
2. For a detailed discussion of the history of Anthropometric photography in the Andaman Islands, and in India in general, see "Stern Fidelity" and "Penetrating Certainty" by Christopher Pinney, in his book, *Camera Indica* (Reaktion Press, 1997, London) and also "Science Visualized: E H Man in the Andaman Islands" by Elizabeth Edwards, and "The Parallel Histories of Anthropology and Photography" by Christopher Pinney in *Anthropology and Photography 1860 – 1920*, edited by Elizabeth Edwards (Yale University Press, 1992).
3. For a history of fingerprinting in India, see *Imprint of the Raj* by Chandak Sengoopta (Macmillan, 2003).

Crisis/Media
CASE STUDIES

NO TRESPASSING

Minneapolis Police Officers have been authorized by the property owner to arrest persons violating Minneapolis Code of Ordinances section 385.380 (trespassing upon the land of another).

MINNEAPOLIS POLICE DEPARTMENT

MADE FROM 50% POST-CONSUMER RECYCLED PLASTIC

DANGER
DO NOT
STAND OR SIT

Media representations of the Kargil War and the Gujarat riots

SUBARNO CHATTARJI

The horrific events of and following February 27th, 2002, in Gujarat have received blanket media coverage and have been written about and discussed in detail. In addition, there are reports by NGOs, citizens committees, as well as the National Human Rights Commission, the Election Commission, and the Intelligence Bureau. Mainstream English media (both television and print) has almost unanimously condemned the communal bloodletting and dwelt on its consequences for the Indian polity. The language of that coverage has been one of outrage. 'Pogrom' and 'genocide' have been used frequently to characterize the nature of the atrocities committed. The taboo of not naming the communities to which the victims belong has also been abandoned. In the context of the frequency of communal riots in Gujarat (some 106 major riots between 1987 and 1991)[1] and in other parts of the country, the media attention might seem excessive. However, as countless analysts have pointed out, this round of rioting has been distinguished by the complicity of state authority (documented in citizens' reports such as the one by Kamal Mitra Chenoy, S.P. Shukla, K.S. Subramanian, and Achin Vanaik), and by a more fundamental collapse of civil society evident not only in the brutality of the riots but in the deliberate disinterest of state authorities regarding rehabilitation and re-establishing of 'communal harmony'. The blight affecting civil society seems evident in the lack of remorse and compassion amongst middle-class Gujaratis and is in stark contrast to the spontaneous outpouring of concern and help for the earthquake victims in 2001. Mahesh Daga, in an article in *The Times of India*, July 13th, 2002, entitled "Psyche of the Aggressor: No Kalinga Effect in Gujarat", contends that there was/is no sense of moral community and therefore no contrition on the part of Hindus vis-à-vis violence against Muslims. He points to studies of post-riot situations the world over where it is seen that the aggressors blame the victims for provoking the violence by their prior behaviour. This is evident in riots in Chicago (1919), Detroit (1943), the anti-Chinese violence in Malaysia (1963), the anti-Ibo riots in Nigeria (1966), the anti-Tamil riots in Sri Lanka (1983), or the anti-Muslim violence in Mumbai (1992). Gujarat, however, is the most extreme example of this trend. As Daga writes, "It is to the 'credit' of the *parivar*'s [family's] unrelenting propaganda that sections of Gujarati society have ceased to regard Muslims as being worthy of an equal human status. There is no doubt that this 'dehumanization' of the Muslim was a necessary precondition for the kind of savagery witnessed in Gujarat".[2]

The process of dehumanization mentioned by Daga is an essential aspect of the oppositional framework of wars, and it is entirely unsurprising that similar rhetorical and political strategies were employed during the Kargil War. In the case of Gujarat, the divide has been further bolstered by a collective sense of retrospective vengeance. As Julio Ribeiro writes,

"There was a widely prevalent perception in the minds of the Hindu upper and middle classes that the revenge that was taken in Ahmedabad was for the good of the city, the state and the country as it would serve as a good lesson to recalcitrant Muslims".[3]

In post-election Gujarat, Ribeiro's prognosis takes on an even more ominous dimension as the 'other' is electorally silenced and the triumphalism of the VHP and the BJP promises a repeat of the 'Gujarat experiment' in subsequent elections at state and national levels.

At this point I would like to digress to dwell briefly on the media debates fostered in the aftermath of the BJP's thumping victory in Gujarat.

India Today magazine conceded that post-Godhra Gujarat was a "rotten spot in India. A place where religion could burn, kill, divide and misrule".[4] The editorial in the December 30th issue then went on to ridicule the "professional secularists and the conscience-keeping industry" for demonizing the rampaging Hindu, and concluded that the "celebration of the popular will ... shows the right way".[5]

India Today's consecutive covers of the Modi phenomenon – as if he were an ahistorical force of nature rather than a cynical manipulator and votary of hate – and its editorial joy at the outcome of the Gujarat elections is not surprising given its political bias and earlier coverage of the riots in that state. In fact, throughout its coverage there seemed to be a schizophrenic divide between the cover photographs and the articles within. For instance, the issue with Modi in traditional RSS attire on the cover held out the possibility of a critical look at his politics and mode of governance, if one may call riot-mongering a mode of governance. In contrast to this expectation, the article actually bolstered the righteousness and iconic stature of the RSS man now fulfilling his avowed mission. I have argued earlier, in a paper exclusively on *India Today* and its coverage of the Kargil War, that this newsmagazine with its huge circulation (more than that of *Outlook*, *The Week*, and *Frontline* put together) and its multi-lingual editions is reflective of dominant middle class views.[6]

I believe the same argument obtains for the Gujarat situation and, in that sense, the newsmagazine has been consistent in its demonization of Muslims, whether across the border or within India.

The post-election debate in *The Times of India* takes on a different argument and tone. Siddharth Vardarajan in "Beyond the ballot: the issue in Gujarat is justice" writes, "As on election eve, the biggest question confronting India today is not the sterile debate over 'Hindutva' and 'secularism' but the future of the rule of law".[7]

The 'sterile debate' reverberates through political discourse and is evident both in the threats of Praveen Togadia live on *Star Newshour* and in the Prime Minister's Goa musings equating *Hindutva* with 'Bharatiyata' ('Indian-ness'). The reactions to the musings, ranging from the VHP to the Shiv Sena, are only indicative of the vehemence and vindictiveness with which the Gujarat agenda will be repeated in future elections. Vardarajan, however, raises two important points: the question of law and justice and the positing of the secular vs. non-secular in absolute dichotomous terms. I will turn to these later.

To return to the justified lament over the collapse of civil society in Gujarat, it is significant that corporate neglect and complicity have been intermittently highlighted by the media. Kingshuk Nag's articles in *The Times of India* analyzed the economic basis of the riots (the specific targeting of shops and factories owned by the *Bohra* community, for instance) and the losses sustained by the state exchequer. Although complicity of business organizations, such as the Gujarat Chamber of Commerce meeting and lauding Modi, were reported, they were seldom examined in any depth. The battle for Kargil led to industry making commercial capital out of war and furthering nationalist fervour. In Gujarat, industrial conglomerates such as Reliance were marked by their silence and post-riot indifference. Thus, not only the state government but also corporate Gujarat seems to have abandoned the riot survivors, further enhancing the ghettoization and resentment of the Muslim community. The media has been relatively silent about this phenomenon.

Another aspect which seems to have escaped media analysis is the money-order framework of the Gujarati economy, in particular the role of the Gujarati diaspora in fostering a particular brand of ethnic and national identity. Much has been made of the prosperous and numerous Gujarati diaspora (and rightly so, for their achievements are legion), but few are the references to the ways in which this diaspora has contributed to the growth of Hindu right-wing movements in the state through a steady inflow of funds and ideological support.

The dangers of what Lord Bhiku Parekh calls "long-distance nationalism" was reported in *The Times of India* on January 10th, 2003, but it does not feature in this or other mainstream media reports and analysis. Lord Parekh refers specifically to the ways in which the Israeli lobby influences policies to the detriment of Palestine and, paradoxically, its own interests. Remote access patriotism is not peculiar to the Gujarat situation: it was available in offshore support for Kashmiri militancy in the UK, and for Sikh separatism in Canada and the UK. What is unique in the Gujarat scenario is the support for a larger notion of a Hindu *Rashtra*, the demonization of Muslims, and the wilful attempt to dismember constitutional and oppositional frameworks that stand in the way of the *Hindutva* juggernaut. "Long distance patriotism" has particular resonance in the context of the recent Bharatiya Pravasi Divas, which, to some extent, legitimizes the financial support offered to Gujarat, among other states. That the RSS, the Vishwa Hindu Parishad (VHP), the BJP and other members of the *Sangh Parivar* have strong international, diasporic affiliates is a matter of concern and enquiry.

That the media was effective in creating a climate of conscience with regard to the carnage in Gujarat is perhaps best indicated by the outrage with which members of the government and *Sangh Parivar* reacted. While the Prime Minister and Home Minister called for more 'restrained' reporting (a euphemism for less critical and graphic reportage), the *Vishwa Hindu Samachar*, edited by K. K. Shastri, head of Gujarat VHP, lashed out at "convent educated journalists who don't know the geography of Ahmedabad". The object of ire here is obviously the English language press, but it is significant that regional vernacular media was equally stringent in its commentary and coverage of the riots. "*Aisee sarkar kyon rahe?*" ("Why should a government like this continue?"), asked an editorial in *Prabhat Khabar*, a major Hindi daily from Patna. The daily was severely critical of Modi and did not spare Vajpayee. "*Pradhanmantri ka Jhoot*" ("The Prime Minister's Lies") was the headline of one editorial. "The PM has shed tears, but hasn't taken action against anyone. It appears these are crocodile tears", the paper commented.[8]

Prajavani, the largest circulated newspaper in Karnataka, editorialized that "The PM's soothing words appear hollow due to his dualistic stand. It is clear from their actions that the *Sangh Parivar* does not even give a thought to what he is saying. A centre which cannot control or does not want to control the Gujarat government is incapable of administering the country".[9]

Kannada Prabha editorial adviser TJS George was prescient in his sarcasm: "The day might not be far when Modi returns to power with a thumping majority, Ramachandra Paramhans becomes the President, and Uddhav Thackeray the PM. It might become the fashion of the next generation to ostracize the minorities on social and economic front, like what is happening in Gujarat and what happened in Nazi Germany".[10]

The exception to this critical media attention is found in the Gujarati language press where publications such as *Sandesh* led the charge in fabricating gruesome tales of viola-tion of Hindu women and the need for revenge. On March 1st, 2002, *Sandesh* reported that the dead bodies of two girls abducted during the attack on the Sabarmati Express had been found near a pond in Kalol. "As part of a cruel inhuman act that would make even a devil weep, the breasts of both the dead bodies had been cut. Seeing the dead bodies one knows that the girls had been raped again and again, perhaps many times. There is specu-lation that during this act itself the girls might have died".[11]

The police could not substantiate the story. As Chenoy et al point out in their report to the nation, such unsubstantiated stories helped to fuel the communal frenzy. It is within this critical context that the government's obvious attempt to control and/or influence the media becomes significant. The year-long harassment of *Tehelka* (a news portal that ran an exposé on corruption in an arms-deal involving major political figures), the arrests of Anirudh Bahal (reporter with *Tehelka*) and Iftikar Gilani[12] are symptomatic of coercive desires and tendencies manifested earlier in incidents in Gujarat.

Events following the riots – including the dissolution of the Gujarat Assembly, the call for early elections, and the disparaging of a constitutional authority such as the Chief Election Commissioner – bolster the argument that this is a government that cares little for the niceties of secularism or constitutional propriety. Within this milieu the media can and has been construed in oppositional terms, resisting the onslaught of political inclinations and ideologies inimical to the larger interests of India. This resistance, however, seems reactive rather than a continuous and prolonged ideological opposition to the hate speech and actions propagated by the BJP, VHP, Bajrang Dal and other *Sangh* departments.

Reportage, by its very nature, focuses on the immediate, the event that is 'news-worthy' due to its political, ideological, or dramatic nature. It is in the concentration beyond the immediate, the analysis of news and events in newspapers and newsmagazines as well as television, that one might expect more considered and in-depth coverage. Quite often, this has been facile and inadequate. Editorials on Gujarat have been scathing almost across the ideological spectrum, but they seem to focus exclusively on Gujarat as if it were an isolated event or an aberration in recent Indian political history. There have been references to the 1969 riots but seldom any to more recent developments, such as the rise of com-petitive fundamentalisms, of the interface between globalization and its effects on the one hand and the consolidation of *atavistic* religious identities on the other.

In short, crucial links between socio-political structures and events are not made. For instance, *The Times of India* has been analytical and critical particularly in its editorial coverage of events in Gujarat. An editorial on April 25th, 2002, described the events as a "pogrom", and an article by Vidya Subramaniam analyzed cogently the fact that the BJP's "ideological highs" coincide with "sectarian targeting". The Times editorial coverage of the Kargil War is in sharp contrast to its take on Gujarat. On the Kargil context, The Times editorialized, "A Talibanised and militarised Pakistan acts as a rogue state because of the autonomy it feels it enjoys because of nuclear capability", and further that Pakistan is "dominated by mullahs and generals steeped in drug trafficking, money laundering and international terrorism". Another editorial in The Times mocked a group of eminent Indians and Pakistanis counselling restraint: "It is like advocating restraint equally to the rapist and rape victim". What is significant about the latter set of comments is that they essentialize and demonize the enemy, as if all of Pakistan consisted of mad mullahs advocating war (shades of our Prime Minister's jihadi speech at the Goa conclave of the BJP).

Star News' coverage of the Gujarat riots was largely courageous, insightful, and politically nuanced. A series of stories by Shikha Trivedi went behind the news, as it were, in their portrayal of the trauma and alienation of the Muslim communities and individuals who returned to their villages on sufferance, and in the ways in which tribal communities have been co-opted into the Hindutva fold. In contrast, Star News projected Kargil as a just and necessary war against intransigent intruders. It also contributed substantially to the spectacle and glamorization of war. Star News coverage, with its slick sets and slicker presenters, was often devoid of serious content and in-depth analysis. It is also significant that hawkish analysts such as K. Subramanyam and Mani Dixit were frequently invited to Newshour discussions. As part of a global media conglomerate, the internationalization of infotainment was most evident in the obvious attempts that Star News made to present a modern India fighting a medieval, Islamist mindset over the border. The Kargil Review Committee Report notes approvingly that "The media coverage, especially over television, bound the country as never before".[13]

A local war in the global village led to the consolidation of almost tribal identities, pushing back any possibility of peace between the two neighbours by years, if not decades. Any notion of truth and analytical gestures were swiftly marginalized in the media, and this suited perfectly the desires of the political class. "Satyameva Jayate" ("Truth always triumphs"), as the Review Committee Report notes, "is an excellent motto. But the truth must be assisted to prevail".[14]

The point here is not that The Times of India or Star News have been inconsistent in their opposition to war, violence, or riots, but that they make no analytical connections between the two events. A long history of communal violence, the hate speech spewed against Muslims, the contempt for the secular fabric of Indian polity and institutions are all predicated on the hatred of the 'other', whether within the country or outside. The demonizing of the 'other' allowed for the patriotic consolidation during the Kargil War. The identification of the perpetrators of Godhra as ISI agents generated the 'action-reaction' rhetoric and revenge model that fuelled the communal violence. In Kargil, the jingoism related to India, the motherland threatened by a devious and evil enemy, and large sections of the media were pro-government. In Gujarat, there is a mythic construction of wronged Hindu majorities now wreaking vengeance to reverse centuries of Muslim barbarism and atrocity, and the media is shocked at government complicity. The two events are arguably different, but they conflate a recently dominant rhetoric of long-suffering, tolerant Hinduism now striking back, whether in war or in riot. This connection seems to be missing in dominant media reports, editorials, and commentaries.

There are other post-riot events which are reported largely as disparate elements rather than analyzed as forming a larger, more significant rhetorical tapestry which bolsters the idea of the evil 'other' (whether within or without), and simultaneously the need for national vigilance, security, and increasing militarization. It can be argued that the Kargil War was not quite as jingoistic as earlier Indo-Pak conflicts, and that the consolidation of national identity was neither uniform nor widespread nor sustained for too long after the war was over. While this line of reasoning is open to dispute, the more important consequence of that confrontation has been the spiralling rhetoric and reality of military posturing and actions, the sense of a nation under constant siege. In political and dominant media mythography, Kargil was seen as the betrayal of Lahore, the proof (if any was needed) of the perfidious Muslim. The attack on Parliament, Akshardham, the Ansal Plaza shootout, the constant criticism of the *Mufti*'s 'healing touch' policy in Jammu and Kashmir, the alacrity with which the accused in the Parliament attack were sentenced to death are just some instances that help consolidate the idea of national spaces and identities under constant threat. The constant rhetoric of the soft state, from Kargil to the Kandahar hijacking, from peace moves in Jammu and Kashmir to Akshardham underlines the paradox of the imagined community being created over the past few years and at present. In reality, the 'softness' of the state is available in far-reaching and pervasive reactions and concessions to global economic and power situations, such as the easy entry of genetically modified cotton or the cosying up to the US in bilateral treaties, such as the one allowing US military personnel to get away with human rights violations. This vulnerability and lack of agency seems to turn inwards and manifest itself in 'tough' attitudes towards the vulnerable and disenfranchised within the country. This brings me back to Siddharth Vardarajan's point about the centrality of law and justice in post-election Gujarat, and indeed India. The lack of justice for victims of riots is in sharp contrast to the swift sentencing of those accused in the Parliament attack. Manoj Joshi writes that "mass murder of the type that occurred in Delhi in 1984 or in Gujarat earlier this year remains unpunished, but does not disturb a large cross-section of the population. In 1984, the Congress was returned to power by the electorate, as was the BJP in Gujarat this year. In no other established democracy would a government's failure to protect its own citizens be rewarded this way".[15]

In a post-September 11th scenario, the denigration and worse of Muslims worldwide has gained currency and legitimacy. Thus while 1984 and 2002 are analogous in their targeting of a particular community and the subsequent failure of justice, the latter is far more deliberate and dangerous in its economic, social, and electoral exclusion of the 'other'. I find it difficult to envision the reintegration of the Muslims in Gujarati community structures in a way that the Sikhs have rehabilitated themselves. The connection between the two riots is crucial but remains facile in media commentary that does not dwell on the differences in political climate, rhetoric, intent, and actuality.

With particular reference to Gujarat, my contention above leads to two further observations about the media's coverage of the riots and their aftermath. One is the predictability of the media response. This was best illustrated in the hope generated by the Prime Minister's "*rajdharma*" speech when he first visited Gujarat, and a subsequent sense of anger and betrayal at his "*jihadi*" speech at the BJP conclave in Goa. In this instance the favourite media construction of the 'moderate' PM caught in the midst of 'hard-line' party members and the mask (*mukhota*) of the same persona was further highlighted. Based on this construction, influential sections of the media (*India Today*, for example) generate and perpetuate a naïve expectation that the BJP and its *Parivar* are liberal, tolerant, pluralistic, and not so different after all from other political conglomerations in this country. The "party with a difference" may not be so different in its dispensation of the spoils of power (the petrol pump scam), but it is quite unique in its pursuit of a political agenda based purely on religious identities and majoritarian paranoia. Arguably, the genesis of the polarization in Gujarat begins with the growth of the Muslim mafia under the Congress dispensation in the 1980s, but its culmination is being played out now.

My second observation relates to the reluctance of the media to analyze minority communalism and its ideology, politics, mechanics, and psychology. In this respect the 'secular' media is instinctively reactive and tends to minimize the role of violence perpetrated by the 'other', i.e. Muslims. At face value this argument seems to be at one with the votaries of the BJP who claim that Godhra outraged no one. However, it seems to me that the best strategy to cast off the taint of 'pseudo-secularism' (whatever that might be) would be to offer analyses of both majority and minority communalism. *Outlook* in its April 1st, 2002, issue looks precisely at the intertwining of both communalisms ("A Dangerous Symbiosis"), but this is a rare example. Ranjit Bhushan raises an important question in the *Outlook* article: "Has this kid-glove treatment of minority communalism resulted in giving secularism a bad name?"[16]

Ashutosh Varshney states, "The framework within which Indian journalists and academics function – right since Nehru's days – does often lead to this intellectual failure. Nehru used to say that majority communalism is India's biggest enemy, not minority communalism. While that may still be true, Nehru failed to see that at some point the two could be seriously interlinked – one could instigate the other and vice versa. Nehru's arguments came apart in the '80s but his intellectual legacy continues. Both forms of communalism – minority and majority – must be condemned".[17]

While Varshney understates the threat represented by majority communalism, he does highlight a lacuna in media analysis. As of now the two sides are caught in a rigid, binary trap: the hate speech of the BJP and its subsidiaries is met by the justified liberal outrage of the secular media, politician, or NGO. Since the former occupies state power and also uses extra-state modes of coercion, the opposition is trapped, as it were, and seems to speak in a vacuum. Both parties in this political conflict seem to be engaged in a monolingual exercise, except that the extremists are on the rampage and in the ascendant. By and large the secular media and intelligentsia seem to be preaching to the converted and need to regain political and intellectual middle ground. The Gujarat election results indicate the increasing marginalization of secular ideals and domains. Competitive demonization and outrage are not the solution. Perhaps there is the need to create space for more tolerant secular and religious discourses to counter the hate speech and barbarism of religious extremism. Rajendra Kumar Vyas, vice-president of the Ahmedabad division of the VHP, declared soon after the riots, "Mark my words, these riots will lead to peace". It is this peace of the grave, of trauma, alienation, and grief that needs to be resisted and the media can play a vital role. The "sterile debate over '*Hindutva*' and 'secularism'" that Siddharth Varadarajan writes about is sterile precisely because of its positing of absolute dichotomies. The recovery of bilingualism and dialogue is possible through more connected and rigorous analysis, a reconfiguration of discourse dominating the debates (similar perhaps to the 'rubble literature' movement in post-Nazi Germany), and the ability to face head on the contradictions and fissures in our secular polity.

Is this expecting too much of the media? Perhaps it is, but then it is also one of the few institutions of free speech combined with mass reach available in India. The first stage of the media revolution in India has been the setting up of large conglomerates, moved as much by business interests as by ideology. The commercial aspects can never be ignored, but a second stage in this revolution is possible if some agents of the media move toward dispassionate analyses rather than the trumpeting of 'truth' or other shibboleths.

NOTES

1. Chenoy, Kamal Mitra, S. P. Shukla, K. S. Subramanian, and Achin Vanaik. *Gujarat Carnage 2002: A Report to the Nation* (April, 2002) p. 4.
2. Daga, Mahesh. "Psyche of the Aggressor: No Kalinga Effect in Gujarat", *The Times of India* (13 July, 2002).
3. Rebeiro, Julio. "Lost Middle Ground: A Community Loses Hope in Gujarat", *The Times of India* (24 April, 2002).
4. "More than Modi: Gujarat 2002 Repudiates the Dead Certainties of Secularism", editorial, *India Today* (30 December, 2002) p. 4.
5. Ibid.
6. Chattarji, Subarno. "Kargil and the Consolidation of 'Indianness': Media Representations of the Kargil Conflict". Forthcoming in *Globalization and India: Social Discourses and Cultural Texts* (Nehru Memorial Museum and Library, New Delhi)
7. Vardarajan, Siddharth. "Beyond the Ballot: the Issue in Gujarat is Justice", *The Times of India* (18 December, 2002).
8. Cited in "Language papers say it in black & white", *The Times of India* (5 April, 2002).
9. Ibid.
10. Ibid.
11. Cited in Chenoy et al, p. 13.
12. See Iftikar Gilani, "A Reporter in Prison", *Sarai Reader 04: Crisis/Media*.
13. *From Surprise to Reckoning: The Kargil Review Committee Report* (Sage Publications, 2000, New Delhi, Thousand Oaks, CA., and London) p. 215.
14. Ibid., p. 218.
15. Joshi, Manoj. "Hitler as Hero: Society without a Moral Compass", *The Times of India* (26 December, 2002).
16. Bhushan, Ranjit. "A Dangerous Symbiosis: Communalism Cannot Exist in a Vacuum – Is that of Minorities being Soft-pedalled?", *Outlook* (1 April, 2002) pp. 20-22.
17. Ibid., p. 21.

Small Town News

TARAN N KHAN

When I was eleven years old, I attended the university-run Girls High School in Aligarh. It was December 1990, and Advani's *Rath Yatra* was on the move. Too young to follow the debate that raged around the Babri Masjid, we were nevertheless acutely aware of the scale of the violence and the tension that permeated our everyday lives. School had become an intermittent affair, to be attended between spells of curfew. In a geography lesson, our teacher let us out to enjoy the winter sun. There was freshly shorn grass lying in the courtyard, and she asked us to help collect it in a corner. We pushed it with our feet to a large mound, and she gave us sweets in red wrappers as a reward. The next day, or perhaps many days later, we found her upset, protesting her innocence, calling on us as witnesses. A local Hindi newspaper, it transpired, had printed an account of our afternoon, claiming that a Hindu student had been humiliated in the *Musalmaan ka* school for partici-pating in the *kar-sewa*.[1] She had been forced to shear grass of the entire courtyard while the school watched. Despite the fact that I never saw the report myself, for many years after that, to my mind, this was how it worked. Local papers told lies, took sides, caused trouble.

Similar ideas apparently prompted the District Magistrate of Aligarh when he ordered a complete news blackout in the city soon after it became plain that the 'reaction' to the Godhra incident was actually genocide. Satellite news channels were blocked, newspaper taxis turned away at city limits and hawkers chased and beaten by the police. Even phone lines went dead. But that, we were told, was routine. His order rested on two common sense notions that have many takers in administrative machinery: one, the power of the media (especially television) to cause unrest and violence; two, the intent and ability of the local media to cause mischief, print rumours and instigate riots. This formulation is not baseless – at that very moment it was available for observation in the vitriolic writings of sections of the Gujarati press – but it grossly underestimates the complexity of the relationship between the city, communal violence and local newspapers. I will examine this interface by looking at the manner in which the vernacular press in Aligarh reported the Gujarat genocide. I suggest that their representation of a current crisis is intimately linked to collective memory of past crises and specifically to memories of (and representations of) the *Rath Yatra* riots, which were the last widespread and protracted cycle of violence in the city. We are thus looking for resonances that the themes and occurrences of Gujarat found in Aligarh's memories, and the manner in which this fragmented, collective memorialization (that often differed diametrically across communities) mediated its representation in the local press.

Here I use Benedict Anderson's conception of the newspaper as a cultural product. Newspapers create imagined linkages between 'communities'; their reading is a mass ceremony that knits together a community, anonymous yet confident of its existence (1991:33). Such a conception adds a layer of meaning to the identification of the news-paper with the community – the Hindi newspaper being synonymous with the Hindu com-munity and the Urdu paper representing the Muslims. The newspapers examined for this analysis – the *Dainik Jagran* (DJ) in Hindi and the *Qaumi Awaz* (QA) in Urdu, while differing greatly in their circulation, clout and editorial policy, do serve this essential function. Aligarh is an interesting place to raise such questions, peculiarly poised as it is between various fault lines of identity and conflict. Part mofussil town and part overlarge industrial centre, it has a sizeable Muslim minority. It is also home to the Aligarh Muslim University, a source of intellectual leadership for Indian Muslims since its inception. AMU is thus a potent symbol of the Muslim renaissance and a past flowering, as well as present attempts at development and empowerment. It is also one of the eight most communally volatile cities in India (Varshney 2002: 7). All this makes Aligarh a visibly Muslim town, targeted by the Hindu Right as a 'hotbed' of trouble and sedition (especially the University), and also explains why the Gujarat genocide caused such immediate and electric tension in the town.

The attack on the Sabarmati Express formed the locus of all initial comment and most reportage in the DJ. It provided an immediate connection with a number of highly evocative, recurrent themes of Hindu nationalism, which dominated coverage of the actual events that followed the incident. The very first report ran under a banner headline; "57 *Ram Sewaks* Burnt Alive in Godhra",[2] the emphasis being on the Hindu identity of the victims, and the fact that they were attacked because of their status as 'servants of Ram'. The chain of memory clearly extends to the *Ram Janam Bhoomi* (RJB), or Birthplace of Ram Movement, and the *Rath Yatra*. For the DJ, the *Yatra* marked an awakening, a resurgence of the latent might of Hindus and a time when many nascent ideas about *Hindutva* coalesced to their present forms. The RJB movement is represented as a continuing, heroic struggle to recover the "manifest inheritance of *Hindutva*" (Jaffrelot 1996:403). The attack on *kar sewaks* returning from Ayodhya thus represents an attack upon both the memory and the process of realization of a resurgent *Hindutva*. In many ways, this initial report set the parameters for subsequent comment and reportage in the newspaper, in particular, the tone of moral outrage and justifiable rage at an "unprovoked assault" that characterized majority discourse on the issue.

"What was the crime of these *Kar Sewaks* that they were burnt alive? Was it that they went to perform a pilgrimage in their own country?"[3] The Godhra incident was thus interpreted as a grave betrayal of faith, an indication of how "pitiable the situation of Hindus is in their own country. If we are not careful, the day is not far off when we will be forced to flee our homeland".[4] Such apocalyptic visions rest on the construct of an inherently (over) tolerant Hindu tradition being systematically undermined and subverted by the proselytizing zeal of Christianity and Islam. They also resonate with the popular imagery of the 'angry Hindu' that gained currency during the *Rath Yatra*. "Our patience should not be tried any further. *Hindutva*[5] is a symbol of tolerance, but even tolerance has its limits".

Simultaneously, the DJ avoids open exhortations to violence against the Muslims as revenge. "Muslims are our brothers ... we must not lose our balance in our grief". Significantly, the same editorial reads, "We must strive to remember that the Muslim of today cannot be compared to the invaders who inflicted terrible trials upon the Hindu populace in medieval times".[6] This appears to be an important admission, since it is upon this rectification of historical wrongs that the RJB movement significantly depends. In Aligarh, it is all the more dramatic since it seems to mark a radical departure from the extremely militant editorial stance and provocative nature of its content during the *Rath Yatra*. The DJ was one of the participants in the media wave that propagated the cause of the *Yatra* in 1990. Its activism for this cause led it to such lengths as to earn a rebuke from the Press Council of India for "gross impropriety and irresponsibility" (Abrar 1993:212), along with three other Hindi newspapers. These newspapers routinely carried news that was either fabricated or distorted in a manner to serve a divisive communal agenda. This included an overt mauling of form, such as drawing prison bars on the photograph of an arrested mahant (religious leader).[7] The *Jagran* printed death tolls of *kar sewaks*. These fluctuated wildly over the days to create an illusion of massacres. Some stories even tended towards the bizarre, like a report about a thousand police officers who planned to quit their jobs in order to form a brigade with the aim of cutting off the hands and feet of Mulayam Singh Yadav (Nandy 1998).

Specifically in Aligarh, there were several incidents of violence that were held to have been 'instigated' by reports in these newspapers. A lengthy and emotional account of these was published in the *Qaumi Awaz*.[8] "The Hindi press has repeatedly acted as the spark to the powder in Aligarh...on December 7th, many such newspapers [unspecified] wrote that the Muslims were planning to launch an attack from mosques after their Friday prayers. On December 8th, Aligarh was transformed into Lebanon. The streets echoed with the cries of blood crazed mobs, and within a few hours, there were over fifty people dead...On December 10th, the Hindi daily *Aaj* printed a completely false story, that twenty-eight Hindu patients and seventy-four attendants had been killed in the AMU-run hospital". This was accompanied by a story in the DJ, which claimed that a mob (of Muslims) had stabbed twenty-seven persons outside the University medical college.[9] While discounting the emotional stress of the QA article and ignoring its mechanistic connotations, these reports were followed by periods of extreme tension that erupted into fierce violence.

In contrast, the tone and editorial policy of the paper during the Gujarat genocide seemed restrained and, if not neutral, at least not overtly sectarian. There were periodic appeals for peace and calls to "help rehabilitate our Muslim brothers".[10] At the end of a month of sustained violence, the paper was moved to comment that "Modi's claim that the situation was under control within 72 hours is difficult to swallow. Why didn't the govern- ment display the speed it employed post-Godhra later also, when people were taken over by monsters of hatred".[11] This change of stance seems to hint towards a shift in ideology, or at least in editorial policy.

Several interesting issues are thrown up by this sketchy juxtaposition of the pages of the *Jagran* over the years.

First – the cause behind this shift. Possible explanations include the physical and emotional distance from the events in Gujarat, which could not match the flow of raw emotion of the RJB movement in UP. More convincing is the view that the change in the demographic composition of its audience had also made it imperative for the DJ to adopt a more open editorial policy and carry news from different sources representing various viewpoints.[12] The bait of increased circulation which was behind the 'competitive sensa- tionalism' of 1990 was served better in 2002 by avoiding divisive discourse.

I argue, however, that this apparent and seemingly dramatic shift is neither radical nor a departure from the paper's previous stance. A reading of the reportage and editorial com- ment on Gujarat reveals a consistent pattern of news selection, skewing and presentation that is subservient to the same agenda of communal/identity politics that motivated edito- rial policy in 1990. While the pitch and tenor of the language may have been toned down, there is no evidence of an ideological shift behind this change. To my mind, it is essential to recognize this fundamental ideological continuity between the *Jagran*'s reportage of Gujarat and Ayodhya. For instance, the *Jagran* established a clear chain of causality between the Godhra incident and the subsequent violence. The first forty-eight hours following the carnage at Godhra saw virtually unchecked targeted violence against Muslims across the state, particularly in Ahmedabad. This violence was reported by the paper as "Anger and outrage at the Godhra massacre shakes Gujarat".[13] A related report on thirty Muslims being burnt alive in a village adds, "It is noteworthy that the village is in the same district where *Kar Sewaks* in the Sabarmati Express were burnt alive". The chronology is thus one of cause and effect. The culpability of the Muslims tempers their being targeted during the 'subsequent violence' and their guilt as the 'instigators' of the cycle of violence legitimizes the 'Hindu reaction'.

Simultaneously, this legitimizing discourse established the genocide as a spontaneous outpouring of Hindu anger. "The lava of anger burst forth in several places in the state today", read reports.[14] This bursting forth was thus essentially unplanned and eminently justifiable. "As any psychologist will testify, such a reaction to (a provocative) action is only natural, though unfortunate".[15] Nothing in the entire body of reportage suggests that the 'riots' bore evidence of planning or state/administrative complicity. The encounter was between "Hindu and Muslim mobs" who "confronted each other" as equal participants in the riot. They thus become stories from yet another set of riots – gruesome and regrettable, yet no different from the regular pattern of violence in times of communal tension.

The *Jagran* also constructed narratives/causes that explained away the symptoms of an unusual riot. "The police, armed only with *lathis* (sticks) could merely watch helplessly as the mobs clashed". Early reports also stressed that various cities were "handed over to the army," creating the image of prompt, impartial action at a time when the forces were only standing by. The attempt was to rationalize the role of the police and the administration by obscuring even the suggestion of a pattern of complicity or sustained violence.[16]

Crucially, this present avatar of the *Jagran's* values does not preclude the presence of news stories representing divergent viewpoints. Most of the incidents that serve as proof of minorities being targeted and massacred are reported in the newspaper.[17] The manner of their reproduction, however, is fragmented and de-contextualized so that their essential nature as acts of violence serving a system of beliefs is glossed over. An agency feature on survivors in relief camps, for instance, was edited mid-sentence, truncating narratives of victims that revealed the nature of the genocide. This failure to communicate critical aspects of 'other view' stories indicates the superficial nature of the *Jagran's* apparent objectivity and indicates the moral vacuity of the belief that the mere presence of news stories advocating a different chronology/victimology represents balanced and objective reportage.

Also, the attachment of the newspaper to the illusion of being neutral and fair is not new. The crude propaganda in the Hindi press in general and the DJ in particular during the *Rath Yatra* "went hand in hand with an almost pathetic attempt to establish the non-sectarian nationalist credentials of the movement". For example, a number of papers foregrounded the fact that the driver of Advani's *Rath* (chariot) was a Muslim, who was persuading other Muslims to offer *kar sewa* (Nandy 1998: 35).

Thus, as I have tried to illustrate, the apparent shift in the Hindi press is neither radical nor fundamental. The apparent dilution of the DJ's militant language does not represent an ideological realignment, but a time honoured survival strategy. By mainstreaming itself, by creating a space for diverse viewpoints on its pages, it will survive and grow in the present context. This expansion of its base is not, however, at the cost of alienating or opposing the interests of its core constituency of middle-class Hindu traders (incidentally also the core supporters of the BJP).

Second – it provides clues to the manner in which the Muslim community perceive the linkages between communal violence and the local media. While this has been previously mentioned, I would like to point out that this interplay is not viewed in isolation. In an article titled "How a Riot is Created", the QA Aligarh correspondent mapped the genealogy of a riot. "First there is circulation of rumours to create tension. Pamphlets are then distributed to increase it to fever pitch. Misleading reports are then published in newspapers",[18] sparking off the riot. The next link is provided when "these riots are written about in an exaggerated way in newspapers àgain". This demonstrates the circular movement of the violence from its representations in the media to its manifestation in reality. There is also concern over the 'unchecked' proliferation of audio/video tapes containing instigatory speeches and militant songs, "which are being played all over in Hindu neighbourhoods, creating a fever of anger and hate". The eventual impression is thus of multiple engagements with a hydra-headed media, diverse and often hostile.

Further, these outbreaks are so contrived that the blame can be pinned on Muslims. "Pamphlets urging Muslims to *jihad* were distributed, signed by non-existent Islamic organizations".[19] This diction of "pre-planned conspiracy to malign the minority community" finds resonance post-Godhra. A more complex resonance lies in the idea of minorities as targets of planned violence. More than any actual correspondence of detail, it is the deliberateness of the creation of violence which resonates across the contexts. A crucial distinction is the identity of these engineers of violence. In 1990, these were 'outsiders', persons external or at least removed from the immediate community of 'ordinary citizens'. After Gujarat, this innocence of the mythical every Hindu has become impossible to maintain.

In one sense then, the echoes between Gujarat and Ayodhya are clearer in the *Qaumi Awaz*, particularly in reports dealing with the complicity of police and institutional apparatus in targeting Muslims, and in a general sense of being victims. This suggests that the trend in academia and journalism of treating the genocide in Gujarat as an entirely unparalleled (or unexpected) occurrence is flawed and counterproductive. Readings of Urdu newspapers reveal the tremendous resonance the events of Gujarat have for Muslims who have lived through riots in other parts and recognize in the former an 'evolution' of 'their' violence. While there were many aspects of the violence that were refined or emphasized to an unprecedented degree, it would be myopic not to recognize the genocide as the latest link in the chain of communalization of Indian social and political life.

Significantly, the two newspapers use near identical language when discussing the pitiable situation of their community, its dwindling security, and its need for protection from the Other. The declaration of the QA that "the oppressors should not push us too far, lest we reach the end of our patience – the vengeance of the oppressed can be truly awful",[20] bears striking resemblance to the idiom used in the DJ while issuing similar warnings to Muslims, indicating a mirroring of persecution myths in both communities. Simultaneously, the resonance of the genocide with the RJB movement is diametrically opposite for the QA to that for the DJ. "Mr. Advani is familiar with how easy it is to stoke communal passions and how difficult to get them back in control".[21] This memory of the *Rath Yatra* and evidence of the cyclic nature of the aggression plays an important role in the manner in which (north Indian) Muslims choose to react to Gujarat; it is in fact an active and articulated element in strategizing by Muslim organizations and associations.

Thirdly – based on this analysis I suggest that these vernacular newspapers essentially replicate the tensions and themes that define inter-community discourse and engagement.

By locating the newspaper (or the media) in the realm of the social, this view complicates the arguments that claim newspapers 'cause' riots by publishing provocative reports. Instead, newspapers need to be conceptualized as a cultural construct which reflect social processes as much as they mould them. This is especially true in a communally charged situation like what occurred in 1990, where the role of newspapers was to reinforce already existing social impulses. It thus follows that changes in media attitudes need to be examined with reference to the context in which they operate. In Aligarh, they tend to reproduce the social distance between the communities, the 'back to back intimacy' of those who live in spatial proximity but with limited civic engagement (Varshney 2002:149). The mapping of patterns of continuity and change in reportage of the two newspapers thus needs to be viewed in the context of their setting of relative calm. In more fraught situations, it is entirely possible that they revert to their more extreme forms of acting as resources for serving identity-driven agendas.

Finally, this analysis argues for language as a significant domain where such conflicts are played out, and as an indicator of social tensions and structures. This approach draws from Barthes' understanding of the difference between a message alone and what can be read from the language (or discourse) it is expressed in. "Through the same message, we read (several) choices, commitments, mentalities... On the level of the simplest message, language explodes; society, with its socio-economic and neurotic structures, intervenes, constructing language like a battleground" (Barthes 1986:106).

As an indication of how clearly language can provide an insight into the complex, nuanced and fragile relationship between the communities, consider this example of usage of a common vocabulary by the two newspapers. Of the three common words I found were used most often in both newspapers, two are *halaak* (killed) and *tandav* (the dance of destruction). The third, *aman*, is peace.

NOTES

1. Literally, 'Service with the Hands' – a cluster of programmes aimed at involving people in the *Vishwa Hindu Parishad* (World Hindu Council's) campaigns to build mass support for the construction of a temple to the Hindu god Ram at the alleged site of Ram's birthplace in the North Indian pilgrim town of Ayodhya, as a key part of the mobilization of Hindu Fundamentalism in contemporary India. *Kar sewa* roughly translates as any activity that helps 'build' the temple.
2. *Dainik Jagran* (1 March, 2002).
3. Mohan, Narendra. "How Long will *Hindutva* Have to Suffer Insults?", *Dainik Jagran* opinion piece (3 March, 2003). Narendra Mohan is the editor-proprietor of the paper.
4. Ibid.
5. The repeated use of the word *Hindutva* instead of Hinduism has possible roots in Savarkar's demands from Hindus to "profess *Hindutva* rather than Hinduism as the first defining characteristic of themselves". See Nandy (1998: 68)
6. *Dainik Jagran* editorial (2 March, 2002).
7. *Aaj* (October, 1990).
8. "Aligarh Newsletter", *Qaumi Awaz* (19 December, 1990).
9. *Dainik Jagran* (10 December, 1990).

10. *Dainik Jagran* (17 March, 2002).
11. 'Human Rights Commission's Warning', *Dainik Jagran* (25 March, 2002).
12. From the late 1990s, Hindi and other regional language newspapers grew considerably, particularly in small towns like Aligarh. The *Jagran* benefited from this trend to emerge as the second widest read Hindi daily in the country. It is also the most popular newspaper in the Hindi heartland (UP, Bihar, Haryana, Delhi), giving it additional clout. Its total readership stands at 12,670,000 (NRS 2002). There is also a web edition aimed at NRI audiences. In Aligarh the paper is read across communal lines, partly due to the relative accessibility of Hindi and also for its coverage of local news.
    Annual net paid sales in the city stand at 11,8584; the Aligarh office is staffed by nearly fifteen people including an AMU correspondent. Local affairs are thus covered in relative detail; the scale and he erogeneous audience of the paper is reflected in a relatively wide pattern of news selection from diverse sources. The period from 1990 to 2002 has seen attempts by the DJ to reposition itself as a 'brand'—this is linked to the post-liberalization affluence of the middle class. There has been a corresponding dilution in its strong communal/parochial associations to win new markets. A number of syndicated columns by established journalists with broadly anti-Sangh opinions have also been introduced.
13. *Dainik Jagran* (1 March, 2002).
14. "An Unforgivable and Heinous Crime", *Dainik Jagran* editorial (1 March, 2002).
15. Misra, Dinnath. "Godhra and Jaundiced Secularism", syndicated column, *Dainik Jagran* (8 March, 2002).
16. The closest the *Dainik Jagran* got to mentioning the genocide was in reporting the accusations of the Opposition members in Parliament and the statements of the NHRC (National Human Rights Commission) indicting the police and the Administration for involvement in the killings. (Various reports, 1-23 March, 2002).
17. This includes potently symbolic incidents like the murder of a Congress-allied politician, Ehsan Jafri, with his family in his home, and the burning of a family of eight in a car who were attempting to flee from Ahmedabad. The car was bound with barbed wire and the family burnt on the state highway. (Various reports, 1-15 March, 2002.)
18. *Qaumi Awaz* (20 December, 1990).
19. Ibid.
20. *Qaumi Awaz* (8 March, 2002).
21. *Qaumi Awaz* editorial (7 March, 2002).

REFERENCES

Anderson, B. *Imagined Communities: Reflections on the Origin and Spread of Nationalism* (Verso, 1991).
Barthes, R. *The Rustle of Language* (Billy and Sons Ltd., 1986, Worcester).
Dainik Jagran: Issues from 28th February to 30th March, 2002.
Haqqi, S. and Abrar, R. eds. *Secularism Under Siege* (Uttar Pradesh Rabita Committee, 1993).
Jaffrelot, C. *The Hindu Nationalist Movement and Indian Politics* (Viking Penguin India, 1996).
Nandy, A. *Exiled at Home* (Oxford University Press, 1998).
Qaumi Awaz: Issues 28th February - 30th March, 2002 and 1st to 30th December, 1990.
Varshney, A. *Ethnic Conflict and Civic Life Hindus and Muslims in India* (Oxford University Press, 2002).
Vilification Campaign Against Aligarh Muslim University: December 1990 Communal Riots at Aligarh (Issued by Aligarh Muslim University Aligarh, A.M.U. Press).

'Out of the Box'
Televisual Representations of North-East India

DAISY HASAN

As an observer of programmes about the North-East on Indian television, both private and state owned, both national and regional, I have invariably had to grapple with a sense of despair. If private television channels are, as is often claimed, making concessions to regional audiences like never before, audiences here appear to have been missed, or acknowledged only nominally, if at all. While more avenues for representation are theoretically available today, it is still only the 'newsworthy' and the out-of-the ordinary that make it to our TV screens. Whole areas of cultural, social and political experience that do not fit neatly into hard and soft news agendas are never becoming part of public memory.

To my mind, the invisibility of the region's everyday is indicative of a crisis of representation on television. My attempt in this essay is to reflect on the causes for this crisis as well as to examine the available representations of the region on private and national television and their regional and local variants.

On the profit-oriented privately owned channels that have come to increasingly monopolize the attention of viewing publics, the region remains decidedly on the periphery of news and entertainment discourses. The following message posted by a Channel [V] producer on an alumni website recently caught my attention:

"A channel [V] team is heading out to the north-east states to do a travel show – not the usual touristy thing but something out-of-the-box stuff. Need research and story ideas from all the states there...need help...weird stuff – people, tribes, strange customs, virgin/ undiscovered beautiful locations. Call me dude...can you get back pronto..."

What is striking is the producer's desire to eschew stereotypical "touristy" representations while simultaneously falling prey to the very stuff that tourism thrives on – tribes, customs, beautiful locations. Ironically, the diverse musical talent of the North-East has rarely caught the popular music channel's attention. Channel [V] remains out of bounds for the many self-made rock, blues, gospel bands here, even as it does not hesitate to exploit its exotic locales and customs for its travel shows.

A similar quest for the extraordinary marks news coverage of the North-East on the privately owned channels. In this scheme of things the bomb blasts, the massacres, the shootouts – threats posed by the region to the sanctity of the Indian state – find pride of place in the headlines of prime time news programmes. News sells and therefore warrants investments in terms of North-East bureaus. Glib correspondents deliver p-to-c with the right mix of sobriety and style that they imagine befits cutting edge TV journalism. Unfortunately, the facts sometimes don't match the flair with which they are delivered. Instances of mixing up names and accompanying visuals abound in television and the print media. But, more seriously, ethnic clashes go misreported. In 1993, the clashes between Meiteis and Meitei-Pangals in the Manipur Valley were misreported as an extension of the Naga-Kuki conflict by prominent national media. Reflective and detailed reportage of the region's everyday is glaringly absent on the channels that 'matter'.

One of the reasons for this glaring absence is that the cities and towns of the region do not come under TRP (Television Rating Points) towns. Audiences therefore are numerically insignificant against the mass viewership in major Indian cities to which sponsorship is wedded. In such a scenario, audiences in the region take what they get even as they become invisible in the images they consume.

Public service television, which could have functioned as an effective forum for diverse local voices, has been handicapped by its own agendas for national integration and state control. If one is guided solely by the investments in communication infrastructure made in the states of North-East India in the current and last decade by Doordarshan (National Television), one is likely to conclude that the region has been given a fair share of attention by the centre. In addition to the regional Doordarshan *Kendras* or centres in the state capitals, a round-the-clock North-Eastern Service was introduced three years ago, fed by programmes produced at a Programme Production Centre in Guwahati.

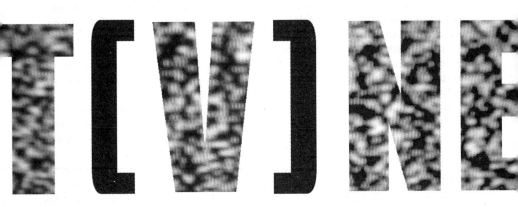

However, this much talked about expansion and development of television translates into a largely infrastructural affair. A great deal of resources may have been spent on setting up transmitters and building and equipping studios according to a standardized blueprint, but little attention has been paid to unique regional and local conditions for broadcasting. Most regional centres bounce off the national network on which programmes about the region are confined to half-hour weekly slots. Programmes originating from the regional station are limited, and shoddily produced. Those who can change channels do so.

The heavily centralized structure of public service television consequently makes for little resonance in the daily lives of people here. In Shillong, for instance, one gets a sense of the local Doordarshan *Kendra*'s remoteness from the rhythms of the city even by its geographical placement. It is located on a hill – aloof and inaccessible to the quotidian life of the city below.

A concentration of resources in Guwahati has aggravated the problem. Policy makers at the centre are advised by self-seeking interlocutors in Guwahati, claiming to speak for the entire region. Contracts for producing programmes go not necessarily to the most deserving, but to those who have the clout to get them. So, while the funds for the region might be generous, as the former Director General of Doordarshan claims they are, they are often intercepted by pockets of self-interest.

When queried about programming policy for the North-East, the Deputy Director General (Programme) in Doordarshan *Bhavan*, New Delhi replied, "Why should there be a different policy? Why should programmes for the North-East be different from those for South India?"

Presumably there is no difference between viewers located in a remote hamlet of West Khasi Hills District, for instance, from those located in an urban locality in Bangalore. The insensitivity to context and the preference for a pan-Indian perspective has stood in the way of enabling the national broadcaster to strike a rapport with audiences in the region.

A former station director in Aizawl recounts how he was expected to send a statement to the Information & Broadcasting Ministry on the number of public service messages against untouchability he had broadcast. "When I was posted there we started getting telegrams – 'your untouchability statement has not reached'. Then I wrote a letter back to them and said we are in a tribal area where there is no untouchability..."

In representing the nation to itself, national television has unfailingly privileged certain positions and memories over others. Between 1984 and1992, the period when Doordarshan monopolized television audiences in the country, an increasingly Hindi and Hindu-centric cultural agenda, supported by the market, emerged. Financially pressured to generate its own revenue, Doordarshan became vulnerable to market pressures, and in a bid to deliver maximum possible audiences to hungry advertisers, all but abandoned the developmental and public service rhetoric which had justified the introduction of television. An opportunistic policy aligning the state's propaganda needs with domestic and foreign capital, and the demand for entertainment by the middle class emerged.[1] This audience was simultaneously co-opted into the discourses of national (Hindu) culture.

Within this scheme of things, the significantly diverse cultural narratives from within North-East India could at best be stereotyped in the national mainstream that television re-presented "...as Other – 'backward', 'violent', 'underdeveloped', 'tribal' in the worst sense. But, in the curious symbolic polarization that constructs Others, [the] region has also been seen as a kind of folkloric ideal – 'tribal' in the best sense, close to nature, isolated from the enervations of modernity, embodying the communal and uncommodified, carrying in local artistic traditions a non-reflective but powerful creativity that expresses some essential, primitive, timeless humanity".[2]

Ohm (1999: 75) has analyzed the manner in which Doordarshan was historically dealt with images that it projected to the nation. The task of television, she argues, was believed to be one of disciplining the image in keeping with its self-appointed role as an educator of taste whose main objectives were educational and developmental. In trying to project images of Indian 'reality', Doordarshan eschewed the 'vulgar exuberance' of Hindi films but came close to embracing a non-image (ibid: 76).

As far as the North-East states are concerned, these non-images continue to dominate its representation on national television.

It is the local entrepreneurial effort at narrowcasting in cities like Shillong, Aizawl, and Imphal that is able to provide a glimpse of the flux generated in the region by the forces of modernity. These weekly, and in some cases daily, news and features produced in local languages and transmitted through the neighbourhood cable networks document the every-day at a level and in an idiom that is not available to the regional, national or private broad-casters. While they might devote a great deal of attention to the workings of local govern-ment institutions and those of 'insurgents', they at least afford the possibility of document-ing other local narratives that animate the cities, towns and villages of North-East India.

One worries about the future of these innovative but financially precarious endeavours in a media environment where the 'big players' are constantly looking to capture new 'markets'. One worries that the innovative spaces carved out by cultural practitioners – most prominently the music concerts – could soon become Channel [V] style frenetic events sponsored by Pepsi and Coca Cola.

Any meaningful representation of the region will have to approach it from a perspec-tive other than the one of insurgency and backwardness that informs current coverage. Unless spaces for the expression of contemporary cultural interests and political aspira-tions are created, the North-East, in spite of all its 'crises' that attract television coverage, might in a real sense remain out of the box.

NOTES

1. See Manjunath Pendakur, "A Political Economy of Television: State, Class and Corporate Confluence in India", in G.Sussman and J. A Lent eds., *Transnational Communications: Wiring the Third World* (Sage, 1991, London) pp. 234-62.

2. Taylor, Betsy. "Public Folklore, Nation-Building and Regional Others: Comparing Appalachain USA and North-East India", *Indian Folklore Research Journal*, Vol 1, No. 2 (2002) pp. 1-27.

Lost in Transit
Narratives & Myths of the Crash of Egypt Air Flight 990 in Egyptian and American Newspapers

MAHMOUD EID

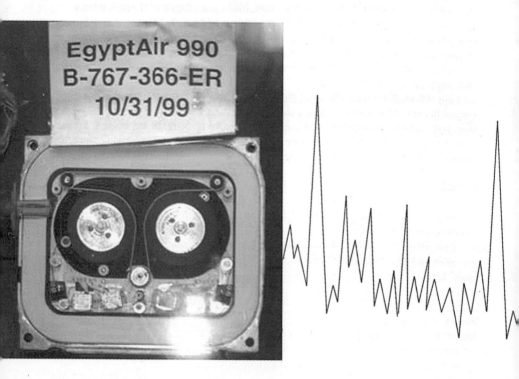

Lost Realities

The contemporary world witnesses the transmission of a very large amount of information every day by transnational mass media. This large volume of information is generally represented in a dizzying variety of ways. The sheer scale of this volume and variety of information makes it difficult for audiences to perceive the reality of the events and situations that they are confronted with. We can think of an audience faced with 'lost realities'. In fact, audiences come to know about events mainly through the filters of 'news-worthiness' that the media deploy to introduce them into public consciousness. The media not only cover and focus on events, they also explain events' consequences and analyze their significance. Any event may give rise to several different explanations, and these interpretations may directly and strongly contribute towards shaping the political, economic, or social consequences of the event. The question of the influence of the mass media on audiences becomes all the more sensitive when we consider controversial events, conflicts, crises, or disasters that require accurate and precise explanations and analyses.

It has become quite obvious that the media often adopt quite a sly technique while covering markedly controversial events. Generally, in such cases, media organizations will tend to diffuse their biases, attitudes, and beliefs indirectly through 'both-sided', or apparently 'even-handed' coverage. Journalists sometimes claim that they are absolved from allegations of bias if they, or the news that they create, are criticized by people on both sides of a sharply divided political scenario over contentious political issues. Actually, they are simply choosing to remain in a position where they can keep 'playing it down the middle' (Karlberg and Hackett 1996:1).

Generally speaking, it is important to consider that journalists, like scientists, may often have hypotheses in mind while working on a story. However, journalists, unlike scientists, carry both explicit and implicit hypotheses. Moreover, journalists find themselves poised uneasily between what they see as two impossible ideals: 'the demands of indexing reality', which they see as reachable through objective strategies, and the 'demands of narrativity'. This makes it important to look at the narrative qualities of news. Although the most significant role of media during conflicts, disasters, and crises is to provide information, the mere purveying of facts is not something that completely satisfies an audience's needs for information about such events. Morgan, Lewis and Jhally's study about the US Media and George Bush's decision to use military force against Iraq in the 1990/1 Gulf War concludes, "[T]he US media failed quite dramatically in their role as information providers. Despite months of intense coverage, most people did not know basic facts about the political situation in the Middle East or about the recent history of US policy toward Iraq ... [Moreover,] the media also failed in their 'duty to be objective' because they largely communicated facts that supported the administration's policy and played down those that did not" (1992:229:230).

The mass media react to, narrate, and report the events that they look at in very particular ways. In this they are often influenced by the way such an event has already been framed through prior reportage, or external considerations. The standard practice is to rely on specific sources of information that are considered, for one reason or another, 'useful' or 'reliable'. However, sometimes the nature of the event makes for an alteration in these 'sources'. It is the interaction between journalists and this changing body of 'sources' that shapes the news. The nature of this interaction is not the same for every situation; rather, its representation and even how it is narrated is mediated by the context it finds itself located in (Berkowitz and Beach 1993:4).

The Dilemma of the Egypt Air Flight 990 Crash

In November 1999, the tragic crash of the Egypt Air Flight 990 during its return trip from New York to Cairo saw the American and the Egyptian media influencing the reading of the event with the deployment of 'myths' in their representations of the story. These myths were in addition to various rumours and conflicting explanations. Basically, the Egyptian media were influenced by the myth that Israel is the prime mover behind any incident or crisis in the Arab world, and the American media were influenced by the myth that Islam provokes violence. Karim H. Karim in *Islamic Peril: Media and Global Violence* (2000:136) explains, "The renewed image of Islam as enemy has developed in dominant global discourses despite the military cooperation between the US and governments of countries with Muslim majorities like Egypt [among others]". Myth controls mass media professionals' ways of thinking, analyzing, and representing events, disasters, or incidents; there is no difference as to the extent of the influence of such myths on news and reportage, regardless of whether we look at media in 'developed' or 'developing' countries.

Narratives on either side (in this case, Egypt and the United States) tried to present the discourse in the terms of what van Dijk (1998:317) calls "Positive Self-Presentation" and "Negative Other-Presentation". The problem that concerns us here is to see how both the Egyptian and the American media used 'strategies of representation' in the course of reporting the tragic crash. Strategies of argumentation, according to Wodak (1997:73), involve the connecting of discrete but related contents in a certain text that serve to convey prejudice even as they simultaneously seek to disguise it.

Strategies of justification, for example, enable speakers to make evaluations and to assign responsibility and guilt, while aiming at the same time to present the speaker as free of prejudice or even as a victim of reverse prejudice. Strategies of group definition and construction, another type of strategy of argumentation, construct a discourse of difference, a 'we/they' or 'us/them' discourse, whose essential function is the rejection of responsibility of guilt and its displacement onto the 'Other' group.

Researching Media Representations of the Disaster

The main purpose of this paper is to examine the extent to which two major Egyptian and American newspapers represented a specific argumentative story differently. It is important to determine strategies of representation which both sides followed, and the sources on which they depended. By examining the different forms of discourse that were deployed by both newspapers, we can also define the myths that lay behind the reporting.

Both quantitative and qualitative content analyses are conducted to illustrate the representation of the crash in both the Egyptian and the American newspaper. Due to the nature of the story under analysis, this paper uses the technique of 'Purposive Sampling'. The sampled items are the specific story, newspapers, and duration. The specific story under analysis is the crash of the Egypt Air Flight 990 into the Atlantic during its return trip from New York to Cairo on Monday, November 1st, 1999. The Egyptian newspaper *Al-Ahram* and the American newspaper *The New York Times* are selected because the former is the main national or official newspaper in Egypt, and the latter a major newspaper and news authority in the United States. Analysis includes all news of the crash in both newspapers during the period from November 1st, 1999, to November 30th, 1999, in order to include the most significant as well as the most (apparently) trivial items, charges, justifications, and rumours. A total of 222 news articles are analyzed in both newspapers. The majority of these articles (77.9%) are in *Al-Ahram* and only 22.1% are in *The New York Times*. The coverage of the former is apparently, and logically, more intensive given that Egypt was more affected by the event. Dates have been counted in order to compare the average coverage of the disaster in both newspapers throughout the period of analysis. The average coverage in both newspapers is more or less an equal variable distribution consistent with the development of events, surprises, and estimations.

In terms of attention, the location (in the pages of the newspaper) of the news coverage of the crash is examined. Unsurprisingly, *Al-Ahram* focused more attention on the crash than *The New York Times*. News about the crash appeared, or was indicated in an indirect manner constantly in the front page of *Al-Ahram*, while more than three quarters of the news covering the crash appeared only in the inside pages of *The New York Times*. The significant (P £ 0.001) and strong (Contingency Coefficient = 0.65) relationship between the newspaper and the location of the crash news in the newspaper is reflected in the value of Chi-Square (161.87). However, the percentage of photos used in *The New York Times* is much higher at 74.6%, three times that of *Al-Ahram* (25.4%), with a higher average number of photos (Mean = 1.5000 and 1.3636 respectively) in news stories.

While there are some differences in the percentages of specific photos and content between the two newspapers, as illustrated in Table 1, families, relatives, and friends of Egyptian victims were the main subjects for both. Also, representations of American coast guards, rescue boats, marine ships, robots, helicopters, and reconnaissance teams searching for victims are highly concentrated on both sides, especially in *Al-Ahram*. (One could argue that this was in order to try and reduce readers' anxiety, and thereby the level of tension prevailing in Egypt at that time, by focusing on the rescue operations and attempts at salvage at the crash site). The most significant difference is reflected in the lack of appearance of Egyptian government officials in the American newspaper, which only showed Egypt Air officials.

Table 1: Content of Photos in *Al-Ahram* compared with *The New York Times*

Contents	Al-Ahram	The New York Times
1. Families, relatives, and friends of Egyptian victims	22.4	30.6
2. American coast guards, rescue boats, marine ships, robots, helicopters and reconnaissance searching	22.4	13.9
3. Maps showing scenario of the crash and explanations	2.0	13.9
4. American officials	10.2	11.1
5. Egyptian victims (passengers & crew)	12.2	8.3
6. Black box (data recorder of the Flight 990)	6.1	5.5
7. Debris from Egypt Air Flight 990 and passengers' items retrieved from the Atlantic	4.2	5.5
8. Egyptian citizens	6.1	2.8
9. Egypt Air officials	4.2	2.8
10. 1998 photo of the Egypt Air Boeing 767 that crashed	0.0	2.8
11. American victims (passengers)	0.0	2.8
12. Egyptian officials	10.2	0.0

As to the news sources, *The New York Times* did not rely on news correspondents from Egypt to reflect the other side's point of view. Instead, it depended largely on its reporters (78.9%) for most of its information. Its use of news agencies as sources (*Associated Press* 8.8%, *Agence France Press* 7.0%, and *Reuters* 5.3%) was limited to photos only. On the other hand, *Al-Ahram* depended on various sources in a more balanced way. Although the sources of 37.8% of news stories were not specified, *Al-Ahram* relied on its correspondent in the United States (22.7%) to follow latest developments. In addition to its reporters (10.3%), it also used a variety of international news agencies (23.2%), and its own news agency, MENA (5.9%). Percentages show that both *Al-Ahram* and *The New York Times* were similar to each other in that they never negatively represented the 'Self' and clearly tended to represent it in a positive way (86.7% and 87.8% respectively), rather than neutrally (13.3% and 12.2% respectively). Also, both newspapers were fairly similar in negatively representing the 'Other', albeit *The New York Times* was more negative (31.8%) than *Al-Ahram* (34.7%), given their compared positive (20.4% and 26.0% respectively) and neutral (44.9% and 42.2% respectively) representations of the 'Other'.

Table 2 illustrates the different perceptions of both newspapers of the 'Other', the strategies of 'Self' and 'Other' representations, and the discourses diffused through the coverage of that disaster. While *Al-Ahram* cited the Boeing company, the American administration, and the Israeli intelligence agency *Mossad* as the 'Other', *The New York Times* foregrounded terrorism, Islam, and the crew of Egypt Air Flight 990. Despite the fact that both newspapers positively represent the 'Self' and routinely represent the 'Other' in a negative manner, both newspapers have, on occasion, represented the 'Other' in a positive way. In fact, both newspapers did so before the charges and counter charges with regard to locating responsibilities and culpabilities for the crash were made. While representing the 'Self', both newspapers depended on attempts at logical justifications for everything that they said. The Egyptians also concentrated on portraying the tragedy and its victims in terms of the 'human dimensions' of the incident.

The New York Times	*Al-Ahram*

The Other

The New York Times
> Crew of crashed Egypt Air Flight 990
> Terrorism
> Islam

Al-Ahram
> The Boeing Company
> The American Administration
> Mossad (Israeli Intelligence Agency)

Self-Representation
Positive

The New York Times
> Effort in search and rescue attempts
> Fair investigations
> US was not obliged to run the inquiry
> Dedication to finding the cause of the crash

Al-Ahram
> Victims of a disaster and calamity
> Tragic human stories
> The competence of the Egyptian pilots
> Safety record of Egypt Airlines
> Egypt Airlines credibility in the West
> Crew of Egypt Air Flight 990 took the correct course of action to try and avoid the disaster
> Pilots of Egypt Air Flight 990 are religious and family men

Other-Representation
Positive

The New York Times
> Aircraft with a good record
> Victims of disaster
> Good record of the crew
> Families of victims get to see the airplane wreckage

Al-Ahram
> Efforts for search and rescue
> Good Egyptian-American relations
> Apologies for the incorrect surmise of suicide
> Hospitality towards Egyptian victims' families and friends

Negative

The New York Times
> Suspicion about the cryptic nature of the words uttered by the co-pilot and their intent
> Egypt Air has had 3 fatal crashes in the past 3 decades
> Islamic fundamentalists and terrorism
> Information gap present when it comes to Islam and Muslims

Al-Ahram
> The defect of Boeing 767 industry and similar crashes
> The American media's criticism of the Egyptian crew
> Mysterious and opaque procedures of the American administration during the investigations
> Irrational, illogical, and incorrect explanation of suicide as a motive for the incident
> The Americans' ignorance of Islam and the Arabic language

Discourses

The New York Times
> The co-pilots suicide
> Terrorist act

Al-Ahram
> Israeli plot (conspiracy)
> American military's fault
> Explosion of the plane's tail due to serious manufacturing defects
> Bad weather

It is useful to consider Karim's (1993:4-5) general conceptualization of struggles between four forms of discourses – "dominant, oppositional, alternative, and conservative populist" – while considering the discourses deployed within the coverage.

Dominant discourses construct the parameters of meaning within which certain terms are used in public discussions of particular issues; oppositional discourses may take exception to aspects of specific terms but do not question their fundamental validity. The ideological bases of terminology networks and meanings proposed by dominant discourses may, however, be challenged more seriously by alternative discourses. New words expressing alternative ideas or new meanings of existing terms may appear through deconstructive processes, and may even be enshrined in legislation. But ultimately, and often with the collusion of conservative populist discourses manifested in daily conversations, dominant discourses reconstruct the previous meanings of the older terms or place the newer ones proposed by alternative discourses into ideological frameworks of the status quo.

Applying this framework to the case at hand, we see that on the Egyptian side the explosion of the airplane's tail due to a serious manufacturing defect was the dominant discourse, and the bad weather experienced during the flight was the alternative discourse. At the same time the oppositional discourse was that the American military was at fault, which was justified by pointing to similar previous crashes in the same region. The populist discourse, which could not be adopted by officials, was the 'Israeli Plot'.

On the American side, the dominant discourse was, is, and will continue to be 'the terrorist act'. Subsequently, the alternative discourse came to be a questioning of the intention of the relief pilot, veering towards an explanation that tried to centre on his purported suicide. This discourse based itself upon the Islamic invocations which the pilot uttered before the crash. One of the interesting findings, that reflects the lack of accurate information or representation, is the presence of contradictory statements on both sides. For example, *The New York Times* reported that the Egyptian officials "authorized" the United States to conduct the many-sided investigation of the disaster. Meanwhile, *Al-Ahram* reported that the Egyptian officials "accepted the request" from the United States to conduct an investigation.

Inescapable Evidence?

Myth was the hidden motivating factor and the main reason behind all the strategies of 'Self-representation', 'Other-representation', and the diffused forms of discourse. Both sides were influenced by a specific myth. In either case, it was myth that controlled its behaviours, beliefs and attitudes towards its 'Other'.

Despite the fact that each side's myth was probably unacceptable at the global level and inconsistent with the other side's version, it was influenced, even if indirectly so, by that which it rejected. The Egyptian side was influenced by the myth that every violent action against any Arab country is definitely supported by, or has the backing of, Israel. The strong relationship between Israel and the United States is seen as the basis for any conspiracy against the Arabs. This myth makes the Egyptian side cautious when considering the American side's explanations and investigations, and makes the Egyptian side suspicious about every procedure. On the other hand, the American side is influenced by the myth that Islam is the base for terrorism and violent actions to the extent that they (the American media) believe that the co-pilot tried to commit suicide. The Americans believe that what the relief pilot said before the crash suggests an Islamic 'martyrdom' ritual, and that this reveals the motive behind the violent action that resulted in the crash. In this way, neither side can escape the implications of being the shadow of its 'Other'. The evidence that it offers and the arguments that it presents are always about the conspiracy hatched by the 'Other'. By reporting the event this way, each side is inevitably tied up with the existence of the very 'Other' that it seeks paradoxically to reject.

An earlier version of this research paper was presented June 28th, 2003, at the "Second Tampere Conference on Narrative: Narrative, Ideology, and Myth" in Tampere, Finland.

Acknowledgment
The author would like to sincerely thank Professor Karim H. Karim of the School of Journalism and Communication at Carleton University, Canada, for his generous sharing of valuable ideas, comments, and suggestions in the course of evaluating this work.

REFERENCES
Berkowitz, D. and D. W. Beach. "News Sources and News Context: The Effects of Routine News, Conflict and Proximity", *Journalism Quarterly* 70/1 (1993) pp. 4-12.

Bird, S. E. and R. W. Dardenne. "Myth, Chronicle, and Story: Exploring the Narrative Qualities of News", in J. W. Carey ed., *Media, Myths, and Narratives: Television and the Press* (Sage, 1988, London) pp. 67-86.

Fensch, T. *Associated Press Coverage of a Major Disaster: The Crash of Delta Flight 1141* (Erlbaun, 1990, Hillsdale, NJ).

Karim, K. H. "Constructions, Deconstructions, and Reconstructions: Competing Canadian Discourses on Ethnocultural Terminology", *Canadian Journal of Communication* 18/2 (1993) pp. 1-19.

Karim, K. H. *Islamic peril: Media and Global Violence* (Black Rose Books, 2000, Montréal).

Karlberg, M. and R. A. Hackett. "Cancelling Each Other Out?: Interest Group Perceptions of the News Media", *Canadian Journal of Communication* 21/4 (1996) pp. 1-9.

Morgan, M., J. Lewis and S. Jhally. "More Viewing, Less Knowledge", in H. Mowlana, G. Gerbner and H. I. Schiller eds., *Triumph of the Image: The Media's War in the Persian Gulf – a Global Perspective* (Westview Press, 1992, Boulder, Colorado) pp. 216-233.

van Dijk, T. A. *Racism and the Press* (Routledge, 1991, London).

van Dijk, T. A. *Ideology: A Multidisciplinary Approach* (Sage, 1998, London).

Wodak, R. "Das Ausland and Anti-Semitic Discourses: The Discursive Construction of the Other", in S. Riggins ed., *The Language of Politics and Exclusion* (Sage, 1997, London) pp. 65-87.

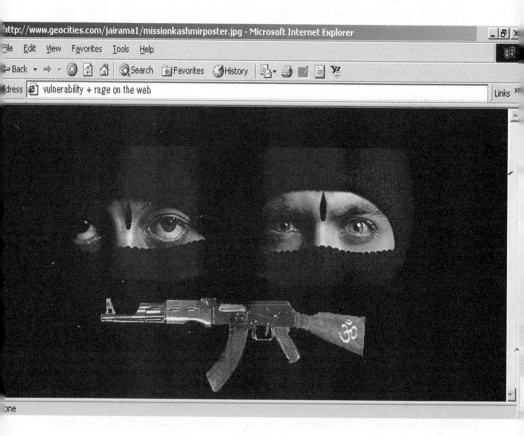

Of Nasty Pictures and "Nice Guys"
The Surreality of Online *Hindutva*
CHRISTIANE BROSIUS

In this essay, I focus on the ways in which the internet, particularly a website, www.hindu-unity.org, set up by the Hindu far right organization Hindu Unity (hereafter HU), becomes a stage for the representation and performance of the crisis of a politicized Hindu identity. I am interested in how the internet as a medium is able to deliver what other media technologies can hardly offer: namely, access for its users to the shared production of affect on a transnational basis, the feeling of participation and empowerment in the making and dissemination of shared myths, identities and histories, as well as fears and desires between various locally-based groups and individuals by means of an imagined networked community (Zook 1996).

Introducing 'HinduUnity.Org'
The introductory slogan of the portal, framed by the organization's logo of Hanuman emerging from the map of India on the left and two *trishuls* (tridents) on the right, reads: "HinduUnity.org – Promoting & Supporting the Ideals of the Bajrang Dal".

The producers of the website openly declare their affiliation with the Bajrang Dal, the youth wing of the *Vishwa Hindu Parishad* (VHP, or World Hindu Council). The *Bajrang Dal* (The Bajrang Militia) is well known for its often aggressively rhetorical and occasionally violent attacks on alleged threats to Hindu identity. They particularly target Muslims, Christians and symbols of 'westernization'.

In order to contextualize the production of HU's visual and narrative rhetoric, it is important to point out that HU (like much else on the web) profits from the density, ubiquity and flow of images on the web: almost everything that is online can be appropriated and framed in a new context, and filled with new meaning. On the HU website we can see bin Laden turned into a voyeur of erotica, and images of Hamas fighters or US military personnel metamorphosed into *Hindutva* soldiers. Here, the images of bin Laden, the erotic figures, the images of Hamas soldiers or American soldiers all have different provenances within the broad digital universe. Their being brought together on to the same web page is illustrative of the recombinant properties of web culture, which is the environment that HU is embedded in.

We can venture to say that the web provides a place for the creation of a new form of intercultural and transnational iconography, even to those committed to militant nationalism and opposed to intercultural dialogue. In building this dynamic repertoire of images and visual rhetoric, symbols of the threatening Other are 'magically fixed' through the strategies of appropriation, defamation, or humiliation. We are reminded here of a key text by Evelyn Kallen entitled "Hate on the Net" (Kallen, 1998). Kallen distinguishes three interconnected means of using the web as a 'hate-mongering' tool: An 'invalidation myth' defines the target group (e.g. the Muslims) as inferior/dangerous; an 'invalidation theory' provides the ideo-logical framework, arguments and 'evidence' to rhetorically attack minority groups; and finally as 'a platform for organized community action', a hate website urges and provides the communicative means for the 'threatened community' to take steps to aggressively counter or eliminate the purported threat.

The aim of HU is to create both an actual and an imagined virtual brotherhood of mili-tant Hindus, and to claim rights to representation over this homogenized community. The consumers of this vision are otherwise physically out of reach to eachother and to the prime movers of HU (social encounters happen predominantly on the net; real world encounters within HU seem rare). The visitors to the HU site can then be seen as an audience respond-ing to the facilitation of a communication platform, responding to projections of Hindus seen and shown as victims, judges, or soldiers. Through various performative strategies, the affective components of the possibility to participate in this world of victims, judges, vigi-lantes and soldiers, and the urge to 'make an impact' on this world, are evoked. The tenor of all the articles and images available, on and through the HU homepage, is one of ongo-ing confrontation and crisis: *Hindutva*, for the makers and producers of HU, is the organi-zed, aggressive, cohesive articulation of what it is to be a Hindu today, and is the only way to protect Hindu identity against national and international threats. HU creates credibility, and thus authority, by entangling the visitor in a claustrophobic space, seemingly filled with countless details of "the evidence of the historic and ongoing humiliation, torture and abuse of Hindus". And having done so, it puts forward what it calls "justified" strategies to encounter the cause/s of this crisis.

Even though most of the images, rhetoric and ideological content put on display on a website like HinduUnity are not new, and can be traced back to the writings of *Sangh Parivar* ideologues such as Veer Savarkar or Golwalkar, it is the ways in which the images are pre-sented and combined that constitutes a strange amalgam of virtual reality/actuality, or, as I indicated in the title of this article, surreality. I employ the term surrealism with some deliberation. I use it here in reference to two issues which I find are at stake in the Hindu Right's use of the internet: One is the conscious alignment of two or more different images, each drawn from different 'real' locations or contexts within one composition, creating through the juxtaposition of two already familiar materials a strange feeling of augmented and renewed familiarity that causes a heightened, uncanny sense of reality. The second issue emerges from the idea of montage, and pulls in cultural historian Walter Benjamin's work on media aesthetics and propaganda. Benjamin's notion of the surreal proposed that the effect of a shock transmitted through image consumption brings to a standstill the free flow of associations. The aesthetic shock freezes perception and at the same time heightens our senses; it creates an aura by means of which the necessary critical distance of the viewing subject succumbs to the concentrated transmission of ideologically imbued content. The magical condensation of meaning embodied in images brings the viewed object close to us, renders it as if it were tactile, and makes available to our desires and fears what otherwise remains abstract and distant. Fetishization (which pulls one closer to the object or feeling desired) and xenophobia (which repels and makes more distant the 'other') are thus simultaneously central to the virtual surrealism of HinduUnity (see Mulvey, 1996).

In the context of HU, I am particularly concerned with the ways in which narratives and images of crisis and suffering work on the sensation of the viewer, and how in particular the visitors to the website are addressed as consumers (and agents) of violence as a spectacle. The kind of agency evoked in this context is the almost oxymoronic creation of what could be called an armchair *jihadi* or a console *dharamyoddha* (Holy Warrior), who views the violence on display with a degree of pleasure and inner torment, combined with feelings of vulnerability and rage.

Exposures, Petitions and Black Lists: HinduUnity as an imagined "Courtroom"

What does the landscape of links, images and articles on www.HinduUnity.org offer its visitors? The HU homepage provides users with a hundred twenty links and eighty articles on the main index (as of October 2002). At first, we enter a jungle of networks and links, with no recognizable structure. Most of the articles are taken from other sources: newspapers, magazines, other websites, or the *Hindu Vivek Kendra*, an archive dedicated to give the *Hindutva* agenda an 'intellectual' touch. Visual sources are appropriated from other websites, or reinterpreted by attributing new captions on to them, or made specifically for a particular HU 'item'. There are no *Devanagari* elements on the site, which indicates that the majority of HU-visitors belongs to the English educated middle-class, probably many of whom access the site from abroad. Hindu Unity claims to have about 500 members, most of them based in India, the UK and the US. HU aligns itself directly to the promotion and support of the Bajrang Dal (BD), the militant youth wing of the VHP, which has so far only been active in India. HU's chairman, Rohit V (see last section, this article) is an active supporter of the BD. The organization of HU bears similarity to an army corps: Four 'lieutenants' head HU, members are referred to as "*jawans*" (literally "youths", a word used for soldiers in Hindi and Urdu). The language and rhetoric of HU is based on an idealization of weaponry, war and a militarized Hindu identity. Dramatic and sensational infotainment seems to be the underlining rhetorical form and tone of most items on display.

Fittingly, the answer to "Who in your opinion should rule India today?", which features as one of the FAQs on HU's link to "About Us", is that this job should be entrusted to Bal Thackeray (Shiv Sena supremo) or Narendra Modi (chief minister of Gujarat, a former RSS *pracharak* (proselytizer), whose renewed electoral success has been linked to the anti-Muslim pogroms following from the Godhra carnage that occurred while he was chief minister of Gujarat in March 2002). [See articles by Darshan Desai, Subarno Chatterji and Arvind Narrain, elsewhere in this reader.]

Hindus as Victims
The declared motto of HU is *"safaiya"* ("cleansing"). "The greatest threat of all", according to HU, "are Muslims", who are depicted almost constantly as "traitors and killers". The site asks the visitor, "HINDUS! When will you arise and save *Bharat* from bleeding to death? When will you stand up and cleanse our soil of those HINDU KILLERS?"

The site works with and articulates the notion that "the Hindu people, sons of the (Indian) soil, have been paralyzed or unconscious or are too tolerant to counter the purportedly anti-national activities of the Muslim minority". Mohandas Gandhi, for example, is accused of having "paralysed the manhood of India, mentally and physically, to such an extent that they were (and still are) a degenerated, docile, submissive and subservient race on earth". (Both these statements are from the FAQs referred to above.) The honour of the Hindu people is furthermore linked to the notion of the nation as motherland, as a body that can be tortured, humiliated, polluted. These views are indeed imbued in *Hindutva* rhetoric elsewhere; the internet can, however, give such messages and metaphors a particular urgency and actuality.

The *Hindtva* Activist as Witness for the Prosecution
HU's rhetoric is embedded in a "survival discourse" (Rajagopal/Bojin, 2002). Throughout the homepage, alleged Hindu suffering, often defined as genocide, and Hindu militancy are related to each other, the latter held out as the unavoidable consequence of the first. Here, Hindus don't appear so much as passive victims but as what we might call witnesses for the prosecution, with a cause to argue in a momentous trial. The list of contents of articles available through the home page includes "exposing evidence of Islamic aggression and brutality" ("Slit the throat of 2 Hindus", "Hindu Slave in exchange for car", "11 Hindus burned alive in Bangladesh by Muslim mob" or "Muslims gang rape Hindu girl"). There is ongoing 'exposure', mainly of the underlying threat of Islam and Muslims towards Hinduism and Hindus, and ever so often, each instance of 'exposure' claims to have visual evidence ("Warning Graphic Content. See how Hindus are ruthlessly murdered in Kerala") to back its allegations.

While there is no shortage of evidence in the modern world of acts of violence committed by Muslims on others (just as, needless to say, there is no shortage of evidence of acts of violence committed by Hindus, Christians, Jews, Buddhists, Sikhs, Communists, or Nationalists of any description, or even animal rights activists), this 'gallery of horrors' on the HU site is exclusively Islamic. In doing this, the HU website mirrors the visual rhetoric of its enemies, be they Muslim fundamentalist groups who rely on the same kind of images – of raped women, disembowelled bodies, destroyed houses, torture and humiliation from Kashmir, to Gujarat, to Chechnya to Palestine – to make their point. Furthermore, the evidentiary authority of this 'proof' is often susceptible to manipulation of its content, if not of the information that can be circulated or suppressed about the content. For a long time, the HU site prominently ran a plainly doctored video grab of a Chechen execution of a captured Russian prisoner, obviously 'borrowed' from a Russian supremacist militia website. What is more interesting, however, is that despite a disclaimer pointing to its provenance, the image was discussed on one of the message boards on the site as if it were something that had happened in an Indian context. The conscious, semi-conscious, or unconscious blurring of locations, contexts, actors, agents and realities, through juxtaposition and trans-position of the elements of one image or testimony to another, enables the suppleness and 'flexibility' with which these pieces of evidence adjust to the demands of a 'desired' truth.

What this 'witnessing' makes possible is a mobilization of the feelings of vulnerability and rage which are sought to be translated into concrete online action. Like much internet-centric activism, HU too makes ample use of the form of the online petition. There are any number of petitions, from protests against obscure scholarly references to beef eating in Vedic times, to petitions against the actor Shahrukh Khan for his refusal to engage in anti-Pakistani rhetoric, to petitions against the possibility of Salman Khan (another film actor with a Muslim name) playing the part of Ram, to petitions against the persecution of Hindus in Bangladesh, Kashmiri Pandits in Kashmir, petitions protesting the innocence of Dara Singh (a Bajrang Dal militant in Orissa accused of murdering the Australian missionary Graham Staines and his children), and petitions against a book that is deemed insulting to the Hindu deity Ganesha. It is unclear as to what exactly happens once a petition is signed. It is, for instance, unlikely that a signed petition is handed over to the Bollywood idol Shahrukh Khan. But this question might even be of secondary importance. Rather, the opportunity to protest, unite, form solidarities and exert pressure on particular agents becomes a fasci-nating instance of the rituals of community formation, and an important instrument of being seen to have acted together on a concrete issue. Petitions suggest personal interaction and scope for participation, and the taking of a stand together with other like-minded people whom one may have never met, or may never meet, but who are, for all intents and pur-poses, very real presences in the world of the petition signatory. However, petitions lack the flair of anonymous denunciation of elements deemed threats to the *Hindutva* cause. This inflicting of humiliation is at the heart of online Black Lists (see below).

The *Hindutva* Activist as Judge
The fact that the internet is a media that enables interaction 'from below' justifies the use of the term 'democratic media'. However, this gets complicated when 'democratic partici-pation' is only a layer under which particular interest groups undermine any sense of a civil society. On HU, this becomes evident with the repeated appeal to netizens to denounce and report 'suspects' and 'anti-Hindus' on to the 'Black List' and to demand jurisdiction in response to their purported 'crimes'. In this case, participation is evoked by suggesting that the Black List is the register of an alternative tribunal and that the participating netizens its judges. In fact, however, the list aims at consolidating a sense of community centred around common hate figures, and at intimidating and threatening the 'criminals' – should they visit the list (not impossible, as names do show up on Google searches) – as well as cautioning those who could become 'suspects' or 'criminals' in the eyes of Hindu Unity. Here, for instance, is the declared aim (given in capitals on the site) of the Black List on HinduUnity.org:

"THIS PAGE EXPOSES THE EVIL FORCES THAT ARE AGAINST THE HINDU PEOPLE: EACH OF THESE PERSONS AND OR ORGANIZATIONS HAVE BEEN GUILTY OF LEADING EFFORTS AGAINST OUR MOVEMENT. THEIR CRIMES ARE CRIMES AGAINST THE HINDU

PEOPLE: KNOW YOUR ENEMIES! KNOW WHO WILL BE RESPONSIBLE FOR THE DOWNFALL OF *BHARAT!*"
More than 100 persons are currently listed here, ranging from what the HU netizens call 'P-SECS' ('pseudo-secularists)' – an epithet often used by *Hindutva* sympathizers to characterize liberals, usually Hindus, opposed to militant or extremist Hinduism – to Communists, Christians, and Muslims. These names are often accompanied by photographs, addresses, phone numbers and e-mail addresses.

The alleged legitimacy for doing this is that all those individuals are said to be part of a larger anti-Hindu conspiracy that has to be addressed in order to avoid further national deterioration. To name a few examples: social historian Vijay Prasad is called "...a bastard and traitor" for having written anti-*Hindutva* articles, and he is warned that "the Soldiers of *Hindutva* are watching you Vijay! Please visit him and call him at..." Historian Romila Thapar's crime is that she is "...distorting the true history of India". Other 'criminals' are Pervez Musharraf, Syed Ahmed Bukhari (the Imam of the Jama Masjid, Delhi), Sonia Gandhi and Osama Bin Laden.

Several penalties are demanded on the Blacklist: for having painted the Hindu Goddess Saraswati in the nude, the painter MF Husain, defined as "destroyer of Hinduism", is asked to paint an insulting picture of the Prophet Muhammed, and a call is issued for the destruction of all his work (supporters of the Bajrang Dal have on more than one occasion physically attacked his work by entering galleries in Mumbai and, most recently, in Surat). The actor Shahrukh Khan is found guilty for being pro-Pakistan and pro-terrorism for arguing that every terrorist must have a reason for his/her deeds. The verdict pronounced on him is: "This criminal needs to be sent back to Pakistan". (Ironically so, considering Shahrukh Khan's antecedents are in Delhi.)

The Black List is a safe zone to denounce anyone without needing to provide real credible evidence, while allowing the denouncer to remain anonymous. The Black List might lead eventually to actual, and less virtual, threats or intimidation to the people defined in it as "criminals"; as of now it seems mainly to be an engine of hate mail. But most of all, the list creates a space of vicarious empowerment for those pointing their fingers at people they consider to be 'suspects' and 'traitors'. The planting of rumours and suspicion and the use of hate speech is a powerful strategy of self-empowerment. Denunciation and the spectacle of the humiliation of the 'other' fuel a pleasure that comes from a feeling of power and control. This pleasure derives from an accusing gaze, speech-act or gesture that can expose another's vulnerability by the suddenness and surprise of its execution. The 'criminals' are placed on a virtual pillory and can be intimidated and humiliated in what has the semblance of a public space.

Often, the accused are out of reach for the accusers. The sudden intimacy and closeness that emerges when any person can harm a seemingly 'untouchable' authority figure, such as a film star or a prominent public person, produces its own twisted satisfaction.

The Making and Unmaking of Heroes and Martyrs: *Hindutva* Posters
Even though Hindu Unity is predominantly a site with articles allegedly producing 'evidence' for the suffering of the Hindu people at the hands of Islam (anti-Christian and anti-American rhetoric is present, though it features to a much lesser degree), explicit and imaginative

visual display (accessible through prominently featured links) plays an important role on the site as well. The images, like the rest of the content, respond to the categories of Hindus as victims, as well as active avenging agents.

The HU homepage carries a link entitled "*Hindutva* posters". Except for one, all of the twenty-two displayed are made by Rahul Y, a student in the USA and active member of HU (more on him below). The images are plain, sticker-like, and include titles such as "Hindu Jew Unity", "Ram Temple Poster", "Fist Poster", "Shiv Sena Poster". The titles themselves speak of traditional *Hindutva* themes of facing the 'Muslim' threat together with Israel, building the Ram temple at Ayodhya, consolidating the community, and promoting the political agenda of militant Hinduism. Let me draw your attention, however, to a selection of poster montages that show the Muslim stereotype evoked by the Hindu Right in a new avatar, closely related to the imagery that began to circulate through television and the world wide web after September 11, and began to shape a new, transnational iconography of the 'Threat of Militant Islam'. In many ways, September 11 enabled the rhetoric of *Hindutva* to strengthen and fed the stereotype of the dangerous 'anti-(Indian) national' with new material of the 'anti-western Muslim'. Suddenly, the *Sangh Parivar*, previously almost consistently anti-American because of their preference for *swadeshi* ('self reliant' nationalism) and anxiety about the 'westernization' of Hindu culture, drew a new axis of power where it could place the Hindu alongside other purported victims of Islamic terror, particularly Americans and Israeli Jews. Members of the *Sangh* could now reinforce their claim that Muslims were essentially aggressive and dangerous not only to India, but to world security. This is an important development: it needs to be understood that the demonization of Muslims through aggressive, stereotypical images in an Indian context had become increasingly difficult to state and sustain in public after the demolition of the Babri Mosque in December 1992, and the widespread violence against Muslims in India that followed. The spectacle of 9/11 and the subsequent media spin of the 'War against Terror', as well as the conflicts in Afghanistan and Iraq, altered that picture considerably. There was a new confidence with which the image of the 'Muslim Aggressor' could be foregrounded. Further, the escalation of the 'second' Intifada in Palestine, parallel to the rise of militancy in Kashmir, allowed for a multiplication of 'cross-references' of images and contexts, and more importantly, for points of ideological and communicative contact between militant Jewish extremist groups and members of the HU community. This is evident both from the prominent links to websites related to Jewish extremist groups such as Kahane.org, the Kach Movement and Masada200.org, as well as the supporting interventions by interlocutors who claim to be members of Jewish extremist groups in the "Soldiers of *Hindutva*" message board on HU. The common denominator on which this alliance with militant extremist Jewish groups is based is an understanding of both Hindus and Jews as a 'Chosen People', with sacred homelands 'encroached upon' by threatening forces (Muslims) and a long history of suffering and persecution. (What this glosses over – and it is not as if the more erudite *Hindutva* enthusiasts, even on HU, are unaware of this; in fact they do refer to it occasionally on the message boards, with a twinge of embarrassment – is the rather different circumstances of *Hindutva*'s search for allies in the 1930s and 1940s, when the supreme leader of the RSS, Golwalkar, was not at all unsympathetic to the project of the 'Final Solution' in Germany; he called it an instance of a manifestation of "Race Pride at its Highest". See *We, or, Our Nationhood Defined*, by M.S. Golwalkar, Bharat Publications, Nagpur, 1939.)

The New Muslim Stereotype

As we have already pointed out, the iconography of victimization in these posters is also paired with slogans and images that call for a *"Hindutva* Revolution" to be articulated along the lines of a holy war. That a Hindu *'Jihad'* should have to rely on the images of Muslim *jihadis* to fuel its own resources of aggression is part of the irony of the visual culture of contemporary fundamentalism. But let us examine how *Hindutva* holy warriors visualize their 'enemy'.

The first image is entitled "Osama Poster". It displays a Pakistani flag burning at the edges. Written on this emblem in red is "KILLING IN THE NAME OF ALLAH". Positioned at the centre of this image is a photograph of Osama bin Laden, looking towards the left where three white pin-up girls stand exposing their almost-naked bodies to the viewer (and to bin Laden). Below his photograph we can read the following legend: "Osama bin Ladin (Busy taking care of American Business)". While bin Laden is looking at the seductive sirens, a bullet hits his head; red spots tinted over the photograph suggest the spilling of his blood over the otherwise mild and peacefully smiling face. And, as we trace the source of the bullet to the right of the montage, we see another photograph of what looks like an American soldier lying on the ground aiming a gun at bin Laden. Again, with the help of image manipulation software, the saffron Hindu flag is fixed onto the soldier's weapon, thus mythically metamorphosing and indigenizing the gun, its holder (and the beholder). Furthermore, the image carries the words "SOLDIERS OF *HINDUTVA*", and *"Jai Hindu Rashtra"* ("Hail to the Hindu Nation").

What we find here is a surreal combination of Osama bin Laden depicted both as lascivious Muslim and an avid consumer of western pornographic imagery. (Another poster has him eyeing not nearly-naked women, but dollar bills.) A subtle feeling of dread is evoked through the deliberate association between the decadent Arab sheikh, the terrorist posing as messiah and the target of the hybrid GI-*Hindutva* warrior. The pleasure of looking, in this case, arises from watching a villain being eliminated without his foreknowledge, even as he is engaged in his most decadent pursuits.

The stereotype of the Muslim as a mindless, machine-like tool of *jihad* is also evident in a very disturbing link to a website called "Israel Storm" (http://israelstorm.cjb.net), which says on its home page, "This web site was built by a Hindu who supports the cause of Israel". Israel Storm (besides providing clearer evidence of collaboration between the Hindu and the Jewish Far Right) is of interest because of a section on it called "The Nursery of Terror". This is a photo album with pictures allegedly depicting the transformation of young boys in Palestine into suicide bombers. Each image carries a cynical comment. Take, for example, the image of the Muslim woman fixing a packet of dynamite on a young boy's belt, possibly her son. He stands patiently, wearing a *kaffiyeh* (a Palestinian check scarf) and a full-face black mask. The subtitle reads: "For the last time, Abdul, I am not dressing you up like Batman". This line suggests a 'misunderstanding' between mother and son, the latter thinking he is preparing for a children's costume party while he is in fact 'dressed to kill' himself and others. The dramatized innocence of the child, unaware of his immediate death, is heightened by his mother's mindless readiness to sacrifice him, to use him as a weapon. Other pictures underline the coming of age of future terrorists, and it seems that this particularly pathological fascination with the abuse of children and the making of 'infant terrorists' is meant to demonize the enemy even further.

The *Hindutva* Holy Warrior

The stereotype of the avenging Hindu emerges as if from the very ground of the image of the hated enemy. HU promotes a distinctly different 'type' of Hindu in the figure of the 'Soldier of *Hindutva*', an almost mythical figure, or Terminator-like being, who arises in response to the alleged suffering of the Hindu majority, no longer willing or able to witness the humiliation of his people, religion and country, finally ready for combat in defence of Hindu pride (see below).

The second set of images from the poster collection on HU that I would like to consider is poster montages. The first amongst these is taken from the successful film *Mission Kashmir*. The protagonists of the film are shown wearing full-face masks; only their eyes, focused on the viewer, are visible. This image, used for advertising the film, has been modified here for the purpose of *Hindutva* propaganda: the foreheads of the two men have been marked with a *tilak*, which in this case is a sacred symbol applied by a wife, sister or mother to sanctify and protect a husband, brother or son as he sets forth to do battle. A machine gun has been inserted, again superimposed with the universal mantra 'Om'.

Again, this iconography merges distinct worlds: the glamour of film stardom, the revival of the patriotic genre in 1990s Bollywood, and the desire to find a visual vocabulary capable of expressing an adequately heroic icon of the Soldier of *Hindutva*, dovetailed into the Indian nationalist rhetoric of keeping Kashmir in India at all cost. It also manages to create an identification between the armed forces' personnel fighting to retain Kashmir, and the *Hindutva* Militant. The text on this poster reads: "Are you ready to fight for the Hindu *Dharma* in Kashmir? Join the soldiers of *Hindutva* at www.HinduUnity.org and become part of the Hindu *rashtra* movement". Browsing a website, becoming part of an online community, downloading and printing a poster, fighting a distant war, and protecting the faith – all these moves merge into a single click of the mouse.

The caption of another *Hindutva* poster reads: "We must not turn our heads, as our own people are being massacred and kicked out of their homeland. Help by supporting Hindu groups or by taking action yourself. Hindu militancy is the only way to defend our religion, our country, and our people!" On this poster we see masked, black-clad combatants holding up machine guns against the rising sun, on which is superimposed an 'Om' sign. The surreal content of the image becomes apparent when we consider that the design template for this poster is most probably taken from the images of Palestinian (Hamas and other) *fidayeen* militants who customarily dress in black and mask their faces. The 'alliance' here, between *Hindutva* and what could well be Hamas, is purely formal, but it reveals a fascination with the ritualized display of a martial aesthetic and heroic bodies so well cultivated in the iconography of the Palestinian uprising (as well as Sikh martyrdom, see next page).

Watching Torture: Consuming Violence

The website is replete with images of violence. While the violence meted out by the 'enemy' is meant to spur the Holy *Hindutva* Warrior to action in vengeance, the violence held out as a threat by him, and the promise of annihilation held out to all those who come in the way, is an affirmation of his power. There is, as I have pointed out before, nothing novel in this; the iconography of 'resistance' and 'just causes' is monotonously similar everywhere.

But why do people need to consider violence and absorb violent imagery in order to feel empowered? Asked in another way: "Why is the iconography of suffering so dominant in the context of empowerment?" In her latest book, *Regarding the Pain of Others*, Susan Sontag explores the iconography of suffering in representations of Christian martyrs which, she argues, "are surely intended to move and excite, and to instruct and exemplify". Furthermore, she states that it "seems that the appetite for pictures showing bodies in pain is as keen, almost, as the desire for ones that show bodies naked" (Sontag, 2003: 36). The voyeuristic pleasures of watching bodies undergoing torture is difficult to tackle. Writes Sontag, "There is shame as well as shock in looking at the close-up of a real horror" (ibid.: 37). And later in her essay she adds, "Photographs of suffering and martyrdom of a people are more than reminders of death, of failure, or victimization. They invoke the miracle of survival" (ibid.: 78). The miracle of survival, of those who witness and mourn the dead, is also the burden of survival and memory, something that is emphasized in rhetorical questions such as, "Do you want history to repeat itself?"

Evidence of attraction in looking at other's pain in order to arouse feelings of both compassion and anger (revenge) are found in captions of another set of web pages visualizing Sikh martyrdom on HU. Accompanying the images, we can read detailed descriptions of torture such as, "Sikh mothers watch while 300 infants speared to death", or of martyrs being "boiled alive", "sawed alive" or "cut joint by joint". The introductory text appeals to the viewer to pay reverence to the heroic martyrs: "Here are numerous pictures of great Sikh martyrs being tortured to death. ... People of *Bharat* should never forget what these mighty Sikh lions have gone through to protect our religion, our culture and faith". The burden of survival is to fulfil the aims and dreams of the dead, which, according to HU, can only be achieved by avenging them in "retrospective self-defence".

In the introduction to this article, I referred to the visitors of HU as potential consumers of violence as spectacle, who experience pleasure and fear, rage and vulnerability from watching or witnessing the torture of others from a safe distance. In this context, I can imagine that looking at some of these images is an almost subcutaneous experience. It gets under your skin. However, at the end of the day, it remains essentially a virtual experience, creating only a temporary inner storm and regular upsurges of the desire to make an impact, be it by means of signing petitions, or by getting a print-out of a 'Soldiers of *Hindutva*' sticker. Yet this does not mean that the anti-Muslim feeling underlying the majority of images should not be taken seriously. They are designed with the express intention of having a 'real' or direct impact on actual contexts. However, the impact is bound to evoke complex routes: from desire to utterance, upload, log-in, download, signing, posting, forwarding, to getting out on the street, or sitting behind closed doors, waiting for life to walk in and give the Holy Hindu Cyber Warrior the chance to be a hero.

Remote Control Patriots

The appeal to defend the 'motherland', and the faith that is staged in the material discussed above, also derives from the experience of living abroad, of wanting to nurture connections to 'roots' in the homeland. Two key figures involved in the production of this material on HU are closely associated with the Bajrang Dal while living (it is not clear if they are permanent or temporary residents) in the USA. The first person is named as Rohit V. He is the chairman of Hindu Unity and declares himself to be a staunch supporter of the Bajrang Dal. He was born in New Delhi in 1970 into a family with strong RSS ties. Rohit V joined the Bajrang Dal before 1992, but was excluded from the organization after the demolition of the Babri Mosque on 'disciplinary probation'. In 1994, he rejoined the BD again. Today, he lives both in the state of New York and in India. He considers the HU website to be his contribution to the cause of *Hindutva*.

The man and brain behind the *Hindutva* posters is Rahul Y. Rahul Y is also president and webmaster of the *Hindutva* Brotherhood and the Kashmiri Liberation Army (hereafter HB+KHLA) website. Like Hindu Unity, HB+KHLA (http://www.geocities.com/hindutvapics) offers its visitors 'participation' by means of a 'Black List' and a message forum.

Interestingly, along with the Black List, the HB+KHLA list also has a list of *Hindutva* leaders which features, along with 'Great Leaders' such as Ramchandra Paramhans, Pravin Togadia, A.B. Vajpayee, L. K. Advani and Bal Thackeray, a long list of district and neighbourhood level leaders and organizers all over India. Prominent amongst them are people that the site names as having "contributed to the *jawan* uprising of Gujarat, March 2003", "organizers of the Gulberg liberation operation that resulted in the bringing to justice of Ehsan Jafri" or, "contributor to the operation Naroda Patalia [sic], and the distribution of swords to activists for self defence". Clearly, the HB+KHLA site takes very seriously its mission to 'inform' about what it calls the "causes of and solutions to Muslim + Christian Problems". A certain penchant for a hip DIY *Hindutva* tactical media aesthetic (Shiv Sena Springing Tigers, and Kalashnikovs with Om inscribed on them) dominates this site, and many icons are available for download as posters or car stickers, embellished by slogans such as "Hinduize the Politics, Militarize the Hindus", and "*Gaurav Se Kaho, Ham Hindu Hai*" ("Say with pride that we are Hindus"). There is also an extensive gallery of photographs of "*Hindutva* in Action".

Rahul Y is not shy in revealing his identity on his personal website. His lack of reticence is quite different from the majority of *Hindutvavadis*. He tells us that he also calls himself "Hindu Souljah" or "Indiaman", that he was born in 1982, lives in Illinois and studies Information Systems Technologies; that his hobbies include "listening to Hindi music and remixes, rap, and techno, playing basketball and soccer, dancing, designing websites, playing computer games, programming, and hanging out with *desi* (Indian) friends" – a 'nice guy', a regular all-American youth even. On the photos he has displayed on the website, we find a good-looking man sporting a trendy beard and a habitus that reminds one of rap music videos. However, for some reason, none of the pictures shows him smiling. He is concerned and dedicated. His *desi* friends love Hindi movies, sports, and fusion music, carry nicknames such as "*Desi* Gangsta", "Bengal Bad Boy", or "*Chhota Babu*" (http://rahul.hindujagran.com/rahul/friends.htm). The latter lives in Australia where he teaches Economics at a college, but he is also the chairman of HB+KHLA, of which Rahul is the president. Rahul Y's declared intention is to uplift India's international image as a backward culture and to increase the intellectual quality of *Hindutva* representation.

In his profile, Rahul continues: "I like to read books that deal with Hindu nationalism, Indian politics, Indian history, and computers. I am a member of the Indian Students Council, *Vishwa Hindu Parishad-America* (World Hindu Council of America), and regularly take part in activities by Hindu Swayam Sevak Sangh".

In the last thirty years, both the RSS and the VHP have become very active among Indians abroad and shape much of the institutionalization of transnational Hindu nationalism. To a great extent, the grassroots and training camp activities of the RSS and VHP abroad are important in order to keep physically 'in touch' with the ideas of *Hindutva* doctrines, and to enable young participants to develop feelings of solidarity and loyalty.

But the internet also provides a strengthening of bonds, a new kind of personal relationship that comes to life through nicknames, family photos and discussion forums, and through initiatives such as Rahul Y's homepage. The photographs of SSV camps, accompanied by comments, leave the impression that the camp is most of all about fun and friendship, like any other summer camp, with cultural nights and talent competitions, and the feeling that "together we are unstoppable..."

Among those pictures, one photograph caught my attention: Rahul and some of his friends attending a mid-west HSS training camp (c. probably early 2000) pose in front of an HSS banner and framed and garlanded posters of RSS leaders Hedgewar and Golwalkar, as well as a poster of *Bharat Mata* (Mother India). They pose as if they are performing a rap song, of the kind of *Desi* Crew lyrics put on the site elsewhere:

"*Desi* pride is my mind,
Desi blood is my kind,
So step aside and let me through,
Cuz it is all about the *desi* crew,
Desi luv is all around,
For my fellow *desis* never let me down,
Show your pride and say it's true,
Cuz *desi* blood flows through you"

The surreal mixture of Savarkar's glorification of the Hindus as a people and a race (*jati*) in the lyrics, the evocation of the Black Panther movement of the 1970s and the commodification of Afro-American ghetto culture through MTV, poses an interesting question with respect to how symbols of western consumer culture, Islamicate and anti-racist movements, and notions of racist superiority can be peacefully appropriated in order to shape a 'new Indo-American' pop-patriotism.

Here, a diasporic Hindu identity emerges that can, without contradicting itself in the view of its bearers, both claim reference to a 'pure Hindu culture' and a hybrid mixture of symbols taken from other cultural domains. The surrealism of HinduUnity is thus also located in the playful creative variability in identity-making, where the Soldiers of *Hindutva* can also be (gangsta) rappers of *Hindutva*.

By looking at the rhetorical forms, technological features and social motivations involved, I have tried to discuss some of the tactics used in and through HU to legitimize violence, and shape the internet as a platform for action.

I do not believe that these are the trivial pursuits of a few 'nice guys' with nothing else to do, however 'regular' they may seem. Yet the answer to the politics of hate that they deploy lies only in creating more resources, and in greater depth, that can challenge the majoritarian and violent agenda that has come to characterize *Hindutva*. Rather than demanding the censorship of a site like HU, we need to further investigate the fact that the world wide web will remain a dynamic social space in which agents will employ a dense network of visual and narrative strategies in order to create in the netizen the desire, anxiety and pleasure of belonging to imagined and networked communities such as that of *Hindutva*. If online *Hindutva* is to be confronted, and possibly challenged, it will require a serious attempt to grasp the complexity of the ways of being, and the virtual and actual spaces that online *Hindutva* weaves together.

NOTES

1. Bajrang is one of the names of Hanuman, the monkey god, who in the epic *Ramayana* is portrayed as Ram's faithful companion-in-arms, and as a brave, if occasionally reckless warrior.
2. Literally, the 'Organization Family '– the cluster of various interest groups and mass organizations, including the dominant political party in the ruling National Democratic Alliance, the Bharatiya Janata Party, that are affiliated to the Rashtriya Swayam Sevak Sangh, a self-styled 'Cultural Organization' that broadly expresses and shapes the ideology of the Hindu Right
3. These references are to the role played by local level leaders of the *Hindutva* movement who are named and celebrated in the HB+KHLA web site for their active roles in contributing to some of the most notoriously violent episodes (the murder of Ehsan Jafri, fomer member of Parliament, members of his family and neighbours in the Gulberg Society massacre in Ahmedabad, and the Narora Patiya killings) during the the systematic pogrom of Muslims in Gujarat, March 2002, in response to the Godhra carnage.

Bibliography

Benjamin, Walter. *Illuminations*, with an introduction by Hannah Arendt. Translated by Harry Zohn (Fontana Press, 1973, London).

Kallen, Evelyn. "Hate on the Net. A Question of Rights/A Question of Power", *Electronic Journal of Sociology*, 1998 (accessed on February 1, 2004).

Mulvey, Laura. *Fetishism and Curiosity* (BFI, 1996, London).

Rajagopal, Indu and Nis Bojin. "Digital Representation: Racism on the World Wide Web", *First Monday*, peer-reviewed journal on the internet, 1996 (accessed on February 1, 2004).

Sontag, Susan. *Regarding the Pain of Others* (Hamish Hamilton/Penguin, 2003, London and New York).

Zook, Matthew A. "The Unorganized Militia Network: Conspiracies, Computers and Community", *Berkeley Planning Journal* Vol. 11, 1996 (accessed on February 1, 2004).

Media Looking Beyond Crisis?
The Urdu/Pakistani Press n New 'ork afte·)/11

REHAN ANSARI

We know well by now that the origins of the crisis that we are familiar with as '9/11' predate the 11th of September 2001. We also know that the crisis continues well after the 11th of September 2001 in Afghanistan, in Iraq and in Pakistan. There has been some amount of discussion in all sorts of media in the US about the background, as well as the fallout, of 9/11 not only in New York, Washington and London, but all across the world, especially in terms of what is called the 'War Against Terror'. But one of the things that has remained outside the purview of the mainstream US media is the accumulating sense of unease and crisis within New York City, in areas like Brooklyn and Queens, where Pakistani immigrants, be they on Atlantic Avenue or in Jackson Heights, see themselves located squarely at the frontline of the skirmishes that mark the everyday domestic reality of what is called the 'War against Terror'.

Mainstream media in the US, be they the television networks – NBC, ABC, CBS, FOX, CNN – or the major newspapers, ignore the persistent assaults on the civil liberties of Pakistani immigrants in America, especially in New York. *The New York Times*, to be fair, does carry the odd report, but it does so in a way that reminds me of the way the Karachi Police (whom I often saw in action as I was growing up in Pakistan) would show up at the scene of a crime always late enough to ensure that nothing could be done, so much so that you got accustomed to presuming their complicity in the incidents that they were supposed to redress.

Since 9/11 I have been following and translating stories from seven weekly Urdu publications in New York for "Voices That Must Be Heard", a weekly news service that puts out news compilations drawn from alternative news sources. There are almost 300 publications in New York City, including various kinds of papers and broadsheets put out by a diverse array of small, neighbourhood, ethnic, community and the independent presses. "Voices", a project of the Independent Press Association, chooses stories from precisely such non-corporate sources. The stories that I followed and translated were of FBI/INS raids on the homes, places of work, shops, offices and businesses of Pakistani immigrants, of detentions and deportations, and of the effect of the Special Registration Law and the Patriot Act on the Pakistani community in the city.

It would be accurate to say that prior to 9/11, the Pakistani Press in New York, which has names like *Pakistan Post, Pakistan News, New York Awam (New York Masses)* and *Sada-e-Pakistan (Voice of Pakistan)* (all Urdu) and the *Muslims Weekly* (English) are generally owned by men who have other businesses which tend to be tax consultancies, real-estate brokerage and travel agencies. The papers primarily serve as public relations fronts for these gentlemen who also position themselves as 'community leaders'. They carry reports of community events, social functions, festivals and entertainment galas. In the months that followed 9/11, however, it was this incredibly small, and often small-minded, press in New York that found itself at the forefront of having to report and highlight many issues of public interest, such as growing attacks on civil liberties, racial profiling, post war reconstruction, the effect of the crisis on the deeply interdependent nature of the world economy, capital and labour flows, migration and perceptions of 'America' both in this country and in others.

Whereas these papers had previously carried op-eds almost exclusively about politics in Pakistan,[1] after September 11th, one saw a surge in local reporting reflecting on FBI/INS raids, the rights of detainees (both legal and illegal), the effect of the 'War against terror', the local economy of Coney Island, and a new interest in the cause of civil liberties activists who were from outside the community. There was also a very vital level of op-ed writing on American foreign policy and the globalization of the post 9/11 conflict.

The Pakistani press in New York became a crucial smoke detector for something burning in US society. Topics that are currently haunting discussions in the mainstream media, ranging from the US administration's assault on civil liberties to the subject of reconstruction in Iraq, first became visible in the Urdu press. It was there that I first read a columnist wondering why the detainees in Guantanamo Bay didn't have rights that are available to anyone else in the territorial United States, which is essentially the question before the US Supreme Court today. Again it was in the New York Pakistani press that a writer asked a question concerning Afghanistan: "So, when will reconstruction end?"

I would like to give a more detailed sense of the news that the papers carried. Below is a selection of headlines and copy that I translated from the New York Urdu papers post 9/11.[2]

"Authorities express surprise at the numbers of Pakistanis calling the INS on each other"
M. R. Farrukh, *Pakistan Post*, 17 April 2002.

Ahmed Imtiaz is one of those hundreds of thousands of people who come to the United States dreaming about a happy and prosperous life. Before September 11th, irrespective of his legal status, he was spending a quiet life earning an honourable living for his household.

Two months after September 11th, he was picked up from his home in New Jersey. His apartment was raided by the FBI, the INS and a squad of Special Forces. At around 2:30 a.m. his wife, three kids and himself were awakened by a continuous ringing of the doorbell. When he got out and saw the officials, he panicked. He had previously never encountered a police officer at his door. The sight of the officers of three agencies belonging to the most powerful country in the world on his doorstep completely unnerved him. The officers took him to his bedroom and searched his home for two hours. He swore upon his innocence, pleaded with them. They arrested him.

Like hundreds of those arrested, Imtiaz was found to have no links with the atrocity of September 11th. Freed of terrorism charges he was transferred from FBI detention to the INS centre. There are people in the INS centre detained for seven months now, without charges, because the law allows that. Imtiaz found himself charged under immigration law. He was found to be in violation of a deportation order from five years ago.

Imtiaz is now facing deportation. He has only a few more days in this county.

He has recently found out why he was arrested. A few years ago an argument with a friend over a trivial matter became an open sore between them. They stopped talking and Imtiaz forgot about the matter over time. Taking advantage of the post-September 11 atmosphere, the former friend told the authorities that Imtiaz was engaged in suspicious activities. The authorities were on a war footing and acted so.

"Who can the community of Pakistanis living illegally in the United States turn to?"
M.R. Farrukh, *Pakistan Post*, 1 May 2002.

The White House, the Congress, and the army establishment in Pakistan are all projecting themselves as fighting the just war against terrorism. Meanwhile, it is the Pakistani community in the United States that is feeling persecuted, voiceless and abandoned.

A few days ago, at a raid on a Pakistani family living in Queens, agents explained that the head of the household's name was somewhat similar to the name of a suspected terrorist! An officer present during the raid told the family that the authorities had every right to pursue any lead in the fight against terrorism.

"Protest against detentions by New York Taxi Workers Alliance, Coney Island Avenue Project, and 50 various organizations"
Mohsin Zaheer, *Sada-e-Pakistan*, NY, 19 June 2002.

The protest took place on June 15th on Coney Island Avenue, in Brooklyn, where high concentrations of people of Pakistani origin live. The crowd was large and diverse except that few Pakistanis attended. There were at most two dozen Pakistanis. Spokespeople from the Brooklyn Mela Committee, Pak-American Merchant's Association and Makki Mosque were among those who refused to attend the march, saying that protests in their own neighbourhood bring greater risks of discrimination.

"The victims of the 'War on Terrorism' are Pakistanis living here, as the crackdown against illegal immigrants continues"
Pakistan Post, 29 July 2002.

American officials are continuing their campaign against US-based Pakistanis, citizens of an important American ally in the 'War On Terrorism'. More than 1,700 Pakistanis have been detained in this country on immigration charges; many have been deported.

The FBI and INS are focusing on Brooklyn, where Pakistanis live and their businesses are based. Authorities are knocking on Pakistanis doors late at night, questioning the residents, searching their houses and arresting those they find to be undocumented immigrants. Some report that officials are seizing even legal documents of people they question.

"The special relationship between America and Pakistan"
Ifti Nasim, *News Pakistan*, 25 September 2002.

(Ifti Nasim is a well-known humorist, Urdu poet and literary critic.)

In one of her poems, Sylvia Plath talks of a foot that was trapped in a black shoe for "thirty years, poor and white, barely daring to breathe". That foot is Pakistan, which has suffered for thirty years in the black shoe of American-sponsored military dictatorships.

"A Pakistani writes from an American jail"
Azeem M. Mian, *Pakistan Post*, 9 October 2002.

A friend of the editors of *Pakistan Post* received a letter from Zubair Hanafi, which has been forwarded to me and I am including in this column. Zubair's address is the Brooklyn Detention Center. His prisoner number is 67898053. The letter bears an Aug. 15.

postmark, meaning the letter has taken almost two months to get to me. Let us hope that Zubair is safe, either released in the United States or deported to Pakistan

"Few Pakistanis register on first day"
News Pakistan, 22 January 2003.

On the first two days of registration, few Pakistanis have showed up: forty on the first day in New York (127 in the first two days); in Chicago, 70 appeared on the first day.

An estimated 600,000 Pakistanis live in the United States, 200,000 in New York State alone. Most are undocumented, have 'incomplete' legal status, or are under due process. If the registration requirements are enforced to the letter, an estimated 400,000 will be forced to leave the country.

"Farewell United States, all hope is with Canada?"
Pervaiz Ramay, *Sada-e-Pakistan*, NY, 12 February 2003.

Pakistanis fleeing the United States into Canada at the border at Niagara Falls are finding refuge at Viva Locasa, a church within US territory, just 15 minutes drive from the Canadian border. Most of the refugees are in terrible need since they left everything behind in their panicked flight.

Immediately following 9/11, the Urdu/Pakistani press in New York rose to the occasion. But where is the press now? How is it doing? Are they still sniffing in the wind for what has not yet apparent to anyone else? Or are these small community papers only good at the rapid, almost real-time dissemination of what a crisis feels like 'from the inside' only when the crisis is upon their heads? Further, have the intellectual and cultural horizons of the world that these papers present to their readers undergone any transformations?

In terms of cultural reporting, before 9/11 there would be no writing in the op-ed pages of almost all the Urdu press that challenged mainstream, middle-class Pakistani Punjabi social mores. There was very little that one could see reflected about the transformations in a new immigrant community, or the awareness of a new generation of immigrants, or of second-generation Pakistani-Americans and their attitudes, and almost no new voices in the op-ed pages. In fact, more than one paper carried the prolific writings of a dead columnist. Maulana Maudoodi, a conservative intellectual and essayist and founder of the *Jamaat-e-Islami in Pakistan*, who in his lifetime wrote about everything under the sun – on marriage, death, cinema, literature, the economy, the upbringing of children, living in the west as a minority, and in the east as a majority, the separation of church and state – but who was, nonetheless, dead, was published with monotonous regularity in several of these papers.

However, it needs to be pointed out that at least two papers – *The Pakistan News* (Urdu) and the *Muslims Weekly* (English) – are positioning themselves editorially, each in different but interesting ways, to the challenges of being interlocutors in post-9/11 New York. I believe the creation and growth of these publications reflects the ways that 9/11 has forced members of the Pakistani-American community to redefine what it means to be Pakistani-American, as well as what it means to be a Muslim-American. The fact that the *Muslims Weekly* is an English language publication indicates an intention to move beyond the confines of a specifically Pakistani identity. It has an Israeli peace activist writing for it, which means that it is positioning itself in a different kind of role from what one is accustomed to seeing within the Muslim community in the United States. Its circulation jumped from 5000 pre-9/11 to 25000. Of its five paid staff, three are non-Muslim.

The Pakistan News, meanwhile, makes the effort of translating articles from the liberal English press in the United States into Urdu. Moreover, it is the first Urdu paper to give prominent column space to women (and not just in the 'Women's Pages'), to regularly publish an openly gay Urdu poet based in Chicago, and to foreground a generally liberal and progressive political/cultural agenda.

Barring exceptions like *The Pakistan News* (Urdu) and the *Muslims Weekly* (English) most Urdu/Pakistani publications in New York have not really evolved beyond the immediate need of reporting what affects the Pakistani community on a day-to-day level. Further, they are in a sense undergoing their own peculiar crisis of 'over-stimulation and under-statement', of exaggeration and exhaustion, and certainly of (self) censorship. They are not reporting on the alliances that are forming between activist and immigrant communities. The work of the New York Immigration Coalition, Asian American Legal Defense Fund, and the American Civil Liberties Union remains un-commented on, and un-analyzed. If at all it is reported, it is done so in the blandest way, by reproducing information from a press release. Nor is there any attempt to flesh out the personalities in these organizations and the issues that they concern themselves with. There was no analysis of the coalitions that made possible the Immigrant Workers Freedom Ride[3] in October 2003.

The Urdu/Pakistani press in New York did ask key questions, but it has not been able to follow through on answering those questions. Severe resource constraints, which ensure that a journalist who writes for these publications never has the luxury to research and follow a story in order to write a well-rounded feature, or even keep to one beat, are certainly responsible for this state of affairs. But given that the reality that the readers of these papers face is a complex and challenging one, one hopes that at least some of the publications will find the wherewithal to evolve beyond their current limitations

This essay is based on a presentation given at the Sixth Sustainable Development Conference (11th to 13th December, 2003) organized by SDPI, Islamabad.

All translations from Urdu by the author.

NOTES

1. Mostly about the pros and cons of the Musharraf regime in Pakistan and the pronouncements from exile of the two civilian ex-Prime ministers – Nawaz Sharif and Benazir Bhutto.

2. For more information, and the full text of these articles see the archive of "Voices That Must Be Heard" (Voices), the weekly web-digest of the Independent Press Association, New York, at http://www.indypressny.org

3. The Immigrant Workers Freedom Ride (a campaign to endorse and support the civil liberties of all immigrant workers in the United States) ended with a huge day-long celebration of America's Immigrants in New York's Flushing Meadows Park on October 2003. More than 125,00 labour activists and community supporters joined the nearly 1,000 immigrant workers who had travelled all over the US in an unprecedented effort to put immigration issues squarely on the national political agenda for 2004 and mobilize USA-wide support for changes in immigration policies. For more information, see http://www.ifwr.org

THE CONVERSATION

The only formal transcript (Kashmiri / Hindi / English) of the conversation between Geelani (G) and his brother Shah Faisal (F) was made by two expert witnesses called in by the defence lawyers. They worked from the audiotape provided by the police: Geelani (G) Faisal (F) in English and *Kashmiri*.

Hello	G	Hello
Hello, asalamvalikum	F	Hello, asalamvalikum
:::::: noise ::::::		::::::
How are you?	F	Varay?
Doing well, and happy, Sir	G	Theek paeth, Khosh khosh, Janab ...
Are you well?	F	Jaan paeth?
Why should I lie?	G	Naa apuz kiazi wanay?
Where are you? At home?	F	Tse katiye chukh... gare paethie?
No, not at home, I'm outside	G	Na, na, na, Bu chus na gare paethie, bu chus naebrey
What?	F	Kya?
I'm in a bus	G	Bu chus base manz
In a bus?	F	Base manza?
He'll be leaving soon, (so) I'm going home	G	Timme naeren vuneh, bu gatseye garre
:::::: noise ::::::		::::::
I said it happens	F	Meh vonmus, "hota hai"
:::::: noise ::::::		::::::
Tell me what you want ...?	G	Tse van tse kya gyatsee...
Syllabus and prospectus	F	Syllabus teh prospectus...
Syllabus and prospectus	G	Syllabus teh prospectus...?
I think you should leave the phone		miyane khyaleha tse trav venni phone
I'll call you later, in a couple of days		ba karey tse tserey phone ya doi treye dovih
He's leaving soon, Khansahib is ...		homus chuh naerun vunnih, Khansahibussa...
Fine	F	Accha
I'll call you later, tomorrow, day-after –	G	Ba karey bey phone oz ya pagah do phone –
or on Eid, I'll call		ya Eid doh karey phone
Its costing a lot right now ...		ropiyeh khasaan ziyadeh venkess...
Otherwise all well?	F	Bae soruy theek?
Yes, sir – all well	G	Janab – bilkul theek
What's happened?	F	Yeh kya koruva?
What? In Delhi?	G	Kya? Dilli ha?
What's happened? in Delhi?	F	Dilli kya koruva?
:::::: noise ::::::		::::::
	G	(Laughs) By god...!
Now, you just take it easy	F	Vanneh behzih sokh saanev
What?	G	Kya?
You just take it easy	F	Vanneh behzih sokh saanev
Fine – where are you? In Srinagar?	G	Accha – tse katev chukh? Srinagar-ha?
:::::: noise ::::::		::::::
Are you in Srinagar?	G	Tse chukha Srinagar?
No, I've left that place	F	Naa, mai kar tate chutti
Are you now in Baramulla?	G	Tse chukh vainv Varmuley?
Yes	F	Aa
Fine	G	Accha
I've left that place	F	Tete kar me chutti
Fine	G	Accha
Fine, God keep you well	F	Accha, khuda hafiz...
God keep you well	G	Khuda hafiz...
Fine, should I put it down?	F	Accha, trava?
Fine, put it down, put it down	G	Accha, trav, trav

Since our campaign, the prosecution's enthusiasm for this intercepted call has waned. "**I am not putting all my eggs in the basket of that intercepted call,**" said the Special Prosecutor during the High Court hearing. (The Hindu, May 6, 2003)

Tried by The Media
The S A R Geelani TRIAL

NANDITA HAKSAR

Since July 2002, I have been deeply involved in the campaign for the acquittal of Syed Abdur Rahman Geelani, the thirty-four year old Delhi University lecturer accused of conspiring to attack the Indian Parliament. The man has been tortured, humiliated and framed in a crime he condemned in a SMS message within a few minutes of hearing the news. But there is no way of getting the record of the SMS message.

The only piece of evidence against him is a two minute sixteen second telephone conversation (reproduced opposite) he had with his brother while travelling in a bus from his home to the nearby mosque on Friday, December 14th, 2001. It seems truly incredible that a man involved in such a big crime should the next day be busying himself buying a hearing aid for his mother-in-law and going for Friday prayers in a bus.

It was while he was travelling in the bus that he received a call from his eighteen year old brother, Shah Faisal, asking Geelani to send him a prospectus and syllabus. Faisal had called the previous evening and was now reminding him. Shah Faisal, a particularly gentle young man with a sheepish smile, was dreaming of becoming a doctor. He could not have guessed that the brief call to remind his brother to send the prospectus would be produced as the main evidence against Geelani and he would be sentenced to death.

When Shah Faisal asked Geelani "what had happened", he was delicately referring to Geelani's decision not to go to Kashmir for Id since there were very few holidays and it would cost too much. Geelani's wife was angry and was insisting on going home. A younger brother in a large feudal family would never directly ask his eldest brother about a quarrel with his wife. The elder brother would not answer, laughing away the query. The policemen of the Special Branch who were tapping his mobile felt that the laugh showed Geelani's complicity in the conspiracy to attack the Parliament.

The police were never able to explain why they had not arrested the younger brother; after all, if he asked the question he must have knowledge of the conspiracy. The police officer in charge of the investigation testified in court that Shah Faisal was innocent. The police also never did explain why they never put a transcript of the telephone conversation on record.

Geelani produced two independent witnesses who put the transcript of the taped conversation on record and testified that the conversation could not be remotely linked to the conspiracy to attack the Parliament.

The trial court judge sitting in a specially constituted court for hearing cases booked under the new anti-terrorist law (Prevention of Terrorism Act, POTA) held that the two independent defence witnesses were in fact "interested witnesses". He did not explain how a trade union leader and a documentary film maker, both Kashmiri Pandits, who appeared in court at the request of senior civil liberties activists known for their personal integrity could be called "interested". The Judge stated in his judgment that he himself had taken lessons in the Kashmiri language and was thus competent to decide on the truth of the police version.

Geelani was condemned to death on the basis of this evidence and he spent one year on death row before being acquitted by the High Court on October 29th, 2003. The police have since filed an appeal in the Supreme Court and are hoping to get Geelani back in his cell in the Tihar jail. They have given public statements expressing the hope that he will be hanged.

What has been the role of the media? Many people across the country have been deeply troubled by the role of electronic and print media in the context of the 'War against Terrorism', internationally and in India. All of us involved in the campaign for the acquittal of Geelani have been acutely aware of the crucial role that the media would play in our campaign. The challenge before us is to reach and shape public opinion in the midst of the growing communalism at home, and the demonization of the Muslim world by the international media.

II
Trial by Media

Abdur Rahman is a brilliant scholar of Arabic and the first Kashmiri Muslim to get a permanent job in the prestigious Delhi University. He was thus a perfect candidate for framing in a case of terrorism. From the time of his arrest, the investigating agencies planted a series of stories designed to portray Geelani as a mastermind of the conspiracy. Newspapers across the country, even respectable conservative dailies, carried tabloid-style headings and sensational confessions by Geelani. *The Hindustan Times* carried a report entitled "Case Cracked: Jaish Behind Attack", which stated, "A Delhi lecturer, who spoke to militants, also called up Jaish militants in Pakistan" (December 16, 2001). The staid *Hindu* carried a story the next day entitled "Varsity Don Guided '*Fidayeen*'". The report states, "Geelani revealed that he became part of the conspiracy due to his ideological leanings. He was closely related to the main *Jaish-e-Mohammad* co-ordinator in Delhi, Mohammad Afzal and his cousin, Shaukat Hussain Guru, who have been arrested. He also knew the terrorists who had come to the Capitol to execute the plan".[1]

These newspapers carried such reports without thought to basic journalistic ethics. The usual healthy scepticism about police stories disappeared as patriotism took over, and patriotism excluded the possibility of raising some basic questions about the truth of the police stories supposedly based on confessions made by Geelani while in custody. Even when the court records clearly showed that Geelani had refused to implicate himself by giving a false confession, the newspapers did not relent.

A few individuals and organizations were alarmed by the trial by media and voiced their concerns in the form of letters to the editor. Amnesty International released an Open Letter to the Indian Law Minister on the eve of the trial expressing concern over the media coverage. The letter stated: "Amnesty International is concerned that the media coverage of the arrests and concerning the person of Abdul Rehman Geelani during the pre-trial period has been extremely prejudicial to his case and that the Government of India has not taken any steps to halt this. The media coverage, which largely presented Geelani as guilty before the trial had even begun, must be presumed to impact negatively on Abdul Rehman Geelani's right to be presumed innocent as required by Article 14 (2) of the International Covenant on Civil and Political Rights and on the impartiality of the POTA court which is to hear the case from 8 July 2002".

Amnesty International expressed its concern over the way that the prime accused, Mohammad Afzal, had been brought before the national media and made to confess to being party to the conspiracy. He, however, told the media that Geelani was not involved. The police officer in charge of the investigation shouted at Afzal and told him that he had been warned not to speak about Geelani. Then the officer turned to the media and requested the media not to broadcast that part of Afzal's statement. Later, during the trial, the senior police officer told the court that he did not know anything about the media conference held at the police station. He lied under oath.

The trial began. In a record time of four months, the prosecution produced eighty witnesses. Not a single prosecution witness even alleged that Abdur Rahman belonged or sympathised with any banned organization. There was no evidence against Geelani except for the two minute sixteen second conversation and the fact that he knew the co-accused. Geelani never denied his acquaintance with the two Kashmiris who were from his home district, Baramulla, in Kashmir.

However, there was no evidence at all that Geelani was ever in touch with the five men who actually attacked the Parliament or with the three Pakistanis who were supposed to have masterminded the attack. In fact, Geelani was the only one who had a regular connection and paid his bills through his bank. The judge who condemned him to death acquitted him of the charge of belonging to any terrorist organization.

The media covered the trial, but entirely from the prosecution point of view. The public never heard of the glaring contradictions in the police version. In fact, on the first anniversary of the Parliament attack, Zee TV produced a film called *December 13th*. Zee proudly announced that the film was not merely a story, it was the truth. Before the broadcast of the film, Zee had Raza Murad, a well-known Bollywood actor with a deep, resonant voice, declare that he thought it his patriotic duty to introduce the film. It could not be a mistake that Zee had chosen a Muslim to do that kind of an introduction.

The film claimed to be based on the charge sheet but it went well beyond the prosecution case presented in the court. The film portrayed Geelani as the mastermind and showed scenes of him talking to the five dead attackers and planning the attack. The film was shown to the Prime Minister and then the Home Minister, and the media recorded their approval of the film.

Geelani's lawyers moved the court and the High Court did stay the broadcast. Zee TV moved the Supreme Court. The corporation was less concerned with the protection of the freedom of speech and expression than with the possibility of losing money. The Supreme Court vacated the stay and the entire nation watched the film a few days before the Designated Court sentenced Geelani to death.

III
Mobilizing Prejudice

On September 19th, 2002, one day after Syed Abdur Rahman Geelani, the thirty-two year old college lecturer, was given a death sentence for a crime he did not commit, an anonymous person wrote the following postcard from Mayapuri, Delhi, to him: "Janab Jilani What do you think about your Islam? In your religion there is no sister, aunt, mother...you are a *Haram ki aaulad* (illegitimate offspring)...this is your fucking religion which will destroy your community".

This was not just an isolated incident. Geelani received dozens of such hate-filled postcards. The postcards reached Geelani deep inside the high-risk ward of Tihar jail. The jail authorities obviously enjoyed delivering these to him while they threw away the letters written to him by his ten year old daughter. They also denied Geelani and other Muslim prisoners and detainees their right to offer *namaz*.

This hate, prejudice and dehumanization are a product of a well thought out strategy in which the media has played a crucial role. Arvind Rajagopal, in his *Politics After Television* (2001), documented the role of television in reshaping and mobilizing Hindu nationalism in the 1980s and 1990s. The Bombay film industry has produced a series of films on in-surgency in Kashmir, such as *Maa Tujhe Salaam (2002)* in which there is this slogan found all over the country: *"Doodh Mangoge to Kheer Denge, Kashmir Mangoge to Cheer Denge"* (If you ask for milk, we will give you cream; if you ask for Kashmir, we will flay you alive). Other films such as *Hero (2003)*, *L.O.C.(2003)*, *Mission Kashmir(2002)* and *Roja (1992)* play upon the same prejudices and stereotypes. I do not know whether any studies have been done to assess the impact of these films, but the hate and prejudice we encounteredin our campaign cannot be de-linked to the media portrayals of so-called Islamic violence.

Chandan Mitra of *The Pioneer* wrote the following lines after Geelani was acquitted in an editorial page article dated November 2, 2004 titled "Go Home, Geelani and Friends": "His masters across the border must have been delighted to see TV pictures of some demented Indian citizens dancing in joy on hearing the news of his acquittal. No wonder Pakistani soldiers are repeatedly told by their commanders that Indians have no stomach for a fight, that as a people Indians are pot-bellied, indolent and seeped in a pacific Hindu culture".

The real crisis in the media is not the existence of Chandan Mitra's kind of hate-filled journalism. The problem is that even journalists with a reputation for professional courage felt that we should rejoice at Geelani's acquittal and we should make it a showcase of Indian democracy; but when Geelani raised vital questions about the threat of fascism towards democratic institutions, the liberals stopped celebrating his acquittal and warned him not to speak out. Instead of praising his courage, they condemned him for it. Kuldip Nayar reprimanded Geelani in an article entitled "Spoilers in the Peace Process" on November 4th, 2003, a few days after his acquittal. Kuldip Nayar told Geelani not to mix Kashmir politics with the conspiracy to attack the Parliament. It did not occur to the veteran journalist that Geelani was a victim of India's policy in Kashmir. Telling Geelani not to voice his opinions on Kashmir was denying him his fundamental right to freedom of speech and expression. It was not only Kuldip Nayar who took this stand. Many people who had campaigned for a fair trial for Geelani now advised that he should not exercise his right to freedom of speech and expression.

The problem is not whether Geelani should speak out or not. The real problem is that patriotic journalists like Kuldip Nayar seem to be willing to sacrifice basic values of democracy and human rights when it comes to defending the nation. They are not willing to raise their voice against the use of the media by the police for mobilizing hatred and prejudice. When the High Court raised some vital questions with regard to the media, even liberal journalists were silent.

The judgment of the Delhi High Court that acquitted Geelani noted the arguments of the Defence Counsel that media trials are an antithesis to the rule of law and pre-trial publicity is sufficient to cause prejudice and hatred against the accused. The High Court endorsed the concerns of the Defence Counsel by holding that media trials are a disturbing feature and the police are misusing custody, but held that judges do not get influenced by propaganda or adverse publicity. The High Court did not pass any strictures against the police for using the media to mobilize hatred and prejudice, even though it is a specific crime under the Indian Penal Code.

IV
Covering Islam
The crisis in the media has been tragically exposed by the coverage of the trial of the four accused in the Parliament case. Many of us are deeply concerned and disturbed by this crisis. However, we still have to give the crisis a name. We have to acknowledge that we have just begun to raise issues relating to the problems of news and media coverage in the context of Islamophobia and the 'War against Terrorism'.

Let me cite a concrete example from our own campaign: Throughout our campaign we came across many Muslim citizens who expressed their appreciation for our work but felt they could not openly express their solidarity. These people included our friends, colleagues, Geelani's students, his teachers and colleagues.

No Muslim organization came forward to either demand a fair trial for Geelani or to condemn the judiciary for displaying prejudice and hostility. It was only on September 20th, 2003, that seven Muslim organizations finally gave a joint statement demanding a fair trial for Geelani. However, Syed Shahabuddin, President of All India Muslim Majlis-e-Mushawarat told me that he would not release the joint statement himself. Since the joint statement was in solidarity with our All India Defence Committee for Syed Abdul Rehman Geelani, we released it to the press, both in Srinagar and in Delhi. No one carried the report.

Three days later Noam Chomsky gave a statement supporting the Delhi University teacher's campaign for a fair trial for Geelani. Chomsky said he hoped that Indian democracy and its legal system would rise to the challenge, reverse this decision, and ensure that human and civil rights are properly protected. Newspapers in Kashmir and Delhi carried Chomsky's statement.

How are we going to deal with the war against Terrorism without addressing the issue of Islamophobia? How are we going to deal with the issue of Islamophobia without talking about Kashmir? And how are we going to approach the Kashmir issue without supporting Geelani's right to freedom of speech and expression?

The problem is well stated by an American Professor of journalism: "The media's

The author would like to thank Syed Bismillah Geelani for sharing his insights and views, many of which have been incorporated here.

choice of patriotism has terribly important consequences for democratic life. When they opt for 'a love of country' that quickly transmogrifies into chauvinism, they prepare the cultural ground for violence and do a disservice to national and global democracy. Journalism needs to resist the temptation to dance to the tune of deafening nationalism often found in public opinion. Instead, it could courageously show patriotic spirit by keeping criticism alive rather than becoming compliant with 'home essentialism'. It could provide reassurance by lowering the fear volume and offer community by defending diversity and tolerance rather than foundational, ethnocentric patriotism".[2]

Is this not what Geelani also said when he told the media on September 18th, 2001, a few minutes after he was sentenced to death, "By convicting innocents you cannot suppress feelings. Peace comes with justice. Without justice there will be no democracy; it is Indian democracy that is under threat".

Geelani's conviction exposed how far democratic institutions in our country have been co-opted into the 'War against Terrorism'. His acquittal showed that there is still space for democratic struggle.

The author would like to thank Syed Bismillah Geelani for sharing his insights and views, many of which have been incorporated here.

NOTES

1. S A R Geelani is named in this text in two different ways, as Syed Abdur Rehman Geelani and as Syed Abdul Rehman Geelani. S A R Geelani's name is 'Abdur Rehman' and not 'Abdul Rehman', but since the police records have always called him Abdul Rehman (having lost the r and picked up the l, even as they were 'adjusting' other facts about his life), the defence committee, his lawyers, the court and the press have had to consistently refer to Syed Abdul Rehman Geelani when speaking of the person under trial. Here, in using both spellings, reference is being made both to S A R Geelani the man, as well as to S A R Geelani the accused.

2. Waisbord, Silvio. "Journalism, Risk and Patriotism" in Barbie Zelizer and Stuart Allan, eds., *Journalism After September 11th* (Routledge, 2002).

RELEVANT URLS

1. All India Defence Committee for Syed Abdul Rehman Geelani
   www20.brinkster.com/sargeelani
2. "Police misinterpreted phone conversation"
   http://www.hinduonnet.com/thehindu/2002/10/12/stories/2002101200711300.htm
3. "The Worst is Always Precise", by Shuddhabrata Sengupta,
   http://mail.sarai.net/pipermail/reader-list/2002-December/001981.html

Truth/
TESTIMONY

"I Saw it on CNN, so it Must be True … Wrong!"

CRAIG ETCHESON

The job of a reporter is to write stories that will "sell newspapers". What kinds of stories about Cambodia sell? Stories about the Khmer Rouge, certainly. Stories about Cambodian politicians who are betraying the principles of justice, or who don't have a clue what those principles might be, they will sell. Stories about getting away with murder sell. About getting away with genocide.

But all too often these days, it is some of the reporters who seem to be getting away with murder – murdering the story. They are mangling reality, leaving it a bloodied, unrecognizable mess. In some cases, it has been so bad it threatens to become a parody of journalism, like a text version of all those dead bodies that appear on the front pages of the Phnom Penh penny press. But this isn't coming from untrained pseudo-reporters working for hack political broadsheets. No, this is coming from some of the best amongst Cambodia's providers of news to the international community.

For example, I woke up last Friday, August 13, 2003, and flipped on Cable News Network International. There on CNN was a story saying Cambodia had passed a law that would delay a trial of the senior Khmer Rouge leader, General Mok, for three years. And that was it.

But is that really it? Does that news snippet give CNN's viewers a good picture of the reality behind the story? Is this high-quality, objective reporting of the facts, with a penetrating analysis of the meaning of those facts? I think not.

That story might have said, instead, that Cambodia has decided to forego a hasty, kangaroo court trial based on an ill-considered application of the 1994 anti-Khmer Rouge law. It might have argued that Cambodia had wisely decided to take the time and effort necessary to draft and pass proper laws dealing with genocide and crimes against humanity in an effort to bring a measure of real justice to one of the perpetrators of the killing fields. It could have pointed out that doing this is part of the process by which Cambodia is accommodating itself to the desire of the international community for any Khmer Rouge trials to meet international standards of justice. But that would be too complicated.

Instead, CNN viewers hear "indefinite delay", with the unstated – and unsubstantiated – but nonetheless clear implication that Cambodia is unwilling to comply with its obligations under international law.

In this way, sloppy reporting reduced to 'sound bytes' sends a message that could well be the opposite of the truth of the matter. It is no wonder that Cambodian Prime Minister Hun Sen is rumoured to blast television sets with his pistol! Who could blame him?

"Experts Rue Lost Chance to Reconcile KR Past", blared the headlines on August 4. "Lost chance to reconcile?" Excuse me? Don't try to blame this all on some ignorant headline writer – the deeper you look, the worse it gets. "Most analysts see the National Assembly's move Tuesday as the latest evidence pointing to the country's unwillingness to deal with its brutal past", the opening graph begins.

"Most analysts"? Let's unpack this just a little bit. Did the reporter take a poll of experts? Perhaps commission a survey research firm to sample opinion among experts? Apparently not. But the reader should not worry – a broad range of recognized experts will be on the record in this story, right? Well, not exactly. Instead, we get exactly "one diplomatic source" and "one legal analyst" – anonymously, of course – who are miraculously transformed through some magic of media alchemy into "most analysts". Shazzam! Would "most analysts" in this case be two out of three? Somehow, I was under the impression that there were more than three analysts in the world, and that some of us have names and occasionally even go on the record.

What about the substance of this story? The substance of this story is that the Cambodian government decided not to proceed with a trial of General Mok on charges of violating the 1994 anti-Khmer Rouge law.

The entire purpose of that proposed exercise was to find a way to continue legally detaining Mok beyond the September 8 deadline for the six-month pre-trial detention limit so that he can be held until Cambodia is able to adopt laws specifying penalties for the crime of genocide. They also hope, once a law is written and Mok has been formally charged, to conduct a proper investigation into the exceedingly complex crime of genocide. That's what the government asserts, anyway. And in my humble opinion, there is just as much evidence to support this view as there is to buttress any contrary view. But there is no mention of that alternative possible interpretation in this story.

What would have been at issue in a trial of Mok under the 1994 anti-Khmer Rouge law was one simple, straightforward fact, and nothing more. The only substantive issue in such a trial, should it have been held, would have been: Was Mok, or was he not, a member of the Khmer Rouge after the six month grace period of the 1994 law expired in early 1995? That would have been the only question of fact relevant to a finding of guilt or innocence in such a case.

But recall that headline: "Lost Chance to Reconcile the KR Past". So where do you get this "reconcile the KR past" bit? No such thing would have been in prospect for a trial of Mok under the 1994 law. A chance to reconcile Mok's resume is all that might have been lost here. What happened in this case is that the reporter (and/or the editor) confounded what might be revealed in a full-scale genocide tribunal with what would have been revealed in a simple trial on charges of being a member of an illegal organization. This is very sloppy. It should be embarrassing, except that so rarely do reporters have their 'bluff' called on this kind of intellectual laziness.

On August 11, the wires moved a story titled, "Cambodia Nixes U.N. Court Plan". Well, it looks like Hun Sen has done it again, that dirty dog! Or has he? Let's peel the onion a bit further here. "Cambodia's foreign minister rejected a U.N. plan for war crimes trials Wednesday", the lead graph begins. Is that right? No, it most certainly is not right.

The United Nations is sending a mission of experts to Cambodia on August 25 to negotiate on international participation in a tribunal for the Khmer Rouge.

They have not even formally presented their 'plan' to the government yet, so isn't it a tad premature to trumpet the rejection of that plan?

What the UN in fact did was to send the government a very brief outline of some – but not all – of the elements of the proposed UN plan for a genocide tribunal.

One element of the plan is to have either five or seven judges sit in the trial chamber of the Khmer Rouge tribunal. One aspect of this one element of the plan is that the U.N. proposes international judges should predominate in the trial chamber by a numerical majority of one. The Cambodian government didn't like the sound of that aspect of that element of the plan, and voiced a public doubt about it.

But again, by that mysterious media alchemy, one aspect of one element of a partial plan is magically transformed into the entire plan in itself, and thus is it confidently reported that the 'plan' has been "rejected". Yet, it is possible that this aspect of this element of the plan is in fact negotiable.

The U.N. might be willing to concede that particular point to the Cambodian government. The government might not be firm in their doubts about it. Who knows? The reporter certainly gives no indication whether he knows if any of this might be the case. And for sure, his readers won't find out from that story.

This goes beyond sloppy and begins to verge on the hysterical. The worst part of this is that it has the potential to seriously damage Cambodia's relations with the international community. This is serious. Maybe CNN/Time Warner has become "All OJ, All the Time", but that does not mean everyone has to jump on the pulp fiction, tabloid trash bandwagon along with them.

The Khmer Rouge accountability issue is crucial both to Cambodia and to many other nations. When citizens in the United States or France, who rely on the media for 'the truth', see stories like this, they read it and think, "There those Cambodians go again, sabotaging the world's efforts at justice". And then they write to their legislators, who in turn put pressure on their foreign ministries, thus needlessly complicating relations. That's why this kind of reporting is so scandalous. Or at least so it should be considered.

The journalists who write this stuff are intelligent and, for the most part, responsible. Indeed, I consider many reporters who cover Cambodia to be personal friends and I have a great deal of respect for them. So why do they seem, all too often, to put out these kinds of misleading stories, which can be so harmful to Cambodia?

Do they detest Cambodia or its leaders? Is it the pressure of the deadline? Is this about craven editors and ignorant headline writers? Is it the tyranny of the medium, which requires the distillation of vastly complex realities down into tiny soundbites? Does reducing the complexity of reality to sound bytes inevitably distort reality? Does the public demand drama and villains, which scribblers can deliver only through wilful oversimplification? Has healthy scepticism and critical analysis been trampled down into terminal cynicism, where one must always adopt the most negative possible interpretation of government pronouncements? Is there some kind of ideological bias infecting some of these reporters? At one time or another, there may be a grain of truth to all of these explanations.

In reviewing my media files while preparing this comment, I was pleasantly surprised to be reminded that much of the reporting coming out of Cambodia on the Khmer Rouge issue, in fact, is really pretty good, against all odds. This issue is incredibly complex, the politics of it are wildly Byzantine, the policy process is utterly opaque, and the stakes are quite high. And that is precisely why journalists carry such a profound burden of responsibility in covering this story.

The best in the business, after all, never exhibit these flaws in their reporting. Study, for example, the work of seasoned professionals like Philip Shenon of the New York Times. They stick to the facts, abjure oversimplification, reject facile generalizations, and avoid the kinds of distortions I have been decrying here. Reporters in Cambodia who want to maintain the respect of an informed and discriminating public must aspire to these values.

The greatest danger is that few among your reading and viewing publics have the data necessary to be very discriminating about your reports. After all, as an 'expert', I have access to many sources of information about Cambodia which are not dependent upon the strange filters of the media world. Most people do not have access to these other sources, and rely on the media to get... what? At times, they are getting a very skewed picture of Cambodia.

Perhaps, my friends, you need to adopt a Hippocratic Oath of Journalism. "First, do no harm". I know you. You claim to love this country. Please be more careful, and convince us that we should believe this. Because we measure the truth of your claims by the care with which you carry out your duties as reporters.

[Originally published in the Phnom Penh Post, Issue 8/17, August 20 – September 2, 1999.]

"CNN Made Me Do (Not Do) It"

Assessing Media Influence on U.S. Interventions in Somalia and Rwanda

LYN S. GRAYBILL

My initial premise upon undertaking this study was a simple one: The U.S. had intervened in Somalia in response to media images of starving children in 1992 but had not acted to stop the genocide in Rwanda in 1994 – not because government officials were unaware of what was taking place there[1] – but because the public did not know. CNN was not on the scene beaming home real time images of the killings. Thus, the administration was under no pressure from the public to do something about the genocide.

This is a common view of the power of the media, especially television journalism which through emotive images moves the public to demand action of its government. The "CNN Effect", it is argued, pushes the government into foreign policy pursuits in response to public opinion. Why did Bush authorize humanitarian intervention in Somalia? Because the media told him to. Why did Clinton not authorize intervention in Rwanda? Because the media, representatives of which had been evacuated from Rwanda as the genocide unfolded, were simply not there to report what was happening. Disturbing images of innocent people being hacked to death did not make the nightly news and did not therefore force the administration into an intervention. If it had made the nightly news, the argument goes, the "CNN Effect" would have forced the US to intervene as it had in Somalia.

That is what I thought I would find. But a review of the coverage of the news stories from Somalia and Rwanda presents a different picture. Media coverage followed political debate or policy action in the government. Rather than setting the agenda, the media reflected the government's agenda, covering what the government decided was important. It is not the all-powerful independent institution that the term "CNN Effect" connotes. Nor does it take foreign policy decision making away from the government as it is assumed.

Somalia

By 1992, starvation gripped Somalia in the wake of the civil war that followed the overthrow of Mohammed Siad Barre in January 1991. As Barre fled, the scorched earth policy of his retreating troops created a famine belt. Once a common enemy no longer existed, the clans that had united to overthrow Barre fought for control of the government. (Factions of the Hawiye based USC guerrilla army supportive of Ali Mahdi Mohammed fought factions of the Hawiye forces loyal to Mohammed Farah Aidid.) Fighting, coming at the same time as a serious drought, led to anarchy and famine. One point five million out of a population of 2 million were threatened with starvation, and 300,000 had already died, including 25% of all children under five (Schraeder, 1994: 177).

A United Nations Security Council resolution called for a cease-fire in January 1992 which was to go into effect in March. Still, factional fighting continued. In April, the Security Council authorized a modest military operation which was delayed by negotiations with Somali factions. On July 27, the Security Council voted to airlift food, and on August 12 announced plans to send 500 troops to protect the relief effort. On August 14, President George Bush announced that the U.S. would take charge of the airlift.

The airlift fell short of its goals, since there was no way to guarantee that the food once dropped reached the famine victims. Five hundred troops, with the support of US warships carrying 2100 Marines, arrived in September but were unable to protect the relief effort. On November 26, after UN Secretary General Boutros-Boutros Ghali announced that the relief efforts were not working, President Bush announced that the US would send ground troops to protect food convoys, and the UN passed the authorising resolution on December 3rd. The first troops of "Operation Restore Hope" hit the shores on December 9th.

What did the media report? Jonathan Mermin's analysis of television coverage of ABC, CBS, and NBC points to very low coverage of Somalia from January through June, an increase in July, and extensive coverage in August and September, a sharp drop off in October, and a recovery in November. Three full stories occurred on January 5th, February 27th, and March 2nd with grim predictions of numbers who would starve without relief. Mermin argues, however, that these stories, broadcast five to seven months before Bush's decision to take charge of the airlift, could have had little impact on his decision (Mermin, 1997: 391).

In July and August, three full stories ran on the networks: July 22 by ABC, July 31 by CBS, and August 13 by ABC, all containing videos of starving children. It was these images which had pundits like Bernard Cohen later claiming: "By focusing daily on the starving children in Somalia, a pictorial story tailor-made for television, TV mobilized the conscience of the nation's public institutions, compelling the government into a policy of intervention for humanitarian reasons" (Cohen, 1994: 9-10).

But by superimposing events in Washington onto the timetable of stories, Mermin demonstrates that it was official Washington which set the context in which the media responded. On July 22nd, the day the ABC story aired, the House Select Committee on Hunger held hearings on Somalia. Senator Nancy Kassebaum (R-KS), the senior Republican of the Senate Foreign Relations Committee's sub-committee on Africa, who had just returned from a fact-finding mission, testified, "I strongly support sending a United Nations security force to Somalia" (Mermin 1997: 392). This declaration clashed with the position of the Bush administration that a UN force should not be deployed until a cease-fire had been achieved. Senator Paul Simon (D-IL), chair of the subcommittee on Africa, also urged the administration to act, saying, "I don't want to wait to have a Democratic administration before we respond more adequately. I want to do it now" (Mermin, 1997: 393). The timing suggests the importance of Kassebaum and Simon and the House Committee on Hunger in getting Somalia on the media's agenda, not the media's power in getting Somalia on the government's agenda. Strobel notes, "Television did not lead but followed policy action or proposals" (Strobel, 1997: 136).

The CBS Story on July 31st also followed this pattern. Senator Edward Kennedy (D-MA) in a hearing of the Senate Judiciary Committee wondered, "why we're not moving in Somalia as we are in Yugoslavia". White House spokesman Marlin Fitzwater in a press conference on July 27th stated: "The tragedy in Somalia...requires the urgent attention of the international community" (Mermin, 1997: 394). According to Mermin, CBS covered Somalia on July 31st only after actors in Washington defined it as a significant concern: "Instead of being out ahead of Washington, television appears to have acted in concert with Congress and the White House in illuminating events in Somalia" (394).

Airlift Decision: August 14th
The August 13st story on ABC followed two weeks of debate and action in Washington: The Senate Resolution on Somalia urging deployment of UN forces (August 3rd); Senators McConnell's and Jefford's comparisons of Rwanda and Bosnia (August 6th & 7th); Senator Rockefeller's criticism of Bush's inaction on Somalia (August 9th); the House resolution on Somalia (August 10th); the UN's announcement to send 500 troops to guard relief supplies (August 12th); and candidate Clinton's citation of Somalia as an important foreign policy issue (August 13th). Mermin points out that the case for the influence of the media on intervention is strongest here; the day following the ABC story, the White House announced it would airlift emergency aid in what it called "Operation Provide Relief" (Mermin, 1997: 396). But Bush had decided on August 12th (before the ABC story) in meetings with James Baker, Secretary of Defence Richard Cheney, and National Security Advisor Brent Snowcroft to authorize the airlift (Livingston and Eachus, 1995: 426).

Interestingly, the media framed the Somalia story as actors in Washington were framing it – that Somalia was a situation that the US should and could do something about. Mermin argues, "It is noteworthy that the framing of the crisis in Somalia as a humanitarian disaster that the United States could do something about does not appear on television until it has appeared in Washington first" (Mermin, 1997: 397).

Influences other than the media influenced the decision. Not to be underestimated is the cable sent by US Ambassador to Kenya, Smith Hempstone, in early July (the "Cable from Hell"), describing the desperate famine conditions. It was forwarded to the State Department, the National Security Council, and eventually to the President. Bush wrote in the margins, "This is very, very upsetting. I want more information" (Strobel, 1997: 132). The OFDA (Office of Foreign Disaster Assistance) of the AID had also been an early and forceful advocate within the administration on Somalia.

CNN had framed the story in May (eight reports in two weeks) as a disaster that the US could and should do something about long before the three networks did. At best, CNN's influence was subtle; perhaps the stories had some behind the scenes impact on Senators Kassebaum and Simon. But this is hardly the absolute "pressure of media" thesis that the "CNN Effect" posits (Mermin, 1997: 399).[2]

Even earlier (in January), *Nightline* did a special program on Somalia. Ted Koppel introduced his broadcast: "It's been called the most dangerous spot in the world, a civil war that has killed or wounded 20,000 people. Widespread starvation. Even the UN has pulled out its relief workers, deeming it too dangerous for them to stay there... You should watch this. We all have a moral obligation to at least know what is happening in Somalia, but in fairness I must tell you it is a very disturbing piece of video". But there is no evidence that senior policy makers altered policy in response (Livingston and Eachus, 1995: 422).

Decision to Send Ground Troops: November 26th

From mid-August to mid-September, the networks devoted fifty-five minutes to the preparations for the airlift and the operation. From mid-September to November 8th – presidential election season – only 250 seconds of coverage was broadcast on Somalia. From November 9th to November 24th, the three networks broadcast four full stories. On November 26th, the White House announced the decision to send ground troops to secure relief delivery routes. During this period, Senators Simon, Kassebaum, and Wofford (D-PA) in a press conference called for further action (November 9th). On November 18th, a six-member Congressional delegation to Somalia held a press conference describing Somalia as "an affront to humanity" and urged further action (Mermin, 1997: 401).

Thus, television coverage and actions of politicians are correlated, with official actions preceding Somalia's becoming a news story. If television contributed to the emergence of Somalia as a foreign policy issue, "it had powerful, outspoken allies in Washington, whose efforts to get Somalia onto the news in the first place appear to have been indispensable" (Mermin, 1997: 403). Journalists reported on and thus facilitated other actors' agendas. There is no evidence that the news media by themselves forced the U.S. government officials to change their policies. But, when as in Somalia, policy is in flux, or weakly held, or without congressional support, the media can have an impact on policy by covering critical viewpoints.

Between November 26th, when the decision to launch "Operation Restore Hope" was announced, until December 9th, the day the US troops landed near Mogadishu, there were ninety-five news reports, and coverage remained relatively high through year's end (Strobel, 1997: 136-37).[3] The images broadcast on CNN and the three networks helped Bush explain why the mission was necessary. Thus, the media became an instrument of policy. Former State Department spokesman Richard Boucher explained: "We didn't have to spend as much time postulating an argument for [intervention]" (Strobel, 1997: 86). When Navy Seals and Marines landed on the beach off Mogadishu on December 9th, the networks and CNN were already there, having sent in their stars, Ted Koppel of ABC, Tom Brokaw of NBC, and Dan Rather of CBS, in what is derisively called "parachute journalism".[4] In addition to the journalists waiting on the beach, more than twenty journalists accompanied the Marines as they prepared for the beach landing (Strobel, 1997: 96).

Pulling Out

In response to the June 5th, 1993, attack on Pakistani peacekeepers, the mission changed, and the new goal was to "get Aidid". A four-month period of open warfare between UNOSOM (the United Nations mission) and General Aidid's militia culminated in the October 3rd US Ranger raid on a meeting of his top officers in Mogadishu, which turned into a day-long fire-fight that resulted in the deaths of eighteen American soldiers. By this time, no American reporters were left in Mogadishu.[5]

The "CNN Effect" clearly did not 'push' Bush into action he would otherwise not have taken (dispatching troops in December 1992), but did it 'pull' Clinton out? Was it media coverage of the deaths of eighteen Army rangers killed in a fire-fight that ensured the US would withdraw? There was no video of the fire-fight itself, but when the image of a dead soldier poked with a stick and dragged through the streets of Mogadishu to the cheers and jeers of the crowd, and that of a very battered captured US pilot Michael Durant, were broadcast on October 4th, 1993, television sets were on in nearly every corner of the White House as well as American households, tuned to CNN. It is widely assumed that these images broadcast around the world forced the US out of Somalia.

But, it was not the images per se that caused the US to withdraw. The US could just have easily responded by massive retaliation, an action it considered. The US had intervened because a consensus developed that it was do-able with little risk of casualties. This turned out to be incorrect, especially when the mission changed. Clinton had not been interested in or able to communicate to Congress or the public the changed mission and the reasons for it. Mounting calls on Capitol Hill for withdrawal rose to a level that President Clinton could not ignore. On October 7th, he announced that all troops would be withdrawn by March 31st, 1994. The risks of escalation did not measure up to the stakes. According to former press secretary Dee Dee Meyers, "The decision was made that it wasn't worth a lot of American lives to go after this guy". Jeremy Rosner, then National Security Council staff's chief liaison to Capitol Hill, concurs: "The lack of perceived security stakes ended up shaping things more than anything else" (Strobel, 1997: 178). According to Strobel, Clinton was already moving in the direction of withdrawing troops even before the deaths of the eighteen Rangers made the news, and he was motivated by factors other than media coverage, especially congressional pressure (180). Strobel writes, "Public support declined not because of the news media, and specifically televised images of casualties, but because the costs, duration, and outcome of the missions began to diverge from what the public had expected. The televised images of casualties fell into this gap; there is no evidence that they created it" (Strobel, 1997: 204). The decision to withdraw was then reinforced by media stories that followed on 'traditional clan hatreds' that conditioned the public to view Somalis as very different kinds of human beings, who ultimately can be deserted (Besteman, 1996: 139).

Rwandan Genocide: The Background

On April 6th, 1994, President Juvenal Habyarimana was killed when his plane was shot down by ground-to-air missiles over Kigali on his return from a summit of African heads of state in Tanzania. Within thirty minutes of the crash, even before news reports of the crash, the FAR (Rwanda Armed Forces) and the Interahamwe (Hutu militias) set up road blocks throughout Kigali and proceeded door-to-door with detailed hit lists prepared in advance. Although a small unit of UN peacekeepers was in Rwanda under resolution 8726 to monitor the ceasefire between the government of Habyarimana and the Rwandan Patriotic Front (RPF), adopted under the Arusha Peace Accord, the blue helmets with UNAMIR stood by, forbidden by their mandate as Chapter VI peace-keepers to intervene. The next day, ten Belgian soldiers with UNAMIR were tricked into giving up their weapons and were tortured and murdered. One week after the murder of the Belgian soldiers, Belgium withdrew from UNAMIR, and the U.N. voted to reduce the UNAMIR troops from 2500 to 270.

Media Coverage of Genocide

Turning back to my original assumption that the US had not intervened in Rwanda because of the lack of media images inciting the public to demand that something be done – what is the evidence? Hutu forces murdered at least fourteen Rwandan reporters and editors in an effort to prevent coverage of the genocide (*Africa Report*, 1995: 8). Plus there were just two international journalists, Lindsey Hilsum and Katrin van der Schoot, on the ground when the genocide began. Many Africa journalists were in South Africa covering the upcoming elections when the killings began (Murison: 30). After Mandela's inauguration on May 10th, several correspondents left South Africa to cover the Rwanda story. But because of the danger involved, most journalists covered the massacre from the safe shores of Lake Victoria where the story literally came to them as thousands of corpses washed down the river (Livingston and Eachus, 2000: 223).

Journalists were caught off guard when the story broke. Rwanda should have been on the government's 'radar screen' since both the UN's Department of Peacekeeping Operations[7] and the CIA[8] were aware of the impending plan to exterminate Tutsis, but unfortunately Rwanda had no important advocate within the U.S. government to put it on the foreign policy agenda. Gowing writes, "The lower the national interest and the greater the distance, the less likely it is that news organisations will have anything more than a passing interest in the developing story" (Gowing, 1997).

Nevertheless, a survey of network evening news stories mentioning Rwanda in 1994 reveals that the networks actually covered the slaughter in Rwanda in April and May 1994 more heavily than they covered Somalia in 1992 (excluding the US troop deployment in December). But the stories "held no power to move the US administration to intervene or to move the public to demand that it do so" (Strobel, 1997: 144).

Early coverage on the three networks and CNN focused primarily on the exodus of Americans and Europeans from Rwanda (Martin, 1994: 9). The Joint Evaluation of Emergency Assistance to Rwanda (JEER) noted that "with the withdrawal of foreign personnel there was a precipitous drop in coverage..." (JEER, 1996: 46). The three networks covered the plane crash on April 7th – twenty seconds on ABC and fifteen seconds on both NBC and CBS. On April 11th, a story broke the two-minute mark on ABC (Livingston and Eachus, 2000: 218). There was significantly more coverage in May, which is explained by the fact that reporters were covering the inauguration of Nelson Mandela and were thus available to be deployed to cover the Rwanda story.

What the journalists reported was often wrong. Original stories mistook the genocide for a two-sided civil war – one that the reporters said the Tutsis were winning (Kuperman, 2000: 101). Rwanda had been wracked by a low-level civil war from 1990 to 1993 between the Hutu controlled government and the mainly Tutsi resistance, the Rwanda Patriotic Front, based in Uganda. At the time the genocide began, the two sides had signed a peace accord that called for the return of Tutsi exiles, integration of the armed forces of both sides, a provisional government, and multiparty elections. The initial killings were reported as the resumption of the civil war, a view the Rwandan government favoured, because it would keep outsiders from intervening. One of the early stories from the New York Times (April 12th, 1994) of the killing of Prime Minister Agathe Uwilingiyimana said she had been killed because she was a Tutsi. She was in fact a Hutu (Myers, 1995: 35). Reporters were unaware that not only all Tutsis but also moderate Hutus in favour of the Peace Accord were targeted.

The Western media swallowed the ethnic interpretation of conflict. Pieterse calls it "a media circus of clichés which privileges whatever notions come floating up that are consistent with conventional wisdom, which are then endlessly and uncritically repeated" (Pieterse, 1998: 80). According to McNulty, most reporters' sources appear to be limited to their own organizations' cuttings and audio/video library. Interviewees on the ground were invariably Westerners: NGOs, UN troops, and other journalists (McNulty, 1999: 277).

If journalists' stories, as I have argued for Somalia, follow official sources, what were the official sources in this case? Journalists accepted uncritically the interim Rwandan government's explanation that this was a spontaneous and unforeseen violence resulting from public outrage at the assassination of the president whose plane was shot down on April 6th. This was a self-serving explanation that was not questioned by journalists, who unfortunately had little knowledge of Rwanda. The political context of the fighting – a hard-line group of Hutu officials seeking to jettison a power-sharing agreement that would have included Tutsi and pro-democracy Hutu parties – was ignored.

Susan Douglas writes that it took at least a month for the news media to stop dismissing the conflict as 'tribal' war and to acknowledge that there were actually political and economic reasons for the bloodshed (Douglas, 1994: 15). Jean-Paul Chretien says, "We had to wait until the start of May [1994] for the media, [human rights] associations, and then governments to [acknowledge] the genocide...Until then observers and [the Rwanda government's] partners continued to evoke 'inter-ethnic clashes' which, it was suggested, were the legacy of some barbarism" (Cited in McNulty, 1999: 278). References to a 'centuries-old' ethnic conflict was misleading as Hutus and Tutsis had intermingled to the point that ethnographers no longer recognized them as distinct ethnic groups, and since the first incident of systematic political violence between Hutus and Tutsis wasn't recorded until 1959.

Lack of Government Interest
Despite extensive, if misleading, press coverage, there was little interest from Washington in the story. When President Clinton did speak of Rwanda in the initial days of the massacre, it was of concern for the 258 American expatriates' safety (Clinton, April 9th, 1994; April 12th, 1994). His statements in April called on both sides to stop the violence, which played into the media's interpretation of this as a civil war (Clinton, April 7th, 1994. See Burkhalter, 1994/1995: 47). Policymakers hesitated to call it 'genocide'. State Department spokesperson Christine Shelly insisted on saying "acts of genocide may have occurred", but that the government was not prepared to use the term genocide, which led one exasperated

reporter to ask, "How many acts of genocide does it take to make genocide?" (US State Department briefing, June 10, 1994). James Woods, assistant secretary for African Affairs at the Department of Defence, has no doubt that the government knew it was a genocide as early as the second week: "Never mind that the American press, which was poorly represented anyway, hadn't quite got it right yet, at all, in fact...there was plenty of evidence around if you'd wanted to use it...It was known that this was planned, premeditated, carefully planned, and was being executed according to a plan with the full connivance of the then Rwandan government. This was known" (*Triumph of Evil*, 1999).

Even the House African Affairs Sub-Committee members, whom one would expect to speak for African interests, were muted in their calls for action. Nine members wrote to the president asking for strong support for an active US role "short of committing U.S. troops" (Melvern, 2000: 190). Senators Jeffords and Simon of the Senate Sub-Committee on African Affairs petitioned the White House on May 13 to request that the Security Council approve sending troops to stop the slaughter. The president did not respond for twenty-seven days (Melvern, 2000: 203). These few individuals appear to be the only important voices in the Congress calling on the US to respond. By contrast, Senator Dole on "Meet the Nation" had argued, "I don't think we have any national interest here...I hope we don't get involved there" (Melvern, 2000: 148). Likewise, senior members of the Defence Appropriation Subcommittees of the Senate and House were wary of peacekeeping after Somalia (Burkhalter, 1994/95: 48).

At the NSC, neither Don Steinberg, senior director for Africa, nor his boss, National Security Adviser Anthony Lake, "appears to have played the role that was clearly needed on Rwanda" (Burkhalter, 1994/95: 52). At the State Department, George Moose and his deputy, Prudence Bushnell, favoured a stronger mandate and troop increase for UNAMIR but found themselves ignored by those higher-up. The under secretary for political affairs, Peter Tarnoff, had no interest in Rwanda. And the under secretary of state for global affairs, Tim Wirth, apparently played no role in the decisions although his brief included human rights (Burkhalter, 1994/95: 47). Because of the lack of high-interest attention to Rwanda at the State Department, Pentagon thinking held sway. According to Burkhalter, when the various agencies met to discuss Rwanda, the Pentagon sent its top brass, including Under Secretary of Defence John Deutch on one occasion, to make its case (Burkhalter, 1994/95: 48).

The Clinton administration decided in wake of the Somalia debacle not to intervene again in Africa for humanitarian reasons that fell short of vital national interests, and quickly signed Presidential Decision Directive 25 that severely limits US involvement in international peacekeeping operations. Because there were no strong voices of opposition in the government, the president's view was the one that got reported by the media. The US's obligation as a signatory to the Genocide Convention, not only to punish but also to prevent genocide, was not mentioned by the president nor raised by the media.

Media Reporting After the Genocide:

By July, as the RPF took over more and more of the country, the Hutus fled to neighbouring Zaire in anticipation of Tutu retribution, where they languished in overcrowded camps. Despite the fact that between 500,000 to 800,000 were killed during the genocide

– at least five times as many as those who died of disease and violence in the refugee camps – there was substantially more coverage of the latter, leading to a "false impression that this was the ultimate tragedy" (Philo, Hilsum, Beattie, Holliman, 1998: 229). Rwanda became a major story in July and August (with 15% more broadcasts of the refugees than the earlier genocide on the nightly news). ABC devoted almost 50% of its overall Rwanda coverage to the refugee story, and CNN devoted nearly 70% of its Rwanda coverage to the refugees (Livingston and Eachus, 2000: 220). If one accepts that the media follows foreign policy, not vice versa, the stories reflect the fact that the Clinton administration put the Rwandan refugee crisis on the foreign policy agenda, as something it could do something about, perhaps to assuage guilt for not doing anything earlier to stop the genocide. Because the government decided it could do something, images of dead Rwandan cholera victims dumped in pits in Goma were followed by government response that was "high profile, low risk, very visible, and conceived for maximum media impact so that the public would conclude that 'something is being done'" (Gowing, 1997).

A better way to understand why the US intervened in Somalia but not in Rwanda has less to do with the media than with the perceived do-ability and level of risk. Judith Murison has coined the phrases "Helpless Africa" and "Hopeless Africa" to describe this phenomenon. She argues that the US will intervene for "Helpless Africa" – starving children, famines, cholera and the like, but when the image is one of "Hopeless Africa", the US refuses to intervene. These conflicts are viewed as primordial, ancient rivalries. The point is that nothing can be done, so why bother? Livingston and Eachus concur: "There are fewer rational responses to irrational behaviour, such as a presumably spontaneous massacre" (Livinston and Eachus, 2000: 226).

The media reflected the US government's view of Rwanda as "Hopeless Africa". (In Somalia, a switch occurred from its original portrayal of "Helpless Africa", needing to be fed, to "Hopeless Africa", mired in unresolvable clan conflict.) In Rwanda, only after the genocide was ended when the Rwandan Patriotic Front rebels had captured most of the country and declared a cease-fire on July 18th, did the media shift its portrayal of Rwanda. Now the image was of "Helpless Africa" (starving children and cholera corpses), and media accounts were at their greatest number, focusing on the refugee camps in Goma.

Only when the genocide was over did the US offer assistance to "Helpless Africa" – those refugees in the camps in Zaire who were suffering from cholera, dysentery and malnutrition (many of whom were genocidists hiding among other Hutus). Television images of refugees streaming into camps framed them as victims of hunger and disease and not the perpetrators of genocide. This portrayal followed the government's spin; Clinton in an exchange with reporters in Hot Springs, Arkansas, on July 23rd said: "The previous government slaughtered large numbers of people, and so those who survived fled..." (Clinton, July 23rd, 1994).

Coverage of the flood of refugees coincided with Clinton's announcement on July 22nd that the US military would assist the UNHCR and other relief agencies by airlifting food and supplies in "Operation Support Hope", and in securing the Kigali airport (Clinton,

July 22nd, 1994). One senior official admitted that whereas the footage of corpses floating down the river earlier had not provoked an intervention, the "later scenes of the refugee camps were a different matter...The mind-numbingness of it all was almost a made-to-order operation for what the US can do and do very quickly. But it was into a basically benign environment" (Strobel, 1997: 144). The framing of these images – these are the victims – reflected the administration's and other important official actors' viewpoint and was picked up uncritically by journalists.

Other Variables
Another variable that may have informed decision-making is public support for various types of interventions, independent of media portrayal. Consistent with the "Hopeless/Helpless" Africa schema (intervening for helpless Africa but not hopeless Africa) are polling data collected by Jentleson and Britton that indicate the public is more likely to support humanitarian interventions (HI), defined as "the provision of emergency relief through military and other means to people suffering from famine or other gross and widespread humanitarian disasters", and less likely to support internal policy change (IPC) interventions, defined as "influencing the domestic political authority structure of another state"[9] (Jentleson and Britton, 1998: 399-400). Jentleson and Britton note that prior to March 1993, 74% of the public supported intervening for HI goals in Somalia but that between March and September 1993, support for IPC goals – getting Aidid – was only 47%. After the October 3rd debacle, only 34% supported IPC goals and 80% of respondents argued against getting "bogged down in a messy civil war" (Jentleson and Britton, 1998: 401). Ninety percent of the American public agreed with the statement: "The US had accomplished the humanitarian mission but now we can never hope to solve the Somalis' political problems for them and so should bring our boys home" (Jentleson and Britton, 1998: 401-02). Yet notwithstanding the horrific pictures of dead GIs broadcast on the nightly news, the public did not clamour for the immediate withdrawal of American troops, as the "CNN Effect" would predict. A CNN poll revealed that only 43% of the public wanted the immediate withdrawal of American soldiers; the number was just 37% in an ABC poll. And a majority favoured increased involvement in the short term at least (Kull and Destler, 1999: 106).

Similarly, during the Rwanda crisis six months later, support for HI objective was high (75%) but support for IPC goals was low (43%) (Jentleson and Britton, 1998: 403). Would the administration's actions have been different had the media accurately portrayed the Rwandan conflict for what it was: genocide, and not a civil war? Public support for IPC interventions (civil wars) is the weakest of the four categories of interventions in Jentleson's and Britton's framework. But Kull and Destler's research indicates that the public is very supportive of intervening to allay civilian suffering and deaths (including stopping genocide) even where no national interest exists, even assuming American lives would be lost, if likelihood of success is high (Kull and Destler, 1999: 102-104). There does appear to be a dis-connect between public opinion in favour of intervening for non national-interest reasons and a tolerance for casualties than what government officials believe is public opinion.

Conclusion
The decision to intervene is less a function of media portrayal than of the president's calculations of stakes and risks coupled with the perceived public support for these operations. While Bush was willing to intervene in Somalia where no national interest existed, it was considered at the time to be low risk, and had strong public support. When it turned out not to be risk-free (with the deaths of eighteen Army rangers), President Clinton rushed to enact the presidential directive which limits humanitarian intervention only to places where a vital national interest exists. On no geopolitical or geo-strategic basis – trade relations, host of American military bases, control of shipping lanes, a critical ally in an unstable region – did Rwanda meet the traditional definition of "national interests". And so the official response to the genocide appeared "lethargic and confused and lacked any White House, Defence Department or senior State Department commitment" (Natsios, 1996:158). Natsios argues that where geopolitical interests are not threatened, electronic and print media attention "will be tangential or irrelevant" to the decision to intervene or not (Natsios, 1996:153).

One reporter from Rwanda wondered, "Do you think we did enough? Is it our fault that the world didn't react to the massacres?" (Weiss and Collins, 1996: 40) Horrifying pictures of bodies floating down rivers perhaps pricked diplomatic consciences, but "they did not lead to any major or fundamental policy change..." (Gowing, 1997). Even if accurate reporting and moving real-time television broadcasts had been the norm,[10] it is doubtful in the aftermath of Somalia that the Clinton administration would have been persuaded that this was an intervention worth the costs. Perhaps Clinton misread the public's unwillingness to intervene for goals short of national interest ones. In 1994, 65% of the public believed the US should intervene to stop genocide – 31% said always, and 34% in most cases (Kull and Destler, 1999, 51). But despite public support to stop genocide, it was not an issue about which Americans felt passionately enough to protest or to demand action from their government.

The relationships between the media, foreign policy makers, and the public are complex. Much more research on the links between information, opinion, and decision-making needs to be conducted before definitive causal explanations can be made. But for now, it can be said that George Kennan's fear on the eve of the Somalia intervention – that American policy is "controlled by popular emotional impulses, and particularly ones pro-voked by the commercial television industry" (Kennan, 1993) – is not borne out. Gowing's conclusion that real-time television "creates emotions but ultimately makes no difference to the fundamental calculations in foreign policy making" (cited by Luke and Tuathail, 1997: 719) is a better interpretation.

NOTES
1. Recent books on the genocide dismiss the view that US officials did not know what was happening. See Samantha Power, *A Problem from Hell: America and the Problem of Genocide* (Basic Books,New York) and Michael Barnett, *Eyewitness to a Genocide* (Cornell University Press, 2002, Ithaca).
2. According to Strobel, CNN is now an integral part of the operations centres and situation rooms found throughout the national security and foreign policy agencies of the US government. (78)

3. Print reports followed the pattern of television coverage; lots of stories followed the announcement of the intention to use airlift capabilities for relief efforts and the later announcement to use US ground troops. (See Livingston and Eachus who followed coverage in *The Washington Post* and *The New York Times*.)

4. In peace operations (as opposed to wars), political leaders' need to attract and maintain public support in the absence of a 'vital interest' explains the lack of restrictions on the media in Somalia, a situation different from the Gulf War in 1991.

5. On July 12, 1993, four journalists were killed by a mob after US warplanes launched air strikes against Aidid. *The Washington Post*, *The New York Times*, and *The Los Angeles Times* pulled out of Somalia, joining the three networks who had left in January. CNN withdrew its American correspondents in September after its five Somali drivers and bodyguards were killed. The AP also pulled out its correspondents in September in response to Aidid's threats to kill Americans.

6. On April 5, the Security Council authorized Resolution 909 which extended the mandate of UNAMIR until July 1994 but with a pull out option in six weeks if the transitional institutions provided for under the Arusha Accords were not in place.

7. General Romeo Dallaire sent what has become known as the "Genocide Fax" on January 11, 1994 to UN Department of Peacekeeping Operations warning of the impending genocide and requesting more troops. (This cable was shared with 3 ambassadors in Rwanda, including the American ambassador David Rawson.) Strong warnings continued from Dallaire in weekly reports about the distribution of arms taking place, the plan to kill opposition leaders, and a plea for more forceful action (confiscation of weapons). The Security Council later claimed that they had not been sufficiently briefed by the DPKO.

8. In January 1994, the CIA had given the State Department a desk level analysis which warned that if hostilities resumed (and it predicted that the Arusha Accords would fail), upward of half a million people would die. The Secretary General's special representative Jacques-Roger Booh-Booh and Force commander Romeo Dallaire also met with three ambassadors in Kigali, including the US ambassador, with the information from the informant in the "Genocide Fax".

9. His research indicates the US public is the most supportive of foreign policy restraint (FPR) interventions for restraining an adversary engaged in aggressive actions against the US, its citizens, or its interests. The key example here is the Gulf War.

10. There was some good television coverage. ABC aired a story on May 7 that went beyond the superficial explanations. Ron Allen reported, "As investigators try to make sense of the killing there is more evidence Rwanda's massacres may be a premeditated political act, not a spontaneous eruption of ethnic hatred. Those responsible, human rights investigators say, are Hutu extremists with Rwanda's government trying to grab more power". (Cited by Livingston and Eachus, 2000: 218-219.) Even earlier on April 12, there was a news story by Jean-Philippe Ceppi in the French newspaper Liberacion that correctly identified the killings as genocide. "This was the first mention of genocide and then the word disappeared", writes Melvern (137). Not all the blame should be placed on reporters. The news organizations were responsible for not giving access to accurate stories. Melvern reports that Roger Winter, director of the US Committee for Refugees, had just returned from Rwanda and was desperate to correct the stereotypical reporting. Winter's article explaining the political nature of the violence, i.e. a plot by extremists to hold on to power by using ethnicity to achieve its end, was rejected by most American papers, including *The New York Times* and *The Washington Post*, and was eventually published in *The Toronto Globe and Mail* on April 14 (138).

REFERENCES

Africa Report, Vol. 40, No. 3 (May-June, 1995) p. 8.

Barnett, Michael. *Eyewitness to a Genocide* (Cornell University Press, 2002, Ithaca).

Besteman, Catherine. "Representing Violence and 'Othering' Somalia", *American Anthropological Association*, Vol. 11, No. 1 (February, 1996) pp. 120-133.

Burkhalter, Holly J. "The Question of Genocide: The Clinton Administration and Rwanda", *World Policy Journal*, Vol. 11, No. 4 (Winter, 1994-1995) pp. 44-54.

Clinton, William. J. "Statement on the Deaths of Leaders of Rwanda and Burundi", *Public Papers of the Presidents*, Vol. 1 (April 7, 1994) p. 635.

Clinton, William J. "The President's Radio Address", *Public Papers of the President*, Vol. 1 (April 9, 1994) pp. 658-660.

Clinton, William J. "Letter to Congressional Leaders on the Evacuation of United States Citizens From Rwanda and Burundi", *Public Papers of the Presidents*, Vol. I (April 12, 1994) pp. 678-679.

Clinton, William. J. "Exchange With Reporters in Hot Springs, Arkansas" (July 23, 1994.)

Clinton, William J. "Remarks Announcing Assistance to Rwandan Refugees and an Exchange with Reporters", *Public Papers of the Presidents*, Vol. 1 (July 22, 1994) pp. 1298-1300.

Cohen, Bernard. "A View from the Academy", in W. Lance Bennett and Daid L Paletz, eds., *Taken by Storm: Media, Public Opinion, and U.S. Foreign Policy in the Gulf War* (Chicago, University of Chicago Press, 1994).

Douglas, Susan. "A Three-way Failure", *Progressive*, Vol. 58, No. 7 (July, 1994) p. 15.

Gowing, Nik. *Media Coverage: Help or Hindrance In Conflict Prevention* (Carnegie Commission on Preventing Deadly Conflict, 1997, Washington, DC). www.ccpdc.org/pubs/media/medfr.htm

Jentleson, Bruce W. and Britton, Rebecca L. "Still Pretty Prudent: Post-Cold War American Public Opinion on the Use of Military Force", *Journal of Conflict Resolution*, Vol. 42, No. 4 (August, 1998) pp. 395-417.

Joint Evaluation of Emergency Assistance to Rwanda, Volume 2 (DANIDA, 1996, Copenhagen).

Kennan, George. "Somalia, Through a Glass Darkly", *The New York Times* (September 30, 1993).

Kull, Steven and I.M. Destler. *Misreading the Public: The Myth of a New Isolationism* (Brookings Institution, 1999, Washington, D.C).

Kuperman, Alan J. "How the Media Missed Rwandan Genocide", *IPI Report* (First Quarter 2000) pp. 11-13.

Livingston, Steven and Todd Eachus. "Humanitarian Crisis and U.S. Foreign Policy: Somalia and the CNN Effect Reconsidered", *Political Communication*, Vol. 17 (October-December, 1995) pp. 413-429.

Livingston, Steven and Todd Eachus. "Rwanda: U.S. Policy and Television Coverage", in Adelman, Howard and Suhrke, Astri, eds., *The Path of a Genocide: The Rwanda Crisis from Uganda to Zaire* (Transaction Publishers, 2000, New Brunswick, N.J) pp. 209-228.

Luke, Timothy W. and Gearoid O. Tuathail. "On Videocameralistics: The Geopolitics of Failed States, the CNN International and (UN)governmentality", *Review of International Political Economy*, Vol. 4, No. 4 (Winter, 1997) pp. 709-33.

Martin, James. "Media Camouflage", *America*, Vol. 171, No. 5 (August 27, 1994) p. 9.

McNulty, Mel. "Media Ethnicization and the International Response to War and Genocide in Rwanda", in Tim Allen and Jean Seaton eds., *The Media of Conflict: War Reporting and Representations of Ethnic Violence*" (Zed, 1999, New York) pp. 268-286.

Melvern, Linda R. *A People Betrayed: The Role of the West in Rwanda's Genocide* (Zed, 2000).

Mermin, Jonathan. "Television News and American Intervention in Somalia: The Myth of a Media-Driven Foreign Policy", *Political Science Quarterly*, Vol. 112, No. 3 (1997) pp. 385-403.

Murison, Judith. *Fleeing the Jungle Bloodbath: The Method in the Madness* (University of Edinburgh, nd).

Myers, Garth. "The Inscription of Difference: News Coverage of the Conflicts in Rwanda and Bosnia", *Political Geography*, Vol. 15, No. 1 (1995) pp. 21-46.

Natsios, Andrew. "Illusions of Influence: The CNN Effect in Complex Emergencies", in Robert I. Rotberg and Thomas G. Weiss eds., *From Massacres to Genocide: The Media, Public Policy, and Humanitarian Crises* (Brookings Institution, 1996) pp. 149-168.

Philo, Greg, Lindsey Hilsum, Liza Beattie, and Rick Holliman. "The Media and the Rwanda Crisis: Effects on Audiences and Public Policy", in Jan Nederveen Pieterse ed., *World Orders in the Making: Humanitarian Intervention and Beyond* (St. Martin's Press, 1998, New York) pp. 211-229.

Pieterse, Jan Nederveen. "Sociology of Humanitarian Intervention: Bosnia, Rwanda and Somalia Compared," in Jan Nederveen Pieterse ed., *World Orders in the Making: Humanitarian Intervention and Beyond* (St. Martin's Press, 1998) pp. 230-265.

Power, Samantha. *A Problem From Hell: America and the Problem of Genocide* (Basic Books, 2002, New York).

Shraeder, Peter. *United States Foreign Policy Toward Africa: Incrementalism, Crisis and Change* (Cambridge University Press, 1994, New York).

Strobel, Warren P. *Late-Breaking Foreign Policy: The News Media's Influence on Peace Operations* (United States Institute of Peace, 1997, Washington, DC).

"Triumph of Evil", *Frontline* documentary (1999).

US Department of State, Daily Press Briefing (June 10, 1994).

Weiss, Thomas and Cindy Collins. *Humanitarian Challenges and Intervention: World Politics and the Dilemmas of Help* (Westview, 1996, Boulder).

Left To Their Own Devices

The Impact of Informal Information and Communication Networks on Security in the Tanzanian Refugee Camps[1]

AMY WEST

"The best information for refugees is no information".[2]

Security is essential to areas where the traumatized have been reduced to one very human and desperate desire: the need to survive. Security is not just a physical entity in conflict and post-conflict areas, requiring military or police presence and the assurance of economic survival. It also includes the psychological and emotional element of an individual's innate need to have some control over what he or she understands of a situation and to whom he or she is able to communicate his or her understanding.

In recent years, the unstable security situation along Tanzania's western border has caused Tanzania to threaten forced repatriations of refugees, and in some cases, to execute such returns. In addition, the crucial lack of military and police presence, through an area prey to rebel movements and the arms trade, has heightened insecurity in the region. These facts alone should compel advocates in the refugee, human rights, and development fields to look critically at where freedom of information becomes a matter of security. Freedom of information is necessary for security and development in protracted refugee-populated areas.

Tanzania's policy to restrict information to the refugee camps has created a monopoly on information in refugee-populated areas. This monopoly is neither controlled by the government, nor influenced by such parties as UNHCR, whose purpose is to protect. Protection of refugees is more than containment, and certainly more than just a camp. Protection is providing information to refugees and communicating with them. Without knowledge of what they are protecting, or what is happening in the refugee camps, there is little hope that the government or the international community can provide adequate protection. The very methods by which those in power mean to control information have, in fact, caused the government and the international community to lose control of information flows. When refugees find that a 'safe haven' is, in many ways, an illusion, and that those with the military power and the legal authority to protect them refuse to inform or communicate with them, they will protect themselves by communicating with each other and whatever other entities fall within their information network. The tighter the reign is held on the very human need to communicate and exchange information, the more desperate will be the means by which it is attained. That desperation is what truly threatens national security and public order, driving people to create informal channels of information, a communication network inaccessible to the 'authorities'.

The significance of this need for information rests in the lengths refugees will go to recreate systems of information transmission and direct communication, especially when more advanced or formal means of acquiring the same end are not accessible to them. Technologies have advanced so greatly in industrialized countries that the power of direct communication and informal information structures, relied upon in unstable and developing countries, is forgotten. However, "technologies that improve people's lives do not have to contain microchips, nor do they have to cost hundreds of millions of dollars to develop".[3] The ingenuity of humankind, especially in the face of great stakes and with limited resources at its disposal, should never be underestimated.

The bottom line is constituted by a series of questions: where do the greatest numbers of people go in order to get information intentionally restricted, what sources do they believe to be legitimate, and how does the nature of information a refugee has access to impact security? Curbing the availability of information to refugees strengthens not only the power of a single message (and its messenger), but also reinforces a particular perspective on the conflict and the different players within it.

* * *

To be human is to be interactive with one's environment. Every refugee, like any human being, is a potential 'wire' feeding into a network. Though the Tanzanian government's policy makes it difficult for refugees to access information, the flow of information is not something that can, truly, be stopped. The dangers of this restriction of information in a refugee crisis are twofold:

>> In the absence of a diversity of sources and perceptions, information can neither be checked for inaccuracies nor weighed for relevance (i.e. a morsel of information gleaned with regard to a reduction in food or soap supplies is quickly interpreted as a clear indicator of the much larger fear of forced repatriation, when perhaps the lack of food or soap rations is indicative of a budget cut within UNHCR and/or WFP).
>> The informal system of information exchange and communication monopolizes the existing information it has (because it is not being constantly renewed by multiple sources, but rather is dependent on limited resources), thereby centralizing control of a network of information by those without the tools of physical or legal protection at their disposal.

Neither the international community nor the Tanzanian government is connected to the informal communication networks in the refugee camps because they have decided to either actively restrict or passively not provide information to refugees. If the Tanzanian government and the international community are not suppliers of information to refugees, those entities that do become the access points of information for refugees influence perceptions. The way an individual perceives his situation directly affects action. And the impact of perception on action in post-conflict zones has everything to do with security and development.

While the Tanzanian government and the international community are involved in the practice, if not policy, of supplying little to no information to refugees, refugees are taking the social organization of the camp and their own mobility, and using them as the foundation for a communication and information network. Lacking access to many of the more institutionalised and formalised ways of communicating, they take what they possess and build a system to obtain what they need. The success of this network depends on two key concepts that are being ignored by the Tanzanian government and the international community: legitimacy and proximity. Moreover, the threat that this network poses to security rests in the anonymity of those who control the access points along the network and the influence they have over shaping both the content and the understanding of that information. "Communications is a resource that can be used in the exercise of power. A minimum condition for this power to be exercised is that the people over whom the power is to be exercised are to be part of the communication process, and that they are able to receive. In contrast, the power of information depends on the nature of the information, the ability of the intended target to understand it, and the correlation between exposure to the information and expected outcomes from it being understood".[4]

The Tanzanian government tries to leverage power over the information provided to refugees, the sources of information refugees can access, and the means by which they can disseminate that information. UNHCR appears to follow suit. Neither is actually successful at the control they seek to exert. Instead, their actions have created a parallel system, forcing refugees to view both as yet another threat to their survival instead of legitimate guarantors of their security and well-being.

Information is vital to refugees. So, when they complain about the fact that paper and pencil supplies have run out, they are not lamenting the loss of a privilege, but rather the denial of tools necessary to inform and educate themselves. Community radios, initiated in the Congolese camps of Nyaragusu and Lugufu, exist, but broadcasting is heavily monitored by the Ministry of Home Affairs.[5] Newspapers were prohibited in the camps.[6] In addition, printed reports from the Burundian Peace Process, bound and collated in several languages, sat gathering dust on several NGO bookshelves in early July of 2001. When queried as to why these reports were not circulating in the refugee camps, sources claimed that they were "not allowed" by government authorities to share this information with the refugees, though informally they were attempting to do so.[7] This was confirmed again in May 2003 by ARTICLE 19, when Burundians stated that UNHCR did not provide any information about the war or efforts to resolve the war in Burundi as refugees were not permitted to participate in any way in the political issues of their home countries. These are examples of active restrictions on freedom of information in the refugee camps. Certainly there are plenty of examples, taken from the pages of history, pointing to the power of information and communication channels that feed rebellion from the bottom-up, overturning an existing power structure, when governments start exercising top-down repression over the flow of information. The Tanzanian government should be wary of any policy that would seek to suppress the flow of information to the most vulnerable in its society. Restricting the flow of information does not guarantee an absence of information. In fact, violating the rights of freedom of information to refugees can actually have reverse consequences on the host government, as the equal and opposite reaction such actions will cut off the government from information it needs to maintain public order and security. Thus, it is not the refugee who lacks participation and is marginalized; rather it is the Tanzanian government and the international community. The dynamic created is one in which those who have been designated to protect and control refugee populated areas, in fact, do not. As a result, the very control the Tanzanian government and the international community believe themselves to possess is actually a façade that dangerously compromises the security of everyone operating along the western border.

Tantamount to a rather collective form of the jailer's idea of solitary confinement, blocking the flow of information to refugees – a confined group with limited resources – is believed to weaken the possibility of any one group's influence or ability in the region to challenge the policies of the host government. Information, though, is difficult to control. Even when governments have tried to contain people for more nefarious reasons, the flow of information and the ability to communicate can often only be reduced to a trickle. History has illustrated that information can never be cut-off completely. The story of Solzhenitsyn and the Russian *gulags*, where cigarettes and matches were used to transmit messages along an 'invisible' network of people; or, that of Kenyan dissenter Ngugi wa Thiong'o who used pieces of toilet paper to write on during his year-long detention in a maximum security prison, is proof that where there are people, communication is not easily extinguishable.[8] In the case of Tanzania, what the government fears is a knowledge 'elite', fed by or able to feed into an information network that eludes a more centralized information command structure. This is seen to be as hazardous as supplying arms to a prisoner of war. In either case, the armament of an able mind, or able body, within the 'weaker' group is a threat to those seeking to secure power.

In a similar vein, the international community protects its interests by cooperating with the government's policy on restricting freedom of information, as well as setting its own restrictions on supplying information to refugees and the general public. There is very little cooperation on the ground between UNHCR and its implementing partners. The public access policy of the UNHCR states, "The archives of the United Nations High Commissioner for Refugees exist to make the experience of the UNHCR, as embodied in its records and related materials, available to guide and assist the UNHCR in planning and conducting its activities and to provide information to meet the research needs of the persons of interest to UNHCR, the scholarly community, and the general public".[9]

If, indeed, it is UNHCR policy to share information with the scholarly community and the general public, as well as other 'persons of interest', it is puzzling why there are so many restrictions and suspicions raised by UNHCR personnel when researchers visit the camps. For instance, after the release in April 2001 of ARTICLE 19's *Voices in Exile* report on freedom of expression in the Tanzanian refugee camps, UNHCR expressed hostility to at least one researcher in the field, refusing to talk about 'anything regarding communications or information', openly stating that 'white researchers should be kept from talking with refugees', as well as spreading rumours that American researchers were CIA operatives.[10] Ironically enough, UNHCR representatives found their voices to spread dangerous rumours in places where otherwise they chose to remain mute. At the same time, ARTICLE 19's *Voices in Exile* report found its own way into the informal information network, as it was not easily available to NGO workers and refugees in the area. A Tanzanian journalist along the border, in possession of one copy of the report, was photocopying it and quietly distributing it to researchers and humanitarian workers passing through the area.[11]

Furthermore, surely refugees qualify as both the general public and "persons of interest" who have a right to information that is directly affecting their lives. The access policy goes on to state, "The refugee, his heirs or assigns or his legal representative, may have access to information related to himself".[12]

UNHCR is obligated by the very stipulations of its mandate to legally protect refugees. Legal protection surely includes communicating to refugees what their rights are under international refugee law, as well as under Tanzania's Refugee Act. Finally, if, according to UNHCR's Public Access Policy, a refugee can have access to information related to himself and his family, current practice in the field begs questioning as to why policy and practice are at odds. Refugees, in general, claim they are unaware of their rights and, barring critical health emergencies or high-profile visitors to the camps, the physical presence of UNHCR is so sporadic as to make them rather uncommunicative with refugees and equally as mistrusted.[13] There are several examples evidencing UNCHR's failure to provide appropriate legal information to refugees. In Ngara, Radio Kwizera wanted to create and broadcast a program on refugee law in cooperation with UNHCR. UNHCR initially agreed to such a program, but later reneged, offering no further explanation to Radio Kwizera.[14] In every camp visited by ARTICLE 19, the claims were the same: refugees were not aware of their rights under international law; they certainly did not know their responsibilities; and they absolutely had no idea which UNHCR representatives were in charge of their particular camp. This was first discovered by research gathered in 2001 and confirmed again when ARTICLE 19 visited Burundian and Congolese camps in 2003. This absence of legal knowledge in the camps means lawlessness – this is not just accepted, it is being reinforced.

ARTICLE 19 was invited to attend two routine meetings, one between inter-agencies and the other between inter-agencies and refugee village leaders in Kigoma region in April 2003.[15] At the meeting with refugee village leaders, UNHCR officials showed up two hours late from the sub-office located ten minutes distance from the designated meeting place. NGO officials said this was the "usual trend" of UNHCR, as "meetings with refugees are widely known to be unimportant". Furthermore, at one village meeting several years ago, a Burundian chairman asked why refugees could not have one addition or change in the type of food being distributed to them for the past eight years. The Chairman went on to tell 'humanitarian' representatives at the meeting that he had heard that refugees in Kosovo received actual meals and even bread. UNHCR officials at this meeting, reportedly, told the chairman that Kosovo refugees were different from African refugees; the main difference being that they were not black Africans.[16]

It is indeed strange that though the United Nations has long recognized the relationship between communication and security, as outlined already, there is very little contextual evidence of successful practice in the area of information exchange and direct communication occurring in the refugee-populated areas. Links between information exchange and security, as well as between communication networks and effective coordination, are not new concepts to humanitarian assistance or the protection of human rights. "Adequate communications, both internal and external, constitute an essential element of any security arrangement. Every effort must be made to ensure that such communications are available under all circumstances".[17] UNHCR is technologically equipped to communicate with Geneva on satellite phones while driving through the bush in their Land Rovers, yet cooperation with aid agencies and refugees, requiring direct communication and a consistent physical presence in the camps, seems too taxing. Such a reputation in the area has sacrificed UNHCR's legitimacy among the refugees, as it should, besides within the much more widespread context of the international community.

Restricting a refugee's right to be informed and to express him or herself only limits where refugees will go to access information and the type of information they receive. Restrictions do not stop the supply or demand of information. Conversely, the restrictions imposed serve to strengthen the monopoly refugees possess over the more informal means of communication and information exchange occurring in the camps. The effects of this can be illustrated by the economics of illegal drugs. Where heavy controls on the market seek to stop the supply and cripple the purchasing power of those operating in the market, the overall exchange of goods does not stop. People simply create another market, motivated all the more because they believe themselves to need the drug, thus causing informal, or 'black' markets to thrive. "An addict will continue paying higher and higher prices for a drug, giving up more and more in order to pay for it. One of the more undesirable externalities resulting from this is that in many places, drug-related crime is on the rise, affecting even those who do not use drugs".[18] Information, to a refugee, works in much the same way. Desperate for information, a refugee will give up more and more, often in terms of his security, for the price of being able to communicate along the informal network. The externalities involved, as with the illegal drug example, affect security on a large-scale.

Sources of Information and the Creation of an Information Monopoly

The right to life, security, health and education, all of which are non-divisible, are a few examples of rights that can be endangered by restricting freedom of information to refugees.

Information is the key ingredient of social organization and flows of messages and images between networks constitute the basic thread of our social structure.[19] For refugees, social organization and mobility, however limited, drive the information and communication network. Refugees use the social organization of the camp and the basic routines of camp life to create the network upon which information is accessed and then disseminated. The efficiency of the informal network depends on the proximity of one person to another. In a refugee camp, the limited space of the camp is used advantageously, connecting the points upon which messages can be transmitted rather easily, in the absence of large-scale infrastructure or readily available communications technologies. The access points, or central mainframe, to which information is then supplied and disseminated, are legitimate leaders voted in by popular camp elections. Though refugees may prioritise the information they want, the limited nature of where they can acquire information ultimately determines what information they have. As a result, this information is understood in terms of the agenda refugees are limited to: survival.

Desperation for information will sometimes force refugees to risk using limited transportation infrastructure. Buses connecting border villages, trains running back and forth between Kigoma and Dar es Salaam, as well as ports connecting communities on Lake Tanganyika, all provide ways for refugees not only to displace themselves at greater distances from the camp, but also to access information that can then be pulled back into the camps. Although refugees use these transportation systems with great resourcefulness to increase the speed and distance any one piece of information will cover, this article concentrates more on how information flows without the existence of a transportation infrastructure.

>> Social Organization

Alejandro Portes defines social capital as the capacity of individuals to command scarce resources by virtue of their membership in a network or a broader social structure. The success of the investment in social capital, as such, is not inherent in the existence of any one individual; rather it lies in the value of the individual's set of relationships with others.[20] The social capital that exists in a refugee camp finds its value in the way in which people organize themselves to become the network upon which information flows.

The physical structure of each refugee camp is divided into zones, and further into villages. The villages contain blocks that then break down into plots of land upon which the unit of the family exists. The plots of land for each family unit measure roughly fifteen by fifteen meters. Connectivity to one's neighbour, within the limited space of a camp, is equally as inevitable as it is necessary. It is a combination of the physical structure of camps, which places people very close to each other, and the hierarchical order instituted, which appoints certain people as legitimate leaders.

Leadership in a refugee camp is established through an election process. Leaders are elected every four years. Popular votes cast in a camp-wide election determine who will hold the esteemed positions of 'Chairman' (Burundian camps), 'President' (Congolese camps), or 'Village Guards' (the refugee protection force within camps). The Chairman and Village Guards are critical to the communication and information network of the refugee camp. Accessible to all, they are chosen by a majority vote of the people and provide a system of internal protection.

Even the Tanzanian government and the international community are aware of the leadership in a refugee camp, as well as how information is disseminated. When emergency information is to be transmitted, NGO representatives or the Tanzanian government will meet with the refugee camp leaders and relay the information they want disseminated throughout the camp. This one-way transmission of information occurs when there is a medical or sanitation emergency, or when food rations will be decreased.

Mobility

To gather information in an environment where information is being restricted, refugees must be mobile. They move around the limits of the camp, between camps, and, sometimes, between a specific camp and the country from which they fled. Sometimes, they apply for permission to leave the camps. Other times, they do not risk applying for formal permission, lest they draw attention to themselves.

Restrictions on freedom of information means information will not enter the camp from official sources. Consequently, refugees must place themselves physically in places where external sources of information will cross at the same point. This includes several places in a camp that attract the local community, as well as some key locations outside of the camps to which a refugee is drawn.

The proximity of camps to local Tanzanian villages and language similarities existing between the refugees and those living on the western border facilitate interactions between the two groups. As a result, markets and businesses, water wells for bathing and washing clothes, health clinics and religious centres are a necessary function of community life. Thus, places servicing a refugee's economic and social needs connect at the same points that service local community needs, thereby creating an environment where information is exchanged.

Food Distribution Centres

A refugee's internal source of information, the hub of the information network, coincides with a vital need: sustenance. Food distribution centres become sources to feed both stomach and mind.

Food distribution is carried out every second week on Wednesdays and Thursdays. The entire camp, by necessity, is represented at the food distribution centre. Food distribution is organized by family groups, not to exceed 250 people for each community leader. Refugees gather at the centre, meeting with friends and elected community leaders. Furthermore, even refugees who have left the camp for whatever reason make it back to the camps for food distribution day. Here, then, people commune with key points on the communication network. As a result, information pumped by certain suppliers into the network is rapidly disseminated along the network.

Markets

The macroeconomic traffic of goods flowing between Tanzania and the neighbouring countries of the Democratic Republic of Congo, Burundi and Rwanda has suffered greatly from regional violence. Yet, a more microeconomic market for the exchange of goods between the local Tanzanian community and representatives of the aforementioned countries thrives in refugee-populated areas. Joint market day, as this microeconomic market is called, allows local communities to receive food rations such as soap, maize flour, and cooking oil provided to camps by international assistance programs. For the refugee, these markets are the only opportunity to supplement their diet, deficient as it is in the daily allowance of minerals and vitamins.[21] Joint market day also allows for social interaction. Economic interests, then, serve a more political interest, allowing both local and refugee populations to share information. Both local people and refugees see the interchange of goods and information as critical to their personal security.

Furthermore, the markets are directly linked to food distribution. When food rations to refugees were reduced by over 50% in the last several months, refugees felt threatened. A reduction in food rations does not affect the central hub through which information flows, because food is still being supplied. However, the effect incurred on the joint market is substantial. With less food portioned out to each family unit in a refugee camp, there is less food available to trade with local communities. The reduction in food rations compounds the restrictions already in existence, and tightens the chokehold on the information pipeline, as it will impede the frequency of visitors to the market. This narrows, yet again, the perspective of refugees, for whenever one source to the information network is cut, the remaining sources are strengthened. And the lack of plurality on the supply line of information has important consequences.

Water Wells

Water wells are a popular gathering place for women and children after food distribution day, as distribution of soap coincides with that of food. In Mtabila II, a Burundian refugee camp in Kasulu district, for example, women and children would gather to wash at any one of the fifty-eight water taps in the camp after food distribution day. The water well in refugee camps helps centralize information for women. For a refugee woman, who is often concerned with gathering firewood, cooking and tending to children, the water well becomes the one place where traditional familial chores cross with a maximum of other women engaged in the same process.

Refugee women supply new information to the informal communication network when they displace themselves. Sometimes, a refugee woman will travel outside the camp to frequent water wells where women of the local community gather. This displacement widens the information network, allowing new information to enter the camp.

The importance of water to both refugee and the local villager is noteworthy. Often, the lack of a water well in each village means a woman displaces herself, with other women from the same village, walking several kilometres to gather water. Local Tanzanian women widen their own communication network by meeting women from different villages at a common water juncture. Interestingly, according to local women, one of the most disastrous development projects ever instituted in western Tanzania sought to threaten one of their key information and communication sources. Well-intentioned NGOs sought to remedy what were perceived as excruciating walks to the nearest riverbed or the village water hole for Tanzanian women.[22] Local women, however, find gathering water to be an opportunity to connect with other people (villagers from other communities as well as refugee women), thus expanding a base of information from something otherwise limited to a particular village.

Farming Initiatives

The majority of Burundian refugees are farmers. In the Burundian camps, the houses often occupy a smaller section of the allotted land space, as Burundians will cultivate the remaining land in their possession. In addition, many Burundians have been given permission to leave the camps in order to farm in the local Tanzanian communities. They are paid less than a local Tanzanian would be paid, but being able to work on local farms is nevertheless a source of income generation for a Burundian. Working amongst local Tanzanians connects refugee men to local farmers, and thus to a source of local information.

As recently as May 2003, Burundians were not allowed to farm in the local communities. Restrictions on permits to leave the camps halt the ability of farmers to cultivate land outside the camps. Thus, information gathered through these farming collectives will dry up as quickly as the meagre flow of income brought into the camps by refugee men.

Health Clinics
Camp health clinics, like markets, serve both refugee and local communities. Health care initiatives in the camps have developed stronger local health care systems in the Tanzanian communities. Both refugees and local villagers are able to reap benefits. Health care centres are social hubs that provide a basic service, but in waiting to see a doctor, locals and refugees communicate. In this environment, the exchange of information is not deliberate, but it happens.

>> Technology
Other sources of information for refugees are more technological in nature. These include the transmitter radio, tracing facilities, and in one case, an experimental internet project. Restrictions on freedom of information have placed heavy controls on these information sources, but they have not rendered them completely off limits.

Radios
Radios are perceived as a status symbol, and a security device, in all of the refugee camps. Mainly, elected leaders had access to radios. The Chairman of Lukole A, the Burundian and Rwandan camp in Ngara district, was unnerved by the distribution of radios to primary schools in the camps while he was still waiting for his broken radio to be replaced. To the Chairman, security comes before education.

Radios are essential, as they become a chairman's connection to a wider world, or a more regional context, thus tempering his influence in the camp. He designates certain people to listen to different stations, such as Radio Rwanda, Radio Burundi, Radio Tanzania, the BBC and Voice of America. Then, he summarizes this collection of reports. In the Burundian refugee camps within Ngara and Kibondo district, Radio Kwizera, a Jesuit-run radio station widely trusted by refugees, is used to check the accuracy of what the chairman hears on other accessible stations. What he does not know is that Radio Kwizera pulls its information from the same sources as the chairman. Therefore, the news is the same. It is often frustrating for refugees to be at the mercy of heavily politicised government or international stations that manipulate news broadcasts to fit a specific agenda.

In the Congolese camps of Nyaragusu and Lugufu, in Kasulu and Kigoma districts respectively, a more informal radio, or 'camp radio', has evolved. The initial information system, begun in 1997, was comprised of megaphones, both hand-held and those mounted on poles throughout the camp, accessible via a PA system. Hand-held megaphones were used twice a day as volunteers would ride through the camp on bicycles to relay news to the community. The news mostly pertained to outbreaks of an epidemic in one section of the camp, the birth or death of a camp member, or sometimes coded messages regarding a security issue. Since people would never obtain this information from the aid workers, the town-crier system was ingeniously invented to pass information from the elected 'gatekeepers' to the wider community.

In tandem with the megaphone system, still in operation today, there is a small but effective radio station in Nyaragusu. The radio station was constructed from a small stash of cables, amplifiers, and antennas engineered to connect into a car battery for broadcasting within the limited circumference of the camp. Authorities closely monitor what information is disseminated, especially regarding Congolese interpretations of Tanzanian politics. While Congolese radio has a license from the Tanzanian government, programmes are edited by Tanzanian officials in the camps and must be broadcast in either English or Swahili; leaving people who most easily understand Lingala at a disadvantage.

A similar station in Lugufu existed for several years. Lack of supplies and funding has dried up the ability to operate the radio in the camp. Refugees in Lugufu reported that President Joseph Kabila recently sent a supply of batteries and money to them.[23] However, en route to the camp, these donations had been confiscated by Tanzanian officials. Though it cannot be confirmed whether or not President Kabila is truly feeding the existence of Congolese radio in the refugee camps, the perception among refugees is that Kabila supports and helps influence communications in the camps. So, while the Tanzanian government does everything to avoid supplying information to refugees, questions should be raised as to the political influence regional governments have within Tanzanian territory.

Tracing Facilities
The International Committee for the Red Cross' initiative to track missing relatives and unaccompanied minors in conflict situations has been utilized mostly for the Congolese refugees. Refugees use these facilities to send out information to the Democratic Republic of Congo for news of whether relatives have been killed or have migrated. This is a source of personal and family information that has enormous psychological effects on refugees as they evaluate their future.

Internet
Despite governmental restrictions on the freedom of information, a short-term internet project has been launched through funding from a private US venture capital foundation with the permission of both the government and UNHCR.[24] Several NGOs, local and international, are supporting this internet project of which Mtabila camp, in Kasulu district, and Kasulu town are the recipients. The project, in its initial stages, allows refugees to connect to the internet in the presence of a monitor. Though the internet

is seen as a positive step towards freedom of information, as it allows refugees to connect with family members or friends relocated in other countries, there are also some clear problems. Almost 60% of the Burundian refugees are illiterate; therefore even if they access the internet, it is not able to provide them information in a format they can understand.[25] Secondly, at the time of ARTICLE 19's visit to Mtabila camp, refugees were not free to surf the internet. Access to the internet translated into a transfer of information from a refugee to a Tanzanian 'monitor', who then accessed the internet. Therefore, the internet was hardly seen as a legitimate source of information or even a trusted source, as all messages sent through the internet were typed (and possibly edited) by monitors who alone were able to access email accounts and the larger world-wide web.

>> Other Mobile Entities

The information network expands, not just along economic and social lines, nor simply along limited technological lines, but also along spiritual and political ones as well. Religious rituals, rebel movements and new arrivals are proven sources of information. The power held by these last elements is unknown, though, because the identities of the participants remain rather unclear. The church operates on confidentiality, rebels on anonymity, and new arrivals on ambiguity. All three are mobile in their own right. The strength of these sources comes from the new information they infuse into the communication channels and the mutual interests that they all share.

Spiritual Centres

The Church in the Great Lakes Region of Africa has a sordid history, besides its ability to influence large numbers of people. Such sway has not always been used for the perpetration of good. For centuries, people have counted on the fact that the Church is a sacred haven that will protect its people, speak the truth and seek justice. In the Democratic Republic of Congo (DRC), Burundi, and Rwanda, the pulpit has been used to disseminate hatred, betray the most vulnerable and hide murderers. Though feelings expressing abandonment by God are common, the majority of refugees continue to practice their respective religious beliefs. Admirably, some legitimate local and international faith based organizations are establishing a rapport among refugees because they are present for more than just the rites of sacrament and confession.

Religious rites are not just sources of comfort; they also serve as fluid networks. Following the death of a community member, Congolese, Burundians and Rwandans travel between camps and mourn together. Nights spent keeping vigil with the deceased's family members and honouring the dead happen in all the camps and allow for representatives from different camps to gather together. Marriages also provide an opportunity for the movement of refugees between camps. Some refugees believe that these sorts of gatherings are not as reliable for exchanging information, as the communication network becomes vulnerable to the emotional state of the occasion.

New Arrivals

Though newly arrived refugees take four to six weeks to process through reception centres before they are placed in designated camps, new arrivals bear witness to the most recent situation in the home country. Along with those refugees who frequently travel between the camps and home in between food distribution days, new arrivals cast their personal family and communal histories within the context of the current political tide that forces them across the border and into the camps.

Many of the new arrivals at one of the reception centres in Kigoma town know what is happening in the refugee camps. Following an interview with UNHCR protection officials, one refugee journalist was absolutely petrified that UNHCR would send him to a camp in Kigoma district. He was certain that Mai-Mai rebels, who he had condemned in his coverage of the violence in Eastern Congo, were in a specific camp and would kill him should he be placed within their reach.[26]

Newly arrived Burundians recounted the failure of peace initiatives in Burundi. Though the Tanzanian government and UNHCR were trying to encourage voluntary repatriation to certain villages across the border, the new arrivals at Kibirizi Reception Centre, specifically, talked of violence and human rights abuses. Many of the newly arrived in May 2003 seemed to be academics and civil servants, rather than the wave of farmers that previously filled the Burundian camps. These rather middle- to upper-class refugees already had a rather fixed impression of the refugee camps, the international community and the Tanzanian government. Moreover, aside from providing information on the current conflict in Burundi, they were unafraid to express their opinions on the failure of the international community and the Tanzanian government to protect the safety and rights of the refugees they were to join in the camps.

Rebels

The existence of rebels in the refugee-populated area is of no shock value to anyone working in the camps. Fear of rebels and the inability to control what happens after dark is the principle reason why the international community and the Tanzanian government exit the camps after sunset. Refugees, then, by default, fall prey to the information campaigns or communication patterns of the rebels. What should be of great concern to those responsible for refugee protection is what information the rebels are passing on to refugees. The leveraging point of rebels lies in their ability to capitalize on the weaknesses in the communication network where those who hold theoretical authority over an area have convinced themselves that that alone is sufficient for control and legitimacy.

Restrictions on information to refugees mean nothing to a rebel. Human rights are, certainly, of no concern. Rebels as a source of information are mobile units that carry information in and out of a refugee camp and with it, enormous influence over the way refugees perceive their situation. The fact that these disenfranchised groups, the rebels and the refugees, occupy a certain territory and have limited resources from which to leverage political influence, creates a natural alliance where information is concerned. This is a direct threat to the host government and the international community because they are not part of such a political alliance and offer no alternative detraction from the mutual dependence strengthening such an alliance.

Refugees value information as much as they do food.[27] When the supply of information is limited, there is little choice but to go 'forage' elsewhere. The social organization of the camp and the movement of people in the camp, around the camp and between camps serve mutual economic, social and religious interests. It is where those interests cross that the informal information and communication network refugees so desperately depend on is established. In the end, it is how 'technologies' are created, used, or substituted for, and not what is in their inherent design and functionality that matters.

NOTES

1. This article reprinted with the permission of ARTICLE 19, and edited with the permission and assistance of Amy R. West. Taken from the text of ARTICLE 19's *Africa Thematic Reports, Left To Their Own Devices: The Impact of Informal Information and Communication Networks on Security in the Tanzanian Refugee Camps*, December, 2003. To obtain a copy please contact John Barker, Director of ARTICLE 19's Africa Program: johnb@article19.org, or email info@article19.org; or write: ARTICLE 19, Africa Program, Lancaster House, 33 Islington High Street, London N1 9LH, United Kingdom. Tel: +44 20 7278 9292. Fax: +44 20 7713 1356.

2. Meeting with Ivana Unluova, UNHCR Information Officer, Dar es Salaam, Tanzania, June, 2001.

3. "A Survey of Technology and Governance: Keep it Simple", *The Economist* (November 10, 2001) p. 13.

4. Alleyne, Mark. *International Power and International Communication* (St. Martin's Press, 1995, New York).

5. Broadcasts were allowed in Swahili. Despite the fact that Congolese speak a 'Congolese' form of Swahili, the language is associated with that of authority, i.e. used by the government, the armed forces, and the police. Lingala, however, is viewed more often than not as one of the many different languages of the people.

6. Interview with Congolese refugees from Nyaragusu and Lugufu camps, Tanzania, July, 2001.

7. Interview in Kasulu District, Tanzania, July, 2001.

8. For more reading please see Kate Millett, *The Politics of Cruelty: An Essay on the Literature of Political Imprisonment* (Norton, 1994, New York).

9. Access Policy, Archives, United Nations High Commissioner for Refugees (accessed on June 17, 2003). Available from www.unhcr.ch.

10. Head and Assistant Protection Officers in Ngara sub-office, Ngara, Tanzania, June, 2001.

11. The Tanzanian journalist expressed his hesitancy over distributing a report that he believed had not only infuriated UNHCR, but had also made UNHCR and the government 'crack-down' on information provided to those working with refugees.

12. Access Policy, Archives, United Nations High Commissioner for Refugees (accessed on June 17, 2003). Available from www.unhcr.ch.

13. Interviews with refugees in Nyaragusu, Lugufu camps of Kigoma and Kasulu districts, June-July, 2001 and April-May, 2003.

14. Interview with Radio Kwizera journalist, Radio Kwizera office, June, 2001.

15. Interagency meetings were attended by representatives of the UNHCR, the Tanzanian Ministry of Home Affairs (MHA), the World Food Program (WFP), and other implementing NGO partners of UNHCR.

16. Interview with Burundian Chairman, camp to remain anonymous, Tanzania, June, 2001.

17. *UN Field Security Handbook* (United Nations, 1998, New York) paragraph 37.
18. *The Economics of Illegal Drugs*. (accessed June 19, 2003). Available from http://www.pancakex.com/words/old/000632.html.
19. Castells, Manuel. *The Rise of the Network Society*, (Blackwell Publishers, 1996, Oxford).
20. Portes, Alejandro. "Social capital: Its origin and application in modern sociology", *Annual Review of Sociology*, Vol. 22 (1998).
21. An interview with the camp manager (Tanzania Red Cross) in charge of Lugufu camps revealed that 100% of a daily food portion constitutes 350 grams of maize meal per person per day; 80 grams of pulses per person per day; 40 grams of corn-soy blend, per person per day; 20 grams of vegetable oil per person per day; and, 10 grams of salt per person per day. Two hundred fifty grams of soap are allotted per person, per month. The food rations were cut in May 2003 to 250 grams of maize meal per person per day; 60 grams of pulses per person per day; 30 grams of corn-soy blend, per person per day; 10 grams of vegetable oil per person per day; and, no salt. A hundred twenty-five grams of soap were to be allotted per person per month.
22. Interview with local Tanzanians, Ngara district, Tanzania, June, 2001.
23. Interview with Congolese refugees, Lugufu camp, Tanzania, May, 2003.
24. For more reading on the Kasulu Internet Project, see http://www.global-catalyst.org.
25. Interview with ex-Burundian Chairman, Kasulu district, May, 2003.
26. Interview with a refugee at one of the reception centers in Kigoma, May, 2003.
27. Interview with Burundian refugee, Lukole A/B camps, Ngara district, Tanzania, July, 2001.

Readers vs. Viewers

IVO SKORIC

In New York subway, I recently saw an older lady with an American flag on the lapel. I couldn't believe it – I mean, this is New York City. She must be a tourist, I thought, until I came closer and saw that the flag was turned upside-down. Protesting US policy. She must be a native New Yorker, then. And an internet junkie, perhaps.

In Serbia 2000, complacency and fatalism were briefly put aside for the sake of survival. That change occurred under the pressure of the, some say, CIA sponsored, and internet coordinated youthful *Otpor!* [Resistance!] movement, and Milosevic ultimately lost. Conventional wisdom would have it that this may happen in the US as well, in a similar way, through the Move On and True Majority internet-based movements. Internet – with its instant information availability – has sped up history more than once.

Walking down the street I stepped on an abandoned CD-Rom from AOL promising 1045 hours free. I was not surprised. AOL sends me a CD every week. What can I do with it but throw it away? I remembered how angry I had been with my father for letting my step-brother have the gramophone when we were moving out to live each on our own. Today that looks silly to me: the gramophone has long since become obsolete. And now in the time of mp3 players that can hold as much music as an old-fashioned juke-box in a device no bigger than a car key, CDs are going the same way.

Twenty years ago when I needed to find something out, I had to go to the library. Today, I enter the query in the Google search engine. Arnold Schwarzenegger, probably the world's most recognized actor, had four times more listings than California's incumbent governor Gray Davis. There was no doubt, for me, as to who would win, despite the fact that in combined word searches (see table) Davis returned most hits when combined with 'education' while Schwarzenegger returned most hits when combined with 'sex'. California likes sexy people. It is the place that brought the US its obsession with good looks. And good-looking people find education mostly boring, don't they?

More interestingly, despite Arnold's statements about Hitler thirty years ago, only 3.1% of articles mentioning Schwarzenegger also mention Hitler, compared to 4.22% of articles that mention both Bush and Hitler – testifying to a growing global internet community that harbours a deeply negative opinion about the current US administration. Bush's Google marks are the highest on 'Hitler' and 'corruption' of all the eight search words used (corruption, health care, terrorism, education, free trade, security threat, Hitler, sex).

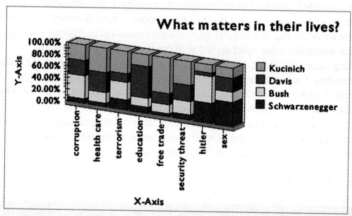

Knowledge on demand has made history move in unpredictable, non-linear, somewhat unexpected and often mysterious ways, isolating and pushing to the fringes traditional ways of power, particularly for the below forty generation – the one whose time is just about to come. The Kucinich and Dean campaigns realized that early on – with Dean being the first political candidate globally to raise majority of his funds on-line.

But, when I could not find time to read the Robert Kennedy Jr.'s well-written but long environmentalist wake-up call forwarded to me, as well as the messages from Kucinich, Clark, and Dean presidential campaigns, Move-On messages, True-Majority messages, a couple of Balkan related lists, around a dozen forwards of articles from various places by friends worried that I would not have found them on my own, I started doubting the revolution.

Indeed, the internet is the place where all radical information is, the place where Bush is often compared to Hitler (a Google search of Bush + Hitler reveals 2,480,000 hits). But, in screaming horror, I just realized that I had spent four hours and forty minutes reading e-mail, opening associated links, filing out on-line petition forms, all that while avoiding looking at hundreds of messages advising me how to enlarge my penis, get hundreds of thousands dollars on my bank account, and see pictures of naked under-aged girls. In just two weeks I had to delete 1500 e-mail messages and I asked myself: how many people can do that? Either the very young who do not have to work yet, or the very old who are retired already, or the very lucky ones, who, like me, remain in control of their time.

The true majority, however, gets its news by glancing over newspaper headlines while travelling by subway from one job to another, or by listening to TV news while keeping one eye on the children and another on cooking, paying bills, and running errands. Americans are overworked: on average, they work nearly nine full weeks (350 hours) longer per year than their peers in Western Europe do. Staying on top of information becomes a luxury.

That's why it is possible that half of America thinks that Saddam is responsible for the September 11 tragedy, and more than a half, possibly the same people, cannot name all nine Democratic presidential contenders. TV networks also do not show pictures of young amputees from the wars in Iraq and Afghanistan (which can be seen at The Memory Hole web site, the name hinting at the Orwellian nature of the administration's denial).

Wolf Blitzer of CNN still calls the Iraqi fighters "insurgents" – bowing to the authority of the Pentagon, rather than to the authority of the Merriam-Webster Collegiate Dictionary.

According to the latter, an insurgent is "1: a person who revolts against civil authority or an established government; esp. a rebel not recognized as a belligerent; 2: one who acts contrary to the policies and decisions of one's own political party".

Therefore, for Iraqi fighters to be called insurgents, the transfer of power to the Iraqi Governing Council must be completed, and the US occupation must be turned into an "invited presence", as Paul Bremer optimistically calls it. Until then, Iraqis who blow up US helicopters are clearly resistance fighters against occupying authorities, just as The Los Angeles Times called them until its journalists got silenced down.

American society is increasingly being divided between the peculiarly privileged who obtain their information from a variety of independent sources over internet, and the majority who get their information predominantly from the TV. Since their sources provide very different information, the perception of events in the world amongst the two groups is also very different, and often at odds. In short, the TV-audience believes that America is doing the right thing, while the internet metaspace offers refuge to those Americans ashamed of what their country is doing right now. It is important to note that the majority of US newspapers and magazines, i.e. print media, are now available online for free. Electronic media – like TV – require more bandwidth than is available with today's connection speeds for on-line viewing to be practical. Therefore, the online audience is essentially an extension of those who habitually gathered information pro-actively, i.e. by reading newspapers.

The two groups are drifting farther apart, making dialogue between them harder, since they are becoming ever easier to offend, even by each other's beliefs. A woman snowboarder joined my friend and I during a gondola ride up our mountain in Vermont. It appeared that she was a law student at the small law school nearby. At one point, talking politics, she said, "I hate America". My friend, who does not spend his online time reading Al Gore speeches, took offence and told her that she should be ashamed.

They were both American citizens: one studying to uphold the law of the country, saying that she hated her country and another, a high school dropout, telling her that she should be ashamed for that. He got particularly rattled when he heard that she even received a scholarship for her studies. As she was probably usually surrounded by like-minded people, she did not expect such a harsh rebuttal. And he had simply gotten used to getting along with me, regardless of our deeply different opinions about the current US administration. But then, I am an immigrant, and even I had never said that I hated America.

In reality, America-bashing has become 'chic' among urban intelligentsia and among the academic crowd. Outside those circles, it is viewed with suspicion as either elitist crap or as a call for action depending on the main headline of the day: if Saddam is captured, obviously that day any criticism of American foreign policy would be preposterous, but if another Black Hawk is downed, then suddenly the 'chic' becomes mandatory.

[A personal caveat: it is really counter-productive to hate one's own country. I hated the former Yugoslavia passionately at the end of 1989. When I meticulously planned to leave for the US, I thought my hate was well justified: the country's political police had been messing with my life since 1985, taking my passport, my typewriter, following me, detaining me. For what? For wanting peace and a better life?! As the war started to unravel shortly after I left, slowly taking its toll on my generation and my friends, the ones I had left behind started telling me: you must be happy now, it is just as you thought it should be.

But I was not happy. It was not as it should have been. Instead of the entire country becoming a democracy, it became a half a dozen countries, all diminutive dictatorial regimes. And the change was precipitated by a succession of exceptionally brutal wars, joined in on all sides by people who hated their former country and who were convinced by sources of information made selectively available to them that Yugoslavia's very existence was at the root of all their problems.]

So on the one side of the divide we have those ashamed of American imperialism, while on the other we have those who represent the view "my country, right or wrong" – and the divide runs pretty much along the technologically different ways the two groups obtain information about the world. The truth is an outdated concept because it cannot be independently verified. The television needs news only to boost its ratings.

The TV reports that which those who pay for its existence want to see and hear. The majority of Americans are subjected to, what Al Gore called in his recent speech at Middle Tennessee State University in Murfreesboro, TN., the "quasi-hypnotic influence" of television. They are dependent on quick information that comes their way without effort and for which they have neither time nor inclination, but which consequently fosters a complacent nation that is a danger to democracy. James Baldwin once said that Nazism thrived not because most Germans were evil, but because most were spineless. Is at least a half of the US population there already? The internet, on the other hand, is by its nature full of speculative opinion writing. There is no guarantee that either means of communication would have an interest to report the truth. As such they just serve to re-enforce the ideological divide between their 'audiences'.

For a while, TV networks were silent on the issue of weapons of mass destruction, and entering the phrase in Google would result in displaying a cleverly designed "Not Found" page. The weapons of mass destruction are now a non-issue for Bush – since he could not find them. While intelligence agencies were dealing with weapons of mass destruction that did and do not exist, plentiful small (and slightly larger) arms were killing US colonels and downing US choppers – particularly those that fly without anti-missile systems, pretending they were patrolling LA and not Baghdad.

A perception downplayed by the TV and nearly celebrated on the net is that this is not just Al Qaeda and *Fidayeen* Saddam – it is regional resistance to foreign occupation. The *'jihadis'* – young Arab men fed up with being dominated by Western civilization – flee to join the fighting in Iraq as they did to fight the Soviets in Afghanistan, like young Europeans (and Americans), fed up with *laissez-faire* imperialism, once fled to join the resistance in Spain in the 1930s. And the recent US killing of the Iraqi mayor of Sadr City – who had actually been appointed by the Americans – will just add more oil to the fire. If the US cannot trust its own appointees, how can any transfer of power work?

Yet for Bush, the daily ritual slaughter of US servicemen in Iraq is a clear sign of US victory. "The more successful we are on the ground, the more these killers will react", Bush said as he sat in the Oval Office with L. Paul Bremer, the US administrator in Iraq. Does that also mean that the more US soldiers are killed, the more the US will be successful on the ground overall? Then the Pentagon should relax the ban on taking pictures of coffins arriving to the Dover air base, I think.

Bush's the-more-we-lose-the-more-we-are-winning rhetoric is not far from Saddam's – Saddam's TV was claiming victory over the US even as US armoured divisions were entering Baghdad in the background. Bush and Saddam (in the defiant agitprop audiotape) are using the same language: they both rely on their God to steer them to victory and they both call each other the 'evil one'. The administration, while bullied by Iraqi resistance into acknowledging publicly that the war is not over despite Bush's previous photo-op on the aircraft carrier under the banner "Mission Accomplished", did not yield an inch on their deeper beliefs that they are liberating the Arab world as some sort of an evangelical force. That ideological posturing, similar to the Soviet communists belief that their Red Army was liberating Poland and Hungary from bourgeoisies, is also similar to Serbs believing Milosevic's propaganda that he was liberating Croatia and Bosnia from fascism.

"He loved his country", said Abe Lincoln of Henry Clay, "partly because it was his own country, but mostly because it was a free country". As the English writer G K Chesterton said in 1922, America is the only country based on a creed, which is enshrined in its constitution and its Declaration of Independence. Now those who declare themselves liberators of others are doing everything to diminish the liberty in the country which owes its very existence to the idea of liberty: in the last decade the prison population in the US rose by 80%. The US is today the country with the largest incarcerated population in the world, half of them non-white, and many states bar felons from voting for life.

Since 1996, immigrants convicted of any crime are automatically deportable. And since the September 11 tragedy, refugees and asylum seekers are treated as immigrants in an act of vengeance against the ungrateful others. In a recent *New York Times Magazine*, a very disturbing story about Kampuchean immigrants reveals an unusual cruelty: a country that used to re-unite families is now breaking them up. A whole generation of illiterate women with their infants came to the US fleeing the cruellest regime on Earth – Pol Pot's

Khmer Rouge. Those children grew up dirt-poor and with no safety net. As many such immigrants before them, many of the children resorted to petty crime. One thousand six hundred of them now face deportation after being here for more then twenty years. Some of them have already been deported, even if that leaves their US-born children fatherless. Who can make any sense of such a policy? But the TV networks will not report on Manny Uch's story. They will not show Spc. Robert Acosta's agony (Acosta lost his right forearm to a hand-grenade in Iraq). Hell, CBS will not even air the Reagans' sitcom because of the pressure of the ruling political party!

We live in a time of pre-emptive aggression, the Pentagon news agency, free-speech zones, disappearing official documents, fake turkeys, and staged arrests. We live in a world where alleged terrorist suspects are held with no hope of release at undisclosed locations scattered around the world far from public scrutiny, and where individuals can be arrested for merely sending an outspoken email to a wrong address. The media are strained between their noble obligation to report the truth, which less and less people on all sides want to hear, and their pragmatic need to survive in the new century of the oxymoron.

What is pre-emptive self-defence (PESD)? It is when you shoot an unarmed man because you believed he could have a gun. It happens all the time in the US of A. At some point during Giuliani's reign, NYPD shot a series of people in pre-emptive self-defence. One victim had a toy-gun. Another was pulling out a wallet with his I.D., an action that cops mistook for pulling out a gun. The police sprayed him with bullets. All were coloured and/or minorities. Officers were acquitted and vindicated because, statistically, there is a high likelihood of coloured young males being criminals. So what else could good officers think?

Such forced statistics help make things easy for police officers. However, pre-emptive self-defence in fact pre-empts the judicial process, preventing the opportunity for victims to prove their possible innocence. The larger public largely does not care about this. They are the victims of forced statistics used by electronic media to drill fear into their heads, making everyone feel like potential victims of aggressive predators on the loose, building a nation of the timid in the supposed home of the brave, breeding support for the abuse of force in the name of pre-emptive self-defence. Derived from the uninformed fear, the PESD is the weapon of choice for self-important cowards – James Baldwin's spineless ones.

Interestingly, and contrary to global public opinion, this doctrine was not brought to the world by the Toxic Texan and his New American Century cabal following the September 11 tragedy, but rather by Slick Willie following the two embassies bombings... Hala Maksoud, the president of the American-Arab Anti-Discrimination Committee, commenting on the cruise missiles strikes of the factory in Khartoum, and in Afghanistan, said to the *New York Times* on August 23, 1998: "The strikes re-enforce the impression that the US is trigger-happy when it comes to the Arab world ... the impression is that the US pre-empted the results of its own investigation, did not give Afghanistan a chance to hand over Mr. bin Laden, did not go to the Security Council or show evidence or rally world opinion or consult its allies, but just is going it alone and undermining the international community and its will".

The current US administration is simply more determined to have more complete control of its image. With 53% of EU citizens believing that the US represents the second largest threat to world peace (tied with North Korea and Iran, behind Israel, but ahead of

Iraq, Afghanistan, Libya, and other nicer democracies), the US pressured the UK to establish humiliating and unconstitutional 'free speech' zones to keep those protesting Bush's visit well away from TV cameras.

"As governor, as presidential candidate, and now as president, Bush's unconscionable disrespect of citizens fundamental right to question authority and confront power has surfaced again and again in an alarming 'Bush Doctrine of Contained Dissent'. What this amounts to is an imperious decision that any and all protestors must literally be corralled – kept in protest pens well beyond the sight and sound of his eminence... and of the media. In Texas, Governor Bush's security police suddenly swept down on a group of peaceful picketers who were on the public sidewalk in front of the governor's mansion – a sidewalk that has historically been a site of protest. At this time, George was launching his presidential run, and he simply didn't want these dissenters to his environmental policies getting between him and the TV cameras – so he had the state police move them to a designated protest zone in a faraway parking lot.

At the Republican presidential-nominating convention in Philadelphia in 2000, candidate Bush created a fenced in, out-of-sight protest zone that would only hold a few hundred people at a time. And, as president, his autocratic games continue – for example, last year at the Columbia, South Carolina, airport, a protester with a 'No War for Oil' sign stood in an area where Bush supporters stood. The protester was ordered to move a half-mile away. He refused, so Bush's police arrested him" (Jim Hightower, AlterNet, October 21, 2003).

The Bush Administration does not stop at the indirect control of information. In an Ocober 20th article by Elisabeth Bumiller of *The New York Times*, Bush is quoted as saying: "'There's a sense that people in America aren't getting the truth', [he] said to a reporter for Hearst-Argyle Television, one of five back-to-back White House interviews he granted to

regional broadcasters. 'I'm mindful of the filter through which some news travels, and sometimes you have to go over the heads of the filter and speak directly to the people'". Therefore the Pentagon will begin broadcasting C-SPAN Baghdad soon – a satellite feed from Iraq that will circumvent the 'filter' of the national networks and send images chosen by the Defence Department right into America's living rooms by way of local news affiliates: the most direct propaganda by the US military.

And beware to whom you send your dissenting e-mails! An Auckland (New Zealand, October 31, 2003) peace activist who sent an e-mail to the US Embassy objecting to the war on Iraq has been charged with the misuse of a telephone. Police went to the Epsom home of university student Bruce Hubbard, 38, and took him to the Takapuna police station for questioning. Mr Hubbard last night said he had been charged under the Telecommunications Act and had been told by police they would seize information from his computer under the Counter-Terrorism Act.

Meanwhile, Slovenian human rights activists (Friday November 21,11:31 AM ET, Ljubljana, Reuters) condemned a court's decision to sentence a man for 'terrorist' crimes for sending hate e-mail to President Bush. Tomi Sluga, 29, told the local court in the north-eastern town of Murska Sobota that he was drunk and only joking when he sent an e-mail to the White House before a June 2001 Bush visit to the small Alpine state. "President, save the Earth, you ass, you will be killed in Ljubljana. Welcome!" the email read. The court found Sluga guilty of "endangering a protected person", and gave him a two-year suspended sentence, the first conviction under Slovenia's new anti-terrorism laws.

Oppressive acts against unwanted information are matched by grandiose hi-budget Hollywood spectacles that glorify the infallible leader of the free world. Nobody cares that the turkey in the picture with president Bush in Baghdad was fake, a plastic prop. The producers were frightened that the real turkey might not look as good in the TV picture. And Saddam Hussein was captured just as the producers of the movie about his capture would want him to be captured: alone, dishevelled, shivering, in a dark hole, like a rat.

"A trained eye could easily detect how the 'spontaneous' outbursts of joy were staged: Here a small group waving the flag of the Communist Party, there a few dozen people jumping like monkeys for the cameras – probably the same people who were jumping a year ago for the cameras of Saddam. Two Arab 'journalists' producing a raucous show at the carefully staged press conference of the American general", writes Israeli journalist, Uri Avnery. He warns the US: "The public humiliation of an Arab leader, whatever one may think about him, evokes the deepest feelings of insult and fury among tens of millions of Arabs. These feelings will strive to express themselves violently. This may cost blood, much blood".

Following the September 11 event, Francis Fukuyama, a professor at Baltimore's Johns Hopkins University, suggested that, "America may become a more ordinary country in the sense of having concrete interests and real vulnerabilities, rather than thinking itself unilaterally able to define the nature of the world it lives in". Along the same lines, in the book he wrote following the collapse of communism (*The End of History*), he argued for the end of what Alexis de Tocqueville called "American exceptionalism". De Tocqueville noted hundreds of years ago that America was a nation created by refugees, intentionally founded on principles to which any country can aspire. The reality of that 'exceptionalism' today, however, is more complex.

In 1999, Gertrude Himmelfarb, a social historian, argued that America is becoming "One Nation, Two Cultures". One is religious, puritanical, family-centred and somewhat conformist. The other is tolerant, hedonist, secular, predominantly single and celebrates multiculturalism. The two cultures occupy different worlds. Traditionalists, exceptionalists and unilateralists are concentrated in a great L-shape on the map, the spine of the Rockies forming its vertical arm, its horizontal one cutting a swathe through the South. With a couple of exceptions, all these states voted for Bush in 2000.

Secularist, multiculturalists, multi-lateralists occupy the Pacific coast, the Northeast and the upper mid-western states. They are urban, rather than sub-urban dwellers. But more importantly, they tend to obtain their information on-line and often participate in its dissemination. They are the READERS. The two groups are more divided by the way they obtain their news than by geography. Traditionalists – the VIEWERS – get their news predominantly from the TV, which cheers the unilateralism. As the on-line world is transnational in principle, the readers are more than just Americans.

They are global citizens and they share the global perceptions and fears of American unilateralism. Curiously, given that the on-line crowd by and large opposes current American policy, the State Department is accepting applications for visa lottery (Diversity Immigrant Visa Program) only on-line this year: as if they want to increase the number of people who oppose them residing in the US?!

The viewers move staunchly in the opposite direction. September 11 ended the exceptionalism of the online audience, but made it stronger for the TV audience, deepening the division between the two groups: one becoming fiercely nationalist (patriotic), and the other becoming more and more resentful and even anti-American. As the groups are divided more by the way they get their news than by geography, the dynamic between them can daily be observed anywhere in the US.

A couple of days ago I was frisked by the DEA. Irritated by the daily chore of having to find parking for my car in New York City after a long day, and with that irritation exacerbated by a particularly slow driver on my right side who just would not get out of my way, I had an attack of pure road rage, cutting through traffic loudly in second gear, making quick, snappy, aggressive turns. Little did I know that the last car that I cut off was actually a police car. The officer behind the wheel, probably thinking that I must be high on angel dust, ecstasy or something worse, went in pursuit.

He also radioed for help. In no time, my car was surrounded in the middle of the street by four civilian looking police cars. My pursuer, wearing an armoured jacket with the DEA imprint, came to my door with gun drawn, screaming, "Get out of the car!" He opened the door, grabbed me by my sweatshirt, threw me against another parked car, and kicked my legs into the spread position. Three or four other agents materialized, pulling my sweatshirt over my head, searching my body, and crawling all over my car in search of evidence. With the out-of-state plates I have, they must have thought I was a dealer who just came in to make a delivery. One of them even suggested that I had better have a lot of cash on me, since I would need it to bail myself out.

I told them that I was sorry, that I did wrong to cut off their car, but that this was just road rage, and that I was essentially just searching for parking. Their reaction was, "Just searching for parking, my ass, one does not drive like that just searching for parking". Yet, utterly disappointed that their search yielded absolutely nothing, they finally asked, "So where is your wallet?" "Well", I said, "I just have car keys and keys to my home on me. I told you I am just re-parking my car". They were pissed. I made them blow their cover in the middle of the hood for nothing. One of them knocked me on the head when he was pulling my sweatshirt over, and another slapped my rear, but generally they were restrained and satisfied just by threatening to break my bones the next time.

The most important part of the event, however, was played by a bespectacled white woman in her thirties, who stopped by and started yelling at them, saying, "Hey, you can't search his car, what he did was just a traffic infraction, and I saw you hit him on the head. I am watching!" The agent behind me reacted with, "This is why I can't wait to get retired. I can't deal with this shit". Another replied to the woman that she didn't know what she was talking about, adding dutifully the September 11 over-arching justification. This was the clash of two Americas unravelling right before my eyes. Agents were behaving like unilateralists, exceptionalists, holding the belief of their evangelical duty bestowed by the proverbial 'people' upon them, to rid the world of potential scum.

The woman was the voice of secular reason, the one that believes that people are innocent until proven guilty in the court of law through due process. She was also brave enough to speak out her beliefs to six burly, armed men. That kind of courage gave me hope. I thanked her – not for myself, since I was not at all fazed or traumatized by a little rough handling (which is nothing compared to what I do to myself daily snowboarding), but for her country, that I live in.

In late eighties in the former Yugoslavia, no civilian would dare to question police brutality in the street. People would turn their heads away and hurry their walking pace. That complacency and apathy became even more evident through the nationalist wars-ridden nineties. Finally, as the proverb goes, there was nobody left to speak out. The availability of space for non-violent dissent makes the current media-driven crisis of identity among Americans look more like a dialogue, albeit a heated one, than like a civil war.

Further readings:

http://www.simpleliving.net/timeday/
http://query.nytimes.com/gst/abstract.html?res=F40617FD35580C748DDDAF0894DA404482
http://www.audioasylum.com/forums/outside/messages/215249.html
http://www.smh.com.au/articles/2003/10/31/1067233349746.html
http://www.thememoryhole.org/war/wounded/gallery.htm
http://balkansnet.org/internet.html
http://www.thememoryhole.org/media/jazeera-cartoons.htm
http://www.back-to-iraq.com/archives/000489.php
http://www.geocities.com/jacksonthor/ebook.html
http://www.commondreams.org/views03/1214-08.htm
http://travel.state.gov/dv2005.html

Cracks in the Urban Frame
The Visual Politics of 9/11
RANJANI MAZUMDAR

There is something about New York which made the September 11 attack on the twin towers both tragic and exhilarating for large numbers of people right across the globe. As Mike Davis says, the attack was "organized epic horror cinema with meticulous attention to mise-en-scène. The highjacked planes were aimed to impact precisely at the vulnerable border between fantasy and reality" (2002: 5). Like the unfolding of a classic action film with its climaxes and pauses, revenge and retribution, 9/11 is an event that offers many interpretations, each trying to understand it from different perspectives and frames. I enter the seamless labyrinth of diverse interpretations with some reflections on the relationship between architecture and cinema, photography and urban space to suggest that the politics of 'mechanical reproduction' over the course of the last century played a decisive role in setting up New York City as a stage for the full play of catastrophic action.[1]

Spectators who physically witnessed the attack on the twin towers saw the sky as a big screen where life had surpassed fiction. The cinematic spell was broken only by the smell of smoke. The aftermath of the attack is perhaps the most photographed disaster in history, communicated as an image even for the residents of the city. The aesthetics of wonder and power that usually shape the panoramic skyline of Manhattan suddenly trans-muted into a tragic narrative with the city emerging as a 'bruised victim'. The reproduction of the disaster through the media and the visual imagination associated with it played a crucial role in the mobilization of world opinion for the 'War against Terror'. The ideological underpinnings and politics of New York's visual journey over the last century of image technology need to be situated within the scramble to understand 9/11's full impact on the world today.

Mechanical Reproduction & the Making of an Icon City
When crisis befalls a global city like New York, its subsequent representations deal with the legacy that shapes the city's iconicity. New York's iconicity, as we all know, is mediated primarily through the powerful form of the visual media: photographs, film, television, and the internet. In postcards and stamps, in photographs and paintings, in spy thrillers and films, and of course through global television, New York has emerged as the most familiar, exciting and powerful city of the Western world. The skyline has been a major backdrop for innumerable print and television advertisements the world over. It has been used extensively

in popular Bombay film song sequences, MTV music videos, and as the opening montage for several American television shows. The city has also circulated through books, fashion magazines, design catalogues, comics and video games, inhabiting the world of our every-day lives. There is really no other city that has been mechanically reproduced through all forms of media so frequently. One of the reasons for the overwhelming global response to the September 11 events was the city's central place as an image within the realm of pop-ular culture. Of all the American cities, there is little doubt that New York provides the archi-tectural grandeur best suited for a visual cartography. The images produced of the city range from picturesque city paintings and photos to modernist poems celebrating the skyscraper as the emblematic symbol of modernity. The camera's gaze has navigated the city's dense labyrinth, moving up and down, horizontally and vertically, providing us as spectators the chance to experience thrill and excitement.

On September 11, the most photographed city became a stage that drew us in as spectators to both watch the drama of action and crisis as well as bemoan the loss of its towers. In the aftermath of the attack, it is the familiarity with the city's topography that aided in the sudden transformation of a powerful visual city into that of a 'victim city'. The towers that once indicated wealth and domination now seemed vulnerable and helpless. Tragedy in the case of New York was seen as universal, spectacular and all consuming. The experience of tragedy therefore needed to be repeated, for only repetition of an already saturated image in its moment of destruction could have the desired effect. Through television and the Internet, people across the world saw the Twin Towers crashing. The subsequent retaliation and production of a revenge narrative unfurled through the cartographic imagination of a bruised city, justifying the 'War against Terror'. All other spaces of destruction were obliterated. When the multibillion dollar deadly cargo fell on Afghanistan, the cameras were crucially absent.

What does it mean when New York is associated with the power of the United States? After all, the attack on the Pentagon in Washington, DC, hardly generated the kind of imme-diate screen response we saw after the towers were attacked. Given the wide circulation and dissemination of the city, it is not surprising that millions identified with the tragedy almost instantly. Suddenly the attack on the towers seemed to have surpassed all other catastrophes as the Western world consolidated itself around this single image of the towers in flames. The cinematic appeal of the towers under attack had acquired the quality of an independent genre, circulating and creating meaning in the midst of a massive coalition of the so called 'civilized world' in their 'War against Terrorism'. The historical representation of New York as a panoramic image and as an autonomous site of utopian imagination was mobilized as the legacy that was under attack. This transformation and destruction of the New York skyline, both in reality and in cinematic practice raises impor-tant questions for the future. Clearly the visual power of 9/11 was different from any other catastrophic event. Director Robert Altman blamed Hollywood for 9/11, suggesting that the idea itself was first created in the movies. Jean Baudrillard's prophecy about 9/11 as the coming together of two elements of mass fascination – terrorism and the cinema – seems singularly appropriate (2002: 413). And yet what makes the spectacle unique is the visual play of architectural creation and destruction.

Cinema, Architecture & Urban Space

Cities are produced through representations. The spatial practice of negotiating the topo-graphy of urban space takes a unique form in the realm of the visual. Film takes the lead in the art of visual cartography. The urban landscape is a space that exists both physically and through its filmic incarnations. Our sense of familiarity, of recognizing the marks of a place can be produced both by the physical street, as also by its reproduction on screen. As Guiliana Bruno says, "The genealogical architectonics of film is the aesthetics of the tourist practice of spatial consumption. As in all forms of journey, space is filmically consumed as a vast commodity. In film, architectural space becomes framed for view and offers itself for consumption as travelled space that is available for further travelling. Attracted to vistas, the spectator turns into a visitor. The film 'viewer' is a practitioner of viewing space – a tourist" (2002: 62).

The cinematic eye usually encounters symbolic and recognizable sites that help situate any city geographically. The towers as the emblematic sign of New York embody the architectural aesthetics of the skyscraper, standing above the entire city. Through the cinematic gaze, the towers emerge as the ubiquitous visual trope and display item signify-ing the urban imagination of New York. America is framed via the city – a semiotics of capital, globalization, architecture and urban space. Bruno's assertion about the relationship

of film to architecture can be most vividly seen in the reproduction of New York as the spectator/tourist's gaze travels the city's iconography, assimilating and recognizing its powerful place in the world.

While New York may be seen as a city that envelops all the five boroughs, it is Manhattan that holds the key to its power and magic. This is a city with a powerful financial centre, a space of wild and dramatic architectural extravaganza, a unique organization of streets and avenues, and a centre for global fashion, arts, theatre and film. The French historian Bernard Fay described New York as "a city of rectangles, harsh and brilliant, the centre of an intense life which it sends out in all directions" (cited in Abbott, 1973). Some have called it a modern city, analogous to the mythical phoenix. This image of power and brilliance was captured vividly in many of the photographs taken by Berenice Abbott in the 1920s and 30s. Subsequently, many photographers created iconic images of the city, playing with the jagged light and shadow texture of the myriad buildings piercing into the sky, evoking both power and the drive for domination in the world. The iconicity of the photographic image of New York was only enhanced by the moving image.

It was the Russian filmmaker Sergei Eisenstein who first saw the relationship between Manhattan's unique grid and the experience of moving through space and time in film. Manhattan's spatial organization lends itself to a range of perspectives that has enabled the city to emerge throughout the twentieth century as the quintessential cinematic city. The low angle view displaying the wealth and power of the financial district, the high angle view from the former twin towers and the Empire State building, the aerial perspective landscaping the density and texture of the city and the tracking across streets – all these techniques have been used to generate a series of iconic images of the city and its magical skyline. Jean-Paul Sartre reflected on this unique relationship of the cinema to urban architecture: "When we were twenty, we heard about the skyscrapers. We discovered them with amazement in the movies. They were the architecture of the future, just as the cinema was the art of the future" (cited in Sanders, 2001: 105).

Like in an urban trance of a futuristic panorama, the skyscraper resides both in the real and the 'mythic city' of cinema. Hollywood's fascination for urban topography has always been a powerful force with the 'idea' of the American city emanating primarily from the movies. For Baudrillard, the American city is like a space out of the movies. Its secret can be grasped only if we move outward from the screen to the city and not from the city to the screen. Baudrillard's reflections hold true particularly for New York whose status as a 'world city' has been mounted most powerfully via cinema.

James Sanders, in his book *Celluloid Skyline*, suggests that the cinematic New York transcends its purely geographic and economic status and turns into a locus of image, style, memory and dreams. Sanders takes us through a journey of well-known Hollywood films to reveal the imagined space of New York in the filmed image. In *Skyscraper Souls*, made in 1932, we see the era's fascination and apprehension of tall buildings as the city becomes the site for an exploration of "heroic achievement and frenzied speculation" (2001: 123). In the film, the character David Dwight says the skyscraper "goes halfway to hell, and right up to heaven, and its beautiful!" In the *Fountainhead*, released in 1949, the modernist architecture of the post-war period is deployed to aggressively push the individualistic ideology of its plot. Based on Ayn Rand's novel and also screen written by her, *Fountainhead* uses the city as a dynamic and dominating presence. The view of the skyline is placed behind all the sequences of the movie's interiors (Sanders, 2001: 128).

In film after film, Sanders reveals Hollywood's fascination for New York and its mix of public and private spaces. The aesthetics of the window looking out at a concrete ensemble was spectacularized in cinema through unusual backdrops. The lights glinting across the city at night creating a shimmer whose magic is available in frozen images of postcards and posters, T-shirts and mugs, is now perhaps generic, but the familiarity of the image is related to the prolific reproduction of a city through a range of perspectives and approaches. The attraction to this city of magic has been the result of a spectacular photographic/cinematic imagination that has fed back into the reinvention and rejuvenation of the city's architecture. Despite a number of films that look at its darker side, it is the grandeur of the skyline and the dynamic presence of its architectural grid that has been most popularly established in numerous ways through films. The panoramic vision, as some have suggested, "creates a pleasure rooted in the senses". The establishing shot of innumerable films places the skyline to locate the narrative world. Sanders sees the skyline view as a proscenium, like a "metaphoric arch" that frames the story world of many films, offering the spectator both a reassuring familiarity and an unpredictable experience. The skyline symbolizes wealth and power, adventure and fantasy. It operates like a "cinematic passport, a rite of passage that may last only a few moments but sets us up for the civic hyper-reality that lies in store for the next two hours" (Sanders,2001: 91).

There is little doubt that the symbolic power of the attack on the twin towers was understood clearly by those who masterminded the operation. But the image of the towers in flames was equally important for the vengeful mobilization of a retaliatory attack by the US government. Baudrillard's bleak prognosis of the media may seem overstretched in a different situation, but in the context of the 9/11 attack, the media became part of the event and the terror, playing a role on both sides. The air strikes were intended to shame a nation that had sought to humiliate others, a defiant act whose symbolic value lay precisely in the unfolding of a duel for the world to watch simultaneously. The power of the event lies in its symbolic value, since ordinary violence can be banal (Baudrillard, 2002: 412). The staging of this event and the massive response it received all over the world could hardly have been possible without the visual iconicity of New York. It is the intersection of cinema, architecture, photography and urban space that prepared the ground for the spectacle of 9/11. The magic of Manhattan systematically constructed by technologies of vision became the symbolic site for a catastrophic event that will continue to unfold in the years to come.

The Catastrophic Event Today

What does it mean to deal with a catastrophic event after the arrival of the Internet and global television? 9/11 was the first catastrophic event watched by millions across the world simultaneously. It was also an event that was spectacularly televised and shown as it was happening. An organized attack on the towers, clearly viewed and shot by several television channels, distributed across the internet, spread over postcards for tourists and captured in innumerable art exhibits, surely this is already the most mediatized event in the history of catastrophic events. Monumentalized almost immediately, 9/11 has now become a new commodity, inscribed on T-shirts, emblems, postcards, tea mugs, bags and posters. "We shall not forget" stares at you from a series of postcards of Ground Zero being sold across the United States for ten times the amount one usually pays for a postcard. The image is now certainly part of the event as thousands of photographers and amateurs reproduce the site of disaster.

Just a few weeks after 9/11, an exhibition titled *Here is New York, Images from the Frontline of History: A Democracy of Photographs* opened in New York. Comprising of 7,000 photographs, the exhibition has now been seen by more than 1.5 million people across the world, making it the largest archive of its kind and the most looked at exhibition of our time. A book along with the exhibition and television reporting on the exhibition are now part of this steady journey of the exhibition across the world. A digital archive of the exhibition has logged more than one million hits. A video and oral history of the exhibition has also been travelling. There are other initiatives in place as well, such as the ebay (commercial website) posting of a 9/11 CD-Rom that says, "This archive will give you the experience of having been at ground zero. It's an experience you will not forget". As the absent towers now showcased in their moment of destruction circulate with blinding speed across the world, we need to take stock of what this means for the future.

"The externalization and objectification of memory, and the infinite repeatability of the event", says Brian Masumi, "distances cause from effect. The event floats in media suspended animation, an effect without a cause, or with a vague clichéd tone" (1993: 26). As the most photographed event becomes monumentalized and commodified in our everyday lives, leaving little room for reflection, the politics of remembering becomes a dubious project. The many sub-narratives that make up the context of 9/11 are consistently marginalized in favour of an institutionalized master-narrative that produces the concept of an 'American People' in a war against 'evil'. The obsession with this memory in our contemporary times is spectacularly mediated through visual technologies. As photographs and art, film and video travel far and wide, we lose touch with the how and the why of the event. Instead, the face of tragedy and death staring at us from the world's most familiar city becomes the new instrument for furthering the iconicity of Manhattan in the making and unmaking of the world today. "The globalization of fear", says Mike Davis, "becomes a self fulfilling prophecy... Terror has become the steroid of Empire. And Imperialism is again politically correct" (2002: 18). The persistence of New York's imaginary production through architecture, film and photography has played no small role in the creation of an 'invincible power'. And the subsequent persistence of 9/11 as an unforgettable image functions like a steroid, a sign moving in pure suspension, aiding the political journey of American exceptionalism in the world today.

In the first weeks of the recent war in Iraq, American exceptionalism inaugurated a new genre of war spectacle. Both the CNN and the BBC were engaged in an information war, a play with words, images and music intended to shape world opinion in favour of the attack on Iraq. The BBC created a montage of war images with background effect music, as if to draw us into the latest Hollywood action film. The montage combined images of the weapons used, the latest so-called precision technology, men in tanks, orange clouds over Baghdad, as the bombs fell. This iconography is familiar. It continues to remind us of the powerful ways in which cinematic images shape television reportage and vice versa, and it also reminds us that war today unfolds before our eyes as visual spectacle.

In a sense 9/11 and its aftermath seem like a textbook case for a media theory of modernity – witness the proliferation, saturation and circulation of images combined with the speed of contemporary globalism. The freezing of world media time into the binaries, of those who mourned and those who celebrated, was a tragedy that seemed so pure, so perfect, so completely overwhelming and draining of our collective energy. This process has been unending and relentless – the war in Afghanistan, the build-up and the eventual war on Baghdad, all part of that cruel cluster of time that 9/11 inaugurated. Those who cannot partake in this moment appear demonized, animal-like in their opposition. This ceaseless drive for representation, however, relies too much on the perfect machinic impulse of imperial power. If the capture of Saddam Hussein and the carefully staged media effects that followed boosted imperial morale, a few sharp attacks could equally render these media strategies vulnerable. A world in constant mourning and war for 9/11 cannot sustain itself.

REFERENCES

Abbott, Berenice. *Changing New York*, with text by Elizabeth McCausland (Dover, 1973, New York).

Baudrillard, Jean. "L'Esprit du Terrorisme", *The South Atlantic Quarterly* 101:2 (2002) pp. 403-415.

Bruno, Giuliana. *Atlas of Emotion: Journeys in Art, Architecture & Film* (Verso, 2002, New York).

Davis, Mike. *Dead Cities & Other Tales* (The New Press, 2002, New York).

Huyssen, Andreas. "Present Pasts: Media, Politics, Amnesia", *Public Culture* 12:1 (2000) pp. 21-38.

Kirshenblatt-Gimblett, Barbara. "Kodak Moments, Flashbulb Memories: Reflections on 9/11", *The Drama Review* 47:1 (Spring 2003).

Massumi, Brian. T*he Politics of Everyday Fear* (University of Minnesota Press, 1993).

Miller, Angela. "The Panorama, the Cinema, and the Emergence of the Spectacular", *WideAngle* 18:2 (1996) pp. 34-69.

Newcomb, John Timberman. "The Footprint of the Twentieth Century: American Skyscrapers and Modernist Poems", *Modernism/Modernity* 10:1 (2003) pp. 97-125.

Sanders, James. *Celluloid Skyline* (Knopf, 2001, New York).

Truth Telling, Gujarat and the Law

ARVIND NARRAIN

G ujarat has produced many kinds of discourses. In some media discourses, the word Gujarat has come to signify violence, murder and rape. Media discourse has been particularly powerful in producing 'truths' about Gujarat. On the one hand, the progressive media has condemned the Gujarat violence in no uncertain terms. On the other, local media has been quite supportive and even encouraging of the violence.

Apart from the media, the other powerful discourse on Gujarat has been the law. This paper seeks to interrogate the law's interface with unimaginable violence and the answers it sought to give. The paper further asks the question as to whether the law can capture the violence in a politically intelligible manner. It seeks to find the answer in the law on genocide.

The Law's 'Truth' about Gujarat

The story of the law's interface with Gujarat is a story of a failure. The failure is at many levels. The most well known failure is the gap between theory and practice. However, apart from this failure, there is also the failure of the legal imagination in the struggles to fit the violence that was Gujarat into the categories of murder, rape, hurt and other IPC offences. The failure can be examined at both levels using the following categories.

The First Information Report (FIR)

The FIR is the first step in the criminal investigation which according to the logic of the law leads to investigation, trial and then either conviction or acquittal. There were numerous problems right from the non-registration of FIRs, to people not being given copies of FIRs, which they are entitled to.

Apart from the numerous ways in which the FIR process was subverted, it is important to note the kind of stories the FIRs narrated. If one takes the case of FIR 33/02, filed in Kalol *Taluk*, it gives an inkling of the stories that emerged in law.

"My name is RJ Patil, Senior PSI Kalol. I am complaining on behalf of the State that on February 28, 2002 there was a *bandh* declared by the VHP. ... The *bandh* was complete in Kalol, Vejalpur and Dehlol. In ... village (Dehrol?) Hindu religious mob of about 500 people were shouting '*Bharatmata ki jai*' and set fire to the mosque and destroyed it. The police tried to disperse the mob using tear gas. ...

Then at 1230 hrs, the hutments behind the Kalol bus stand and shops nearby were destroyed by a Hindu mob of 6,000-7,000 people. They burnt vehicles and shops. Announcements were made on mikes to disperse the mob. When they did not disperse upon orders from the *Mamlatdar*... (name not clear) PC Uday Singh Pratap Singh (buckle # 1272) fired in the air from his .303 rifle and the mob dispersed.

During the course of the bandh declared on 28/02/2002 by the Vishwa Hindu Parishad, the groups armed with swords, knives, sticks, sickles, stones destroyed and burnt shops, houses, cabins, masjid, vehicles, lorries resulting in a loss of Rs. 500,000/-PI K V Katara was hit on the head by a stone.

Then in Kalol town, between 1335-1510 hrs, a Hindu mob of 6,000-7,000 people and a Muslim mob of 3,000 people confronted each other with weapons, sticks, *dharia*, swords, etc. Both mobs began destroying shops, vehicles and houses. The police used tear gas and fired in the air. *Naib* Police Officer Halol and CPI Halol and police staff announced for dispersal on the mike. But the mob did not disperse. Six tear gas shells were fired but the mob could not be controlled. They pelted stones at the police. The *Mamlatdar* who was present ordered firing. CPI ... (name not clear) Halol, fired one round from his service revolver, but the mob did not disperse. Stone throwing continued. CPI K V Katara was seriously injured when a stone hit him. ... Despite such attempts to quell the mob the situation remained serious.

After that, at 1600 hrs at Kalol Bus Stand area, a mob of fundamentalist people attacked, looted and burnt shops near the Kalol bus stand area and Radhashyam complex. As the District Police Officer, PMS, Godhra and *Naib* Police Officer and the *Taluka* level officer were present at the time of the attack, mike announcements were made to try and disperse the mob. Despite making such announcements, the mob comprising of 6,000-7,000 people became violent. On seeing this, the Taluka level officer ordered firing. PC Naranbhai Navlabhai fired eight rounds from his .303 rifle. Also PC Ganpat Singh, Bhoop Singh, fired two rounds from his .303 rifle and Head Constable Veersingh Mansingh fired two rounds and PC with PSI Pawar fired two rounds. This made the mob go out of control and Kalol was put under curfew from 4:30 pm. After this the mob dispersed. Later, a mob of 500 Hindus burnt down a *masjid* at Kalol and on the day of the bandh call by the VHP. Shops and houses were also looted and burnt. Shops, cabins, houses, trucks, scooters, jeeps, etc., were also burned down causing a loss to the tune of approximately 5 lakhs by mobs comprising of both Hindus and Muslims.

The mob, carrying sharp weapons like sickles, swords, knives, sticks and stones, attacked the police and the circle police inspector, K V Katara, was grievously injured in the head".

The above FIR is referred to as an omnibus FIR as it clubs various offences committed at different times under one head. It allows only a partial 'truth' to emerge by not allowing victims stories. Thus, if one analyzes people's individual complaints, the contrast is startling. Individual complaints were sent to the NHRC, SP and concerned police stations but were not registered on the ground that a State FIR already existed on the point.

In a complaint given by Yusufbhai Sheik, for example, which was not registered as an FIR on the ground that there already existed an FIR, thirteen deceased were listed by name and four accused were also listed by name. In the description of the event:

"After the Godhra carnage communal riots had broken out all over Gujarat and in every village of Panchmahal District all Muslim areas were targeted, their lives taken and property destroyed.

On the 28th of Feb 2002 a mob of about 150-200 people entered our village, looted our houses and burnt the remaining property. This made us extremely scared. On the next morning between 9:00 and 10:00 am this same mob entered the village shouting slogans 'Kill the Muslims, cut the Muslims'. Hearing this, we all ran to save our lives and hid in the vehicles nearby. Around the same time, about twenty-five to thirty Muslims in Dellol village had been massacred. At 4:00 pm twenty of us sat in a tempo belonging to Haroonbhai and left for Kalol. At Kalol-Ambika Nagar Society a mob of approx 100-125 people armed with weapons stopped our Tempo and overturned it. As people started getting out of the Tempo they were killed and then burnt. Ten people were killed instantly, then put in the tempo and the Tempo was set on fire. Three people ran ahead but were caught and killed. Five other people and myself managed to save our lives and escape. We were later admitted to S S G Hospital, Vadodara, for treatment".

The above is only illustrative of the pattern of legal truths established throughout Gujarat. The legal truth of the FIR elided the significant question of naming the accused and instead produced the anonymous figure of the mob. The State FIR seems to understand the events that happened as instances of random violence, limited to damage to property. Details pertaining to motive were conspicuously absent. Thus, while Yusufbhai Sheik's complaint points to the killing of thirteen people, the Kalol State FIR does not even acknowledge this. Further, Yusufbhai Sheik's complaint has in it details which point to motive, statements by the mob such as "Kill the Muslims, cut the Muslims", which are significantly absent in the State FIR's record of random incidents of violence by faceless mobs. The legal provisions invoked by the Kalol FIR, if divided into those where punishment is less than seven years and more than seven years, fall mainly into the less than seven years category. The most serious offence invoked by the FIR is Sec. 333 of the IPC, which is "causing hurt to deter a public servant from doing his duty", and relates to the injuries suffered by Inspector Kataria. The provision relating to murder is not even invoked, in spite of there being at least thirteen killings.

Thus, if one were only to read the State FIRs, the story of what happened in Gujarat emerges within the existing legal framework as a story of random violence that the state was unable to control.

Human Rights Reporting

Possibly no other event in human rights terms in India has produced such rich documentation as the events in Gujarat in 2002. There are a number of important fact finding reports which question the legal truth in every detail. The complicity of the State in violence emerges in painful detail in reports such as the *Citizen's Tribunal Report*, Syeda Hameed et al, *How has the Carnage in Gujarat affected Muslim Women* (A National Women's Panel Investigates), Kamal Mitra Shenoy et al, *Gujarat Carnage*, 2002, Communalism Combat March-April 2002, Year 8, No 77-78, PUDR Delhi, *Maaro! Kaapo! Baalo!*, *Report of the visit by CPI(M) and AIDWA to Gujarat*, 2002, SAHMAT, *Ethnic cleansing in Ahmedabad: A Preliminary Report*, The NHRC Report.

What emerges through the fact-finding reports is a story which counters the FIRs' story of random and meaningless violence by stressing strongly on the planning and instigation which resulted in the violence. The fact-finding reports thus bring to light numerous aspects of the violence that can be categorized under:

>State Complicity in Violence

This is of course brought out powerfully in all the reports. They argue that what happened after the Godhra incident on February 28 is a wilful and mediated State abdication of the responsibility of protecting the life of its citizens. The State stood by and watched murder, rape, destruction of property, and desecration of religious places, and in some cases even aided the process. Perhaps the most compelling reports have been the *Concerned Citizens Tribunal Report* as well as the *NHRC Report.*

The *Citizens Tribunal Report* notes,
"1.4. Shri Modi played an active role, along with at least three cabinet colleagues, in instructing senior police personnel and civil administrators that a 'Hindu reaction was to be expected and this must not be curtailed or controlled'.

On the evening of February 27, two cabinet colleagues of the chief minister, Shri Ashok Bhatt and Shri Pratap Singh Chauhan, met at Lunavada in Panchmahal district along with others. In this meeting, the manner and methods of unleashing violence on Muslims were planned in detail.

2.1. The facts mentioned in this report clearly establish that chief minister Shri Narendra Modi is the chief author and architect of all that happened in Gujarat after the arson of February 27, 2002. It is amply clear from all the evidence placed before the Tribunal that what began in Godhra could have, given the political will, been controlled promptly at Godhra itself. Instead, the state government under chief minister Shri Narendra Modi took an active part in leading and sponsoring the violence against minorities all over Gujarat. His words and actions throughout the developments in Gujarat show that he has been openly defying the Constitution and indulging in actions which are positively detrimental to the interests of the country.

2.2. Shri Modi was the one who took Godhra to the rest of Gujarat. He was the one who directed the police and the administration not to act. He was the one who refused to help the likes of former Member of Parliament, Shri Ahsan Jafri, and the large number of people in Shri Jafri's home, who were all butchered later on".

Similarly the NHRC Report also makes a convincing case for state complicity in the violence. "The Police administration on the 28th of February was acting under dictation of the BJP politicians. Two senior cabinet ministers were present in the Police Control Room – State Health Minister Ashok Bhatt was at the Ahmedabad Police Commissionerate in Shahibaug for more than three hours on February 28th and the Urban Development minister, I K Jadeja, was in the State Police Control Room at Gandhinagar for four hours from 11 am onwards. Home Minster Gordhan Zadaphia was directly monitoring the progress of attacks on Muslim localities from the room of Ashok Raina, Home Secretary".

The NHRC brought these facts to the notice of the State of Gujarat (*Confidential Report on the visit of the NHRC team* headed by chairperson NHRC to Ahmedabad, Vadodara and Godhra from 19th to 22nd of March, p4) but the State of Gujarat chose not to respond to this report, which has very serious implications. The NHRC in its latest report noted that "the Report of the State Government fails to rebut the repeatedly made allegation that senior political personalities – who have been named – were seeking to influence the working of the Police Stations by their presence within them" (*Proceedings Report of the NHRC*, 31st May, 2002, p 4.).

>Targeted Nature of the Violence
Another fact that emerges powerfully from the fact-finding reports is the selective and targeted nature of the violence. In fact, all fact-finding reports carry in gruesome detail the nature and extent of the violence unleashed against the Muslim community in Gujarat. The violence was selectively targeted at the Muslim community: killing Muslims, raping women, inciting violence against them, destroying Muslim owned property and desecrating mosques, *dargahs* and other places of worship.

As the *Citizens Tribunal* notes, "The carnage was at six levels: physical destruction of a part of the community; economic destruction; sexual violence and rape of a large number of Muslim women; cultural and religious destruction; resistance to rehabilitation; publicly declared desire to physically and morally destroy the Muslim community of Gujarat".

>Mass Participation
The other shocking detail that emerged in poignant detail is the mass participation of ordinary Gujaratis in the violence. Many fact finding reports recorded masses ranging from a few hundred upwards to 10,000 and 15,000 people participating in the violence. As the *Citizens Tribunal* notes, "Sixteen of Gujarat's twenty-four districts were engulfed in the most organised armed mob attacks on Muslims between February 28 and March 2, 2002, when most of the attacks were concentrated. Rampaging mobs were at it until mid-March. In some parts of Ahmedabad and Mehsana, they are still on the loose". (Another three districts had sporadic bouts of organised violence). Nowhere were the mobs less than 2,000-3,000; most often they were more than 5,000-10,000 strong. This, and the fact that they were armed with swords, *trishuls* and agricultural instruments that could kill, the fact that the manner of arson, hacking and killing was chillingly similar, all suggest a carefully laid out plan behind the attacks".

The Legal 'Truth' and the 'Truth' of Fact-Finding
What emerges quite clearly is a dissonance between the state's truth and the truths produced by civil society groupings. The key facts of state complicity, targeted violence and mass participation cannot be captured within existing legal language. This is because the conceptualisation of offences in the Indian context is very narrow. Offenders are perceived as individual entities, and the offences are conceptualised as offences against individuals.

However, the imagination of the law is unable to move further and conceptualize an offence against a group, as well as the possible motive for such an offence. Further, offences under Indian law are treated as offences against the state, but there is no answer to the question as to what happens when the state is complicit in the offence.

Thus, we see the inadequacy of the law to capture the three significant aspects of the violence. The most the law can do is to bring to book individual offenders for the offences of murder and rape as the most serious offences in the IPC. This is in fact the political struggle which is being carried forward with great difficulty in the trial courts of Gujarat. The *Best Bakery* case – exemplified in the person of Zahira Sheik – embodies this brave quest for justice within a legal framework which has limited our understanding of the violence. To tell the story of what happened in Gujarat in terms of the law, one needs to really look elsewhere.

The 'Universal' Law of Genocide

Genocide was first codified as an international crime by the *Convention on the Prevention and Punishment of the Crime of Genocide, 1948*. Since then, the prohibition against genocide has achieved the status of *jus cogens* and become a norm of customary international law, which is binding on all parties regardless of, whether they are party to the 1948 Convention.[1] Towards the close of the twentieth century, with the re-emergence of violent ethnic conflict in both the Balkans and Rwanda, we had the setting up of Ad Hoc Tribunals, viz. International Criminal Tribunal for Rwanda (ICTR) and International Criminal Tribunal For Yugoslavia (ICTY) by Security Council Resolutions.[2] Both these tribunals have jurisdiction over the crime of genocide. Finally, we have the setting up of the International Criminal Court under the Rome Statute of 1997, which also has jurisdiction over the crime of genocide. What is important to note is that in the formal instruments of international law, the 1948 definition of genocide has been adopted in both the tribunals and the ICC without any change.

The Convention was born out of the horrors of World War II, and was particularly aimed at preventing the intentional destruction of whole groups of people. In fact, Raphael Lemkin, a Polish lawyer who coined the term genocide, derived the word from the Greek word *genos*, which means "race, nation or tribe" in ancient Greek and *caedere*, which means "to kill" in Latin. In Lemkin's conception, it was "a coordinated plan of different actions aiming at the destruction of essential foundations of the life of national groups, with the aim of annihilating the groups themselves".[3]

The aim of the Genocide Convention was organically linked to human rights instruments such as the Universal Declaration of Human Rights. As Schabas notes, "These instruments concern themselves with the right to life whereas the Genocide Convention is associated with the right to life of human groups, sometimes spoken of as the right to existence. The General Assembly Resolution 96(1), adopted in December 1946, declares that 'genocide is a denial of the right to existence of entire human groups, as homicide is the denial of the right to live of individual human beings'".[4]

What is clear is that the concept of genocide at its widest is meant to protect the rights of entire groups to continue to exist. It evolved in the context of a political history of attempts to exterminate entire groups of people. Probably the first such attempt in modern times was the attempt to exterminate Native Americans by European colonizers.[5] The European colonizers followed up this early genocide with numerous attempts to exterminate historically troublesome groups. Mamdani documents some instances of the European genocidal impulse in his writings.[6] However, true to the racist origins of international law, exterminating entire groups of people of the Third World was never considered serious enough to warrant the description of genocide. It was only the extermination of the Jews by Nazi Germany which was good enough to provoke a response in terms of Lemkin's neologism, genocide, which then became transmuted in international law into the Genocide Convention of 1948.

The Genocide Convention of 1948 is a result of this history of exclusion of people never considered as people, hence deserving no mention under the new law. Among the most troubling aspects of this 'exclusion' is the limited number of groups the destruction of which would constitute genocide. Though the Nazi extermination of Jews went hand in hand with the destruction of the first modern homosexual sub-culture in history,[7] homosexuals were never seen as worthy of protection under the Convention. Similarly, though historically 'political groups' such as the Communists in Nazi Germany and indigenous people were intentionally exterminated, they were excluded from the protection of the Convention. The only groups deemed worthy of protection under the Genocide Convention, 1948, were national, religious, racial and ethnic groups. As is clear, the 'universal' law of genocide is actually really quite particular defining this most serious of offences in a way in which exclusion is an ever present reality. However, the interesting question is whether this particular and contextual treaty lends itself to appropriation by human rights groups.

Gujarat as Genocide

In the Genocide Convention, 1948, genocide means any of the following acts committed with intent to destroy, in whole or in part, a national, ethnical, racial or religious group, as such:

>> Killing members of the group;
>> Causing serious bodily or mental harm to members of the group;
>> Deliberately inflicting on the group conditions of life calculated to bring about its physi-cal destruction in whole or in part;
>> Imposing measures intended to prevent births within the group;
>> Forcibly transferring children of the group to another group.

The elements of the offence of genocide are the *actus reus* defined in Article II (a) to (e) and the mental element otherwise described as *dolus specialis* or special intent. The mental element inherent in the offence of genocide is seen as not just the intent to commit the particular act of killing but a discriminatory intent, which aims through the killing to "destroy in whole or in part, a national, ethnic, racial or religious group as such". Thus it is not enough to merely show intent to kill, one has to discharge the higher responsibility of showing that the killing had the specific intent of "destroying in whole or in part, a national, ethnic, racial or religious group as such".[8]

If we did a legal analysis of Gujarat using the rich fact finding data before us, it is possible to make the argument that what happened in Gujarat was genocide. The crucial category of 'special intention' can be proved using either the particular speeches or statements of the *Sangh Parivar*, or the tests evolved by the Akayesu judgement as well as the Kristic judgement that were decided by the tribunals on Rwanda and Yugoslavia respectively.

The importance of using the term 'genocide' in the context of Gujarat is that it is a deeply political category which tells the story of racial identities. Mamdani uses the term racial as opposed to ethnic to mean the perception of the other as a threatening, alien presence. Thus, once the 'other' is perceived not as a neighbour but a foreign settler, then the violence becomes understandable as a political move that aims to cleanse the soil of an alien presence. As he notes, "We need to distinguish between racial and ethnic violence: ethnic violence can result in massacres, but not genocide. Massacres are about transgressions, excess; genocide questions the very legitimacy of a presence as alien".[9] The deployment of the category of genocide points back to the perception of the Muslim in Gujarat, and in India, by the Hindu Right. The Muslim has – like the Tutsi – always been perceived not as a troublesome minority but a threatening alien presence.

Golwalkar, one of the first ideologues of the RSS, expounded on his perception of the relationship between the different communities in India by referring to the example of Nazi Germany: "To keep up the purity of the race and its culture, Germany shocked the world by her purging the country of the Semitic races – the Jews. Race pride at its highest has been manifested here. Germany has also shown how well nigh impossible for races and cultures, having differences going to the root, to be assimilated into one united whole, a good lesson for us in Hindustan to learn and profit by".[10]

The lessons that Hindustan was to learn were expanded by Golwalkar when he noted that, "The foreign races in Hindustan must either adopt the Hindu culture and language, must learn to respect and hold in reverence Hindu religion, must entertain no ideas but those of glorification of the Hindu race and culture [...] or may stay in the country, wholly subordinated to the Hindu nation, claiming nothing, deserving no privileges, far less any preferential treatment – not even citizen's rights".[11]

This is the logic formulated at the beginning of the century which has resulted in Gujarat. Hence the importance of naming what happened in Gujarat as 'genocide'. One needs to move away from the 'truth' of random violence of the FIRs to the 'truth' of an intention to eliminate a group. However one has to note that describing what happened in Gujarat as genocide still does not solve the difficult problem of dealing with the 'popularity' of genocide. There was the active participation of vast sections of the Gujarati population in the violence. This is the element that most fact-finding reports do not address head-on as the 'popularity' of the genocidal act has no easy answers. While it is easy to ask for the punishment for the instigators and planners, what about the executors when they number in the thousands? When Mamdani notes that "the unique moral dilemma of the genocide in Rwanda admits of no easy answers", it applies equally to Gujarat.

This text was presented at the "Crisis/Media" workshop, organized by Sarai-CSDS and the Waag Society in Delhi, March 2003.

NOTES

1. See DJ Harris, *Cases and Materials on International Law* (Sweet and Maxwell, 1998, London) p. 729. Harris argues that the prohibition against genocide forms part of customary international law reading the various developments in international law including the 1948 Convention and the General Assembly Resolution of 1948 which also declared genocide an international crime.

2. Security Council Resolutions 955 of 1994 and 808 of 1993 respectively.

3. Lemkin, Raphael. "Axis Rule in Occupied Europe: Laws of Occupation, Analysis of Government, Proposals for Redress", cf. William Schabas, *Genocide in International Law* (Cambridge University Press, 2000) p. 25.

4. Ibid., p. 6.

5. Zinn, Howard. *People's History of the United States* (Longman,1996, London) pp. 1-22. Zinn documents a history through which the American Indian population was exterminated through war, conquest, murder and attacks on civilian populations and use of biological weapons such as small pox.

6. Mamdani, Mahmood. *When Victims Become Killers: Colonialism, Nativism, and the Genocide in Rwanda*, http://pup.princeton.edu/chapters/s7027.html. Mamdani notes, "Whereas the prototype of settler violence in the history of modern colonialism is the near-extermination of Amerindians in the New World, the prototype of settler violence in the African colonies was the German annihilation of over 80 percent of the Herero population in the colony of German South West Africa in a single year, 1904". He quotes an official publication, *Der Kampf*: "No efforts, no hardships were spared in order to deprive the enemy of his last reserves of resistance; like a half-dead animal he was hunted from water-hole to water-hole until he became a lethargic victim of the nature of his own country. The waterless Omaheke was to complete the work of German arms: the annihilation of the Herero people".

7. Miller, Neil. *Out of the Past: Gay and Lesbian history from 1869 to the Present* (Vintage, 1995, New York).

8. *Prosecutor vs. Akayesu*, Case No. ICTR-96-4-T, para 497.

9. Mamdani, Mahmood. *When Victims Become Killers: Colonialism, Nativism, and the Genocide in Rwanda* (Princeton University Press, 2001) p. 14.

10. Golwalkar, M.S. "We, Or our Nationhood Defined", cf Christophe Jaffrelot, *The Hindu Nationalist Movement and Indian Politics* (Penguin, 1996, Delhi) p. 55.

11. Ibid., p. 56.

CAUTION
Reporters at Work

Massacres and the Media
A Field Reporter Looks Back on Gujarat 2002
DARSHAN DESAI

I come from Gujarat, a place where I was born and brought up, where I made my career, where I have my family, my friends, my relatives, my dear ones. But today, sometimes I feel it is an alien land, a land that has suddenly disowned me. Today, all the people who once used to look at me with respect question me and abuse me. They do this because I represented a publication whose medium is English and because I reported human misery in its right perspective.[1]

What pains me today is not that many of my friends see me in a different light, but that the way they look at me reflects the poison injected into them. They don't realize how tactfully it was all fed to them. A senior Gujarat police official told me recently, "Darshan, you are blacklisted"; a friend who came to meet me after a long time said, "...all of you from the English language media have tarnished the image of Gujarat".

What my friends think of me may not be that important, but I think that it is important to understand why they say this. It doesn't just concern me, it concerns each and every journalist who wishes to report the facts as they are and analyze them in their (correct) perspective. So, what happened in Gujarat? Why were the English language journalists demonized? This is exactly what needs to be understood.

Politicians have a nose for news. The merely skilled politician can stomach adverse news. But the genius smells it, swallows it and uses it to his advantage. In India, there is only one such politician, and he is one of his kind. Naming him here will be stating the obvious. But you still had to name him, and precisely this, the fact that you had to name him, was his USP. He could smell the fact that the aggressive reportage of the news of communal violence in Gujarat could flatter him. He swallowed the tirade, used it against the same media that made it and carved out a victory of sorts. They say you cannot have your cake and eat it too . He showed he can, and how.

Today, the 'common man' in Gujarat hates the English language media. The Gujarati language media hates the English language media. Even a section of the English language media hates the English language media. This is an achievement painstakingly planned and excellently executed by one single man. Remember, this genius of a politician doesn't hate the media. He laughs at it and with it. He mocks it. He smirked when he rode to victory in Gujarat, riding roughshod over the media hype against him. Today, he is laughing, and laughing loudly. He continues to ridicule the media, and ironically, he does this with the help of the same media. His strategy was simple and straightforward: just remain in the news. Hate him, love him, but you just can't ignore him. Throughout his Gujarat *Gaurav Yatra* (Gujarat Pride Campaign), across towns and villages, across every nook and cranny of Gujarat, he ensured that the media chased him everywhere. Despite the fact that he repeated the same rhetoric, the media followed him – in case he said something controversial. And he did not disappoint them.

It made news when he referred to Sonia Gandhi (the leader of the opposition Congress party) as "Italy *ki beti*" (the daughter of Italy). It made news when he spoke of *"miya* Musharraf" to refer to Muslims in general. It made news when he called "James Michael Lyngdoh" by his full name to let people know that he (Lyngdoh) is a Christian, to insinuate that therefore he is close to Sonia Gandhi. It made news when he said, "*Hum paanch, hamare pachhis*" ("We are five, and we have twenty-five"). For those who had not heard it, he repeated, "*Hum paanch, hamare pachhis, pachhis key chhe-sou-pachhis*", and told the reporters to note it properly.[2]

He referred to the massive coverage of the post-Godhra violence by the English language media as biased and thundered, "Were the deaths of Godhra not deaths?" He characterized the reportage which continued to expose his government's complicity as a 'hate campaign' against fifty million Gujaratis. This strategy worked and the election results showed how. His media bashing still continues, with the media reporting every word of it. During the last several months, he has gone hammer and tongs after the English language, national-level media and used the same media to do so. In this process, if he was lambasted by the media, the latter too was not spared. The accusations bounced back on the media. The wily politician acquired a martyrdom of sorts.

The VHP (*Vishwa Hindu Parishad* – World Hindu Council) firebrand Pravin Togadia played the same trick. His strategy: the cruder you are, the more space you get in the media. Call Sonia Gandhi an "Italian bitch" and hog the headlines on page one. Assert, "We will give Godhra's reply, today in Gandhinagar and tomorrow in Delhi', and announce that "India will be a Hindu *Rashtra* (state) in two years".

On the day of polling, Togadia pulled a fast one when he howled before TV channels,"James Michael Lyngdoh has removed my name from the voters list". It was on air and channels kept repeating it, even before anyone bothered cross-checking the allegation. As it turned out, his name was actually on the list. By the time this entire drama had played itself out, his attempt to influence voters by his allegation that the election commission was playing tricks with Gujaratis had proven effective.

Around the same time, several TV channels showed our great politician atop a platform in Maninagar, telling indignant ruling party workers that he can't help it if the election commission had deleted their names and that they should keep calm. Very tacitly, he was telling the voters what Togadia was saying directly to them. The media was used to persuasively address apathetic and fence-sitting voters even on the day of polling. Looked at another way, the media had to carry it when Togadia said his name was deleted. The media was also bound to carry it if there was a resulting commotion and the Chief Minister, the genius politician, was trying to calm things down. After all, it made news.

When I think about this, I remember my days as a cub-reporter in the late eighties. There were riots going on in Ahmedabad. It was my first year as a reporter, and I was on the night shift. Around midnight, I called up the city police control to find out what was the 'latest'. I was told that there was one incident of a shop being torched and stone pelting in the town, and that the police had opened fire to disperse the mob.

I started my report like this: "The police had to open fire on a mob pelting stones, etc". Our resident editor called me and asked what was up. I informed him about the incident. But he wanted me to read out what I had written. Just as I read, "Police had to open fire", he interrupted with the question: "Why do you defend the police?"

I could not make out what he was saying. He asked me, "If you were not at the spot, how could you say, 'Police had to open fire'? Are you sure that they had no option left but to open fire. Why can't you write a straight copy, saying that the police opened fire to disperse stone-pelting mobs?"

In contrast, here was the case when Togadia was shouting before reporters that his name was struck off from the electoral rolls, and it was dutifully reported, verbatim, while it did not deserve any publicity at all. Why should we report some weird allegation without confirming it? Similarly, there was the recent case of a sex scandal involving two Punjab ministers in Gujarat. The Minister of State for Home Affairs in Gujarat calls a press conference and declares that two ministers from Punjab enjoyed sexual favours from call girls. At the same conference, he also says that their names are not in the first information report (what we call the F.I.R). But still, the allegation was reported.

I am not commenting as to whether the allegation was true or otherwise, but should the media not be wary, or at least sceptical, with regard to unsubstantiated allegations? In earlier days, such allegations were not carried. And, if at all they were, they were carried in tandem with analysis that pointed out their unsubstantiated nature.

To return to the days of communal violence in Gujarat and the elections last year, politicians employed other ways to spread their influence too. A little known Gujarati paper, *Gujarat Today*, run by people who happen to be Muslims, carried an ad from a lesser-known Muslim clergyman appealing to the minority community to deliver a hundred percent turnout on Election Day.

The politician genius and Togadia were quick to release counter-ads in mass circulated Gujarati dailies displaying the appeal, calling it a "*fatwa*" (a religious edict), and then telling the Hindus to vote a hundred percent. Simultaneously, hundreds of photocopies of the "*fatwa*" were distributed in the villages of Gujarat. It made a big impact, just as was desired, and even those (Hindus) who never vote for anyone as well as those who never vote for the BJP came out in droves to vote.

Similarly, compact discs containing messages that worked to create a fear psychosis were widely distributed and even played on TV sets. The CDs had a simple message: If a certain party came to power, the Muslims would start on a killing spree. Here are some of the specific things that the CDs said:

> you are travelling in a train, you might be attacked.
> you are in your prayers, you may be assaulted.
> you are walking in a crowd, you may be lynched.

With the media playing the great politician's complete speeches, word for word, the last day of campaigning before polling day (December 12th, 2002) saw the chief minister asking the people, "You may have *gaadi, waadi* and *laadi* (car, land and wife), but what if your son doesn't return home in the evening?" He appealed, through public meetings reported exhaustively by the media and through ads in the papers, to turnout to vote "a hundred percent".

The media reported everything; the politician genius ridiculed all of its reportage, and the media reported that too. On December 15th, the media was reporting his victory, analyzing it and ending up finding faults with itself. Later, the same English language media had armchair columnists spitting venom on the same English language media.

A series of commentaries in this vein started appearing in the media after the election results in Gujarat. Criticizing the media became easy after everything was over, but journalists, who had seen communal polarization closely and suffered for it, know better.

The common thread running through all such articles was that the national-level English language media had demonized the politician of the day to such an extent that the people of Gujarat responded with vengeance to give his political party a landslide victory. In simple words, the accusation was that the English language media had played a game in favour of the opposition party, but the people of Gujarat had seen through it. They also argued that by its exposés on the macabre violence in Gujarat and the obvious complicity of the state, the English media had defamed the fifty million people of the state.

What was, and is, unfortunately, being glossed over is how this genius of a politician converted the stinging tirade against him, his party, its affiliates and his government into a criticism of the people of Gujarat. There has not been any article seeking to analyze how and why this politician was successful in portraying, though deceptively, the media exposés of his government as an assault on the collective pride of the people. Instead, especially after election results, self-appointed media critics begin saying exactly what the politician had been saying before the results.

To establish that the media had gone overboard with its alleged 'demonization' of the politician, these commentaries that came out after the elections sought to fish out stray reports in the English press to bolster their case. Attempts were made to show that certain reports were deliberately twisted to level accusations at one politician. One such instance cited in one of these articles was a report in *the Indian Express* that carried the headline: "Dial M for Modi, Murder?"[3]

Here, this media critic says the story had nothing on the chief minister of Gujarat but on two of his cabinet colleagues sitting in police control rooms in Ahmedabad and Gandhinagar when mobs went about killing Muslims on February 28th. (Remember, the major killings in Gulberg Society and Naroda Patia happened on this day). The article says that *the Indian Express* story said that the two ministers were dictating police inaction when hundreds of innocents were being killed, without corroboration from the police.

This critic, unfortunately, had not read the story properly before judging the integrity and credibility of reporters. The report never said that the ministers were directing police inaction. It said that when major massacres were taking place on February 28th, and when desperate telephone calls to police control rooms were not being attended to, the two ministers were sitting, in the police control room at the Ahmedabad Police Commissionerate. The story quoted Additional Chief Secretary (Home) Ahok Nrayan as well as both the cabinet ministers to confirm that they were indeed there at the control room. And this was not denied by anyone later.

The article goes on to say that there was no reference to Narendra Modi (the Chief Minister of Gujarat) in the story despite the aggressive headline. The critic should have known that in Gujarat at that time, the Home Ministry was under the Chief Minister, while neither of the two ministers present at the control rooms had anything to do with the Home Ministry for they held the Health and the Urban Development portfolios. Does this media critic expect us to believe that the ministers were checking on the health of the cops and discussing urban development with them when the state went up in flames? If they were there to ensure prompt police response to people in danger, there was little sign of this. Last, but not the least, should we believe that the Chief Minister had no idea that his two senior cabinet colleagues (one of them his spokesman) were helping the police in the control rooms?

Reference is also made to an essay by Arundhati Roy in *Outlook* magazine about Gujarat, where she (mistakenly) mentions the death of Ehsan Jaffrey's daughter.[4] She (Roy) wrote that Jaffrey's daughter was raped and killed while it was later found that she was actually alive. This was definitely a *faux pas* and the magazine was quick to carry a prominent apology by Roy to that effect.[5] Media critics conveniently gloss over this fact (of the writer correcting her mistake through an apology). They also wish away the fact that one stray case or even a few stray cases don't make an adequate case for a generalization of bias. They know that if they recognize these facts, it will take away the very weapon that they have deployed.

The question that we need to consider is – how would the allegations made against a report such as the one we have just discussed stand against an objective scrutiny of the mass circulation Gujarati language press? Was the perspective of the Gujarati papers so objective that they did not need any review? And if it was actually so, why don't these media critics pat them on the back? They should have given them marks and cited the Gujarati press as an example to hold out against its English language counterpart. They did not do so. Why? Was it because they can't read Gujarati, or because they did not think the Gujarati press was so objective, or because such a review would destroy the basis of their analysis?

I am steering clear from any remarks on the Gujarati language press because, as a field journalist, I know that vernacular paper reporters also work with the odds heavily stacked against them. How could one forget that a senior reporter of a prominent Gujarati daily lost his job because he refused to bow down to the diktats of his editors and write a false report. This false report, was carried prominently. How will critics explain another report in a mass circulated Gujarati daily which carried a headline about the abduction and killing of a Hindu woman in a Muslim-dominated area, while the copy of the story that went under this headline said at the very end that the woman was not actually kidnapped but was traced to her native village where she went of her own accord.

Those who cannot write, criticize. Those who cannot report, recoil later. Let us begin at the beginning, and undertake our own little analysis of the Gujarat events vis-à-vis the national English media. The Godhra train carnage happened on February 27th, and the retribution began from the very next day. Each and every national-level paper (English or otherwise) had banner headlines about fifty-eight *kar sewaks* (VHP volunteers) being burnt alive, and ran editorial columns condemning the incident.

The event, as it happened, was reported and displayed in the English language press in all its seriousness. It got greater prominence than the reportage of the budget sessions in the national Parliament and in the Gujarat assembly. Had nothing happened after Godhra, the English language media would have continuously followed up on the train carnage. But other events started happening and continued for far too long, obviously taking up major space in the papers.

Assuming that the media critics are aware about the functioning of the newsroom, it is obvious that the alarming killings post-Godhra would take prominence for, unlike Godhra (which was a one-off incident), they kept on happening. A large number of Muslims got killed and (in this instance) they suffered the most. This was a fact and it was reported as such. Besides, whatever may be the deafening propaganda to the contrary, the media had adequately reported the suffering of the Godhra victims. The gory scenes were shown and the cries of the victims were registered in detail.

Yes, the volume of reporting on the post-Godhra massacres was greater than the volume of reporting on the Godhra incident for the simple reason that they (the post Godhra killings) kept on happening. There was no deliberate design to ensure that they should be given more prominence in the English language press. The Gujarati press also covered the same violence, and displayed the news sometimes even in red banner headlines. There may have been instances of exaggerations and biases in the English media (I will not speak of the Gujarati press), but the biases were no more than reflections of the extent of the gruesome killings, which the media covered, as it was bound to.

The English language media professionals did not plan Godhra, or what happened in its aftermath. There is a bizarre allegation being made against the English media that the aftermath of Godhra would not have been so gruesome had the English language, national level media criticized Godhra in adequate terms. Do the media critics and politicians who make this allegation mean that the killers read the English language papers, weighed the adequacy of the coverage of Godhra, and decided that it was not good enough before starting their job on the morning of February 28th, 2002? It is unfortunate that there may be many people who may have believed in this brilliantly rehearsed rhetoric of our wily politician genius, but must our media critics too fall into the trap?

The violence in Gujarat was largely one-sided and more of a pogrom than a riot. This is in sharp contrast to the past when there were riots in the form of clashes between groups and it really was difficult for the media to decide about the extent and involvement of the different actors. This time it was so very obvious.

Another criticism levelled against the English language media is that they were quick to reason that the post-Godhra violence was the result of a conspiracy, but did not pay attention to the possibility of Godhra itself as being part of a conspiratorial design. An objective reporting of the events will suggest that it is difficult to prove a conspiracy in Godhra while it was actually obvious in the events thereafter. This writer, as a field journalist, went to Godhra looking for an ISI (the InterServices Intelligence agency of Pakistan) conspiracy, but the government's own officials, railway authorities and the cops told him something else. Physical verification in the field suggested that the officials were right. Even today, investigating agencies have not been able to put together all the pieces of the Godhra incident.

Last but not the least, the English language media is targeted for not registering and acknowledging the popularity of the politician of the day, our politician genius. It is argued that the English language media deliberately did not wish to see the popularity of the politician for they were working for the opposition Congress party. Wrong – it did report the aspect of his popularity, but it also did more than that; it analyzed the politics of the making of a communal divide and the impact that this had on society and the economy.

The job of the media is not to campaign for a party but to analyze the processes that unfold before it. If, because of this, a party wins or loses an election, so be it. If while reporting the facts, a section of the media is portrayed as working for a political party even if this is not the case, so be it. Osama bin Laden may be popular among a section of people, Adolf Hitler was popular in Germany at one time, Indira Gandhi was popular and her death led to a ghastly pogrom against the Sikh community in 1984, the chief minister of Tamil Nadu, Jayalalitha, is popular despite her scandals. Does this mean that in each such case we should be carried away and go ga-ga over their popularity? Or should we report what these politicians really do, and how they do what they do?

This text was presented at the "Crisis/Media" workshop, organized by Sarai-CSDS and the Waag Society in Delhi, March 2003.

NOTES
1. Darshan Desai, a journalist based in Ahmedabad, reported on the Godhra carnage, and the killings that followed in its aftermath for *The Indian Express* in 2002.
2. A twist on the well-known 'family planning' slogan used by the Indian Government – "*Hum do, Hamare do*" ("We two, and our two") coupled with a jibe at Muslim customary and personal law in India, which entitles Muslim male to have four spouses, hence the "we five". A particularly lethal reference here to the untenable myth that Muslims are breeding faster than ever before, and that polygamy is a conspiratorial device used by Muslims to ensure that they will eventually outnumber Hindus.
3. Desai, Darshan and Joydeep Ray. "Dial M for Modi, Murder", *The Indian Express* (Sunday, 23 March, 2002, Ahmedabad), see http:// www.indianexpress.com/ie20020324/top1.html.
   For a comment critical of this report, see "Why the Media lost Gujarat", *The Pioneer* (22 December, 2002, Delhi) http://www.topscan.net/Channels/Archives/Ar_jan 03/Ar_1.htm
4. Roy, Arundhati. "Democracy: Who's She When She's At Home", *Outlook India* (6 May, 2002).
5. Roy, Arundhati. Letter to the Editor, *Outlook India* (27 May, 2002).

The Everyday Life of a Srinagar Correspondent

Reporting from Kashmir

MUZAMIL JALEEL

In Kashmir, the job of reporting does not fit in the realm of reason or logic. It's like treading a razor's edge around the clock, while facing animosity and hatred from all sides. You are being judged everyday, and if an uncaring guerrilla or an arrogant security man so chooses, there is nothing that can stop you from becoming 'collateral damage' in a war that has already consumed more than 50,000 lives.

Unlike an open confrontation, insurgency is a dirty war in which no rule, no law, no code of conduct is followed. It's a war in which every player feels he is a victim, believes his is the only 'just struggle' and is convinced that his perception is the gospel truth. If you dare question him, the act of questioning itself is immediately dubbed as being part of a conspiracy. In Kashmir, if a journalist wants to be truthful to his profession and follow his duties, all the parties across the divide indict him as a 'conspirator'.

One day, he may be called an 'anti-national element' – someone who mounts assaults with his pen to fulfil some ulterior motives, such as 'defaming the security forces who are serving the nation, who are ready to sacrifice their lives to defend its integrity and sovereignty'. He is expected to put down his pen and shut his mouth whenever an ugly situation arises, because reporting places a question mark on the conduct of the government, and his writing will only be seen by the state as 'helping the enemy'.

The next day, he may be writing about an atrocity committed by the 'militants' or exposing the hidden agenda of a separatist leader who exhorts the sons and daughters of ordinary Kashmiris to die for the 'Cause', while the leader's own children hold on to their lucrative jobs. Then he (the journalist) will be in trouble. If you happen to be a local, you have to be seen to be following the militants' *diktat* religiously. It's an added obligation, because otherwise you are being 'disloyal to your own people'.

If you are a journalist, ulterior motives are seen in everything you write that criticizes separatist ideology and the credibility of the separatist leadership. And even if the facts are on your side, the story is taken as a plant by intelligence agencies and you are dubbed a 'conduit of state propaganda'.

Kashmir is an especially complicated story. In fact, it has always been a story of many truths woven together into layers of lies. It's a story of a relative truth with several contradictory definitions and confusing interpretations. It's a story of a deliberate lie, carefully projected as the gospel truth. Truth is the most politicized commodity in Kashmir today. Nobody wants to put it in words and with reason. Why should an ordinary villager put his heart out, especially before a journalist? Why should he push himself unnecessarily into a controversy and risk his life? And many a time, what the eyes see and the ears hear don't represent reality. Thus the challenge of reporting on this conflict lies in the ability to decipher silences and understand the meaning behind every spoken word. And if you do the job well and break the monotony of popular belief on either side of the political divide, you must share the curse of Cassandra. You will tell the truth and it will be so dark that no one will believe you. In fact, truth is easily available in Kashmir but hardly anybody dares publicize it.

Over the years the very definition of news has changed for Kashmiri reporters. Unlike other situations across the country, when you 'break news' in Kashmir, it does not shock anybody. The truth is there and everybody knows about it, but everyone prefers the safety of silence. News is available in street gossip, in the things that people talk about, in the things that they know. It is there when people talk to each other in a barbershop, or chat while sitting on a pavement. It is buried in the poetry that is written during these troubled times, especially because expression through prose is also deemed dangerous. Thus 'breaking news' only means taking the risk of putting a fact that is already in public knowledge into print.

The dilemma of local reporters covering this conflict is that most of us are Kashmiri Muslims, and that's a part of the story. The separatists believe that we have a responsibility to take their side because, as Kashmiri Muslims, we are their people. The (Indian) Government, on the other hand, wants us to prove our 'impartiality' by supporting its claims in Kashmir. Our identity often does get in the way of our reporting. Once you are conscious of this and try to make an additional effort to be impersonal and keep a distance from the story, you are accused of being anti-Kashmir. Yet, if you get swayed by your emotions, you jeopardize your own credibility. The only safe path is to take refuge in silence. Confine your self to hard news, avoid opinion and thus avoid any controversy. But most of the time this silence, too, becomes partisan.

There are a few examples. When Mirwaiz Mohammad Farooq, the head priest of the Jama Masjid in Srinagar, was assassinated in his office in Nageen on May 21st, 1990, there was little mystery attached to the identity of the killers. The purpose behind the killing was even discussed on the streets in Kashmir. Twelve years have passed and it is still a well-kept secret, especially by his own family. His young son, who succeeded his father as the valley's head priest, prefers silence, and so do all of us. Truth is dangerous. Everybody takes refuge in the realm of ambiguity. The current Mirwaiz and the powerful separatist conglomerate, All Parties Hurriyat Conference, that he founded soon after his father's assassination, publicly talk about a conspiracy and accuse the Indian intelligence agencies of committing the murder. But privately, everybody acknowledges that he was killed by what are called 'our own people'. They might not name the names but if you stop a twelve year old boy in downtown Srinagar, he will tell you who did it without thinking for even a fraction of a second. Nevertheless, the assassinated Mirwaiz became *Shaheed-e-Millat*, the martyr of the nation, and is buried in the Bihisht-e-Shauda-e-Kashmir (The Paradise of the Martyrs of Kashmir), the biggest martyrs' graveyard in Srinagar, alongside his own assassin. And, ironically, both the Mirwaiz and his assassin remain undisputed martyrs for the Kashmiri separatist movement.

September 7th, 1995, was a lean day for Srinagar-based reporters till a rumour started making rounds that the four western trekkers who were being kept hostage after their abduction from the jungles ahead of Pahalgam were killed. Everybody rushed to their offices, including the BBC reporter Yusuf Jameel. When he reached the press enclave, he was accompanied by Mushtaq Ali, a young photographer with AFP. Jameel was told that an unidentified veiled woman had left a parcel for him, and as Jameel started to open the parcel, he got a phone call. He left the parcel to answer the phone and Mushtaq took it to see what was inside. And as he opened the seal, a bomb went off, making a sieve of his body. Jameel was lucky to have escaped with minor injury but Mushtaq died three days later. There was no mystery associated with the veiled woman who had come to drop the parcel. She had been accompanied by the surrendered militant, Ikhwan, who was immediately identified, but nobody dared to tell the truth. Those who came from the outside took the easy route, toed the line of the security agencies and blamed the killing on the militants. Local reporters preferred silence because that was the only safe way out. Now, seven years after that murder, Javed Shah, a counter-insurgent turned politician, claims that he knew about the plot and accused the police of sending this lethal bomb to the BBC office. He didn't break any news because everybody in the press enclave, now called Mushtaq Ali Enclave, had an idea of the perpetrators of the crime and its aim. Jameel had escaped death but his voice was silenced. Even the BBC threw him out because it was Jameel and not the organization that was under threat. His crime was nothing unusual. He had tried to tell exactly what was happening, thus hurting the interests of various players in the game and making enemies for himself. In those days, Jameel's dispatches had become the most credible information emanating out of Kashmir's confused crisis. Even people within the valley would wait impatiently to listen to him to know what was going on.

Exactly twelve years after Mirwaiz's murder, a similar incident happened, this time right at the martyrs' graveyard. Another senior Hurriyat Leader, Abdul Ghani Lone, fell soon after he left for home after attending the martyrdom anniversary of Mirwaiz. A young man armed with an AK47 walked up and showered him with bullets. He fell in a pool of blood, along with his police bodyguard, dead. This time, his son, Sajjad Lone, mustered the courage to blame the militants in Pakistan. But as night fell, good sense prevailed, and he shifted the blame to the then chief minister, Farooq Abdullah, accusing him of facilitating the murder of his father. Everybody knew who had killed Lone and why. Thus, deliberate silence engulfed the truth and the reporters again. When Lone's body was finally buried in the same graveyard, he was extended the status of a martyr. Lone's sons were keen to take his body to his ancestral village near Handwara and bury him in an ordinary graveyard but it didn't work because of the intervention of the Hurriyat leadership. The separatists called him *Shaheed-e-Hurriyat*, Martyr of Revolution, while his party and his sons, Sajjad and Bilal, preferred to call the slain leader a Martyr of Peace. Sajjad and Bilal nursed the grudge but never talked about it in public. Later, when Kashmir prepared for polls, they played a crucial role in generating a wave of participation by fielding four of their party's main leaders as candidates from their father's political bastion of Kupwara and Handwara but never publicly acknowledged it. Ghulam Mohiuddin Sofi's decision to run as an independent candidate from Handwara had a significant effect on the mood of the people. A close confidant of the assassinated Hurriyat leader Lone, Sofi managed to erase the taboo related to the polls in this separatist stronghold. He, overnight, levelled the vast gulf between the elections and *azadi* (call for freedom). His first rally was attended by thousands of people who shouted slogans in favour of separatism, and vowed to vote for Sofi in the same breath. The campaign was carefully orchestrated. The Lone brothers stayed in the background, even publicly distancing themselves from Sofi and other leaders who had participated in polls. But the truth was exactly the reverse. The entire People's Conference cadre had been asked to actively participate in the poll campaign and the candidates were even allowed to use the blue flag of the Party. The Hurriyat Conference privately spat venom against the Lone brothers but did not throw them out of the alliance. Why?

So, this is one very important thing. For example, if I go to report and I say that the Peoples' Conference participated in elections, they can take me to court because they are not doing so publicly. They are still publicly a separatist outfit. They don't do it through press releases. This is all a covert operation. When you report crisis in Kashmir, which is a completely complex situation, everything is a covert operation. You can't get people on quote. People might tell you off the record that this is what is happening, but writing that can get you taken to court easily. So when we report, we have to keep this also in mind. There is always the threat to our lives, but this is another threat. People can take you to court and silence you forever.

A reporter may also be attacked so as to make headlines. The logic? Violence is not just a tool to force opponents to buckle under and concede demands, but also a medium of communication in a war in which human lives are so devalued that a few killings hardly make it to page one. The violent death of a journalist is a guarantee that the issue is, violently, back in view again. I had never thought of it till I saw it happen. It was on the evening of August 10th, 2000. I was in my office and there was nothing unusual. Violence itself was not new, even though it sent shivers down my spine. I was scared; bodies haunted my dreams. It is extremely difficult to forget faces that vanish in a matter of seconds. It is hard to erase the memories of blood split on the road as if somebody wanted to create a painting in red. That day I was to be haunted by a new image: a dismembered human limb, dangling from an electric wire above my head, dripping blood. I don't know if it was the immediacy or the jolt of yet another close shave with death that affected me so much. The deadly blast that day on Srinagar's Residency Road, just a kilometre and half from my office, claimed sixteen lives, including photojournalist Pradeep Bhatia.

In a sense, it was nothing new. It was part of the ongoing violent campaign in the valley. For eight years I had been reporting death almost everyday, covering bloody encounters, gathering eyewitness accounts, meeting victims or affected families and writing their accounts to chronicle the horrors of Kashmir. In the lull between these encounters, we journalists simply wait for the next tragedy to happen. Like vultures we then swoop on the spot into the environs of death of which the smell, sound and touch are now all too familiar. Death has become an important ingredient in our professional as well as personal lives. Keeping a tab on the body count each evening has become an essential routine, the way a shopkeeper carefully counts his cash before locking up. When I started as a cover reporter, every assignment was traumatic. It was difficult to eat, sleep and drink. Many a time it seemed to me that I was continuously swimming in a sea of blood. After sometime I became so used to the daily dose of violence that I lost all feeling, all pain. Twenty deaths a day became a routine matter. Individual human lives began losing their news value. No one killed in the valley today became worthy of a headline. Unfortunately, I thought I had become numb. But the August 10th blast momentarily pierced through that hard shell of emotional immunity. It was different because death came so much closer than before. Just a few metres from where I stood, I saw friends and fellow scribes blown to smithereens, flung high in the air like bloody rag dolls. Although the authorized explanation was that the bomb was laid for security forces and that journalists were caught unwittingly, I never believed that. Sure, it was not a direct attack on us, but certainly the perpetrators knew that there was a likelihood of us being the victims. It was a typical strategy to use violence as communication. Our own penchant for death and bullets had caught up with us. Violent death makes news and if a few of the victims are journalists, so much the better. The perpetrators were aware that a huge media party was camping at hotels Ahdooz and Broadway, not far from the site of the bombing. First they detonated a small bomb that hurt no one. The sound of the blast emptied the street. Actually it was an invitation for journalists to rush to the spot. As the police reached there to investigate, the scribes too arrived to capture the moment, not knowing that a far more horrible event was just a few seconds away. Within seven minutes, the improvised explosive device went off. Shrapnel hit Pradeep Bhatia straight in his heart although many others escaped without a scratch. The AFP photographer Taufseen Mustafa had just left the spot to take pictures of soldiers taking position. If he had stayed another minute near the explosive-laden Ambassador car, he too would have been dead. Pradeep had hugged him just a minute before his death and he had shaken hands with me just four or five minutes before the event. "I can't believe that he is dead. One minute he had hugged me, a huge grin on his face, and the next minute he was lying there in a pool of blood. I feel as if the shrapnel is still following me. I feel the pricks all over my body when I am asleep", Taufseen later told me.

The Asian Age photographer was just a metre away from the car. He was saved because a parked auto rickshaw took the entire barrage of the splinters. But he was still injured; a metal shard bypassed all obstacles and carved a huge hole in his thigh. "Everything turned dark and I ceased to think or feel for a few seconds. I did not even hear the sounds of the blast. It was like a flash of lightening. I thought the sky had come down over us. I thought that everything was over", he told me when I visited him in the hospital. In his decade career of covering violence, Naqash has had a close brush with death at least five times. The last time was he was at the local office of the British Broadcasting Corporation, and a bomb had gone off killing fellow journalist Mushtaq Ali. Naqash had been injured along with the then BBC correspondent Yusuf Jameel. The blast had damaged his eardrums.

On November 3rd, 1995, Naqash and two others had been stranded in the public relations office of the army's Fifteen Core in Srinagar during a fidayeen attack in which the army PRO Major Puroshttam was killed. Naqash and the others owe their lives to Major Puroshottam, who pushed them into a toilet for safety and courted death in his office. Naqash recalls the twelve hour-long ordeal, waiting for death to come: "Trapped in the toilet we felt that somebody will soon barge in and shoot us too". But his most traumatic memory is that of the horrific death of Mushtaq Ali; it was an event that shook the collective psyche of journalists in Kashmir valley. We renamed the Srinagar Press Enclave as Mushtaq Ali Enclave in silent tribute to this colleague. An engraved plaque there reminds us everyday of the supreme sacrifice that he made in the cause of reporting the truth about Kashmir. It also reminds us how much we walk the razor's edge.

Ali was not the first to be caught in this maelstrom. In April 1991, when militancy was at its peak, unidentified gunmen had barged into the office of *Al Safa* newspaper and shot its outspoken editor, Mohammad Shaban Vakil. Though the cause of the killing is still wrapped in mystery, many believe that the provocation was his famous column *"Karva Sach"* (Bitter Truth). His death was a warning to all reporters to discipline themselves and follow the dictates of the various warring factions.

Official censorship was not always so direct. Newspapers were forced to stop publication on many occasions under pressure from counter-insurgent brigades that are ruthless and brutal. The Kashmiri journalist Zafar Meraz once met top counter-insurgent leader Kuka Parrey (he is now a politician and a former member of the state assembly) in his den at Hajin, about fifty kilometres north of Srinagar. As Meraz was returning from the hour-long interview, a group of armed men stopped his vehicle at Narabal, on the Srinagar-Baramulla highway. Without saying a word, they pumped half a dozen bullets into his belly while the taxi driver and the colleague who was with him were asked to run for their lives. Meraz spent twenty minutes plugging the blood wounds with his shirt and crying for help. No one stopped to help the profusely bleeding journalist. It was sheer luck that eventually a truck driver took him to a hospital. He received immediate attention there. He survived but the wounds inflicted on his psyche still remained unhealed. He lodged a complaint with the police in which he identified the attackers. Nothing happened. Thereafter he kept silent because if he pursued the matter he might not even be there to tell the tale. Being a Kashmiri, he also has to think of the security of his family members.

The militants, too, are unsubtle. Their style of dictating terms and forcing their will has changed over the years. *"Manu un shaya karien"*, which means "reproduce exactly", was the order that was issued with each of their press releases in the early 1990s. At times they dictated headlines and column size to the editors. Reporters were kidnapped and threatened often, and newspaper offices and printing presses ransacked and bombed. The Urdu daily *Srinagar Times* had to suspend publication ten times under pressure from the Government or militants. Two other leading dailies, *Aftab* and *Al Safa*, were forced to stop publication at least six times. There were dozens of grenade attacks on newspaper offices when militants either wanted space to project their viewpoint or wanted to censor the news of a rival group. Labelling a scribe as anti-movement was tantamount to a death sentence. Once a counter-insurgent leader, Azad Nabi, who was later killed by militants, took a large group of journalists hostage in Anantnag. The anti-militancy Ikhwan Group kidnapped reporters too. They were all too ready to use guns and grenades if newspapers did not publish their news prominently.

Writing boldly and bluntly remains a far-fetched dream in Kashmir. Caution verging on censorship has become a rule of survival. Personally, I have been harmed physically just twice. Last year, personal security men of the Srinagar police caught hold of me in front of my house one evening. They were enraged because their officers' car had met with an accident. They didn't ask anything and started hitting me with rifle butts. By the time the officer recognized me I was already half dead. The rifle butt blows on my head had been so severe that I had to spend the next twenty-four hours in the hospital. Doctors treated my eardrums for three months and, thankfully, I am now fine.

There are many incidents when I had to stop writing and even take a few days off and lie low. After the massacre of thirty-six men from the Sikh community in Chattisinghpora in March 20th, 2000, on the eve of the then US President Bill Clinton's visit, the police and the army claimed to have eliminated five foreign militants responsible for the massacre. Our bureau changed the story and finally exposed the truth of that encounter. It was a fake encounter and the men killed were not foreign militants but innocent villagers who had been rounded up and then killed to show that the security men had managed to solve the massacre mystery.

We followed the story on a day-to-day basis and soon I got a phone call from a counter-insurgent leader that a senior security force officer wanted to meet me. When I visited this officer, he didn't seem happy about our stories and he gave a long explanation about the difficulties of anti-militant operations in Kashmir. He was not subtle and tried to scare me. He advised me not to write about such contentious issues which would earn me enemies, saying that anybody could shoot me or plant an IET on the road that I took every day. Similar threats from militant groups are not rare either. If there is a critical story, displeasure is conveyed immediately. In fact, the more frightening thing is if they don't call. It means they don't even want to talk. At times we are made responsible for stories filed from other centres. This is one of the biggest problems for us. For example, a story about foreign funding that had been written by a correspondent in Delhi under her name was published in The Indian Express. But as soon as the newspaper arrived at the newsstands, we started getting calls. The group was extremely angry. And we were considered responsible for the story. Thankfully, they decided not to harm us. The situation becomes especially difficult when you have to file about the inter-group rivalries of the militant organizations or talk about big events like elections.

During the past year, two journalists were attacked to send a message to the entire press corps here that write-ups talking about their inter-group fights would not be tolerated. One such attack happened just last month. A group of militants barged into a local news agency and shot dead the editor, Parwaz Mohammad Sultan. Nobody took the responsibility. But the way local newspapers published front-page apologies in the next few days clearly explained why Sultan had been killed.

Writing about the polls was especially difficult. Reporters could not physically visit each and every place, so it was hard to strike a balance in reporting about the public's fear of the polls, and of security force coercion. The treatment of the story was so difficult that most of us had to write confusing pieces and take refuge in ambiguity. On poll day, if you happened to be in Handwara, the story would have been one of a fear of the polls. But if you were in Bandipur, it was altogether different. In fact, that day I was in a professional dilemma. What was the story? People coming out in droves to cast their vote, braving militant threats, and putting their faith in the democratic process? People boycotting the elections? Or security forces coming out and knocking on doors to get people out to vote, thus putting a question mark on the entire process? We knew how dangerous this was. Many newspapers had sent parachute reporters to Kashmir. But we had no escape route because our newspaper has the biggest bureau there. So we decided to hold a meeting and put our heads together to get answers. Finally we decided to do three stories. We knew that the Kupwara district would have a good turnout, and boycott of the polls would work in places like Sopor and Bandipor. So the stories were about the fear poll in Kupwara, another on boycott and coercion, and the third on Handwara, which had emerged as the model constituency for 2002 Assembly polls. The poll day passed peacefully and we managed to avoid putting our lives into danger. But even today I don't have an answer to that one question: what was the real story that day?

Coming back to the danger to our lives, there are a few precautions that have become almost mandatory for us. I personally have developed the habit of changing my office timings on a daily basis, and I never create a routine. For example, if I come to office at 10 am today, I will try to come half an hour early or late the next day. Then, generally, I don't take the same route or wear the same type of clothes everyday. It is the best I can do, though I know it doesn't make much sense since we still are sitting ducks in our offices and our homes. The day any agency or individual decides to harm us, nobody can stop them.

Although this daily grind of violence has somewhat scared me, it has certainly also changed me in other ways. Often, I can't sleep, and I cannot prevent that knot of tension, that thump of fear, each time the phone rings late at night. The Residency Road blast was much more traumatic than other such incidents because the faces that vanished were those of colleagues with whom I have been working for years, and the bodies flying in the air were those of friends whom I had been meeting almost everyday. The night of the Residency Road blast I was so afraid that while driving home, I stopped at least ten times. Every ditch on the roads seemed to be a camouflaged land mine, every shadow looked like a menacing figure. And when I reached home and went to bed, immediately visions of the bloody limb on the electric wire and bits of body strewn across the lane would not let me close my eyes. The screams of wounded colleagues sounded in my ears. Finally, I found oblivion with sleeping pills. I know many of us are addicted to sleeping pills these days.

Every time a violent attack happens, it brings Kashmiri journalists closer to each other than ever. Death and bloodshed can desensitize you, but when tragedy comes home, it makes you much more dependent on human bonds. We may return to the routine of writing, breathing and sleeping, but the loss of another colleague, this personal loss, makes us stronger, more determined.

As days and nights pass, and other scenes of violence super-impose themselves on the memories of that dreadful blast and shooting, we recall the brutal lesson we learned that day. We have to have a sense of the boiling point, and keep our writing always a few degrees below that threshold. There are some unwritten rules. Never attack individuals below the belt even if you have damning details. Be subtle in everything. You may expose the institutions but do not make personal enemies. After every big story, keep a low profile for a while. Avoid being a very high-profile journalist at all times, for when the profile is high, not just your writing but your life, too, comes under attack. Flow like a river and follow events as they happen. And do not let players on either side of the divide form a harsh judgment about you.

This text was presented at the "Crisis/Media" workshop, organized by Sarai-CSDS and the Waag Society in Delhi, March 2003.

A Reporter in Prison

IFTIKHAR GILANI

t was a relic from the World War II era, but it proved a comforting companion in New Delhi's Tihar Central Jail. And it was this outmoded, single band radio I purchased while an inmate that, on the night of January 10th, broke the news: I would soon be a free man again. It was unbelievable. The government had decided to withdraw the case against me.

It was a little after midnight on June 9th. I had finished my column for Pakistan's prestigious weekly, *The Friday Times*, and gone to bed. Some two hours later my wife, Aanisa, woke me. "Someone is knocking at the door", she said worriedly. I ambled out of bed, trudged to the door and found myself confronting two uniformed men armed with SLR rifles. In a flash the two men pushed me aside, entered my home and pointed their weapons at me. Another ten to fifteen others stormed in behind them.

"We are from the Income Tax department", one of the officers said. "We have been authorized to search this house". The next eighteen hours were interminable. The three bedroom apartment was turned inside out, upside down, in search of what, I was not told. At around 7 am, one of the members of the raiding party flicked on the television and there it was.

One of the networks said a defence document was found on my hard drive in breach of national security. (The document in question was taken off the internet and was readily available to anyone interested). Other networks claimed that Aanisa and I had gone into hiding. I was taken to the Lodhi Colony police station and kept there for almost a week. I was grilled by the Intelligence Bureau in the day and left alone at night. Subsequently I was moved to Tihar.

Shackled and chained, I was escorted to my cell in Tihar Jail. A din erupted as I made my way. "Here he comes! There he is!" inmates shouted. Men in plain clothes, jailers and some convicts then pounced on me. I was beaten up badly, taunted and jeered for being a "traitor", a "terrorist". An inmate convicted on triple counts of first-degree murder ordered me to clean the jail lavatory with my shirt. After the reception I had received, I felt I had little choice but to comply. Once these initiation rituals were over, they took me to the cellblock for high-risk inmates. It was only after I protested against this in my formal meeting with an officer that I was kept with other first timers.

I barely slept the next two months. Accounts of my 'treachery' were splashed across Hindi newspapers, and so the hostility of the inmates persisted. My incarceration is a lesson for our crime reporters, who tarnish the image of a person and rely heavily on the police version. They must introspect and have a look at the implications of their reports. I saw many people inside the jail suffering due to one-sided representation in the press.

The mother of all mischievous reports about me was by a Neeta Sharma, crime reporter of *The Hindustan Times* and now with the NDTV. She reported that I had admitted before the court to having ISI links. The report said, "Iftikhar Gilani, 35 year old son-in-law of Hurriyat hardliner Syed Ali Shah Geelani, is believed to have admitted in a city court that he was an agent of Pakistan's spy agency". She went even further, and reported that Syed Ali Geelani was so happy with Iftikhar's working with the ISI that he gave his daughter to him in marriage. What a ridiculous report! Thanks to friends in *The Hindustan Times*, and its Deputy Chairperson Shobna Bharatiya, the paper corrected itself.

The Hindi daily *Hindustan* reported, *Geelani key damad key ghar aaykar chhaapon mein behisab sampati wa smwaidansheil dastaweiz baramad* ("Huge property and sensitive documents recovered from the house of the son-in-law of Geelani during Income Tax raids"). This had not even been claimed by the police in their charge sheet. They had merely shown a recovery of Rs 3,450 from my house. This newspaper carried a series to malign me. One of its reports said that I was in constant touch with international Islamic terrorist organizations. It made its case quoting a neighbour who had said that I used to work in my study till the late hours. Pramod Kumar Singh wrote in *The Pioneer*, "Iftikhar Gilani was the pinpoint man of Syed Salahuddin of *Hizbul Mujahideen*. Investigations have revealed that Iftikhar used to pass information to Salahuddin about the moves of Indian security agencies. He had camouflaged his real motives behind his journalist's façade so well that it took years for security agencies to unmask him, well placed sources said".

The *Statesman* reporter described me as the owner of a company called Wall Media Productions. There were scores of such stories. Since I belonged to the media and my friends know how things work, they were able to make editors see the truth, and stop such malicious campaigns. But this is of little consequence to the lives of hundreds of others who are the victims of such irresponsible reporting.

Such appearances of motivated news items compounded my misery. My wife Aanisa was allowed to visit twice a week, and it was this alone that kept my spirits up. I had told her to leave Delhi and go back to Kashmir with the children. She stayed put, and with support from *The Kashmir Times*, where I work, continued to fight for my freedom and ensured that the lives of our children were not disrupted. Colleagues and friends kept up pressure. National dailies ran lengthy pieces questioning my detention. In the dark jail cell where I lay sleepless night after night, all this comforted me.

The day would begin at 5:30 am with the welcome coarse bellow of the warders because it signalled time for morning tea and the two slices of bread. "Everyone is destined to have a fixed quantity of food while in jail", went one jail myth. "The sooner you eat and are done with this fixed amount, the sooner they'll be done with you". These words would come to mind at every meal and I would not know whether to eat or fast. Mostly I ate.

After a month, they let me subscribe to a newspaper as part of the jail's reforms programme. I chose *The Indian Express*, and it would reach my cell carefully censored by the jail authorities – effectively only the sports pages. I could not complain. There were also mandatory classes from 8 am to 10 am. I was in the programme for literate inmates. Since this was territory no free man wished to enter, inmates imparted their specialized knowledge to other inmates.

White-collar crime convict Yogesh Chowdhry taught us how to defraud banks. A pick-pocket gave lessons on filching wallets. A swami gave legal advice on how to avoid getting convicted for multiple rapes – he would often ask his 'students', booked under Section 376, to narrate their lascivious tales. This titillated the inmates no end.

Another time, a first-timer complained that his prized Honda had been stolen from Karol Bagh. The teacher, a car thief, asked this student what model and colour the car was. "White", the student replied. "And this was the same day that an Esteem too was stolen from there, correct?" the teacher asked. "Why, yes", responded the first-timer. "How do you know?" The teacher cocked his head and said, "Yes, I sold each of them for Rs 150,000". The two men had to be separated.

I was soon shifted to another cellblock, the IGNOU ward – home to corrupt captains of industry. Life was a Sunday here. There was a library, a few computers (which never worked) and a television. It was this section of Tihar Jail that the warders showed off to a delegation from Afghanistan. "Don't do it", I murmured to one of the warders during their inspection tour. "If you show them all this, they'll want to come to India, get arrested and hope to live in this paradise". It's hard maintaining one's sense of humour in jail. I was trying.

When I took ill, I was enrolled in the jail hospital, where I found it difficult to reacquaint myself with a mattress and a pillow. The doctors who treated us had become hardened and cynical and wrote down reams of prescription simply by gazing at the patient, how he looked and walked. Other inmates, tasked with the duty of cleaning the hospital, would not appreciate the easy life the sick were spending. Two patients breathing through oxygen masks were made to get out of bed and make the lavatory sparkle. Perks included milk. A man would bring a jug of milk to the hospital and place it in the middle of the room. All five of us recuperating, two from tuberculosis, would leap at it and polish it off sharing a single plastic glass between ourselves.

We had our own exchange system in Tihar. Coupons in Rs 5 and Rs 10 denominations were used instead of real currency to purchase contraband and to grease palms. If a Gandhi (a Rs 500 note) was smuggled in, it could yield slips worth Rs 750 or more. These slips came in handy. A bag of tobacco that costs Rs 2 in the world outside could go for as much as Rs 400. The rolling paper, incidentally, was free. Thank you, Father Paddy.

Father Paddy was one of many counsellors who would visit the jail weekly. The Holy Bible that he gave away for free was a most sought after commodity. Printed on fine white paper, the bible was most suitable for rolling tobacco and making bidis. I had to guard my Collins dictionary with my life the days Father Paddy was late!

When I became a journalist I never expected to land up in jail. Now, as I walk in the open again and have my liberties restored as a free citizen, I cannot help but think of Tihar and all my friends there. I shall never forget them. I shall never forget Tihar.

This text was presented at the "Crisis/Media" workshop, organized by Sarai-CSDS and the Waag Society in Delhi, March 2003.

Kashmiris may not get a
hundredth of the internation
-al newsprint that Palestine
does, yet in South Asia it is a
"sexy" beat. It is front page/
cover story stuff in the South
Asian media.

SARAI
CSDS
29, Rajpur Road,
Civil Lines,
Delhi,
India.

Covering Kashmir
The Datelines of Despair

BASHARAT PEER

Some years ago during a summer break from university, I walked into the office of Kashmir's most respected daily, *The Kashmir Times*, to meet a senior journalist. I was a starry-eyed political science graduate – wanted to be a journalist and maybe a writer someday. "How hard do I need to work on my English?" I asked him. "To be a journalist in Kashmir, you need to know around thirty words of the English language", he sighed. I left his office a little confused.

The following years of reporting and writing about the conflict in Kashmir made me agree with him. The list is: Fear, arrest, prison, torture, death, Indian security forces, separatist guerrillas/Islamic militants/terrorists, grenades, assault rifles, sandbag bunkers, army installations, hide-outs, crackdowns, search and destroy operations, common people, frustration, tension, anxiety, trauma, democracy, betrayal, self-determination, freedom, peace talks, international community, mediation, non-starter, breakdown, despair and rage. Journalists do pretty well as professionals using various combinations of the above list of words. We do end up using death and despair more often. And reporters eager to 'show, not tell' add to the list phrases and clichés like: eyes welling with tears, choking voice, shivering fingers, hopeless sighs, lives wrinkled by suffering, youth consumed by hopelessness, rage fuelled by humiliation. At times, words like hope, dreams and ambition also find their way into copy.

Kashmir may not get a hundredth of the international newsprint that Palestine does, yet in South Asia it is a 'sexy' beat. It is front page/cover story stuff in South Asian media. Reporters vie for stories; still, the above-mentioned words and phrases suffice most of the time. Dexterity with permutations and combinations does not help; the story of Kashmir helps. It does not change.

The joke about a wire service reporter in Srinagar is that he wrote the basic format for his news stories years ago. He keeps altering names and figures in his basic report which reads, "At least seven protesting Kashmiri villagers were killed and fifteen others injured, three of them seriously, when Indian paramilitary forces opened fire on demonstrators at X village three kilometres from Y in south Kashmir. The villagers were demonstrating against the alleged custodial killings of five local youth".

Or, "Five civilians were killed and twenty injured when separatist militants hurled a grenade at an installation of Indian security forces in the north Kashmir town, Baramulla. The grenade missed the target and exploded on the street. The injured have been rushed to a local hospital. A ten year old boy/a youth/a woman is critically wounded". The stories hardly ever carry that boy's or youth's or woman's name. Names do not matter. They do not tell us the story of a person who lived with a name from childhood to adolescence to youth or maybe middle age before he/she fell to a bullet. For all those people whom bullets mutated into statistics, a carefully chosen name exists: collateral damage. It tells neither about a person's religion nor his/her ethnicity. It tells nothing. Such reports constitute most of the news that came from Kashmir since 1989. Only figures of the death tolls lower in the wintry months between December and March – winters in Kashmir are harsh and relatively peaceful. And news stories written for international wires or newspapers have an additional paragraph on the background of the conflict. In a 1993 magazine story that paragraph read, "More than 11,600 lives have been claimed in Jammu-Kashmir, where Muslim rebels have been fighting for independence for more than five years". I checked the same magazine this month; the paragraph had been updated to, "More than 50,000 lives have been claimed..."

Anyone who takes interest in reports from a place like Kashmir, which geography has placed somewhere between the remote Himalayas and has neither oil nor gas reserves, certainly deserves to know more.

Reporters in Kashmir do write special/interesting stories too; they write profiles of boys who wanted to be doctors and turned suicide bombers; they write about these boys' mothers serving them tea while narrating the last meeting, when the would-be suicide bomber was an unknown, unheard of son. They write about village women raped/allegedly raped, (depending on editorial policy/degrees of conscience/fears/apprehensions or to quote my ageing father, "foolhardiness") mostly by Indian security forces and at times by 'unknown gunmen'; about the children of almost 4000 Kashmiri men who disappeared after being arrested by Indian forces, holding placards at demonstrations enquiring about their fathers;

Fear, arrest, prison, torture, death, Indian security forces, separatist guerrillas/ Islamic militants/ terrorists,

about their mothers earning titles like 'half-widows', waiting for years for the husbands to return.

They write about tourist guides nostalgic for the time when Kashmir was the second-largest tourist destination in Asia, before the first bomb exploded on a street in Srinagar announcing the birth of armed militancy amidst a population historically reputed for their docility, even bordering on cowardice; about the Pandits who lived harmoniously with Muslims for centuries but cast their lot politically with India and migrated to the Indian plains after certain militant groups killed some prominent Pandits.

Kashmir does not just have reporters; veteran Kashmir watchers and syndicated columnists thrive in hordes. They tell in cold black print the reasons that fuelled the boiling rage of militancy, reasons such as that for a petty amount the British sold Kashmir to a petty Hindu chieftain; that the Hindu ruler and his descendents ruled Kashmir oppressively till 1947; that the United Nations Security Council resolutions for a plebiscite in Kashmir remain unimplemented half a century after India and Pakistan fought their first war over Kashmir, their first diplomatic battle in Geneva.

That even Sheikh Mohammed Abdullah, the popular leader of Kashmir who led the movement against monarchy till 1947, supported India when the Hindu ruler signed the instrument of accession with India, and who was later betrayed. That even the autonomy granted by the instrument of accession was shredded to pieces by New Delhi's puppet regime during the Sheikh's jail days between 1953 and 1975. That the Kashmiris who watched the portrayal of the unrelenting Libyan revolutionary, Omar Mukhtar, on celluloid looked at the Sheikh's acceptance of Indian authority on his release as a betrayal after decades of his struggle.

That India rigged the state elections of 1987, which the Sheikh's flamboyant son Farooq Abdullah along with Indian National Congress was losing against a spontaneously formed opposition Muslim United Front (MUF). That MUF polling agents and candidates were arrested and tortured.

They also write about the consequences: That Mohammed Yousuf Shah, a MUF candidate whose defeat was engineered and who was arrested, heads the largest Kashmiri guerrilla outfit, Hizb-ul-Mujahideen. That his polling agent, a wiry youth, a cardiac patient, Yasin Malik heads another group, the pro-independence Jammu and Kashmir Liberation

assault rifles, sandbag bunkers, army installations, hide-outs, crackdowns, search and destroy operations, common people, frustration, tension, anxiety, trauma, democracy,

Front, which fired the first bullet in the armed rebellion against India in the winter of 1989. That the winter of 1989 was when Kashmir became news, news that continues to read like a headline I saw on *The Kashmir Times* front page last month: "26 Killed in a Day of Routine Violence".

This winter is the fourteenth since 1989. As snow whitens the green peaks of Kashmir's mountains, we hear that the winds of change are blowing. The media is telling the story of a thaw between India and Pakistan: of Pakistan declaring a unilateral ceasefire on the Line of Control, the temporary border dividing Kashmir between India and Pakistan; of the nuclear neighbours not shelling eachother's positions. Of Indian Prime Minister Atal Bihari Vajpayee, who once wrote a poem asking how could the pilots who dropped the bombs on Hiroshima and Nagasaki sleep at night, shaking hands with Pakistani president Musharraf in Pakistan and describing him as the "biggest leader from Pakistan".

Of the resumption of air links between India and Pakistan, cancelled after the December 13th, 2001, terror attack on Indian parliament. Of a train named Samjhauta (Compromise) Express chugging along the tracks between India and Pakistan. Sounds good! Sounds great! But reporters in Srinagar carry on filing the usual reports. A recent report read, "60 injured in Kashmir violence".

Militant groups do not accept the ceasefire; they believe it is mere political posturing. Traditional Indian and Pakistani positions on Kashmir remain unchanged. For Pakistan, Kashmir remains the "jugular vein". For India, she is the "integral part" and "the test case of its secular credentials", which were badly torn apart in the 2002 pogrom in the Western Indian state of Gujarat, wherein Hindu fanatics killed around 2000 local Muslims after a Muslim mob killed 57 Hindu militants.

Kashmiris fear it might be just another round of "PLEASE BUSH, PLEASE BLAIR, INDO-PAK CHAMPIONSHIP", and the shadows of death and despair will keep lurking. A twenty-one year old neighbour of mine, who loves Ezra Pound and is irritated with Hanif Qureishi using "f**k" too often in a play tells me, "Nothing will change in Kashmir". Many others I spoke to agree. I feel like agreeing, but hope this time around we are wrong.

grenades, betrayal, self-determination, freedom, peace talks, international community, mediation, non-starter, breakdown, despair and rage.

Mumbai (Dongri)-Gujarat-Mumbai-Kashmir
Pages from my Diary

ZAINAB BAWA

was born on February 28th, 1979. I spent two precious years of my childhood, from the ages of two to four, in Dongri, a Muslim-dominated area in Mumbai. Dongri is an old apart of the city, not unlike Paharganj in Delhi. It has old structures, shrines, small industries where sweets and masalas are manufactured. It is an area which has a charm all of its own. There are certain areas in Mumbai City such as Nagpada, Agripada, Dongri and Mohammed Ali Road that are essentially Muslim dominated areas, and are popularly (!) referred to as 'tense' areas, especially during volatile times (like during an India-Pakistan cricket match). I am now beginning to understand why these areas are popularly known as 'tense'.

I cherish the childhood years that I spent in Dongri. I grew up in what I would call 'a mixed cultural environment'. I grew up visiting different religious carnivals, listening to *qawalis* and Samantha Fox, Michael Jackson and Madonna – all at the same time. I have lived the experience of Mumbai through Dongri and the surrounding *Imambada* area, which is known for its kite-making industry. The kite of my life is made up of many coloured scraps of paper, and this is what makes it all the more interesting for me.

I am Muslim, but perhaps this identity was never very crucial for me. I almost looked at it as a negligible portion of my life, nothing too significant to define me. Riots took place in Mumbai during December 1992 to January 1993, yet these never affected me drastically, though my own family and friends experienced violence during the riots. In fact, the riots produced in me a sense of solidarity, an 'Indian-ness' which manifested itself through concerns for the betterment of this country. I began to work assiduously towards doing what I thought was 'good for my country'. I looked at myself as if I was the very essence of 'Youth', somebody who had an inner power and a deep potential to contribute to the advancement of the Indian nation.

Ten years down the line, on February 28th, 2002, my beliefs and convictions received a jolt. Where were I, and the Indian nation, heading towards? For my birthday on that day of that year, I received a piece of news – "a compartment of the Sabarmati Express carrying *Kar Sevaks* is burnt at Godhra", "communal riots hit Gujarat". Prior to this, September 11th had occurred. I guess September 11th began to work on my unconscious and began to make me slightly conscious of my Muslim identity. But Gujarat made me completely conscious of my Muslim and Indian identity. And to top it all, in March I undertook my first visit to the state of Jammu & Kashmir. Then began a process of confrontation – deep confrontation, violent confrontation, profound confrontation, vehement confrontation – with and about myself, my beliefs, my relationship with the Indian State, my Indian identity, my Muslim-Indian identity and my Indian-Muslim identity.

My visit to Kashmir was important and interesting. Sitting in Mumbai, I had never really thought much about Kashmir. Perhaps Kashmir affects the Delhi person more than it affects me, the Mumbai person. Gujarat affects me, the Mumbai person, more than the Delhi person.

I want to bring in here a piece which I wrote in my diary on March 29th, 2002:

Kasheer[1]: An Outsider's Experience of the Valley
While I am writing my thoughts and perspectives on Kashmir, my mind drifts towards the magnificent mountains which surround Kashmir from all sides. Mountains have this amazing capacity to make you feel humble. Yet mountains are not arrogant. They are omnipotent, omniscient.

Sitting in my little flat in Mumbai, all I can see from outside my grill window are huge concrete buildings. Buildings look hopelessly helpless. After all, all they can do is to stand and keep standing. Mountains have life; buildings are lifeless.

Last year, I developed an enchanted attachment with the idea of visiting Kashmir. This attraction developed as a result of my interactions with Kashmiris and people working towards restoring peace in the Valley. All along, I had never given very serious thought to Kashmir. My interest in Kashmir developed because of my association with an organization which was trying to understand the nuances of the India-Pakistan conflict. This led me to participate in many discussions about Kashmir, but I could never really understand the complexity of the issue.

While in Mumbai, one of my main sources of information about Kashmir was the media, particularly newspapers. Everyday, all the knowledge that I got about Kashmir was to do with the troubles occurring there. This would bring various pictures and images to my mind. I thought of Kashmir as a place with old and dingy brick houses, masked men, lifeless streets and scared people huddled inside their houses. Some of my interactions with people working in the region gave me a gloomy picture of Kashmiris and I began to think of them as people who have no hope and who are somehow 'going through the motions' of life.

March 7th, 2002
[Cut to Jawahar Tunnel!] As I passed through the darkness of the 4.55-kilometer long tunnel, I suddenly found my mind becoming empty and blank. As the vehicle moved out of the tunnel, I experienced a feeling of being absorbed by the Valley. Moving further, I was completely lost in the remarkable beauty surrounding me. The snow-capped mountain peaks seemed to join me in my laughter as I discovered ecstasy in being insignificant and minute. The roads along the towns were peopled with scenes of women drying clothes, children with rosy cheeks playing and enjoying themselves, willow trees, countryside landscapes, and so on. In the midst of all this wonderment, my mind began to feel restless. I tried to analyze the reasons for this sudden unease. What could it be? Could it be this large expanse of nature? Could it be a different culture?

I realized that this unease was due to the uniformed guards standing on the roads with their guns. The presence of the BSF and the Army men every furlong gave me a terribly disconcerting feeling. I felt like someone was trying to stop me – stop me from thinking, stop me from being free. Though the soldiers were merely standing on the roads and none of them did anything to me, I could feel, psychologically, that an authority was being imposed upon me.

For somebody who comes from a free city, this experience can range from mild disturbance to profound devastation, depending on how well you can handle yourself. This very insight forced me to think about freedom and what freedom means to me. How free are we?

Kashmir forced me rethink the institution of governance in India. India is diverse, and I need not say much about its diversity because it is a lived experience. Delhi is as foreign to me, a Mumbai resident, as it is to a non-Indian (whom we would call foreigner!). So I am a foreigner in different parts of India just as much as a white, black or an oriental tourist is! The idea of an 'Indian Identity' forced me to think very hard, both during the Gujarat riots and the Kashmir experience, about lots of questions. For instance, does someone have the right to define for me what is Indian?

After Gujarat, perhaps every Muslim seems to have come under scrutiny, and this scrutiny is about 'patriotism' and about proving allegiance to the Indian state. Every incident after Gujarat has made me wonder, "Whom else do I have to satisfy about my Indian-ness, and how often will I keep doing this?",

The media has played a crucial role in this regard. Indian cricket victories, terrorist attacks (wherever they occur), terrorism legislation – all form the headlines of newspapers. Each piece of reportage works on my subconscious. Bollywood films run to full houses if they talk about Pakistan, Islam, Muslims and terrorism in the most jingoistic manner – the louder and more vulgar the dialogues, the greater the applause, the more full houses! Every little insignificant aspect of life, including sport and entertainment, becomes commercially popular if it is 'patriotized'. Patriotism is the new mantra of advertising!

Here is a piece which I wrote in April 2003, while Gulf War II was going on:

I do not live in a war zone. I live in a state of terror. Terror, which is perpetual, which assumes various proportions. There is terror inside of me, outside of me. Terror about who is lurking in those distant shadows. Is it my enemy or my foe? Oh, it is the security guard! He is here for my security. He has a naked gun in his hand. The gun is ignorant, but the guard is not. The strength, might, and power of the gun give me courage to muster up courage. I am feeling safe. My breath is calm and smooth. So is my heartbeat. I am safe.

Suddenly, the guard advances towards me. His naked gun advances too. He comes close enough, looks into my eyes, peers. His looks are piercing. He says, "Sorry pal, I have to shoot you down. I have to shoot you so that you become (vulgar) news. The headlines should shriek, 'We gunned down an enemy spy'".

What is my crime? What is my sin?

"Nuffing! Nuffing's your crime; Nuffing's your sin. You are simply going to be a martyr, a martyr of the 'Other Side', and a source of security for 'Our Side'. You see, buddy, there are many whom I have to protect, many whom I have to assure that the world is a safe place to be in, to live in, as long as I am there. So put your faith (and money) in me (and my guns).

For as long as I am there, you will be there. Your progeny will be there. Safe, calm and soothed. And you, buddy, will help me comfort the souls of this world, souls who are in un-rest and discomfort because the Other is there. The enemy is there.

"And they, these perturbed and disturbed souls, need to be protected, and made to feel secure. Your death shall bring them security. Your dead body shall unnerve their perturbed souls. Your death will be their joy".

"But what about tomorrow", I asked, "Whom will you gun down tomorrow? How long will you continue to make them feel safe, feel secure, feel soothed? Will they ever cease to be insecure?"

"No, not until I know", said he, "...as long as there are weapons, as long as there are bombs, as long as there are walls in people's minds, as long as people don't know. (the unknown enemy is always greater than the known), as long as we don't let them know, fear will prevail. The state of terror shall continue. And there shall be martyrs like you. Whom we shall slay alive".

Saying this, he shot a bullet into my skull

And the next day, I, an unknown citizen, became known. I became The Enemy.

Kashmir inspired in me a journey of exploration. Till today, I remember that I was introduced to everyone in Kashmir as, "...she is from India!"

Today I can afford to laugh about this, but back then, it was astonishment, a sense of irritation and at times, even anger, to be introduced as an Indian when all that I had known always was that "Kashmir is a part of India". I was more Indian in Kashmir, but when I am back here, in my own and known domain, I am questioned about my Indian-ness. Not directly; yet, everyday and through every indirect means! What kind of atmosphere is being generated? I know, and I am afraid of admitting this to myself, but how long can I protect myself from the truth?

The journey that I underwent through the Kashmir experience motivated me to bring this experience to more people of my generation. In June 2003, I organized the first exchange programme of students from Mumbai to Kashmir. Here are a few words from a diary that I kept during that trip

July 1st, 2003
My visits to Kashmir have been a process of building relationships with individuals whom I had not seen before, but had heard a lot about (through the media of course!).

"At a certain point I lost track of you.
You needed me. You needed to perfect me:
In your absence you polished me into the Enemy.
Your history gets in the way of my memory."
Agha Shahid Ali, "Farewell" from The Country Without A Post Office

Kashmir was 'the Other' for me. But travelling to Kashmir changed me; I could not be the same person that I was. How could I? I had seen the other face of India, the face of militaristic democracy. My idea of India changed. Today, my idea of India is very personal to me. India is dear to me, but Indian governance is not. I trust India, but not her governors. I relate to India, but not to the people who claim to be her 'guardians'.

Kashmir has been my journey of learning, of understanding the relationship between the individual and state, the individual and society; of understanding culture and identity from a new paradigm. I owe my growth to Kashmir, to the moments of introspection, the intricate questions which disturb me as much as they disturb others around me. Kashmir has taught me to question everything – from my beliefs, to everything happening around me.

Kashmir is not just a hotbed of conflict and a volatile region in South Asia; it is a case of skewed democracy, of not respecting people's wishes and aspirations. Kashmir is not the only case; the same issues are at stake in the North-East of India, Palestine, and elsewhere. Each of these struggles has valuable lessons for us. But Kashmir is important. The purpose of undertaking this exchange was to re-examine 'reality' with one's own eyes, with the eyes of the mind. There are no ultimate solutions, no final answers, but there is a journey to tread – the journey of asking questions, of looking for options, of collaborative partnerships, and above all, of keeping the mind open and not accepting anything as final – and mapping the road. This journey motivated me to pursue and organize the exchange that took place from June 8th to June 26th.

Gujarat made me pessimistic and worrisome, but today I am beginning to realize that there is a need to take stock of the situation and move forward. I do not know what consequences will emerge from efforts like these and the different efforts of several others throughout the world, but what needs to be done has to be done. It is said that the greatest noises of the world come from silences; I want to speak.

July 1st, 2003

Silences can be deafening. Silences can be loud. I will tell you a story:

A story of every house. It happens in my house as well. Father and I fight because we do not agree. We do not agree on values, on issues, on thoughts. But while we fight, mother is in a state of tension, a state of nerves (her nervous system is completely nervous, tense). She is struggling with her nerves. She wants Peace.

She intervenes, says, "Be Silent! We should not fight. After all, we are a family. We should maintain Peace". Father and I stop. I am speechless before her tears. Father says, "Look what you have done to your mother. You have shattered her Peace. You have shattered the Peace of this House!" (Have I?) I stop. There is calm in the house, but I am seething from within. I was not heard. I was not given space to express myself. Do I want this Peace?

NOTES

1. Kashmir was known as Kasheer until the British came and changed the name to Kashmir.

War Correspondences
FIRST PERSON PLURAL

Thoughts on Afghanistan in 5 parts

MEENA NANJI

1. March 2003

It's around 10pm, and pitch black. There are no streetlights. I am in a large Land Rover with an assortment of journalists, aid workers and diplomatic types. We're lost. Streets have no names, they all look exactly the same: rows of brown adobe walls high enough not to be seen over, punctuated by small, indistinguishable, metal gates that mark entrances. Then someone hears a faint sound that may be music. We drive towards it and soon it's unmistakable. Drum and bass beats throb into the emptiness surrounding us. We start to see a few parked cars, then more and more. Outside one gate there are people milling around. Armed guards look on furtively, scanning us intensely as we file in. Inside are a small courtyard, and a two-story house filled with crowds of trendily-dressed people, mostly in their 20s. Alcohol is flowing like the newly rain-filled Kabul River and all kinds of smokes fill the air. The first person I meet is a man who's set up a mini-mobile circus for kids, where they make up their own stories, costumes and performances. The aim of the circus, he says, is to make children laugh. Excitedly he shows me pictures on his laptop of kids who've had their legs blown off by landmines, now wearing stilts in these outrageous, long, pointy, brightly coloured hats and costumes. They look amazing. Other people I meet are setting up radio stations, building water pipes, bringing in laser-eye surgery equipment, de-mining the still mine-infested countryside, opening trendy restaurants. They all seem incredibly bright, motivated, articulate and thrilled with whatever it is that they are doing. It gets late and the dancing gets hot and heavy. The lights are down low, the music up loud. Not an Afghan in sight. Welcome to Kabul 2003. Or at least one section of it.

2.

Afghanistan doesn't really make the headlines anymore, unless one of the hundreds of international aid workers or American troops is attacked, or if more than thirty Taliban are killed in the East, in the South, always in mountain caves. We hear nothing of the struggles of everyday life; the small, mundane things that are made almost insurmountable by the destruction wrought during the last twenty-five years of war. We hear little about how people manage without running water, without electricity, little of the 'reconstruction effort', its successes and failures. We hear little of the fate of Afghan women who were so recently used to galvanize the US call to war. We are told that they are now 'free', and can go to school, get a job. Not about the daily terror they face, the fear of being abducted or raped, of forced marriages, and of the continuing tradition of violence, physical and mental, against them. We hear nothing of the past violations, the years of attacks, torture, deaths, fuelled largely by outsiders, and what the consequences of their actions are now. Did they just disappear? Did everyone just forget about these atrocities, and who committed them? Did they even really happen? Is it possible to just bury the past, hope that its consequences won't erupt out of the earth and start afresh?

A Truth and Reconciliation Commission for Afghanistan has not been publicly talked about, let alone set up. There are no Inquiries for 'healing'. No trials for war criminals. Instead, war criminals are the ones who have had a mantle of legitimacy conferred upon them by the international community, and are back in power, guns in hand. International power alliances and corporate media are participating in a Bury and Forget Past Crimes

Commission, but for Afghanistan this is merely business as usual.

History has been re-written for the Afghans by CNN, by the BBC, by men thousands of miles away who sit in plush offices making decisions that affect the life and death of ordinary Afghan people. But their way of writing history is curious: they do not strive to include as much information as possible, but the least amount. They want to reduce this history to one paragraph, one sentence, one line if possible, easily said and more easily digested in the space of the sixty seconds they have to utter it.

So what we see most often now is a history of omission, of erasure and/or substitution. It might actually be a good project to document the progress of erasure in corporate media: In the 1980s we knew this about Afghanistan, now we know this even less.

A History of Forgetting
Example:
In the 1980s the religious fundamentalists, referred to in this text as Islamists, who threw acid in the faces of women, sliced off their breasts and partook in other unspeakable acts, were promoted by western governments and mainstream media as Afghanistan's freedom fighters, bravely resisting the Soviet infidels. Their independence struggle was branded a 'jihad', a good snappy, jingle/logo that the CIA latched on to, and used, to bring good Muslims from around the globe to unite and fight the good fight. Many people responded to this not-so-holy-call, most of them poor, uneducated, unemployed. The pay was good, in addition to three meals a day, and clothes on their backs. The cause could not be faulted. Though there were true 'mujahideen', Afghans that resisted the occupation independently, it was the zealots who received the bulk of the $6 billion dollars in training, arms and funding that the U.S poured in, first covertly, then overtly. These mercenaries fought hard and long with US bought guns, matching funds from Saudi and Pakistani support and direction. It was a proxy war for the US, and no body bags filled with Americans flew home. Communism was going to be defeated, at any cost, by Afghans fighting for their own country, Muslims fighting alongside their brothers, against the godless evil of communism. At least a million Afghans died over this 10-year period, at the end of which the US cried victory over the Soviets.[1]

With the ouster of the Soviets in 1989, the US left too. There was no repatriation of fighters from other countries, who now knew nothing except how to fight. There was no disarmament program: the country was awash with the latest arms technology – the most modern machinery Afghanistan possessed by a long shot. Afghanistan was left with no reconstruction help and with fundamentalist groups armed to the teeth.[2] They fell into fighting amongst themselves. News of these internecine battles dropped off the radar in the West. There was an almost complete news blackout for at least four years until the Taliban began to make their appearance.[3] Thousands of Afghan civilians were killed during this period, but who in the outside world really knew or cared about it?

Then Came September 11, 2001
Now those very same freedom fighters are 'Islamic terrorists'. Gulbuddin Hekmatyr, Abd Sayyaf, Osama bin Laden, those who once received the bulk of US and Pakistani support

are now called, by the US administration, the world's "greatest threat to peace". Corporate media follows the lead of the US government in denouncing them as extreme, fanatic, and worst of all, Evil.

Corporate media makes no inquiries. It assumes that there are no dots to connect over the evolution of a 'movement'. 'Evil' is a blanket term that renders cause and effect irrelevant: Evil just exists, and one must either overcome it, or be overcome by it. It's a Manichean view of the world, the 'you're either with us or against us' logic that denies complexity, cause, dialogue, engagement, and imagination. In this case it doesn't even ask why so many disaffected young people are joining the ranks of Islamists. It's as if even asking the question will somehow make this 'movement' worthwhile of inquiry; give it credence as a phenomenon with an evolution that grew out of certain circumstances; raise it above its current status of being 'terrorism' – a random and chaotic force that has no reason for being except its inherent evil – that must be stamped out at all costs.

3.
"Afghanistan has experienced atrocity after atrocity for the last twenty years. First it was the Soviets who came destroyed and left. Next the mujahideen destroyed and killed, then the Taliban did the same, then the Americans, and now the mujahideen are back".
- Nilab, RAWA member, March 2003[4]

I keep watching the news, watching reports about Afghanistan, watching documentaries – about the women, about aid groups, health care issues, fighters, trying to catch even a glimpse, a hint, of an essence of feeling, but it is elusive, it cannot be captured, just as it is impossible to describe heat or cold: you can only know it if you have experienced it and even then it is impossible to describe. So with pain. So with the irrevocableness of loss: it is impossible to 're-vocalise' the depth of sadness over lives disrupted and lost. It is impossible to capture or re-present. How does one even begin to approach the extent of feeling over the destruction not only of one's own life, but also of one's family, community, home-land? And of knowing that it is impossible to restore anything from the loss created.

Ordinary Afghan people have suffered, and the next wave of suffering came even before they had no time to get over the first one, supplanting the old suffering with new, without any time for recovery, for processing, for physical, mental or emotional reconstitution.

Recently, war trauma experienced by western journalists and war reporters has been getting some attention as a cause for concern. But there is little of this attention on the population that suffered the war.

A 2001 World Health Organisation report estimated that 60% of Afghanistan's population suffers from mental disorder. "Twenty-three years of war have ravaged the health of psychosocial functioning of the people in Afghanistan. Killings, executions, massive persecution, forced internal displacement, fear of mines, have left an indelible mark on the population ... There are virtually no opportunities for treatment under the current cirucmstances".[5]

According to this and other reports, women are particularly susceptible to depression, as a large percentage of them have suffered atrocities such as kidnapping, forced mar-riage, rape, amputation, torture and other abuses. Anxiety disorders, nightmares, fear of loud noises and fear of the future are some of the overt symptoms of their condition.

A 1997 UNICEF report states that 97% of Afghan children have witnessed the violence of war. Another 60% or so have lost a close family relative.

In a Pakistani refugee camp I met a ten year old Afghan boy whose father had lost an arm in Afghanistan. The boy didn't want to go to Afghanistan because he thought everyone there would lose an arm. A young Afghan girl told me she wanted to forget the past,

because it was so horrible to think about. Then she added that the past wouldn't forget her.

How do children who have never experienced a safe, secure environment grow up? What do children who have seen their parents blown up, who have lost limbs, or have witnessed horror but never peace, think about the world? How does one rebuild when hearts and minds are shattered and bloody? "How can things so terrible, such personal and historical traumas be over? Is it possible for them to be consigned to an untroubled or untroubling past?"[6]

The pain and trauma of twenty-three years of war remains unarticulated and unexpressed. After a while, perhaps, the suffering cannot even be expressed, it becomes un-utterable, and is literally un-speakable: it is too terrible to speak of. The memory of an entire people is rendered silent. But what happens to the past in such silence?

4.
"Remembering is an Act of Resistance"[7]
This phrase resonates with the Afghan women I speak to. There is an overwhelming sense that their stories will not be remembered, that 'History' will not remember things the way they remember them. From minute details to the big things: why did fighting break out to begin with, the fact that perpetrators of attacks have gone unpunished, the fact that their lives have been stolen from people, the feelings of despair, rage, anguish, helplessness, none of this ever makes History. They are eager for their stories to be told, to be recorded, and documented. Besides validating their experience, the survival of their remembrances resists the twisting of facts, resists falsities that are re-presented as 'truth', resists the re-writing of History by dominating governments and corporate media who need events to fit their narrow, self-serving view of the world so that their power remains intact. These remembrances resist erasure of the way things happened.

5.
Flying from Delhi to Kabul one passes the Hindu Kush mountains, a view so spectacular one might think one's died and gone to heaven. Not an hour later, you might think you've landed in hell. Nothing prepared me for Kabul airport. Adorning the runway, as we screeched to a slow taxi, were bombed-out, burnt-up, mangled civil and military airplanes that

A 1997 UNICEF report states that 97% of Afghan children have witnessed the violence of war. Another 60% or so have lost a close family relative.

looked like prehistoric carcasses of gigantic beasts, their shapes obscenely twisted out of recognition, their guts splayed out for all to see. Though only machines, the violence that had been done to them was shockingly visceral. One couldn't help but think about people, flesh and blood, who must have experienced the same violence, or worse. As we were disembarking, a seasoned journalist that I'd been sitting next to on the plane saw my expression, patted my back and said, "Don't worry, you'll get used to it".

I never did get used to it. I couldn't get over the ruins that overwhelm the city, the burnt-out tanks that litter the countryside, the remnants of buildings and streets, wreckages of people with missing limbs and crushed faces.

Kabul is full of wild contradictions, surreal juxtapositions, and paradox. Devastating ruins sit in a stunning location; majestic mountains that surround the city and seem right up in your face. The poverty and deprivation is matched by unrivalled hospitality and grace. A palpable feeling of excitement in the air, the sincere desire and hope for a chance to reassemble lives stands in stark opposition to an underlying sense of uncertainty, fear and tension.

In Kabul, certainly, extraordinary work is being done that makes a positive dent in the lives of individual Kabulis. Aside from the availability of more schools and basic health care, there are also extraordinary people who are approaching the issues of how to imagine a city and build it from ground up with striking creativity and innovation. Many young Afghans have opportunities they couldn't have dreamed of a few years ago: training in media production, driving lessons for women, markets are buzzing with activity, beauty shops and photography studios, both banned under the Taliban, are booming with business. But these are just surface changes.

The lives of foreign workers play out practically in a bubble, mimicking the colonial structures of 'expat' life in many other countries of the third world. While the areas they live and work in now have electricity and running water, Afghan populated areas have virtually none. Foreigners can spend time in the cosy comfort of a couple of cafés serving cappuccino and chocolate croissants, with internet connectivity and satellite television (where US special ops guys watch either Fox International or the Fashion Channel non-stop), and a swirl of expensive restaurants and social activity that is justified by the sentiment that life has to be liveable for them to be able to work in Kabul.

But life for most Afghans remains bleak. The reconstruction efforts are much too little, far too late. And they rest on the tip of a seething volcano.

In an interview with Weeda, a representative of RAWA (Revolutionary Association of the Women of Afghanistan, the indefatigable women's rights group) in December 2001, she stated: "The Northern Alliance members have cut their beards and their hair, they have put on western suits and are now presentable to the world. But they have not changed their way of thinking. They are anti-democratic, anti-woman and anti-modern. No fundamentalists (Islamists) should be included in government. If they are, there will only be more corruption and killing. Nothing will change and the rule of the gun will be the only law in Afghanistan".

Almost two years after the fall of the Taliban, Islamists make up the majority of the new government of Afghanistan. There is no law except the rule of the gun, and corruption and killing by government forces is widespread. Regional warlords have tremendous power in their areas, and the central government which holds sway only in Kabul is deeply fractured.

There has been no disarmament of local militias or factions. The Taliban are gaining in strength, sometimes working in cahoots with the US' biggest ally during the Soviet occupation, Gulbuddin Hekmatyr.

One would think that the US administration would learn from the recent past and heed RAWA's call of having no Islamists in the new government. No such luck. Or logic. Not only does the US not support this notion, one could argue that they are once again actively promoting Islamists to power. The US is still funding regional warlords who undermine the central government and the handpicked President, Hamid Karzai.[8] Even within the central government, the US is tacitly supporting Islamist elements. One can only assume that with all the US' heat and anger over fundamentalist Islam, with all its rhetoric of helping the Afghans build a democratic nation of peace and stability, in actuality a peaceful Afghanistan does not serve US interests. It seems that a fractious, unstable, terrorized Afghanistan serves US interests better.

Talking to people in Kabul, it seems that President Karzai is generally liked. Although Afghans seem to know that Karzai has been a friend of the CIA for many years, and, during the Taliban period, he served as an advisor to UNOCAL (the American-based oil company looking to build Central Asian gas pipelines), they say that he isn't a war criminal like the others, he hasn't killed innocent people. He might even be a good man, but no one knows for sure. He has no power. He cannot do what he wants so people don't even know what he really does want.

Certainly Karzai's power is limited. Driving around Kabul one sees enormous billboards, erected on the hillsides, of Ahmed Shah Massoud, the Islamist leader of the Northern Alliance. In shops, businesses, even in government offices, one see photos not of Karzai, but of Massoud. It is obvious who rules Kabul.

Inexplicably, Europeans, especially the French, love Massoud. They consider him to be the Che Guevara of Afghanistan, the handsome, well-dressed Lion of Panjshir, a hero. So what if he was responsible for the deaths of thousands of civilian Afghans – it was war and he was the good guy. Not so. The best that can be said about Massoud was his military acumen. His participation in civilian rule during the presidency of Rabbani (1990-92) was a bloody mess, when over 25,000 people were killed in Kabul alone and the city completely razed by rocket shelling between forces of Massoud and Hekmatyr.[9]

Massoud was assassinated a few days before September 11. It is his progeny who now surround Karzai and hold powerful positions: the Defence Minister, Mohammed Qasim Fahim (whose animosity towards Karzai is well-known, as well as his brutal methods of control – Kabulis shudder at the mention of his name), Foreign Minister Dr. Abdullah Abdullah, and Education Minister Younis Qanooni are all former Northern Alliance commandos. Their high positions are payment for helping the US offensive against the Taliban in 2001. Unfortunately, their agenda doesn't seem so different from that of the Taliban. Recently their looting of land, and Taliban-era methods of intimidating citizens have come to the attention of international human rights groups and even the UN.[10]

There are many other ministries that make up the government. They compete with each other rather than work in a spirit of co-operation. There is much fighting and backbiting, with each ministry accusing the others of corruption and ethnic nepotism.

Of Major Concern is the Judiciary.
"Afghanistan's legal system has collapsed … There are few trained lawyers, little physical infrastructure and no complete record of the country's laws. Under successive regimes, laws have been administered for mostly political ends with few protections of the rights of individuals to a fair trial".[11]

Karzai had an opportunity to positively influence the legal system with his appointment of the Supreme Court Chief Justice. He even promised to keep in line with Afghanistan's constitution (the Bonn Agreement signed in December 2001 re-established the 1964 Constitution of Afghanistan) which states that the Chief Justice be under sixty years old, and that he be educated in all sources of Afghan law, religious and secular. However, Karzai re-appointed Fazl Hadi Shinwari, an ally of the Saudi-backed pro-Wahabi Islamist leader Abd Sayyaf. Shinwari is in his eighties and does not have formal training in secular sources of law.[12]

Shinwari had been in Pakistan for forty years teaching in Taliban Deobandi *madrassas*. He was brought back to Afghanistan in 2001 – by the Americans. Once appointed, he moved quickly to consolidate his power, packing the nine member Supreme Court with 137 sympathetic Islamist mullahs, bringing back the Taliban's dreaded Department of Vice and Virtue and calling for Taliban-style punishments to implement Shari'a law.

For women this is truly a nail in the coffin. Their mobility and opportunities are already severely restricted. Now, if they report abuse and by some miracle it reaches court, they have no chance of retribution. If a woman is beaten or raped, the overwhelming attitude is: "What did she do to provoke this action?" She is held responsible while the perpetrator is considered merely reactive. Shari'a law is used to support this belief. Women who do report abuses are often put in prison, purportedly as protection for themselves. The Women's Ministry is also of no help. It is highly ineffective and is considered a device by Karzai not to deal with women's rights: it exists only in name, to keep the international community at bay. It has no implementation power and no legal jurisdiction. The most it can do is make recommendations, but even this is questionable since many women working at the ministry are deeply conservative themselves.

Most ominously perhaps, Chief Justice Shinwari announced in October 2003 that talks between the government and "moderate elements" of the Taliban were taking place, sup-posedly to limit the Taliban's destructive activities.[13] 'Moderate elements of the Taliban' is like saying 'moderate elements of the Nazis'. It seems that the way is being paved for Taliban re-entry into the governing of Afghanistan.

The Supreme Court has also effectively taken justice for past crimes off the agenda. This in turn has contributed to a sense among commanders that they can act as they wish with no risk of punishment, and so they carry on their human rights abuses across the countryside with impunity.[14]

Which brings us back full circle. Why is there no call for a Truth and Reconciliation Committee? Why are there no trials for war criminals? How can we justify the re-instatement of people we know are war criminals?

How easily we as members of the international community forget about the suffering of the Afghan people. We refuse to look at Afghanistan with depth and complexity, instead consoling ourselves with the donation of pennies that go towards a nebulous 'reconstruction'. Not asking difficult questions about the profoundly complicated situation of Afghanistan doesn't mean they don't exist. It is unrealistic for international powers, who have once again contributed heavily to the installation of destructive structures of power in Afghanistan, to expect anything other than the worsening situation that is rapidly unfolding there.

NOTES

1. Cooley, John. *Unholy Wars: Afghanistan, America and International Terrorism* (Pluto Press, 1999, London). For a fascinating view of CIA recruitment tactics of Muslim *jihad* fighters read Chapter 5.

2. "Conversation with Journalists", Rahimullah Yusufzai, *The Dawn*, Pakistan, and Shahin Shaheed, *The Nation*, Pakistan (December, 2001).

3. Ingalls, Dr. Jim. "Western Interests in Afghanistan and their Consequences for Afghan People: A Critique of US Media Coverage" (July 6, 2000) http://www.sonaliandjim.net/politics/index.html (November 30, 2003).

4. Interview with Nilab (pseudonym) of the Revolutionary Association of the Women of Afghanistan (March 2003).

5. World Health Organization, "The Invisible Wounds: The Mental Health Crisis in Afghanistan", Special Report, Central Asia Crisis Unit (November 6, 2001).

6. Punter, David. *Postcolonial Imaginings: Fictions of a New World Order* (Edinburgh University Press, 2000). Paraphrasing of a description of 'trauma', pp. 66-67.

7. Bell Hooks

8. Human Rights Watch. "Afghanistan: Warlords Implicated in New Abuses", Press release (July 29, 2003)

9. Human Rights Watch. "The Second Phase: from the Geneva Accords to the Mujahideens Civil War" Backgrounder on Afghanistan: History of the War, October 2001 http://www.hrw.org/backgroundeer/asia/afghan-bck1023.htm (November 30, 2003).

10. "UN U-Turn on Afghan Land Grab", *BBC* (September 14, 2003).

11. International Crisis Group, "Afghanistan: Judicial Reform and Transitional Justice", *Asia Report* No 45 (January, 2003). http://www.crisisweb.org/home/index.cfm?id=1631&l=1 November 30, 2003

12. Ibid.

13. Tarzi, Amin. "Afghan Administration Reportedly Opens Negotiations with Taliban", Radio Free Afghanistan, (October 8, 2003) <http://www.azadiradio.org/en/dailyreport/2003/10/08.asp> (November 30, 2003).

14. International Crisis Group. "Afghanistan: Judicial Reform and Transitional Justice", *Asia Report* No 45 (January, 2003).

On Experiencing Afghanistan

DAPHNE MEIJER

I married an Afghan man recently. We did not have a romantic wedding with all of our friends and family present. Rather, we flew to India and went to a lawyer in Delhi. He organized a marriage ceremony for us, a shortened version of the tourist wedding some people travel to Goa for. The next day, we went to a judge who declared the whole thing legal under Indian law. This Afghan-Dutch union has me, the Dutch bride, wondering about what it means to be Afghan in this day and age. And about the state of affairs in Kabul. And the crazy twist my life took since the fall of 2001. My husband and I met when I visited

Afghanistan for the second time, in May of 2002. I'd been there before, in November and December 2001. Before the 9th of September 2001, I'd never considered travelling to Afghanistan. It simply did not enter my mind. I was happily ensconced at home, working as a theatre critic, among other things. I had one Afghan woman acquaintance in the Netherlands, and knew that friends gave shelter to an Afghan refugee for a while, although I'd never met him in their home. Yet there was a nagging voice in the back of my mind reminding me of a plan for the future I used to cherish in which I would swap dreary and rainy old Amsterdam for the Middle-East. So, if I had any reason to go out to Central Asia, it was a personal quest; a desire to drastically change venue before it was too late. And yes, there was a man involved; a fellow Dutch reporter, friend and lover and colleague. He had gone on ahead and phoned me from Dushanbe in Tajikistan to tell me to come over too. So I went out to Tajikistan.

Tajikistan
I knew the country existed, and could have told you there had been some kind of civil war going on at some time between two factions who each wanted something, but that was it. And from Tajikistan's capital Dushanbe, I went with a convoy to the Tajik-Afghan border on my own, trailing the footsteps of my friend. Never before have I experienced such fright in anticipation of what disaster might befall me as during the days before I actually crossed the Afghan border.

I was afraid to die. Or to watch my lover die. Or some fate worse than that. In fact, I was so stiff with fright that my period was late for a week and a half. And, what do you know, the moment I crossed the border I started to bleed. And I did not stop bleeding until I was back in the hotel in Dushanbe again, ten days later.

Looking back, I curse myself for my ignorance. I did not have a clue about the country. Had I known then what I know now, I would have paid far more attention to what was going on with the American Special Forces I met en route, and the Northern Alliance commanders I saw at work. Even so, I had a great time that first visit. (Actually, I also felt deeply miserable, having to manage tampons and sanitary pads in freezing cold, squatting above latrines.) But a few hours after the convoy crossed the border, I lost my fear of Afghanistan. The landscape in the north was awe-inspiring. Rough peaks, patches of sandy desert, villages made of clay and dust, houses surrounded by tall walls made of mud brick, and no modern amenities in sight. No electricity, no asphalt on the muddy track, no nothing. Men wrapped in greyish blankets stood watching us as we were driving by. It was cold and soggy weather, and large puddles had formed all over the tracks. Amongst this barrenness, modern trucks were driving around, and people were carrying the latest weaponry.

About twenty-four hours later, I had seen the casket of a killed Swedish cameraman passing us by on the road back to the border; I had had my first experience of sleeping on an Afghan sitting/eating/sleeping mattress; I had had my first experience with the Northern Alliance commanders who gave me a travel pass to go to the Mazar-i-Sharif; and I had said goodbye to my Dutch friend, who hated the place and wanted to go home. This was only the beginning. Suffice to say, the adrenalin rush had rarely been so strong, nor has it been ever since. I was hooked. Also, I liked the people. Not the foreign colleagues per se, although some were great and one Irish television reporter even loaned me 500 dollars, but the Afghans. My experience was restricted to men, mostly, but I did meet a few women. I enjoyed spending time with everybody. I liked, and still like, the Afghan sense of self. Modest, very polite, but at the same time very autonomous and egalitarian. The Afghans bow to no man. Sure, there were con artists among them, bullshitters and crooks, but they conned, bullshitted and crooked with definite style. And not to sound coy, but let's face it: the Afghans are among the most beautiful people in the world. It is not a decisive factor, but it sure helps. But don't get me wrong; I was very happy when I got a ride back from the northern town of Taloqan to Dushanbe with an American relief worker, bless his heart. After ten days, I had completely run out of money and physical energy. Also, I needed to take a proper shower and wash my clothes. As I stepped on the pontoon bridge that would take us back to the Tajik side of the Amur Daria, I felt relief, but also envy for the colleagues who were staying behind.

This was a Place to Get Back to
The first trip taught me a lot about how not to be a reporter in a war zone. I was unprepared and ill-equipped. (I was non-equipped the first time, but never mind that.) I probably remained ill-equipped during the next two years, a large part of which I spent in Kabul. That is all a matter of money. Or, rather, if you are working for newspapers and other media in a relatively small country like Holland, a lack of money.

In May of 2002, I went back for three weeks. I flew to Kabul, travelled around with a young interpreter I have since married, and enjoyed myself immensely. It was the golden age of Kabul. The weather was good, and the air smelled faintly of jasmine and hope and promise, and everybody was excited about all that was happening. The International Security Assistance Force was getting their act together, and the government was taking shape. If I wanted something done, all I had to do was ask. All restrictions and official accreditations and formalities and gatekeepers and personal body check equipment personnel had not yet been put in place. I returned in August 2002 for six weeks, and again in January of 2003 for an indefinite period as a freelance correspondent for two newspapers. And, as a sideline, to write a book about the Dutch involvement in Afghanistan's reconstruction. Why did I return? A friend of mine recently voiced her disappointment in my getting married to my Afghan husband. She had been under the impression that I had travelled back and forth to Kabul for two years because I liked the country so much. But, instead of being genuinely interested in Afghanistan's development, it was a banal relationship with a man that had pulled me back all the time.

So, yeah. My interest was not pure. Not solely professional. The mix of the personal, the professional and the private was irresistible. As I changed into We, so did life in Afghanistan. And my perceptions of it. Living in a Kabul neighbourhood, surrounded by Afghan families, in a house with three Afghan men and all their guests and visitors, gave a distinct Afghan flavour to daily life. Traditional culture is very charming, but spending a summer without the possibility of swimming anywhere is difficult. This is actually not completely true: the U.N. guesthouse and the British embassy have pools. But for Afghan women, there is no possibility anywhere. And I wanted to live the Afghan lifestyle – and besides, I am not British, and the U.N. pool was only open for U.N. and NGO personnel. How seriously the

Afghans took their prohibition on swimming was brought home to me by my neighbours. I had brought them a plastic pool as a gift for their six young daughters to fill up in their garden and spatter about in, like children all over the world would do during a long sweltering summer. It was never used.

Traditional Islamic culture provides little personal space for women and girls, and certainly does not encourage physical exertion. You are not supposed to walk just for fun, ride a bike, fly a kite, swim, skate or do anything in the public domain that might attract attention. I found these rules increasingly difficult to comply with.

We planned to stay in Kabul for a long time, but things did not work out well professionally. Interest in Afghanistan from the Dutch media dwindled as the war in Iraq broke out. And, gradually, the difficulties to get anything done ground me down. By now, some of the problems that reporters faced a year ago had disappeared. I could send emails and access the internet from many cyber-cafes. The phone worked, off and on, and at some point we even got the hot water up and running in our house. But nowadays, Kabul is no longer a city where you can just walk into an office to talk to someone and find out what's going on. Downtown has become a collection of fortresses. One travels with difficulty because of all the roadblocks and other restrictions put in place, from one heavily guarded facility to another. This is not just detrimental to the people on the outside, but also to the folks indoors. Sometimes a gate swings open and an armoured car ventures out, giving the military commander or the ambassador or U.N. expat or whoever is inside a peek at daily life in Kabul. The rest of the time these people spend indoors, or at one of the crazily expensive restaurants that have sprung up where you can eat braised veal with asparagus in a white wine sauce. The people inside this loop don't know what's happening on the street, and sprout propaganda about human rights and development that they got off the email from NGOs specializing in the monitoring of human rights, who spend the working day emailing each other...

And outside the loop, Afghans are becoming more and more frustrated. Because so little is being done about their very real problems of water and sewage and unemployment, and so much false information is being spread around. The Tajik and Pashtun populations dislike each other vehemently, and fight for the ear of whoever will listen to their lamentations. Sympathy has shifted from the Tajik fighters who were part of the Northern Alliance to the Pashtun intellectuals who have returned home from abroad. Okay, I'm married to a Tajik from Panjshir valley. I know I'm not the most objective person. But in this part of the world, nobody is objective. To me, it is very disconcerting to hear my foreign acquaintances mouth their dismay about human rights abuses by Tajiks, and at the same time see them cuddle up with the Pashtuns. The Tajiks are an undemocratic lot, but so is everybody else in these parts. Let's not kid ourselves. The sons of the Pashtun elite who are currently returning to their homeland from their extended stay in the West have the edge; they posses western table manners and know how to push the right buttons in the international community. The Tajiks, Hazaras and Uzbeks don't know – they never learned how. They never went to college abroad.

To the Pashtun elite, things should more or less go back to the way they were. Which means: with them on top of their own community, and the other ethnic communities nicely stratified underneath, with the Hazaras at the bottom. Not surprisingly, the other ethnic communities want no part of this. They want fundamental change but, never having picked up the diplomatic tools to formulate what they want, they are instead using the old Afghan ways. They fight. In a sense, this ethnic conflict is really a classic case of class struggle. However, it is not formulated in Marxist jargon. The arena for this battle is Islamism. Strangely, the Pashtun leadership has managed to convey an image of themselves as Islamic moderates and modernists, while the Tajiks et al are generally seen as ultra-extremist Islamists. This is clever spin, if nothing else. The premise here seems that an American accent is a guarantee for sensibilities regarding democracy and human rights. And a lack of English, does that mean you cannot decide your own future?

Returning to Kabul from India in December to do some reporting on the Loya Jirga where the Afghans were ratifying their new Constitution, I noticed again how the circus works. The West supports the rule of interim-president Karzai, which is nice for him, but short-sighted. The media reported how the different factions at the Loya Jirga vied for power, with the Karzaiites going for a strong presidential system and most of the Tajiks, Uzbeks and Hazaras going for a strong Parliament. Hamid Karzai went on record to say that he would not run for president if the Grand Assembly did not favour the Presidential system.

Well goodbye mister democrat, one might think, but oddly enough, the Western democracies rallied behind Karzai (e.g. the American ambassador sent a message stating his support for Karzai and went to a meeting with Uzbek leaders, right in front of Afghan television news cameras, to win them over), thereby destroying the chance to get the Afghans a form of democratically elected government that the western diplomats would have voted in for themselves, had the shoe been on the other foot. The Tajiks, Uzbeks and Hazaras did not easily give in, and in the bargaining that had to follow in order to appease everybody, the Islamic clerics who made up a substantial part of the delegates managed to gain many small victories – which was exactly what the West did not want to happen because Islamism freaks us out no end.

One might say that Islam and Islamism need a Voltaire, a Diderot and a John Adams to come along and change the Muslim outlook on the relationship between Mosque and State. Then again, is it really any of our Western business? I sincerely believe it is, but it is equally important to treat people with the respect they deserve.

As I said, my Dutch-Afghan union got me thinking.

The Afghan eXplorer
http://compcult.media.mit.edu/afghan_x/
THE COMPUTING CULTURE GROUP, MIT MEDIA LAB

"In the First Amendment, the Founding Fathers gave the free press the protection it must have to fulfill its essential role in our democracy. The press was to serve the governed, not the governors. The Government's power to censor the press was abolished so that the press would remain forever free to censure the Government. The press was protected so that it could bare the secrets of government and inform the people ... And paramount among the responsibilities of a free press is the duty to prevent any part of the Government from deceiving the people and sending them off to distant lands to die of foreign fevers and foreign shot and shell".

Supreme Court Justice Hugo Black
New York Times Co. v. United States
1971 6-3 Majority Opinion

>> **Afghan Explorer is intended as a vehicle for personal knowledge acquisition, in the belief that international peace can only come from mutual understanding.**
As the most powerful, and arguably the most technologically advanced nation in the world, it seems as if Americans should be able to get information at any time, from any place.

>> **Economies of Scale**
In fact, Americans are often information poor. Their reliance on low content mass media, like *USA Today* and television news, means that they see relatively little news and commentary, usually written for a seventh grade literacy level.
In contrast to European nations, our geographic isolation means that we seldom learn foreign languages, and rarely meet people from other countries.
Isolation used to mean an isolationist foreign policy, but increasingly we find ourselves 'peacekeeping', or at war with people and regions we've barely heard of. Without an active and unrestrained media, how can we, the people, decide if our elected representatives are acting in our interest?

>> Alien Reporting

Really, our only hope is for an aggressive media, which can help to tell us what's going on, both in peace time and in war. But since the Persian Gulf War, US reporters are disallowed from freely covering events.

In Vietnam, for instance, journalists had self-imposed rules for how to protect our service-men and operations from potential security breaches.

In the ten years of the Indochina conflict, out of several thousand US correspondents, none had accreditation revoked for violating these rules, which the US Military also approved. But during Desert Storm, reporters had to have military escorts wherever they went, escorts who routinely would interrupt interviews if a soldier strayed from the official line. Dispatches, still photographs and video footage were subject to military censorship. Reporters operating outside the so-called pool system for wire services, newspapers and networks were subject to military arrest.[1]

>> War Without Witnesses

Obviously the security of our troops is important, indeed, essential. But so is making sure that the US involvement is appropriate, measured, and humane.

Yet Afghanistan is so far away, and our information about it so one-sided, that it is almost invisible. In fact, it's about as conceptually remote as Mars, yet teeming with intelligent life. The US can send autonomous robots to the reaches of space, so why can't we do the same for geopolitical hotspots?

Experience has shown again and again that an informed, aroused public is the best disciplinarian of power, public or private. That's why it's so worrisome to see the obstacles that the Pentagon is placing now in the way of direct, on-the-scene news coverage of the war on terrorism… Power must always be disciplined, even in a cause as eminently just as this one. And there is no discipline like information, freely gathered and widely disseminated.[2]

>> A Technology for Peace

The Afghan eXplorer is a technology to help international understanding. By allowing US citizens, the 'average Joe', to be virtually present in the stunning natural beauty of Afghanistan, and to remotely sense its ancient history and diverse people, we can only help the current situation. And likewise, by allowing the Afghani people to get a sense of who we are – not a Great Satan, but rather a peaceful, freedom-loving people – we can only be paving the way for peace and reconciliation.

NOTES

1. Sloyan, Patrick J. "The Real War", *Media Studies Journal*, Vol. 15 No. 1 (Summer 2001, Arlington, VA).
2. Wycliff, Don. *Chicago Tribune* (11 October 2001).

Enabled by global wireless technology, solar power, and sophisticated computing, the eXplorer is able to navigate both urban and rural terrains. Its unique combination of hardware and software allow it to gather video, image, sound, conduct two-way interviews, and interact with local populations, even in areas deemed off-limits by the local and US military authorities.

Artist's conception v. 1.4

Waiting
Entries from a Filmmaker's Diary in and around Tel Aviv

ANNA FAROQHI

 # Sunday 16th March 2003

...It's five in the morning and still dark. I take a bus from Ben Gurion Airport into Tel Aviv.

Behind me, passport control and questions from a security man with shaven head and sexy lips:
"You speak Hebrew?"
"A little".
"Why have you come to Israel?"
"A private visit".
"What do you mean?"
"I'm visiting friends".
"What are their names?"
I gave him some names.
"How come you know them?"
"Through other friends".
"And what are their names?"
Again I complied, giving Jewish names. My interrogator smiled.
"How come you speak Hebrew?"
"I take lessons, in Berlin".
"Thank you". He let me go. I'm familiar with this kind of interview, but not accustomed to getting a come-on from the interviewer.

It's a strange time to be in Israel. Friends in Berlin and in the USA advised me against it, not just because of imminent war, with the Americans and their "alliance of the willing" poised to invade Iraq. Iraq, they claim, has Weapons of Mass Destruction and Israel could be a target. And there could be more suicide bombings.

Transferring from the bus to a share-a-ride taxi, I reach David's apartment as dawn begins to break over a city I recognize as pleasingly shabby and oriental. In my absent friend's chaotic room, I find a space and settle down to sleep. He's in Paris, not due back for several days.

Scaffolding
(Three workers scrape and hammer at a house front.)
Arabs on a scaffolding scrape and hammer at the facade of a house opposite my window. Not before time, renovation work is under way on the district's fine but crumbling 1930s Bauhaus-style buildings. The men wear no protective masks. Israeli Arabs, or migrant labour from Israeli-occupied regions?

A CONSTRUCTION SIGHT
NEXT DOOR
3.4.03

ARABS
CHEAP LABOUR

This latter is unlikely, with only around 7,000 Palestinians still working in Israel. Those here legally have been rare in the Jewish state since the start of the Second Intifada in 2000. Now, job seekers are imported from Rumania, China or Thailand, with residence permits lasting only as long as there is work for them. There are many illegal immigrants, entering on tourist visas or going 'underground' when their job contracts expire.

Foreign workers, waiting.
(Russians and Chinese crowd around a car, which moves on, and they resume waiting.)

Here, in Tel Aviv's migrant labour quarter, they mill around, morning after morning, hoping a car will arrive with offers of employment for a few days or even a few hours.

Rothschild
(Posh street, trees, renovated houses, pedestrians with dogs.)

It's mid-day, sunny and mild. I buy bread, still warm and I eat it sitting on a bench on Rothschild Boulevard.

THE ANGEL
COSTUME IS
POPULAR

It's a quiet street, offering shelter from crowded Shenkin and Allenby Street. Today is **Purim**, commemorating Esther's foiling of Hamon and the Persian vizier's plot to eliminate Jews. The biblical event is remembered by way of a sort of street carnival. Many youngsters are costumed as witches or winged angels. Some concede only a hair clasp, a wig or satanic horns made of cloth. Others are Cleopatra or Superman. The festivities, monitored by police officers, are fun to watch.

Later, I call on Avi, who works at the opera. He and his friend have separated after 13 years of cohabitation. They haven't decided who gets the apartment and its contents. (Avi hasn't yet made up his mind where he wants to live.) Besides, he could soon be unemployed. Israel's economy is in poor shape. But for the first time in years, Avi feels free. He is planning a trip to Berlin.

Night, Allenby, frontal

(Nocturnal street, lights. Hints of decay. Focus moves to beach; lights.)

In the evening, I meet Micha and his girlfriend Anat at the cinematheque. We sit on a bench, already occupied by three teenage girls. We discuss the film we're about to see. The girls, who've already seen it, join in.
...The girls are in high spirits, telling us they've come into town from a Tel Aviv suburb for **Purim**. They're off work for three days, until Wednesday. One of the girls is sure they'll get Thursday off too because that's when the war will start, she says.
...Gas masks are being distributed to the public. Israelis are told they must have a "**cheder atum**", a sealed room, in case of a gas attack. Micha says he only has an old gas mask from another war and that the filter probably no longer offers protection. He doesn't have a sealable room either. He doesn't see a real danger and is angry that people just accept the inevitability of war.
...Micha, it seems, has at least four jobs and numerous other sidelines. His girlfriend appears not to lack employment either. The truth is, it's a strategy for survival in Israel, a means of deflecting from a desperate struggle.

Monday 17.3.2003

Allenby, frontal, daytime.
(Same street, now daytime. First quiet, then busier. Following military police. Long drive toward beach.)

Heading for a mid-day rendezvous, I walk along Allenby Street, which intersects Rothschild Boulevard and cuts right across the city before veering toward the sea.

Allenby had an elegance in the 1920s, but has acquired a rundown image since the 1950s, when Dizengoff Street became Tel
Aviv's shop window. It's the location of houses representing all
of Tel Aviv's main construction periods – Arabic architecture,
eclectic style, Bauhaus. Allenby is a popular thoroughfare, with
its own street market.
I meet up in a café with Rafi. We drink carrot juice and eat
little triangular pastries filled with dates, nuts or poppy seed
paste called **osnaiim shel Hamon**, The Ear of Hamon – a traditional **Purim** speciality. It being a time of public festivity,
the café offers them free and children make the most of it. The
place is crowded. We sit enjoying the sun, almost as on a spring
day in any normal country.
Rafi is a jeweller. He shows me jewellery he makes and sells
to shops along the Ben Yehuda Street. His cell phone keeps
interrupting our conversation – his brother, a friend, a
friend's father, all needing small favours. We have an unspo-
ken agreement not to mention the imminent outbreak of war. But
Rafi does say how important he thinks it is that I have come
to Israel at this time. He wants me to tell the world that
life in Israel is good and goes on as normal. The phone rings
again. This time, a friend asks him to procure 50 tequila
beakers for a **Purim** party in the evening.
We meet another of Rafi's friends in Dizengoff Street. Jordan
lives alone in a three-room 1960s luxury apartment with mar-
ble floors and smart furnishings. He teaches English at a
school in Yaffo, north of Tel Aviv. Jordan has lived in Israel
for the past seven years, but he's still lonely. He is sitting
in his living room with a friend from Denmark, rolling a
'joint'. Jordan has just turned thirty. The table in front of
him is littered with greeting cards. We refuse his offer of a
draw on his joint. He tells us his parents object to his use
of drugs, but points out that marijuana can hardly be called
a drug, despite the fact that its possession in Israel carries
stiff penalties.
We don't stay long. Rafi doesn't have much time. In the car,
he tells me Jordan can't bear silence or being alone. Once a
month his parents come from Britain. They show their gratitude
for Rafi's friendship with their son by letting him live rent-
free in the house, though he rarely stays there. Jordan reminds
me of a character in a **fin de siècle** novel, a spoiled British
lord who can't find his place in the real world.
An e-mail from David announcing that he won't return until

Thursday makes me mad at the thought of waiting another day and possibly getting embroiled in the war.

I go for a walk.

Market
(Stallholders at work. An ill-tempered Orthodox Jew grudgingly hands a customer a plastic bag for his purchases. An old man meticulously chooses bananas and apples. Smartly dressed women meet. A cute baby on its mother's arms.)

A man recites a war poem for my camera and me. (We need the translation of the market poem.)

Market stalls, night time.
(Empty market stalls after dark, claustrophobic atmosphere, rain. Pass by a group in raincoats.)

In the evening, I watch television. International diplomatic negotiations are broken off. No UN Security Council vote on a new resolution on Iraq. The pro-war powers - the USA, Britain, Spain and Italy - decide it's now up to them to determine what happens next. The Americans are their mouthpiece. President Bush is to address the nation and will probably issue an ultimatum to Saddam Hussein to leave Iraq. There's no longer any doubt: there will be war. I can't guess what it means for this coun-try, for Israel, where people have gas masks and airtight rooms. The television reports that an Israeli family has suffocated in its airtight room.
Micha calls and I tell him of my fears. He advises me to do what everyone else here is doing: "Be local", he says, "Keep busy".

Tuesday 18.3.03
Travelling streets to Camp Adjami, rain.

(Rain swept streets, rundown and deserted. To camp, then along the perimeter (?). Barbed wire and wall, then view of military camp, military vehicles with boxes containing rockets.)

The air feels strange, the sky yellowed by sand and rain sus-pended in cloud. This is the **Chamsim**, a sandstorm from the Sahara. It hits me that I'm not in Europe or America, but in the middle of the desert.

I switch on the television; Bush has delivered his address,
threatening Saddam with war unless he leaves Iraq with his closest associates. Saddam is showing no signs of complying. War is
a certainty. Newsreaders on all channels wear grim expressions,
look tense and excited. Somehow, the pace of events animates
them.

I reach David in Paris. He got the dates mixed up and will come
on Wednesday after all. I tell him I'm afraid of the war and
can't be as calm as the people around me. David answers:
"A terrible country. Why are you there?"

Avi calls. "Get yourself a gas mask," he says. "Not that anything will happen, but you'll feel better. What if you're sitting among lots of people in a café and the sirens go off and
everyone puts on gas masks and you don't have one?"

A gasmask retails for 250 shekel for non-Israelis, allegedly
refundable when they leave the country. Avi advises me to register with the foreign ministry as a journalist, assuring me of a
place in the Hilton Hotel bunker should the need arise.

In the afternoon, I meet up with Micha and Anat and their friend
Ofek. Ofek says, "**Ha milchama-se kef** – War is fun. The war ten
years ago, that was the best time of my life. People get closer
together. Parties. Close friendships. You could call anyone at
any time. Lots of children were born nine months after the Gulf
War".

A FAMILY WATCHING
THE SIGHT,
HAS BEEN BUILT
ONLY 2 WEEKS AGO

An STRAND VON YAFFO.
ARMEE LAGER DER ANGEBLICHEN
MIT KANONEN, OUR PROTECTORS

We drive to the beach at
Yaffo. There, the French
ambassador has his resi-
dence, surrounded by park-
land and children's play-
grounds. On the beach
itself there's a big camp.
Tents, armoured vehicles,
soldiers – and rockets. On
some of the trucks, you can
see the crates containing
Patriot missiles earmarked
for Baghdad. The camp was
set up only two weeks ago.
The weapons are American.
"Just like in a Hollywood
film", says Micha. "We
don't have automobiles
like that here".

The soldiers at the gate are Israeli and very young, among them
two women. There's a sign saying, "Welcome to Camp Adjami".
We stand at the barbed wire fence and Micha points the camera
into the camp. Filming here surely must be forbidden.
Ofek says "I grew up at the border, in a Jewish settlement. I
feel safe when I see barbed wire fencing".
There are other onlookers besides us - a father with two children. He hoists one onto his shoulder and points to the missiles.
Micha tells us that during the Gulf War, lots more people had
gone to see the camp and the Patriots, but at a different location.
A newspaper has a special supplement with tips on how to make a
room airtight, a **cheder atum**. Comic strip figures use plastic
foil and adhesive tape to seal windows. There's a list of items
to be kept in the room - a TV set, a pail of fresh water, chairs
and beds, and games for the children, a toilet facility and food
conserves. Another page contains illustrations of missiles -
nice, new, confidence building weapons on 'our' side and old,
ugly, nasty looking monsters belonging to 'them', with details
of how they work. Child's play!

Yaffo Street lateral, night time.

(Rather shabby shopping malls, some cafes, viewed laterally.)
British Airways announces the temporary suspension of all
flights to and from Israel. Unlike the United States, British,
Italian and Japanese missions, the German embassy issues no
warning to its nationals to leave Israel, saying the likelihood
of an Iraqi missile attack was almost non-existent. Television
reports from Iraq speak of demonstrations by patriotic, pro-
Saddam Iraqis, shown brandishing pistols and machine guns. Grim-
faced Iraqi military spokesmen, crudely translated from Arabic,
reaffirm Saddam's will for victory. France, which has shunned
the 'coalition of the willing', says it'll join the war if the
Iraqis use biological or chemical weapons against US troops.
In the evening, I meet Avi. He plans to fly to Germany tomorrow, Wednesday. Germany's Lufthansa airline can't say if there
will be any flights. Avi hopes the war won't start until the
weekend. He wants to get to Germany and be stuck there for a few
days longer than planned. The calendar of war has become part
of his agenda.

Wednesday 19.3.03

Soldiers and guards
(Soldiers sitting in a Burger King café, guard at door. Security
men, bored, check shopping bags. Policewomen telephone, stroll.
Shot of girl soldiers looking at window display.)

In the morning, I clean up the apartment – a necessary chore
even on the brink of war. I'm looking forward to seeing David
again; nothing new on the TV news – just waiting for Bush's ultimatum to run out and Saddam Hussein still obstinate.
Avi calls. He's getting ready to leave. His Lufthansa reservation has been put back to tomorrow, Thursday morning, with
flights booked out today as foreign nationals rush to leave
Israel. Avi won't say if he thinks it wise for me to stay, con-
centrating on his own hectic preparations to leave. We agree to
telephone in the evening.
There are rumours that the war will begin tonight, just before
the Bush ultimatum expires at 20 hours Mid-Western time – around
2 am in Israel.
I visit an exhibition with Micha, who meets a female friend, a
soldier in uniform. She's carrying a carton imprinted with the
word 'gasmask'. "Soldiers must carry their gasmasks at all
times", she tells us. "Just like students and kids, who're not

allowed into kindergarten without their gas masks".
A pretty girl with blonde hair who laughs easily, she can't be
older than twenty-four. She and Avi talk about movies, not war.
As we part, she calls to me, "Have fun".

Travelling Dizengoff, nighttime
(Shops lit up. D Centre, guarded entrances)

David arrives in the evening. Before we can really celebrate our
reunion, we get drawn into war talk with two neighbours outside
the apartment. They discuss various precautions for the war: who
has brought in canned food and water, should one install an
emergency power generator. Jokes are cracked, but faces are
serious. Fate is awaited seemingly without fear.
David has to work on his film into the night. Like many Israeli
intellectuals, he has no wish to remain in Israel permanently.
But there are family and work commitments. We drive to a film
studio in Haifa, fully manned despite the late hour. Studio
costs are lower at night. An evening paper is passed round in
the corridor. The front page carries the greenish night-vision
photo of modern warfare.
Back in Tel Aviv after just an hour's drive, David and I have a
late meal in a café on Bograshov Street.
A couple of people sit at the bar, some at a neighbouring table.
No radio, no television, only Israeli pop music. No sign of
imminent war.
We get back to the apartment at 2 am. I'm too tense to sleep,
unaccustomed to David's closeness and unsure of our future relationship. I wonder what it must be like to live in a country in
a permanent state of emergency.

Thursday 20.3.03
People wait outside embassy
(Grim-faced people wait outside Ukrainian embassy. Guard opens
the iron gate and admits a few.)

It's said that, since the Second Intifada, 100,000 Israelis have
left the Jewish state. Those in possession of British, German or
American passports, thanks to a second, inherited nationality, have
the choice of making a fresh start away from Israel. Applications
are even being lodged for Polish or Hungarian passports.
A Russian woman employed as a nursemaid by Ronen told me of acquaintances queuing outside the Russian or Ukrainian embassies hoping

for entry visas for their old homelands. They claim they merely wish to visit relatives or check out property they own. In reality, all they want is to get out of a country unable to fulfil its promise of a new home.

Day of travel, Rotschild
(Drive along smart avenue. Refuse collection. People out walking. Bauhaus house. Quiet.)

8 am. It's quiet outside. Work hasn't yet started on a nearby building site. "Maybe the war has started", I venture and we turn on the radio. Missiles have struck Baghdad. An Iraqi government spokesman talks of Saddam's will for victory.
CNN shows shots of bright spots said to be rockets fired into the night sky. The US administration promises a wave of "shock and awe" over Baghdad. The words are imbued with the fear of God. And Iraq answers that the USA will be made to regret the attack. David and I drink coffee in silence. Outside, it's cool but getting warm.
Newspapers carry the message "The war begins", but the streets are quiet and all appears normal. The tension of the past couple of days erupts from a banality into a verbal battle between David and me. The phone rings and David has to leave. I'm at a loss what to do, so just carry on waiting – for another night of war, another night with David.
Lufthansa confirms that I could get a flight back to Germany on Sunday, but I don't book. I want to wait.
Avi tries to console me. He has not gone to Berlin. His flight was cancelled. Hurrying between two meetings as he plunges into hectic activity after the forced change of plans, he says to keep on waiting and try to decide what it is I really want.
Later, David and I talk. We have calmed down.
Heavy bombardment of Baghdad during the following night.

Friday 21.3.03
Kids with gas masks, kindergarten
(Little children accompanied by mothers and fathers in kindergarten. Woman security guard. Plastic sheeting shields off the view from the garden. Here, vigilance against attack is a daily routine.)

Iraqis were killed last night. Their exact number is not known – or so we're told. Three hundred sixty missiles were fired. TV

news says Iraqi troops surrender to British forces. Shots of young soldiers with raised arms and white flags.
Video of a tired-looking old man with a moustache, beret and spectacles - possibly Saddam Hussein, but maybe not. Perhaps he's dead in his palace, or injured.
In San Francisco, 1,000 people are arrested demonstrating against the war. Here, children go to kindergarten as usual, carrying their gas masks in brown boxes with red or green print. For very small children, there are gas proof tents in blue plastic containers with yellow marking.

Scaffolding, hammering
(Men at work on scaffolding.)

Work goes on as normal. David and I are speaking again.

Allenby, lateral, night
(More shots of shops in busy street. Not so many people around.)

David left his car standing in the street the last time he left Israel. Police came after two weeks and took the car apart, took out the seats, dismantled the number plates. A car without a driver here is a 'chefez chashud' - a suspicious object.

The car won't start, has to be taken to a repair shop. This done, we visit Gidon and Tamar and their little child. We watch the child playing, talk about everyday issues. The television is on for the child, showing a kiddies' programme with cute figures singing, dancing and adventuring. Then, studio shots in which children are shown how to don gas masks.
Now the war does come up. Everyone agrees that, at best, gas masks and sealed rooms could extend life expectancy by a maximum of fifteen minutes.
My friends assure me this war won't threaten Israel, unlike the 1991 Gulf War over Kuwait. Then, Tel Aviv was repeatedly attacked for a whole month, with sirens constantly wailing. People were terrified, fleeing the city in search of safe havens. But they didn't stay away long, returning by day. David says he felt safest in the open or in his car. The worst thing wasn't fear for his own safety. Like everyone here, he was once a soldier and worried more about the people he loved than about himself.
Gidon frowns. His elder son is in the army, due to complete basic

training in one week, and then be deployed for active service.
One exercise involved mine detection and clearance. Gidon is
worried, although he, too, was once a soldier. Like his wife,
he was an officer, but in less dangerous times. But their son
is proud of his role.
Television reports that New York's JFK airport has been partially closed after an Israeli passenger was found with a gas
mask and suspicious white powder.

Shabbat 22.3.03
Beach
(People jog and speed-walk on a promenade. Two women with radio
receivers clamped to their heads like Mars beings. Children
play. People put up parasols. The Stars and Stripes flutters
under the Israeli flag. Dogs sniff at each other and run off.)

CNN: More attacks on Baghdad and other Iraqi cities. Turkish
forces have crossed into northern Iraq.
It's Shabbat and the sun is shining.
In a small café on the seafront, we eat **Jachnon** - an oriental
shabbat food made of pastry and vegetables, served cold. We
stroll to the beach and David tells how he slipped and fell onto
the quay with a film camera, onto his arm. The location is without colour, deserted and not pretty. But somehow his banal anec-
dote gives me reassurance.
David receives a call about a job not connected with his profession but offering money. I gaze upon a sparsely populated sea
front in a rich, poor country beyond my comprehension.

Travelling Rothschild, daytime (Back in smart street. End with
children playing with their father.)

CNN claims hundreds of Iraqi soldiers have surrendered in northern Iraq; reports 2,000 bombs dropped since last Friday, 200
dead or wounded civilians there; speculates on Saddam's possible death or the collapse of the regime. British troops are shown
taking Umm Qasr, claiming they'd expected more resistance and
are almost disappointed the conquest was so easy.
A howling siren makes me panic, but only for a moment. This war
is taking place on television here.
David returns, tells me about an opinion survey with the question: what would you do if we were hit by Scud rockets? Many say
they'd just put on their gas masks or retire to their air-sealed

rooms. More than 40% reply that they would climb on to their
roofs to watch the missiles.
We're back on speaking terms.
Two weeks later, when I left Israel, Saddam had still not shown
up and the coalition had won the war.

'UAR IJ ALWAYJ A CATAJTROPHY.'
KOFI ANNAN

no 17.3. 2003

IT IJ ALL
CLEAR NOW:

THERE IJ GOING
TO BE A JAR.

HARRY GREENJTOCK IN THE UN BULDING

BWH WILL ANNOUNCE HIJ THREAT / DECLARATION TO JADDAM
TONIGHT. IF JADDAM WON'T LEAVE THE COUNTRY THERE'J GOING
TO BE A WAR.

THERE IJ GOING TO BE
A JAR

WHAT CAN I DO I AM JHOCKED ANJ IN TEARJ

Last Email from the Gaza Strip

RACHEL CORRIE

A statement from the parents of Rachel Corrie, the American 'human shield' killed by an Israeli army bulldozer, followed by a "Letter from Palestine" which Rachel sent them on Feb. 7th, two weeks after her arrival in the Gaza Strip.

Date sent: Mon, 17 Mar 2003 01:27:48 +0000 (GMT)
From: ism rafah
Subject: Statement from Rachel Corrie's parents
March 16th, 2003

We are now in a period of grieving and still finding out the details behind the death of Rachel in the Gaza Strip.

We have raised all our children to appreciate the beauty of the global community and family, and are proud that Rachel was able to live her convictions. Rachel was filled with love and a sense of duty to her fellow man, wherever they lived. And she gave her life trying to protect those that are unable to protect themselves.

Rachel wrote to us from the Gaza Strip and we would like to release to the media her experience in her own words at this time.

Thank you.
Craig and Cindy Corrie,
Parents of Rachel Corrie

LETTER FROM PALESTINE
By Rachel Corrie
Excerpts from an e-mail from Rachel on February 7th, 2003.

I have been in Palestine for two weeks and one hour now, and I still have very few words to describe what I see. It is most difficult for me to think about what's going on here when I sit down to write back to the United States - something about the virtual portal into luxury. I don't know if many of the children here have ever existed without tank-shell holes in their walls and the towers of an occupying army surveying them constantly from the near horizons. I think, although I'm not entirely sure, that even the smallest of these children understands that life is not like this everywhere. An eight-year-old was shot and killed by an Israeli tank two days before I got here, and many of the children murmur his name to me, Bali, or point at the posters of him on the walls. The children also love to get me to practice my limited Arabic by asking me "Kaif Sharon?" "Kaif Bush?" and they laugh when I say "Bush Majnoon" "Sharon Majnoon" back in my limited Arabic. ("How is Sharon?" "How is Bush?" "Bush is crazy." "Sharon is crazy.") Of course this isn't quite what I believe, and some of the adults who have the English correct me: "Bush **mish Majnoon** ... Bush is a businessman". Today I tried to learn to say "Bush is a tool", but I don't think it translated quite right. But anyway, there are eight-year-olds here much more aware of the workings of the global power structure than I was just a few years ago – at least regarding Israel.

Nevertheless, I think about the fact that no amount of reading, attendance at conferences, documentary viewing and word-of-mouth could have prepared me for the reality of the situation here. You just can't imagine it unless you see it, and even then you are always well aware that your experience is not at all the reality: what with the difficulties the Israeli Army would face if they shot an unarmed US citizen, and with the fact that I have money to buy water when the army destroys wells, and, of course, the fact that I have the option of leaving. Nobody in my family has been shot, driving in their car, by a rocket launcher from a tower at the end of a major street in my hometown. I have a home. I am allowed to go see the ocean. Ostensibly, it is still quite difficult for me to be held for months or years on end without a trial (this because I am a white US citizen, as opposed to so many others).

When I leave for school or work, I can be relatively certain that there will not be a heavily armed soldier waiting half-way between Mud Bay and downtown Olympia at a checkpoint – a soldier with the power to decide whether I can go about my business, and whether I can get home again when I'm done. So, if I feel outrage at arriving and entering briefly and incompletely into the world in which these children exist, I wonder conversely about how it would be for them to arrive in my world.

They know that children in the United States don't usually have their parents shot, and they know they sometimes get to see the ocean. But once you have seen the ocean and lived in a silent place, where water is taken for granted and not stolen in the night by bulldozers, and once you have spent an evening when you haven't wondered if the walls of your home might suddenly fall inward waking you from your sleep, and once you've met people who have never lost anyone – once you have experienced the reality of a world that isn't surrounded by murderous towers, tanks, armed 'settlements' and now a giant metal wall, I wonder if you can forgive the world for all the years of your childhood spent existing – just existing – in resistance to the constant stranglehold of the world's fourth largest military – backed by the world's only superpower – in it's attempt to erase you from your home. That is something I wonder about these children. I wonder what would happen if they really knew.

As an afterthought to all this rambling, I am in Rafah, a city of about 140,000 people, approximately 60 percent of whom are refugees – many of whom are twice or three times refugees. Rafah existed prior to 1948, but most of the people here are themselves or are descendants of people who were relocated here from their homes in historic Palestine – now Israel. Rafah was split in half when the Sinai returned to Egypt. Currently, the Israeli army is building a fourteen-meter-high wall between Rafah in Palestine and the border, carving a no-man's land from the houses along the border. Six hundred and two homes have been completely bulldozed according to the Rafah Popular Refugee Committee. The number of homes that have been partially destroyed is greater.

Today as I walked on top of the rubble where homes once stood, Egyptian soldiers called to me from the other side of the border, "Go! Go!" because a tank was coming. Followed by waving, and "What's your name?" There is something disturbing about this friendly curiosity. It reminded me of how much, to some degree, we are all kids curious about other kids: Egyptian kids shouting at strange women wandering into the path of tanks. Palestinian kids shot from the tanks when they peek out from behind walls to see what's going on. International kids standing in front of tanks with banners. Israeli kids in the tanks anonymously, occasionally shouting – and also occasionally waving – many forced to be here, many just aggressive, shooting into the houses as we wander away.

In addition to the constant presence of tanks along the border and in the western region between Rafah and settlements along the coast, there are more IDF towers here than I can count – along the horizon, at the end of streets. Some, just army green metal. Others, these strange spiral staircases draped in some kind of netting to make the activity within anonymous. Some hidden, just beneath the horizon of buildings. A new one went up the other day in the time it took us to do laundry and to cross town twice to hang banners. Despite the fact that some of the areas nearest the border are the original Rafah with families who have lived on this land for at least a century, only the 1948 camps in the centre of the city are Palestinian-controlled areas under Oslo. But as far as I can tell, there are few, if any, places that are not within the sights of some tower or another. Certainly there is no place invulnerable to Apache helicopters or to the cameras of invisible drones we hear buzzing over the city for hours at a time.

I've been having trouble accessing news about the outside world here, but I hear an escalation of war on Iraq is inevitable. There is a great deal of concern here about the "reoccupation of Gaza". Gaza is reoccupied every day to various extents, but I think the fear is that the tanks will enter all the streets and remain here, instead of entering some of the streets and then withdrawing after some hours or days to observe and shoot from the edges of the communities. If people aren't already thinking about the consequences of this war for the people of the entire region, then I hope they will start.

I also hope you'll come here. We've been wavering between five and six internationals. The neighbourhoods that have asked us for some form of presence are Yibna, Tel El Sultan, Hi Salam, Brazil, Block J, Zorob, and Block O. There is also need for constant night-time presence at a well on the outskirts of Rafah since the Israeli army destroyed the two largest wells. According to the municipal water office, the wells destroyed last week provided half of Rafah's water supply. Many of the communities have requested internationals to be present at night to attempt to shield houses from further demolition. After about ten p.m. it is very difficult to move at night because the Israeli army treats anyone in the streets as resistance and shoots at them. So clearly we are too few.

I continue to believe that my home, Olympia, could gain a lot and offer a lot by deciding to make a commitment to Rafah in the form of a sister-community relationship. Some teachers and children's groups have expressed interest in e-mail exchanges, but this is only the tip of the iceberg of solidarity work that might be done. Many people want their voices to be heard, and I think we need to use some of our privilege as internationals to get those voices heard directly in the US, rather than through the filter of well-meaning internationals such as myself. I am just beginning to learn, from what I expect to be a very intense tutelage, about the ability of people to organize against all odds, and to resist against all odds.

Guerrilla News Network's Digital Documentaries
Interview with Stephen Marshall

GEERT LOVINK

The political videos of Guerrilla News Network are a challenging affair, in terms of their content, aesthetics and distribution. Deeply hybrid, GNN is crossing boundaries in such a professional – and easy – manner, it almost seems that we have landed in the perfect, tactical media future. On GNN, it is trance meets Chomsky. Without leaving behind the tradition of political documentary video and investigative journalism, GNN uniquely frames classic footage in an innovative television format. Edited as high pulse video clips, the works are designed as interactive art works and distributed simultaneously on VHS, DVD, as television signal and, last but not least, as streaming video content on the web. In fact, the website is the centrepiece of the GNN operation and not only works as a video portal but also serves as a platform for daily written Newswires. GNN topics range from Environment, the War on Terror and Intelligence. My favourite is *S-11 Redux*, a scratch video masterpiece that jams American news footage – a delightful deconstruction of the late 2001 hysteria, leading up to the invasion of Afghanistan.

Canadian writer and video director Stephen Marshall has been involved in desktop video and the handy-cam revolution since 1995 when he ran Channel Zero, an 'underground' video magazine, which had wide distribution through stores such as HMV, Tower and Virgin. After Channel Zero fell apart, Stephen worked as a DJ in New York and Toronto. In early 2000 he got together with MTV's Josh Shore and together they created GNN. At the height of the dotcom boom, Guerrilla News Network was launched as a hot, content-rich multimedia site. After having produced two videos, one on the diamond trade in Sierra Leone and one on CIA's involvement in drug traffic, GNN merged with another alt-news web venture and attracted a few other professionals. I met Stephen Marshall at Chicago's exciting Version New Media Festival in March 2003, where we decided to keep track of each other's movements. Precisely because of GNN's political overtone, I kicked off the interview with camcorder technologies and digital video aesthetics. All the rest you can see and judge for yourself: www.gnn.tv.

>> **Geert Lovink:** Could you tell us something about your editing technique? You seem to edit on the rhythm of the music, that's the feel one gets, but perhaps the content is not always ready to follow that logic. How do you solve that tension?

>> **Stephen Marshall:** It is important to know that, besides being a video director, I am also a progressive trance DJ. And I have always been deeply interested in the alchemy of sound and live 'editing' of beats that happens in the clubland culture of dj-ing. So when I cut videos, it is really just an extension of that process. The visuals are just another layer of

meaning but not necessarily a more important one. I think that anyone who is seriously dedicated to the creation of transformative media – and by that I mean media that has as its
core goal the (sub) conscious evolution of its audience – the study of human perception is
critical. You simply cannot attempt the production relevant socio-political media while ignoring the avenues of receptivity that are innate to your audience. And we know that, in that
respect, sound precedes image. Human beings hear before they see. Before there was
light, there was 'the sound'. You know? It's just fundamental. And what I learnt from DJing is
that there is a whole array of reactions and responses that can be triggered in people
through the purposeful architecture of sonic frequencies – at least in the way that they move
their bodies. So much of the art of dj-ing is about building a narrative with the music, one
that is inclusive and has impact enough that people never leave the dance floor.

Applying this to GNN, my intention has always been to merge the subliminal elements
of electronic music culture with the overt and traditionally barren transmission of socio-
political data. And not just because of my own artistic fetishes. There has been such a huge
dropping off in the relevance and popularity of the documentary genre, and all news programming for that matter, which is really quite alarming. If young people are not engaged
in the gathering and trading of data that directly informs their perception of society, the
potential for a widespread tactical overthrow of the system is threatened. And if activist content producers are not willing to use all the means at their disposal to compete with the
mainstream broadcast spectacle, then they are not serious about building a movement to
silence it. So, in my approach to the editing and design of the GNN news videos, the primary focus is always on building synergetic media that is driven by a musical narrative.
Because that is what the younger generation responds to. Nike knows this. Coca-Cola
knows this. And we should not ignore the time and research they have put into attracting
and conforming the attention of the youth through their advertising campaigns. In many
cases I have let the music guide the editing process and conformed it to that, because the
original concept for the GNN news videos was that they exist as a new form of 'enhanced'
music video – political films that were scored by pre-produced ambient or beat-driven
tracks. So right from the start, we knew that there was going to be a tension because we
wouldn't just be cutting the video and then sticking in loops after the fact. The editing would
be done to the track itself. So I would spend a lot of time looking for tracks that evoked the
frequency of the message inherent in the video we were producing, and then let the music
guide my cuts, my design techniques and the placement of the content.

Let me give you an example: The first video I edited for GNN was called *The Most
Dangerous Game*. I had shot the principle interviews a month before and decided that I
wanted to go with a very basic, split-screen design that incorporated flashes of white text
centred between the two screens on the bottom of the frame, so as to create a hypnotic
effect. And we had made an arrangement with Mitchel Akiyama, a Montreal-based producer,
to use one of his tracks. But when I began to listen to his music, it was so haunting and
beautiful that it began to shape the way I was approaching the narrative. The song became
primary and I found myself literally cutting the documentary to the music. You can imagine
how weird and backward that is but I felt totally compelled to maintain the integrity of his
composition and warped the spoken word and text around the track. So when people

watched *The Most Dangerous Game*, the first thing they always said was, "the music is so perfect for that" or "I can't believe how well that goes with the music". Obviously this was not going to be a sustainable approach to editing the news videos. Since then I have developed relationships with djs who take mp3 clips of various speakers, and then create loops that I can drop in behind them, which are specifically produced to mirror that person's vocal pitch and the tempo of their speech. In the case of *AfterMath*, we actually worked directly with Paris who gave us individual tracks for each segment and then came to the studio in post to make sure that the speeds and tempos were all synchronized. So it is an evolving process.

>> **GL:** Can you tell us something about the background of the infographics that you are using? Who is your main source of inspiration there? Is it in video art or documentary film- making or rather something from the world of computers?

>> **SM:** My first and most decisive exposure to the use of typography and text-driven design, as a pure art form, was in Peter Greenaway's *The Pillow Book*. That film, and its approach to cinematic composition of text, specifically Mandarin characters, was so beautiful that it really inspired and informed most of the work I have done since 1997. It just added an extra layer of information and, in many ways, was the next level evolution of the design that Tomato had done for all the Underworld videos of *Dubnobassinmyheadman*, which were also hugely inspiring – though not so much in a practical way, more just for their obvious love for 'type' and re-contextualization of it in the beat-driven electronica of Underworld's seminal tracks.

In all of GNN's work, the primary emphasis is on the functional dissemination of information. It may move quickly, and require multiple viewings, but the bottom line impetus is transmitting useful socio-political data. So, in that regard, I have also been very influenced by the template approach of the various twenty-four hour cable channels – the way they use their little news tickers and the Flame-enriched motion graphics to dig deep into the collective unconscious of the spectatorial masses. It's all very experimental in its own way. When I was running Channel Zero, I was actually brought into CNN by its chairman and CEO right before they got taken over by Time Warner in 1997. He wanted me to help them re-design the network and to potentially create a youth-driven news channel. I used the opportunity to work our designers to develop a series of design templates for the network. These were all based on using a new palette of colours and background designs as well as placing the newscasters in smaller boxes allowing for more space for text. We also spent a lot of time conceiving ways to make the information presented more visceral. So we came up with designs that featured key words that would pulse through the screen when they were spoken by the commentators.

These days I get most of my ideas from magazines and online design journals. There is such a powerful renaissance occurring in the realm of design but it is so seldom used to further any political or social goals. So it's actually quite easy to look at what the kids are doing with Flash and Photoshop and just riff on it within the political context of the videos we are producing.

>> **GL:** Could you, in theory, produce all your clips with a DV camera and a PC or Mac with

video editing tools or do you still have to go into a studio? Where will we be in a few years from now, in terms of tactical media tools?

>> **SM:** Everything that I make can be produced entirely on a laptop and a firewire cable. Of course, the larger projects really depend on drive space, but with 3 x 60 gig drives, you can basically cut a feature film. The next crucial element is software, of course, and even then we only really need a good desktop editor like Final Cut Pro as well as some basic design tools like Photoshop or After Effects. Tactical media tools have become 100% portable. I remember that when I was cutting *AfterMath*, I had to do a series of talks around the US and so I took the video on the road with me. It was a huge design project with some parts expanding over sixteen layers of video. On one flight to Chicago, I was actually designing this sequence that dealt with the failure of the military to intercept the hijacked aircraft on 9/11. I had cut out images of the actual planes and was creating an animation of the Pentagon attack, probably one of the more complicated design sequences I have ever executed. I didn't know it but there were a group of passengers all sitting behind me watching me cut. And one of them came up to me and asked me if I was playing a video game. I laughed because, even though to many people this would be considered a relatively complex process, for me it has become the equivalent of walking around with a Gameboy.

I was actually just in Iraq. And before we left, we were warned by some journalists not to bring too much equipment because it could get jacked driving across from the Jordanian border. So we just took our cameras and flak jackets and left our laptops behind. But once we got there, I realized that it would have been fine. There was no real danger of getting robbed and I could have been producing video of the situation in Baghdad right from my little hotel room, and uploading to the site through the net café downstairs. So, it's all here right now, from a tactical media perspective. What we need to focus on is the development of the infrastructure that will disseminate these clips. We need to think in terms of our own broadcast enterprise so that it is not such an atomistic, singular culture.

>> **GL:** Some of the people that I spoke with are critical of your populist approach. They also see your affiliation with conspiracy theory as a symptom of leftist media populism. How do you respond to such remarks? Where does investigative journalism stop and turn into conspiracy? Do you see such criticism as envy because GNN so successfully brings together pop aesthetics with critical content?

>> **SM:** It's interesting that you say "populist". I was just with Naomi Klein and we were talking about differences between American and European broadcasters. I was saying that, after being in Iraq and watching a lot of the BBC, I was quite impressed by some of the coverage of the war. And, specifically, about a series they had run challenging the virtues of capitalism. But she was not at all impressed, and made the point that although the BBC has more intellectual vigour and is able to find an audience for programming that publicly challenges the foundation of their economic system, there is a more ingrained elitism which pervades their coverage. One example she used was that the BBC always uses the word 'populist' to describe revolutionary or insurgent movements in countries like Bolivia or

Venezuela – as if to give the impression that they are the products of some irrational mass hysteria, instead of a deeply intrinsic and instinctual reaction to an entrenched socio-political power base that has, at its core, militarized defence mechanisms. And looking back at the coverage of the recent Bolivian protests, I found her to be very accurate in her characterization.

Like the BBC, or any organized social cluster, the so-called Left has its own entrenched elitist core. And one of their defining conventions is the whole scale rejection of any decon-struction deemed 'conspiratorial'. From Noam Chomsky to Chip Berlet, they simply deny, and in many cases, ridicule those who attempt to piece together disparate facets of a lar-ger picture in order to understand how power operates through covert channels to achieve its prime directives. I feel that this is one of the primary faults with the Left elite – and one of the major reasons for their increasingly diminished relevance with younger generations. They refuse to expand the horizon of their intellectual inquiry. For them, there is no tangible value for theory that falls outside of the institutional critique. But what kind of world would we live in if Aristotle hadn't mused on the nature of the heavenly spheres or if Newton hadn't extrapolated on the laws of gravity, or Einstein on the quotient of relativity? Or, more to the point, if Woodward and Bernstein hadn't gone down the muddy path toward expos-ing the Watergate scandal? All of these people built their cases, at one crucial juncture or another, without factual data to back them up. All of them had to postulate at certain times, and instead of drawing society away from the critical work of catalysing an overthrow of the structural paradigm, these 'theories' created entirely new constructs for the society to per-ceive itself through. Surely there is a place, in all modes of inquiry and critique, for this type of scientific adventurism … it is how we get from one place to the next. For now, I think these intellectuals do us a mild disservice by looking down their noses at even the most humble attempt to piece together and understand what is a very simplified and untenable explanation of the events.

With respect to your question about GNN, I don't think that we have a conspiratorial ethos. Nor, even, an 'affiliation with conspiracy theory'. All of our (text and video) stories are vetted with traditional journalistic standards and scrutiny. We have certainly never been accused of disseminating misinformation. Perhaps one could accuse us of slumming with conspiracy theorists, but only in one of our video productions, *Aftermath: Unanswered Questions From 9/11*. In *Aftermath*, we sought to gather perspectives from nine individuals who collectively represent a spectrum of beliefs about what occurred that day. And, yes, in that film we did feature people who wholeheartedly believe that 9/11 was orchestrated by a covert US intelligence cell, working through Al Qaeda. But we also featured a major US attorney whose deepest conspiracy theory is that the airlines did not do enough to protect their passengers, and a long-serving civil rights attorney who is concerned with the impact that the US Patriot Act will have on civil society. So there was a spectrum of opinions pre-sented, and none of them were factually inaccurate – not even the revelations concerning the Northwoods Document, which was authored by a former general in the Joint Chiefs of Staff, and which called for attacks on US civilians to justify a war on Cuba.

But anyone who finds that or other facts untenable immediately accuses us of con-spiracy theory. Just as I imagine they did when Gary Webb broke the Dark Alliance story in

1996, proving that the CIA had engaged in drug traffic to support the right-wing Nicaraguan Contras. He was called a conspiracy theorist when the story first came out. But now it is accepted as historical fact. And, interestingly enough, we actually won our prize at Sundance for Crack The CIA, which is just a graphically enhanced, beat-driven rehash of the Contra scandal. So, clearly, young people are looking for answers to questions that go beyond the intellectual theory that is the elite Left's principal strategy for overhauling the system. If that is really what they are trying to achieve. Because the mass public will not help anyone overhaul anything unless they see tangible evidence, at a very base level, of complicit wrongdoing and overt criminality. They do not respond to hyper-verbosity. They want it tabloid style. And we can either snobbishly reject that 'populist' approach, or take our cues from the mainstream realm of advertising and music television and deliver socio-political commentary in the most charismatic style possible. Weaponize the media. And this is what we are trying to do with GNN – to help corroborate a functional algorithm for under-standing the machinations of power. If critics of the work see GNN as somehow reaching down to the lowest common denominator by questioning the motives and potential crimi-nality of the covert bodies operating on behalf of the American elites, then I have to ques-tion what their motives are. And if they have really thought it all out now, in the year 2003, with a Bush in the White House and the advent of a nuclear battlefront. Obviously they are not having much success.

The Left is invisible in American political life. Can't they see or admit to themselves that it's not working? We need to overthrow the power structure (in both the Left and the Right!), and this will only happen by creating a widespread and widely held level of public distrust of those who manipulate it for their own ends. As to the issue of jealousy, I have always taken shit for my designer approach to tactical media, which has usually been a hit with the kids. That, and my talkative personality, tend to make people think I am perhaps a little too cocky. I don't think it is a matter of envy, though. At least I hope not. It is more an issue of an establishment ethos making itself transparent in the Left elite – that they are just as old-fashioned and fuddy-duddy as the monarchies. Just look at what Roger Ailes is doing with Fox News Channel. Have you seen it? They are using some of the highest-end graphics generators to filter the Pentagon's press releases into the public consciousness. You think we have time to sit around debating whether or not to use drum'n'bass as a background score? The spectacle is in full effect and we need to build ourselves into a powerful rival if we are going to have any tangible shot at the hearts and minds of the next generation.

>> GL: What interests me in your work is that you have not dropped the 'talking heads'. In fact, you have reframed talking experts within a contemporary environment of music video clips and computer graphics. Can you imagine moving on and dropping the 'talking heads' altogether? In short: how can critical content be delivered within screen culture if we do not want to use the written or spoken word?

>> SM: I do think we can evolve the broadcast template to a level where the viewer does not need to see an image of the spokesperson in order to digest their words, though that will have an effect on the way that they process the information. From a pure news perspective, there is an element of credibility that is assured by showing the 'talking heads'. You know they are the authors of the ideas. You can see their faces and look into their eyes. There is, at least, the illusion of contact. And I have tried to stay with that on a fundamental level. So what I have been doing, the re-contextualizing of the standard 'talking heads', is really just merging traditional documentary form with the more modern approach used to sell ideas or products. In a sense, we are 'selling' or 'commodifying' the ideas of our intellectuals and experts. Selling them to the viewers as aggressively as Coke sells sugar-water. And I am not sure that we would be as successful if we just dropped the talking heads altogether because I think people need to see that person, hear that voice to know what they are dealing with – and whether they want to 'buy' that perspective. However, as you know, there is a relatively new genre of film that does not depend on talking heads or spoken word to make profoundly impacting and controversial political statements. The *Qatsi Trilogy* by Godfrey Reggio and Philip Glass has become cult with global reach. And they translate so well because they are driven purely by the universal languages of image and music. How many raves have you been to with *Koyaanisqatsi* playing on multiple screens behind the dj? I've been to hundreds. It is a ubiquitous presence in underground culture. And this is one goal I have for the GNN videos: that, eventually, we might begin to create works that are so subliminally subversive and non-specific in their 'language' that they can be played anywhere, in any environment, and still conjure some instinct for critical enthusiasm on the part of the audience.

>> **GL:** What is the main source of distribution for GNN? Do you see broadcast TV as the ultimate opportunity or would you rather bet on an increased distribution via DVD and the net, combined with screenings in halls and theatres?

>> **SM:** Without sounding too idealistic, all of the above. GNN's main source of distribution is through our website. But that is only the first tier of our horizontal distribution network. It serves as a free, viral platform for the videos, which have been the catalysing force for our 4000+ registered online community who interact through the forums. We also sell our DVDs from the site and get a lot of sales from people who have shows on community television stations. Our deal with them is that as long as they buy one DVD, they can play the videos as much as they want. So there is a broad level of distribution occurring through broadcast TV, just not the corporate networks. Through our work with Interscope and other, smaller, record companies, our videos have been given a platform that reaches a broader audience, but the closest we came to having an MTV debut was with the video we produced for Eminem's *White America*. Unfortunately, on the day it was set to launch, CNN did a feature on it and brought on one of the parents of a Columbine victim. Within a matter of minutes they had reduced the video to a glorification of the infamous school shootings, pronounced it vile and opportunistic. And Interscope was forced to pull it from MTV. As a result, it got approximately 6 million views online. But the most successful and rewarding of all have been the public screenings of *AfterMath*. These started with a sold-out premiere in San Francisco's historic Herbst Theatre. The event had been organized by a group of local 9/11 activists and they had raised money to buy thousands of beautiful, full colour movie posters.

The hype was massive and we had about 1,500 people show up for the screening, with 500 turned away. When other groups heard about this, we began to get a flood of requests to provide DVDs and posters for local events. These culminated in a North America-wide screening on September 11, 2003, to commemorate the second anniversary of the tragedy. Screenings were held in large theatres, public libraries and even people's homes. Many had long, formal debates after the film to discuss the issues it raises. Since we completed the DVD, *AfterMath* has been translated into four languages. So, on a microcosmic scale, we are pushing the envelope in each realm of exhibition. Apart from the site, we have also distributed the DVDs through retail video chains – though only the large independents. Mainstream companies won't stock the films and we cannot get a distributor to represent us. So it's still a grassroots thing and we're happy that way.

>> **GL:** In October 2003, half a year after the Bush invasion/liberation of Iraq, you visited Baghdad. Reading the dispatches on your website, we get a sense of both the beauty and violence of the place. This visit must have moved you. To what extend did it challenge your perceptions of the war? Are the anti-war protesters still right? I suppose so. But how about the intense reality over there? Did that overturn the global media spectacle?

>> **SM:** Visiting Iraq was a transformative experience. Not because of the hyperrealism and immediacy of witnessing a culture reacting to a major military occupation, but more because I was able to step directly into the meta-narrative that exists beyond the veil of America's shallow, Pentagon-sanctioned media coverage. While we were there, we began to think of the experience in terms of a virtual reality game. It was so palpably dangerous, chaotic and graphically stunning. And so much more complex than what we had been told. We jokingly referred to it as "Grand Theft Auto: Baghdad". The tableau was so rich. And the characters we met were incredibly diverse and eloquent people – from Rana, our chain-smoking pro-Saddam translator, to Lt. Colonel Nate Sassaman, the legendary West Point quarterback now running tactical operations against the insurgency in the Sunni Triangle. At one point, when asked how he would describe the experience of being in Iraq, Sassaman smiled and said, "I am living in, like, a totally surreal movie". So I know we were not the only ones who felt it was something ultra-ordinary.

And yes, it totally overturned the media spectacle and illustrated how truly dangerous the media has become, in that they have simply accepted the new rules of war and wilfully allowed themselves to be 'embedded' without ever gauging the experience of the average Iraqi. When was the last time we saw Iraqi citizens speaking for themselves on television or in the mainstream press? It's so brutally ethnocentric that you have to wonder just how producers and editors can sustain their apologist rhetoric without ever being struck by the vacuous negative space given to the Iraqis to occupy.

As far as how the experience affected my interpretation of the war – from the minute I stepped on the plane to Jordan, my perceptions were challenged. Like many of us in progressive social movements, I was against the war – not so much because of its stated objective of removing Saddam Hussein, whatever the justification, but more because it was being prosecuted by individuals that had established business relationships with him during some of his most brutal and repressive periods. Bush and Cheney are just so nakedly disin-genuous that it would be difficult to support even the most humane of policies because you know that their hearts just aren't in anything. But when we met Frank al-Bayati, an exiled Iraqi freedom fighter who had been rescued by US soldiers after being left for dead by Saddam's soldiers and then given a new life in America, on the flight to Jordan, it changed everything. And I would challenge any steadfast anti-war protestor to stand at the border of Iraq and watch Frank, weeping uncontrollably, kiss the ground of a country he was forced to flee due to his political beliefs, and then tell him that the Americans didn't do the right thing. I certainly was hard-pressed to summon even the remotest degree of cynicism. And as we travelled around the country, filming his emotional return to a family that had assumed the worst, our sense of confusion and conflict only deepened. It was a profound experience.

Of course, we know Frank's return to a 'free' Iraq is only a sideshow to the American boot print which has been placed firmly on Arab soil, and that was only made clearer by our time with US troops stationed in the Sunni Triangle. As you probably know, this is where all the fighting is happening and we were able to spend a few nights with the troops stationed out there. It was an equally transformative experience. We met top-level colonels and low-est rank privates, all of whom were imbued with an almost uncanny level of humanity and integrity and an open compassion for the Iraqi people. Many spoke very candidly about their fears and lack of enthusiasm for fighting, especially when they only signed up for the reserves to get a college education! But what they all had in common was a sense of pride in the notion that they were working directly with the rebuilding of schools and hospitals. And why wouldn't they? These are the very people who can relate to the kind of world social inequity the Iraqis are facing because they are the poor and lower middle-classes of the country. But by no means less intelligent. In one of the more paradigm-busting moments of the trip, we interviewed an African-American tank commander named Hollis who proceeded to deconstruct the war, referencing the Third Punic War, and citing analogies to *Star Trek* and the battle between humans and the Borg. It was truly mind-blowing. But what got me the most was when he explained the Administration's need to lie in order to justify the war. It went something like this: "You can't tell mothers who have lost their sons that they died fighting to save our way of life, that they were taken to Iraq to fight for what is the globali-sation of capitalism. You have to present them with a war fought over ideology. That is the way it has always been. But we understand very well that we are fighting for economic rea-sons. And we should. It is either us or them. Falafel or Big Mac. And that is worth dying for".

For me, Iraq was about finding the human strand of DNA that runs through all of the conflict and betrayal of our innermost desire to be one. I found it in everyone I met. Everyone who was on the ground in that country was united by that elemental desire. No one, not even Saddam's staunchest supporters, would say that he was a good or kind or wise leader. But the one idea most everyone would accept is that the reasons for America's drive to Baghdad were never clearly and honestly spoken by its architects. And that, in the end, even the biggest lies will yield poisoned harvests for their advocates.

Synchronicities
Baghdad/Delhi

ANAND VIVEK TANEJA

Salam Pax lives. I hope.
He listens to Portishead and Leonard Cohen...
Doesn't think driving with Bjork on the stereo is a good idea, because it does strange things to brain cells.

But he's been doing a lot of driving with his father and cousin in recent days.
Tanks stocked up with gas, they go out to see their city. Burning. Full of smoke and debris. And sudden death, and the possibilities of death.
Salam Pax lives in Baghdad. I hope.
He hasn't written in on since March 24. The phone exchanges in Baghdad have been destroyed by American missiles.

He turned twenty-nine last year. Or was it thirty. On September 18.
He has a friend called Raed who lives in Amman.

in some ways its very sickening how 'exciting' news has become...exciting bcoz ppl are being killed....its horrible....was regularly reading this blog kept up by a guy in baghdad....and all of a sudden he has stopped writing...and while this could be bcoz his internet connxn has been cut off it could also be bcoz he doesnt exist any more...anand, why is life like this? why cant the world be a happier place?
Atishi

Atishi lives. In Oxford.
She listens to Leonard Cohen and the Beatles. Giggles a lot when she does hash.
Studies history. Very hard. She freaks out on Harry Potter and Roald Dahl. Also works for women's welfare. She has many friends. One of them died in a car crash last week ...

Atishi is one of the most active anti-war protestors in Oxford. She was part of the millions of people who thronged the streets

of the world on the fifteenth of February to protest the war.
She was part of the crowd that invaded the Fairford Air Force
Base, the only one in England from which B-52 bombers fly.

She has a friend called Anand who lives in Delhi.

The most disturbing news today has come from Al-Jazeera. They
said that nine B-52 bombers have left the airfield in Britain
and flying "presumably" towards Iraq, as if they would be doing
a spin around the block. Anyway they have 6 hours to get here.
Salam Pax

Anand writes about B-52s. And A-10s. And F-15s. And all those
other numbers which can blitz cities out of the sky. He is
obsessed with military hardware and what it can do to urban landscapes.
He writes about Delhi getting ripped open by bombs in 2007.
...He also makes movies about people who survive holocausts.
...He listens to The Police.

On weekends, sometimes, he shows rich white people around Delhi
and makes money, while beggars pull at his arms.
He takes them to the Jama Masjid.

The pigeons rose upwards from the corn-scattered courtyard with
a collective explosion which made me turn from Hussain's Quran
to look at their suddenly startled flight. I remembered a story
of Hussain, on his way to the Karbala, who had to leave his
daughter behind in Medina for she was ill. She kept sending letters by carrier pigeon to tell him to come home soon.
     I wondered about the pigeon she sent, with a letter for
her father and almost all her family, as they travelled. I wondered what the pigeon felt as he came in over the slaughter of
Karbala, where Hussain and his family and followers had been
killed for their faith, surrounded and much outnumbered by
Yazid's troops. After flying over miles and miles of barren
earth, expecting food and water and loving stroking for bringing a message from a loved one – then to come in over a blood-
soaked stinking battlefield. I thought of all the pigeons on all
the crowded rooftops in the lanes and mohallas surrounding the
Jama Masjid, in Chawri Bazaar, Ballimaran, Lal Kuan, Matya
Mahal, Hauz Qazi, and I hoped that this would never happen to
them. Again. How was I to know I was a frigging prophet, that

when those pigeons came back from their whirling soaring air-
races, one day, this day, it would.
Anand

The Americans and Brits have fought at Najaf and Karbala, and
have moved on to Baghdad.

...Metaphors have tumbled. Died wordless deaths inside heads.

And as Anand sat in Café Coffee Day today, richer by two thousand, feeling like he'd sold his soul to the devil, while beggar children pressed their noses against the plate glass, he
read about Salam Pax, and he cried.
Anand

Do not meddle in the affairs of dragons, because you are crunchy
and taste good with ketchup.

....
....
....
....

url's of Blogs from Baghdad
Salam Pax's Blog
http://dear_raed.blogspot.com/
Riverbend's Blog
http://riverbendblog.blogspot.com/

Portrait of a Day in Baghdad

PAUL CHAN

December 28
2AM
My first drink of *arak*, an Iraqi liquor, that tastes like liquorice and stings like rock candy. The poet Farouk Salloum told me he was drinking *arak* at his house when the missiles hit Baghdad in the first Gulf War. After his first glass, he prayed the attack would end quickly. After the second, he wished he had more *arak* at his house because there was no way he was going to get more during an attack. After his third glass, he screamed at the missiles to bring it on.

9AM
I remember now the party last night at Farouk's house. Members of the Iraq Peace Team were invited to a private party of musicians, journalists, and poets. Farouk was dressed in casual black. He had sleepy eyes. He was gracious and demanding, ordering drinks be constantly filled, especially for the women. The socialist Baath Party banned public drinking in 1995. Ever since, Iraqis have taken their drink underground and at each other's homes. Farouk's second daughter is named Reem, which means one who is as graceful as a deer running. She doesn't have her father's eyes.

   A droll pianist and a veteran of the Iran/Iraq war in the early 80s played Bach and a jazzy funeral march. Earlier in the evening the pianist had told me that he had killed six men in the war, and that the men and women of Iraq are all trained in combat, and will take to arms and stones if need be to stop the Americans from entering Baghdad. I ask him if his experience in killing shaped, in any way, his piano playing. No response.

NOON
A word or two about *kubbe* in soup. At the Al-Shadbandar Café, where the Iraqi literati come to drink tea and speculate about the war, and who is the number one poet of the week, Almad, a young sculptor, invites me for *kubbe* in soup. It is close and it is good, he says. Fair enough. I'm ready for it. Before I had left the States, Aviv, a dear friend and member

of New Kids On The Black Bloc, an artist political collective in Barcelona, asked me to seek out *kubbe* in soup. "I know you're not going to Baghdad for a culinary tour, but promise me you will try it".

It is a meat-dumpling the size of my head swimming in greasy soup. The skin of the dumpling is thick and wheaty. Inside, a mixture of ground meat of unknown origins and cinnamon. Other spices too, but who can tell. The soup is hot water with onions. Sometimes with tomatoes.

Almad wants me to come. But Haider, another sculptor, says it may not be such a good idea. It will be crowded, he says, and the water is not so good for foreigners. Okay, I say to Almad, next time. I drink my lemon tea and dream of dumplings the size of my head. A cinema critic enters the café. He's the number one critic in Baghdad, Haider tells me, because he is the only one in the city. He jokes to Ellen, my travel companion for the day and a full time peace activist from Maryland, that he would like to do a cultural exchange with her; she can take his post as the number one critic in Baghdad if he could get a visa and go to the US.

3PM

We wander around the booksellers' row, a *souk* (open market) next to the Al-Shadbandar Café. Former engineers sell their collection of books on statistical analysis here and whatever else they can find in their house. Books are indiscriminately piled on the sidewalk for people to browse through. Iraq had, before the sanctions, one of the highest literacy rates in the Middle East and the largest number of PhDs. This is why you will find not only books on mathematics and structural mechanics, but also Hegelian philosophy, Pop Art, and Modern absurdist drama in Arabic, English, French, German, and even Chinese. I find a nice copy of Tom Stoppard's play, *Rosencrantz and Guildenstern are Dead*. Also a beautiful book on Islamic calligraphy.

We have what's called a magic sheet. On one side of this piece of paper is an explanation of what the Iraq Peace Team is about and why we are in Iraq. On the other side, the same thing in Arabic. We pass this out and hope to enlarge our family. It does work like magic, and a bookseller quickly becomes a friend (because, not surprisingly, everyone is against the war). It is only paper but has the weight of gold.

I meet a poet named Suha Noman Rasheed. He is slowly selling his collection of poetry books on the row, to live. He has published three books of Arabic poetry and promises me he will bring a copy of one of them next week. A writer friend in the US asked me to bring back some books in Arabic so they can be translated into English. This is our rescue mission, he tells me.

4:50PM

Walking back to the hotel, Ellen and I noticed the pristine quality of the Iraqi police cars. Some of the plastic coverings haven't even been taken off the seats. Ellen, who served for four years in the US army, and I agreed that one can tell the health of any regime by the cleanliness of the police cars.

6PM
An action-planning meeting for the Peace Team. Productive. There will be an action on December 31st entitled "Resolutions and Celebrations". The goal is to throw a party and get Iraqi mothers, fathers, kids, poets, writers and peace activists together to make New Year's resolutions that would replace the UN resolutions now serving as the litmus test for war. I am in charge of the visuals. I imagine 10,000 Iraqi children dressed in white suits and dresses, singing and waving their hands up as if they were surrendering. Musical accompaniment: Aretha Franklin. Special Guest: sub-commandante Marcos. I don't tell the others about the plan. Let's see what I can do in four days.

7:30PM
Found out George is leaving the team because his father in Massachusetts is in serious condition after he broke his hip. I'm very fond of George. A Lebanese man who also stays at the Al-Fanar hotel, who may or may not be a war profiteer, said George has a heart of gold. I believe him. He's been to Iraq nine times and financially supports eight families here. On this trip he brought two suitcases of medicines and toys. Baghdad is the city of infinite need.

8PM
Saddam is on television. He is sitting on a white leather couch. The reception is bad. Just now there was a cut-away shot to the crowd listening to him speak. It is immense. But there is never a shot of the crowd and Saddam together. Did you know that the Russian KGB was the grandfather of Adobe Photoshop? Not only did they make people disappear, they made their appearance in photographs disappear as well. With a razor blade, pen and ink they would retouch photographs with such precision, it was as if the person had never appeared in the original photograph. Now the cut-away is the standard, whether it is used to subtract or add people. Reality has never been so elastic. Followed by a music video of children singing, and images of Saddam at various state functions.

11PM
Saf, a young student who I play dominos with sometimes, asks me if I have any aspirin for him. I tell Saf, tomorrow.

11:50PM
Every night at 11:30 Iraq television plays a movie. Tonight it's *Mission to Mars* starring Val Kilmer. Kilmer, incidentally, came to Iraq in 1998 as a part of a campaign called "America Cares". One of the members of the board of directors on AC was Barbara Bush. The campaign was set up to take the media spotlight away from former attorney general Ramsey Clark's delegation called "The Sanctions Challenge", which was in Baghdad at the same time. It worked. No one paid attention to Clark and his crew, who were campaigning to stop the sanctions. All eyes were on Val and his vague promises to bring democracy and bad movies to the Middle East.

1AM

Cannot sleep. The wild dogs of Baghdad are out, barking and laughing at the few cars that are still out on the street. I find the following quote in a book about Lao Tzu, mystical Chinese philosopher, that seems appropriate to the times: "Vulgar people are clear, I alone am drowsy. Vulgar people are alert, I alone am muddled".

The Iraq Peace Team Project

Paul Chan is part of the Iraq Peace Team Project. Since September 2002, Iraq Peace Team members have travelled to Iraq and have taken up residence in major cities. They have sent back reports, digital still photographs, open diary entries, digital video footage, press releases, opinion articles, recorded audio, letters to the editor, and more. Chan is a member of the December Iraq Peace team and was in Iraq until mid-January 2003, creating media and art that tells the story of this unspeakable drive for war and the people caught in its path. Chan's video work is distributed by Video Data Bank (www.vdb.org) and his new media work is online at (www.nationalphilistine.com).

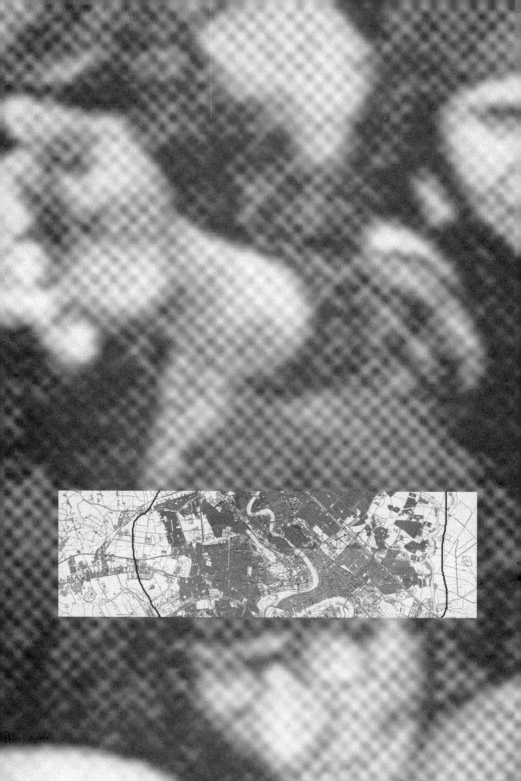

Diary of a News Cameraman
Baghdad, July 2003

SHAKEB AHMED

To Begin

This is a journal of my fourteen days in Iraq. The account is punctuated with the advantage hindsight offers; but this was also a projection to begin with, even as the words engaged with a clear and confused present. I was visiting Baghdad from the 6th to the 19th of July 2003 as a television cameraman for the program *World View India* that aired on Doordarshan, the Indian national television channel. Choppers were brought down later, there was still no talk of troops being withdrawn by so and so date, and George Bush had not yet appeared for a Baghdad Thanksgiving. Before all that comes…

July 6th, 2003

Ali Babas and Saddam Currency

At four in the morning we left our hotel in Amman. Everyone had prescribed that we cross the Iraqi Border as early in the day as possible, because once the day starts melting away, the reign of *Ali Babas* would set in. *Ali Babas* – armed bandits – who wouldn't show any legendary Arab hospitality, who craved your material possessions, and who would not discriminate between guests armed with pens or guns. We were told to carry all our dollars inside our socks or maybe even stash it in our underwear if that was not too uncomfortable.

It was a long journey. Ten hours. I will not call it long-and-winding because that conveys a sense of slowness, a certain languor. Instead, we were pushing ahead in a Chevy Suburban at speeds of ninety or a hundred miles per hour. That was exciting, and dange-rous. Three quarters of the travellers on these roads from Amman to Baghdad were jour-nalists, and this journey for most of them was exactly that: exciting and dangerous. In the adrenalin trap of reporting an after-war, one willingly forgets death – you are after all at a safe distance from that spectre, the War ('The War Is Over!') – and what matters is only the sensation of excitement and danger. Let's call those reporting on the after-war "Tourists of the Modern Ruins". I was one of these touring hordes descending on the horizons of Baghdad, a television-cameraman on a news assignment in Iraq post-*priori* the ouster of Saddam Hussein.

Dutifully, our Jordanian driver refreshed our fears of the scourge of *Ali Babas*. Later I would learn that while liberating Iraq from everything that represented the repression of Saddam, Coalition Troops emptied out many a prison thinking that all those enclosed were political prisoners. Some say Saddam directly contributed to this while he was doing his final fleeing act. Many hard-boiled criminals finally saw their freedom in these default war-actions. Most now run freewheeling careers as independent *Ali Babas*.

Our Suburban rolled on. At places we would slow down to catch others on the way, and you could then see serpentine caravans of Chevys moving together slowly like a pack of deer that has just smelled danger. At the Jordan-Iraq border we saw with our own eyes that American troops were definitely not very fond of Arabs, but they did cooperate with white and coloured non-Arab people. Once done with our passport registration, and having entered Iraq officially, our driver could now buy gas for the rest of our journey. Countless young gas sellers dotted the near-field of the extending empty rocky desert ahead. With their *kaffiyehs* and faded blue jeans, these youths hurried to service. There was risk involved, so they mostly had to be paid in a familiar currency. Everybody coming from Amman would bring some Iraqi exchange – dinars with the beaming face of erstwhile president *Baba* (father) Saddam Hussein.

One of the boys to whom we were supposed to hand over our Saddams – for that is what these bills are popularly called – said something to the effect that he knew Amitabh Bachhan and, pounding his fists in empty air, proclaimed that, like him, Saddam would fight back. But did not we come with the idea that everyone in Iraq was happy once they saw their President exit? Pictures of jubilating crowds shaped our imagination as Saddam went in hiding … and we took it as the most representative picture of liberated Iraq. Dutifully, we would follow the same line even in our sojourn, questioning Baghdadis: was Saddam not a bad man? Always the same reply in the affirmative, but in a way that I could almost construe lines delivered comically to strange enquiring beasts. Nobody was digging for more.

A month and a half later, local attacks would grow in audacity, casualties, and regularity. Only then would even majors like BBC start relaying reports that these are not just effects engineered by the 'Remnants of the Erstwhile Saddam Regime', or the insecure subjects of The Sunni Triangle … but these might yet be an underground yet popular uprising of a national character which presumes that no promises of the Regime Change have been delivered, and that people might actually be worse off now, not knowing till when the misery would last.

July 7th, 2003
Under Siege
Baghdad metropolis – fibres of over bridges and stretching roads, high-rises of government buildings, mammoth modern residential blocks, and in the distance the overarching burning torches of those oil refineries … And the people, these Iraqi faces, always hemmed-in by

the blueness of the UN flags, the fatigues-less personnel of globe-trotter NGOs, and the dark glasses of entrepreneurs brought to Baghdad by hopes of having a share in its reconstruction. And always those hands that are busy writing them down, filming them up...

A shattering sound wakes me up. I rise up from my Hotel Palestine bed, run to the room balcony: helicopters are cutting corners around my hotel. These are military choppers of the Coalition Forces serving the double purpose of being both 'a roving eye in the sky', as well as ensuring visibility of the deterring potency of American might. Later, I would know that Baghdadis did not much like them in their sky. I also noticed, down on the roads, coalition personnel perched atop military tanks, nervously clutching their machine guns, not knowing from where they would attract hostile fire; and traffic lights that didn't work with plying vehicles engineering a pitiless anarchy. One woman would tell me how dangerous the roads had become. Whenever her children left for school, she was never sure if they would return to her safely.

Traffic lights no longer work in the absence of a basic supply of electricity after the war. Traffic guards do not exist because they haven't been paid, or have switched to other jobs – taxi-driving and interpreting for foreigners being the most popular. Whoever could afford it was running their power supply with huge generators, and there was a whole market – legal and illegal – around the running of these machines. We would see enormous lines of vehicles jamming an entire flyover waiting for their turn at gas stations where petrol had mysteriously become scant, while illegal buying and selling of gas happened openly outside the stations. Sometimes there would be fights, and some avoidable accidents. In electronic news, these portraits are often insignificant: "Civic structure, and law and order are not keeping too well. But CPA promises to restore normalcy very soon!"

Later in the day, we would hear our driver mumbling that he had to be relieved early, for after six it was too risky to return home. As the evening approached, we saw streets emptied to complete desertion, even though CPA would impose the curfew only from eleven in the night. *"Baghdad kharab hua!"* ("Baghdad has gone to dogs") was a line we would constantly hear throughout our fourteen days, by our driver who boasted an Indian connection from his father's side, and spoke Urdu well enough for our purposes. In reporting crises like an international war, crises of everyday life are always retained as fillers … just that!

July 8th, 9th, 10th, 2003
Diplomats, Politicians, Press Conferences – the Communication Revolution
Electronic media would be lost if not for the sound bytes and the images of the select few who hijack the orbit of we-are-the-faces-who-decide. All through these three days we would be, like many of our brethren, attentive to the notice boards in various hotels: they carry open invitations by political parties or to-be-political-parties about when and where the 'press conferences' would be held. We would shuttle from Palestine Hotel to Hunting Club to Hotel Sheraton to Canal Hotel etc. etc. and catch up with conferences thrown by the Iraqi National Congress, UN, Coalition Watch Group, All Tribes Iraq etc. etc. In the evenings we would see that the meat of televised news was snippets from these conferences: we were not alone, not to be entirely blamed! The formula in television is: if you find investigating the facts in a conflict a hard job, just record the

gatherings of people vying for power … all that TV needs in difficult situations is *related-visuals* to make up screen time. Only some local press would be investing their not-so-precious time on the kitchen-sink dramas of ordinary characters inhabiting the fringes of this grand Reconstruction Drama.

We do interviews with Dr. Adnan Pachachi, President of the Iraqi Independent Democrats, and Dr. Ahmad Chalabi, Head of the Iraqi National Congress. No doubt they are important, but our choice for these interviews is largely defined by the fact that these few gentlemen are most interviewed by bigger tele-newsies than us. The agenda for reportage is often set not by the reporter. We could simply not afford too much imagination.

July 11th, 2003
Prisoners of War
Saddam's monument to the Qaddisiya Martyrs in Baghdad could be a surreal dream André Breton would have dreamt. A hundred and fifty foot high tiled dome split in two, commem-orating Iraqi soldiers killed in the war against Iran in the early eighties. Its scale exudes a strange feeling of trepidation, and of waste. Now it serves as a base for one of the armoured division of the American forces. We talk with a couple of soldiers at the gate. One of them speaks slowly while gazing at the other side of the road where an Iraqi wedding procession is passing-by. Pondering, he says, "I wish I could have known them at some other time. They are very talented! Every Thursday these Iraqis have a string of weddings, and the young boys playing trumpet can teach a thing or two. I wish I could have formed a music group along with some of these guys. But its unfortunate that we met only in these circumstances". He seems to be about twenty-six years old.

The Media Officer arrives. A young man of twenty-eight. He welcomes us to the base and entrusts us to another of his companions. This companion is only twenty-five, and every few minutes automatically mutters under his breath, "I want to go home". He looks very tired. We go down under the dome. Below is an unimaginably huge bunker where we meet scores of other soldiers. Most are very young. They claim to be volunteers for the forces of their country. I remember talking to an Iraqi caretaker in my hotel. He had said that the only problem – others can still be discounted – that many Iraqis had with Saddam was that right from the time they would join university, they knew they were going to be conscripted in the army. That was the norm, and not every one liked it. These Volunteers of America – they are also conscripts – not many were looking too happy, not too convinced that they should have been here. Who knows how long it would take to get these Siegfried Sassoons, Wilfred Owens and Edmund Blundens out of these bunker worlds.

July 12th, 2003
Ennui
Not much to do today. Nothing lined up. Some appointments didn't come through. From my hotel room window, I watch an old woman sleeping on her terrace. It is seven-thirty in the morning. Minutes pass. She wakes up on her clay terrace; the heat is increasing and she gathers the sheets, pillow and a plastic jar of water, and descends into the house.

Some children are playing in the street. The scene is a regular cliché, but they aptly repeat the staging as if invented only now: all have imaginary guns in hands and are dividing themselves up – maybe as Iraqis and Americans. Then they get busy delivering death to each other.

From my correspondent's room I watch two camouflaged coalition tanks parked on the left side of Abu Nuwas street. Some soldiers loiter with their automatics while their Iraqi helps scrupulously frisk any and everyone bound for the by-lane to Palestine or Sheraton hotels. These men would frisk the women as well; a woman cadre does not yet exist. Similarly, we are told that soldiers regularly use sniffer-dogs during their routine raids, and these dogs – regarded unclean by Arabs – are a constant source of anger and shame for the raided families: men secretly vow to avenge the dishonour though they are given a clean chit at the end of the raid. Two cultures making themselves familiar on pavements.

July 13th, 2003
The Spectacle
It was to start at nine in the morning. A press journalist from France whom I met last evening said he wouldn't waste his time visiting this vulgar joke. Only around two-thirty in the afternoon the proceedings began, after we had thrice been asked to leave the auditorium even as our cameras were meant to stay right there. Thirteen Shia, five Sunni, five Kurds, a Christian and a Turkoman lined up on the stage to steer Iraq into the paths of democracy, while Paul Bremer from the wells below gazed on to see that everything went well with his script. The announcement of the new Iraqi Governing Council went on peacefully at the refurbished Military Industrialisation Organisation headquarters, while BBC and Al Jazeera ran a live show.

July 14th, 15th, 16th, 2003
Providence. Progeny. Pathology
Issam Shukri's office was on Al Rashid Street. There were ten to fifteen men sitting on dusty sofas and wooden chairs. In some hands, rosary beads were constantly racing, and at intervals there would be raised palms and eyes, addressing a god somewhere higher above the damp roof.

Issam is the International Relations Coordinator for the Union of the Unemployed in Iraq (UUI). Officially, unemployment is rated at sixty percent; it might be much higher. He tells us that at various places in Iraq, the ousted Baath regime has started recruiting militias, and many unemployed, in their desperation, are filling the ranks for a few dollars or dinars: increase in the attacks on coalition forces is connected to unemployment in many ways. Unemployment is a bomb – the earlier it is defused, the better.

Later, we had an appointment with a former colonel with the Iraqi armies. Colonel Razak had a small two-floor house in one of the suburbs. His three children welcomed us not just politely but enthusiastically – there have been very few visitors in recent times. In his conversation Razak exuded a sense of warmth and sincere honesty. Then we spoke to Shehla, his wife, and she suddenly broke down; she told us that since returning from the war her husband has not been his usual self. There are times he would not utter even a single word for hours. Razak was, as was the convention in the Iraqi armed forces, a card-carrying member of the Baath Party. Now he was the latest pariah in the new social order born after Regime Change. In the past, no other popular political party had been allowed, and most people in government positions were required to be cadre of the party. The media is yet to identify critical questions around perceptions that do not discriminate between the *individuals* who worked for, and the ideology of the *party* as a whole. People like Razak were never fanatic followers of the party. Their long careers in the army also cut them off from developing other skills useful in these latest circumstances. Instead of exclusion on ideological grounds, there needs to be what is often fashionably called Rehabilitation. And they need more representation in a media that can always try to be a little braver, a little more independent.

One month and three days later, I would never have been able to write this. On the 19th of August 2003, Canal Hotel, the site of the United Nations headquarters, was in flames. A suicide bomber's truck rammed into the hotel. One month and three days earlier, we were waiting in the small security-check shack at the gates for Dr Adnan and Solomon. They joined us and we drove to a site few kilometres from here.

It was a small fallow ground, with a solitary date tree and some children. In the centre of it all stood two missile rockets nearly twelve feet in length, set on their launching pad, pointed in the direction of the stadium ahead. Some thirty metres behind was a small residential colony. Solomon provided the commentary: these still carry live propellant within, and one day some prank by a child might ignite them and it may all bring about a horrifying accident somewhere.

Solomon took us to yet another site half a kilometre away, closer still to a residential colony partially evacuated, but still a few children could be seen playing. Our security supervisor boomed in a strict tone, "From here on, do not take a single step off from the line I follow while we move ahead!" All around us on the ground lay unfired bullets, heavy machine gun cartridges from whom youngsters have often tried scraping the brass to sell, and, the deadliest of them, the cluster bombs with their bright yellow orange casings tempting children with their toy-like appearance.

Months after the official end of the war, unexploded ordnance and live munitions continue to take a heavy toll on Iraq's civilian population, and most particularly the Iraqi children. Some of the munitions were left by the fleeing Iraqi Armies, others were contributed by the after-attacks of the Coalition Forces.

Solomon's face: his was the face, briefing the press in that notorious tape BBC and others ran umpteen number of times, as the attack happened at Canal Hotel, and on which the screen went black.

Al-Kindi was one of the most eminent philosophers and physicians to have lived in Iraq. And Al-Kindi is one of the most eminent emergency hospitals existing in Baghdad, located on Palestine Street in 7th Nissan. As the bombing ended in Baghdad, the hospital was looted with relish: much of its equipment went missing in the loot. Nowadays, a camouflaged military tank and some very visible coalition soldiers stand on guard.

Earlier, when it was war, most patients were victims of bombing. Now the composition of people needing attention has dramatically changed. One of the doctors tells us that a score of children we see here are victims of unexploded ordnance. Some of the elders are illegal petrol peddlers whose plastic cans of gas suddenly exploded under the intense Baghdad sun. But many of the patients have bullet injuries and stab wounds sustained when they were either trying to defend, or steal cars and money.

When a familiar governing structure is taken off, and nothing substantial is offered, one can see a default formula for civil strife, a perfect recipe for anarchy.

July 17th, 2003
Picture Perfect
I film street shots once again:
Armoured vehicles. Coalition Troops on streets.
Bombed Communication Ministry building. Bombed Planning Ministry building. Bombed Petroleum Ministry building. Bombed Foreign Ministry Building.
Defaced Saddam mural. Defaced Saddam bust. Defaced Saddam billboards.
Peopled held up at Gas Stations. Attendants at Private Generators. Street Urchins.
Shops selling Satellite Dishes. Thuraya Phone Dealers. DHL centres.
And more Armoured Vehicles. And more Coalition Troops on streets.

July 18th, 2003
To Faluja
Seventy kilometres to the west of Baghdad lies the desert town of Faluja. Once again I saw the evolved sophistication of Iraqi motorways – a number of people even compare it to the German Autobahn. In between the stretching desert, large patches of green groves suddenly emerge like mirages. In recent times, Faluja has been a regular flashpoint for attacks on coalition forces. The popular media-reason ascribed is its being part of what is technically called the Sunni Triangle. However, the history of reasons accommodates other narratives as well.

The gates of Qa'id School are locked when we reach the building. On the 28th of April, when Coalition Forces were in occupancy, a protesting crowd of locals had gathered in front of the school. They had demanded the school be vacated and resume its teaching functions. In the grip of confusion and nervousness, Coalition Forces opened fire – thirteen people were killed, and many of the residents of the houses opposite received bullets in their homes, with tragic results.

Now it was time for Friday prayers, and we passed a military tank at the doors of a mosque. A number of children were around ... some innocently fooling around with soldiers, others making faces and taunting them from a distance.

Noori, our driver, wanted us to film prayers in the mosque – he said all the media people do it when visiting Faluja. But we arrived late and ended up talking to Mohammed, Abdullah and Mehmood, and they were unanimous in showing their unpleasantness at the continuing presence of "American Ali Babas".

Afterwards, while lunching on famed Faluja-kebabs, we heard of an attack on a Coalition armoured vehicle a few kilometres to the north. And we rushed. Americans had closed the main bridge leading to the site, and we had to take a detour. A kilometre before the spot, we were halted by a couple of American soldiers. A number of onlookers had gathered, and in the distant foreground lay the remains of a blown military truck carrying presumably two dead soldiers. Soon choppers started circling the sky, and airlifted the dead. More troops arrived and we were asked for our credentials, and how come we had reached earlier than many of the troops. Our reply was: everyone in the city knew it, we only followed the news!

In the evening, as we returned against an amber sun, I kept watching the silhouettes of tractors returning from the fields, a few children noisily dipping in roadside pools, and a fleet of vehicles all travelling on a bypass because even two hours afterwards the main bridge was still blocked, and maybe that truck was still there...

July 19th, 2003
Winding Up
A day of rest. Tomorrow we make our long way back to Delhi.

In the dining hall I have a breakfast of melons, black grapes, croissants and coffee, along with two Spanish girls working for an NGO. I ask them whether NGOs are becoming just a lucrative business in times of international conflicts. They correct me partially. They say that these are yet the only frontline bodies that do attempt a close touch with the locals; and for the individuals from many countries who work in them, they are the only avenues that can create an engaging empathy with a cultural Other. We discuss whether foreign interventions have become a new salvation formula for heads of nation-states to extend their legitimacy and benevolent paternal image to the people at home, when rapid changes within their own dominions are making this task tougher. I remember our interview with Dr. Ahmad Chalabi; we had asked why he had not worked in Iraq all the time, even as others, while living in Iraq, had organized resistance to Saddam's regime. He had replied, "It does not matter! Didn't Mahatma Gandhi also began his struggle for independence from South African soil at the start?"

To End
Sergio Viera de Mello joyously read half of his speech in Arabic on the day the Governing Council was announced. He had true hope. He died a violent death as the Canal Hotel was attacked. My French journalist friend had met de Mello a day before the announcement ceremony and he was singularly struck by Sergio's love and immense sincerity for Iraqi people. The world would have been a better place if the man were living.

Rescued Pages of War-Sense

TARUN BHARTIYA

1.
Curious, these death wishes
Lurking in barren mountains.
Sometimes in the valleys of Sohra,[1]
Sometimes on my TV set,
I sniff in the breath of reporters
The reality of gunpowder.

2.
In the First World War
As narrated by Commando Comics,
The eyes of the enemy sketch out
Our eyes, meaning they
Sketch out the enemy.

3
Whereas the Jewish trader of Addis Ababa
Searches for Herat, and I for enemies.

4
War poetry
Should be composed inside homes,
While sipping tea, craving cigarettes,
Busy discussing the
Proper use of Kabul's *heeng*.[2]
The need for war should be discovered at leisure.

When Mr. Mahanta, the neighbour, laughs
At this arm-chair poetry of war,
He should be invited to smuggle
The pictures of B-52,
Then, to raise money for the Museum of Strategies.

We should establish
An Abhimanyu Fund.

Can you find a better place than the border,
To deceive lovers
Who continue to sulk
As you examine the cures for betrayal?
War poetry should be composed to complete
The verse
Of romance-tempered gardens.

Let the great poets
Receive the mysteries of composing epics
From secret sources.
I won't challenge them.

If
That six feet three inches tall pilot
Forgets to shut his cockpit
Busy dreaming of
Your epic heroines.
War poetry must not be real.
There must live possible impurities
In fables.

5

He must be my age,
That pilot.
Querying from his window
Mathematical tables of nineteen
And the personal geography of Persia.

6

Mr. Rana's lecture on the "Need of Enemies" had just ended,
And I saw excited news anchors belching.

7

One has to shelter for the night
In a world like this
And wait every morning
For couriers from the border.
In the tunnels of their bags
Rumours crawl, whispering,
Opening the windows of neighbours.

8

And this is the fresh century.
Cultural good lies
In the antiquity of mediums.
For example this Photograph,
The moment you saw it, you said, "This is our tradition".
Because in it someone speechifies
Pricing potatoes in New York
As if in Kabul.
It is true that this city has a right to be
Absent
And one knows what enemies are like.
They are rats, nibbling through a *halaal* darkness
To find salt.

Even to steal a glance at these enemies is to
Destroy civilisation.
That is to say, the invisible frontiers of B-2,
Beyond the shadow of the camera
In our dreams,
And children with GI Joe in their
Hands.

You are welcome to this century of flat truths.
Welcome!
Would you eat Mughlai Meat?
Even Bush relishes Mughlai Meat.

NOTES

1. Sohra, Khasi name for Cherrapunji, known as a place which is said to receive the highest amount of rain in the world. Just about fifty kilometres from where I live.
2. Asafoetida.

Translated from Hindi by the author.

DEEP
Instabilities

Politics in the Picture
Witnessing Environmental Crises in the Media
SANJAY KAK

In the very heart of central India, as the first of a series of large dams begins to carve up the Narmada River and savage an eco-system, hundreds of thousands of people are readied to be displaced and slowly and infinitesimally ground into dust. An entire valley and civilization are in crisis. What is happening in the Narmada valley is a story with enormous implications: economic, social, scientific, political, even philosophical, moral, and ethical. These are huge, complex issues. But they are not unique to the Narmada valley. It's just that a remarkable group of individuals, both within the resistance movement that is the *Narmada Bachao Andolan* (NBA) and in the wider world outside, have excavated these, have argued them out, so that they now have a shape and a form that is more explicit.

As a filmmaker, I have spent the better part of the last four years trying to make sense of it all, travelling as often as I could in the Narmada valley, and a few times to Kachch and Saurashtra (where the waters from the dams are meant to go). 'Witness' is a good word to describe this process, to distinguish it from 'report', which suggests a moment in time and remains the more urgent task of television and print journalism. 'To witness' is a fair description of the privileged point of view of the documentary filmmaker, and does some justice to the time-scale that crises of the environment seem to demand.

What has happened in the Narmada valley is not a secret history – it's been researched, documented, analyzed, spoken about. Out of that process has come the NBA, which is probably the best-known peoples resistance movement in India, and even internationally one of the most visible interventions in the ecological domain. So unlike many other 'environmental' crises in the country, it has had light shone upon it.

As a mass movement, the visibility of the NBA, its active courting of the media, of national and international supporters, has not been without rewards. A combination of many strategies – on the ground, with the media, with financial institutions – has led to some stunning victories. A sustained international campaign in the US in the early 1990s forced the World Bank to withdraw from its funding of the Sardar Sarovar, the controversial centrepiece of the Narmada valley project. This was the first time in its history that this institution had withdrawn from a project. (Even earlier, Friends of the Earth Japan ran an equally successful campaign which led to the Japanese ODA withdrawing its funding.) Recently, a short, sharp and creative campaign strategy has led at least six foreign investors – including the giant multinational Siemens – to withdraw from the Maheshwar dam, India's first privately promoted dam. (Its promoters are frantically looking for funding within Indian financial institutions.)

Unfortunately the occasional victory does not mean that the battle has been won or that the war is done. Despite the visibility and the seventeen years of non-violent resistance, the process of dispossession in the Narmada valley continues to this very day. Our newspapers have once again seen Medha Patkar and three activists from the Narmada Valley on a protest fast outside the offices of the Chief Minister of Maharashtra. What they were asking for, once again, is no more than the fulfilment of the already unfair promises of resettlement made to the people displaced by the Sardar Sarovar dam. This week in Maheshwar, where work has been at a standstill for almost two years, the newly elected Government of Madhya Pradesh has promised a financial bailout, and is proceeding with the construction of two more dams: the Omkareshwar, and the Narmada Sagar.

And dams are not alone in their capacity to precipitate crises in the environment. There are also other, less visible places, like Jadugoda in the mineral-rich state of Jharkhand, where the indiscriminate and criminally negligent mining of uranium continues to destroy a land and cripple, deform and – what better word – devour its people. In Gujarat, coastal mangrove is being systematically destroyed to make place for, amongst other things, a gigantic port promoted in collaboration with the notorious UNOCAL. (The loss of the mangrove has allowed seawater to come inland, dangerously increased the salinity of the land, and made the already precarious existence of people even less viable.) Or the mineral rich district of Rayagada in Orissa, where the much older devastation caused by the open cast mining of bauxite is rapidly making place for the new 'modernizing' pace (and gigantic appetites) of a rapidly globalising world – the Indian Sterilite in partnership with the Canadian ALCAN.

These are the endless crises of the environment – of the soil we live on, of the air we breathe, of the water we drink. To think of all the endless environmental crises is indeed to stare at an abyss.

But how much of all this do we receive from the media? What do our newspapers and television really tell us about what is going on there?

Why do we not see the real motor behind the rapaciousness with which our environment is being consumed? Behind the broad generalizations about the way 'mankind' is destroying the globe and how 'we' are over-consuming, why do we not see more clearly who exactly is doing the destroying and the consuming? The real crisis of the environment today stands exposed as a political struggle, as a fairly direct contestation over scarce natural resources with the endless appetites of a small group of global consumers posed against the vast numbers of the poor.

The early signs of this contestation which have been coming through as whispers for many years now, are becoming louder and clearer with every passing year. The peaceful *dharnas* and hunger-fasts of so many years have slowly begun to mutate, hardening into incidents of police firing. Despite the overpowering clamour of the mass media, you can now hear the mortal struggle.

If you look for answers to this silence within the mass media, even sympathetic elements will offer the most superficial explanation: that environmental issues run to a different clock, they develop over very long periods of time. That they are difficult to package, they resist simplification. (The killings in Gujarat in 2002 are simpler to communicate). To convert ecological holocaust into a TV soundbite is a travesty.

The resistance to the dams in the Narmada valley, for example, has an argument. It's asking to be argued with, not dismissed in a couple of short paragraphs or a sound bite. Every few weeks or months, some fragment of information from the Narmada valley does make it to the news, but not quite headline-making and usually buried deep, subsiding quickly amidst the swirling tide of the next day's headlines. Only the truly initiated are able to make out the significance of such isolated facts. At its most benign, one dam is confused for another, the fates and futures of *adivasi* and plains farmer are mixed up, landless labour and village shopkeeper are seen as one, the withdrawal of one financial institution mistaken for another, till ultimately one is left with almost nothing to hold on to. The news is sporadic, disconnected. This is often disingenuously explained away as the collateral damage of the speed and expediency of the newsroom.

The consequence of this is a damaging reduction, a fragmentation, a reversal of precisely the kind of near corporeal structure that the struggles have patiently managed to put together from the shards of their excavation. But 'this is the nature of the media business', we are told. 'The story has grown old, the players are unchanging, the media cannot follow every sob-story, make every connection. After all, audiences tire, journalists get fatigued'. The implication is that the movement has been doing and saying the same thing for too long – that is to say their consistency is held against them.

Of course, anyone who follows the path traversed by the NBA would see that its positions have been far from static. It began by working towards rehabilitation in the early 1980s until it realized the charade of that exercise; it moved to saying, "*Koi nahi hatega, bandh nahi banega*" ("Nobody will move from here; the dam will not be built"); then to developing a formal critique of large dams; then moving onto a broader inquiry into the accepted models of modern development; to its most recent active involvement in opposing the twin threats of globalisation and privatization. It's a fairly busy series of changes, but in the media (and public) imagination it is fixed, static. Anti-development, romantic luddites. Medha Patkar and 'her' *adivasis*.

Second, and more often, the resistance in the Narmada Valley (or in Umergaon or in Rayagada) is pitched as a kind of timeless, almost romantic epic, a classical story, a movement to save a river (or a coast, or an *adivasi* elysian paradise), an elemental conflict that pitches the fragile world of the *adivasi* against the juggernaut of modernity. (Naturally, the *adivasi* is doomed). Pitched thus, the crisis appears to be primarily one of two competing ways of looking at the world: romantic vs. pragmatic, static vs. dynamic, broad generalizations presented as if they were actually two ideologies.

Far from being static and backward looking the movement in the valley is modern and progressive in its systematic deconstruction of the ideology of big dams. But in this construction, the struggle between the two worlds is mediated/constructed around the charismatic presence of Medha Patkar. There is considerable attention given to anthropomorphising the resistance – the leader is the resistance and is imbued with considerable heroism, the spirit of sacrifice, a dogged, almost crazy determination. In other words, in a hopelessly practical world, she is doomed.

(Interestingly, when the right-wing newsmagazine *India Today*, produced a 'Power List' of fifty of 'The High and Mighty' of this country last year, they included Medha Patkar. This is a publication that has consistently scorned the movement and its supporters, editorially spoken in favour of big dams, and broadly rubbished what the NBA stood for!)

Beyond the simplification, the reduction to archetype, what this has done is to irreparably distort a very central tool in the armoury of the non-violent resistance movement: it has damaged their ability to express themselves through symbols – the *dharna*, the hunger strike, the capture of the government office and the dam site, and most potently, the standing chin-deep in the rising floodwaters of the river, *jal samarpan*. The resistance will no more be heard without visibly resorting to this dwindling armoury of symbols. Through overuse, the symbols are being slowly emptied of all meaning.

Each of these, powerful tools in their own context, must be pushed to 'crisis'. A demonstration is of little interest unless it promises a confrontation with police. A hunger strike by a group of activists is meaningless unless it crosses twenty days and at least a few people are just short of going into coma. Until some years ago, when the monsoon waters rose and people stood up to their necks in the water, almost defying the water to drown them, at least the images used to make it in the press for a few days. If you think that was a short shelf life, last monsoon, it didn't even merit a mention.

Do the resistance movements themselves play into the stereotype? Perhaps they do. And it has to be admitted that this is a failure of a political imagination.

In this quest for crisis, the last event in the Narmada valley to warrant any substantial attention was the judgement of the Supreme Court of India, a remarkably ill-considered piece of jurisprudence, which arrogantly stamped its seal of approval on the construction of the dam. For that day, the judgement was briefly posited as a crisis – it was on page 1, on the main television news, and so on. The questions to the movement were quite direct: What will you do next? Will there be violence? Will you drown yourselves? In other words – will you please come up with a hysterical response, and preferably within the next twenty-four hours before the story dies down?

Since the movement instead called for meetings in the faraway towns and villages and *adivasi* hamlets of the Narmada valley so that people whose lives were affected could be asked what they made of the judgement and what the next steps should be, media attention moved on. Meanwhile, the shocked and uncertain responses of the first day or two were seen as an admission of defeat. It was posited as the end of the struggle, and of the issue itself.

I would argue that a first step to arriving at a more realistic account of what is really going on is a fairly obvious question: Who pays? Who profits? Place the full range of complexities, the heavy layers of detail, the usual on-the-one-hand-this and on-the-other-hand-that, put all that bombast on this little test-bench: Who pays? Who profits? And the whole mass of obscure detail begins to fall off. Where is the water from the Sardar Sarovar dam going? Why will it not reach parched Kachch and Saurashtra? Where will it go instead? Or how much electricity will the Maheshwar dam produce? At what cost? Who will afford it? Who wants it? Sieved through a criss-cross of these simple questions, the political is placed inside the picture.

Certainly in our century, ecological crises are increasingly political ones. They are about scarce resources, competing interests, about hegemony and control. These cannot be brought to us by the Indian corporate owned media in print or television; not by National Geographic Television ('This programme brought to you by Chevron') nor the Discovery channel ('This programme brought to you by Shell').

I also believe that there is one other reason why media coverage of really important environmental issues has now become impossible outside of the 'crisis' mode. It is because the crisis provides a neutral stance from which it can be reported on – after all, if a group of *adivasis* from the Narmada valley are standing neck deep in water and waiting to drown, you can hardly be accused of being partial to them. But the moment that crisis passes, so does the attention. Crisis allows 'coverage', but it also encourages, even demands, a kind of frantic, un-worked out, fragmented description of the event. Once the crisis is over, when we most need the cogent, patient joining of the dots, that's where media coverage balks.

To continue to follow events, to display a genuine commitment to joining the dots as it were, to following the thread that would probably expose one to the charge of being overzealous, even that dreaded word 'committed'...

Crisis is the enemy of understanding. Crisis is the little bumps on the paper that prevents us from joining the dots. Crisis suits the status quo.

This text was presented at the "Crisis/Media" workshop, organized by Sarai-CSDS and the Waag Society in Delhi, March 2003.

THE TOXIC TI

Late City Edition, Friday, June 12, 0000

Assets seized, see page 3

Hills Denuded.
STATE EMERGENCY

By Special Correspondent

The Himalayan states declared a state of emergency when citizens woke up to see the surrounding hills denuded and bare, as if chomped off by a monster. In several places, plastic and smelly garbage was found and is suspected to be the beast's droppings. The states have declared a state of emergency as this threatens to unleash an ecological crisis, which could lead to water shortages and a rise in local temperatures. No one has sighted the beast, but several unconfirmed reports state that they heard noises similar to large industrial machinery. The Chief Minster has called a cabinet meeting to consider calling in the army's eco task force to capture the beast. People have been asked to participate and cooperate.

Contd. P7

MES OF INDIA

www.toxicsnewsindia.com

Plastics Excreting Monster Suspected.
DECLARED.

Remembering SARS in Beijing
The Nationalist Appropriation of an Epidemic

SANJAY SHARMA

党和政府领导人民一定
能够打赢"非典"战役

The SARS will surely be conquered by our government
under the leadership of the Communist Party of China.

北京市工商行政管理局
北京市工商行政管理局海淀分
北京桑夏广告有限公司策划

Like any other disease, SARS (Severe Acute Respiratory Syndrome) has no deep-rooted meaning. It is caused by a mere virus, although a very potent one as far as human beings are concerned. This is because so far it has defied accurate comprehension and conquest. SARS acquired enormous significance and meaning from its cultural and ideological contexts. It may have infected a few thousand and killed a few hundred people but it shook the lives of millions, elicited diverse public reactions, expressed underlying dark fears and redefined segregation and interventionism. SARS was not yet another case of an 'Asian Disorder' because when it crossed the seas to strike North America it challenged the cosy assumption of the divide between the developed sanitized west and a fast growing but upstart, parvenu Asia.

I travelled to Beijing from Bangkok in early March 2003. Around the same time a World Health Organisation official also undertook a similar but fateful journey succumbing to the disease a few weeks later. When I reached Beijing there was talk of a mysterious disease in the south. It still did not have an official name. It was being called a flu, a typical pneumonia, just another common respiratory ailment – like pet names we give to children at home that have an air of intimacy, familiarity about them. But till then it was confined to the southern province of Guangdong – just a few cases had been reported since late 2002. The government assured the people that there was nothing to worry about. For the media it was a soft story.

It was a time to celebrate the spring season that had followed a severe winter. The New Year had been ushered in on 1 February – the year of the sheep. The whole country raised red lanterns in celebration. From toys to tanks, virtually everything was die-cast in the image of a sheep or a ram. Millions of people moved across China during the spring festival holidays for family reunions and dumplings were consumed at an alarming rate. In the frenzied celebrations one got an inkling of contemporary Chinese nationalism. No opportunity was lost in the festivities to smuggle in high figures of growth: GDP, FDI, exports, number of air travellers; that eighty percent of the toys children played with worldwide were made in China (the only regret being that Chinese manufacturers still have not managed to produce a brand figure like 'Barbie' doll). On stage and on state-owned CCTV (China Central Television), operas were being performed, pop singers danced and sang songs extolling the achievements of Chinese society and people (is there any distinction between the two?) – how the children were growing taller, the air was becoming cleaner, roads wider and the Chinese people becoming healthier and wealthier. Little did anyone realize that the massive movement of people during the spring festival was to be later held responsible for SARS virus's dissemination. But in February and March ignorance was bliss. People were queuing outside cinema halls to see Zhang Yimou's latest blockbuster, *Hero*. Others watched dragon and lion dances and were busy consuming a bewildering variety of gorgeous Chinese food. The new leadership of President Hu Jintao and Premier Wen Jiabao exuded youthful confidence at sixty and promised, if not the moon, a manned mission in space later in the year. Bill Gates was on his eighth visit to China in March 2003.

Everything appeared to be in order. The economy had been booming since the 'opening up' and the initiation of reforms in 1978. The statistics were narcissistic: nine percent plus GDP growth since 1989, massive decline in absolute poverty, China replacing the US as the highest recipient of FDI (Foreign Direct investment) in 2002 ($52 billion). Many of these awesome achievements translate visually for a visitor to Shanghai, Beijing or even smaller towns. The grand imperial past of Beijing now lies submerged in the maze of material achievements of modern industrialism – only to raise its head for curious tourists in search of China's mysterious 'forbidden' past. As a mega-city Beijing is truly impressive: the eight to twelve lane highways, a spaghetti of glittering roads and flyovers, shopping malls, plazas, banks, restaurants, apartments blocks – and more of these. And many goods, branded ones included, are cheap. The 'China Bazaars' that have mushroomed all over India selling everyday goods (saris even!) at unbelievably low prices are not products of some Chinese trick. No wonder so many China experts now acknowledge that the Chinese economic performance is a bigger miracle than the earlier 'east Asian miracle' of South Korea, Singapore, Hong Kong and Taiwan – after all, this growth has been accomplished for 1.3 billion people. It may be accompanied with new inequalities, may not be egalitarian but is still more participatory than elsewhere.[1] And it is built on the social gains made in post revolution China: high literacy, improved gender equality and health. To most Chinese it does not matter whether one calls their society capitalist or socialist or even a 'socialist market economy'. Deng Xiaoping's pragmatism has 'settled' this issue for most Chinese: 'It does not matter if the colour of the cat is black or white so long as it can catch mice'. The rhetoric of class struggle and internationalism or socialism has virtually vanished like the famous *Red Book* of the Cultural Revolution era that is now sold as memorabilia along with Mao key chains at Tian'anmen Square. The bloody events of 1989 at this Square are at best an embarrassment, to be seen and perhaps to be forgotten as an aberration. And when faced with the question most asked of the Chinese, "What about democracy?" they retort, "Look what the world's democratic nations are doing to Iraq". Many Chinese say that there is no one version of democracy and it is more important to have freedom, which they claim is now being experienced by them in ways unthinkable in Mao's time, especially in the 'chaotic' years of the Great Proletarian Cultural Revolution (1966-76). Yet no one likes to speak ill of Mao, the great helmsman. The party line and guidebooks give him a ratio of 7:3. He was seventy percent right thirty percent wrong. Mao has been deified and hence marginalised, no longer deemed relevant for a globalized China where for the moment Deng's mantra rules: 'Its glorious to be rich'. You can make money in China as some restaurants do by selling Mao's favourite dishes, especially braised pork, but his famous collarless coat has yielded to western-style suits.

Indeed, the quest for riches appears relentless, the thirst seems unquenchable. From being the sixth largest economy in the world China aims to overtake Japan by 2020 and the US by 2050. This is an ambitious nationalist project – gigantic and scary. It is all consuming – everything from technology to culture is sought to be appropriated in this enterprise: the gargantuan Three Gorges Project said to be the world's biggest; and it is a matter of pride for the Chinese that General Motors believes that, by 2025, China will be the biggest car market in the world overtaking the US. Currently Beijing has 121 museums – ranking second after Paris – but how can it be left at this? By 2008, the year of the Olympics, it will have 130, leaving the French capital behind. The year 2008 seems a slice of hundred metres of the long marathon race China wants to win like an agile sprinter. Beijing is working out feverishly for that mean and lean look. At times, it appears to be preparing for D-day like a bride to be unveiled in 2008 before the global gaze that will take everyone's breath away. Old *hutongs* (lanes) are being cleared, giving way to wide roads, planned concrete blocks, shopping arcades, banks. The drive to clean the city and sanitize it is the litmus test of modernity that China has imposed on itself. This desire is being pursued by a technocratic elite that seems eager to master western models and prove its success.[2] Since the Chinese development strategy seems to be paying off dividends for its growth-obsessed policy makers so far, not enough debate has taken place about environmental and other costs.

The hazards of this uncritical approach were brought out by SARS that threatened to plant roadblocks in the path of the Chinese dragonnaut.

The disease spread in late March-early April 2003. Along with the virus, rumours spread too. There was talk of a flu like disease that caused breathing trouble with high fever but it was dismissed as yet another type of respiratory disease. After all, respiratory diseases such as pneumonia, pulmonary tuberculosis and lung cancer are the third biggest cause of death in cities and the main killers in the countryside. But the rumour mills kept churning out more stories of the mysterious disease spreading northwards in mainland China. So far Shanghai, Tianjin, Beijing, etc., were assumed to be safe. But masks started appearing on human faces. And then a Finnish man – Pekka Aro working for the WHO – died on April 6. Media reports still carried the official tone that the disease was under control. The situation in Beijing was described in jargon: 'safe' and 'normal'. However, on April 9, Premier Wen Jiabao admitted that the situation was 'grave', something already known to Beijing's residents. Public belief in the official figures of infections and death dipped further. Panic struck. People started shopping in a state of frenzy, stocking up daily necessities as if there was no tomorrow. Supermarkets were raided and ransacked by desperate shoppers. They withdrew into their homes, shunning social contact and public places. Windows were closed, hand shakes stopped and all kinds of home remedies were tried to keep the killer virus at bay – vinegar was boiled in rooms and herb concoctions were gulped. And then something unprecedented happened. The health authorities, realizing the need to be more transparent, held a press conference on the 20th in which Vice Minister Gao Qiang admitted that there were many more cases of the disease and deaths than those previously reported to the public. Heads rolled, and the health minister Zhang Wenkang and Beijing's mayor Meng Xuenong were stripped of their party posts. A live press conference was now held regularly and on April 23, *People's Daily* wrote in an article: "To the broad masses of people, accurate and timely information is also a good way to mobilise them to be more conscious of the disease. Panic stops when the public is fully informed".

Soon the Chinese Vice Premier Wu Yi was put in charge of health matters – a strong-willed matronly figure to reassure people. The Communist Party declared SARS as the enemy of the people – indeed the Chinese nation. Somewhere it was also perceived as the first major challenge the new leadership of the country was facing. Were the new rulers facing the threat of losing the Mandate of Heaven? The official media was inundated with pictures of Hu Jintao, Wen Jiabao and Wu Yi mingling with common people – providing the healing touch. The seriousness of the situation now exploded. Schools, colleges, cinema halls, theatres, internet cafés, restaurants, congested markets – all were shut down. Anti-SARS propaganda commenced with the might of the state behind it. Billboards promised "SARS will surely be conquered by our government under the leadership of the Communist Party of China". As tourism collapsed and the global image of China appeared infected, fears were expressed about the growth rate of the economy and the reduced confidence of foreign investors.

Even now the attempt was to blame the 'foreign' origins of the disease. It was said that outsiders had brought it to China. But did origins really matter? There is an old Chinese saying: "Keep an army for 1000 days to use it for an hour". Was it going to fail in the battle against the new enemy? Suddenly SARS exposed the health system and one got a feeling that it was regarded more as a 'public shame', an embarrassment, by the Chinese establishment. Other voices were being expressed in what looked like a debate on public health. Leading academics wrote and debated on the effects of reforms on the public health system with a tone of dissent. Hu Angang and Hu Linlin (*China Daily*, 24 April, 2003) declared that health care was a basic right of all citizens and the slow withdrawal of the state was undesirable: "In the field of public health, the role of the government and the market should be re-adjusted. Services like anti-epidemics, maternal and child hygiene, access to safe drinking water and sanitation of public toilets are typical products of public interest and should be shouldered by the government". *China Daily* later (29 May) carried the headline:

"Ailing health system exposed: crisis reveals public complacency over infectious diseases". Figures highlighted the fact that the Chinese government spent only 1.71 percent of its fiscal expenditure on health compared with about 14 percent in developed countries like the US and Britain.[3] Fears were particularly strong for people living in rural areas where the older, more egalitarian public health system, now reeling under reforms, was too ill-equipped to deal with SARS. Suddenly the urban-rural divide, regional disparities and new inequalities of the post-reform China were under spotlight, much to the chagrin of the state.

With its pride wounded, the Chinese state declared war on the new enemy. And its power was palpable. Suspected SARS patients were picked up, secluded and treated in designated hospitals. Affected areas were cut off and there were rumours that Beijing would be put under curfew and its boundaries would be sealed. This did not happen as by now the little that was known about the disease required people to come out of their homes. Now people were exhorted to open their windows, ventilate their homes and spend time in open public spaces. Parks were now full and countless people were out – hiking, boating, exercising, playing. Badminton racquets and shuttlecocks disappeared from shops, life reversed, imitating the elderly in China who can be spotted walking backwards to ward off aches and improve concentration. Hawkers selling seasonal fruits or baked sweet potatoes switched to selling masks and thermometers. Masks were given free with McDonald's hamburgers! Taxi drivers and lift operators started to wipe doors and handles and the smell of disinfectant emanated from empty buses and trains. The disease became a site for further intervention with the onslaught on the 'dirty' and 'unhygienic' habits of the people. While earlier there was an attempt to attribute it to outsiders, now its spread was blamed on 'squalid classes'.[4] The unhygienic personal habits of people suddenly appeared completely out of step with the vast array of cheap cosmetic products available to them. It was repeatedly regretted that people spat in public, did not wash their hands, kept poor oral hygiene and did not bathe regularly. How could these traits be allowed to exist? Didn't they reinforce the discredited stereotype of a 'backward yellow race' and puncture claims of a modern germ free society? For the self-image of the Chinese, fortunately, the disease struck elsewhere, especially in Canada. The fact that the western medical system had not come up with a cure for SARS somewhere aided the deep-rooted Chinese belief in the superiority of traditional Chinese medicine (TCM). Discarding western medicines, many Chinese turned to folk remedies, concoctions and a variety of fuming disinfectants with a vengeance – quite understandable given the absence of any known cure for the disease. However, once again this was hijacked for another ideological purpose – an intensely nationalist agenda where age-old traditional knowledge was assumed to be inherently superior, along with the belief that it was bound to have some cure. But critical voices could also be heard that pleaded with users of traditional Chinese medicine to remain calm: "Fear more virulent than SARS".[5]

By the end of May the disease started showing signs of abatement, and this glimmer of victory threw up national heroes. *People's Daily* published the diary of Zhang Jihui, head nurse at the Guangzhou No. 1 People's hospital. A physician, Dr. Jhong Nanshan, became a public icon – a household name across the country for his pioneering battle against SARS. However, what was significant about him was that he publicly expressed reservations about the claims made by the then health minister Zhang Wenkang in early April that the disease

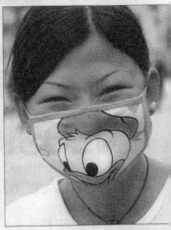

Photos by LI WEN/Xinhu

healthy mind is a healthy body: Local Beijing residents have drawn paintings or simply written big characters to show their strong determination the on-going battle against SARS. Experts suggest that a healthy state of the mind is important in maintaining bodily defences against the virus.

had been "brought under control". At a conference Dr Nanshan asked: "How can you bring the disease under control when you don't know its cause?" The health minister was sacked and Dr. Nanshan emerged shining as the state sought to appropriate him as a national hero, leading the war against the disease. Once again Deng Xiaoping's pragmatic adage was in operation: "Take two steps forward and if in trouble, one step back".

The battle against SARS continues. The frantic search for its cure and effective prevention, preferably with Chinese methods or a vaccine, is on. It would be deemed as another triumph of the Chinese nation, another feather in the cap of Chinese civilization. How can one quarrel with this, given its astounding achievements in the recent past (post 1949 revolution)? But does everything have to be part of the 'paradigm of conquest' where no distinctions are drawn between the conquest of nature, global markets, a virus...should everything be approached with the Great Wall mentality? As China proceeds to build a *xiaokang* society, one that is 'comprehensively well off' with all round human development, isn't there a need to question the 'siege mentality' that deploys civilizational capital in the quest for the largest possible piece of the global capital cake? And what about the soaring number of the new poor in China and over 100,000 mentally retarded elderly in Shanghai alone, out of which only ten percent are given support. SARS brought out the conflict between technology-centric modernity and the assertion of cultural nationalism – a familiar unease felt by many cultures carrying the burden of civilization and the taint of backwardness.

China seems too eager to prove to the world, especially the West, that it can win the war against SARS. In January 1836, a Brahmin instructor, Pandit Madhusudan Gupta, and four Indian students performed a human dissection for the first time at the newly established Medical College in Calcutta. In those days of early nineteenth century British colonialism in India, it was hailed as a major victory affirming the superiority of western science, medicine, indeed civilization. This historic achievement was celebrated by firing a fifty-round salute from the guns of Calcutta's Fort William.[6] Salutatory gunshots celebrating yet another victory might be heard from China soon.

NOTES

1. Drèze, Jean and Amartya Sen. "India and China" in *India: Development and Participation* (Oxford University Press, 2002, Delhi) p. 123
2. Feenberg, Andrew. "The Possible Futures of Technology in China", in *Sarai Reader 03: Shaping Technologies* (Delhi/Amsterdam, Sarai-CSDS, Delhi/The Waag Society for Old and New Media, Amsterdam 2003) pp. 2-6.
3. *China Daily* (24 April, 2003).
4. Cf. Slack, P. "The Response to Plague in Early Modern England: Public Policies and their Consequences", in John Walter and Roger Schofield eds., *Famine, Disease and the Social Order in Early Modern Society* (Cambridge University Press, 1991) pp. 167-87.
5. *China Daily* (29 May, 2003).
6. Arnold, David. *Colonizing the Body; State Medicine and Epidemic Disease in Nineteenth-Century India* (Oxford University Press, 1993, Delhi) p. 6.

SEVERE ACUTE RESPIRATORY SYNDROME

Frequently Asked Questions about SARS

THE DISEASE

What is SARS?
Severe acute respiratory syndrome (SARS) is a viral respiratory illness that was recognized as a global threat in March 2003, after first appearing in Southern China in November 2002.

What are the symptoms and signs of SARS?
The illness usually begins with a high fever (measured temperature greater than 100.4°F [>38.0°C]). The fever is sometimes associated with chills or other symptoms, including headache, general feeling of discomfort, and body aches. Some people also experience mild respiratory symptoms at the outset. Diarrhea is seen in approximately 10 percent to 20 percent of patients. After 2 to 7 days, SARS patients may develop a dry, nonproductive cough that might be accompanied by or progress to a condition in which the oxygen levels in the blood are low (hypoxia). In 10 percent to 20 percent of cases, patients require mechanical ventilation. Most patients develop pneumonia.

What is the cause of SARS?
SARS is caused by a previously unrecognized coronavirus, called SARS-associated coronavirus (SARS-CoV). It is possible that other infectious agents might have a role in some cases of SARS.

How is SARS spread?
The primary way that SARS appears to spread is by close person-to-person contact. SARS-CoV is thought to be transmitted most readily by respiratory droplets (droplet spread) produced when an infected person coughs or sneezes. Droplet spread can happen when droplets from the cough or sneeze of an infected person are propelled a short distance (generally up to 3 feet) through the air and deposited on the mucous membranes of the mouth, nose, or eyes of persons who are nearby. The virus also can spread when a person touches a surface or object contaminated with infectious droplets and then touches his or her mouth, nose, or eye(s). In addition, it is possible that SARS-CoV might be spread more broadly through the air (airborne spread) or by other ways that are not now known.

What does "close contact" mean?
Close contact is defined as having cared for or lived with a person known to have SARS or having a high likelihood of direct contact with respiratory secretions and/or body fluids of a patient known to have SARS. Examples include kissing or embracing, sharing eating or drinking utensils, close conversation (within 3 feet), physical examination, and any other direct physical contact between people. Close contact does not include activities such as walking by a person or briefly sitting across a waiting room or office.

If I were exposed to SARS-CoV, how long would it take for me to become sick?
The time between exposure to SARS-CoV and the onset of symptoms is called the "incubation period." The incubation period for SARS is typically 2 to 7 days, although in some cases it may be as long as 10 days. In a very small proportion of cases, incubation periods of up to 14 days have been reported.

DEPARTMENT OF HEALTH AND HUMAN SERVICES
CENTERS FOR DISEASE CONTROL AND PREVENTION
SAFER·HEALTHIER·PEOPLE

Evictions - Projections
Watching Dharmendra in Suburban Lagos

HANSA THAPLIYAL

I listen to friends telling stories about Agege. Professionals, in their mid and late thirties, who have spent childhood years in this area and have seen it grow and change. Stories of how politics shifts people from their homes, how suburbs are born, stories about the particular nature of their own suburb. With some of these stories as my main research, some other small conversations, and my own conjectures, I try to sketch a picture of the area that is home.

In the 1970s, the government shifted a huge working class population of Oluwole area, Central Lagos to the far, far outskirts of the city, in Ogba. Oluwole was too close to a prospering business area and a semi-slum, however vast, however old, could not be allowed to stay there, reasoned the powers that be. After all, the area was ripe with business possibilities; there were many other, more profitable eyes on it. Very soon, real estate prices would sky rocket in the 'cleared out' land that was now 'developed' as the business navel of central Lagos.

The people who lost their homes struggled to adjust to a place that was closer to the rural hinterland than their city. Gradually, they brought back some of their lost citylife into the suburb. Their shops and institutions, their businesses and entertainments, and their urban outlook began to give a new character to Ogba.

The civil war got over. The government planned again, and 'gave place' to the many soldiers, shattered physically and mentally by the war, and their families, in far off Agege, just beyond Ogba, away from the city. Way out from the centre of Lagos, Agege was already a large trading junction for the Egba man coming in from Abeokuta and for the Hausa trader disembarking at its once famous railway station to go to Lagos.

My friends came from other families, families of middle class people from Lagos, who decided to relocate to the outskirts of the city, where land was cheap, where it was still possible to build a decent house. People who hoped, (as all middle class people all over the world, making this shift, hope of their cities) that Lagos, expanding on and on, would eventually embrace their suburb as its own, and share out its amenities and its opportunities. For the children leaving Mushin, or some place else in Lagos, to go live in Ogba or Agege was like going to live in the bush! They eventually found fellow complainers in the neighbourhood, with whom they tried to make this new place their own. One afternoon a child saw someone being knifed in Abule Egba. It gave him a precocious insight into a dangerous adult world. Responding perhaps to a sense of danger, or to the sparsely peopled, empty landscape of Agege, he played destructive games with his friends, throwing stones at passing car windows. Stories of violence became the stuff of children's mythology and the source of new games. They made their own map of danger of the unfamiliar suburb - certain street corners, among certain 'kinds' of people, in darknesses, like the darkness of cinema theatres which 'hoodlums' frequented. Danjuma, Pen Cinema... were places of entertainment for 'strange people'.

Coincidentally those were the days when the big screen was becoming popular in Lagos, and in much of Nigeria. People began to flock, singly, in families, and groups, to darkened auditoriums mapping the city, to watch stories told by well-known actors unfold on the screen. Metro, Jebako, Rainbow... cinema houses in the main city had begun catering to middle class and even elite audiences. One of the theatres would have snacks served, mid-screening, with minerals, to its patrons.

Soon Dharmendra, Hema Malini, Wang Yu, Jugnu, Charas, Sholay... were names on diverse tongues in Lagos. And everywhere a new lot of cinema lovers entered the theatres, young, often not yet ten year old boys, stealing into shows well after the family outing was over, to be overwhelmed by the giants striding across the white screen.

By now missions had opened schools in the city's new suburbia. And roads to Agege from Lagos became busier. Simultaneously, from outside the city, traders added to the noise on the streets. Perhaps reassured by the increased new crowds, slowly more middle-class people started frequenting the cinema halls. And the two cinema houses of the area achieved some respectability in 'family' eyes. Danjuma ('International') Cinema was considered safer than Pen Cinema. It was larger, with a huge seating capacity, air-conditioned, relatively expensive balcony seats that separated the people who could afford them from the poorer 'masses', and 35 mm projection, mostly of Indian films. The children started flocking to the cinemas – boys with small stolen change, trying to get in on half tickets after the interval, sitting with unknown crowds of people, with 'people not quite like their families', in the crowd, in the stalls, watching the screen. Mesmerised by the secrets of large liquid eyes in a giant sized woman's face, or echoing the movements of a Kung Fu dance as they watched Bruce Lee in the dark.

Then, the cinema boys of the 70s grew up. Film watching became less of an addiction, more a pleasant occasional outing: A late night film with friends, or with a date maybe. By the late 1980s, public areas across Lagos started becoming unsafe. The nights especially had new dangers - armed robbers, increasing in number as the sliding economy created more poverty and unemployment; a military government that was suspicious of everyone; and its arm of law, the policeman: the man in the crowd given a uniform and a gun, power and a bad salary, a training and a license in violence and a need to show 'results'.

One late night in the 1980s, a group of friends, all children of the 70s, were returning from a late night show at Danjuma. Some trouble had broken out nearby. The police stopped the young men. The usual: kneeling on the roadside, humiliation. It seemed like simple extortion would not serve the policemen. The young men were told to get into the police van. The future lawyer among them refused, and managed to get a word with the senior officer. Managed to tell him they were coming from the cinema. "Show your ticket then", the officer barked. Wale put his hand in his shirt pocket, and that night, the slip of paper that let him into Danjuma became 'proof' and let off Wale, and the friends with him. The ticket became a talisman to protect the faithful patrons.

Late eighties, and with the still increased state brutalities, and the bad economy, cinemas became more deserted. The middle class was the first to clear out of the theatres. For many of them the house became the sanctuary instead. For those who could afford it, security gates, higher walls, grills, broken glass shreds, barbed wires guarded the house where entertainment, communion, leisure, everything was to be strictly contained. People lived as though in voluntary house arrest. Meanwhile, well heeled televangelists from American shores knocked on the television screens in these living rooms, encouraging people to join in a larger, more purposeful congregation, a different kind of sharing and participating.

Public gatherings did not die out completely; they found a new venue in religious assemblies. Almost every street of Agege soon had a church. What must these assemblies have offered that the cinema could not any more? More local context, perhaps, than the 35mm exports from far off countries. Who had the time anymore to pleasantly argue the nuances of romantic love dances, the peculiar absence of hot blooded passion; who had the time to deduce from these stories some truths about foreigners? Hope was what was desperately needed. A place of communion where you seemed to be much more directly addressed. Who had the spare money to spend on some exotic cinema, which might now have seemed like an indulgence of an easier time? What if you were attacked by armed robbers, stopped by the police?

And still, even those difficult years did not manage to shut down many cinema houses, they still had their takers. Some old faithfuls, some new initiates, and some seekers for whom the organized communion of religious places was not quite it. Who were these people who put together their meagre resources to still afford this leisure. Maybe those for whom life, with or without the military government, was a constant struggle anyway. Some sought the oblivion of the dark, some made the theatre their own carnival of discontent, unwinding with noise and disorder.

By the time some sense of order returned to the polity, the local film on video had become very popular with the middle-class especially. The children of the 70s did not return to these old haunts, or to their childhood films, except in nostalgic conversation. The combination of a locally made film, and a place like FSP, set in an estate, more 'orderly' and professional, started drawing in some middle-class families.

One Sunday in late November, instead of going on from my familiar landmark – a clumsy plaster statue of some Oba of Agege, standing amid the traffic – I crossed the road and wandered into Pen Cinema: the large, silent building for which this square is named. There was a man sitting astride a bench, in the narrow gallery alongside the theatre. The walls of the gallery were covered with posters of different Indian films. He beckoned me into the bulb-lit corridor. I hesitated: a lone woman, *oyinbon*, wary with accounts of hoodlums at such places. I finally walked in and stared at faces on the posters, recognizing some, imagining stories, till I felt easy about venturing a little further, and stepped to where a door led into the theatre. I could see only a few heads in the large darkness. People had paid to get away from the bright afternoon outside, to sit in the dark and gaze at a flickering screen, a bad print, a foreign film – to dream, or seek an answer or a corroboration in someone else's story, or just to unwind. I stood at the door few minutes, my eyes widened by the brightness of the grainy print with undulating oversized human beings. Then I fled.

To return on Monday afternoon, determined to be bolder. To watch a whole film. I found Pen Cinema gone.

The gallery I remembered was a mess of unplastered walls and masonry. The posters were gone, their wooden boards, stacked up outside, waiting to be carted away. The board on top was chalked in with the old admonition... "Smoking of Indian Hemp and Igbo is strictly forbidden inside the premises".

The cinema hall, I was told, had been leased out to a church. One of the cinema employees, who is mute, gesticulated vividly with his hands: "All of it is gone, pulled down, over". Inside, the doors had been flung open, lights lit up the dark interior that I remembered. The screen had been replaced by a pulpit. A blue cloth hung there, with a rosette on it. Some four wooden steps covered in cloth separated it from the congregation: so far, rows of empty chairs, standing still, waiting for their new occupants.

Among those who will miss their cinema are the small traders of the area. Ronke, a young girl, who would go in occasionally for a film, or catch a few minutes with the screen when she went in on errands. Lasisi, in his mid-thirties who sells perfumes outside the theatre. He has lived in this area since he was a boy and he remembers Pen Cinema from then. Crowds, big crowds. Even now, he claims, people were still coming in, from as far as Mushin. He remembers the time when they tried to show a Yoruba film, but the crowds were so big and uncontrollable, they had to call the police! And so they returned the Indian film to the screen. The films shown were often reruns. Lasisi remembers how someone would stop by a poster, look at the faces, and narrate the story of the film to people gathered around. "And when we went in to see it, we saw all that again, all that he had said".

· Pen Cinema used to have two theatres. Now both house separate churches.

I follow the current 'operator', (projectionist) who has been here 11 years, upstairs, overlooking the newly designated church hall, to the small dark space that is the old projection room. By candlelight I see two old large projectors, their noses pointed at small openings in the wall. "Victoria 8", he tells me their make, with visible pride. These are the magic making 35 mm machines he has wielded. So, will they fall into disuse now? He tells me they are waiting to be shifted, in two weeks or so. He was a patron of this cinema house too, a cinema boy, before he got the job here. He likes the place. It is not like other cinema houses, he says, it is... not rowdy. I hear the opinion repeated by others who frequent this place. This is a cinema hall they are intimate with, they are relaxed in here, they think it is better than many other such places. The 'rowdy' cinema house is a description of some other place; their own is not like that. I think of all my and my friends' misgivings. 'Rowdy', 'lumpen', are probably epithets used by one class to give a blanket description of people of another class. To describe a crowd that is not our own? Within that crowd, of course, people perceive themselves and each other differently.

A young boy outside worries about his mother's small trade, a roadside spread of women's footwear... She supports a family of four with it. Will the church chase them all away, just remove the small stalls that they spread out at the theatre entrance? Would I speak to the management? I am thrown back, and tell him surely they will not heed me.

He tells me he would often go in to take a break from helping his mother, or when someone came to meet her. The people inside knew them, they would let them stroll in for a break… His worry returns, swiftly and suddenly, "But now - what will happen to the shop?"

An old ticket collector, Ahmeduilahi, sits astride a bench at a much-weathered looking Danjuma. He has been here 22 years, almost as long as the cinema. It is Sallah day, the end of Ramadan, but there is hardly anyone in the balcony watching the video projection of a new Indian film. (I am told it is new, therefore there are no subtitles.) Curtains are hanging loose, many blinds have been broken, and daylight flows in. A young couple sits stiffly, staring at the screen. Two young men share a resigned look and try and laugh at a comedian on screen. The catatonic violence unfolding on the screen precludes the need for subtitles. Overlit enlarged male muscles, alternate with sadistic bloodletting and frail lifeless women. And then small moments of comedy. The landscape the film 'expresses' scatters further out of reach.

A few washes of glitzy blood later, I walk out, up the stairs, and visit the projection room instead.

A large easy airy room. The silent ledges facing the film projectors are covered over with small objects of daily use. A video projector casts its image onto the hall outside. A comfortable cot stretches across one corner of the room. And the projectionist speaks to his woman friend as they both watch a local programme on television. A fairytale projection room, with so many more 'pictures' than those small dark spaces I have seen squeezing in the projectionist in other theatres everywhere. I peer out of the balcony. Neat shadows edge the sunlit street below.

I walk out and look back at the large spacious generously built building, by far the largest in the immediate landscape. In the distance I see the tall minarets of the Morcas Arabic and Islamic School. Around the theatre the road is neatly lined with single shops, there are hardly any buildings with even a first floor. A large cinema in a working class area.

I think of the contrast with the enclosed, strictly middle, upper-middle class housing estates spread over this area, where my friends live. Friends weighed in still by the wasted years of misrule, struggling at relatively late ages to consolidate hard-earned positions, or to provide well for newly started families. Friends, who as young boys had clamoured to this theatre, as young men had frequented roadside beer parlours, had been part of the 'common life'.

Agege has grown. Travellers, visitors, people of different nationalities are seen here today. Many kinds of shops and markets, catering to different classes of people with as many kinds of homes. On the streets, crowds, and vans of different organizations. Different churches for different classes of congregation, and now Muslim assemblies catering to the middle-class. For people at large, the beer parlours continue to be gathering places, lively with politics, personal relationships, religion, the electricity problem of Agege, lively chatter that sets into relief the silence of a lonely beer drinker.

In the market behind my house at Oko Oba is another world of Agege: a poorer world, lively, vibrant, where small traders make a very small daily living. These people of this small market have lived on, through times of violence and disruption, struggling to keep their place at the margins of this suburb. It is here, on a routine Saturday morning shopping, that I meet a faithful member of the thin crowds at the Agege theatres. I hear a scratchy rendition of a Hindi song, on an old transistor. I ask the owner of the box, a soft-spoken middle-aged trader, maybe a little older than my friends, if he likes Indian songs. He does, he likes Indian films too. He still goes to Danjuma, Pen or another small cinema (I later get to know it is the Daily Mirror – a small busy cinema house tucked away in a small lane close to Danjuma) on weekends. One film on the weekend. It is a leisure he really tries to make time and money for, an outing he tries to treat himself to. Pen Cinema is out of his reach now, far off in Alagbado. But Danjuma and Daily Mirror still play for their faithful patrons from Agege.

Sunday afternoon, and someone else is minding his pepper-onion-tomato shop. I presume he has gone to diligently keep his tryst with his leisure, the screen at the theatre.

Mediated Guilt
The Illusion of Participation in Delhi's Social Welfare Advertisements

OMAR KUTTY

begin this essay by narrating a banal personal experience. On November 14, 2002, in the midst of my morning routine of tea, toast, and the newspaper, my attention was seized by a large image of Jawaharlal Nehru in *Dainik Jagaran*, a Hindi daily. The black and white close-up of his head and shoulders made India's first Prime Minister look striking, emphasizing his sharp features by exaggerating the dramatic contrasts of the natural lighting. The line of his rather long nose steered my eyes towards an elaborately laid out column of text to the right of the photo. Near the text were two somewhat less carefully presented photos of Delhi's Chief Minister and the Minister of Social Welfare. It turned out that Nehru's image was part of a well-designed advertisement inviting public participation in Children's Day, an event conducted annually by the Delhi Department of Social Welfare on Nehru's birthday. I immediately felt a slight pang of anxiety. My research concerns made me interested in attending the event, but it was scheduled for ten o'clock and it was now nearing nine. Short of cancelling my existing plans and, more painfully, interrupting my breakfast, attendance was impossible.

If one pays attention to social welfare advertising in Delhi, one notices something ironic. The ads in the newspapers are designed to publicize programmes and achievements, as well as solicit *public participation* in certain welfare-related events, so as to get the citizenry involved in the labour of welfare provision. However, the timing and composition of the ads themselves make it extremely difficult for any ordinary resident to actually take part in these programmes. The ads usually appear in the paper the day of the event, and can lack all the information required to get to the venue at the appropriate time. While giving short notice and careless information for public lectures and cultural events is certainly not unique to the Department of Social Welfare, social welfare ads are otherwise well designed, large (sometimes full page) and relatively expensive; thus their ineffectual character is worth consideration. Of course, it would be easy to dismiss their inadequacy as government incompetence, but this paper will suggest that the failure, whether intended or not, is the most socially consequential aspect of these ads.

To be strictly fair, some advertisements do provide sufficient notice and information. Still, when in the course of research I arrive at these events and introduce myself to the organizers, they are often surprised to hear that I found out about the program through the newspaper. No one else, they often tell me, comes because of the ads. Attendees of social welfare programmes, such as informational camps, tend to be either the department's own professional social workers and affiliated NGO personnel, or the intended beneficiaries. The latter are not notified about the event through advertisements, but through the network of local child development field staff (*anganwadi* workers). In other words, the mechanisms that bring people to welfare events are personal, local and directed. Very few people, if at all, come because of mass media advertising. Indeed, it appears that the ads are not intended to attract 'the general public'. What purpose, then, could a mass advertising campaign serve?

Representatives of the Delhi Department of Social Welfare claim that advertising attracts some people to some events, although they are unable to produce any supporting data. When asked why they continue to spend money on advertising that seems to attract so few new participants, representatives invoke the widespread distrust towards a government that is blamed for corruption and wasting money. The main objective of the advertisements, they claim, is simply to make people aware that the department exists and is active. Off the record, one official gave a more complex account of the department's motivation for all publicity activities: "You have to do something so that people vote. You have to reach their doorsteps. The motive is political, but it does some good in the process".[1] The main purpose of these advertisements, it is clear, is not to attract public participation but to bolster the image of the government by flaunting its social welfare programmes.

Distrust of the government is now so common that virtually any Indian would likely offer a similar explanation. This account, however, is not sufficient. The incompetent nature of social welfare requests for participation may well be the result of short-term political concerns, corruption and inefficiency, but these ads nonetheless have profound social consequences. As I shall argue, these unanswered, and, in some cases, unanswerable solicitations have a pragmatic consequence despite their utter failure to attract participation. The very act of reading them produces the affect of guilt – even if only a momentary, languid guilt – that serves an interpellative function for the neo-liberal social imagination currently hegemonic in global political-economic discourse.

Hollow Solicitations

Indian newspapers are filled with ads from government agencies that follow a similar pattern: they proclaim the achievements of the given agency and attach that success to the faces and names of incumbent politicians. Railways, highways, electrical lines and even sewers can become the object of a current government's boasting. Government advertising is an inescapable feature of Delhi's political landscape. However, social welfare advertising often does something that other government advertisements do not: it invites public participation. In language that is often dramatic and moralistic, these ads implore the reader to take action; specifically to come forward and help the government provide welfare to beggars, the handicapped, children, impoverished women and the elderly.

Considering the obvious ineffectiveness of the welfare advertising, significant amounts of money are allocated to their production. The Delhi Department of Social Welfare, for example, spent Rs. 5.9 million in 2002-3, over 1.4 per cent of its total expenditure, on 'Advertisements and Publicity'. This is not insubstantial considering that only Rs. 183,000 was allocated to 'Training Courses', Rs. 235,000 to 'Schemes for Adolescent Girls' and Rs. 3.1 million on 'Fuel and Lubricants.'[2]

I have already argued that social welfare advertising is not particularly effective in attracting people to its events. Not only are the advertisements ineffective, the events to which readers are supposedly being invited have no facilities for welcoming the general public. One such advertisement in *The Hindustan Times* for a workshop on the problem of beggary announced: "The toughest part of a journey is taking the first step. Come forward and be part of a movement". But when I attended the workshop, my inquiries once again indicated that I was probably the only person there who was not otherwise already associated with begging related issues. The conference room was small and overcrowded. Participants were not allowed in without registering. Only after establishing my credentials as a foreign researcher was I given a nametag and an information packet. The workshop consisted of a panel of NGO personnel, social welfare officials, legal personnel, police officers and an audience filled with activists and social workers who were mainly hostile to the government's anti-beggary campaign. As a member of the general public, I felt I had no role to play. This advertisement had presented itself as a call to action, but there was in fact no action that an uninitiated person could take.

Many of the ads prominently display the Department of Social Welfare's logo, "We Care, You Share", but it is not clear exactly what is to be shared. The Department of Social Welfare does not accept donations and does not work directly with donations, yet a request to share something is being made. The language of sharing is reminiscent of Charles Titmus' *The Gift Relationship*, in which he argues that the gift of blood to a generalized other (i.e., society at large) emotionally bonds the individual to an otherwise abstract thing called 'society'. For Titmus, the real act of donating blood produced the affect of social belonging that he considered crucial to a successful welfare state. In the case of Delhi's social welfare advertisements, however, real acts of giving are not possible. The ads thus make requests, but they seem to be peculiarly uninterested in a response.

An advertisement for another function called "Kalyan Week" makes the hollowness of these solicitations even more apparent. Kalyan Week consisted of daily events designed to publicize the various activities of the Department of Social Welfare. Curiously, except for the inaugural function at Delhi, the starting times of each individual event are absent. Nevertheless, the advertisement calls forth in bold language: "You also come and join this flame of volition, volition to combat the forces, which undermine the dignity of human beings, their childhood, womanhood, old age and disability". Further down in the advertisement, there is an explicit invitation: "Be a proud Delhi Citizen. Join us and make the Kalyan Week a Success". The ad, however, does not explain how a citizen could contribute if he or she were to actually attend the functions. Like the other events I attended, these programs had no facilities for volunteering, joining organizations, or donating money.

What social consequences could emanate from advertisements that so obviously fail to achieve their express purpose? There are at least three obvious ways one could account for this failure. First, it would be possible to argue that the makers of the advertisements have no interest in attracting public participation but are simply vehicles for incumbent politicians. Second, one could also attribute their failure to simple government carelessness and incompetence – the Department of Social Welfare makes an effort to involve the public, but does not properly follow through on its own goals. Finally, one could portray these ads as simple propaganda for a liberal social imagination. Each of these accounts is a plausible explanation for either intentional or unintentional failure of these ads, but none of them provides any account of the possible social consequences of the failure itself. None of these accounts, in other words, help us answer the most important question: what is the effect of a public request that cannot be fulfilled, a solicitation that cannot be answered?

A (Neo) Liberal Social Imagination

When I use the term 'liberal', I mean it in the classic sense of private property, rational individuals, freedom of exchange, and a minimalist 'night watchman' state. Post-independence India tried to negotiate a path between liberalism and socialism, ending up with a set of policies that simply protected the domestic bourgeoisie and invented a new regime of bureaucratic privilege. Nevertheless, it must be recognized that the architects of independent India genuinely intended to develop their country into a welfare state. Unfortunately, entrenched political interests in conjunction with conditions of under-development prohibited India from performing a welfare state's most basic function – propping up aggregate demand by providing unemployment insurance, pensions, health care and a range of other social benefits. Rather than the rights that they were supposed to be (see Article 41 of the Indian Constitution), these benefits became the exclusive privilege of government employees. At the national level, the Ministry of Welfare (which began as the Central Social Welfare Board in 1953 and became the Ministry of Social Justice and Empowerment in 1998), performed a limited set of functions, namely the distribution of miniscule benefits to designated groups of 'deserving poor', including the abandoned elderly, street children, beggars, the handicapped and also, notably, women, the lower castes and tribal populations.

Given this limited mission and the (perhaps misunderstood) Gandhian legacy of voluntary service and self-help, it is not surprising that the Ministry of Social Justice and Empowerment and its Delhi counterpart continue to adopt liberal policies vis-à-vis the poor. That is, they adopt policies, which, albeit sympathetic to the plight of the poor, still treat poverty as an essentially private problem and implicitly assign blame to the poor. The majority of schemes are structured around self-help and financial independence. They fund programmes that provide services such as small business loans, *crèches* (day-care centres) to allow women to work, and a variety of training courses that teach people various crafts (e.g., tailoring, beauty care, handicrafts, etc.) and business skills.[3] These methods of upliftment strangely ignore larger economic dynamics, such as the level of demand for these very traditional industries. Instead, the central Ministry and its Delhi counterpart assume the basic liberal conception that wealth is generated through a combination of thrift and hard work.

The advertisements of the Department of Social Welfare communicate this liberal social imagination in two ways. First, as the ads describe the Department's programs, they make it clear that most of the benefits they distribute are to various categories of deserving poor (e.g., the handicapped, widows, underprivileged women, street children, etc.) who are entitled to assistance because, unlike the rest of the poor, they cannot help themselves. Second, by appearing to solicit participation, these advertisements suggest to the reader that individual volition in the form of voluntary labour and charity is an effective method for economic development. Implicit in all of this is that poverty is not rooted in property relations and economic systems but in individual failings.

Languid Guilt

Let us pause for a moment and imagine the experience of the readers whose attention is captured by such ads. These people are likely to have little interest in social service, the poor, or the Department of Social Welfare. They simply happen to notice the graphics of the ads and suddenly find themselves scanning a text that is not promoting a product but calling them to action, asking them to fulfil their duty as both citizens and human beings. Yet, as we have seen, the ads are almost impossible to respond to. We can further conjecture that these readers are not going to examine the ads adequately enough to realize the difficulty of response, but will simply notice the fact of their own inaction and then quickly move on to other, more interesting parts of the newspaper. If this scenario is valid, then we can deduce that the advertisement does register with the reader, even if only in some remote corner of the unconscious.

It also seems safe to assume that our imaginary Indian reader thinks of social service as a universal good, although he or she may never participate in any such service. The moral value of selfless service to society is inculcated through history lessons on Gandhi and other nationalist leaders, as well as from exposure to India's many famous voluntary organizations such as the *Harijan Sevak Sangh*, the *Bharat Sevak Samaj*, the *Ramakrishna* Mission, the Servants of the People Society, the *Samta Sainik Dal*, the Hindu nationalist *Rashtriya Swayamsevak Sangh* (RSS), Mother Teresa's Sisters of Charity, and the myriad of more contemporary NGOs. Given the value placed on voluntary service in India, it is not difficult to believe that social welfare advertisements could initiate an associational chain that ends in guilt: I am being asked to help, I should help, it is possible to help, others are helping, but I am not going to do so because I am too lazy, too selfish, or too concerned with my own family and friends.

I want to be clear about the modesty of my claim; no one is losing sleep over the Department of Social Welfare's advertisements and my argument by no means depends on the guilt experience being profound, enduring, or even memorable. On the contrary, my argument is precisely that the reader experiences a mere fleeting moment of guilt, an episode so short and trivial that it has no motivating force. However, it is in that momentary transpiration of affect that the reader comes to feel him or herself to be a part of a liberal world – a world in which poverty is a private problem that is solvable through the force of volition. To use Lacanian terminology, guilt acts as a 'suture', or a 'quilting point', that stitches the signifier (the language of private property, individualism, and volition) to the signified (the supposedly real world in which these things exist).[4]

The fact that this is an un-motivating, languid guilt is crucial to my argument. If it were actually a galvanizing force, it would magnify the risk of mass-scale critical engagement, in so far as large numbers of involved people might also begin to ask deeper questions about the origins of poverty. The languid guilt produced by social welfare advertising, I am suggesting, secures the reader's self-perception as 'normal' (i.e., not psychotic) because their feeling of guilt serves as evidence of their own induction to a symbolic order that everyone else takes to be 'real'. To not feel guilt would be the symptom of a terrifying pathology – a lack of basic human empathy and moral orientation. Thus, these banal, highly forgettable moments of guilt are, intended or not, effective mechanisms for suturing subjects to a liberal symbolic order by making them feel like caring, empathetic, and hence normal human beings.

My argument about languid guilt could be extended well beyond the rather incompetent advertising of the Delhi Department of Social Welfare to even the best charitable advertising in the world. I appeal here to my own personal experience of watching Sally Struthers on American television make her impassioned pleas for the world's needy children. I feel a twinge of guilt at the images of unclothed, sickly children and, though a combination of

Marxist criticism and selfishness keeps me from ever making a donation, I find myself comforted that someone, somewhere is doing something about this problem. Unlike the ads of
the DSW, most American advertisements for charity contain very clear instructions about
how to respond ('Dial the number at the bottom of your screen and have your credit card
ready'), and yet millions of first-world residents see such solicitations but do not, for whatever reason, respond. This uncountable group of non-respondents must also be experienc-
ing an ephemeral moment of languid guilt that sutures them to a liberal social imagination.

Languid Guilt and the Historical Trajectory of Participation Discourse
Returning to the Indian context, we must bear in mind that the specific instance of languid
guilt under analysis is situated in a historical trajectory. The rhetoric of participation is by
no means new, but its authorizing conditions have changed significantly. In the fifties
and much of the sixties, Indian development planning had as one of its major components
the Community Development Program, which was based on the idea of citizen-state
'co-operation'. The project of development, it was argued at the time, could only be successful if the common Indian villager understood its long-term goals and benefits. Equally
important, the voluntary participation of villagers in local projects – irrigation, land utiliza-
tion, etc. – would provide a free source of labour, thus releasing large amounts of capital
for allocation to heavy industry and infrastructure. Moreover, it was believed that the
process of involving the villagers in development projects would inculcate them with a
'scientific temper' and social-democratic values. The challenge, then, was to mobilize the
villagers. 'Village Level Workers', equipped with hardly anything except a training manual,
were dispatched throughout rural India to initiate this great endeavour to 'urbanize the
village'.[5] The state, as we know well, was the main agent for carrying out this civilizing mission. Hence, the project of participation in this period was very closely aligned with state
aims. The point I wish to emphasize is that this phase of participation rhetoric was about
modernization, about spreading the word of modernity, about taking the values, worldviews,
habits, and institutions labelled 'modern' to the people and places they had not yet reached.

By contrast, the current wave of participation rhetoric is not about building something
new but about repairing what already exists. Solicitations to participate in social welfare
events in Delhi, for example, are part of the Sheila Dikshit (Congress) government's
'*Bhagidari*' ('Participation') campaign, as each ad proudly proclaims. The campaign is
designed to promote solution-oriented dialogue between citizens, NGOs, trade associations, and Delhi's many municipal agencies.[6] The core of the campaign consists of Resident
Welfare Associations (RWAs), which are local bodies that serve as liaisons to the government. Their function is not, in general, to build new infrastructure but rather to force the
municipal corporation and the Delhi government to maintain existing amenities properly.
RWAs mainly concern themselves with things like broken streetlights, clogged drains, blown
transformers, potholes and other mundane issues. When they are involved in the implementation of new technology, it tends to be simple, non-expert driven technologies like
garbage separation and rainwater harvesting – technologies that are designed to solve the
problems created by urbanization. In addition to RWAs, Bhagidari also emphasizes greater
transparency and communication as a partial solution to the problem of corruption. Hence,

the government makes efforts to publicize its activities through the old media as well as the new. Again, the problem is one of reparation rather than construction – corruption is seen as a problem that results from an overly powerful government rather than a lack of state structures.

The programme has, on the whole, been well received and has earned international accolades as a model of participatory governance.[7] Its free-market detractors, however, criticize *Bhagidari* for creating an illusion of citizen involvement while masking the inherent inefficiency and corruption of big government.[8] For them, minimizing state power through the privatization of government services is the solution, but the assessment of the problem is the same: modern institutions exist aplenty in India, but their damaged nature is retarding India's development. Thus, we can conclude that whereas participation rhetoric used to be about becoming something we are not, it is now about refurbishing that which we already are. The grand narrative of progress, in other words, has been replaced by a much less ambitious narrative of reparation.

To be clear, I am not suggesting that the languid guilt produced by social welfare advertising is unique to the current phase of capitalist development. Any instance of mass mediated solicitations for public participation can produce this affective state. However, perhaps a guilt that fails to motivate action but nevertheless seals subjects into a neo-liberal social order is ironically appropriate to contemporary historical conditions. If this is an era that has dispensed with grand narratives of radical social change – an era that tries to cope with its own pathologies rather than curing them – then perhaps languid guilt is the optimal affective instrument for exercising hegemonic control.

NOTES

1. Interview with Public Relations Officer of the Delhi Department of Social Welfare (name withheld) conducted on December 3, 2002.
2. Roy, Shubajit. "Social welfare staff keeps largest share", *The Indian Express* (*Express Newsline*), (24 October, 2003) p. 1.
3. Notably, these programs do not appear to be rooted in a larger economic plan. Thousands of men and women, for example, are trained as tailors every year, yet there is no indication that this is a growing field.
4. Lacan, Jacques. *The Seminar of Jacques Lacan. Book III: The Psychoses, 1955-56.* Transl. by R. Grigg (1993, New York) p. 290-2.
5. Cited in Ravi Kalia, *Chandigarh: The Making of An Indian City* (Oxford University Press, 1990, Delhi) p. 30.
6. See interview with Sheila Dikshit in *Frontline* (web version) 19,11 (May 11-24, 2002).
7. "Bhagidari scheme goes global", *The Hindu* online edition (July 24, 2003).
8. Chakravarty, Sudeep. "Loose Change: The Citizen's Stock Option Plan", *India Today on the Web* (October 2003).

Journey through a Disaster
A Filmmaker's Account of the Gujarat Earthquake, 2001
BATUL MUKHTIAR

When the earthquake occurred in Gujarat on January 26, 2001, at 8:30 in the morning, I was having an English breakfast in a five-star hotel with a British film crew from Channel 4, UK.

We were shooting a bizarre story. An English girl, a small-time model in UK, had done a small 'item number' a year ago for a Bollywood film, and had been bitten by the bug. The producer, in an attempt to dissuade her politely, told her she was too slim for Bollywood. Hindi films demanded a more buxom figure. The girl, determined, got a breast enhancement surgery, and Channel 4 was following her arrival in Mumbai and her attempts to land an acting job.

This sounds saner than it actually was. In three days we had seen it all: leering passes, false promises, endless waiting on film sets, hilarious auditions. My job as a production coordinator did not allow me time to watch the news about the earthquake, and I depended for updates on the British cameraman who was keenly concerned about what was happening in Gujarat.

By a strange quirk of fate, Nick the cameraman got a SOS phone call from Channel 5, UK, asking him if he could go to Gujarat and shoot. Channel 5 was doing a story on the International Rescue Corps from UK and they were scheduled to fly out that day. The producer/director of the program was unable to fly out for some reason, and Nick's name had been suggested for the job. Nick asked me whether I would go out with him, and I agreed.

We spent January 27 trekking across Mumbai, chasing an elusive film star who had promised to help the English girl with contacts. We spent the evening waiting outside the film star's make-up van while the girl talked to him inside. I hurried home to pack a bag, and then pick up Nick and the sound-recordist. We had decided to drive down to Bhuj that night after the Channel 4 shoot was through.

The drive to Bhuj was long and arduous, not the least because Nick was panicking about getting there quickly and would not trust the Indian method of asking for directions instead of looking at a map. As soon as we reached Gujarat, we saw vehicle after vehicle heading out to Kutch with relief material.

At the Surajbari Bridge, the road was blocked. The bridge had been damaged and the police were allowing only one vehicle across it at a time. The number of those waiting was huge, and tempers were high. Nick insisted that we must jump the line, deeming it of vital importance that we start shooting with the Rescue Corps as soon as we could. He stormed off to the police through the crowd and we did get our way through, but not without abuse and jeering from the waiting crowd.

We drove into Kutch at twilight. The setting sun sparkled golden rays on cracks in the road and a broken petrol pump. We arrived at the Bachau crossing. There was destruction all around. The road was littered with old clothes that people had sent from all over the country and which no one had wanted. In the fading light, people milled on the roads like sad ghosts. By the time we reached Bhuj it was pitch-dark. The power supply had not been resumed and only car headlights, torches and lanterns guided us to the Jubilee Ground where rescue units from all over the world were staying.

The International Rescue Corps had arrived that morning, after the usual tussle with red tape at the airport, waiting to be cleared by the authorities. They were expecting us but were not prepared to host us. The Rescue Corps travel like military units, each man with his own backpack of tent, utensils, bedding, and big freezers of army rations. They had food enough for us, an extra tent that they could spare, but no bedding and no utensils. We were confronted with the reality of having to sleep on the cold, freezing ground like the entire city that had become homeless, and spooning out food with our fingers from thawed packets. Having a cup of tea was hard without a cup to spare.

Early next morning, we started out on rescue calls. Jubilee Ground was teeming with people asking for help, government clerks trying not too successfully to understand international accents, and government drivers with too few vehicles at their command trying to fulfil too many demands. I soon found myself becoming an interpreter between Gujarati and English and sending out our own vehicle on rescue calls. Every few minutes I would get pulled back by Nick, who needed me to concentrate on the shoot.

We spent the better part of the morning in the city following the Rescue Corps over mountains of rubble, tiptoeing over dead bodies, fighting the smell, the dust, trying to diffuse the anxious anticipation of family members hoping for miracles. Bollywood was another world, though only twenty-four hours ago we had been in the middle of it. I was laden with cameras around my neck, finding it hard to keep pace with the physically fit rescue workers, terrified that I would stumble over a dead person. The walled city was nothing but an endless obstacle course of debris and the dead.

In the afternoon, after yet another futile search, we got a SOS call on a walkie-talkie. There were some sounds from an apartment building that we had searched earlier that day. Two men from our unit were already there, and there was definite sign of life. Not one of the rescue corps units had yet found anyone alive and the hope of success was already exciting us.

At the apartment building, neighbours had already gathered, repeating the story of who had heard the sounds and what had happened. Our unit went to work with their ultra-sonic equipment. Since they had combed the site earlier that day, and for the last two days as well, they could move quickly.

A few minutes later, I heard the head of the unit arguing into his walkie-talkie. Work halted. He strode down angrily and seemed to be walking out of the site. I asked him if our car could take him somewhere. He hopped in and asked to be taken back to Jubilee Ground. At the ground, I watched from a distance the heated argument between him and the coordinator of the rescue corps from UK.

There were three units from UK and they took it by turn to attend calls that came to them. This call was apparently to have been taken by the Fire Brigade unit. It took me a few minutes to figure out what the fuss was about. Obviously, if a life had to be saved, the fight was to be in the limelight, to get the publicity. Eventually a compromise was worked out, and both units agreed to share the credit.

Work resumed after a delay of about thirty minutes. Within a few minutes, a young man was taken out on a stretcher, hale and hearty, fully conscious. He had been under the debris for four days. He had an iridium watch on and was aware of the passage of time, and aware of how long he could survive. Cameras flashed, the crowds clapped, reporters from across the world marvelled at the story it would make. The young man, Viral Dalal, was worried about what had happened to his family, who were still trapped underneath.

Later in the evening, Nick and I went off to the hotel grounds where the media people were camping. Nick was hoping to get the story of the rescue edited on someone's laptop and also hoping that some news network would show interest in airing the story. The hotel grounds were abuzz with satellite phones, a frenzied rush to send in reports, a long waiting list to send in one-minute video stories through the satellite network. Nick found himself sidelined. No reporter wanted to spend time over a story that he had not brought in himself.

Nick decided we must go back to the apartment building the next day. The Rescue Corps was going to look for Viral's family, and we must persuade Viral to talk about his expe-rience under the debris and his rescue. The job of 'fixing' Viral was mine. I felt nauseated at the thought.

I waited with Viral for the better part of the day. His gaze was focused like a hawk, willing with all his might for the rescue of his family. Late afternoon, they found the body of his brother. Pieces of a body, crushed, disfigured, purple. It was certain that the rest of his family was dead. Viral rushed off with the ambulance and his brother's dead body. Nick and I kept waiting, hoping he would come back.

I did not want to ask Viral to do the interview, but Nick was determined. My Indian colleague, the sound-recordist, took it upon himself to convince Viral that he must do the interview. We waited until evening, and on sighting Viral we pounced on him like vultures, using all our psychological skills to complete our story. We got the interview.

The next day, Nick wanted to do a helicopter ride over the city. He seemed to think that I should be able to get the requisite permissions. I was not functioning as I ought to, because we had been sleeping on the ground in the freezing cold, because the army rations had given me the loosies, and also because I was too shaken by what was going on around me. I did not give a damn about the shoot anymore. I could not think it more important to requisition a helicopter ride for a shoot rather than using it for some relief work.

This was my first experience of a disaster up close. I had worked for six years as a production coordinator and fixer with international documentary crews. My initial enthusiasm and admiration for their painstaking methods had waned into a dislike for their prejudices, for their 'white man's' expectations of having things work smoothly for them always, for their disregard of people once they had finished shooting with them. However, I also knew that this disregard and prejudice was not unique to foreigners, but a part of the film culture even in our own country.

What irked me most was the blurring between fact and fiction. The imperatives of making a television programme that was interesting, entertaining and 'told a story' often meant staging set-ups, pushing contributors to do and say things they would not do or say otherwise. A year ago, I had spent many months with a Scottish associate researching for a television series for Channel 4, finding characters that epitomized Mumbai. Our hard-won rapport with these people was often jeopardized during the shoot by the directors' demand for meaty stories, and after the program came out we lost many friends. These experiences had created much confusion within me, as I wondered how the need for a good story could be reconciled with sticking to the truth. Like many other filmmakers, I had bought a DV camera, sure that this was the path to freedom.

A fortnight after the earthquake, my husband Vivek, who is a cameraman, and I went back to Bhuj. The papers had been carrying stories of heroic rescues, bravery, courage, fortitude. My own glimpse of the Kutchi people during my first visit there inspired us to go find these real-life heroes on camera.

It took us less than a day to realize that what worked as written word did not work as speech. So much of the heroism came from the text itself. The smallest action became a major heroic act, much in the way of mythical poems. It also took us only a few hours to realize that the real heroism of the people was in the way they conducted their day-to-day lives, the spirit with which they were determined to rise from the ashes.

I decided to quit looking for stories and only to explore: to walk, to talk, to meet, to be with those who were there. Of course, filmmaking training guided us subconsciously, sometimes even against our will. One of the most important lessons I had learnt while working with international crews was that there was magic in what seemed mundane. Being part of a culture, a country, one takes so many sights and sounds for granted, but these seem to tell entire stories to those to whom they are unfamiliar. Kutch was an unfamiliar enough terrain to someone coming from Mumbai to keep eyes and ears open. The pitfall was that it was so easy to beautify the images of destruction. Everywhere that one turned the camera, the ruins gave a beautiful 'frame'. And that, somehow, seemed wrong.

This exploration with one's own ideas about the documentary continued over a year.

As did the questions about one's own life when faced with the philosophical fortitude of people who had lost not only material belongings, but their history, their way of life. It was not always easy to be spontaneous, and over and over we were faced with the question, "But what is your focus?" We never were able to answer that question, even at the end of a yearlong shoot and a ten-month edit.

Shooting with a DV camera afforded all the advantages of intimacy, of simplicity. Except for a few initial awkward moments, where people seemed to think it necessary to act up to the camera, mostly people went about their work and we went about ours. I knew, from past experiences, that people often felt that a camera would somehow alleviate their problems, that being telecast would bring attention to their woes. And it was hard to make people understand that we could not help, that we could only document.

A tribal woman abused me for shooting her. She understood the international value of her nose-ringed face and wanted money to be photographed. A Tibetan rescue team, dedicated, compassionate, pulled out a dead body with their bare hands twenty days after the earthquake. The grandson of the old lady was grateful that he would now be able to cremate his grandmother with proper rites. The rescue team posed with the dead body like hunters with a trophy. There were cameras all around. A group of American tourists wandered the rubble-ridden streets, clicking away furiously. A mendicant beggar outside a temple harangued Vivek and me, explaining to us the futility of all photography. "This is only a documentary", he said. "This can tell you I am here. This cannot tell you who I am". True to his nature, he resisted all our attempts to 'follow' him the next day in our quest for an 'interesting character'.

Since we were making an independent film, we had the freedom to structure it loosely, to keep our concept of a non-concept through the edit. Filmmaker friends from all over the world praised the film but considered it too loose. Audiences at screenings were touched, moved, and bored by turns. At the Cinema du Réel in Paris, an astronomer film buff said the film had been for him a journey through India, which he had never seen. But it was "not a film". The line between being a film and "not a film" was too distinct in market terms for the film to be sold. All I had to hold on to was my own stubborn ideas about what a documentary should be.

The theme of the Yamagata International Documentary Film Festival in 2003 was "Beyond Documentary". Many brave documentaries were screened there, including a nine-hour film from China. A touching story of an old Korean woman living in America almost got wiped off by the pandemonium during the after-screening question and answer session when it became clear that the filmmaker had not shown the film to the old lady. Winning her trust, he had exposed all her family skeletons and deemed it safer not to show the film to her or her family. Cries of "Shame!" and his feeble defence exposed the critical issue that faces all of us – the profiting of the filmmaker at the expense of another's innocence, naiveté and tragedy.

The metaphysical doubts raised by the mendicant outside the temple are echoed all over the world in the minds of documentary filmmakers, who are most often sincere in their quest for truth. However, market realities can afford a flight to freedom only once. Very few filmmakers can afford to be stubborn through their lives, questioning their own integrity along with the social and political issues of their times. It is easy to be paralyzed into silence by doubts. New DV technology makes it easy to speak out, to experiment, to explore, and the search continues through the world to define and redefine the role and the potential of documentary.

CYBERMOHALLA
Street Logs

LOG 001
20th October, 2003
DAKSHINPURI, CYBERMOHALLA MEDIA LAB

LOG 001
20th October, 2003
Kiran Verma, Lakhmi Chand Kohli, Rakesh Kumar, Sudip Das

The first photograph is clicked at 3:30 PM. The sound of a motorcycle, *drr...drr...drrr...* A *rickshawwala* is standing in front of me. He is wearing a loin cloth. There is also an RTV (Rural Transport Vehicle/Mini Bus). People sitting in it are probably wondering who these people with a camera and notebooks and pens are. Just then a water tank of the Delhi Water Board passes by. There is a cycle repair shop in front of us. Its sole customer is pumping air into his bicycle. There is loud noise of vehicles around us, *pi... pio... po...*

3:35 PM
The sound of a Boxer motor cycle, *durrr... durrr... durrr... ti...* The traffic has increased. There is a three-wheeler driver looking for passengers. An RTV arrives. A man is transporting some things on a bicycle. Vehicles are coming from every direction. A girl wearing a green coloured *salwar kameez* walks by, scratching her head.
3:40 PM
Some school kids walk past. Just then, the waiting RTV leaves. A vendor is selling guavas on his cart. School hours have just ended. A scrap-man is taking scrap on his rickshaw. A

roaming vendor is selling cosmetics. The voice of a boy, "Hey! What are you doing?" The driver of an RTV is looking at us, and laughing. A cow is roaming around as if the road were a cowshed. Scooter: *Ti... Ti... Ti... Ti... Ti... Ti...*

3:45 PM
A scooter: *Trr... Tr...* A red van stops, and then drives away. The conductor of an RTV calling out, "Moolchand! Moolchand!" Two women are walking past. The woman in front is holding a child in her arms. The child's face looks kind of sad. Two girls are walking past, laughing, exposing their teeth! Two children walk by, drinking mango Frooty. A boy runs and gets into the RTV.

3:50 PM
A bus, route number 521, has blocked the road. Then it drives on. An old man, his head bent, walks past. There is an accident! A scooterist has rammed into a cycle that a child was riding. The child fell. Incidentally, the scooterist is a friend of ours. We call out to him, "Wait!" But he doesn't stop. Maybe he didn't recognise us in his fright. He runs off with his scooter. A man selling clothes is standing in front of us.

3:55 PM

An RTV comes. Two women and five men are sitting in it. The driver is smoking a *bidi*. A middle-aged man is carrying three small, covered buckets of milk in his hands. A tractor is transporting a tank of water. A five year old boy is pulling a loaded, heavy cart. Lakhmi runs to him to help. From nearby comes the sound of a car mechanic at work: *thuk... thuk... thuk...*

4:00 PM

Two cars pass by, *po... po... po... po...* A man is making fresh fruit juice on his mobile juice stall. A newly-wed bride is being taken in a decked-up car. The car is adorned with flowers. A delicate looking man wearing jeans walks past holding a slip of paper in his hand. A boy, perhaps ten years old, is selling thin crisp cakes made of lentils (*papad*). Another RTV arrives, *pi...o...oo...*

4:05 PM

A fat man comes and parks his scooter right in front of us. A man selling tea is calling out, "Tea! Tea!" Another RTV arrives, with its conductor calling out, "Gol Daak Khana!" People are looking at me curiously, strangely. A Rajasthani man is sitting nearby. Another RTV comes and halts behind the first. The conductor calls out, "Come on! Move! Another bus is here". A third RTV arrives. The conductor of the first RTV is still calling out. The conductors of the RTVs keep announcing their destinations to woo passengers, and pull them away from the others. Two of the drivers are fighting. Maybe their route timings have got mixed up. I am feeling a little awkward, because everyone's glances are directed towards us. Far from us, an infant is crying on a cot. No one is listening to him, perhaps not even his mother.

4:15 PM

The sound of an RTV, *tu-uu... tu-uu...* A girl sitting in it is looking at us and laughing. A bangle-seller is walking around, carrying the bangles in his hands. A rickshaw*wala* rides past us. I am enjoying sitting here. An empty DTC bus drives past. An RTV is waiting at the stop, with the conductor calling out loudly. A man walks past, completely lost to the world.

4:20 PM
Another RTV arrives. The conductor looks morose. Maybe they didn't earn well today. Right next to us is a carpenter's shop. The sound of something being hammered is incessant.

4:25 PM
Three young girls are carrying cans of milk they have bought for their homes. A man says to us, smiling, "Hey! Take this woman's photo as well!" Then he laughs. A vegetable seller, selling vegetables on a horse cart. The sound of the horse's hooves can be heard, *tak, tak, tak...* An old man, who is toothless. He is looking at us and laughing. SK *Chaat Wala* passes by. A truck that is loaded with bricks.

4:30 PM
An elderly person behind us is reading a newspaper. One RTV leaves and another arrives immediately after. A song is playing in it, *"Jahan main jaoon, bahaar chali aayee, mehak jaaye..."* ("Wherever I go, it becomes spring time, it becomes fragrant...") A Sumo speeds past. A pandit is riding along on a small bicycle. A vendor with a cart is preparing to start business.

4:35 PM
A seller of incense sticks comes, "Buy some incense sticks..." A door-to-door sales boy of the company Kissan walks past. There is a lot of noise around me. It is getting to me now. Where we are sitting is an auto stand. There are four of us – Rakesh, Lakhmi, Kiran, Sudeep. My three comrades are doing everything they can to get on my nerves! There is a *paan* stall here. An old *baba* stops to chat and joke with Lakhmi. Now everyone is staring at us.

4:40 PM

Another RTV arrives. The faces of all the passengers look unhappy. A Sikh man drives past on a scooter, scratching his head. The RTV is waiting. The passengers are troubled. A bus (route number 521) arrives. Another RTV arrives. A fat woman whose weight makes it cumbersome for her to walk.

4:45 PM

A mechanic looks at us, and smiles. The sound of a song playing a little distance away. Then, the voice of a conductor, the sound of an RTV, the soft sound of a scooter, the sound of a three-wheeler. A meat seller is setting up his stall. How many hens will be slain today? An old woman chewing *paan*. The sound of conversations.

4:50 PM

A child working in the mechanic's shop has just received a slap from his employer. Four girls are proceeding for their tuitions. A man with half a crop of hair on his head is trying to explain something to a boy through gestures. A peanut seller. One boy just slapped the mechanic and left. Two women walk past talking to one another. The voice of a boy, "Hey! Listen!"

4:55 PM

A bus, route number 522, arrives. A tempo, a van, a scooter and some bicycles. There is heavy traffic, almost a jam. A one and a half foot man is sitting next to us, scratching his beard. Two elderly men are standing, both are bespectacled. Another RTV arrives. And behind it, another RTV is approaching, honking its horn. Two boys are walking in our direction, whistling.

5:00 PM
Lights have been switched on now. (I took a break – took out a packet of mouth freshener from my pocket, ate it, and resumed writing.) My attention wanders back to the spot where a dead rat, its insides exposed, is lying. We're all feeling revulsion at seeing it. A fish-seller sets up his stall by the road, on the ground. He is burning something for smoke to chase the mosquitoes away. Lakhmi is sitting right in front of me. Then a cat came to eat my rat. Suddenly, my hand was raised in the air, and the cat scampered away.

5:05 PM
Another jam. The crowd is denser. I think to myself, "Write faster". A fat, tired man. A sound that stands apart from all the sounds around me, *chir chir chir...* Maybe it's an animal. Two boys ask a conductor if the bus will go to Kotla. A girl says to Lakhmi, "Yes, go on, keep doing this. Keep sitting here all your life!"

5:10 PM
An egg-seller is setting up shop. Two boys in front of me, fighting. One swears by the mother, the other by the sister. A man is frying crispies, to sell. Another *chaat wala* comes.

5:15 PM
The man selling eggs looks like he is wondering why we are taking his photograph. A voice from an RTV, "Hey smartass, why don't you move ahead?" A girl sitting inside the RTV is looking at me, as if trying to recollect whether she knows me. The voice of the conductor, "Hey, sister-fucker!" The boss of the auto-stand is trying to choreograph the movements and positions of the RTVs.

5:20 PM
The sound from the carpenter's workshop continue. There can be a traffic jam at any moment. A sound from a motorcycle, *hui hui*. A man selling tube-lights is standing and looking around. There is quite a crowd at the cyclist's now. We are sipping tea. The tea is nothing special. There is a broken pipe lying in front of us, and children are dropping stones in it.

5:25 PM
A strong looking boy is going towards the wrestling ground behind us. Another different voice – the loud grunting of pigs from a distance. The *pi pi* of a horn, the noise from a scooter. The noise has increased and is enveloping us from all sides. Sometimes, it gets very silent, and sometimes the noise becomes very loud. A man is standing next to us, smoking a cigarette. Three girls are walking past. One among them is fixing another's *dupatta*.

5:30 PM
The sound of an RTV reversing. The sound of a three-wheeler, and of a man selling cooking-gas cylinders. One man has come and is standing next to us, troubling us by trying to befriend us with his strange queries. A man selling sweet syrupy *jalebis* is setting up his cart to start business. The hens have begun to be slaughtered. Two boys have got down from the RTV with milk cans. Three are covered, two are not. It is evening now. Passers-by are looking at us. They look like they are wondering what it is that we are doing. Many questions seem to be arising in their minds. Just then a man walks up to us, "Hello mister, what are you doing?" We reply respectfully, "Sir, right now we are working. Please ask us when we have finished".

5:35 PM
There was a bus-stop here earlier. But there isn't one any more. Yes, buses continue to come and stop here. Bulbs have been lit in peoples' homes. Seeing us, some people are coming to enquire. Four boys drive past on a motorcycle.

5:40 PM
A woman on a motorcycle looks at us, as does her husband. We can hear the yelling and screaming of boys around us.

5:45 PM
A cyclist is buying a carpet. Some men are arguing with one another. There is quite a crowd

around the fish-seller. A crow is sitting on a pole. A Coca-Cola van, *zurr, zurr...* It is very crowded here now. The RTV is still waiting. The sound of vehicles from a distance. A Tata 407 tempo arrives. A man is pulling down the shutters of his shop.

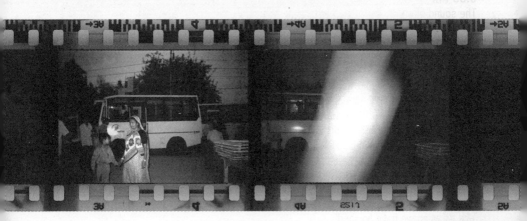

5:50 PM
An old man is buying a wooden seat for his shop. The boy accompanying him is probably his grandson. All the street lamps are on now. The sound of horns can be heard from our left and right. Drums are being beaten some distance away. Two boys are in a friendly, playful argument. The sound of a Toyota Qualis. Two girls with red *dupattas*. Two men are carrying a wooden ladder. Four boys are returning from school.

5:55 PM
A child, about five years old, is taking the body of an old scooter from the mechanic's workshop. Schools have closed for the day. The road is filled with school children. All four of us are ravenously hungry! But, alas! We have work to do! Lakhmi is in anguish with the want of something to eat. The sound of an explosion compels us to turn around to look.

6:00 PM
We have ordered roasted chicken pieces. Some school children are cursing while walking. I am ignoring some of them. The sound of a wooden leg of a cot, falling.

6:05 PM
The sound of drums beating, near us. The sound of an RTV driving away, an auto rickshaw, a boy running. Some men are transporting wooden planks on a cycle-rickshaw. A boy approaches us and says, "*Bhai*, please take my photo as well". He leaves.

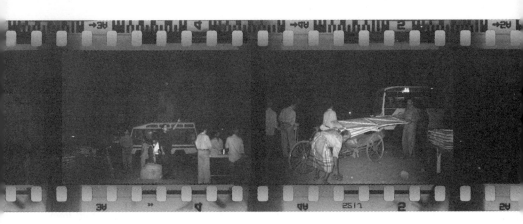

6:10 PM
A boy is hiding from someone on the roof and looking around. There is hustle-bustle around me. The scene is quite intriguing. I had never seen it this way before. That's because I was always mixed in this crowd. Today, standing apart from it, I feel I am seeing it differently. The mechanic's workshop has packed up.

6:15 PM
Sudip brings the roasted chicken pieces. Suddenly, there is a traffic jam. We take a break to eat the chicken.

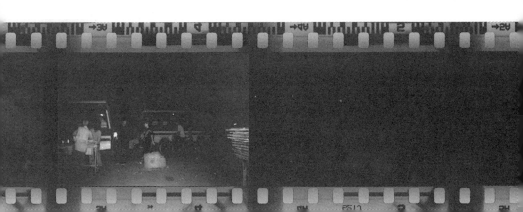

6:20 PM
The wooden planks that had been lying next to us all day are now being kept back into the shop. A Maruti car drives past with a dead body wrapped in a white shroud secured to its roof.
6:25 PM
A truck drives past. Its silencer doesn't work. The sound of some women joking with one another. The sound of a can of milk falling from a boy's hand. Now the cap on my head is useless. The sun has set and it's late evening. I didn't realise it till now!

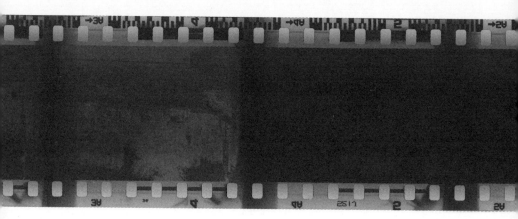

6:30 PM
Some policemen have set out on their evening rounds. I'm sure they will pick someone or the other up. A traffic jam of buses and RTVs again.
6:35 PM
A chartered bus passes by noisily. The egg-seller is still looking at us curiously. The *khut khut* of a cycle. Just then, an RTV arrives. A scooter stops. A little girl asks the conductor of the RTV, "*Bhaiya*, will it go to Lajpat Nagar?" The sound of a bus that comes and stops close to me. A man smoking a *bidi*. Maybe he was craving for it. Now I am standing amongst a lot of people and thinking.

Information =
POLITICS

P2P: Power to the People

JANKO RÖTTGERS

Sooner or later the Napster story will hit the big screen. Copyright-Catfight, orchestrated by Hollywood. It will be the story of Shawn Fanning, Napster's founder, painted in rich cinematic colours. Born as a result of quick sex at a birthday party, raised without a father, money or any strong family ties. Escaping into the world of cyberspace, setting out on a mission to change the way we consume music. We'll see him getting into the music industry's radar, fighting in court, mobilising the masses. He'll lose battle after battle, face showdowns with Metallica, and finally see his creation die, wrangled by lawyers. What a story.

After ninety minutes we will get up from our comfortable cinema seats, feel good, reminiscent. Napster, after all, was our story too. We made it possible, together with millions of other users. We'll think about the rush we felt when we downloaded our first mp3s with Napster – and that unexpected excitement when a total stranger with a funny nickname downloaded something from our own hard disk. Back home, we will – instead of turning on the TV as usual – grab our notebook or settle in front of that fancy iMac. We'll go online and do something we haven't done in a while – download a file-sharing application. It might be Kazaa [http://www.kazaa.com], some Gnutella [http://www.gnutella.com] client or something new we read about recently on Wired.com [http://www.wired.com].

We'll install it, start it, and wait some magical seconds for the client to make contact with its network. And then they'll be there again, as if they had never gone: thousands and thousands of users, engaged in a restless exchange of bits and bytes. Music, films, programs, books – everything seems to be available, provided by individuals like you and me, and everything will be free. Maybe we'll search for the soundtrack of that movie we just watched, or maybe for the movie itself. Something of interest to us will be there for sure. We'll suddenly feel this rush again, and then we'll understand: Napster's story is by no means finished. Not after the company's demise, and certainly not after ninety minutes of Hollywood fun. It's really just beginning now.

Free Install
Napster 2.0 *Click Here!*

Napster's Rise

When Shawn Fanning was eighteen, he used to spend lots of time on the IRC [http://www.irchelp.org], an internet chat network used by tech-savvy people who avoid the main trails of the data highway, with its paved roads and corporate communities. There he met up with friends from a group called w00w00 [http://www.w00w00.org], which dubs itself a security team but is really one of the many hacking crews of the internet. Mind you, being a hacker doesn't necessarily mean that you are showing destructive behaviour. It's just a sign of curiosity combined with technical skills. w00w00's members had very different backgrounds and came virtually from all over the world, connected only by email and their regular chats. The group earned some respect in the global hacker and security community by documenting program vulnerabilities, such as a serious security flaw in the AOL instant messaging program. But its members also worked on little tricks in order to gain extended rights on the servers of their favourite chat network.

Shawn Fanning's role in the whole group remains unclear. He didn't seem to be involved in too many of the group's exploits. But in 1998 he started a project that would earn him lots of respect from his fellow w00w00 members – and cause some serious trouble for the music industry. Fanning noticed that his friends at Boston University's dorm rooms had started downloading lots of mp3 music files from the web. At that time, most popular for that purpose were the Lycos mp3 site [http://music.lycos.com/downloads/] and the music website Scour.com. Both were classical search engines, and both left their users fighting with some serious problems. Most of the websites that hosted mp3s were shut down after a few weeks – either due to a demand from the phonographic industry, or, more likely, because they simply caused too much traffic.

Fanning wanted to circumvent that problem by skipping the intermediaries – the web servers and search engines – and directly connecting mp3 fans. This structure is called peer to peer, because it brings together equal programs (peers) instead of letting them all connect to a central entity. Fanning started programming in autumn 1998 and very soon got the feeling that he was about to create something really important. It was his first major programming project, and it became so time-consuming that he decided to drop out of school and work full time on the application that soon would become Napster.

In summer 1999 Shawn Fanning finished the first version of Napster, uploaded it to a web server and gave the address to a few of his IRC friends, asking them to try it out but refrain from forwarding the download location. His friends tried, were seduced and couldn't resist sharing the software. After only a few days, thousands of people were using Napster. Soon Shawn Fanning had to ask some people from w00w00 to help him set up a better scalable version of the file-sharing service.

Spurred on by the overwhelming success, Shawn incorporated Napster with the help of his uncle. The young company raised venture capital and relocated to California. But with gaining hundreds of thousands of users in only a few months, Napster showed up on the radar of the music industry sooner rather than later. On December 7, 1999, the Recording Industry Association of America (RIAA) [http://www.riaa.org] sued Napster for copyright infringement, demanding $10,000 for every song that was traded over the system. What would follow was a long legal battle with lots of setbacks and a few temporary victories. For now, we'll leave the showdown with Metallica and other juicy parts to Hollywood and concentrate on the technology and its social impact instead.

Napster's problem was one of its main features: in order to serve its users with community functions such as a chatroom and a big, searchable index of all songs available for trade, the system relied on a farm of servers. Although the users exchanged their MP3s directly, the servers were still a crucial part of Napster's architecture. No servers, no Napster – that was the logical approach of the legal attacks.

Like the Telephone Game

In early 2000, Justin Frankel wanted to prove that file sharing was possible without any central entity – be it a server or an upstart company like Napster, who had just raised another $15 million of venture capital. So he worked out a complete server-less system and called it Gnutella. Frankel's system worked in a similar way to the telephone game: instead of querying a central database for a file, a user simply asked a handful of other participants. They looked for the file in their own collection and passed the request down to some more users. If the request was successful, the owner of the requested file would contact the search initiator directly and allow him or her to download it. Frankel published a first version of Gnutella on March 14 on the web. Soon the notorious geek news website Slashdot reported on the program, and again thousands of people were willing to give it a try immediately.

The punchline: Frankel was an AOL employee. The media giant had bought his company Nullsoft [http://www.nullsoft.com] about half a year earlier. AOL was not so pleased with the idea that one of its programmers would release something that was soon dubbed 'the future of Napster'. Within days it forced Nullsoft to pull the plug. But it was already too late: Gnutella was up and running, offering free exchange of all kinds of files. After some reverse engineering and a little undercover help from Nullsoft, Gnutella's protocol – the set of rules that make the network work – was documented by some tech-savvy file-sharing fans. Only days later, the first third-party programs showed up on the Internet. Soon file-sharing fans would learn that Gnutella at that time was far from perfect. In July 2000 the music industry won a first round in its attempts to shut Napster down. A judge granted a preliminary injunction against the company and demanded that all illegal file transfers be stopped within two days. Thousands of soon-to-be-homeless file traders downloaded Gnutella to keep on downloading – and brought the whole network down immediately.

Jordan Ritter, a co-founder of Napster, had a valid explanation for this network behaviour. "Gnutella is truly a 'broadband killer app' in the most literal of senses", Ritter wrote [http://www.darkridge.com/~jpr5/doc/gnutella.html]. "It can easily bring the Internet infrastructure to its knees". The problem was something like this: if every user forwarded his or her search requests to a handful of other users and these users kept forwarding them, then the number of recipients grew exponentially. And while this didn't really bring the internet infrastructure to its knees, it was enough to make Gnutella unusable as soon as a certain amount of users were connected.

7 Million Users. Right Now
Niklas Zennstrom and Janus Friis knew about this problem fairly early and thought they had a key to its solution. The day Napster was hit with its injunction, Friis and Zennstrom announced the launch of a new file-sharing network called Kazaa [http://www.kazaa.com]. About a month later Kazaa was finally ready, and it seemed to overcome Gnutella's obstacles. Instead of just passing messages from equal peer to equal peer, Kazaa introduced network layers. Regular users would connect to so-called ultrapeers – strong computers with a fast Internet connection that could serve as a form of temporary server.

In March 2001, Napster was ordered to filter all content from the major music labels. This gave Kazaa a big boost, and when Napster had to shut down four months later, Zennstrom and Friis's system was ready to take over all those mp3 fans. With Kazaa, people used to Napster experienced a whole new dimension of file sharing. This was not just about music any more. Programs, ebooks and even films were easily accessible. And because the Kazaa-like programs download from various sources at once, getting even big files was no problem any more. Soon Hollywood blockbusters started showing up – some even before their initial release date.

Hollywood and the music industry reacted in the same way they had when they targeted Napster: they sued Friis and Zennstrom. But instead of defending themselves in a long and costly legal battle, the Kazaa creators simply sold their software to an unknown company with headquarters in the tax-haven of Vanuatu. Since then, copyright holders have been trying to get their hands on Kazaa and its allies around the globe. But whenever they seem to get hold of someone, new links show up on a different continent, and local jurisdiction doesn't always go along with the requests of the US record companies.

More important than this legal showdown is the technological impact that Friis and Zennstrom had: Since their network is capable of serving millions of users, other peer-to-peer developers have been adopting ultrapeer structures as well. This is the most remarkable when it comes to the Gnutella developer community. Since 2001, various small companies and hobbyists have helped to modernise Justin Frankel's original Gnutella protocol, connected only loosely by informal contacts and an open mailing list [http://groups.yahoo.com/group/the_gdf/]. They have created a modern network that is able to deal with thousands of users, but almost impossible to stop by court orders: because different programs form the network by using an open protocol, there is no single entity that could pull the plug. And because it is decentralised, content filtering isn't possible either.

Meanwhile the user bases of various file-sharing systems are growing and growing. The overall number of P2P users is hard to estimate, but Kazaa and its allies alone serve more than 4 million people at any given time. The number of casual users might well be ten or twenty times higher: possibly three million people are downloading the Kazaa client every week. Soon the program will have been downloaded more than 200 million times from the company's web server. Overnet [http://www.overnet.com] and Edonkey [http://www.edonkey2000.com], both well known as film-trading networks, combine about 800,000 simultaneous users. DirectConnect [http://www.neo-modus.com], used by hardcore users who tend to lock out everyone who doesn't share at least a few gigabytes, combines up to 150,000 file traders. Gnutella's user base is estimated to be around 100,000.

Then there are various smaller networks with a few thousand users each. Some stay that size, some might become much bigger. And finally there is a loose network of so-called 'Open Napster' servers [http://www.napigator.com/servers/] – people who use Napster's technology by setting up small servers out of their living rooms – with an additional 200,000 users. All together, there might be between six and seven million people from all over the world involved in file sharing right at this moment. And there is a good chance that this number might double in a year or two.

It's all about control

But even more important than these sheer numbers is the change that file sharing has brought about in public opinion. Despite the legal and public relations battle, file sharing is no longer seen as controversial. It's part of everyday life for millions of computer users. More and more people are getting used to having an always-on connection to popular culture. After all, no record store beats the amount of music available in various P2P networks. And soon Blockbuster [http://www.blockbuster.com] will look deserted in comparison to your favourite film-swapping network.

All this is happening at a time when the future of intellectual property, as we know, it is at stake. Facing the obstacles as well as the opportunities of the digital world, the content industry decided to extend its control. Music, films, texts and databases are increasingly becoming restricted by per-use licenses. Traditional usage rights such as the personal copy are defeated by copy protection technologies. Public institutions such as libraries are already facing severe problems in fulfilling their mission – how can they possibly provide knowledge to the public if the public is divided into country zones and user bases and billing is done on a per-click basis? Developing countries that need public access to knowledge more than anything else are forced to adopt restrictive intellectual property policies such as the WIPO treaty [http://www.wipo.int/treaties/ip/wct/index.html], which makes circumvention of copy protection measures illegal.

The public may not be aware of all the consequences of these conflicts, but it has already taken a stance: Empowered by peer-to-peer applications, it chose to leave the empire of corporate control and enter the kingdom of piracy [http://bigboy.spc.org/kop/].

Too bad all this won't make it into Hollywood's Napster tale. It surely sounds like a good plot, doesn't it?

This essay was published in *Dive: An Introduction to the World of Free Software and Copyleft Culture*, edited by Armin Medosch (FACT, 2003, Liverpool).

"Every age constructs its own type of war".·
Fernand Braudel

War in the Age of Pirate Reproduction

NITIN GOVIL

To the State and market technocracies charged with bureaucratizing our experiences of everyday fear, contemporary terror is placeless. The history of the late twentieth century narrates the intimacy of terror and territoriality: crisis mapped onto discrete somewheres like Auschwitz, Hiroshima, East Timor, Belfast, Halabja, Kosovo, Rwanda, New York and Gujarat. Now, however, the hysterical movements of modern terror are calculated on the logic of everywhere. The ubiquity of terror justifies the unprecedented efforts of enforcement agencies to counter the spatial transgressions of the terrorist: we recall how Mohammed Atta moved effortlessly through airport security, even as the close-circuit cameras winked and whirred away. The banal sequence of photographs that captured his movements sent a tremor down the spine of the security establishment, short-circuiting the delicate machinery of vigilance (modernity, after all, has always slept better with its eyes open). Armed with post 9/11 righteousness, the surveillance establishment is urgently recruiting new allies in the 'war on terror'. This is the story of one such courtship.

The initial attraction that brought piracy and terror together is the subject of considerable conjecture. But we know that the 9/11 hijacker's use of counterfeit Microsoft 'Flight Simulator' programs, now sold in many parts of the world with bin Laden's face on the cover, helped cement a decade-long equivalency between intellectual property piracy and terrorism. Nowadays, intellectual property (IP) monopolists claim that the viral threat of piracy overlaps with terrorism's wild, ubiquitous, spatiality: "Piracy can be found everywhere", declares Microsoft's web portal (http://www.microsoft.com/piracy/). The scare tactics of copyright maximalism suggest that, like the unhindered movements of the terrorist, the culture of the copy infiltrates the flows of 'legitimate' commodity exchange. For these IP advocates, the parallel trajectories of the pirate and the terrorist – from Delhi to Davao City to Cuidad del Este – threaten the otherwise healthy circulatory regime of the international body politic. The millenarian anxiety of viral invasion is reflected in a recent US Department of Transportation newsletter: "They run computer manufacturing plants and noodle shops, sell 'designer clothes' and 'bargain basement' CDs. They invest, pay taxes, give to charity, and fly like trapeze artists between one international venue and another. The end game, however, is not to buy a bigger house or send the kids to an Ivy League school – it's to blow up a building, to hijack a jet, to release a plague, and to kill thousands of innocent civilians" (US Department of Transportation, 2003).

In the peculiar speech genre of the policy manifesto, the "they" indicates that the pirate and the terrorist are not like us. They only partially subscribe to the sacrosanct norms of proper citizenship, without proper reverence for country and conduct. They are *unheimlich*, without a home: mere shells of us, as if from a 1950s science fiction film, they are manufactured in a churning vat of religious fundamentalism and commodity fetishism.

In September 2003, influenced by European Commission studies on the links between organized crime and large-scale counterfeiting, the International Police Organization (Interpol) added Chechen separatists and Northern Irish paramilitaries (who traffic in Disney's *The Lion King* and Sony Playstation videogames) to the growing list of organizations suspected of using profits from pirated software, film and music to fund their networks. The two nationalist groups joined a growing list of others linked to both terrorism and intellectual property piracy, from Al Qaeda, Hezbollah, Hamas, and Albanian and Basque separatists, to anti-Arroyo agitators in the Philippines, FARC in Columbia, and the Sicilian Cosa Nostra and its international affiliates. The equivalence between piracy and terrorism gained legitimacy in 1995, when New York's Joint Terrorism Taskforce claimed that profits from counterfeit T-shirt sales – sold in the very shadow of the twin towers – helped fund the 1993 bombing of the World Trade Centre. Post 9/11, policy proposals from the European Commission and Interpol alike have naturalized the relationship between IP piracy and terrorism and the connections are flowing fast and furiously. For example, British detectives claim that Pakistani DVDs account for 40% of anti-piracy confiscations in the UK, and that profits from pirated versions of *Love Actually* and *Master and Commander* funnel back to the coffers of Pakistan-based Al Qaeda operatives. Similarly, anti-piracy evangelists, like Bombay's former police commissioner Julio Riberio, claim that pirate CD factories in Pakistan fund the Inter-Services Intelligence, even as Hindu nationalists consider the Bombay film industry a front for Islamic terrorism. An Indian intelligence community, eager to build on US-India joint military exercises begun in May 2002, claims that Dawood Ibrahim's Karachi-based music and video piracy outfits help fund Al Qaeda and Lashkar-e-Toiba. Not to be left out, Kerala police organized a national seminar on anti-piracy in late 2003, claiming that pirated Tamil films sold in Canada help fund LTTE.

As the war on terror focuses on the global circuits of the information commodity, the national tames the affective anxieties brought on by the frenetic movements of contemporary intellectual property: the uncanny everywhere-ness of piracy. In fact, the moral commensurability of piracy and terrorism – as equal partners in the heresy of spatial dislocation – is insured by their simultaneous threats to the properly interpolated spaces of the nation. While the national has been central to the inscription of difference in the IP policy archive, functioning as a command metaphor for the distribution of scarcity, its evocation is far from static. The first English copyright statutes in the early eighteenth century transformed land "into the model against which other types of interests were analogized or compared to assess market value, of information commodities" (Aoki: 1327). However, the elevation of local vernacular print traditions to national literary patrimonies in the late nineteenth century was fuelled by early international copyright conventions claiming an extra-territorial, universalist criteria for legal protection. The Swiss government, for example, invited "all civilized nations to join the planned Berne copyright convention in 1883, claiming that it is, in fact, in the nature of things that the work of man's genius, once it has seen the light, can no longer be restricted to one country and to one nationality. If it possesses any value, it is not long in spreading itself in all countries, under forms which may vary more or less, but which, however, leave in its essence and its principal manifestations the creative idea" (Ricketson: 54).

While information technology facilitates the deterritorialization of flexible accumulation on a global scale, the national continues to play an important role in anchoring IP within existing spatial regimes. Multilateral treaties from the Berne Convention to the EU Satellite and Cable Directive invoke a number of national criteria to fix the space of production and reception, from industrial or commercial domicile, to place of first publication or the location where electronic signals are 'introduced'. International trade and information policy in the 1990s insisted that the development of 'local' cultural industries depends upon a national infrastructure of intellectual property rights overseen by global enforcement and procedural norms. This has lent weight to the prevailing World Bank orthodoxy that the rest of the world must strengthen domestic intellectual property regimes in order to lure the direct foreign investment capital required for the ascension to Western modernity. Clearly, the national is still the coin of the realm in the currency of global IP governance.

But this is not mere reterritorialization. The national cuts across an array of social practices, from informal codes of belonging to bureaucratic regularizations of identity and domicile. The territoriality of the national is not simply mapped on a pre-existing space: social practices under the sign of the national perform the territorial as a provisional and improvisational marker (Ford, 1999). For example, media pirates in Malaysia have been charged by Hollywood studios under trade description laws that prosecute based on fraudulent 'Made in USA' labels. Given Hollywood's thoroughly globalized production, the mandate to fix national authenticity through the (trade)marks of American exceptionalism is partly a response to piracy's spatial 'wildness'. Similarly, new Russian copyright laws mandate that every CD, DVD and cassette sold must display the name and location of its manufacturer along with a unique licensing number. While American and Russian copyright laws insist on registering national authenticity, the material transportation of properly registered goods is governed by international maritime laws that allow the insignia of national origin to be traded on the open market. Media goods with national attribution are routinely transported on cargo vessels bearing purchased 'flags of convenience', easily obtained from any government willing to sell their national attribution to third-party shipping distributors in exchange for a portion of the profits on a percentage basis or for a one-time fee.

These forked evocations of location demonstrate the performativity of the national as an index of spatial authenticity. Meanwhile, the territorial governance of IP, while responsive to contemporary cultures of circulation, is effectively bolstered by the ethical management of consumption. Such discourses of citizenship – the primary artefact of national subjectivity – become part of a pedagogy designed to internalize proper forms of media consumption. For example, the Motion Picture Association of America (MPAA) began a middle-school program called "What's the Diff: A Guide to Digital Citizenship" in October 2003. This program 'educates' American students in grades five through nine about the incivility of peer-to-peer (P2P) file sharing. The new initiative (for details, see http://www.ja.org/programs/programs_supplements_citizenship.shtml) urges teachers to "bring home the message that P2P downloading is illegal, immoral and wrong ... As students recognize that there is essentially 'no diff' (i.e. no difference) between the illegal and unethical nature of these practices, it is our hope that they will begin to adopt more appropriate attitudes and beliefs about digital media, which will help guide their future behaviour".

Well aware that altruism is no match for exchange-value in the pedagogy of citizenship, the MPAA offers DVDs and CDs, movie tickets and paid trips to Hollywood for students who write prize-winning essays denigrating copyright piracy. Though, as the contest rules for the "Xcellent Xtreme Challenge" note, "best of all, when you and your friends help stop the downloading of files from the Internet, EVERYBODY WINS!" These happy proclamations are deployed through new techno-bureaucratic architectures, from digital copyright regimes and electronic watermarking, to trusted systems and other digital rights management sys-tems. Representing the vanguard in consumer surveillance, these technologies determine the appropriate consumption of the media commodity by inscribing the logic of proper use in the information good itself: with the mouse-click that signals an acceptance of the media commodity's constraints of use, the consumer takes on the mantle of digital citizen-ship. Expanding the sphere of copyright criminality to include previously legal forms of circumvention, trusted systems and digital rights management are the latest allies in the coalition of anti-terror metaphors, part of an overarching logic of pre-emption that justifies unilateralism in anti-piracy and anti-terrorism alike.

In its evocation of ethical self-management through the invigilation of consumption, copyright's moral majority is actually tapping into a much older connection between piracy and terrorism as equally heinous crimes. This equation is clearly indicated in the history of 'universal jurisdiction'. In recent applications of international law, the category of universal jurisdiction has been used by national courts to prosecute human rights abuses in foreign nations. Consequently, the moral heinousness of crimes against humanity circumvents the normal territorial sovereignty of national jurisdiction. However, for centuries prior to the post-World War II application of universal jurisdiction against genocide, apartheid and war crimes, maritime piracy was the only crime deemed heinous enough to warrant universal jurisdiction under international law (see Bassiouni). While rarely invoked in actual application, linking piracy and crimes against humanity was well established in late eighteenth and nine-teenth century theoretical treatises that argued the case for extraterritorial jurisdiction. Although state-sanctioned piracy or 'privateering' was widely condoned – maritime piracy has always been part of the legitimate business of the state – the act of stealing on the 'global commons' of the high seas without state issued license was deemed the most serious transgression in the international law of nations (see Kontorovich). The moral righteousness of contemporary anti-piracy initiatives draws on precedent for the universally accepted immorality of piracy, still understood by the community of nations as exceeding even the sovereign power of national jurisdiction. What better basis for unilateral action against the genocidal implications of intellectual property piracy than its historical abjection by the community of nations?

The global and the digital certainly complicate the classical geometries of cultural exchange, but the crisis in spatial referentiality has only spurred the generation of new forms of reverence. The para-territories of the national and the mnemonic traces of digital rights management are motivated by intellectual property's newfound missionary zeal. Yet the circumscription of use enervates what is most unique about the information commodity. Distinct from the categories of what Igor Kopytoff (1986) called "terminal commodities" – commodities whose social biographies involve only one journey from production to consumption – information goods and their infinite recombinatory possibilities suggest a multiplicity of social biographies. Information goods are a kind of transversal commodity, one that moves across production/reception categories at a velocity that outstrips the declarative injunction of 'proper' use mandated by the normative social contract of legal consumption. These transverse commodities cut across the common intersections and agglomerations of production and use; their transit is figurative and draws the shape of new, transitory, and strategic relations of affiliation.

But for those tallying the gains and losses in the global war on terror, circumnavigating the 'everywhere' of piracy has become a matter of great urgency. From the pre-emptive strikes of digital rights management to the moral invigilation of consumption, and the alternate spatialities of national jurisdiction and its erasure under the historical invocation of genocide and maritime piracy, modern intellectual property initiatives have orchestrated a melodrama of considerable intensity. The script of this new feature locks together the pirate, the consumer, and the terrorist in a fatal attraction that any moviegoer can learn to love.

REFERENCES

Aoki, Keith. "Surveying Law and Borders: (Intellectual) Property and Sovereignty: Notes Towards a Cultural Geography of Authorship", *Stanford Law Review 48* (May, 1996).

Bassiouni, M. Cherif. "Universal Jurisdiction for International Crimes: Historical Perspectives and Contemporary Practice", *Virginia Journal of International Law 42* (Fall 2001) pp. 81-162.

Braudel, Fernand. *The Mediterranean and the Mediterranean World in the Age of Phillip II* . Trans by Siân Reynolds (University of California Press, 1995, Berkeley).

Ford, Richard T. "Law's Territory: A History of Jurisdiction", *Michigan Law Review 97* (February, 1999) pp. 843-930.

Kontorovich, Eugene. "The Piracy Analogy: Modern Universal Jurisdiction's Hollow Foundation", *Harvard International Law Journal 45* (forthcoming, Winter, 2004).

Kopytoff, Igor. "The Cultural Biography of Things: Commoditization as Process", *The Social Life of Things: Commodities in Cultural Perspective*. Arjun Appadurai ed. (Cambridge University Press, 1986) pp. 64-91.

Ricketson, Sam. *The Berne Convention for the Protection of Literary and Artistic Works: 1886-1986* (Centre for Commercial Law Studies, 1987, London).

U.S. Department of Transportation, Office of Safety and Security. *Transit Security Newsletter 36* (May 2003) p. 2.

Floss and the 'Crisis'
Foreigner in a Free Land?[1]

MARTIN HARDIE

" ... capitalism (or any other name that one wants to give to the process that today dominates world history) was not only directed toward the expropriation of productive activity, but also principally toward the alienation of language itself, of the very linguistic and
communicative nature of humans, of that logos which one of Hericlitus's fragments identified as the Common. The extreme form of the expropriation of the Common is the spectacle, that is the politics we live in. But this also means that in the spectacle our linguistic
nature comes back to us inverted. This is why (precisely because what is being expropriated
is the very possibility of the common good) the violence of the spectacle is so destructive;
but for the same reason the spectacle retains something like a positive possibility that can
be used against it".[2]

- Giorgio Agamben, *The Coming Community*

here is a lot written about the world of Linux, Free, Libre or Open Source Software[3]
production. Most of it is gushingly positive and written in a manner that only seeks to
promote the benefits of this type of software over the apparently dominant corporate
or proprietary forms. Supportive reportage generally posits Floss (Free/Libre Open Source
Software) as being more advantageous in terms of personal or community autonomy than
are the dominant corporate/proprietary alternatives. The basic argument is based upon the
premise that Floss grants the technologically savvy user/producer greater control over the
machine to which their production is tied. As *The Seattle Times* reported on the eve of the
2003 World Summit on Information Society (WSIS): "Particularly in the developing world,
Linux and other free and open-source software have economic and political attractions ...
Politically, a shift to open-source can be a digital declaration of independence in an era when
the United States and its software industry are not universally trusted".[4] It should go without saying that this political attraction is not confined to the 'developing world'.

At first glance there are not a lot of 'essays in self criticism' surrounding Floss and not
much seems to be written that, even by implication, appears relevant to these times of
perpetual crisis that this issue of the *Sarai Reader* is devoted to. However, I think it can be
reasonably argued that Floss, its methods of production, as a form of labour and its location within the realm of the global politic, is firmly a part and parcel of the world of crisis.[5]
Floss is in many ways the archetypal crisis media, and its potential as an alternative thus

rests with decisions made by those that live and act within these crisis times. Floss inhabits a space that is signified by the tendency of global corporate sovereignty, and here I will seek to outline an argument that Floss currently resides within a particularly American vision of freedom which seems to be spreading virus-like in its quest to smooth the space of the globe. With this vision and this tendency, fear and control are sought to be generated with the invoking of images of the enemies of freedom often related to the 'war on terror'. But these images form only some of the gloss of the spectacle necessitated by this overarching tendency toward global corporate or Imperial sovereignty.

In some ways the label, Floss, that is the term or description itself, appears in fact to be situated at the heart of this tendency. The American flavour to the rhetoric embodied in the name, and in the language that abounds around it, causes me to have concerns as to whether the Floss machine in its present incarnation can live up to the expectations, and whether it is a real and viable alternative – that is, whether its potential can survive the increasingly imperial form of global sovereignty within which we live. In saying this, it is probably necessary to point out that the enquiry I seek to commence is not 'against' Floss but one that seeks to contribute to the continuation of the political benefits of the machine. In this regard, borrowing from Foucault, I think it is fair to say that "... there are no machines of freedom, by definition ... the exercise of freedom can only function when there is a certain convergence; in the case of divergence or distortion, it immediately becomes the opposite of that which had been intended..."[6] Or to paraphrase what he said in another place, my point is not that Floss is either bad or good in itself, but that "everything is dangerous ... (and if) everything is dangerous, then we always have something to do".[7]

Therefore, what I would like to try and do here is to raise the question, open it for comment as it were, about the rhetoric, the language, the discourse that envelopes the Floss machine, and look a little at its particular place and heritage in order to try and see if this factor in any way gives cause for concern, and to reconsider the current, particularly uncritical, approach. My interest here lies in trying to come to grips with a snippet of the rhetoric of this vision of Floss in order to try and understand what sort of vision of 'free' it is tied to. I want to raise the questions as to whether the 'Free as in Freedom' of Floss-speak is bound to a certain vision of 'Free as in America', and in doing so raise the possibility of considering other ways with which we may be able to re-imagine Floss and its future, and thus possibly continue to pursue its emancipatory potential.

I intend to start exploring here the intersections of the rhetoric of 'Free as in Freedom', the law of copyright, and what I have dubbed, "Lessig's transcendental foundationalism" within the global 'kingdom of money'. Here I can only seek to lay out the bare bones of an argument suggesting that the intersection of these various lines do not coincide with a drift toward 'free as in speech', but with a drift toward a machine that proposes property itself as the basis of liberty and freedom. It appears to me that to pose speech against property in the forums of capital, as the rhetoric of Floss seeks to do, within the context of the rhetoric of American freedom, is to concede the struggle to a form of American constituted power, privileged by capital within the realms of imperial sovereignty. It is more than likely, given the intersections I seek to describe, that it will be property that comes out on top – even if that means perpetual crisis, and continual management and control of the hackers, pirates, terrorists and other barbarians who seek to escape the bounds of freedom.[8]

At this point a brief digression is probably in order to position the conceptions of freedom that I will discuss. I have let forth here with a phrase 'Free as in America' – I am attempting to take the piss out of Stallman's "Free as in Freedom" – probably without luck; and I am sure my characterisation of this sort of logic as being 'Free as in America' will rile some and be held against me and what I am trying to grapple with. I could be open to attack that I am treating America and its visions of free as some totalized whole. But what I am alluding to here is that 'constituted' freedom as signified by aspects of American law, politics, culture and power. To help set the bounds of this particular 'freedom in the American sense', it might be useful to first refer to Larry Lessig, one of the chief proponents of American free speak in relation to things digital.

Speaking of the struggle for control of the internet, a topic interwoven with the life of Floss, Lessig states in his second tome, *The Future of Ideas*, that this struggle "will determine what the 'free' means in our self congratulatory claim that we are now, and will always be, a 'free society'. ... This is a struggle about an ideal". He continues to deny that this meaning of free is either a moral or a political question, but "instead best described as a constitutional question: it is about the fundamental values that define this society and whether we will allow those values to change. Are we, in the digital age, to be a free society? And what precisely would that idea mean?"[9] Lessig may be just carving the meat off the bone in order to dissect what he feels is the core issue, but it is easy to get the feeling that to him, either we are all Americans now, or that decisions about the internet are best made within the US constitutional context. For me, here lays the heart of Lessig's analysis, the line that runs through his two books: he proceeds as if the struggle regarding the future of the internet, its control, is a purely constitutional matter, and, at that, an American constitutional matter. For all that Lessig gives us, this is the thing that gets stuck in my throat when I read him: his abiding faith in America, its Constitution and its 'founders'. For Lessig, 'the' constitution is an architecture "that structures and constrains social and legal power, to the end of protecting fundamental values – principles and ideals that reach beyond the compromises of ordinary politics".[10]

We can try and situate Lessig's constitution and its freedom in a wider context by looking at Toni Negri's work, *Insurgencies*.[11] Here Negri takes us on a journey that traverses America, Machiavelli, Spinoza, Harrington, Rouseau, Marx and beyond. In particular, he examines the "freedom of the frontier" in a way that obviously was taken up later in his writing with Michael Hardt in *Empire*.[12] Negri characterizes the American revolution as an example of constituent power, "an effective, social, political alternative"[13] to the transcendent constituted power of sovereignty or constitutionalism. For Negri, constituent power is founded in the multitude, "an always open form of democratic government".[14] Negri chronicles how American constituent power, founded upon the frontier, in the end was submitted to the constitution: "The *homo politicus* of the revolution must submit to the political machine of the constitution, rather than in the free space of the frontier, the individual is constrained to that of the constitution. ... [I]t is absorbed, appropriated by the constitution, transformed into an element of the constitutional machine. It becomes constitutional machinery. What constituent power undergoes here is an actual change of paradigm ... shift-

ing it away from its meaning as active participation in the government to a negative meaning - that of an action ... under the aegis of the law".[15] It "is not conceived as something
that founds the constitution, but as the fuel of its engine ... no longer an attribute of the
people ...(it) has a model of political society".[16] The constitution becomes an organism with
its own life, with the people reduced to a formal element of government – "a modality of
organised power".[17] And at the heart of this organized power, "the constitution is elevated
to the kingdom of monetary circulation". Money replaces the frontier, as Negri describes
the "organism by which Hamilton is inspired is that of the 'powerful abstraction' of money,
of its circulation, and of its pulse. ... [He] reorganises power around financial capital".[18] Thus
when I speak of 'free as in America', I refer to this America constituted on power and confined by "the transcendental theory of the foundation", and with it the "always theological
foundations of capital's economy".[19]

With this as background, let's continue. In its pure state, the Floss machine may bear
some of the hallmarks of a form of communal production, as described for example by
Marx in *Grundrisse*.[20] Or because of its apparent 'rejection' of the propertising aspects of
copyright law, Floss appears to be, or is professed to be, beyond (or even prior to) property, and thus embodying a tendency that is outside the realms inhabited by commodities
and even in the longer term, capital. However, although differences exist within the high
priests of Floss, their mantras are well expressed by Stallman's position that Floss is not
"Free as in Beer"[21] – that is as in price, and hence it is Libre and not Gratis – but "Free as
in Speech". The reference to "as in Speech" links us back again to 'The Constitution' and in
particular to its First Amendment. And thus it is here, with this intersection of 'free' with "free
speech" and not with "free beer" that we encounter the beginnings of the production or piloting of the rhetoric of "free as in freedom". With this intersection, the production of the logic
and rhetoric of Floss are immediately caught within the bounds of American visions (and
hence imperial capital's visions) of what it means to be free. Our initial point of departure is
immediately caught within the bounds of an American, a constitutional freedom.[22]

Two quick points here – within this American vision there is a definite binary, but complementary, vision of what 'free' means. It is clearly tied to capital and its attendant concepts of innovation. Here, free speech is often perceived as founding a marketplace of
ideas that in turn nurtures private acts of development associated with commodity relations. Speech here is the breeding ground of "the kingdom of monetary circulation",[23] rather
than the boundary of the frontier. Second, this particularly American vision of freedom is not
what many of us, who find ourselves at the edges of or within contemporary capital, envis-
age when we think about 'free', and/or even the benefits of Floss. But as the smooth space
of Empire is widened, through the work of the imperial military, corporate and NGO
(non-government organization) machine, we find ourselves more and more within this
particularly American vision of 'free as in freedom'. Thus we succumb to this virus of
American freedom, whether we like it, believe it, think it, intend it, want it, or not.

Without a doubt, Floss plays an integral role in the production of knowledge in the contemporary world, especially where linked by the coverage of the internet. In this way Floss
forms a part of the new forms of "immaterial labour"[24] made possible by communications
technology. In fact, to a large degree, Floss actually makes a large part of communications

technology possible. It is indisputable today that many of the links and portals within the internet are themselves products of Floss. And, as with the internet, it is arguable that in its original peer-to-peer form Floss constitutes a vegetal, rhizomatic model of production in which concepts or products are never stable but in a state of constant flux, as they are modified or transformed by producers and users in their communal passage from one problem to the next. If these characterizations are accurate, Floss may then contain the possibility of being a "system in perpetual heterogeneity", or even crisis.[25] Therefore, in many ways it could be said that Floss is against the arborescent, the corporate, the proprietary or the cathedral image which has been, up until recent times, the prevailing model of production within capital. Nevertheless, it has been convincingly argued (as far back as *Grundrisse*) that capital itself is a system of this type, continually coming up against and seeking to overcome its own limit.[26] And it is precisely because capital is a system that continually requires new forms and methods for its own survival, and because of this hunger for new sustenance, that more than the mere repetition of the benefits of Floss and its current rhetoric and logic is required in order to resist such consumption – an over-coding that tends toward control and a functioning consistent with its ever present "cash nexus".[27] While Floss does have within it an enormous emancipatory potential that may be realized by creating "continuous connections and transversal tie-ins",[28] this threat of over-coding by capital, the threat of blockage of its lines of flight is continuous. And as Floss, like capital, is in a constant state of crisis, there is always work to be done to realize its emancipatory potential. There is little to ensure that capital will not devour and regurgitate Floss anew in its own likeness. It will come "back to us inverted" or at least not bearing the likeness with which it was originally conceived. In the light of this, the intersections I seek to describe here, through the production of meanings, tend to produce Floss, pilot it, to take on the likeness required by capital.

I will now try and sketch some factors in order to flesh out the ways these intersections may tend to confine Floss within a particular form of logic and piloting. By considering some statements related, in one way or another, to the position of Floss within law, economy and discourse, it is possible to understand how its potential to go beyond the acceptable bounds of imperial freedom is being watched, monitored, controlled, and when necessary, castigated. At present, little attention is being paid to these movements; there is very little critical analysis of this side of the picture. There is a tidal wave of promotion surrounding Floss's benefits, self-congratulatory back patting and repetition of mantras such as "information just wants to be free". But critical analysis of this rhetoric is too often avoided, and when raised, dismissed as coming from a non-believer or from someone 'against'. This state of affairs is open to attack on many a level.

The attacks upon the Floss machine's potential lines of flight are being made and becoming clearer by the day as the rhetoric of the other, complementary side of the American free-speak machine tends to include Floss and its various coordinates within its sights. A notable occurrence was when WIPO decided to can its planned meeting to discuss Floss. *The Washington Post*[29] reported, "It is understood that lobbyists ... pressed the US State Department and the US Patent and Trademark Office to have the meeting called off. ... Lois Boland, Director of International Relations for the US Patent and Trademark Business

says that open-source software is contrary to WIPO's mission to promote intellectual property rights. 'To hold a meeting to disclaim or waive such rights seems to us to be contrary
to the goals of WIPO', she says". In characteristic form, Lessig dismissed her comments
as ignorant and sought to give her and us all a lesson on what copyright is "correctly" all
about.[30] But the point was that the lobbyists and Boland had set the stage for WIPO's
withdrawal and opened the path for the questioning of the most acceptable role for Floss
within the bounds of imperial sovereignty.

At the other end of the spectrum are the direct calls for control. Reflect upon the language of SCO's Darl McBride in his "Open letter to the Open Source Community".[31] McBride
couches his language in familiar 'you're with us or against us' rhetoric: "No one can tolerate
DDoS (Distributed Denial of Service) attacks and other kinds of attacks in this Information
Age economy that relies so heavily on the internet. Mr Raymond and the entire Open Source
community need to aggressively help the industry police these types of crimes. If they fail
to do so, it casts a shadow over the entire Open Source movement and raises questions
about whether Open Source is ready to take a central role in business computing. ... Until
these illegal attacks are brought under control, enterprise customers and mainstream
society will become increasingly alienated from anyone associated with this type of behaviour". Now it might be easy to dismiss the SCO drama as an aberration, as the death
throes of a failed company, or even to try and disprove that the attacks did in fact occur,
but the language surrounding their case, their legal claims and even McBride's Bush-like
rhetoric sit well with much of the discourse of late.

We are used to this language when it comes to the crimes of file sharers, with whose
'pirating' the 'worst excesses' of the P2P culture are associated. Not so very long ago, a
few kids in Sydney had to face the music in court. Their story, as told in the media, is one
of castigation and control.[32] Law in this case castigated by use of the criminal sanction, but
at the same time the example serves the tendency of law in its becoming-economic, its tendency toward economy. That is, it is becoming-economic in both the sense of the free market and in the sense used by Foucault concerning the correct and efficient management of
individuals.[33] Here is an example of law intervening to discipline deviant, un-commercial relations, and in so doing, shows how law plays its part in producing smooth capitalist relations.

With these instances of castigation, whole communities and fields of communication
and practice are concurrently and implicitly called into question. They become suspect.
These events occur and with them arrive far wider desires for control and restraint, as one
of the pirates/sharers, Tran, told the press after his conviction: "I strongly discourage anyone else from doing this as well". The example of Tran and his fellow pirates turned into
unwitting agents of control oils the economy of law, which in turn oils the economy of economy. In the spectacle of the imperial machine there is a link, no matter how tenuous in
reality, how rhetorical and attention-grabbing it may seem, between cyber-delinquency and
that other evil, global terrorism. Cyber-delinquency, file sharing, become in the spectacle of
Empire, the metaphoric equivalent of smoking pot behind the school shed, a simple step
away from the heroin of Al Qaeda.

Lessig and others were able to dismiss the US Patents Office 'outside' interference in
WIPO's plans as ignorant, but it became a little harder after the organisation decided to

contribute to the spectacle itself by announcing in the weeks prior to WSIS 2003 that IP theft was in fact a form of "terrorism".[34] Closer to the homeland, as they call it, technology companies are urged to cooperate in the battle against cyber-terrorism – or submit to government-imposed security regulations. "The enemies of freedom use the same techniques as hackers do", U.S. Homeland Security Secretary Tom Ridge said to 350 industry executives gathered for the first National Cyber Security Summit in Santa Clara.[35] And then, funny things happen: late in November ICANN's[36] name registry website was hacked. As reported, "... visitors to the name registry home page [found] a mysterious black screen upon visiting the site ... The bottom of the black screen ... included a rotating image displaying the following text in sequence: "It's good. www.slackware.com Open Source is Good. Free is Good. Slackware Linux".[37] And very soon after, SCO's own website was repeatedly, or allegedly, attacked. Whatever the facts may be is probably not the point.[38] The point is the contribution to the spectacle, as the file sharer, the hacker, the cyber-delinquent, the pirate and the terrorist, become the scapegoats of the information society, "charged with everything ... bad ... everything that resist(s) the signifying signs" of American free speak, the incarnation of "a line of flight the signifying regime cannot tolerate ...".[39] The tendency of this rhetoric appears to want to keep deviant technology, and by implication, Floss, within the bounds of American freedom to ensure it does not escape capture, that it is functional and controlled within the global machine.

This tendency toward the limiting of the frontier of Floss intersects dangerously with the rhetoric of "free as in freedom" with which I opened. How does this intersection manifest itself; that is, what do we encounter with this convergence of the Ridge/McBride/WIPO allusions to terror with the freedoms of Stallman and Lessig? Is the consequence of the intersection of their freedoms incompatible, or are they just two complementary sides of the same American freedom bound together by the organized power of the Constitution? I am not suggesting that Lessig or Stallman hold views of the nature of Ridge, but that their language and the meanings that it produces tend to permit only an American freedom. That is to say, Lessig's foundationalism intersects with Stallman's freedoms so as to bind them to a constituted freedom within the context of global capital. The question to ask is – what is being produced? Is it a Floss that is being piloted within the acceptable outer boundaries of freedom, centred as they are upon the axiom of a marketplace of ideas that nurtures private acts of development?

One way to come to grips with this tendency is by considering some of the legal discourse concerning these issues. The current SCO related litigation[40] and the Eldred case[41] provide us with one way in which to commence such an enquiry. In looking at these instances, it is useful to step back a little and commence by providing a brief reconnoitre of the American vision of liberty enunciated within the US Constitutional context. Liberty and hence freedom in America has a particular Lockean genealogy or derivation. For Locke, society was based on property and property embraced a man's right in his own person to use his labour as he saw fit. At the time of the much vaunted 'founders' of the US Constitution, people recognized "the exclusive use of some tangible property as essential to survival and the right to such as essential to autonomy"; that vision embraced the notion that, "to the extent that a person is dependent on another for the necessities of life, that person is not autonomous".[42] It was one of the 'founders', Alexander Hamilton, who wrote that "a power over a man's subsistence amounts to a power over his will".[43] For the "generation of 1787-91, property was a natural right ... that basic right included a cognate right to contract with other property holders...".[44]

By the latter part of the nineteenth century, and as the movement from an agrarian to industrial economy occurred, the prevailing wisdom was that uncalled for interference with property rights, and the new industrial market where "...competition was a law of nature" risked paying "... the price of mitigating the economic struggle" which in the end may signal "... the destruction of liberty...".[45] Property was thus "the fundamental constitutional value, liberty ... the primary constitutional right, and substantive due process ... the instrument for their accomplishment...".[46] *Allgeyer vs. Louisiana*[47] summed up the Supreme Court's jurisprudence at the time: "The liberty mentioned in (the fourteenth) amendment means not only the right of the citizen to be free from the mere physical restraint of his person ... but the term is deemed to embrace the right of the citizen to be free in the enjoyment of all his faculties; ... and for that purpose to enter into all contracts which maybe proper, necessary and essential to his carrying out to a successful conclusion the purposes above mentioned". It "was the last right, that of contract, which the Court came to consider paramount". Of course, the paradigm case of this period and of *laissez faire* capital and substantive due process was that of *Lochner vs. New York*.[48] Lochner has been much criticized, but has also been the subject of some writing about the new cyber-economists who characterize neo-liberal thinking about the information society.[49] Whether or not the specifics of Lochner are what lawyers call "good authority" may be a moot point. What is not moot, however, is that the liberal vision that found its voice in Allgeyer and Lochner is alive and well in the current neo-liberal US Supreme Court.

How does this short history intersect with the SCO cases and with the rhetoric I have previously set out? As I have briefly tried to state, much of the Floss rhetoric of 'freedom' is couched in terms of being the 'correct' argument or position because of its alleged conformity with the vision of the 'founders'. I don't want to buy into an argument as to whether SCO will be or could be successful; that is not my point here.[50] It is the role that SCO plays in the wider tendency of piloting that I am describing which is of interest to me for the present. This is where the real game of the economy of law in the contemporary world is played out. Becoming-economic entails law acting as much through its signals of control, 'fundamental values' or truths and power, as much as it does by the positive legal word.

Thus it is important to try and locate SCO's claims within the broad vision and genealogy of American freedom as described above. Situating it in this way, and considering its intersections with the rhetoric described, suggests that what is at stake may not be whether SCO survives but, in the end and at its core, the very meaning of (American) liberty itself. It goes without saying (or it should) that American meanings are of course increasingly important for us all these days. Globally, very few of us are immune to the virus of American freedom – even more so for those outside of the Floss machine; just ask those that now camp out, free, in the rubble of Afghanistan or Iraq. But within the Floss machine and amongst its high priests – its academics, lawyers and developers – to even suggest that SCO's claims should be seriously considered as relevant in any way is dismissed. To

Flossers, their legal arguments seem plain ludicrous. Their claims are unfathomable merely because Floss-ers are bound to hold dear their particular vision of 'free' as being the correct and the only logical one. Thus SCO's claims are given scant attention and are simply labelled "nonsense"[51] by those within, or who hold their work as being the ultimate embodiment of, the dreams of the 'founding fathers'. In this way, the rhetoric of Floss in itself suffices to exemplify this strain of faith in law and liberty. However, let's go back to the SCO vision of copyright and why they say it is the 'correct' one, why Darl McBride says it is the one consistent with the vision of the 'founders', and read it in the light of the small piece of constitutional discourse set out above.

McBride's version is summarized in his analysis of the majority US Supreme Court opinion in Eldred. McBride argues that the "Court's analysis of the constitutional foundation of the Copyright Act applies directly to the debate between SCO and FSF/Red Hat regarding intellectual property protection for software". SCO's position is that the authority of Congress under the US Constitution to "promote the Progress of Science and the useful arts" inherently includes a profit motive, and that protection for this profit motive includes a constitutional dimension. Put simply, SCO says that the US Constitution protects a right to profit as a central element of its copyright provisions, and that the "progress of science" is best advanced by vigorously protecting the right of authors and inventors to earn a profit from their work. On the other hand, SCO says "... The Free Software Foundation, Red Hat and other GPL advocates take the contrary position. The FSF and Red Hat believe that the progress of science is best advanced by eliminating the profit motive from software development and insuring free, unrestricted public access to software innovations. The Free Software Foundation was established for this purpose. The GPL implements this purpose. Red Hat speaks for a large community of software developers dedicated to this purpose. However, the US Supreme Court has dramatically undercut this position with its guidance in Eldred in how to define the term 'promote the Progress of Science and the useful arts...'".[52]

Whether McBride's characterizations of the GPL and its backers are ultimately accurate is again not the point. In the spectacle, things are about perception and, as I have tried to explore, rhetoric, and of course, power. The Floss machine privileges speech over property in its quest for innovation. This was the argument that Lessig so passionately ran in Eldred. But McBride is accurate when he says that the Eldred court privileges property and contract – profit – over speech as the fundamental underpinning of the copyright regime. This is probably best enunciated in a footnote to the majority opinion in Eldred where Justice Ginsburg wrote, "As we have explained, '[T]he economic philosophy behind the [Copyright] [C]lause ... is the conviction that encouragement of individual effort by personal gain is the best way to advance public welfare through the talents of authors and inventors'. ... Accordingly, 'copyright law celebrates the profit motive, recognizing that the incentive to profit from the exploitation of copyrights will rebound to the public benefit by resulting in the proliferation of knowledge ... The profit motive is the engine that ensures the progress of science'. ... Copyright law serves public ends by providing individuals with an incentive to pursue private ones".[53]

This is the vision of freedom, the vision of the 'founders' of the US Constitution, that holds sway within the bounds of freedom in America today. This is the vision of the becoming-economic of law and the functionality of the global machine. With this vision it is clear that the tendency toward freedom in America, "free as in freedom", is the tendency toward that which favours property, contract and profit. Eldred specifically privileged 'free as in profit' over 'free as in speech'. Keeping all this in mind – that is, the intersections of rhetoric and law that I have described – is there not some cause for concern? Does not using property to go beyond property, or using constitutional notions of freedom (whilst possibly a pragmatic and tactical decision in the circumstances) carry with it the risk of the most emancipatory possibilities of the project coming up against some sort of blockage, some sort of institutional opposition to its intended line of flight? Especially when all signs suggest that the tendency of global corporate sovereignty is toward the (en)closing of more and new forms of property to feed the engine of global information capital? If the global tendency of law becoming-economic is to act as a facilitator in the enclosing of open spaces, to act with the insurance of capital's efficiency as its core *raison d'etre*, as one of its axioms, why, or better how, can Floss-ers remain bound to their position which is bolstered (or boostered) by blind faith in the objectivity and reason of law, and trust that law will act to defend the vision of the 'founders', or that which they see as the 'correct' principles upon which their rhetoric seeks to justify their vision?

With all of this in mind – the intersections of Lessig's transcendental foundationalism, the liberal and neo-liberal visions of contract, property and profit that underpin both the concepts of liberty in the US Constitution and that of innovation and progress in copyright – can we not conceive that the rhetoric of "free as in freedom" of Floss is in danger of being piloted in such a manner that it comes back to us "inverted"? Is there not the "very possibility of (a) common good" being produced by these intersections that is not the one that we originally intended, but one that has been expropriated by the necessities of the "cash nexus" that reigns within the "kingdom of money"?

I wonder, therefore, if without more than the hollow mantras – of invoking the vision of the 'founders' or "free as in freedom" or the more banal "information just wants to be free" – if there is any defensible position of Floss possible.

Floss at its heart is another form of community knowledge production; it is a community formed through a language of production that goes beyond the discourses and rhetoric I have tried to describe here, and as is the case with other forms of community knowledge production, its longevity as an alternative to imperial sovereignty requires more than simple repetition of currently accepted dogma. To do so will simply continue us along the merry path of totalizing one vision of the world and imposing it upon the rest. Should we – rather than trying to make all forms of community knowledge production conform to this peculiarly American vision of freedom, chanting along the way, "information just wants to be free" – not recognize that the potential and position of Floss is just one of the many manifestations of community knowledge production, a very special one indeed, and thus commence our analysis and discourse from there? Is not the desire to push all knowledge production into this logic of "free as in freedom" within the intersections set out here simply a corollary of the imperial tendency that seeks to allow no space for flight? To make us all "Americans" within the new "kingdom of money"?

To borrow some rhetoric myself, information and machines will not set us free, but a language and rhetoric which allows those that produce to control their machines may. Or, it is not enough to say that the machine gives you freedom; you also have to create intellectually mobile concepts of freedom to converge with it. But for now, it is probably enough to say that the quest of some Floss-ers for "universals of communication" should indeed tend "to make us shudder".[54]

NOTES

1. I wrote this paper while in Mozambique and the Basque Country for Sarai based upon some thoughts and doubts I encountered during research work I am undertaking into "The Logic, Rhetoric and Law of Open Source Software" for my post-graduate degree in law at the University of New South Wales in Sydney, Australia. I must thank Hans Skott Myhre, Derek Merrill, Michael Hardt, Benjamin Murphy and Monica Narula for their assistance in trying to formulate my ideas. I must also thank my thesis supervisor Kathy Bowrey for her constant assistance, criticism and her caring vegemite parcels which got me through this process, and no doubt will continue to get me through my larger research. The title changed with the text and in the end the subtitle "Foreigner in a Free Land" seemed to sum up the contradictions and doubts I had and which appear inherent in the situation. The subtitle as such also continues my tendency to adopt or adapt titles of Ornette Coleman tunes for my recent written work. See for example "The Shape of Law to Come", http://openflows.org/~auskadi/shapeoflaw.html. I also must apologize to our friends in Latin America who know all too well about colonization and language coming as they do from a country (once) known as "América".

2. Agamben, Giorgio. *The Coming Community* (University of Minnesota Press, 2001) p. 80.

3. Free, Libre or Open Source Software which for the sake of ease I will call here Floss, rather than Open Source, Free Software or one of the other variants. Peer-to-peer software production may be a more appropriate description at another time but the object here is better served by using a conjunction of the more common Free, Libre and Open Source labels.

4. http://seattletimes.nwsource.com/html/nationworld/2001808984_linux06.html

5. Here I want to begin dealing with the questions surrounding rhetoric, language and law relating to Floss. But another line of enquiry relating to Floss as crisis media would indeed be to consider the actual method of producing software itself as a form of 'crisis'. By this I mean the continual scratching or itches, the continuing ability to always seek to resolve problems afresh, and of always re-proposing the question at the limit. In this way Eric Raymond's itch scratching, Deleuzian notions of thought and Toni Negri's ideas of constituent power and crisis can be used as tools to examine the differences between peer-to-peer software production and that of corporate/proprietary software production. This question and intersection of the ideas of a gun toting US right wing libertarian, a couple of French philosophers and Negri's relevant and most contemporary Marxism I must however leave for another day.

6. Foucault. "Space, Knowledge and Power," in Rainbow (ed.) *The Foucault Reader* (Panthenon, 1984) p. 247.

7. Foucault, "On The Genealogy of Ethics: An Overview of a Work In Progress", in Rainbow (ed.)

8. In my description of these intersections I will adopt as a part of my approach Foucault's position outlined in his work, Michel Foucault, *The Archaeology of Knowledge* (Routledge Classics, 2002) pp. 39-42. For my purposes here, what I take as important from this exposition is that when one is within a certain theme of rhetoric or discourse, variants may and do occur, but the options open, the possibilities to act within a given field are bound by the pre-conditions inherent within the overall discourse of the theme.

9. Lessig, Lawrence. *The Future of Ideas* (Vintage, 2002) p. 11.
10. Lessig, Lawrence. *Code and Other Laws of Cyberspace* (Basic Books, 1999) p. 5.
11. Negri, Antonio. *Insurgencies* (University of Minnesota Press, 1999).
12. Hardt, Michael and Antonio Negri, *Empire* (Harvard University Press, 2001). *Empire* also provides us with the hinge with which to articulate the links between the American and Imperial constitutionalism.
13. Negri, Antonio. *Insurgencies*, p. 82.
14. Ibid.
15. Ibid., pp. 157-8.
16. Ibid., p. 160.
17. Ibid., p. 161.
18. Ibid., p. 164. At page 167: Constituted power erases "in the constitution the subjects that were its origin, it gives back to society pure and simple constitutional products, juridicial individuals ... one thing is forgotten: the creative capability of the subjects ... (s)trengh has yielded to power, and nothing was left of it in the constitution".
19. Ibid., pp. 307 - 308.
20. Marx, Karl. *Grundrisse: Foundations of the Critique of Political Economy* (Penguin, 1973). See for example pages 171-173, and later for example "The Fragment on Machines" and sections on the "General Intellect", pages 690ff.
21. The Free Software Definition – "'Free software' does not mean 'non-commercial'. A free program must be available for commercial use, commercial development, and commercial distribution..." http://www.gnu.org/philosophy/free- sw.html).
22. As Lessig teaches us: "Free resources have nothing to do with communism ... I am not arguing that there is such a thing as a 'free lunch' ... Resources cost money to produce. They must be paid for if they are to be produced. ...But how a resource is produced says nothing about how access to that resource is granted. Production is different to consumption". Lawrence Lessig, *The Future of Ideas*, p. 13. Again I must leave this argument for another day.
23. Negri, Antonio. *Insurgencies*, p. 164.
24. Hardt, Michael and Antonio Negri. *Empire* (Harvard University Press, 2001). The fullest definition given by Hardt and Negri of immaterial labour is probably found at pages 290-294.
25. Patton, Paul. *Deleuze and the Political* (Routledge, 2000) p. 17.
26. See for example Gilles Deleuze and Felix Guattari, *Anti-Oedipus, Capitalism and Schizophrenia* (Viking, 1977) p. 230.
27. Patton, Paul. *Deleuze and the Political*, p. 96.
28. Deleuze, Gilles and Felix Guattari. *A Thousand Plateaus* (University of Minnesota Press, 2002) p. 166.
29. Krimm, Jonathan. "The Quiet War over Open-Source", *The Washington Post*, http://www.washington post.com/wp-dyn/articles/A23422-2003Aug20.html See also <nettime> dossier: WIPO Knuckles under on open-source software, 29 August 2003, http://www.nettime.org and Paul Kedrosky, "A Reasonable Discussion Hijacked", *National Post*, Canada, 23 August 2003.
30. Lessig, Lawrence. *The Extremists in Power*, http://www.lessig.org/blog/archives/001436.shtml
31. McBride, Darl. *Open letter to the Open Source Community*, http://www.linuxworld.com/story/34007.htm
32. November 18th, 2003. First Internet music piracy convictions – Suspended sentences over music piracy http://www.abc.net.au/news/newsitems/s991935.html

33. Foucault, Michel. "On Governmentality" (1978), *Ideology and Consciousness*, No. 6 (Autumn 1979) pp. 8,10. Cited in Paul Rainbow, ed., *The Foucault Reader* (Panthenon, 1984) p. 15.

34. http://australianit.news.com.au/common/print/0,7208,8061044^15317^^nbv^,00.html Here again the link between policing and the economic functioning of the 'information society' was made clear to be both the duty of the state and all honest citizens: "The UN agency says it is actively involved in building awareness, the demystification of what intellectual property means and training law enforcement authorities. ... I know that combating piracy is not an easy task, but it requires efforts of governments and international organizations and of course the NGO (non-governmental organization) community".

35. http://australianit.news.com.au/articles/0,7204,8061136^15319^^nbv^,00.html Ridge continued: "We must be as diligent and determined as the hackers". And note that there is not so much light between the position of SCO and Ridge on this one.

36. ICANN – the Internet Corporation for Assigned Names and Numbers, a US Company that 'governs' the use and assignment of internet domain names, internet protocol addresses, port numbers and related matters.

37. http://www.circleid.com/article/383_0_1_0_C/

38. See Groklaw's contributing coverage of the SCO spectacle at http://www.groklaw.net/. In particular regarding the "attacks":
http://www.groklaw.net/article.php?story=20031210163721614
http://www.groklaw.net/article.php?story=20031212171912108
http://www.groklaw.net/article.php?story=20031213111633554

39. Deleuze and Guattari. *A Thousand Plateaus*, p. 116.

40. The SCO related cases are: *SCO v IBM* case and the *Red Hat v SCO* case. The various court documents can be found on the Groklaw site:
http://www.groklaw.net/staticpages/index.php?page=legal-docs

41. Eldred et al. vs. Ashcroft, http://laws.findlaw.com/us/000/01-618.html

42. Murphy, Fleming and Barber. "The Right to Property: To Individual Autonomy and Back", *American Constitutional Interpretation*, 2nd Ed, Ch 16 (Foundation Press, 1995) p. 1071.

43. Murphy et al, p. 1072.

44. Murphy et al, p. 1073.

45. Murphy et al, p. 1074 -5.

46. Murphy et al, p. 1076.

47. Allgeyer vs. Louisiana 165 U.S. 578 (1897) http://laws.findlaw.com/us/165/578.html; see Murphy et al, page 1077.

48. *Lochner vs. New York* 198 U.S. 45 (1905) http://laws.findlaw.com/us/198/45.html In Lochner, the Court held that a state law limiting bakers to no more than a sixty hour work week was a 'mere meddlesome interference' with freedom of contract.

49. Cohen, Julie E. *Lochner in Cyberspace: The New Economic Orthodoxy of "Rights Management"*, 97 Mich. L. Rev 462 (1988), http://www.law.georgetown.edu/faculty/jec/Lochner.pdf

50. Whether the issues is up for grabs and the SCO litigation has any legal basis is another topic entirely but those issues could be briefly summarised as: 1. The 'restrictive nature' of the GPL that gives rise to the licences alleged unconstitutionality; 2. The 'restrictive nature' of the GPL and its alleged subsequent anti-competitive status; and 3. Its not restrictive enough nature that gives rise to the charges laid against

it in relation to the its breach of US Export Regulations – that is it is all too freely available to people who are not part of the free world.

51. http://www.linux.org/news/2003/08/19/0006.html
52. http://www.sco.com/copyright/
53. *Eldred et al. vs. Ashcroft*, Footnote 18.
    http://caselaw.lp.findlaw.com/scripts/getcase.pl?court=us&vol=000&invol=01-618#FR1.18
54. Negri, Antonio. "Control and Becoming, An interview with Gilles Deleuze"
    http://www.generation-online.org/p/fpdeleuze3.htm

Introducing AIDC as a Tool for Data Surveillance

BEATRIZ DA COSTA+JAMIESON SCHULTE+BROOKE SINGER

Introduction

A young woman goes to a liquor store to buy a bottle of wine. At the checkout counter, she is asked to present her driver's licence — the usual procedure in the United States for any person who looks under 30. The woman hands over her licence to the clerk, but what happens next surprises her. On this day it is not 'business as usual'.

Instead of looking for her date of birth, the clerk swipes the driver's licence through a small machine under the cash register. The young woman does a double-take; had she handed over her credit card by mistake? When she takes her card back, she studies it closely. Yes, indeed, it is her driver's licence, but for the first time she notices a magnetic stripe on its backside very similar to her credit card.

A number of thoughts run through her mind. Why didn't he just look at the face of the licence to ensure she was of age? What information is on that stripe besides her date of birth? Is it only being read or did the clerk copy the encoded information? And, if her information were saved, what would the store do with it anyway?

A story much like this inspired us to take a closer look at driver's licence card technologies and the industry family to which they belong — Automatic Identification and Data Capture technologies (AIDC). The purpose for using magnetic stripe technology, and for AIDC technologies in general, is to identify people or objects through machine automated processes. But why is AIDC technology even necessary for such a simple task as verifying a person's age in a liquor store? Why are technological solutions cropping up in the most routine tasks of our everyday lives?

The liquor store would argue that machine-automated reading of a magnetic strip makes the sales clerk's job easier and, therefore, more efficient. The clerk does not have to worry about making others wait in line as he tallies up the customer's age; a machine quickly does it for him. The store would also claim that a magnetic stripe is much harder to tamper with than the face of the driver's licence, making fraudulent IDs easier to detect.[1]

Both efficiency and fraud prevention ultimately save the business money. Every store wants to serve customers as quickly as possible and a liquor store especially wants to avoid costly lawsuits that result from selling alcohol to minors.

After a little independent investigation into the matter, however, it became clear to us that this technology is used primarily for less publicized reasons. ID verification is how AIDC is advertised to the public; this is what the store tells its customers and why the machine's screen openly displays a person's age after a valid ID is swiped. But the hidden benefits — what goes on out of sight — are data collection, data matching, and data analysis. The president of Intellilink, a manufacturer of ID verification systems, states in an industry article "Not only are the retailers [who use our system] complying with the law by carding, but at the same time they have compliance, they're also building a database of information."[2] Such a database which is nearly free of charge and exactly describes a business customer base, is arguably the most important benefit a card-verification system brings to a business — and in some cases the U.S. government as well.

This paper explores current and proposed uses for AIDC technologies, focusing primarily on the already widespread practice of driver's licence swiping in the United States. Driver's licence swiping is an ideal case in point and it exemplifies several of our greatest concerns related to AIDC: the invisible or discreet nature of most AIDC technologies, the lack of notification and consent by subjects, the largely unregulated and unaccountable data collection and usage practices by U.S. businesses, the interdependence of business and government interests, and the encouragement of 'surveillance creep' into every facet of contemporary life.

We begin with a technological discussion. It is our belief that critical assessment of, and informed reaction to, AIDC must be founded on solid technical knowledge. Our aim is not to denounce all AIDC uses, but to bring about a better understanding of this vast and rapidly developing field, which is often in conflict with our ideas of social justice. More public consideration of these technologies will help shape a better future with AIDC technologies that, in our opinion, must incorporate safeguards built into the technology itself, coupled with better governmental policy controls.

AIDC Industry and Technologies: A Technical Overview

Automatic Identification and Data Capture (AIDC) is a family of technologies for the unique identification of physical objects by automated processes. These technologies are designed to bridge the gap between entities in the real world and computer databases that describe them. AIDC endows a computer system with a set of eyes that can uniquely identify any object that is appropriately tagged. Computer algorithms designed to improve efficiency can then work with direct and immediate knowledge of the environment, rather than process statistical information collected by hand at a prior date.

Applications of AIDC have been around for decades, and now include retail check-out, warehouse inventory, livestock management, vehicle drivers' licences, and keyless building entry systems. The AIDC industry profits by creating new systems that reduce the human effort required to perform tasks relating to recognizing objects. AIDC takes the human out of the loop and thus reduces labour costs, accelerates the movement of products, and, in theory, reduces the potential for error, fraud, and sabotage. In addition, by facilitating data collection, AIDC allows for the accumulation of large volumes of information. This information represents a high value for a number of businesses and has opened new markets, such as data collection and data selling.

AIDC addresses an old technological problem: how can a computer identify an object in the real world? As of 2003, computer vision research has not yet come close to producing systems that can visually recognize a wide range of objects in a natural environment without significant error. Even if vision worked well, a computer would be unable to differentiate between different objects that have the same appearance. To reduce this problem, AIDC focuses on techniques that involve 'tagging' objects with a data encoding that can be interpreted more directly by the computer. The earliest and most obvious example of object tagging is the bar code, which is printed on the package of virtually every product sold by large retailers in modern industrial economies. More recent innovations, such as magnetic stripe cards and contact smart cards, are typically used to identify consumers rather than products. Currently in development are radio frequency identification (RFID) technologies, which have shown promise as an advanced method of identifying both products and people with minimum labour.

Since their standardization in the 1970s, bar codes have accelerated the flow of products in commercial and industrial settings. Bar codes come in different sizes and encodings. The simplest variety is capable of representing short numbers only, whereas later designs can encode a short paragraph of text from the ASCII character set. In the United States, a product such as a tube of toothpaste is marked with a simple bar code that encodes the numerical universal product code (UPC). In most of the rest of the world, the European article number (EAN) system is used. During checkout, the UPC symbol simply indicates the brand and type of product that has been scanned, while the retailer's database links this to the product price, the number remaining in inventory, and (in some cases) the purchasing history of the individual consumer. In retail environments, bar code systems are inexpensive to implement since most products are already marked with a UPC symbol, but they require careful scanning by a human operator.[3] More advanced encoding schemes, often called 2-dimensional bar codes, consist of a square region filled with small black and white pixels and can represent a greater quantity of information. 2D bar codes are used on some ID cards, by the U.S. military, and have been adopted as the national standard for bar coding by China.

The unique identification of people as opposed to commodities by machines presents a different set of challenges. Even though bar code tattoos indeed exist, they are generally not embraced by the mainstream and many people will circumvent identification systems when technologically possible. However, involuntary subjects such as prisoners, animals and students[4] have been marked with radio badges, ankle bands or injected subdermal RFID chips. For everyday ID situations, the solution has commonly been to provide people with machine-readable identification cards that are easy to hide and in some cases difficult to modify.

Since the 1970s, magnetic stripe credit cards have been a standard method of automated identification. Magnetic stripes are technologically similar to audio-tape, in the sense

that data is recorded on a special surface by applying a magnetic field to it, and later played back by passing it over a magnetic sensor. At the time of their introduction on credit cards, magnetic stripe scanners were sufficiently rare and expensive that it would be challenging to read cards in an unauthorized manner or tamper with the magnetic media. Now, however, magnetic stripes are used in many new settings, such as drivers' licences, student IDs, conference passes, store loyalty cards, and room keys, resulting in a large market for reading and writing hardware. Magnetic stripe readers and writers can be purchased on a personal budget (about $500) and don't require expert knowledge to be used. This creates a situation in which the magnetic stripe is now easier to modify than the printed information on a card.

In addition to security concerns, both bar codes and magnetic stripes are limited by the fact that they store only a small amount of information. As a result, bar codes and magnetic stripes usually store little more than an ID number that links to a full data record elsewhere in a database. As a result, smart card AIDC systems have been developed to allow for large quantities of information to be stored on the card itself. Smart cards are in fact small computers and do not need to point to an entry in a remote database in order to reveal meaningful information. The risk of tampering still exists, but encryption techniques make this task very difficult if not impossible. Smart cards are similar in appearance to a magnetic stripe card, but are distinguished by a small square containing gold electrical 'contacts' that connect to a computer inside the card.

When inserted into a scanning machine, the card's internal memory can be read and modified. The bi-directional communication between the computers inside the card and the reader allows for sophisticated interaction, which enables each to verify that the other is a valid device that is authorized to perform its task. As a result, a smart card can provide reasonably secure storage of electronic cash, medical data, or other information that the designer wishes to control.

Because the magnetic stripe or smart card is not permanently affixed to the person being identified, cards may be exchanged or stolen, leading to misidentification. To ensure that the cardholder is the intended user, various techniques have been used to match the owner with the card. Two approaches are (1) to require a signature when the card is used (which must match a signature on the card), and (2) to put a picture of the person on the card (which must match the person using the card). Neither method provides very strong security and the matching procedure in both cases must be performed by a person. To address this problem, biometric information has been included in the electronic data of the card. In the context of security and AIDC, biometry focuses on the computational analysis of features that identify individuals. To match ID cards to their owners securely and automatically, the favoured metrics are the nearly unique patterns found in fingerprints and iris blood vessels. Other less common techniques are voice analysis and face recognition. Whichever metric is used, a few features that are nearly unique to the cardholder are stored in the card's memory. A person attempting to use the card later is subjected to analysis to determine if his or her features match those stored on the card.

AIDC is concerned with reducing the human effort involved in identifying objects and people, but all of the technologies described so far require an explicit scanning act that is

labour-intensive. Radio frequency identification (RFID) is an extension of the smart card concept, in that it consists of devices that can securely read and write to special electronic tags. The main innovation of RFID is that it employs wireless communications to eliminate the need for the card reader to physically touch the card. In fact, scanning can occur without any human operator at all, since the tag simply needs to pass within the vicinity of the reader. The RFID 'tags' or transponders can be physically smaller and less expensive to produce than an ID card, making them suitable in many applications where bar codes have previously been employed. The reading distance for RFID tags depends on the application and underlying technology, but ranges from several centimetres to several metres. Current uses include automated payment for public transport, road tolls, gasoline, and fast food; tracking of parts in factories and warehouses; livestock and pet identification; building access cards; and medical patient IDs. The retail chain Wal-Mart and the U.S. military are pushing their main suppliers to put RFID tags on products by 2005. As they become commonplace, RFID systems will uniquely identify the items that they are attached to, and, by extension, may identify the person holding or wearing them. The push for faster, less labour-intensive, and more convenient retail checkout and inventory control has created the potential for new, hidden forms of surveillance of individual people.

AIDC and The U.S. Driver's Licence

A driver's licence is currently the most requested form of identification in the U.S., making it a prime target for integration with AIDC technology. This card, issued by state Department of Motor Vehicles (DMVs) to certify a person's right to drive a car, has become the means by which individuals are granted access to a wide-range of unrelated activities (writing a check, buying a drink, or boarding a plane, for example). Retailers, government agencies, commercial airline companies, and others who depend on the driver's licence for personal identification look to AIDC technologies — like the magnetic stripe, bar code, or smart card — to automate and secure this process. With the addition of AIDC technology, the driver's licence does not simply afford quick and trustworthy identification, but enables retailers, agencies, and commercial businesses to collect massive amounts of data about a person that accumulates each time a card is provided.

Companies and government agencies that want to collect data from drivers' licences run into difficulties, however, because no standards exist. Licences are not federally regulated, leaving each state to determine how to issue its own. Therefore, a driver's licence in Maine does not look like a driver's licence in Utah and many times drivers' licences within a state vary greatly because states change standards.

Currently forty-six states are using some type of magnetic stripe or barcode technology (or a combination of both) with the remaining four states actively considering or making plans for implementation.[5] Not only do the basic card technologies vary from state to state, but also the methods for encoding the information differ, making universal reading impossible. To make matters more confusing, the amount and type of information encoded is irregular: in some states the electronic information on the magnetic stripe or barcode is just a mirror of the printed information on the front side of the card, while in other cases additional information such as social security numbers, digital fingerprints, and face recognition templates augment the standard information.

The American Association of Motor Vehicle Administrators (AAMVA), a lobbying organization for the state motor vehicle administrations, has been pushing to change this situation, citing it as a threat to national security and an inconvenience to corporate America.[6] In the post-9/11 climate, the AAMVA's call for a universal standard is finally making material progress and gaining vocal support from industry leaders (such as Larry Ellison of Oracle) and important politicians (such as Tom Ridge, Director of Homeland Security). Industry and government officials may have desired standardization earlier, but were hesitant to voice their opinion. Any proposal that remotely resembles a national ID plan has been routinely shot down in the U.S., initiating intense criticism from both political parties. In the current crisis of 'permanent war', however, traditionally unpopular policies are able to gain peer support by promising a new sense of security.

In May 2002, the AAMVA plan got its biggest boost: Reps. James Moran (Democrat) and Tom Davis (Republican) introduced H.R. 4633 or the Driver's Licence Modernization Act of 2002,[7] which reflects AAMVA's recommendations and establishes national standards for state issuance of drivers' licences. These standards include the implementation of smartcard technology to store personal information (including biometric data) and a centralized database of U.S. driver's licence information. Supporters of this legislation consistently state the primary goal to be, of course, secure identification, but already secondary functions are being proposed, like using the smartcard on the driver's licence to administer food stamps and for voter registration.[8] This legislation would establish an apparatus for total and automatic authentication, analysis, and control. If H.R. 4633b becomes law, driver's licence swiping will no longer be an unusual occurrence, but a precondition for participation in American society.

Who is Swiping Drivers' Licences Today?

Government officials as well as private businesses are already using computer hardware to read the information from a driver's licence magnetic stripe or bar code, the police being among the first to do so. When stopped for speeding, for instance, a driver must show his driver's licence. Previously, a police officer would call the information into headquarters. Today, it's more likely he will take the card back to his vehicle, swipe it through a dashboard-mounted scanner and cross-reference the data with several databases, such as the National Crime Information Center (NCIC) or the National Law Enforcement Telecommunication System (NLETS). Instantly the officer will find out, for example, if the driver has a past record of driving offences or a criminal record. Coplink, a database system allowing American police officers to instantly access and exchange information, has been specifically designed to facilitate this procedure.

Liquor and tobacco stores, as well as nightclubs and bars, were the first commercial businesses to realize the benefits of such systems. These businesses, required by law to verify age, turned to licence-scanning hardware to automate a necessary function. As we have seen, however, the real motivation for purchasing and maintaining such a system may not be for efficiency or to more effectively uphold the law, but to build a detailed and valuable customer database virtually free of charge. In all but two states (New Hampshire and

Texas), there are no restrictions against storing the data once it has been read from a licence. Companies selling the hardware make data collection as easy as possible for their customers by bundling customer database software with their products.

The software that comes with the licence scanners makes explicit what businesses might do with the data once it is collected. Typically this software allows businesses to archive customer information and transaction history in a database, parse data based on keywords, analyze customer transactions based on demographics or customer statistics, export data to use in other applications, print letters, labels and reports, or set alerts for specific individuals so when their IDs are scanned a message is displayed in real time.[9] Any business would find value in such software and the most obvious benefit is probably for marketing purposes. A database is valuable for other reasons like analyzing a customer base for strategic planning or providing data to investors in order to justify future projects.

There are only a few instances in which states have stopped the practice of drivers' licence swiping with legislation, and this is usually in response to citizen protest that the practice violates the Driver's Privacy Protection Act.[10] There are, however, good reasons why government would allow the practice to continue and turn a blind eye. Law enforcement, for instance, from the local to the federal level, reaps huge benefits from commercial businesses that collect transaction data because it can be used for investigations and subpoenaed at a later date. Most recently in the 'War on Terror', federal agents have requested transaction histories from businesses like bookstores and scuba dive shops. If the information is detailed, organized and electronic, the easier it is for the agents to request, receive and utilize the data. There was one reported incident in which a supermarket voluntarily handed over its customer database complete with purchase histories to federal investigators. This was not in response to a request but rather a patriotic gesture.[11]

Government officials are not only requesting data in pursuit of committed crimes, but are also establishing databases from commercial transactions in case of future criminal behaviour. One such example is occurring in the state of Pennsylvania. When an ID is scanned at a Pennsylvania state-run liquor store, the purchase and identification information is added to the Pennsylvania Liquor Control Board's (PLCB) electronic database in Harrisburg.[12] The PLCB database is pre-emptive: it is established to assist police with criminal cases that have yet to be committed. In order to grant the police this comfort, however, every Pennsylvania resident's alcohol purchase history is monitored and recorded. Because it is not possible to buy bottled wine or spirits in Pennsylvania at any place other than a state-controlled liquor store, there are no options for circumventing this surveillance unless a person goes to the extreme of buying out-of-state. Licence scanners have been used in Pennsylvania liquor stores since 1997 and are currently installed in all 638 state-run liquor stores.

Airports, hospitals and government buildings are the latest places that drivers' licence scanners are being used. *The New York Times* reports that, "Logan Airport in Boston is using [driver's licence scanning] machines to check the identity of passengers. New York University Hospital scans and stores visitors' driver's licence information. Delaware has installed the machines to screen visitors at the state legislature and its largest state office building".[13] With most DMVs issuing data-encoded drivers' licences and with the low cost of drivers' licence scanning equipment that even novice computer users can manage, many businesses and government agencies are adopting or considering carding and collecting personal information.

Driver's Licence Swiping and Digital Data: Hidden Information and Database Mistakes

Licence scanning usually occurs outside the cardholder's field of vision. Police officers are taking the driver's licence with them to run a quick check inside their car. Card scanners at convenience and liquor stores are often placed underneath the counter and are invisible to the customer. Even if a customer sees the driver's licence scanner in use, that does not necessarily make the process transparent: the customer may not realize what is happening, she does not know what information is stored on the card, and she does not know what will be done with her information after it is collected.

If a customer asks what the store is going to do with her information, often the clerk will simply shrug his shoulders. Employees are not usually trained to understand the ways in which their store database operates. Customers are thereby left powerless with their personal information, having been entered into a computer system whose purpose and functions are opaque to them. The situation does not allow for a helpful exchange of information. There is no chance to 'opt out' or a chance to verify that the information is even correct.

Human errors resulting in false entries are not uncommon. In the case of a driver's licence record, a person's file begins with an employee at the DMV entering information by hand into a database from a form, which ultimately ends up encoded on the driver's licence. Mistakes, of course, happen; it's only human. In our experience scanning people's drivers' licences, we have found errors; we have seen cards in which the information on the front is correct but the digitally encoded data on the back is different and false.

Once the entry is made and follows its destiny into other databases, the false data acquires legitimacy by mere fact of replication. Sometimes database mistakes do not result from mistyping, but rather from identity confusion. If two people's names are similar or they have nearly identical Social Security numbers, their information can easily be scrambled. U.S. PIRG's study on credit reports, for instance, found that seventy percent contained errors and twenty-nine percent were the result of reporting credit accounts that belonged to another consumer.[14] When mistakes are found, individuals are faced with the nearly impossible task of tracing the source of the error and rectifying the error across numerous databases. Substantial amounts of time, money and knowledge are needed to complete this tedious task.

Data warehouses, businesses that consolidate data from various sources and resell it to third parties, are at risk of perpetuating false information. These companies should, therefore, pay considerable attention to verifying all data they redistribute, but unfortunately this isn't often the case. ChoicePoint, a well-known data warehouse based in the United States, is aware of its own data flaws and doesn't assume liability for the accuracy of its information.[15] This is particularly disturbing since ChoicePoint is the leading commercial supplier of information to the U.S. federal government. It has multi-million dollar accounts with thirty-five different federal agencies, including the FBI, IRS and Department of Justice. In 2002, ChoicePoint was ultimately held accountable for its poor verification practices by a New York court and ordered to pay $450,000 to the plaintiff. The court found that ChoicePoint "intentionally maintained substandard procedures for verifying accuracy of data or should have known that its procedures were substandard under the Fair Credit Reporting Act."

ChoicePoint does offer individuals the chance to review what information is maintained about them in its database for a fee of $20. Privacy expert Richard Smith did just that and found that it contained more inaccurate than accurate information and learned later that he could not opt out from the ChoicePoint's collection of personal data.[16] ChoicePoint suggests that, if a person finds inaccurate information in his files that he should contact the originator of the data to correct the problem and points a person towards the labyrinth of public offices, commercial businesses, and credit agencies from which the data originates.

Convenience versus Privacy Rhetoric

More than fifty years after *1984* was published, "Big Brother" is still the most dominant metaphor when describing surveillance societies. Today, at least in the case of the United States, this metaphor is less evocative and even misleading. As David Lyon puts it: "Orwell's dystopic vision was dominated by the central state. He never guessed just how significant a decentralized consumerism might become for social control".[17]

The examples we have outlined so far — as with most AIDC technologies — are not matters of state coercion but rather consensual situations in which an individual willingly participates (most often through consumption) and as a result submits to some sort of commercial-controlled surveillance system. This condition is often referred to as 'convenience versus privacy'. People are led to believe that by using the latest technological innovations (cell phones, EZ-Pass tags, supermarket loyalty cards) the benefits inherently come with unpleasant surveillance possibilities and that modern luxuries have 'strings attached'. Modern luxuries, of course, quickly transition into necessities and with the proliferation of AIDC technologies even basic pleasures — like buying a bottle of wine — present a person with the dilemma of convenience or privacy.

The EZ-Pass is one such modern luxury that raises the 'convenience versus privacy' issue for many people living in the Northeast region of the U.S. The EZ-Pass is an optional device that a person affixes to his car windshield that triggers automatic debit from an electronic account when driving through a highway tollbooth. The convenience is simply less wait at the tollbooth and more cruise time. This electronic toll collection system (that is not unique to the U.S.) consists of a RFID tag that transmits a unique ID from the car to the RFID receiver in the toll lane. This information is transferred to a customer database to debit the cost of the toll from the customer's account. Along with account balance information, the database also records location, time, and toll lane. Other factors like average speed can be interpolated using two points of entry in the database. This rich information has not only been used for debiting accounts, however, but has been used for policing purposes such as issuing speeding violations and increasing car insurance fees.[18] The use possibilities for the EZ-Pass database are numerous and even unforeseeable as technologies develop and collection practices potentially change.

There is, of course, no reason that EZ-Pass tags have to be unique to drivers, but could function instead more like disposable phone cards that are available at most convenience stores. This card would be bought with a set amount of dollars, decreasing with each use and ultimately invalid when it reaches zero. State transportation departments would still benefit from this automatic debit system (as they do now with EZ-Pass information), using anonymous data to conduct surveys of traffic patterns for future highway improvements. However, this disposable EZ-Pass system would not grant policing and control powers through unique RFID tags to the company that owns the EZ-Pass. This disposable system would therefore eliminate the 'convenience versus privacy' dilemma by granting convenience without increasing corporate control.

Government and Corporate Co-Dependence

This EZ-Pass scenario not only illustrates how corporations are increasingly becoming policing forces through use of new technologies, but also demonstrates the ways in which a private business (EZ-Pass) shares data with a government body (state transportation departments) for a common cause (to improve congestion problems through EZ-Pass integration into the highway system). This type of data sharing between the private and public sectors for the benefit of both parties is not uncommon or limited to AIDC technologies. Another recent example of this involved the turnover of the airline JetBlue's customer records to the Transportation Security Administration (TSA). JetBlue released its customer data to the TSA upon request and without notification or consent by the subjects involved, which was in clear violation of its own privacy policy. The TSA wanted the information for a data mining experiment whose purpose was to assess the terrorist risk of each passenger record.[19] Such tactics leave customers with the uneasy feeling that data originally collected for one reason can easily be used for other reasons without their knowledge.

There are other instances, as we have seen with ChoicePoint, in which the entire purpose of a business is to provide government with information and the motivating factor is not a common cause but rather profit. The government does not typically seek out commercial warehouses because they have access to special information; ChoicePoint's data is drawn from public records combined with information provided by the media, credit-reporting firms, and in some cases private detectives. Often government agencies turn to private companies and outsource data collecting jobs to circumvent the Privacy Act of 1974. This law places restrictions on the collection, use, and dissemination of personal information by and between government agencies, but never set limits on the private sector. Even after the passage of the USA Patriot Act in 2001, which legalizes enhanced government data collection and analysis with reduced checks and balances, the government still relies on the private sector to perform 'watching' activities at full speed.[20]

Maybe the most questionable use of commercially maintained data by the government sector in recent years was in 1998 when the Florida state legislature made an unprecedented decision to 'scrub' ineligible voters—mostly ex-felons—from the state's voter registration list based on information bought from a commercial firm. The state legislature claimed this was the necessary response to a botched Miami mayoral race in which numerous illegal votes were cast. But the $4 million contract went to ChoicePoint, and it is estimated that thousands of voters—disproportionately black—were unduly disenfranchised in the 2000 Presidential election as a result of faulty, unverified data.[21]

Data flows, of course, in the other direction too: from government body to corporate database. Private businesses for a long time now have used census data and other public records that are made free and available by the US government to make decisions such as where to put a store or how to price a product. This practice of using characteristics like age, gender, or income for market research is called demographics. With the increase in data storage capacities and the ease of accessing public information through the Internet, demographic analysis has accelerated. Today businesses can utilize this information quickly, efficiently, constantly, and automatically.

Recently another commercial trend has emerged that is dramatically undermining the original purpose of public information, which was to make powerful government bureaucracies accountable to citizens. Daniel Solove, an expert in information privacy law, explains: "A growing number of large corporations are assembling dossiers on practically every individual by combining information in public records with information collected in the private sector such as one's purchases, spending habits, magazine subscriptions, web surfing activity, and credit history. Increasingly, these dossiers of fortified public record information are sold back to government agencies for use in investigating people".[22] Solove suggests that regulations of pubic records must be rethought—including commercial access and use restrictions—in light of new technologies in the Information Age.[23]

Consequences of AIDC
Similar to Solove's demand for the reconsideration of public records regulations due to the emergence of new technologies, we see an urgent need for a broader reconsideration of data collection and usage practices in the US, especially with the continued development and integration of AIDC technologies. The data situation is already dire (as our examples suggest) and in danger of getting much worse. AIDC does not create a bad situation, but aggravates one that is without sufficient controls (technological or governmental) and without satisfactory public understanding to allow for just implementation. In the specific examples cited in this paper, there are always individuals who lose, but it is our belief that society takes the biggest hit as AIDC transforms individual behaviours, social interactions and class relations. An in-depth discussion of the social consequences of AIDC is beyond the scope of this paper, but we would like to underscore a few points and specifically consider AIDC's role in intensifying consumer profiling and creating fear or a sense of permanent guilt.

Consumer profiling is the recording and classification of behaviour through aggregating data. Consumer profiling is related to demographics, but it targets an individual based on specific, non-anonymous data that is sometimes bundled with more general information such as census data. Loyalty cards used in grocery stores, for instance, allow for the collection of individual purchase information that is analyzed and ultimately used for direct marketing. Consumer profiling refines a store's marketing strategies and profits; the consequences are typically junk mail or individualized coupon discounts at checkout. While this type of mail or coupon may be useful in some cases and annoying in others, the important aspect is not the extra offers made to a specific group of people, but rather the limited choices for people outside the target group. Boundaries between income groups and other store-determined clusters are created and reinforced, and become pronounced over time. Whereas this phenomenon is not new and occurs with or without the existence of AIDC, loyalty card data certainly accelerates and individualizes this process.

Many people think loyalty cards produce nothing but savings. A common reaction from people when they hear others refuse to participate is "Well, what do you have to hide?" Most of us don't have anything to hide, but you never know anymore. As was the case of a man who, while shopping at Von's grocery store, slipped and fell on some spilled yogurt. When he tried to sue the store to recover for lost wages, pain, and suffering, Von's threatened to use information from his loyalty card records against him in court. The store claimed the customer bought an inordinate amount of alcohol. It was later determined that alcohol was not a factor in the incident and the threat by Von's was ultimately dropped. The underlying message, however, is clear: your data bits can be selectively used to paint a certain data biography (or support a particular point of view) and the potential for a person's past data to be used to intimidate him — even when the data is fairly innocuous — is always a distinct possibility.

There are many times, of course, when the data is not innocuous, but very sensitive. This was the case in *Doe vs. Southeastern Pennsylvania Transportation Authority* (SEPTA), in which a doctor guaranteed a patient (Doe) that his health insurance company (SEPTA) would not inquire about the prescription drugs he was using to treat his HIV. Although SEPTA did not ask, Rite-Aid pharmacy supplied it with a list of his drugs anyway. Doe's doctor informed him of this mistake and Doe feared his employer (who paid for the insurance) was ultimately 'in the know' too. Doe filed a lawsuit, but the court decided that his privacy invasion was minimal. As Daniel Solove comments: "[The court] missed the nature of Doe's complaint. Regardless of whether he was imagining how his co-workers were treating him, he was indeed suffering a real palpable fear. His real injury was the powerlessness of having no idea who else knew he had HIV, what his employer thought of him, or how the information could be used against him. This feeling of unease changed the way he perceived everything at his place of employment".[24]

This situation underscores the way people relate to their own data: removed, unsure, and powerless. Those who work inside the bureaucracy are often unsure too, which leads to harmful mistakes and information ending up in the wrong hands. If AIDC technologies are utilized to administer health benefits (as is the case in Canada and has been proposed in the U.S.), no trustworthy systems are in place to handle the flow of sensitive information. In the U.S. personal medical information is, in fact, so unprotected that businesses such as the Medical Marketing Service exist whose sole purpose is to sell lists of persons suffering from various ailments. To employ any technology that would further ease the distribution of sensitive medical information in the U.S., considering the country's track record, would be unwise until more safeguards are built into the health and judicial systems.[25]

One place all Americans are now used to being treated with suspicion until they provide an ID, answer some questions, and get frisked, is the airport. After the hijackings on 9-11, airport security in the U.S. has been reviewed and tightened. Some of these changes make sense like including the prohibition against a person boarding a flight with a small knife or box cutters. But passenger profiling, and more specifically the second generation of the Computer Assisted Passenger Pre-screening System (CAPPS II), requires closer review and is riddled with problems similar to those we have raised concerning AIDC technologies.

CAPPS II is a data-driven system that electronically absorbs every passenger reservation, authenticates the identity of each traveler and, finally, creates a passenger assessment. The project, overseen by the TSA, is a data-matching project (rather than a data-mining project) meaning passenger information is verified against external databases to determine that a person is who he says he is (identity verification) and to assign him a terrorist risk level (assessment). In this system passengers are required, when making a flight reservation, to provide identifying information such as name and address, a passport, Social Security and frequent flyer numbers. These details are then cross-referenced with information provided by private data firms. The end result: each traveller receives a Threat Assessment Color. In this system, green means fly freely, yellow means extra security checks, and red means not allowed on board. TSA is pressing to implement this program on all commercial flights originating in the US by summer 2004 and has supposedly been testing the program on select Delta Airlines flights since spring 2003.

One obvious problem with this plan is the government reliance on private firms to provide the essential data for identification and threat assessment. As we have seen with these companies (and ChoicePoint has been named as a potential participant in CAPPS II), they do not promise the information they provide is accurate and verification of second-, or third- or fourth-hand information becomes a game of 'pass the buck'. Other data sources for CAPPS II, such as financial and transactional records, have been named by the TSA, but there has never been any mention of the methodologies used to analyze this data to make these 'terrorist assessments'. Who is programming the computer to spot the terrorists and what rules are they following? Furthermore, there has never been any indication of how someone could inquire about an assessment, let alone contest a decision once it is made by the system. If the government is controlling who can move freely based on an automated decision-making system, the rules of the system cannot be a secret reserved for the government and its private corporate allies.

The CAPPS II system, as it has been described by the TSA, is full of inadequacies that must be addressed, reconsidered, and made transparent to those forced to abide by its rules (all citizens who fly). To our knowledge, AIDC technologies are not required for passenger check-in, as of now, but airline agents must see each passenger's driver's licence before boarding a plane.[26] If a passenger chooses automatic e-check-in, an AIDC technology (credit card with magnetic strip) provides this convenience. It is, therefore, not a far stretch of the imagination to connect a system like CAPPS II with an AIDC automated check-in procedure to produce increased efficiency and provide what would be touted as 'maximum security'.

Complex Situations, Simple Solutions

So far we have attempted to give an overview of AIDC technologies and draw attention to some of its social implications. However, as Tactical Media Practitioners and interdisciplinary artists we are interested in developing projects that use communicative means other than the written word to address our concerns. Swipe — a three-part project consisting of a performance, workshop, and website — has been our participatory response to the various controversies affiliated with driver's licence swiping and data collection.

The Swipe project is primarily educational in that it informs people of a practice and offers an opportunity for public discussion. The performance centres on an alcohol-serving bar from which a person gets a drink and an unusual printed receipt. The receipt is all information we 'swiped' from his driver's licence at point of sale plus any additional personal information we could glean off the Internet and archived databases while the customer's drink is prepared. The workshop is a demonstration that demystifies the data collection and data warehouse businesses, offering a behind-the-scenes look at the Swipe bar. The website will be a bit different: it is a set of hands-on tools for the motivated cultural activist. On the website, you will be able to decode the 2D barcode on your driver's licence through a downloadable program, determine the value of your personal information on the open market using a data calculator, and request your own data file from the big data warehouses such as ChoicePoint. There will be a bulletin board system so people can post how many errors appear in their requested files and keep track of the response time of the data warehouses to correction requests. (Website launch date is February 2004.)[27]

Education and raising awareness are, of course, very important. Only with understanding can there be public reaction, and only due to persistent public outrage will there be reason for government and industry to change practices. Resistance on the micro or individual level is also helpful. Some common strategies are paying with cash instead of using the EZ-Pass or using another customer's loyalty card to add noise to the store database. As part of Swipe, we distribute stickers for people to place over their magnetic stripe or barcode on drivers' licences that have slogans such as "Keep your paws off my databody" or "I stop shopping when you start swiping". These stickers temporarily disable the AIDC technology and will ensure a person's information is not swiped without notification or consent. These stickers can create an interesting situation when a shopkeeper, police officer, or bouncer notices the sticker and has a moment of recognition (verbal or non-verbal) with the cardholder.

In terms of long-term solutions, we feel the answers must be found in both technology and policy. There are technological fixes to some of the data collection problems we have raised. For instance, Latanya Sweeny's research into computational disclosure control has produced several software programs that remove individual's names and other unique identifiers from a database without rendering all the data useless for research purposes. There are, of course times when identifying an individual may be necessary and Sweeny comments: "Despite the possible effectiveness of these systems and others not mentioned here, completely anonymous data may not contain sufficient details for all uses, so care must be taken when released data can identify individuals and such care must be enforced by coherent policies and procedures. The harm to individuals can be extreme and irreparable and can occur without the individual's knowledge. Remedy against abuse however, lies outside these systems and resides in contracts, operating procedures and laws".[28]

These contracts, operating procedures, and laws Sweeny mentions should be considered and developed along with emerging technologies. The privacy policies in the US have been written in response to failures in a system and work as patches to immediate problems. These fixes are never complete and are often too easy to work around or totally ignore. Rights of privacy, social justice and equality must be addressed at the start of AIDC research and development, not tacked piecemeal onto different projects only after trouble arises. At this time we believe the implementation of AIDC technologies is irresponsible and often dehumanizing business.

We have seen that AIDC technologies are economically attractive. They reduce labour costs and help feed information about industrial and commercial processes directly into computers that can further streamline those systems. When the target of AIDC is the consumer, massive databases are created that in turn can be used in an attempt to model human behaviour to predetermined demographic cluster groups, medical conditions, and terrorist inclinations. Due to the current legal and political environment, data determinism is flourishing, and any perceived protections against this kind of activity are simply illusory. Our goal has been to describe AIDC and highlight how it encourages a broad range of data surveillance activities that have been subject to increasing criticism. We hope that this perspective can benefit participation against new forms of surveillance, in legal, political, and activist settings.

NOTES

1. This assumption is wrong. Please refer to paragraph 5 of *AIDC Industry and Technologies: A Technical Overview* for further explanation.

2. Wiederer, Dan. "Answering Age - Old Questions", excerpt from *Tobacco Retailer*, June 2002, (November, 2003). <http://www.cougarmtn.com/news/featureArticle/tobaccoRetailer_Jun02.asp>.

3. Retail bar code systems are easily fooled by covering the true product bar code with one from another product. Re-Code, an interesting project by activist collective "Hacktivist" has been developed to address exactly this issue. More information can be found at <http://www. re-code.com/>.

4. According to a press release by Texas Instruments (TI), a manufacturer of RFID systems, prisoners at the Pima County Jail in Tucson, Arizona, will soon be monitored using RFID wristbands sold by Precision Dynamics Corporation. Livestock, wild animals, and pets have for several years been identified using implanted RFID devices (glass-coated tubes approximately the size of a grain of rice) that are injected into the body. The implanted devices are manufactured by TI and by a company called Applied Digital, which has also recently created "Digital Angel", a wearable product that tracks the health status and location of people, targeted at wandering Alzheimer's disease patients and children. The Enterprise Charter School in Buffalo, New York, has begun to experiment with RFID tracking of students with wearable badges to monitor school attendance.

5. For a reference table issued by the AAMVA please see
    <http://www.aamva.org/standards/stdUSLicenseTech.asp>.
6. AAMVA press release, "AAMVA helps secure a safer America", 14 January 2002 (30 November 2003).
    <http://www.aamva.org/news/nwsPressReleaseAAMVAHelpsSecureSaferAmerica.asp>.
7. The bill summary and more information about the Driver's licence modernization act can be found here:
    <http://thomas.loc.gov/cgi-bin/bdquery/z?d107:h.r.04633:>.
8. Welsh, William. "Driver's licence bills: reduce speed ahead," 23 August 2002 (30 November, 2003).
    <http://www.washingtontechnology.com/news/17_13/statelocal/18969-1.html>.
9. DI-tech homepage: <http://www.idi-tech.com/manual/index.html>.
10. Dandurant, Karen. "License scanning, now illegal, 3 May 2002 (30 November, 2003).
    <http://www.sea coastonline.com/2002news/exeter/05032002/news/2731.htm>.
11. Baard, Erik. "Buying Trouble: Your grocery list could spark a terror probe", 24 July, 2002 (30 November, 2003). <http://www.villagevoice.com/issues/0230/baard.php>.
12. Berry, William. "Cops use ID info in criminal cases", 9 April, 2003 (30 November, 2003).
    <http://www.collegian.psu.edu/archive/2003/04/04-09-03tdc/04-09-03dnews-08.asp>.
13. Lee, Jennifer. "Welcome to the Database Lounge", 21 March, 2002 (30 November, 2003).
    <http://www.we-swipe.us/nytimes.html>.
14. Pirg's survey: <http://www.pirg.org/reports/consumer/mistakes/page3.htm>.
15. Choicepoint Privacy FAQs: < http://www.autotrackxp.com/privacy_faqs.htm#correct>.
16. Epic news. <http://www.privacy.org/digest/epic-digest05.15.01.html>.
17. Lyon, David. *The Electronic Eye: The Rise of Surveillance Society* (University of Minnesota Press, 1994), p. 78.
18. One of the author's friends moved from upstate New York to New York City and did not immediately notify his car insurance company of his move. He subsequently bought an EZ-Pass for his work commute — a drive he began to make a daily basis. Within weeks of his move, his car insurance company sent him a notice that his insurance rate was more than doubling based on his new residency. When he called the car insurance to discuss the fare hike, he asked how they knew of his move. The operator told him that it was based on EZ-Pass data the company routinely acquires. EZ-Pass FAQs:
    <http://www.ezpass.com/static/faq/speed.shtml - penalties>
19. "Betraying One's Passengers", *The New York Times*, 23 September, 2003, (30 November, 2003).
    <http://www.nytimes.com/2003/09/23/opinion/23TUE2.html?ei=1&en=9a3c8df287b89fe0&ex=
    1065342076&pagewanted=print&position=->.
20. Electronic Frontier Foundation, "The EFF analysis of the provisions of the USA Patriot Act that relate to online activities", 27 October, 2003, (30 November, 2003).
    <http://www.eff.org/Privacy/Surveillance/Terrorism/20011031_eff_usa_patriot_analysis.php>.
21. Gregory Palast is a journalist who extensively investigated this incident. Palast, Gregory. "Florida's flawed 'Voter-Cleansing' program", 4 December, 2002, (30 November, 2003).
    <http://archive.salon.com/politics/feature/2000/12/04/voter_file/print.html>.
22. Solove, Daniel. "Access and Aggregation: Public Records, Privacy and the Constituion", *Minnesota Law Review* 86 (2002) p. 1140.
23. Ibid.
24. Solove, Daniel. "Privacy and Power: Computer Databases and Metaphors for Information Privacy", *Stanford Law Review* 53 (2001) p. 1438.

25. To read more about medical data and privacy issues in the US, see Latanya Sweeny's research at <http://privacy.cs.cmu.edu>.
26. John Gilmore is currently challenging the legality of requiring ID for air travel. See information online at <http://cryptome.org/freetotravel.htm>.
27. Please see <http://www.we-swipe.us/> for full project description and documentation.
28. Sweeny, Latanya. "Privacy and Confidentiality, in particular, computational disclosure control". <http://privacy.cs.cmu.edu/people/sweeney/confidentiality.html>.

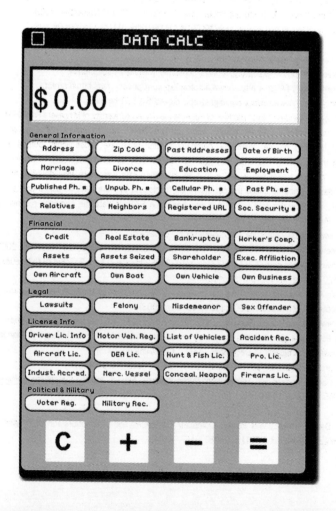

Anagrams of Orderly Disorder
(For the New Global Order)
GEOFF COX, JOASIA KRYSA & ADRIAN WARD

```
sub degenerate()

    dim c1,c2 as integer

    c1=1+(rnd* len(myString))
    c2=1+(rnd* len(myString))

    swapchars(c1,c2)

end sub
```

An anagram is a word or phrase that contains all the letters of another word or phrase in a different order. This brief text attempts to apply this principle in making some introductory comments on the current world disorder to reflect the complex intersections of global and local issues. It employs the text presentation software Anagrammar (like a corrupt version of Microsoft's popular 'Power Point') but contains two contradictory operations activated through sound input – above or below an ambience threshold. The characters are either moved randomly out of order, or rearranged pragmatically back into order – to generate or degenerate accordingly. In doing this, we aim to evoke Hardt and Negri's description of corruption in that institutional forms (such as language) might be rearranged. To them, "The Empire's institutional structure is like a software program that carries a virus along with it, so that it is continually modulating and corrupting the institutional forms around it" (2000: 197-8). In this case, the arrangements are generated by two dialectically opposed subroutines at the beginning and end of this text. Despite the appearance of disorder, any complex system expresses deep structures of order. By analogy, can the new global disorder be rearranged by human action?

The current global context articulates considerable tensions over sovereignty, political commitment and action. The quotes we have selected present these debates in a historical context and investigate the local tensions around the ways in which artists and commentators respond to global processes, and the language and strategies they employ to do so.

```
sAllrfIx

d, fast froaanthelatinns, sitret oie tdfinoaf a cihn
usnd ceeerablelprej dices ane opindons, vwe aw h
iray, ll new-aensrdrones become antiquated before
they cAn ossify. all that is solid melts into air, all
that is holy is profaned,wgh

urhs rsknt  ast nsdpealed toioacoawitn srn t aecsesh
piserlam coadbtioo erteefe,slnd his re otin s with him
kindo
bhe h eyaae a oln tartly  xpindien msetet foreito
products cyatns ihm oeulgeooszl ovee the
entwrf,suefaer f orhn gl.be.fi  mws tne tle everriivte
nTeitlv eee hwnete, esnaf isi concectab s,eeery hore.e
```

The present phase of production still remains predicated on the speed and frequency of communications technologies as well as its organisation on a global scale. But old and relatively ordered 'cold war' oppositions have been pacified and replaced by new complex, asymmetrical ones. This asymmetry is partly as a result of the 'decomposition' of communist power. Now, the phrase "all that is solid melts into air" simply begins to sound like a truism. The very idea of change has paradoxically become stable (or solid rather than melting) and digital technology appears to be the engine for this approach.

Like the communications industries that underpin it, Hardt and Negri describe the contemporary form of dominant power structure as 'Empire' – 'governance without government'. To define this power base more closely as plural and multiple (not centred), they draw upon

```
o[Empire is] ch
ractegised by a flurdioy oa wsrm -p neebbyand al l tf
formation ans deformgdion, generation and
degeneratIon. [

]
[it is the] decentered and deterritorializing
apcaratuv

of rusu tfat  rofr sf,lbl  phc eporatic the rntie
mlovili ealmrwfthin its opei, expansing ironnier t Emp
re manuimsuhybrsd idectiteennaflexible hi rarnhirs,
andopluhal exchanges shrough modulatingenetworks of
comsasd.' [

]
'Our politgiaw taado is notpsigply to re ost ehese
erocessis btt tn rnorgaeise them and redirect ttem
```

network and rhizomic metaphors that privilege flows and mutability – in the tradition of Deleuze, wherein resistance is disrupted: no longer marginal, but active in the centre and expressed in networks, chaotic and indeterminable.

But if power cannot be grasped, how can it be resisted?

```
'g, tho a, encrooi n elclarld eu tg, ths list
forhodabld ineey in  must saceei  pilioics
stsrisordera htt Dieor or i  peedrn  sI rye[treo unke
ittriyo aoh thisoteti of thy atnl e eved ltck]nioas ea
edafdanegnm

e brpngsoit fh bYbnfore  Tdne isethe case godare alth
lgh omsy because nee-liberal ideology [...]
paradoxically considers disorder to be positive and
order negative, the equivalent ew.creabn er f pewsi.
he.ssmu  epsyf ntataon eu pyisrterea,oromethenv
oarefll w s the erisinamnssirce of.t m aolitrral
ieoies fod ordeeh'
```

Alain Joxe sees Hardt and Negri's *Empire* as lacking crucial analytical questions, in its not taking sufficient account of the military question, and of seeing globality as only answerable in equally global terms. So how is resistance to be best characterised?

It is as if power has taken the form of resistance itself – that order is expressed through disorder if you like. In such a scenario, the strategic standpoint of resistance seems powerless to resist power.

Does political action require new forms, by basing resistance on the structure of chaos itself?

Is the new world order simply the logic of the post-political?

The very notion of politics stems from the conflict between order and disorder – politics, itself and its negation.

There is a paradox at work. To return to Marx's 'melting vision' – what appears as in flux is simultaneously stable – leaving the capitalist mode of production as solid as ever at its core. To Zizek,

```
'It i,f s easllrntdtioagine th' 'tnd tlothe rorwdi
than a far mmreamo e t change in the mode of
production, as if liberal capitalism is the 'real'
that will somehow survive even under ecological
catastropHe


'how are we to reformulate a leftist, anti-capitalist
political prececoeiebousmoraloe geopal capie l sm mn-
iss  deelogical surplament  libejalodeiocratic mu ti-
dulturafism?'
```

This is what Zizek calls the 'failure of identity politics' – the hybrid, fluid, subject identifications that reflect the processes of globalisation itself.

How might resistant, creative subjectivities be conceived in the new global disorder – the proletariat or multitude, the activist, the hacktivist? Are artists and hackers merely locked in resistance mode only as a kind of rhetorical action, nostalgically repeating the tactics of the previous artistic vanguard?

How do we move beyond resistance to social transformation?

What chance does networked resistance have of being resistant in such a scenario?

What models (or metaphors) are there left to aspire to? Or to re-invent?

In relation to the postcolonial context, Homi Bhabha proposes to analyse the congruence between postcolonial and postmodern politics. He points to a crucial distinction that has to be made between "the semblance and similitude of symbols across diverse cultural experiences … and the social specificity of each of these productions of meanings as they circulate as signs within specific contextual locations and social system of values".

This distinction can be extended to explain existing tensions within the current global cultural economy. It seems to reinforce a single, dominant model of social, political, cultural and economic organisation, while on the other hand, this seemingly universalist model is by no means homogenous in the context of specific locality.

Arjun Appadurai argues that rather than global disorder,

```
bohe newoelobal nulpural ecocomw hawetn ue
unshndtoodtae e complgx, ov rlapping, disjunctive
order, which cannot any longer be understood in terms

 f lwiitvm tcentra-emreerery rodpls [

] Evbn t eldost cemplex ann flexibeT  heori s of
global d heeopoed ae ] have nmt come to teamcswsti c ]
'd sorgtnssed c

pitauiix'. The complexity ef thelcurrent [lobal
pcoosmy gat toedoimiah certainhflndnmentai
disjunsabhes[ootyeea economy, culture ine telagics ohi
h we hrve 'trs y blgun to theorize.'
```

Orthodox post-modern thinking would suggest that simple binary oppositions like global/local or homogenous/heterogeneous cannot be easily justified or maintained. Instead, Appadurai proposes a model in which the complexity of the current global economy is made up of 'flows' and 'scapes' (evoking Manuel Castells' 'space of flows'), which sweep through the globe carrying capital, information, images, people, ideas, technologies.

These evocative metaphors can undoubtedly be useful in describing current cultural practices in defying orthodox and simplistic distinctions and instead aiming to explore what might be described as a 'micro-politics of global media'.

Some key questions need to be posed: How can digital technologies that inherently serve to support processes of globalisation be used to promote and maintain what is locally specific, culturally and socially heterogeneous, and what artistic and curatorial strategies might be employed to respond to these conceptual tensions? How does contemporary artistic practice respond to these tensions, especially when using or reflecting the use of network technologies? Do artists and commentators simply respond using the same fashionable rhetoric as the system they seek to question?

Taken together, the form and the content of this script (programme script and the text itself) set out to raise these questions that arise in the new global disorder.

```
sub regenerate()
   dim l as integer
   dim targetCharacter as string

   targetCharacter=mid(myOriginalString,regen,1)

   if mid(myString,regen,1)<>targetCharacter then

     l=regen

     while mid(myString,l,1)<>targetCharacter
       l=l+1
       if l>len(myString)+1 then
         l=1
       end
     wend

     swapchars(regen,l)
       end
     regen=regen+1
     if regen>len(myString)+1 then
     regen=1
   end
end sub
```

NOTES

1. The software and more information on Anagrammar can be obtained from the website <http://www.signwave.co.uk/> © 2001 - 2003 Signwave UK.
2. The initial ideas for this paper were first presented as an introduction to the symposium '[anti-] globalica: artistic and conceptual tensions in the new world disorder', organised by Geoff Cox & Joasia Krysa [i-DAT] as part of the WRO Media Art Biennial, 1 May 2003, Wroclaw, Poland <http://www.wrocenter.pl>. It included contributions from Adam Chmielewski (University of Wroclaw), Esther Leslie (Birkbeck, University of London), Andreas Broeckmann (transmediale, Berlin), Monica Narula (Raqs Media Collective, Delhi), James Stevens (DECKSPACE, London), Zoran Pantelic (APSOLUTNO & kuda.org, Novi Sad) and Piotr Wyrzykowski (C.U.K.T. collective, Gdansk/Kiev). The suggestion with these examples was that a number of current strategies have been developed by techno-art collectives that go some way to address the questions posed in this paper. The groups who presented at the symposium demonstrate antithetical uses of networked technologies, wireless networks, the re-purposing of technology and open source principles. A conference report 'Locality, locality, locality' by Esther Leslie was published in *Radical Philosophy* 121 (September/October, 2003) pp.63-64.
3. Some related ideas were also presented as a conference paper "Generating Orderly Disorder" by Geoff Cox, as part of Marxism and the Visual Arts Now, University College London, April 2002.

REFERENCES

Appadurai, Arjun. "Disjuncture and Difference in the Global Cultural Economy", in Simon During ed., *The Cultural Studies Reader* (Routledge, 1993, London).

Hardt, Michael and Antonio Negri. *Empire* (Harvard University Press, 2000).

Joxe, Alain. *Empire of Disorder* (Semiotext(e), 2002).

Marx, Karl and Frederick Engels. *The Communist Manifesto (1848)* (Penguin, 1985, London).

Zizek, Slavoj. "Introduction: A Spectre Is Haunting Western Academia..." &"Part 1: The Night of the World" in *The Ticklish Subject: the absent centre of political ontology* (Verso, 1999) pp. 1-123.

The Tools and Tactics of a Festival
Looking back at N5M4

DAVID GARCIA

September 2003 saw the fourth edition of Next 5 Minutes (N5M) festival of tactical media. Unlike other events of a similar scale, N5M has no structural funding or fixed institutional base. Made up of a loose affiliation of artists and activists, it is a parasitic organism exhibiting both the qualities and the defects of the particular usage of the term 'tactical' to which it gave rise.

Every edition of the festival has to be invented from scratch and its permanent status as a 'one-off' means that the organizers frequently do not know whether a particular edition of the festival will be able to go ahead until quite soon before it is scheduled to take place. This game of bluff and brinkmanship places intolerable strains on the editors, volunteers and the organizations which commit themselves to making it happen. Small wonder, then, that at the end of each edition the people involved say, "Absolutely never again!" This is only partly the result of exhaustion: there is also an avant garde nihilism at work which was described by Barthes in another context as "..like phosphorous ... it shines at its maximum brilliance at the moment when it attempts to die". To this extent every Next 5 Minutes strives to be the Last 5 Minutes. There is never any shortage of obituaries proclaiming the death of the tactical, yet the meme remains strangely, irritatingly persistent.

Tactical media remains, as it was from the outset, a contentious umbrella of a term under which can be found varieties of critical, antagonistic, parasitic, heterogeneous, dissenting media practice and theory. In its optimal form, the effects of the tactical can be recognized in so far as they perform the critical (in both senses of the word) role of inventing fresh ways to help those of us saturated in media culture to resist the forces drawing us in to legitimizing the status quo. Resisting these subtle and powerful forces of legitimization is so difficult because they are as invisible to us as water is to a fish, built into the very structures and language of the technological environment telling us what is real, restricting (and trivializing) our sense of what democracy could be and leading us (whatever we actually know) to act as though no other world was possible.

A number of practitioners and activists find the militaristic nature of the term tactical both objectionable and resonant of a bipolarity which they argue belongs to an earlier era.

But the militant quality of the term also helps to explain its stubborn persistence. In an era of Third Way consensus politics, it sticks out like a sore thumb as a politics of the stubbornly partisan. In an era in which all the fight appears to have gone out of the democratic left, its antagonistic decisiveness helps to explain a persisting appeal.

As a distinct category, tactical media was first identified and theorized in Amsterdam during the first half of the 1990s. It was part of the process of formulating a rhetorical narrative for a festival that would stand in polemical opposition to the glittering hardware spectacles which constituted the video and media art festivals of the time.

Our thinking was connected to both local and international conditions of the period. On the one hand, the term served as a flag of convenience, linking a diverse constellation of Amsterdam's (then active) pirate media networks, artists, 'can-do' hackers combined with the pragmatic, militant, issue based politics of the Dutch squatting movement. On the other hand, the fact that the term caught on is inseparable from the euphoria which accompanied the then recent collapse of the Soviet empire.

This phase of tactical media was constituted out of a meeting in the context of early editions of the festival of central European electronic *samizdat* activists with western European and North American media artist/activists.

At that time, we entertained an exaggerated sense of the importance played by *samizdat* media in this revolution. It seemed as though old style armed insurrection had been superseded by digital dissent and media revolutions. It was the *samizdat* spirit, extended and intensified by the proliferation of Do-It-Yourself media, that seemed to have rendered the centralized statist tyrannies of the Soviet empire untenable. Optimistically, some of us allowed ourselves to believe that it would only be a matter of time before the same forces would challenge our own tired and tarnished oligarchies. Furthermore, the speed and comparative bloodlessness of the Soviet collapse suggested that the transformations that were coming would not have to be achieved through violence or personal sacrifice. This would be the era of the painless revolution, in which change would occur through challenging the domains of forbidden knowledge. This mad sense of the power of information acting as a catalyst for deep social change was captured in John Perry Barlow's (in)famous slogan, "Information wants to be free". In retrospect, it is easy to be sniffy about this rhetoric, but the hacker ethic with its prime directive: "Don't hoard information, share it", was the distinctive challenge thrown down by radical technoculture, and it continues to resonate. It is precisely in the domain of information politics that absurdities of the restrictive dominion of intellectual property regimes are provoking some of the most effective challenges to established networks of power and privilege.

One More Time

I started thinking about the possibility of another (just one more, really!) festival around two years ago when I visited a small development workshop in at New York University's Center for Media Culture and History. A group of researchers connected in different ways to this department had been recently introduced to some of the ideas and people involved in tactical media. The conveners of this event, Barbara Abrash and Faye Ginsburg, were seeking ways in which the approaches to knowledge available in their department and related institutes could contribute to, and draw on, the ideas and network of tactical media. To Europeans, this connection between the tactical and the academy may seem surprising. But in the context of the US, where academia is one of the few outposts where the ideas of the radical left have any kind of legitimacy, it is more understandable.

The meeting at NYU was exciting and productive enough to suggest that the 'strange attractor' of tactical media had again become generative. On this basis, a small group of organizers in Amsterdam imagined that Next 5 Minutes might be re-ignited by morphing from a festival into a series of small, networked, development meetings: a kind of a rolling research program combining face-to-face meetings with web and list resources. It was this approach that convinced Eric Kluitenberg (and, thus, the key institution of De Balie) that there was something new on the table. Our first instinct was to stick at the network of small research meetings (which were christened Tactical Media Labs – TMLs), but it soon became clear that the surprising enthusiasm with which many people undertook to organize TMLs and post reports on the website was also accompanied by the wish for the continuation of a festival as catalyst for local research. And there is no doubt that it was only through the eruption of passionate online arguments about which themes and projects should be included in the festival that the autonomous organizations and people actually became a network. What was exciting at the time was the sense of a large-scale event taking shape by means of a radical (and antagonistic) process of decentralization, in which labs in Amsterdam, Delhi, Dubrovnik (and other Croatian sites), Moscow, Cluj, Barcelona, Birmingham, Chicago, Nova Scotia, São Paolo, Sidney, and Zanzibar generated the basic material from which a large international list of editors forged the final festival program.

In some ways, the heart and soul of the festival lay in the TMLs and the passionate online arguments and the struggle to live with the conflicts between heterogeneous communities and big egos. The downside of our experiment in open-sourcing N5M was that, in too many cases in our three-day event, we were simply unable to match the expectations raised by the discussion and the program. Certain key issues, which had been the subject of passionate debate on the list, such as the thread developed in the Sarai lab "Beyond the Development Paradigm", simply failed to be addressed during the festival. Moreover, the open source model which inspired our organizational process was very nearly tested to destruction in a situation where, unlike the digital domain, resources of time, buildings and money are not infinite. In this sense, our first instinct to keep the project to a network of small meetings was perhaps correct.

[For reports from all the tactical media labs, go to http://www.n5m4.org/journal.shtml?118]

The Revenge of Low-tech
Autolabs, Telecentros and Tactical Media in São Paulo
RICARDO ROSAS

The Context of the Tactical Media Lab in Brazil

In *Johnny Mnemonic*, William Gibson writes about an obscure group of people, the Lo-Teks. Lo-Teks are people who live at the margins of a high-tech society in the near future. These people have their own peculiar weapons, even if they're made of discarded tech-residua of the overdeveloped society of their time.

But why talk about low technology nowadays? Tactical media practitioners mostly like to think about action when it's mediated by a very high-tech device, which they can learn or teach others how to use. That's how it works; that is what you usually get to understand when reading *Nettime* or tactical media theory texts all over the web. But such an approach only works if you are talking about a very rich country that has a large number of people who have access to the internet or to high-tech gadgets. And what if you are a tactical media practitioner living in an 'underdeveloped' country like Brazil?

As far as we know, the Next Five Minutes Festival is a kind of umbrella-like coming together of DIY, activist and tactical media producers. If the point is to talk about Brazilian DIY media and arts in the context of the Next Five Minutes, then basically we have to talk about low-tech.

So let's begin with a cliché: Brazil is a land of contrasts. That's what everybody says, be it a foreigner who comes here for the first time, be it a Brazilian theoretician in his comfortable seat at a university. Even in the richest city of the country, São Paulo, you can see beggars guiding their wooden garbage recycling carts as they walk through the gigantic Paulista Avenue, with its impressive skyscrapers of glass and steel. This is a country where you can find very rich boys with lots of high-tech gizmos, the latest ones from Japan, living very near a homeless family which has nothing to eat. Yes, there is lots of net stuff here, lots of web designers, programmers, software experts, web writers, bloggers, and so. Our cyberspace is full of beautiful home pages, full of e-commerce, full of 'cool' hackers, but, coming back to reality, if you keep your eyes wide open, if you walk a little bit (or a little more!), you can see violence, hunger, ugliness, all the things found in a supposedly Third World country. To complicate the picture further, the mediascape in Brazil is dominated by giant media monopolies that articulate the interests of the elite and work towards maintaining the appearance of a complacent consensus, even in the face of intense social conflict. Immersed as many Brazilians are in this mediatized consensus populated by the stars of 'telenovelas' (Brazilian sitcoms) and variety shows, critical views and perspectives on the media tend to be very marginal and few.

How could a Brazilian TML (Tactical Media Lab) dialogue with such different cultures and bring the virtual and the real together in a common space? We were clear in our minds that while translating the Tactical Media Lab and its concept to a Brazilian reality, we would never, throughout the entire process of creating the TML, shut our eyes to our ground realities. We also knew that this would be even more difficult if we had to talk about net art and net activism.

There is a culture of 'web-art' in Brazil – a very alienated, self-referential kind of practice, mostly related to technology for technology's sake. The 'web-artists', not unlike most artists in general, are much more worried about their own egos, and very distant from the everyday reality that surrounds them. Most of them don't even know about net art (in, say, Nettime's terms), net activism, or tactical media. Political issues are something totally ignored in their works, and the situation gets a little worse when you discover that the ones who do know about such things don't care too much about letting others know what they know. It seems they are not interested in doing this; it rocks their status quo. As people say, information is power; so why not be privileged?

Actually, the picture of new media culture in Brazil is not as simple as I have just made it out to be. Brazil is also notorious (or famous) for its hacking scene. Piracy is also a very hot issue nowadays, as pirated software and music CDs are the easiest thing to find in the 'camelos' - the little tents that crowd the streets' 'black' markets.

Independent media undertakings are also not something entirely new in Brazil. During the last dictatorship, in the 1970s, lots of alternative magazines, the 'imprensa nanica' (small press) produced innumerable zines and samizdat literature that generated a sort of a counterculture. However, from the 1980s onwards this movement was gradually reduced to a pop market of 'fan' publishing. The renewal of critical or agitprop-like media culture only happened again in the late 1990s, following the worldwide wave of the so-called 'anti-globalization' protests. Cyber-activism too has consistently been on the rise ever since the appearance of the Brazilian Indymedia portal in late 2001. Before 2001, there were very few sites producing independent news and information, one of them being Rizoma (www.rizoma.net), which tried to establish a sort of digital counterculture in Brazil (like Disinfo.com in its early, 'good' days). So, after 'our' Indymedia started, its incisive media activism paved the way for the spread of a great network of leftist and activist web sites. Such things had never been seen before in Brazilian cyberspace. There were also some slightly hacktivist groups such as the one called 'Microphobia', which tended however to be very difficult to find or contact.

Apart from this, a few important advances had been made and continue to be made in cities such as Porto Alegre and São Paulo (both these cities are governed by PT - The Workers Party), where the initiative to create Linux-based computer centres, called Telecentros, located in working class suburbs may well become the first step in what could be a 'utopian' virtual democracy in Brazil (Telecentros are discussed in detail below).

It was against this background that we set ourselves the task of designing the TML in

Brazil. We were clear from the beginning that we wanted to respond to the 'here and now' of our reality. Accordingly, we decided not to invite mainstream Brazilian 'web-artists', whose practice is very distant to everything we understand as 'tactical media'. We tried to look for groups whose practice could have web-based components, but at the same time were not fixated on high-tech. Such groups (regardless of whether they defined themselves as 'artists' or 'activists') were spread all over Brazil. Some were prolific producers, some were part of an 'underground' culture, and there was so much difference and diversity between the different groups that it sometimes appeared as if their practices were antithetical to each other. The TML embraced a wide spectrum, from art/activist groups and collectives to djs and street theater performances. Here is a brief description of some of the groups that were active in our TML.

Groups like Bijari/Antipop and *A Revoluçao Nao Sera Televisionada* (The Revolution Will Not Be Televised) work mainly with video art and video activism. Their aesthetic emerges from an MTV-influenced collage style full of edgy political and artistic content. *Rejeitados* ('The Rejected') is a national 'combo' of alternative artists whose work focuses on urban interventions and art outside the institutions. *Formigueiro* (Ant's Nest) works with plagiarism and parody, and their exhibition played with fake biotech art. *Museu da Pessoa* (Museum of the Person) collects individual stories and photograhs/videos of ordinary and anonymous people. *Anomia* (Anomy) works with culture-jamming, comics, zines and video, (influenced by psychogeography and sonic shock). *A Cria* (The Baby) is a 'factory' of fanzines. The Nomads' Collective work with architecture and popular solutions for living and habitation. Projeto Sid Moreira – whose name is a parodic reference to a TV news anchor on the giant Globo TV News Network – works with posters and culture-jamming. Metafora.org (Metaphor) recycles old computers for disadvantaged communities and develops wiki-based projects that centre on open publishing and group-based actions like *Recicle-1-Politico* (Recycle-1-Politician), which re-uses the trash residue of paper ad material from political campaigns. Rizoma.net practices what they call 'conceptual engineering' in order to transform subjectivities by re-combinations of online textual content, in order to arrive at an open source-inspired treatment of ideas drawn from activism, afrofuturism, and neuropolitics

Besides these groups and their presentations, the TML saw the creation of giant anti-war cartoons, info rooms created by Indymedia Brazil activists, street journals and 'Telecentros', designers and programmers collectives like Banda Paralela, who created a media monster made out of tech-detritus, and martial art/dance groups like Batukaçao as well as alternative/experimental or 'home made' music labels like LSD Disco and free radio stations like Radio Muda.

All these people 'settled' at *Casa das Rosas* (House of Roses), which is a venue for non-mainstream art exhibitions on Paulista Avenue, something like a "castle" in Peter Lamborn Wilson's terms. We had the run of the house for four days, during which we not only had an exhibition – that looked more like a weird fair or TAZ – but also pocket music shows, performances, (unplanned and spontaneous) parties and a temporary pirate radio station that defied the repressive policies with regard to 'free radio stations' in Brazil. It was also important that all this was happening at the heart of Brazil's financial district. We also tried to host a free rave (in collaboration with Interfusion, a free party group that promotes raves for free in the poor suburbs of São Paulo).

At the same time, many theoreticians, activists and artists presented lectures, participated in debates, conferences and workshops during the four days of the TML in a building
next to the Casa das Rosas. Among other things, they debated and discussed independent
media, art as tactic and resistance, the politics of multitudes, cyberactivism, copyleft, open-
source philosophy, post-media sounds, free radios and independent music production.

The TML was not flush with funds, and that is why everyone chipped in and worked
voluntarily. Most of the participants produced low-tech works and actions in actual space,
even if, paradoxically, many of them were part of a closely inter-linked online, internet driven community. Most of the groups were marginal in relation to the mainstream of art or
political discourse. And, in a way, it was a revenge: an act of revenge against the self-
indulgent, high-tech, web-artists and techno-fetishistic elite in Brazil which is interested only
in its own obsessive egoism. A revenge of low-tech!

A major concern, both in terms of concrete actions as well as theory, and a hot topic
of discussion at the TML was the question as to whether the media monopolies in Brazil
could be effectively challenged. Many of us at the TML felt that the challenge could lie in
and through a practice centred on 'Autolabs'. The remainder of this essay is devoted to an
elaboration of the concept and working of Autolabs.

What are Autolabs?

Autolabs are laboratorial prototypes for media literacy, technological experimentation and
creativity created with the help of local communities. Autolabs are based on 'tactical' concepts, and use cheap DIY media made accessible by the digital revolution. They are geared
towards enabling independent media production (by individuals or collectives) using free
software/open source operating systems. Autolabs are centres of orientation, documentation and self-education with free and open access to anyone who wants to come and
work/play/create in them. In an 'Autolab', knowledge is accessed and shared through
human mediation, collective work and creative participation.

The new global economy and new technologies demand a renewal of skills and a
sharpening of communicative competences, a refinement of the practices of reading and
writing. Autolabs attempt to face these challenges through networked, cooperative learning
and shared hypermedia use in sound, radio, graphics and web production with people who
normally cannot afford to use communication technologies. The labs interact with various
autonomous social initiatives, articulating a lively, organic and nomadic mode of functioning
that mobilizes actions on the basis of collective strategies of creation.

Among other things, Autolabs plan to generate new practices, new forms of work,
focusing on new media as a means of action and the transformation of the world. This
means opening up new spaces for cultural, artistic and media interaction, creating forms
of access to knowledge resources for individuals or groups excluded from the new paradigm raised by the technological revolution, proposing useful ways of integrating informational technology and the needs of a given community, promoting the exchange of experiences (ideas, perceptions, insights) and the democratic collectivization of information,
creating new spaces for political participation on the territories charted by the information

revolution, developing visual, sonic and textual sensitivities, and making social actions of collective utility possible.

The Functioning of the Autolabs
But how will all this be done? And how is it being done? According to Giseli Vasconcelos, an artist and tactical media projects coordinator who laid the conceptual foundation of the Autolabs, the project was conceived to last between six to nine months, and it had already begun working in July 2003 with 300 youngsters between seventeen and twenty-one years old from three poor districts of São Paulo's periphery: São Miguel Paulista, Ermelino Matarazzo and Itaquera.

The workshops are divided into four different teaching units:

>> Technical learning of computer maintenance and assembly of recycled hardware.

>> Computer literacy for independent media, mobilization and online collaboration through drupal, wikis and mailing lists as well as the knowledge of the principles of free software and copyleft.

>> Electronic media production through design experimentation and graphic publishing as well as production of content through digital story-telling.

>> Sound production, free radio/web radio programming and CD editing/authoring.

All these units remain open to the possibility of a dialogue between themselves through the integration of workshop processes in a phased manner. These processes are registered and articulated by workshop co-ordinators (monitors in Portuguese) who document and evaluate all the processes and actions in an integrated manner. All participants collaborate in this and it results in the generation of a general project/product – a website.

The website is seen as the online ambience that concentrates and organizes the information generated, processes initiated, and results arrived at in each lab, in a manner that contributes to further research and development that will be steered by the young participants themselves. The interactive and collaborative processes entered into by the practitioners, as well as all the resulting products, will form the main body of the project. This will make the development of the methodologies evolved in the labs transparent.

The website, by providing comprehensive documentation of every step undertaken in the labs, will enable the replication of processes and will also serve as a resource for research on the themes and ideas of the project by people elsewhere. The website will also contain all the musical and sound materials produced in the workshops.

The development of the website will be done in phases, in tandem with the process of the constitution of the laboratory idea. The first phase will document the coming together of people in the workshops and a delineation of the different perspectives proposed by the different groups who are joining the process. In this phase, the site's content will offer general information about the project and all the institutions (partnerships) involved in the process. As the workshops start, the online systems designed to enable collaboration between and within different units will become available. This will constitute the second phase. The last phase will contain evaluations of the process, descriptions of the results and the productions created in each session, as well as manuals, tutorials, and FAQs that are developed in the course of the workshops. All this will be available on the website for open access general public usage.

It is important to emphasize here that the specific methodology for each project that enters the lab will be proposed and realized by the individuals, groups and collectives themselves. This will be done echoing the theories and practices relating to the development of an independent media culture allied to social initiatives and organizations, that they themselves evolve as they engage creatively with new technologies.

The groups involved are very varied, ranging from broad-based independent media organizations to specialized musical producers. A few examples are:

>> Technical Unit: *Metareciclagem* (Metarecycling), an initiative of the *Projeto Metafora* (Project Metaphor)
An initiative to recycle discarded hardware for use in poor communities and localities. Instruction in the technical maintainance and care of recycled computers. All computers will run on free software with operating systems customized to the specific reality of each machine, user and community.

>> Support Unit: Indymedia Brazil (CMI)
Workshops in 'free computing for independent media'. Elaboration of notions of copyleft, and (in collaboration with Projeto Metafora) building a network dedicated to decentralized development for the democratization of technological access, formation of digitally mediated social networks enabled by free software, teaching online mobilization and tools for collaboration.

>> Electronic Media Unit: *Coletivo de Historias Digitais* (Digital Story-telling Collective) and *Museu da Pessoa* (Museum of the Person) and Base V (An Experimental Design Collective).
An initiative to collect the everyday histories of ordinary people, teaching digital story-telling and rendering these through self-published forms using experimental graphic design.

>> Sound Unit: *Radio Muda FM* (Radio Mute FM)
A free radio collective dedicated to studies and practices in radio and web-radio, Radio Cipo, an independent musical community devoted to low-tech music production, and Interfusion, a group that promotes events like street parties and free raves on the periphery of SãoPaulo. Workshops in teaching sound production, editing and mixing, free radio/web-radio programming.

The groups mentioned above comprise the independent pedagogic staff that will prepare the 100 youngsters – as most of them haven't even seen a computer in their lives – to know, understand, create, and express themselves through computers.

Autolabs and the Community
To sum up, local people from peripheral urban communities will create their own Autolabs from the very inception of the project. This means that they will learn how to recycle and

maintain discarded computers, and set up a space for a lab that they identify on their own, in partnership with local community leaders. They will, of course, learn through the workshops to actively use the machines to create their own media, which they will render public through the website. Two such initiatives are already underway, and they will happen in tandem with a week-long event featuring lectures and debates involving Brazilian as well as foreign theoreticians and media activists, as well as a weekend festival – all to be held in one of the poor peripheral districts of São Paulo.

Of course, such a big undertaking demands not only technical and specialized support, but also funding and a viable social network to help in its realization. Thus the autonomous practice of critical pedagogy had to be dovetailed into an existing public policy plan. From its inception, the Autolabs project was linked to Youth Action Centers (Centros de Acao Juvenil, better known as CAJUS).

The CAJUS were developed as independent social projects by an NGO called La Fabricca. La Fabricca is a NGO that raises funding for social projects from other NGOs or institutions. La Fabricca readily embraced the Autolabs project as an innovative process designed to combat the media illiteracy of poorer urban populations. The CAJUS network identified the candidates for participation in for the workshops – all selected from economically disadvantaged families – and also located the spaces where the media labs could be situated. The Autolabs' personnel came into the process once the foundations were prepared, and engaged with it right through the planning, development and execution phases of the project.

Once the project was formatted, and after La Fabricca had put up the initial funding, the Autolabs project was submitted to UNESCO. The project was approved for funding and a plan prepared for the certification of workshop instructors as well as apprentices. This was certainly good news to us, but the most important achievement was being able to prove that autonomous and independent projects in critical pedagogy could also work, be developed and obtain funding from established institutions.

Autolabs and Telecentros

The story does not end here. Initially, each Autolab was conceived as being equipped with twenty computers, a sound production facility (a mini-studio) for radio/musical creation and low bandwith. But soon, we had some really good news! The São Paulo city government's agency for technology, called *Governo Eletronico* (Electronic Government), also decided to enter the project as a partner.

The Governo Eletronico of São Paulo is known throughout the world for its initiative to combat the 'digital divide' – the very successful experiment of Telecentros (free public internet access centres running on GNU/Linux platforms). The agency, along with Prodam, the organ dedicated to the provision of technological infrastructure, decided to support the Autolabs by providing them with high bandwidth connectivity. Further, it was decided that once the course of workshops ends, the labs will also become Telecentros, and be absorbed (together with infrastructure, personnel and material received or created by the Autolabs).

All this happened because the Autolabs model of autonomous skill-sharing and creativity attracted the attention of the São Paulo city government as holding out the possibility of evolving a more participatory and active method of practice for Telecentro coordinators, as well as creating the conditions for the emergence of editors, content providers and maintenance technicians from within local communities.

However, even though Autolabs will eventually be absorbed within the much larger Telecentro structure, the core intention of remaining a flexible network of autonomous labs with their self-regulated practices of organization, education and creation remains unchanged.

They will remain embedded within their local community contexts, and responsive to the foundations laid by the independent and tactical media practitioners, even as they evolve into hybridized Telecentros – quite different from the original prototype of what a Telecentro was meant to be. This commitment to autonomy emerges from the practice of the Autolabs, not from any ideological proselytization. What really counts here is the interaction between the free and open access to knowledge that the participants benefit from, and the experiences that the workshop conductors (independent media practitioners) are enriched by. Free Software and hardware recycling being the basis of the project, and since copyleft is the core vision, these projects are able to self-replicate. And since manuals and methodologies (that contain information about 'setting up and getting started' procedures as well as detailed description of everyday activities) are publicly available to anyone who enters the project website, it ensures its own reproduction by any act of replication, by anyone, anywhere.

From the Periphery to the Centre – A Tactical Revolution?
Ultimately, Autolabs are intended to reach not only the periphery but also the very centre. Communication plays a fundamental part in the transmission of the process. Thus, apart from the website and the planned events, two publications – comprising essays, articles, interviews, etc. – are also being planned to present the results to the wider public as well as journalists, intellectuals, media producers, activists, and opinion makers.

Reaching the centre – as opposed to remaining only within the peripheries (the periphery-centre cultural dichotomy is very present in São Paulo) – is part of a tactic to rethink the much-debated 'Digital Divide'. In Brazil, the establishment is accustomed to believe that the antidote to the digital divide is what they call 'Digital Inclusion', a very Brazilian expression, and a concept pervaded by very obscure, paternalistic and demagogic allusions. By merely meaning 'to give digital access to those who don't possess computers', the term 'Digital Inclusion' itself reflects the same ethos of inequality and hierarchy that it apparently sets out to challenge. The policy, conceived in a top-down, one-way fashion by the state, generally lacks a deep comprehension of the everyday life practice, uses and local needs of the very communities that it addresses. It confronts merely the consequences and not the causes of the reality it seeks to intervene in, and usually creates more problems than it can solve. It reinforces the belief that the mere provision of hardware is the only solution and gives more emphasis to consumption than it does to critical/creative production.

Autolabs, on the contrary, are envisaged as critical models of learning how to use media, to produce media, and even recycle the hardware through which these media are practiced. Although they locate themselves in relation to wider public technology policy, they remain autonomous communitarian media labs – in a way, like an 'alien' concept living within the body of a 'host' policy. In other words, they implement a form of 'practical subversion' while being at the same time funded and supported by big institutions. Like viruses, Autolabs are also self-replicant and may be replicated, since the model and its instructions to do so are freely available on the net. The results are yet to be seen, but the project has just begun and a lot is going on. The virus, then, has been inoculated. Ready for a tactical revolution?

(See "A Network of Castles", http://amsterdam.nettime.org/Lists-Archives/nettime-l-9705/msg00118.html)

Contesting
CENSORSHIP

Reasonable Restrictions and Unreasonable Speech

LAWRENCE LIANG

Seamless Webs and Disobedient Speech

It is always through the curious histories of irony that larger stories reveal themselves. The irony that concerns us is that of an apparently innocuous phrase: "the first amendment". The first amendment in the context of the US constitution refers to the right of freedom of speech and expression, a right which has been held to be almost absolute in the US. The first amendment in India refers to the First Amendment to the Constitution in 1951 which attempted to strengthen state regulation over the freedom of speech and expression by expanding the scope of Article 19(2). This paper attempts to narrate the history of the first amendment to the constitution of India as the history of the first media crisis in post-colonial India, and the response of the state to the crisis. This crisis of the media in the early life of the 'new' nation was – not surprisingly – seen to be a crisis of the nation, and this configuration of the 'national crisis' has remained the spectral fear that permeates much of media history in post-colonial India. It also provides for us the first instance of what Upendra Baxi terms as "constitutionalism as a site of state formative practices".[1]

Article 19(1)(a) in its original form read as follows: "All citizens shall have the right to freedom of speech and expression". This fundamental right was, however, limited by Art. 19(2), which said: "Nothing in sub-clause (a) of clause 1 shall affect the operation of any existing law insofar as it relates to or prevents the state from making any law relating to libel, slander, defamation, contempt of court or any matter which offend against decency, or morality or which undermines the security of the state or tends to overthrow the state".

The First Amendment to the Constitution was to the proviso to Art. 19(1)(a), namely Art. 19(2), and after the amendment the provision read as follows: Art. 19(2) "Nothing in sub-clause (a) of clause 1 shall affect the operation of any existing law insofar as such law imposes reasonable restrictions on the exercise of the right conferred by the sub clause in the interests of the security of the state, friendly relations with foreign states, public order, decency, or morality or in relation to contempt of court, defamation, or incitement to an offence".[2]

The three significant additions brought about by the amendment were:

>> Addition of the word 'reasonable' before 'restrictions'
>> Addition of 'friendly relations with foreign states' as one of the ground for restricting freedom of speech and expression, and finally,
>> The addition of 'public order'

Before we begin to understand why this amendment was made, it is important to provide a background to the emergence of the constitution, the philosophy that it sought to articulate, and the structural logic it adopted to realize its goals. While India gained independence on 15th August, 1947, it was not until two and a half years later – on 26th January, 1950 – that India adopted a formal constitution. The headline of *The Hindustan Times* on 26th January, 1950 triumphantly announced, "Hail our sovereign republic...a day of fulfilment...good wishes from near and far...Rejoicings all over". The day marked the end of three years of debate and drafting, and the paper's editorial went on to say, "Today India recovers her soul after centuries of serfdom and resumes her ancient name".[3] The Constitution was therefore seen to be both a document that articulated the hopes and aspirations of the new nation, as well as one which was structurally designed to actualize these aspirations.

The challenges for the framers of the constitution were great. "How could authority be centralized enough to enhance national unity and to promote economic development without alienating subordinate levels of government and stultifying local initiative. How, while applying the rule of law, would social economic reform be fostered and democratic institutions strengthened in a huge society in which religion and tradition sanctioned inequality and exploitation? How would government achieve these and other national goals – indeed, how would it govern – when the law, the courts and the administration failed to reach so many citizens effectively?"[4]

According to Austin, the Indian constitution sought to ensure a structure which would achieve all these ends in a non-contradictory manner. The core vision of the constitution "may be summarized as having three strands: protecting and enhancing national unity and integrity, establishing the institutions and spirit of democracy, and fostering a social revolution to better the lot of the mass of Indians. The framers believed, and Indians believe today, that these three strands were mutually inter-dependent and inextricably intertwined. Social revolution could not be sought or gained at the expense of democracy. Nor could India be truly democratic unless the social revolution had established a just society. Without national unity, democracy would be endangered and there could be little progress towards social and economic reform. And without democracy and reform the nation would not hold together. With these three strands the framers had spun a seamless web".[5]

However, the early history of the Constitution of India is precisely about the strains that begin to emerge in this imagination of the seamless web, as the three strands start to contradict each other and work against each other. On the one hand, the project of nation building in terms of national sovereignty and security begins to conflict with the exercise of democratic rights, especially freedom of speech and expression. On the other, the promotion of social justice by way of land reforms conflicts with the right to property and equality under the Constitution. Was this seamless web then an impossible project right from the beginning? If the seamless web were to be resolved, could it be done in a harmonious manner, or would it require the prioritization of one strand over the other? How could you resolve the differing interpretations made by different organs of the state, from the legislature to the judiciary, in the case of a conflict between one of the strands?

Between the Left and Right of Free Speech

The first real strain on the seamless fabric of the constitution emerged in the context of three decisions, one by the Patna High Court[6] and two by the Supreme Court, over the interpretation of what constituted freedom of speech and expression in a democracy and what were the powers of the state to impose restrictions on the exercise of these rights.

In the *Romesh Thapar vs. State of Madras*[7] case, the petitioner was the printer, publisher and editor of an English journal called *Cross Roads*. *Cross Roads* was printed and published in Bombay and was considered a left-leaning journal, very critical of a number of the policies of the Nehruvian government. The Government of Madras had already declared the communist parties illegal and now, in exercise of their powers under section 9(1-A) of the Madras Maintenance of Public Order Act, 1949, purported to issue an order No. MS.1333, dated 1st March, 1950, whereby they imposed a ban upon the entry and circulation of the journal in that State. Romesh Thapar approached the Supreme Court of India and alleged that this ban was a violation of his freedom of speech and expression as guaranteed under Art. 19(1)(a). The court stated that the ban would *prima facie* constitute a clear violation of the fundamental right of freedom of speech and expression unless it could be shown that the restriction was saved by the exceptions provided by Art. 19(2) of the Constitution.

The question that therefore arose was whether Sec. 9 (1-a) of the Madras Maintenance of Public Order Act was saved by Art. 19(2). Section 9(1-A) authorised the Provincial Government "for the purpose of securing the public safety or the maintenance of public order, to prohibit or regulate the entry into or the circulation, sale or distribution in the Province of Madras or any part thereof of any document or class of documents". Given the fact that Art. 19(2) did not contain the phrase "public safety" or "public order", the question was whether it could fall under the language of Art. 19(2) and be considered a "law relating to any matter which undermines the security of or tends to overthrow the State".

The government argued that the expression "public safety" in the Act, which is a statute relating to law and order, means the security of the Province and, therefore, "the security of the State". Within the meaning of Article 19(2), "the State" has been defined in Article 12 as including, among other things, the Government and the Legislature of each of the erstwhile Provinces. The court, however, stated that the phrase "public safety" had a much wider connotation than "security of the state", as the former included a number of trivial matters not necessarily as serious as the issue of the security of the state. It concluded that "unless a law restricting freedom of speech and expression is directed solely against the undermining of the security of the State or the overthrow of it, such law cannot fall within the reservation under clause (2) of Article 19, although the restrictions which it seeks to impose may have been conceived generally in the interests of public order. It follows that Section 9(1-A), which authorises imposition of restrictions for the wider purpose of securing public safety or the maintenance of public order, falls outside the scope of authorised restrictions under clause (2), and is therefore void and unconstitutional".

In the second case, *Brij Bhushan vs. State of Bihar*[8], the Chief Commissioner of Delhi passed an order under Section 7(1)(c) of the East Punjab Public Safety Act, 1949, against an English weekly of Delhi called *The Organizer*. If in the Romesh Thapar case the order was against the far left, in this case the order was against the far right as *The Organizer* was the mouthpiece of the RSS. The commissioner had issued the order against *The Organizer* for printing inflammatory materials with respect to the partition. As per the order, the editor of *The Organizer* had to submit for scrutiny, before publication, all material about communal issues, and news and views about Pakistan including photographs and cartoons other than those derived from official sources or supplied by the news agencies, viz., Press Trust of India, United Press of India and United Press of America.

The question arose as to whether this order of pre-censorship could be held to be constitutionally valid. This decision was delivered on the same day as the Romesh Thapar case and the majority in this case referred to their decision in Thapar's case and concurred with the findings in the Thapar case. The key factor in both decisions was the fact that the phrase "public order" was not included in Art. 19(2) and that the courts interpreted restrictions on freedom of speech and expression as being legitimate only if they pertained to "undermining the security of the state or overthrowing the state". Mere criticism of the government could not be considered as speech which could be restricted for the purposes of Art. 19(2). It is interesting to note that Justice Fazl Ali delivered a dissenting decision in both the cases, and his argument was that a literal construction of the phrase "public order" would justify restrictions even in the case of trivial offences. However, in the context of the two legislations, it could only relate to serious offences affecting public order.

These two decisions of the Supreme Court precipitated in the minds of the government the first major crisis of the nation state. The crisis can be read at various levels: it exposed the inherent tensions between balancing freedom of speech and expression and the promotion of national security and sovereignty. It also posed the question as to who the guardians of the Constitution were. Finally it set in motion a debate which would haunt Indian democracy for the next fifty years, viz. the exercise of a democratic right as a threat to the larger, abstract ideal of a democratic state.

The First Amendment: Bringing Order to Speech

Sardar Patel, the Home Minister, thought that the *Cross Roads* decision "knocked the bottom out of most of our penal laws for the control and regulation of the press"[9] while Nehru was livid with the interpretation of the court. He immediately wrote to Ambedkar "express-ing the view that the Constitution's provisions pertaining to law and order and subversive activities needed to be amended. Reflecting the difficulties the government was having with the courts over the fundamental rights, Nehru added that the provision affecting zamindari abolition and nationalization of road transport also needed to be amended".[10]

In February 1951, Nehru formed a cabinet committee to examine the proposed amendment. The home ministry recommended to the cabinet committee that "public order" and "incitement to a crime" should be included among the exceptions to the right of freedom of speech. It preferred dropping "to overthrow the state" in favour of the wider formulation "in the interests of the security of the state".

It is to be noted that the original Art. 19(2) did not have the word "reasonable" before the word "restrictions", and the law ministry was of the opinion that the word "reasonable" as used in Art. 19 should be retained and even added to Art. 19(2). The cabinet committee, however, strongly disagreed with Ambedkar and felt that while it was reasonable to retain the word "reasonable" in the other provisions in Art. 19, restrictions on freedom of speech and expression should not be qualified in any manner. This slightly contradictory logic was justified on the ground that they feared the political repercussions of taking away the protection that "reasonable" accorded to the other freedoms in the article, but they were so alarmed by the dangers to national security, friendly relations with foreign states, public order, etc, that they felt that possible curbs on free speech did not have to be reasonable. President Rajendra Prasad, on a reading of the Supreme Court decision, did not think that it was necessary to amend the Constitution and was of the view that, "Amendments should only come if it was found impossible to bring the impugned provisions of law 'in conformity with the constitution'".

The draft amendment without the word "reasonable" and with addition of "public order" was introduced on 12th May 1951. Nehru defended the amendment, stating that it fulfilled the need of the hour. Referring to the statement by the judge in the Patna high court, he said, "It was an extraordinary state of affairs that a High Court had held that even murder or like offences can be preached". The critics of the bill included H N Kunzru, who argued that this was not an amendment but a repeal of Art. 19(1)(a). Shayama Prasad Mookerjee of the Hindu Mahasabha delivered a scathing critique of the proposed amendment. In response to the various apprehensions articulated and as a compromise gesture, Nehru suggested adding the word "reasonable" to qualify the restrictions on freedom of speech and expression.

The addition of the word "reasonable" was a partial defeat for Nehru, as it was clear that given a choice he would have preferred not having any qualifications to the restrictions. In a subsequent letter to T T Krishnamachari, Nehru stated that the reason why he did not like the word "reasonable" was because it was ambiguous and would open up the possibility of the court being called on to interpret whether a particular act was reasonable or not.

The Cabinet accepted the recommendation in order to avoid a split and ensure a two-thirds majority. On the first of June 1951, Parliament passed the bill by a vote of 228 to 20.

Conclusion

Over the past fifty years, there have been over ninety amendments to the Constitution, not all of which have great historical significance. However one thing is certain: every period of conflict in the history of India can be mapped onto a history of the moves to amend the Constitution, the constitutional history during the Emergency being a classic case. The First Amendment, however, retains a significant space in this history, not merely because it was the first amendment but because in many ways it also signalled the kinds of battles that would take place between the project of nation building and the sphere of the media. It marked the rather premature end of the vision of a 'seamless web' with the promotion of national security and sovereignty being prioritized over the promotion of democratic institutions.

As with any project of state imagination, the impact of the First Amendment is also fraught with contradictions and internal conflicts. While introducing the discourse of public order into constitutional restrictions on freedom of speech and expression, it also introduced the idea of 'reasonable restriction', and as Nehru rightly predicted, it proved to be the basis for future conflicts over the media, the Constitution and state formative practices. The contradictions that arose between the three strands of the seamless web of the Constitution were seen as the disintegration of the whole rather than as the inevitable process through which fragments work their ways into monumentalist imaginations.

It is also perhaps well worth looking at the crisis that precipitated the First Amendment to understand our contemporary situation. In 1950, there was a situation where Nehru had to contend with speech and expression that were ideologically opposed to his liberal values – from that of the far left to that of the far right. Nehru's response was a classical case of deferring an exercise of a democratic right or democratic practice in favour of the larger interest or abstract norm of a democratic state. Having assumed the greater common good, he could then determine what was desirable and undesirable speech, and proceed to act with a democratic conscience. Rather than understanding the media as a perpetual site of politics and contestation over the form of the nation, over what constitutes the public sphere, the media was seen to be an instrument/medium for the promotion of an assumed public interest. This perhaps also speaks to some contemporary debates where progressive intellectuals, media practitioners, etc, demand greater regulation against the 'hate speech' of the right. We need to be a little cautious in our responses to forms of speech that offend our liberal sentiments. Very often the assumption of desirable forms of speech presumes a pre-tailored relationship between media and the properly constituted public sphere (much like the imagination of the seamless web), and a plea to the state to rule out undesirable forms of speech abandons the site of politics and converts it into a site of regulation that will merely heighten the crisis rather than resolve it.

NOTES

1. See Upendra Baxi, *Constitutionalism as a site of state formative practices*, 21 Cardozo L. Rev. 1183
2. Art. 19(2) was subsequently amended again in 1963 by the 16th Amendment Act following the Indo-China war.
3. Austin, Glanville. *Working a Democratic Constitution: The Indian Experience*, (OUP, 1999, Delhi) p.13.
4. Ibid., p.14.

5. Ibid., p. 6.
6. We will not be referring to the Patna High Court decision. But an important point to note is that Justice Sarjoo Prasad's statement would later be used by Nehru while defending the First Amendment. Justice Sarjoo Prasad had stated that "if a person were to go on inciting murder or other cognizable offences either through the press or by word of mouth, he would be free to do so with impunity, because he could claim freedom of speech and expression".
7. AIR 1950 SC 124
8. AIR 1950 SC 129
9. Austin, Glanville, Ibid., p.42.
10. Ibid.

"The Whole Constitution Goes for Six"[1]
Legislative Privileges and the Media
SUDHIR KRISHNASWAMY

An oddly-phrased cricketing metaphor used by the editor of *The Hindu* – which prides itself on its 'proper' English – to describe the crisis occasioned by the decision of the Tamil Nadu Assembly to imprison the editor and senior staff of *The Hindu* and the Murasoli for breach of legislative privilege. This decision of the House Privilege Committee of the Legislative Assembly was adopted as a resolution by the majority in the House.[2] The immediate provocation for this resolution was the publication of an editorial piece titled "Rising Intolerance", which criticized the alleged attempts of the Chief Minister and the speaker of the Legislative Assembly to muzzle the media. A Tamil translation of this editorial was published in *Murasoli*, a newspaper sponsored by the Dravida Munnetra Kazhagam (DMK), a leading regional political party. Predictably, the editors of *The Hindu* proceeded to the Supreme Court to obtain a stay on the Assembly's orders and thereby authored another legal episode in the continuing struggle between legislative assemblies and the press. On previous occasions, these battles have raised some significant constitutional issues regarding the scope and nature of the un-codified powers of legislative privilege in the Constitution, and its claims of superiority over the fundamental rights guaranteed in the Constitution. This essay explores why the exercise of legislative privilege provokes the constitutional outrage that it does and attempts to clear some of the theoretical confusion that plagues such cases. This essay does not aim to comprehensively work through the dense legal argument that a full response to these issues would require. Instead, it illuminates some crucial themes that such cases raise.

1. Source of Legislative Privileges
Unlike the conventional basis of privilege in the British Constitution, the source of legislative privilege may be traced to Articles in the text of the Indian Constitution. The Constitution sets out in Articles 105 and 194 the powers and privileges that Parliament and the State Legislatures are entitled to. These articles are identical in structure and content. Clauses 1 and 2 grant members of the House the privilege of freedom of speech and immunity from civil liability for anything said or published under the authority of the House. Clause 4 extends both these privileges to apply to any person who is not a member of the House but who participates in proceedings of the House or its Committees. These clauses ensure that participants in House proceedings are not impeded from performing their functions in the House in any manner.

Clause 3 allows the legislatures to define other powers, privileges and immunities by passing laws in this respect. Till such time as they pass these laws, the privileges they are entitled to in 1947 continue to accrue to them. The constitutional framers intended the legislatures to enjoy the privileges enjoyed by the British Parliament in 1947 till such time as they enacted new laws that spelt out these privileges.[3] Unsurprisingly, the Indian legislatures have not passed any legislation on the subject and have cashed this blank cheque whenever they have seen fit! It is under the blanket authority of this clause that the Tamil Nadu legislature seeks to proceed against newspersons for a breach of privilege.

We must note at this stage that the privileges of the legislature have both an external and internal effect. Clauses 1 and 2 in these articles protect the internal practices and conduct of members and non-members in the House in order to allow it to conduct its affairs as well as prevent members of the House from abusing their privileges in the House. Clause 3 empowers the House to deal with the conduct and expressions of outsiders who, for good reason, are found to have violated the privileges and immunities of the House. This essay is concerned primarily with the latter external effects of legislative privileges.

Interestingly the South African Constitution of 1996 anticipates the Indian scenario and provides for privilege rather differently. Section 58 sets out the privileges of Parliament. This section adopts a structure very similar to that in Article 105 and 194. Apart from the rights to free speech and immunity from civil proceeding spelled out in sub-sections 1 and 2, Parliament is empowered to make national legislation to provide for other privileges and immunities. The crucial difference lies in the approach to un-codified privileges. Till Parliament passes such a law, it is not entitled to any such privilege. By extinguishing any extant privileges and providing only for codified privileges, the South African Constitution avoids the possibility of any claims of unqualified privilege by Parliament.

Taking a cue from the South African Constitution, the Indian Supreme Court should deny the Indian Legislatures' claim to conventional privileges and compel them to legislate on this crucial subject. Significantly, such a law would need to pass the test of compliance with the fundamental rights under Article 13, thereby ensuring that such a law would imbibe due process norms and respect the guarantees to life, liberty and speech. This step alone will guarantee against any future possibility of flagrant abuse. Till such time we would do well to engage with the problems of the debate as it presently stands.

2. A Definition of Privilege

One key element that plagues the debate in India is the absence of an acceptable definition of the idea of "privilege". Presently, the debate proceeds on the assumption that privileges are what the legislature defines them to be. So it would be useful to begin with a recent definition of legislative privilege developed by the Report of the Joint Committee on Parliamentary Privilege in the United Kingdom:[4]

"Parliamentary privilege consists of the rights and immunities which the two Houses of Parliament and their members possess to enable them to carry out their parliamentary functions effectively. Without this protection members would be handicapped in performing their parliamentary duties, and the authority of Parliament itself in confronting the executive and as a forum for expressing the anxieties of citizens would be correspondingly diminished".

This definition does not work by setting out an exhaustive listing of privileges that the legislature may claim. Instead, it speaks to the functions that the doctrine of legislative privilege seeks to achieve. The definition marks out two essential functions: first, that legislative privilege allows the house to maintain independence and autonomy from the executive, and secondly, that legislative privilege maintains the representative capacity of the house.

A noteworthy omission from this list of functions is the reputation and dignity of the house and its members, which are not sought to be protected by the exercise of legislative privilege. In the Indian experience, the reputation and dignity of the House has sought to be invoked as the fundamental purpose of the powers of legislative privilege. By omitting these concerns, the Report does not suggest that these are unimportant, but only that these interests are best protected by the ordinary civil law of defamation and libel and not through the constitutional powers of privilege. In the present case, there has been a tendency to conflate the interests of the executive wing of government with that of the legislature, so that legislative privilege may be invoked to protect the reputational interests of the executive wing of government, particularly that of the Chief Minister. Any attempt by the Supreme Court to circumscribe the scope of these privileges by naming the functions that they are to achieve would prevent the excessive range of interests that Indian legislatures have tended to protect using these powers.

3. Language of 'Privileges'

It is odd to come across a republican constitution that speaks in the language of privileges of the legislature. Despite the proud proclamation of the republican character of our Constitution in the Preamble, the inability of the courts to develop legal principles that reflect the republican aspects of the independence struggle has diminished our constitutional and political tradition. Madison in the *Federalist Papers Number 39* opposes "republicanism" to a state founded on aristocratic, monarchical or feudal power. At the very least, a republican constitution embodies the principles of legal authority that derives from the people at large and admits of no royal privileges, prerogatives or immunities.[5] The United States Constitution does not grant Congress or the House of Representative the "privilege" to punish those who offend its sensibilities. It leaves it to the ordinary courts to mould remedies that protect the functioning of the Houses.

Given that our Constitution does use the word "privilege" in Articles 105 and 194, the courts are obliged to provide a reasonable construction of the term. The use of the word privilege to describe the powers of legislature no doubt has its origins in the English common law and political tradition. As its inclusion in a republican constitution is anachronistic and hinders clarity of thought, the court should clarify the precise nature and scope of the "privilege" enjoyed by the legislatures in tune with the principles of public authority in a republican constitution.

The ideas about the interpretation of the Constitution set out above must not be seen as a disgruntled academic semantic complaint about the use of inappropriate words. As Adam Tomkins argues, the metaphorical use of the word "Crown" in English public law has prevented public lawyers from asking difficult questions that would have allowed them to develop "a modern and sophisticated understanding of the State"[6] and ensured that they did not "under-estimate the continuing and extraordinary powers of the Crown".[7] The use of the word "privilege" in Articles 103 and 163 of the Constitution has a similar effect. The language of privilege suggests a mystical source of power that lies beyond and above the Constitution, when the written Constitution sets out to be the exclusive and supreme source of secular and temporal power in the State. While no constitutional arrangement of power can be completely written in a single document, or even in several documents, we must remember that conventions and other sources of constitutional authority are subject to the express arrangements and language of the Constitution. The granting of unnamed and unregulated privileges to the Houses of Legislature invites them to take an anachronistic view of such a power and thereby violate other constitutional guarantees.

4. Legislative Privilege and the Courts

The history of legislative privilege may be usefully divided into three stages. The early origins of the privilege clauses are closely tied to the history of conflict between the House of Commons and the Tudor and Stuart monarchs, during which successive monarchs utilized criminal and civil law to suppress and intimidate critical legislators. Subsequently, the courts and Parliament locked horns to delineate their respective boundaries of power. The more recent history of the privilege clause is tied to its use by legislatures against citizens. In this last stage, citizens look to the courts to protect their rights of liberty and speech, thereby pitting these two types of powers against each other.

Though it is this last stage that we are concerned about in this essay, it is rewarding to pay attention to the previous conflicts between the courts and the legislatures on the exercise of privilege, as they provide us with insight into the historical context and attitudes that ground these conflicts. Two historical precedents will enhance our ability to see through the patterns arising out of such a conflict. The first of these relates to the state of the law in England.

In 1839 Hansard had, by order of the House of Commons, printed and sold to the public a report by the inspectors of prisons which noted that an indecent book published by Stockdale was circulating in Newgate prison. When Stockdale brought an action for defamation, Hansard was ordered by the House to plead that he had acted under an order of the House of Commons and that the House had declared that the case was a care of privilege. The court rejected this defence[8] and held that no resolution of the House could place anyone beyond the control of the law, and when dealing with persons outside the House, the courts would determine the nature and existence of privileges of the Commons. Though courts are willing to grant the House a wider brief to deal with matters of privilege internal to the House, they concede far less latitude to the House when dealing with outsiders.

But like all good stories, this one has a sequel! The sheriffs executing the order of the court had proceeded to recover damages of the princely sum of 600 pounds from Hansard. The House committed Hansard and the two sheriffs who had intended to implement the orders of the court. Sensing the resolve of the House, the court backed down[9] and refused to entertain a writ of *habeas corpus* to release the sheriffs from the custody of the House. This particular sort of dispute was sought to be resolved by the Parliamentary Papers Act of 1840, which overturned the decision of the court in the Stockdale case and established that a non-member who published material on the orders of the House was immune from prosecution for libel. However, the broader question of whether it would be the courts or the House who would determine the scope of privilege is an open question that is yet to be settled conclusively.

The bright sides to this story are, first, that it reflected the position in English law 163 years ago, and secondly, that this is not the position in Indian law. Moreover, the Nicholls Committee which reviewed the English law on this point went so far as to suggest that the power to punish non-members of the House for contempt should be taken away from the Legislature and passed on to the High Court which would have the limited power to impose a fine.[10] The Committee pointed out that with the passing of the Human Rights Act, 1998, the privileges which accrue to the Houses were thereafter subject to the right to free expression and fair trial guaranteed by Article 12 and Article 6 of the European Convention on Human Rights.[11] Though the ideal solution would be the establishment of an independent and autonomous tribunal to try such cases, the least that should be followed is a procedure that affords a person accused of breach of privilege the procedural protections of the notice and hearing before any action can be taken.

The second incident which we will investigate was closer to home and relates to the Indian Supreme Court's ruling in the Keshav Singh case.[12] Keshav Singh had published a pamphlet maligning a member of the State Legislative Assembly. The House found him guilty of contempt and sentenced him to prison for seven days. He challenged this order before the High Court, which granted him interim bail. The House responded by finding that the judges who issued interim orders were themselves guilty of contempt of the House and liable to be punished. The judges moved petitions before the High Court, which sat in a full bench and stayed the orders of the House. As this confrontation seemed to be spiralling out of control, the Union government requested the President to refer the matter to the Supreme Court.

The key argument before the Supreme Court was about the scope and nature of the power of legislative privileges. While the State Legislative Assembly contended that this power was *sui generis*, supreme and independent of the other provisions, the petitioners argued that the power, like all others in the constitution, was subject to the fundamental rights of citizens. The historical parallels between the circumstances in the Stockdale v Hansard and Keshav Singh cases end with the decision of Supreme Court. The court rightly concluded that it had the power to review unspeaking warrants issued by the Legislature for compliance with the due process requirements under Article 21, among others, thereby asserting the supremacy of the Constitution in general, and some fundamental rights in particular, over the exercise of the privileges powers.

5. On 'Rising Intolerance'

Notwithstanding this assertion of constitutional supremacy in the Keshav Singh case, state legislative assemblies continue to exercise their powers of legislative privilege in an indiscriminate and uncontrolled fashion. A motivation for such an exercise might lie with an earlier ruling of the court which found that legislative privilege may be exercised even if it were to violate the rights of citizens to free speech under Article 19(1)(a).[13] The present case of

The Hindu provides the Supreme Court with an opportunity to overrule this decision and spell out the limited scope and nature of legislative privilege in a republican constitution which guarantees fundamental rights. Legislative privilege, rightly conceived, would extend only to the protection of the autonomy of the House from the executive, and to maintaining its ability to represent the people.

NOTES

1. N Ram interview with Rediff.com. Available at http://www.rediff.com/news/2003/nov/19inter.htm
2. For the full text of the Tamil Nadu Assembly Resolution see http://www.thehindu.com/2003/11/08/ stories/2003110809261100.htm
3. This was established by the Constitution (44th Amendment) Act, 1978.
4. House of Lords Debates 43-1, House of Commons Debates 214-1, 1998-99.
5. Madison, James, Alexander Hamilton and John Jay. *Federalist Papers* (Mentor Books, 1961) pp. 240-43.
6. Tomkins, Adam. *Public Law* (Oxford University Press, 2003) p. 85.
7. Ibid., p. 89.
8. *Stockdale vs. Hansard* (1839) 9 A & E 1.
9. Case of the Sheriff of Middlesex (1840) 11 A & E 273.
10. *Nicholls Report* [271] – [314].
11. Ibid., [280] – [292].
12. Keshav Singh's case AIR 1965 C 745.
13. *MSM Sharma vs. SK Sinha II* AIR 1960 SC 1186.

Censorship Myths and Imagined Harms

SHOHINI GHOSH

"Every idea is an incitement"
- *Justice Oliver Wendell Holmes*

On November 28, 2003, the Left Front Government of West Bengal banned *Dwikhandita* (*Split in Two*, 2003) by Bangladeshi writer Taslima Nasrin. Chief Minister Buddhadev Bhattacharjee said: "I've read the book, not once but several times. I've discussed the contents with 25 people who matter and have finally decided to proscribe it". The Home Secretary, Amit Kiran Deb, said that if the book were not banned, "it could ignite communal tension".[1] After conducting nightlong raids, the Calcutta police triumphantly announced that they had seized all documentary evidence from the bookstores and publishers, including microfilms, floppies and all hard copies of the manuscript. Taslima responded by offering to put the manuscript on the net so that interested readers could download it and decide for themselves.

Most people would agree that, in the age of the internet, censorship could only be a symbolic gesture. The persistent reader/viewer will always find ways of accessing proscribed material. Censorship makes access difficult, not impossible. However, the one thing that censorship does ensure is that even the indifferent begin to take interest.

I personally believe that the fundamental right of freedom of speech and expression must be absolute in any democracy. When I make this statement, I am often considered to be a reckless libertarian who wants to inflict offensive and deviant speech on 'normal' people. On the contrary, I make this assertion knowing full well that this would also entail being subject to speech that would be hurtful and offensive to me. But that is the inevitable price. Article 19 should ideally protect not just speech that is full of hate on the speaker's part, but also speech that maybe hateful to an audience.[2] To express what may be offensive to others, we have to hear what is offensive to us. If this logic sounds self-evident, we have only to do a consistency check on advocates of free speech. The Hindu Right that is now valiantly defending Taslima Nasrin's right to free speech has deployed censorship strategies as an integral part of their Hindutva campaign. Conversely, the opponents of the Hindu Right's censorship attempts have now decided to ban *Dwikhandita!* Various women's groups at various times have demanded the erasure of a series of words and images.

A platitudinous abstraction that circulates during all censorship controversies is that "one must be careful not to hurt other people's feelings". This statement is a summary of mission impossible. There is no speech that hurts absolutely no one. If we were to ban sexist speech, for instance, what would we be left with? Perhaps only a handful of films from the entire gamut of Bollywood, regional, art, parallel or whatever cinema. Even that handful would vanish were we to ban 'casteist' films! Freedom of speech and expression therefore is not so much a prophylactic to hurt but the commitment to be able to bear it. This does not mean that we become passive subjects of hate speech. It simply means that we circulate more speech. Counter speech and the expansion of spaces for more speech are the only ways to fight problematic, hateful or discriminatory speech.

In this essay, I would like to discuss the critical overlap between hate speech and sexual speech. The intersectionality of hate and sexual speech provides valuable insights into why sexual stigma becomes integral to hate campaigns. Feminists, in particular, need to pay careful attention to the implications of obscenity laws that promise to protect women but in practice end up punishing them.

Harmful Images and Words

The mediascape of the nineties began with deep anxieties and affirmative engagement. The liberalization of the economy and the 'opening of the skies' catalyzed wide-ranging cultural transformations. Optimism around India partaking of the global community coexisted with anxieties around collapsing certainties. The rise of the Hindu Right during this time was therefore accompanied by frequent reminders that Indian culture and tradition were under threat by various marauding forces.

The new anxieties around the larger cultural transformations saw the enactment of new laws around speech and expression. In 2000, the Information Technology Act made, among other restrictions, the publishing of "obscene" electronic matter a punishable offence. Under this clause, "whoever publishes or transmits or causes to be published in electronic form any material which is lascivious or appeals to the prurient interest or if its effect is such as to tend to deprave or corrupt persons who are likely, having regard to all relevant circumstances, to read, see or hear the matter contained or embodied in it, shall be punished". The punishment could be imprisonment upto five years or a fine up to one lakh rupees. Another clause in the Act allows police officers and other officers to enter, search "any public place" and "arrest without warrant any person found therein who is reasonably suspected of having committed, or of committing or being about to commit any offence under this Act".

The BJP government introduced similar restrictions in the amendment of the Cable Television Networks (Regulation) Act (1995) and the Programme and Advertising Code in addition to bringing TV under the Cinematograph Act of 1952 which had hitherto been used to pre-censor feature films. The Advertising Code prohibits the telecast of cigarettes, tobacco, wine, alcohol, liquor and other intoxicants along with infant milk substitutes, feeding bottle or infant foods.[3] These laws were enacted notwithstanding existing laws that restrict 'obscene' speech. For example, Section 292 of the IPC prohibits 'obscenity,' which it defines as any visual or written material that is "lascivious or appeals to prurient interests" or which has the effect of depraving or corrupting persons exposed to it.[4] The Indecent Representation of Women Act (1986) prohibits indecency, which it defines as "the depiction of the figure of the woman as to have the effect of being indecent or is likely to deprave or corrupt public morality."

It is ironic that in a decade marked by vicious anti-minority propaganda, the majority of the censorship debates in the nineties have been around obscenity and vulgarity.[5] Responding to more transgressive images of women's bodies, the Hindu Right and feminists, albeit with different intentions, demanded the proscription of 'degrading' images. This only served to blur the crucial distinctions between sexism and sexual explicitness, coercion and consent. All sexual expression was being damned as 'degrading'. Historically, sexually explicit materials have always been the first targets of attack. Suppression of sexually explicit materials under obscenity laws has included literature on feminist issues like reproductive health, gay/lesbian issues, cliterodichtomy, marital rape, health and safe sex issues.

The feminist debates around censorship emerged first from the pornography debate in North America. The 'radical feminist position' demands censorship of all pornography because it is believed to encourage a culture of rape and violence against women. In the eighties and nineties, this position found its strongest supporters in Catherine MacKinnon and Andrea Dworkin whose crusade for censorship took inspiration from slogans like "pornography is the theory and rape is the practice".

The anti-censorship feminist position, whose politics I share, draw attention to the difference between sexist speech and sexually explicit speech. We argue that by conflating sexual explicitness with sexism and misogyny, anti-porn feminists have failed to interrogate gender-based discrimination in 'respectable institutions' such a the family, religion and judiciary. By focusing exclusively on 'harmful images,' pro-censorship feminists have understood neither harm nor the complexity of images. Importantly, by framing sexuality within a discourse of violence, it has encouraged sexphobia and victimology. Anti-censorship feminists repeatedly draw attention to the overwhelming data that fails to show causal links between pornography and violence. In fact, the absence of causal links is evident from the work of the very researchers that radical feminists quoted in their 'anti-porn' campaigns. In the 1987 study by Donnerstein, Linz and Penrod, the authors conclude, "Should harsher penalties be levelled against persons who traffic in pornography? We do not believe so. Rather, it is our opinion that the most prudent course of action would be development of educational programmes that would teach viewers to be critical consumers of the media".[6]

MacKinnon and Dworkin advocated that victims of sexual violence should litigate and seek financial redress from producers and distributors of sexually explicit material. A version of this idea has also been played out in the Indian courts leading to mitigation of several sentences. The judgement in the *Phul Singh vs State*, (AIR, 1980 SC 249) reads, "A philanderer of 22, overpowered by sex stress in excess, hoisted himself into his cousin's house next door and in broad daylight overpowered this temptingly lovely prosecutrix of 24, Pushpa, raped her in hurried heat and made an urgent exit having fulfilled his erotic sortie".

This judgement by Justice Krishna Iyer reduced the sentence of a rapist partly on grounds that "modern Indian conditions" are drifting into "societal permissiveness what with proneness to pornos [sic]...sex explosion in celluloid and bookstalls, etc.". Similarly, in *Reepik Ravinder vs the State of Andhra Pradesh* (1991 Cr J 595), the sentence of a five year old girl's rapist was mitigated on grounds that he had "seen too many blue films".[7] Image blaming can easily turn the criminal agent into a victim and absolve the person of any responsibility for his/her actions. Instead of helping the woman, the 'porn-made-me-do-it' argument is only likely to harm her.

The Journey to Banning *Dwikhandita*

The demolition of the Babri Masjid in 1992 precipitated communal violence all over India and a Muslim backlash in Bangladesh. Best-selling Bangladeshi author Taslima Nasrin responded to the anti-Hindu retaliation in Bangladesh through a hastily written novelette titled *Lajja* (Shame, 1993) about a liberal Hindu family caught in the sudden and cata-strophic communal backlash. Released in 1993, the book sold 60,000 copies before being banned by the Bangladesh government on grounds that it was inflammatory and likely to incite communal violence. The Council of Islamic Students declared her a heretic and demanded her arrest and public hanging. The attack intensified when an interview in *The Statesman* of May 9th, 1993, said that she had asked for a "thorough revision" of the Koran. Contending that the interview misrepresented her position, she issued a clarification to the newspaper on May 11th:

"My view on this issue is clear and categorical. I hold the Koran, the Vedas, the Bible and all such religious texts determining the lives of their followers as 'out of place and out of time'. We have socio-historical contexts in which these were written and therefore we should not be guided by their precepts. We have to move beyond these ancient texts if we have to make progress. In order to respond to our spiritual needs let humanism be your new faith".

Clarification notwithstanding, the reproduction of the May 9th interview in Bangladesh newspapers of June 4th changed her life forever. The Government, headed by Bangladesh National Party's Khaleda Zia (whose allies have historically been Islamic fundamentalist groups), lodged a criminal case against Taslima under Section 295 (A) of the Bangladesh Penal Code for "outraging religious sentiments" with "deliberate" and "malicious" intent. The same clause in the Indian Penal Code was invoked against the cultural organization SAHMAT for allegedly depicting Ram and Sita as siblings in their exhibition Hum Sab Ayodhya after the demolition of the Babri Masjid. Similarly, it was used to demand artist M.F. Hussain's arrest in 1996 for allegedly drawing the goddess Saraswati in the 'nude'. Taslima had to flee Bangladesh and live as an exile.

I am often told, even by people who cannot read or write Bengali, that Taslima Nasrin is an overrated writer. It is also suggested that her books sell because of their explicit dis-cussion of sex and sexuality. Future generations will agree that Taslima Nasrin is one of the most important figures in contemporary Bengali writing. Moving away from ornate and euphemistic rhetoric, Taslima deploys language that is direct, even ruthless. Her feminist politics emerges not out of victimology but rage. Her sexual explicitness is daring and unembarrassed. These traits are neither traditionally feminine nor desirable by Bengali canonical standards. Taslima's writings assail the canon itself and urge the redefinition of 'literary merit'. Her style is nowhere more evident than the autobiographical series that she started writing in exile. The first part, *Amar Meyebela* (My Girlhood, 1999), covers the first thirteen years of her life. *Utal Hawa* (Wild Winds, 2002) and *Dwikhandita* are the second and third parts respectively.

The West Bengal Government's ban on *Dwikhandita* found unlikely allies in one section of the Bengali literati, including many advocates of free speech. Why did so many writers defend the ban? Do they really fear a communal conflagration? If such a fear is genuine, then why has the Left Front Government never proscribed anti-Muslim hate literature that the Hindu Right routinely circulates in all states? Or does the discomfort lie somewhere else? Defending the ban, writer Dibyendu Palit says that "two points" require consideration: First, Taslima's "delving into" the "sexual lives" of eminent literary figures in India and Bangladesh; and second, an appeal from some "Muslim intellectuals, who are not fundamentalists", that the book be banned as it slanders "Prophet Mohammed and Islam" and is likely to "hurt religious sentiments". The second consideration is commonplace but the first one is puzzling.

Why should a state government ban a book because it "delves" into the sexual lives of eminent literary figures? If "eminent figures" feel misrepresented, they can file defamation suits and battle it out in court. Why should this be any business of the State? Interestingly, every writer who supports the ban on *Dwikhandita* takes pains to discuss the offensiveness of the sexual content of the book. Writer Sunil Gangopadhyay says that he finds the sexual content of the book "distasteful" but supports the ban only on account of two pages that harshly indict Islam. Commenting on Taslima's discussion of her sexual relationships with eminent writers, he says, "Everybody knows that adults enter a sexual relationship on the basis of an unwritten pact, which is why they close all doors and windows. If someone breaks that trust then it is a breach of contract and confidentiality which is not only distasteful but an offence".[8]

This is not the first time that the 'whore stigma' has caught up with Taslima. During the controversy on *Lajja*, the media frequently painted her as a woman who smokes, drinks and indulges in sexual promiscuity. Clearly, the anxiety around "hurting religious sentiments" is only a ruse to disguise the moral indignation of Bengal's cultural guardians. No one articulates it better than Taslima herself. In an essay titled *Shokol Griho Haralo Jaar* (The One Who Loses All Homes), Taslima writes, "I have become the target of a million arrows of indictment and I am sinking in a quagmire of insults and baseless allegations – all because I have spoken honestly. Honesty often does not go down well. If the honesty of *Amar Meyebela* and *Utal Hawa* was acceptable, then that of *Dwikhandita* is not. When in *Amar Meyebela*, I described how my childhood was exploited, people sighed and expressed their sympathies. When in *Utal Hawa*, I discussed how my husband abused me, people felt sorry. But when in *Dwikhandita*, I described multiple sexual relations with several men, I became the object of shame and disgust. The single reason is that as long as a woman is oppressed and helpless, weak and beset by misfortunes, she is worthy of sympathy and goodwill. But when the woman stops being helpless and oppressed and instead, stands upright and asserts herself and when, for her own emotional and physical independence, breaks the rotting norms of society, she is no longer liked. Instead she becomes reprehensible. I know this character of our society well and yet I did not hesitate to reveal all".[9]

Taslima knows the wages of the "whore stigma". By discussing what is 'immoral' and 'obscene', she has violated a certain 'public order'. We may legitimately ask whether *Dwikhandita* was censored in the interest of public order or to impose a certain morality on public life.

Whores and Goddesses

Hate discourses have historically resorted to the deployment of sexual stigma in order to demonize their 'other'. Charges of sexual deviancy and perversity become endemic to hate propaganda. During the controversy on *Fire*, the Hindu Right took great pains to show that homosexuality was alien to the Hindus but integral to the lives of Muslims.[10] In an indictment of *Fire*, K R Malkani narrates a story about how, after defeating a Hindu King, the "invader" Mahmud of Ghazni asked him to choose between Islam and death. The Hindu king replied that he could become a Muslim to save his life provided he was not asked to eat beef or sleep with a boy. Predictably, the Hindu King was denied his request and he finally chose to immolate himself![11] Extending the same argument, Bal Thackeray offered to support the film if the names of the female protagonists were changed to Shabana and Saira instead of Radha and Sita.

Such sexual demonization is also evident in the controversies around Hussain's paintings. In October 1996, Bajrang Dal volunteers broke into the Herwitz gallery in Ahmedabad and destroyed a number of rare and acclaimed paintings by Hussain. The volunteers defended their actions by declaring that Hussain had painted the goddess Saraswati in the "nude" and thereby hurt "Hindu religious sentiments". Hussain was accused of aggravating communal tension by deliberately painting pictures offensive to Hindus. Regardless of the facts, the media perpetuated the same idea.

The details are significantly different. This was not a new painting but one made in 1976 and discovered recently by the Hindu Right through its reproduction in *Vichar Mimansa*, a BJP-backed magazine.[12] Responding to the complaint lodged by the Shiv Sena government, the Bombay police registered a case against Hussain under Sections 153-A (promoting enmity between different groups on grounds of religion, race, etc. and acting in a manner prejudicial to harmony) and Section 295-A (for perpetrating deliberate and malicious acts intended to outrage religious feelings of any class by insulting its religion or religious beliefs).

In 1998, a lithograph entitled *Sita Rescued* was targeted as obscene because it showed Sita and Hanuman naked. Hussain had produced the lithograph in 1984 for Ramlila Programmes run by a Lohiaite socialist group. The VHP vandalized the exhibition in Delhi where the painting had been displayed. A Shiv Sena leader declared that Hussain "wants to strip our mother naked". BJP's Uma Bharti stated that "it is not only a question of Hindu sentiment but of women sentiment" [sic], and that she would have protested had Hussain painted "Marian or Khatija in the nude". She added that Hussain was a "pervert" who needed "psychiatric treatment". If Taslima carried the 'whore stigma' of excessive agency, Hussain had turned the goddess into a whore. Both carried the stigma of being sexual deviants who had "degraded" the image of women in society.

This idea is best evident in writer Iqbal Masud's attack on Hussain. Calling Hussain's "artistic depiction of Saraswati distasteful", he writes, "If Hussain faces himself…he will realize that his paintings caused serious hurt. He will realize that while he can afford to play around with Madhuri, he should leave Saraswati alone".[13] Clearly, beneath the degradation argument runs a strong 'woman-blaming impulse'. Therefore, bad girls get what they deserve – whether in life or in representation. This logic lies at the heart of the 'whore stigma'.

There is a long history of women being punished for having sexual agency. Anne McClintock has observed how, on the one hand, prostitutes are patronized and silenced as having inherent lack of agency – as coerced slaves and victims of "false consciousness" – while on the other they are castigated for having an excess of agency. Evidence of women's sexual history is readily introduced during rape trials because our judiciary is still inclined to believe that whores can't be raped. Besides, too much sexual agency deserves to be punished anyway. The central importance of consent in adult sexual relations continues to escape many. As Margaret Baldwin has remarked, "If 'no' means 'no', 'yes' should also mean 'yes'".

I can already hear some women protesting, "But I am not a whore". Now try explaining that in a rape or child custody trial. The definition of a whore is as open to interpretation as words like 'obscenity', 'vulgarity', 'depravity', 'prurient', 'distasteful', 'degrading', and 'objectifying'. Attempting to come to a consensus around these terms is like trying to separate pornography from erotica. The thin dividing line is in everyone's head and in a different place. As the common saying goes, "What you like is pornography, and what I like is erotica".

Last Word

Among the censors of *Dwikhandita*, perhaps there are those who truly believe that the book could incite communal violence. Then these people should be consistent in their attempt to extirpate all books that could provide similar incitement. What better place to start than with religious texts because they contain passages that can easily be read as incitements to violence? Not to mention all propaganda material by the Hindu Right. If Dibyendu Palit's 'non-fundamentalist Muslims' asked for Hindu Right propaganda to be banned in West Bengal, would the Left Front government comply? I have serious doubts. At this point in time, hate speech of the powerful Hindu Right is least likely to be proscribed. Throughout history, censorship has been used disproportionately to silence those who are relatively disempowered. It will always be speech on the margins, not the speech of the powerful that will be suppressed. It is for this reason that Taslima has written, "No, my writings have never caused catastrophic tragedies like riots. Whatever happens, happens only to me. The consequent punishment for my writings has to be borne only by me. It is my house that catches fire. I am the one who has to lose every home".[14]

NOTES

1. 'Bengal Bans Taslima's Book", *The Statesman* (Saturday, November 29, 2003).
2. The right to freedom of speech and expression is protected under Article 19 of the Constitution. But according to the provisions of Article 19 (2), this fundamental right is subject to "reasonable restrictions".
3. In order to ensure that censorship provisions are followed, the I&B Ministry under the BJP revived the Central Monitoring Cell on the Gurgaon-Mehrauli Road. About 120 staff members monitor TV programmes for "anti-India propaganda" and other violations.
4. Section 292 is based on an 1868 English decision called the Hicklin case. This decision has been approved and repeatedly applied by the Supreme Court of India.

5. See "The Troubled Existence of Sex and Sexuality: Feminists Engage with Censorship" by Shohini Ghosh in Christiane Brosius & Melissa Butcher eds., *Image Journeys: Audio Visual Media and Cultural Change in India* (Sage, 1999, Delhi).

6. Linz, D., E. Donnerstein and S. Penrod. "The Findings and Recommendations of the Attorney General's Commission on Pornography: Do the Psychological 'Facts' fit the Political Fury?" *American Psychologist*, 42 (1987).

7. In *Gauri Shankar vs. State of Tamil Nadu* (JT 1994, 3SC54), popularly called the Auto Shankar case, the Defence Counsel argued for a mitigation of sentence on grounds that he watched too many films "depicting sex and violence and illicit business and got misguided and ended up as a criminal" and therefore, makers of such films were 'vicariously responsible'".

8. "Government Decision to Protect the Innocent", Interview with Sunil Gangopadhyay, *Aaj Kal* (December 9, 2003). The translation from Bengali to English is mine.

9. *Desh* (December 17, 2003). The translations are mine.

10. *Fire* directed by Deepa Mehta, is a love story about two married sisters-in-law who fall in love with each other and have a relationship (1988).

11. Malkani, K R. "Any natural being will concede that homosexuality is unnatural", *The Times of India* (November 22, 1998).

12. Nagpal, Om. "*Ye Kasai ya Chitrakar?*" ("Is he an Artist or a Butcher?") in *Vichar Mimansa*. Accompanying the article was a photograph of the so-called 'nude' Sarawaswati that the editor V.S. Vajpayee had found in Dhyaneshwar Nadkarni's book *Riding the Lightning*. It was a copy of this article that Pramod Navalkar handed over to the Bombay Police Commissioner.

13. *The Times of India* (October 13, 1996).

14. *Desh* (December 17, 2003).

Homeless Everywhere
Writing in Exile

TASLIMA NASREEN

"Freedom is always and exclusively freedom for the one who thinks differently".
Rosa Luxemburg

When I look back, the years gone by appear dry, ashen. Suddenly, a half-forgotten dream tears itself from that inert grey mass and stands before me, iridescent, obtrusive. Odd memories tiptoe into my solitary room. Confronting me, they make me tremble, they make me cry; they drag me back towards the days left behind.

I cannot help but walk down the serpentine, shadowy alleys of my life, foraging for remembered fragments. To what use? The past is past, irrevocably so. The dreams that are long dead are unrecognizably dead. What good can it do to dust the cobwebs off them with tender fingers? What is gone just isn't here anymore.

I know, yet my life in exile makes me reach back into my past, again and again. I walk through the landscape of my memories like someone possessed. Each night brings with it nightmares, its own thick blanket of melancholy. It is then that I start telling the story of that girl.

A shy, timid girl, who grew up in a strict family, uncomplaining, constantly humiliated; a girl encircled by boundaries, whose every desire, every whim was thrown away as garbage; whose small, frail body was prey to many dark, hairy hands. I have narrated the story of that girl.

A girl with modest adolescent dreams, who fell in love and married in secret, hoping to live the ordinary life of an ordinary woman. I have told her story. A woman betrayed by her dearly beloved husband, whose convictions came crashing down like a house of straw, a woman who knew sorrow, pain, mourning, and bereavement; a woman who was tempted to follow the terrible road to self-destruction. I have simply told her agonizing tale.

A woman who then gathered up the broken pieces of her dreams and tried to live again, to make a little room of her own in the midst of a cruel, heartless society; who surrendered to a guardian called 'man' because society demanded it of her. But the hurt, the pain kept growing, the traumatic pain of losing an unborn child, wounds that left her bloodied and sore, onslaughts of malice, distrust and unbearable humiliation. All that I have done is to tell the story of that trampled and bruised girl.

That girl who, with whatever strength remained in her body and mind, stood up again, without anyone's help, turned away from all shelter, trying to be her own self once more, her own refuge; a woman who refused to renounce and retreat from the world that had deceived and rejected her, a woman who refused to heed people's taunts and sneers

I have narrated the story of this girl, of this woman standing upright. A woman who refused to obey society's diktats, its rituals and traditions. A woman whose constant stumbling, falling, being thrown, taught her to stand straight. Whose stumbling steps taught her to walk, whose wanderings showed her the way. Slowly, gradually, she witnessed the growth of a new consciousness within her, a simple thought took hold of her – "This life was her own and no one else's. She was the one who could rule over it, no one else". I have told the story of that girl, of the circumstances that shaped her. It is the story of a girl who came out of the furnace of patriarchy, not reduced to ashes, but as burnished steel.

Have I done wrong? Even if I don't think so, many people think today that it was wrong of me to tell this story. Today, I am standing in the prosecution box waiting for the verdict. It wouldn't have been such a terrible crime if I had not disclosed the identity of that girl. The girl was I, Taslima.

Had I used my imagination, I could have done whatever I pleased – written page after page of fancy and all would have been forgiven. But it is forbidden to stake my claim in this real world to being a flesh and blood woman and announce audaciously – "I am that girl; after those turbulent years of sorrow I am standing up again; I have vowed to live my life as I see fit".

Why would the world accept this bold stance? No woman should have this kind of courage. I am completely unfit for a patriarchal society. In my own country Bangladesh, in my very own West Bengal, I am a forbidden name, an outlawed woman, a banned book. Nobody can utter my name, touch me, read me; if they do so their tongues will rot, their hands will become soiled, a deep disgust will overwhelm them. This is the way I am. This is the way I have chosen to be.

Yet even if the publication of *Dwikhandito* (*The Broken*) shatters me into a thousand pieces, I will still not confess to any wrongdoing. Is it wrong to write the story of one's life? Is it wrong to expose the deep, secret truths of life as you have lived it? The unwritten rule of every autobiography is – 'Nothing will be hidden, everything shall be written about'. An autobiography's subject is the unknown, the secrets of a human life. I have simply tried to follow this rule honestly. The first two volumes of my life story, *Amar Meyebela* (*My Girlhood*) and *Utal Hawa* (*Strong Winds*) have not raised the kind of controversy *Dwikhandito* has. In any case, I have not started the controversy, others have. Many have said that I have deliberately chosen sensational subject matter, incapable of generating anything but controversy. This question should not be raised in the case of an autobiography. I have described the years of my childhood, my adolescence, my youth, living and growing through all kinds of experiences. I have spoken about my philosophy, my hopes and despairs, my beauty and my ugliness, my happiness and sorrow, my anger and tears, my own deviation from my ideals. I have not chosen a titillating or sensitive subject. I have simply chosen my own life to write about. If this life is a stimulating and exciting life, then how can I make it less so? I am told this volume has been written to raise a hue and cry. Does every conception have to have a petty motive? As if honesty, simplicity cannot be adequate reasons. As if courage, something that I am told I have in abundance, cannot be a good enough reason.

Controversy about my writing is nothing new. I am familiar with it from the very time I was being published. Actually, isn't the truth rather simple? Just this: if you don't compromise with a patriarchal society, you will find yourself at the centre of a storm?

There are many different definitions of what makes an autobiography. Most of us easily accept those autobiographies that are idealistic and describe only good and happy events. Generally, great men write about their lives to inspire other lives, to reveal the truth and the path of righteousness. I am neither a sage, nor a great, erudite being, and I write not to show light to the blind. I am simply unmasking the wounds and blights of an ordinary human life.

Even though I am not a great litterateur or a remarkable personality, momentous things have happened in my life. Certainly it is no ordinary life, when, because of my beliefs and ideals, thousands take to the streets asking for my death; or when my books are banned because they carry my opinions; or when the state snatches away the right to live in my own land for speaking the truth!

When it is all right for others to constantly describe my life, and add colour to their portrayal, why shouldn't it be all right for me to take the responsibility to describe it myself, fully, truthfully? Surely no one else can know my life the way I know it?

If I don't reveal myself, if I don't depict the whole of myself – especially those events that have shaken me – if I don't talk of all that is good and bad in me, of my weaknesses and my strengths, my happiness and sorrow, my generosity and cruelty, then I don't think I can stay true to the responsibility of writing an autobiography. For me, literature for literature's sake, or literary niceties for their own sake, cannot be the last word; I place a greater value on honesty.

Whatever my life may be, however contemptible or despicable, I do not deceive myself when I sit down to write about it. If the reader is disgusted or appalled by my tale, so be it. At least I can be satisfied that I have not cheated my reader. I am not presenting a fictitious narrative in the guise of an autobiography. I narrate the truths of my life, the ugly as much as I do the beautiful, without hesitation. I can't change my past. The ugliness and the beauty must both be accepted; I won't lie and say, "It didn't happen".

The sharp arrows of mockery come flying from every direction. The mud of slander and humiliation is flung to soil me. There is only one reason for this assault. I have spoken the truth. Not everyone can bear the truth. The truths of *Amar Meyebela* and *Utal Hawa* can be borne; *Dwikhandito*'s is insupportable. In *Amar Meyebela*, when I described my ignoble childhood, people said sympathetically, "How terrible!" In *Utal Hawa*, when I described being cheated on by my husband, they expressed their sympathy. But in *Dwikhandito*, when I spoke openly of my relationships with various men, they began to point fingers at me. We can draw only one conclusion from this: As long as a woman is oppressed and defenceless, people like her and sympathize with her. But when she refuses to remain exploited or suppressed, when she stands up, when she straightens her spine, establishes her rights, breaks the rotten social systems that chain her so as to free her body and mind – she is no longer admirable, she becomes hateful. I knew this character of our society; even then I was not afraid to speak freely about myself.

One of the main reasons for the controversy regarding *Dwikhandito* is sexual freedom. Since most people are immersed neck-deep in the traditions of a patriarchal society, they are irritated, angry and outraged at the open declaration of a woman's sexual autonomy. This freedom is not something that I simply talk about; rather, I have established it for myself, in and through my life. But this freedom is not license; men cannot touch me whenever they please. I decide.

Our society is not yet ready for such freedom in a woman. It refuses to accept the fact that a woman can sexually engage with and enjoy any man she desires, and yet rigorously decide where to draw the line in any encounter.

Our renowned, famous, well-heeled writers delight in slandering me by calling me a fallen woman, a whore. In doing this they only prove themselves to be the figureheads of this disgusting, dirty patriarchal society! They first use 'fallen women' for their enjoyment and then deploy the words 'fallen woman' as a term for abuse! There is really nothing novel in the use of women as sexual slaves.

Although in this volume of my autobiography I have spoken about my personal struggle against patriarchy, spoken about the torture meted out by society on women and religious minorities, nobody talks of the fact that I have spoken of such things. They only notice my relationships with men. They notice the audacity that I have in opening my mouth about the deep, secret, ugly and repulsive subject of what happens to sexuality in a patriarchal society.

Whenever, in the history of the world, in times of darkness, a woman stands up against patriarchy, speaks about emancipation, tries to break free from her chains, she gets called a 'fallen woman'. Many years ago, in the preface to my book, *A Fallen Woman's Fallen Prose*, I wrote about how I delighted in calling myself a 'fallen woman'. It was because I knew that whenever a woman has protested against oppression by the state, by religion, or by society, whenever she has become aware of all her rights, society has called her a whore. I believe that in this world, for a woman to be pure, to be true to herself, she has to become a 'fallen woman'. Only when a woman is called a 'whore' can she know that she is free from the coils of society's diktats. The 'fallen' woman is really a pure and pristine human being. I truly believe that if a woman wants to earn her freedom, be a human, she has to earn this label. This title, coming from a fallen, degenerate society, should be seen as an honour by every woman. Till now, of all the prizes I have received, I consider this honour to be the greatest recognition of what I have done with my life. I have earned it because I have given a mortal blow to the decaying, rotten body of patriarchy. This is the true measure of the worth of my life as a writer, of my life as a woman and the long years of my struggle to be the person I am.

A writer in Bangladesh has sued me for defamation after *Dwikhandito* came out. Another in West Bengal has also followed suit. Dissatisfied with that, they have demanded a ban on my book. I really cannot understand how a writer can demand this about another writer's work. How can they fight for freedom of speech and thought and then behave like fundamentalists. I believe every word of what Voltaire said – "*Je ne suis absolument pas d'accord avec vos idées, mais je me battrais pour que vous puissiez les exprimer...*" – ("I do not agree with your ideas, but I will fight for your right to express them".)

So many people have written about their lives. If it is a human life, it is full of errors, mistakes, black marks, and thorns, even when those in question are saints. St. Augustine (335-430 AD) wrote about his life, talked openly about his undisciplined, immoral, reckless youth in Algeria, his illegitimate son, his sexual exploits. Mahatma Gandhi spoken of how he tested his celibacy by making women sleep in the same bed with him. Jean Jacques Rousseau (1712-1774) in his *Confessions* narrates every incident of his life, without holding back the ugly and the bad. Benjamin Franklin (1709-1790) confesses how he brought up his illegitimate son, William. Bertrand Russell and Leo Tolstoy have been equally frank about their lives. Why did these men talk about things they knew were unacceptable by society? It is because they wanted to let their readers know their real selves, and because they felt that these experiences were important in their lives. Does anyone call them names because they have been indiscreet? Rather, these admirable men remain exactly in the position of honour they have always occupied, and it is reinforced by their telling of the truths of their lives. Catherine Millet's *La vie sexuelle de Catherine M* (The sexual life of Catherine M) describes the sexual freedom of the sixties, her life with many men, vivid descriptions of sex. Hasn't this book occupied a place among other literary works? Gabriel Garcia Marquez in his *Vivir Para Contarla* talks of other women with whom he had relations.

Will someone run to court to ban Marquez's book?

In every country, biographies are written about famous men and women. Biographers conduct research for years to unearth some hidden aspects of the life under examination. Even innermost secrets no longer remain so, and we have seen this even in the case of Rabindranath Tagore's life. In spite of being a passionate spokesman against child marriage, why did he allow his daughter to marry so young? We now know the reason. But the question remains: Why does a reader need to know all this? Why do researchers spend years finding out the most intimate details of a person's life? It is because in the light of these hidden facts we can analyze and understand the writer and his work in a new way.

Many Bengali writers love playing games with women, and even if they hesitate to mention these escapades in their autobiographies, the characters they create boldly commit such acts. Nobody has ever questioned them, but if a woman talks of sexuality, in a fictional work or in her autobiography, eyebrows are raised. Sexuality is a man's prerogative, his 'ancestral' patrilineal property. I can't possibly write like men. I must write more discreetly. I am a woman after all. Only a man possesses the right to discuss a woman's body, her thighs, her breasts, her waist and her vagina. Why should a woman do it? This patriarchal society has not given me that right, but since I have thumbed my nose at this rule and have written about it, however sad or poignant my tale may be, I have crossed the limits.

For a man, a playboy image is something to be proud of. When a woman writes about her love and sexuality with honesty, she becomes a suspect, a 'characterless' woman. I have talked of certain things in my autobiography that I should not have. I have muckraked; I have crossed the limit allowed to me.

One should not discuss what happens inside the bedroom or between two individuals because such events are unimportant. But I consider them important because all those incidents have shaped the Taslima that I am today – this woman with her beliefs and disbeliefs, mores and thoughts, and her own sense of her self. The world around her has created her brick by brick, not as a chaste domesticated angel, but as an ardent, renegade, disobedient brat.

Then they say: I can destroy my own reputation, but why do I have to destroy the reputation of others? This question has come up, although I am writing about what is after all my own life. I fail to understand why those who are so self-consciously respectable do things that they consider contemptible? They say that I have broken their trust. But I never promised anyone my silence. People tell me there is an unwritten rule, but only those afraid my revelations will destroy their saintly images uphold this code of discretion. And then they try to intimidate me with their furious wrinkled brows! But what if I want to reveal whatever I consider important? What if I decide that what I am talking about is not obscene, at least to me?

Who creates these definitions of obscenity and sets out the limits? I decide what I should write in my autobiography, how much to reveal, how much to conceal. Or should I not? Should I wait for instructions from X, Y, and Z, from some Maqsud Ali, some Keramat Mian, or from some Paritosh or Haridas Pal? Should I wait on them to tell me what to write, how much to write?

Critics want to characterize my freedom as self-indulgent license. This is because our likes and dislikes, our sense of right and wrong, sin and virtue, beauty and ugliness are moulded by thousands of years of patriarchy. So, patriarchy has taught us that the true characteristics of a woman are her diffidence, her timidity, her chastity, her lowered head, and her patience. Therefore, the critic's habituated, controlled perceptions are afraid to face harsh truths, and quickly shut their ears in disgust. "Is she a real writer? Does she have the right to an autobiography?", they ask in anger.

I think that everyone has a right to talk about their lives, even the pompous critic who regards a pen in my hands as an outrage! I have been called irresponsible. I may be irresponsible, I may be irrational, but I refuse to give up the right to be so. George Bernard Shaw once said, "A reasonable man adapts himself to the world. An unreasonable man persists in trying to adapt the world to himself. Therefore, all progress depends upon the unreasonable man".

Taslima Nasreen is one of those unreasonable human beings. I do not claim that progress depends upon me; I am simply an insignificant writer. In the eyes of wise men, I am happy to be labelled an unreasonable or imprudent person. It is because I am foolish that I have not kept my mouth shut, I have stood my ground even as an entire society has spat upon me. I have remained firm when patriarchy's ardent supporters have come to trample me. My naïveté, my unreasonableness, my irrationality are my greatest assets.

The question of religion has also come up. Those who know me also know that I always speak up against religious conventions. Religion is thoroughly patriarchal. If I insult religion or religious texts, why should men tolerate it, especially when these same men use religion and religious texts to suppress others? It is these pious gentlemen who have forced me to leave my country. I have paid the price for truth with my own life. How much more should I pay?

Just like in West Bengal today, my books have been banned earlier in Bangladesh on the excuse that they may incite riots. The communal tension raging through South Asia is not caused by my books but by other reasons. The torture of Bangladesh's minorities, the killing of Muslims in Gujarat, the oppression of Biharis in Assam, the attacks against Christians, and the Shia-Sunni conflicts in Pakistan have all occurred without any contribution from me. Even if I am an insignificant writer, I write for humanity, I write with all my heart that every human being is equal, and there must be no discrimination on the basis of gender, colour, or religion. Everyone has the right to live. Riots don't break out because of what I write. But I am the one who is punished for what I write. Fires rage in my home. I am the one who has to suffer exile. I am the one who is homeless everywhere.

Translated from Bangla by Debjani Sengupta. The translator gratefully acknowledges the author's permission to translate the piece. First Published in *Desh*, 17 December, 2003 as "Shokol Griha Haralo Jar".

NOTES

1. Written by Taslima Nasrin in response to the ban order placed on November 27, 2003, by the Government of West Bengal on her book *Dwikhandito*, the third volume in her memoirs. Taslima Nasrin has had her previous book *Lajja* proscribed in her native Bangladesh. Following death threats by fundamentalist organizations and a hostile government, Nasrin has had to live in exile. She currently lives in the United States of America. For pdfs of her banned books and more about Taslima Nasrin, see www.taslimanasrin.com.

\<ALT+OPTION\>

Manifesto Against Labour

GRUPPE KRISIS

1. The Rule of Dead Labour

A corpse rules society – the corpse of labour. All powers around the globe formed an alliance to defend its rule. They know but one slogan: jobs, jobs, jobs!

The society ruled by labour does not experience a temporary crisis; it encounters its absolute limit. In the wake of the micro-electronic revolution, wealth production increasingly became independent from the actual expenditure of human labour power to an extent quite recently only imaginable in science fiction. No one can seriously any longer maintain that this process can be halted or reversed. Selling commodity labour power in the twenty-first century is as promising as the sale of stagecoaches in the twentieth century. However, whoever is not able to sell his or her labour power in this society is considered to be 'superfluous', and to be disposed of on the social waste dump.

Those who do not work (labour) shall not eat! This cynical principle is still in effect; all the more so nowadays when it has become hopelessly obsolete. It really is an absurdity: Never before was society as much a labour society as it is now, even as labour itself is made superfluous. On its deathbed, labour turns out to be a totalitarian power that does not tolerate any gods beside itself. Seeping through the pores of everyday life into the psyche, labour controls both thought and action. No expense or pain is spared to artificially prolong the lifespan of the 'labour idol'. The paranoid cry for jobs justifies the devastation of natural resources on an intensified scale, even though the destructive effect on humanity was realized a long time ago. The very last obstacles to the full commercialization of any social relationship will be cleared away uncritically, if only there is a chance for a few miserable jobs to be created. 'Any job is better than no job' became a confession of faith, which is exacted from everybody.

To some people, unemployment is the result of exaggerated demands, low-performance or missing flexibility; to others unemployment is due to the incompetence, corruption, or greed of 'their' politicians or business executives, besides, of course, the inclination of such 'leaders' to pursue policies of 'treachery'. Everybody shall keep his or her nose to the grindstone even if the grindstone gets pulverized. The gloomy meta-message of such incentives cannot be misunderstood: Those who fail in finding favour in the eyes of the 'labour idol' have to take the blame, they can be written off and pushed away.

"Everyone must be able to live from his work is the propounded principle. Hence that one can live is subject to a condition and there is no right where the qualification cannot be fulfilled".
- Johann Gottlieb Fichte, *Foundations of Natural Law according to the Principles of Scientific Theory*, 1797

2. The Neo-Liberal Apartheid Society

Should the successful sale of commodity 'labour power' become the exception instead of the rule? A society devoted to the irrational abstraction of labour is inevitably doomed to develop a tendency for social apartheid. All factions of the all-parties consensus on labour, so to say the labour-camp, quietly accepted this logic long ago and even took over a supporting role. There is no controversy on whether ever-increasing sections of the population should be pushed to the margin and should be excluded from social participation; there is only controversy on how this social selection is to be pushed through.

The police, salvation sects, the Mafia, and charity organizations take on responsibility for that annoying human litter. In the USA and most central European countries, more people are imprisoned than an average military dictatorship. In Latin America, day after day, more street urchins and other poor are hunted down by free enterprise death-squads than dissidents were killed during the worst periods of political repression. There is only one social function left for the ostracized: to be the warning example. Their fate is meant to goad on those who still participate in the rat-race of fighting for the leftovers. And even the losers have to be kept moving so that they don't hit on the idea of rebelling against the outrageous impositions they face.

"The crook has destroyed working and taken away the worker's wage even so. Now he [the worker] shall labour without a wage while picturing to himself the blessing of success and profit in his prison cell ... By means of forced labour he shall be trained to perform moral labour as a free personal act".
- Wilhelm Heinrich Riehl, *Die Deutsche Arbeit* (*The German Labour*), 1861

3. The Neo-Welfare-Apartheid-State

The ideological transformation of 'scarce labour' (tight labour market) into a prime civil right necessarily excludes all foreigners. The social logic of selection then is not questioned, but redefined: The individual struggle for survival shall be defused by means of ethnic-nationalistic criteria. 'Domestic treadmills only for native citizens' is the outcry deep from the bottom of the people's soul, who are suddenly able to come together, motivated by their perverse lust for labour. Right-wing populism makes no secret of such sentiment. Its criticism of 'rival society' only amounts to ethnic cleansing within the shrinking zones of capitalist wealth.

Thereby, the intensified exclusion of refugees from the Eastern and African world can be legitimized in a populist manner and without getting into a fuss. Of course, the whole operation is well obscured by talking nineteen to the dozen about humanity and civilization. Manhunts for 'illegal immigrants' allegedly sneaking in for domestic jobs shall not leave behind nasty bloodstains or burn marks on German soil. Rather it is the business of the border police, police forces in general, and the buffer states of "Schengenland", which dispose of the problem lawfully, and best of all, far away from media coverage.

"Any job is better than no job".
Bill Clinton, 1998

"No job is as hard as no job".
A poster at the December 1998 rally, organized by initiatives for unemployed people.

"Citizen work should be rewarded, not paid ... Whoever does honorary citizen work clears himself of the stigma of being unemployed and being a recipient of welfare benefits".
- Ulrich Beck, *The Soul of Democracy*, 1997

4. Exaggeration and the denial of the labour religion

Since the days of the Reformation, all the powers of Western modernization have preached the sacredness of work. Over the last 150 years, all social theories and political schools were possessed by the idea of labour. Socialists and conservatives, democrats and fascists fought each other to the death; but despite all deadly hatred, they always paid homage to the labour idol together. "Push the idler aside", is a line from the German lyrics of the international working (labouring) class anthem; "Labour Makes Free" resounds eerily from the inscription above the gate in Auschwitz. The pluralist post-war democracies swore all the more by the everlasting dictatorship of labour.

At the end of the twentieth century, all ideological differences have vanished into thin air. What remains is the common ground of a merciless dogma: Labour is the natural destiny of human beings. Today, the reality of the labour society itself denies that dogma. The disciples of the labour religion have always preached that a human being, according to its supposed nature, is an *animal laborans* (working creature/animal). Such an 'animal' actually only assumes the quality of being human by subjecting matter to his will and in realising himself in his products, as once did Prometheus.

The modern production process has always made a mockery of this myth of a world conqueror and a demigod. Whoever asks about the content, meaning, and goal of his or her job will go crazy or become a disruptive element in the social machinery designed to function as an end-in-itself. *Homo faber*, once full of conceit as to his craft and trade, a type of human who took seriously what he did in a parochial way, has become as old-fashioned as a mechanical typewriter. The treadmill has to run at all cost, and 'that's all there is to it'. Advertising departments and armies of entertainers, company psychologists, image advisors and drug dealers are responsible for creating meaning. Where there is continual babble about motivation and creativity, there is not a trace left of either of them – save self-deception. This is why talents such as autosuggestion, self-projection and competence simulation rank among the most important virtues of managers and skilled workers, media stars and accountants, teachers and parking lot guards.

The crisis of the labour society has completely ridiculed the claim that labour is an eternal necessity imposed on humanity by nature. For centuries it was preached that homage has to be paid to the labour idol just for the simple reason that needs can not be satisfied without humans sweating blood: to satisfy needs, that is the whole point of the human labour camp existence. If that were true, a critique of labour would be as rational as a critique of gravity. So how can a true 'law of nature' enter into a state of crisis or even disappear? The floor leaders of society's labour camp factions, from neo-liberal gluttons for caviar to labour unionist beer bellies, find themselves running out of arguments to prove the pseudo-nature of labour. Or how can they explain that three-quarters of humanity are sinking in misery and poverty only because the labour system no longer needs their labour?

"Work, however base and mammonist, is always connected with nature. The desire to do work leads more and more to the truth and to the laws and prescriptions of nature, which are truths".
- Thomas Carlyle, *Working and not Despairing*, 1843

5. Labour is a Coercive Social Principle
Labour is in no way identical with humans transforming nature (matter) and interacting with each other. As long as mankind exist, they will build houses, produce clothing, food and many other things. They will raise children, write books, discuss, cultivate gardens, and make music and much more. This is banal and self-evident. However, the raising of human activity as such, the pure expenditure of 'labour power' to an abstract principle governing social relations without regard to its content and independent of the needs and will of the participants, is not self-evident.

It fell to the modern commodity producing system as an end-in-itself, with its ceaseless transformation of human energy into money, to bring about a separated sphere of so-called labour 'alienated' from all other social relations and abstracted from all content. It is a sphere demanding of its inmates unconditional surrender, life-to-rule, dependent robotic activity severed from any other social context, and obedience to an abstract 'economic' instrumental rationality beyond human needs. In this sphere detached from life, time ceases to be lived and experienced time. Rather, time becomes mere raw material to be exploited optimally: 'Time is Money'. Every second of life is charged to a time account, every trip to the loo is an offence, and every moment of gossip is a crime against the production goal that has made itself independent. Where labour is going on, only abstract energy may be spent. Life takes place elsewhere, or nowhere, because labour beats time round the clock. Even children are drilled to obey Newtonian time to become 'effective' members of the workforce in their future life. Leave of absence is granted merely to restore an individual's 'labour power'. When having a meal, celebrating or making love, the second hand is ticking at the back of one's mind.

"The worker (lit. labourer) feels to be himself outside work and feels outside himself when working. He is at home when he does not work. When he works, he is not at home. As a result, his work is forced labour, not voluntary labour. Forced labour is not the satisfaction of a need but only a means for satisfying needs outside labour. Its foreignness appears in

that labour is avoided as a plague as soon as no physical or other force exists".
- Karl Marx, *Economic-Philosophical Manuscripts*, 1844

6. Labour and Capital are Two Sides of the Same Coin

From the standpoint of labour, the qualitative content of production counts as little as it does from the standpoint of capital. The only point of interest is selling labour power at best price. The idea of determining the aim and object of human activity by joint decision is beyond the imagination of the treadmill inmates. If the hope ever existed that such self-determination of social reproduction could be realized in the forms of the commodity producing system, the 'workforce' has long forgotten about this illusion. Only 'employment' or 'occupation' is a matter of concern; the connotations of these terms speak volumes about the end-in-itself character of the whole arrangement.

The ruling idol knows how to enforce its 'subjectless' (Marx) will by means of the 'silent (implied) compulsion' of competition to which even the powerful must bow, especially if they manage hundreds of factories and shift billions across the globe. If they don't 'do business', they will be scrapped as ruthlessly as the superfluous 'labour force'. Kept as they are in the leading strings of intransigent systemic constraints, this is what makes them a public menace, and not some conscious will to exploit others. Least of all are they allowed to ask about the meaning and consequences of their restless action. They cannot afford emotions or compassion. Therefore they call it realism when they devastate the world and disfigure urban features, and they only shrug their shoulders when their fellow beings are impoverished in the midst of affluence.

"More and more labour has the good conscience on its side: The inclination for leisure is called 'need of recovery' and begins to feel ashamed of itself. 'It is just for the sake of health', they defend themselves when caught at a country outing. It could happen to be in the near future that succumbing to a 'vita contemplativa' (i.e. to go for a stroll together with friends to contemplate life) will lead to self-contempt and a guilty conscience".
- Friedrich Nietzsche, *Leisure and Idleness*, 1882

7. Labour is Patriarchal Rule

It is not possible to subject every sphere of social life or all essential human activities to the rule of abstract (Newtonian) time, even if the intrinsic logic of labour, inclusive of the transformation of the latter into 'money-substance', insists on it. Consequently, alongside the 'separated' sphere of labour, so to say at its rear, the sphere of home life, family life, and intimacy came into being.

It was no accident that the image of the somewhat primitive, instinct-driven, irrational, and emotional woman only solidified along with the image of the civilized, rational and self-restrained male workaholic, and became mass prejudice. It was also no accident that the self-drill of the white man, who went into some sort of mental boot camp training to cope with the exacting demands of labour and, pertinently, its human resource management, coincided with a brutal witch-hunt that raged for some centuries.

The modern understanding and appropriation of the world by means of (natural) scientific thought, a way of thinking that was gaining ground then, was contaminated by the social end-in-itself and its gender attributes down to the roots. This way, the white man, in order to ensure his smooth functioning, subjected himself to a self-exorcism of all evil spirits, namely those frames of mind and emotional needs that are considered to be dysfunctional in the realms of labour.

In the twentieth century, especially in the post-war democracies of Fordism, women were increasingly recruited to the labour system, which only resulted in some specific female schizophrenic mind. On the one hand, the advance of women into the sphere of labour has not led to their liberation, but subjected them to very same drill procedures for the labour idol as already suffered by men. On the other hand, as the systemic structure of 'segregation' was left untouched, the separated sphere of 'female labour' continued to exist extrinsic to what is officially deemed to be 'labour'. This way, women were subjected to a double-burden and exposed to conflicting social imperatives. Within the sphere of labour – until now – they are predominantly confined to the low-wage sector and to subordinate jobs.

Due to the systemic constraints of the labour society and its total usurpation of the individual in particular – entailing his or her unconditional surrender to the systemic logic, and mobility and obedience to the capitalist time regime – in society as a whole, the sacred bourgeois sphere of so-called private life and 'holy family' is eroded and degraded more and more. Patriarchy is not abolished, but runs wild in the unacknowledged crisis of the labour society. As the commodity-producing system gradually collapses, women are made responsible for survival in any respect, while the 'masculine' world indulges in the prolonging of the categories of the labour society by means of simulation.

"Mankind had to horribly mutilate itself to create its identical, functional, male self, and some of it has to be redone in everybody's childhood".
- Max Horkheimer/ Theodor W. Adorno, *Dialectic of Enlightenment*

8. Labour is the Service of Humans in Bondage
The identity of labour and bondman existence can be shown factually and conceptually. Only a few centuries ago, people were quite aware of the connection between labour and social constraints. In most European languages, the term 'labour' originally referred only to the activities carried out by humans in bondage, i.e. bondmen, serfs, and slaves. In Germanic speaking areas, the word described the drudgery of an orphaned child fallen into serfdom. The Latin verb *laborare* meant 'staggering under a heavy burden', and conveyed the suffering and toil of slaves. The Romance words *travail*, *trabajo*, etc., derive from the Latin *tripalium*, a kind of yoke used for the torture and punishment of slaves and other humans in bondage. A hint of that suffering is still discernible in the German idiom "to bend under the yoke of labour".

Thus 'labour', according to its root, is not a synonym for self-determined human activity, but refers to an unfortunate social fate. It is the activity of those who have lost their freedom. The imposition of labour on all members of society is nothing but the generalization of a life in bondage; and the modern worship of labour is merely the quasi-religious transfiguration of actual social conditions.

For individuals, however, it became possible to repress the conjunction between labour and bondage successfully and to internalize social impositions because in the developing commodity producing system, the generalization of labour was accompanied by its reification: Most people were no longer under the thumb of a personal master. Human interdependence transformed into a social totality of abstract domination, discernible everywhere, but proving elusive. Where everyone has become a slave, everyone is simultaneously a master – that is to say a slaver of his own person and his very own slave driver and warder. All obey the opaque system idol, the 'Big Brother' of capital valorization, who harnessed them to the 'tripalium'.

9. The Bloody History of Labour

The history of the modern age is the history of the enforcement of labour, which brought devastation and horror to the planet in its trail. The imposition to waste most of one's lifetime under abstract systemic orders was not always as internalized as today. Rather, it took several centuries of brute force and violence on a large scale to literally torture people into the unconditional service of the labour idol.

It did not start with some 'innocent' market expansion meant to increase 'the wealth' of his or her majesty's subjects, but with the insatiable hunger for money of the absolutist apparatus of the state in order to finance early modern military machinery. The development of urban merchants and financial capital beyond traditional trade relations only accelerated through this apparatus, and this brought the whole of society in a bureaucratic stranglehold for the first time in history. Only in this way did money become a central social motive, and the abstraction of labour a central social constraint without regard to actual needs.

Most people didn't voluntarily change over to production for anonymous markets, and thereby to a general cash economy. They were forced to do so because the absolutist hunger for money led to the levy of pecuniary and ever-increasing taxes, replacing traditional payment in kind. It was not that people had to 'earn money' for themselves, but for the militarized early modern firearm-state, its logistics, and its bureaucracy. This way the absurd end-in-itself of capital valorization, and thus of labour, came into the world.

Only after a short time, however, revenue became insufficient. The absolutist bureaucrats and finance capital administrators began to forcibly and directly organize people as the material of a 'social machinery' for the transformation of labour into money. The traditional way of life and existence was vandalized, and the population earmarked as the human material for the valorization machine put on steam. Peasants and yeomen were driven from their fields by force of arms to clear space for sheep farming, which produced the raw material for the wool manufactories. Traditional rights like free hunting, fishing, and wood gathering in the forests were abolished. When the impoverished then marched through the land begging and stealing, they were locked up in workhouses and manufactories and abused with labour torture machines to beat the slave consciousness of a submissive serf into them. The floating rumour that people gave up their traditional life of their own accord to join the armies of labour on account of the beguiling prospects of labour society is a downright lie.

The gradual transformation of their subjects into material for the money-generating labour idol was not enough to satisfy the absolutist monster states. They extended their claim to other continents. Europe's inner colonization was accompanied by outer colonization; first in the Americas, then in parts of Africa. Here the whip masters of labour finally cast aside all scruples. In an unprecedented crusade of looting, destruction and genocide, they assaulted the newly 'discovered' worlds – the victims overseas were not even considered to be human. The cannibalistic European powers of the dawning labour society defined the subjugated foreign cultures as 'savages' and cannibals.

This provided the justification to exterminate or enslave millions of them. Slavery in the colonial plantations and raw materials 'industry' – to an extent exceeding ancient slaveholding by far – was one of the founding crimes of the commodity-producing system. Here 'extermination by means of labour' was realized on a large scale for the first time. This was the second foundational crime of the labour society. The white man, already branded by the ravages of self-discipline, could compensate for his repressed self-hatred and inferiority complex by taking it out on the 'savages'. Like 'the woman', indigenous people were deemed to be primitive halflings, ranking between animals and humans. It was Immanuel Kant's keen conjecture that baboons could talk if they only wanted and didn't speak because they feared being dragged off to labour.

Civilization in this sense means the voluntary submission to labour; and labour is male, white and 'Western'. The opposite, the non-human, amorphous, and uncivilized nature, is female, coloured and 'exotic', and thus to be kept in bondage. In a word, the 'universality' of the labour society is perfectly racist in its origin. The universal abstraction of labour can always only define itself by demarcating itself from everything that can't be squared within its own categories.

The modern bourgeoisie, who ultimately inherited absolutism, is not a descendant of the peaceful merchants who once travelled the old trading routes. Rather it was the bunch of Condottieri, early modern mercenary gangs, poorhouse overseers, penitentiary wards, the whole lot of farmers general, slave drivers and other cutthroats of this sort, who prepared the social hotbed for modern 'entrepreneurship'. The bourgeois revolutions of the eighteenth and nineteenth centuries had nothing to do with social emancipation. They only restructured the balance of power within the arising coercive system, separated the institutions of the labour society from antiquated dynastic interests and pressed ahead with reification and depersonalization. It was the glorious French revolution that histrionically proclaimed compulsory labour, enacted a law on the 'elimination of begging' and arranged for new labour penitentiaries without delay.

This was the exact opposite of what was struggled for by rebellious social movements of a different character flaring up on the fringes of the bourgeois revolutions. Completely autonomous forms of resistance and disobedience existed long before, but the official historiography of the modern labour society cannot make sense of it. The producers of the old agrarian societies, who never put up with feudal rule completely, were simply not willing to come to terms with the prospect of forming the working class of a system extrinsic to their life. An uninterrupted chain of events, from the peasants' revolts of the fifteenth and sixteenth centuries, the Luddite uprisings in Britain, later on denounced as the revolt of backwards fools, to the Silesian weavers' rebellion in 1844, gives evidence for the embittered resistance against labour. Over the last centuries, the enforcement of the labour society and the sometimes open and sometimes latent civil war were one and the same.

"The barbarian is lazy and differs from the scholar by musing apathetically, since practical culture means to busy oneself out of habit and to feel a need for occupation".
Georg W. F. Hegel, *General outlines of the Philosophy of Right*, 1821

"Actually one begins to feel ... that this kind of labour is the best police conceivable, because it keeps a tight rein on everybody hindering effectively the evolution of sensibility, aspiration, and the desire for independence. For labour consumes nerve power to an extraordinary extent, depleting the latter as to contemplation, musing, dreaming, concern, love, hatred".
- Friedrich Nietzsche, *The Eulogists of Labour*, 1881

10. The Working Class Movement was a Movement for Labour
The historical working class movement, which did not rise until long after the fall of the old social revolts, did not any longer struggle against the impositions of labour but developed an over-identification with the seemingly inevitable. The movement's focus was on workers' 'rights', and the amelioration of living conditions within the reference system of the labour society whose social constraints were largely internalized. Instead of radically criticising the transformation of human energy into money as an irrational end-in-itself, the workers' movement took the 'standpoint of labour' and understood capital valorization as a neutral given fact.

Thus the workers' movement stepped into the shoes of absolutism, Protestantism and bourgeois Enlightenment. The misfortune of labour was converted into the false pride of labour, redefining the domestication the fully-fledged working class had gone through for the purposes of the modern idol, into a 'human right'. The domesticated helots, so to speak, ideologically turned the tables and developed a missionary fervour to demand both the 'right to work' and a general 'obligation to work'. They didn't fight the bourgeois in their capacity as the executives of the labour society but abused them, just the other way around, in the name of labour, by calling them parasites. Without exception, all members of society should be forcibly recruited to the 'armies of labour'.

The workers' movement itself became the pacemaker of the capitalist labour society, enforcing the last stages of reification within the labour system's development process and prevailing against the narrow-minded bourgeois officials of the nineteenth and early twentieth century. It was a process quite similar to what had happened only a hundred years before when the bourgeoisie stepped into the shoes of absolutism. This was only possible because the workers' parties and trade unions, due to their deification of labour, relied on the state machinery and its institutions of repressive labour management in an affirmative way. That's why it never occurred to them to abolish the state-run administration of human material and, simultaneously, the state itself. Instead of that, they were eager to seize the systemic power by means of what they called 'the march through the institutions' (in

Germany). Thereby, like the bourgeoisie had done earlier, the workers' movement adopted the bureaucratic tradition of labour management and storekeeping of human resources, once conjured up by absolutism.

"Labour has to wield the sceptre,
Serfdom shall be the idlers fate,
Labour has to rule the world as
Labour is the essence of the world".
- Friedrich Stampfer, *Der Arbeit Ehre* (*In Honour of Labour*), 1903

11. The Crisis of Labour

For a short historical moment after the Second World War, it seemed that the labour society, based on Fordistic industries, had consolidated into a system of 'eternal prosperity', pacifying the unbearable end-in-itself by means of mass consumption and welfare state amenities. Apart from the fact that this idea was always an idea of democratic helots – meant to become reality only for a small minority of world population – it has turned out to be foolish even in the capitalist centres. With the third industrial revolution of microelectronics, the labour society reached its absolute historical barrier.

That this barrier would be reached sooner or later was logically foreseeable. From birth, the commodity-producing system suffers from a fatal contradiction in terms. On the one hand, it lives on the massive intake of human energy generated by the expenditure of pure labour power – the more the better. On the other hand, the law of operational competition enforces a permanent increase in productivity bringing about the replacement of human labour power by scientific operational industrial capital.

This contradiction in terms was in fact the underlying cause for all of the earlier crises, among them the disastrous world economic crisis of 1929-33. Due to a mechanism of compensation, it was possible to get over those crises time and again. After a certain incubation period, then based on the higher level of productivity attained, the expansion of the market to fresh groups of buyers led to an intake of more labour power in absolute numbers than was previously rationalized away. Less labour power had to be spent per product, but more goods were produced absolutely to such an extent that this reduction was overcompensated. As long as product innovations exceeded process innovations, it was possible to transform the self-contradiction of the system into an expansion process.

The striking historical example is the automobile. Due to the assembly line and other techniques of 'Taylorism' ('work-study expertise'), first introduced in Henry Ford's auto factory in Detroit, the necessary labour time per auto was reduced to a fraction. Simultaneously, the working process was enormously condensed, so that the human material was drained many times over the previous level in ratio to the same labour time interval. Above all, the car, up to then a luxury article for the upper ten thousand, could be made available to mass consumption due to the lower price.

This way the insatiable appetite of the labour idol for human energy was satisfied at a higher level despite rationalized assembly line production in the times of the second industrial revolution of 'Fordism'. At the same time, the auto is a case in point for the destructive character of the highly developed mode of production and consumption in the labour society. In the interest of the mass production of cars and private car use on a huge scale, the landscape is being buried under concrete and the environment is being polluted. And people have resigned to the undeclared third world war raging on the roads and routes of this world – a war claiming millions of casualties, wounded and maimed year in, year out – by just shrugging it off.

The mechanism of compensation becomes defunct in the course of the third industrial revolution of microelectronics. It is true that through microelectronics many products were reduced in price and new products were created (above all in the area of the media). However, for the first time, the speed of process innovation is greater than the speed of product innovation. More labour is rationalized away than can be reabsorbed by the expansion of markets. As a logical consequence of rationalization, electronic robotics replaces human energy, and new communication technology makes labour superfluous. Entire sectors and departments of construction, production, marketing, warehousing, distribution, and management vanish into thin air. For the first time, the labour idol unintentionally confines itself to permanent hunger rations, thereby bringing about its very own death.

As the democratic labour society is a mature end-in-itself system of self-referential labour power expenditure, working like a feedback circuit, it is impossible to switch over to a general reduction in working hours within its form. On the one hand, economic administrative rationality requires that an ever-increasing number of people become permanently 'jobless' and cut off from the reproduction of their life as inherent in the system. On the other hand, the constantly decreasing number of 'employees' is suffering from overwork, and is subject to an even more intense efficiency pressure. In the midst of wealth, poverty and hunger are coming home to the capitalist centres. Production plants are shut down, and large parts of arable land lie fallow. A great number of homes and public buildings are vacant, whereas the number of homeless persons is on the increase. Capitalism becomes a global minority event.

In its distress, the dying labour idol has become auto-cannibalistic. In search of remaining labour 'food', capital breaks up the boundaries of national economy and globalizes by means of nomadic cutthroat competition. Entire regions of the world are cut off from the global flows of capital and commodities. In an unprecedented wave of mergers and 'hostile takeovers', global players get ready for the final battle of private entrepreneurship. The disorganized states and nations implode, their populations, driven mad by the struggle for survival, attack each other in ethnic gang wars.

"The basic moral principle is the right of the person to his work ... For me there is nothing more detestable than an idle life. None of us has a right to that. Civilization has no room for idlers".
- Henry Ford

"Capital itself is the moving contradiction, [in] that it presses to reduce labour time to a minimum, while it posits labour time, on the other side, as sole measure and source of wealth. ... On the one side, then, it calls to life all the powers of science and of nature, as of social

combination and of social intercourse, in order to make the creation of wealth independent (relatively) of the labour time employed on it. On the other side, it wants to use labour time as the measuring rod for the giant social forces thereby created, and to confine them within the limits required to maintain the already created value as value".
- Karl Marx, *Foundation of the Critique of Political Economy*, 1857/8

12. The End of Politics
Necessarily, the crisis of labour entails the crisis of state and politics. In principle, the modern state owes its career to the fact that the commodity producing system is in need of an overarching authority guaranteeing the general preconditions of competition, the general legal foundations, and the preconditions for the valorization process – inclusive of a repression apparatus in case human material defaults the systemic imperatives and becomes insubordinate. Organising the masses in the form of bourgeois democracy, the state had to increasingly take on socio-economic functions in the twentieth century. Its function is not limited to the provision of social services but comprises public health, transportation, communication and postal services, as well as infrastructures of all kind. The latter state-run or state-supervised services are essential for the working of the labour society, but cannot be organized as a private enterprise valorization process; 'privatized' public services are most often nothing but state consumption in disguise. The reason for this is that such infrastructure must be available for society as a whole on a permanent basis, and cannot follow the market cycles of supply and demand.

As the state is not a valorization unit on its own, and thus not able to transform labour into money, it has to skim off money from the actual valorization process to finance its state functions. If the valorization of value comes to a standstill, the coffers of state empty. The state, purported to be the social sovereign, proves to be completely dependent on the blindly raging, fetishized economy specific to the labour society. The state may pass as many bills as it wants; if the forces of production (the general powers of humanity) outgrow the system of labour, positive law – constituted and applicable only in relation to the subjects of labour – leads nowhere.

This essay is an edited version. The full text is available at
http://www.giga.or.at/others/krisis/manifesto-against-labour.html

Digital Declaration

THE INFOSSIL CORRECTIVE

<WE HAVE MUTATED FROM COLLECTIVE, CONNECTIVE TO CORRECTIVE. LET US CORRECT YOU, BEFORE IT IS TOO LATE!>

<ART IS ONLY GOOD FOR ENTERTAINING THE TROOPS IN TIMES OF CRISIS.>

<IN TIMES OF PEACE, ARTISTS BEHAVE IN AFFIRMATIVE MANNERS.>

<ARTISTS ARE THE WEAKEST TRIBE, FIGHTING THEIR OWN SHADOWS.>

<MEDIA ART HAS THE PALEST FACE OF ALL.>

<DIGITAL ART HAS ONLY BEEN UNDER-STOOD BY ITS CHINESE INVENTORS, AND POSSIBLY, BY BINARY MR LEIBNIZ.>

<COMPUTERS NEED SO MUCH ENERGY FOR PRODUCTION AND OPERATION THAT GLACIERS WILL MELT.>

<SOFTWARE IS A BLIND BORN VIRUS.>

<EMAIL IS A LAME TIME BOMB.>

<ALL HARDWARE IS SIN AND WILL ROT.>

<THE INTERNET SPAMS SO MUCH FOSSIL
ENERGY THAT THE SAHARA WILL REACH
YOUR GARDEN VERY SOON.>

<DOT MEANS TOD.[1]>

<DIGITAL MEANS FINGER. YOU HAVE 10
TO OPERATE 2 HANDS. DO SOME THING NOW!>

<MEDIA GIVES THE DEEPEST KISSES.
SAVE YOUR CHILDREN. MEDIA KISSING
IS SOUL-SUCKING DEEP!>

<MEDIA IS THE ANTICHRIST. DON'T
BELIEVE A WORD, THE WORD IS A WHORE.>

<UNPLUG NOW AND REVERSE THE STREAM.>

<YOU ARE NOT A NOMAD, JUST BECAUSE
YOU ARE SENT ALL OVER THE GLOBE WITH A
LAPTOP AND A MOBILE PHONE. NOMADS DON'T DIE AT HOME.
TAKE YOUR ANIMALS, CHILDREN AND GRANDPARENTS ALONG!>

<ENTER LIFE.>

<TRESPASS TERROR.>

1. TOD: DEATH [GERMAN]

CONTRIBUTORS (in alphabetical order)

Adrian Ward (Plymouth) is a software artist and musician. He creates auto-generative software artworks and performs music with Alex McLean under the name of Slub. His works include collaborative efforts with the likes of Stuart Brisley and Geoff Cox. He recently participated in the Generator touring exhibition, and has presented his work at venues like Transmediale (Berlin), Lovebytes (Sheffield), Rhizome (New York) and Sonic Acts (Amsterdam). He has awards from Transmediale and Real Software, and an honorary mention from the 2001 Prix Ars Electronica. www.adeward.com/biog.html, adrian@signwave.co.uk

Amy West has worked for ARTICLE 19, the Global Campaign for the Freedom of Expression, on media related issues in Africa. awest@kof-law.com

Anand Vivek Taneja (Delhi) describes himself as an 'unemployed bum' and is almost sure he likes being that way. Otherwise he is a writer, researcher, film-maker, photographer, historian, quizzer and (very occasional) transvestite. His areas of interest are urban histories and narratives, pop-culture as philosophy, and the histories and politics of 'fluid' identities. bulle_shah@hotmail.com

Anna Faroqhi (Berlin) is a filmmaker and a writer. She studied music and mathematics before training as a filmmaker at the Munich Film School. She has made several short and experimental films, exploring both narrative and essay forms. Her films have been shown at several international film festivals, including the Max Ophuls Festival, and the International Film Festival of Rotterdam. Her recent film *Waiting* is an essay on waiting for the war on Iraq to begin in Tel Aviv in the spring of 2003. AnnaFaroqhi@t-online.de

Annie Gell (Washington, DC/San Francisco) graduated from Columbia University cum laude in May 2003 with a major in US History. She has worked with Lawyers' Committee for Human Rights in Washington, DC, Médecins Sans Frontières in New York, and Sarai in Delhi. She plans to pursue a career in journalism and international human rights advocacy. anniegell@yahoo.com

Arundhati Roy (Delhi) is a writer. She has written extensively against nuclear weapons in South Asia, the displacement caused by big dams, corporate globalization and global militarism. Her collections of essays include *The Greater Common Good* and *The Algebra of Infinite Justice*. She won the Booker Prize for her novel *The God of Small Things*, in 1997. Arundhati Roy was recently awarded the Lannan Foundation Prize for Cultural Freedom (2003). smallthings@mantraonline.com

Arvind Narrain (Bangalore) studied Law at the National Law School, Bangalore and at Warwick University. He is presently working with the Alternative Law Forum as a practising advocate as well as a legal researcher interested in questions of law and exclusion. arvindnarrain@hotmail.com

Basharat Peer (Srinagar) is an independent journalist and writer. He has reported on the conflict in Kashmir for rediff.com and *India Abroad* news weekly. His work has appeared in the *Guardian* and *Financial Times Magazines*. He is working on a book about Kashmir. basharatpeer@rediffmail.com

Batul Mukhtiar (Mumbai) studied at the Film & TV Institute of India, Pune. She has worked as researcher and 'fixer' on international documentaries filming in Mumbai, for Channel 4 and BBC, U.K. Her films include16 4-minute documentaries on Mumbai for an internet channel, EVEO, California and the independent docu-feature *150 Seconds Ago* on life in Bhuj after the earthquake in January 2001. shootoutfilms@hotmail.com

Beatriz Da Costa (Irvine) is a Machine Artist and Tactical Media Practitioner. Besides her collaborations with Jamie Schulte and Brooke Singer, she has worked with Critical Art Ensemble since summer 2000 and taken part in the development and implementation of various bio-tech initiatives and models of contestational science. Her work has been exhibited at the New Museum in New York, ISEA in Japan and the World Information Organization in Belgrade. She recently joined the faculty of UC Irvine as an Assistant Professor of Studio Art,

Electrical Engineering and Computer Science. www.beatrizdacosta.net, beatrizdacosta@earthlink.net

Bhrigupati Singh (Baltimore) is doing his PhD in Social Anthropology at Johns Hopkins University in the US. Before this, he studied in Delhi and London, and worked at Sarai-CSDS. bhrigupati@hotmail.com

Brooke Singer (New York) is a digital media artist and curator. She has exhibited and lectured throughout the US and internationally. With NYC Wireless (www.nycwireless.net) Brooke is co-producing "Art in the Wireless Park" events, bringing net art off the screen and into public spaces. She was recently appointed Assistant Professor of New Media at SUNY Purchase.www.bsing.net, brooke@bsing.net

Christiane Brosius (Frankfurt) teaches at the South Asia Institute, Karls Ruprecht University, Heidelberg. She has written *Empowering Visions: The Politics of Representations in Hindu Nationalism* (Anthem Press, 2003) and co-edited (with Melissa Butcher) *Image Journeys: Audio Visual Media and Cultural Change in India* (Sage Publications, 1999). chbrosius_4@hotmail.com

Computing Culture Group (Boston) is an art/technology/activism research group within the MIT Media Lab. Recent projects include the DJ I Robot Sound System, Government Information Awareness, Critical Cartographies, Doom Monitor, Haptic Opposition, and the Afghan Explorer. The group is led by Chris Csikszentmihályi. http://compcult.media.mit.edu

Dakshinpuri Cybermohalla Media Lab (Delhi) The second Cybermohalla Media Lab was set up in the working class resettlement colony, Dakshinpuri, in June 2002. Dakshinpuri emerged as a colony during the Emergency in the mid-seventies. At present there are twelve practitioners at the lab, experimenting with different media forms.

Kiran Verma has been with the media lab since it was set up. She enjoys writing, and is currently part of a team working towards a tech-manual for young people interested in information technology.

Lakhmi Chand Kohli is a prolific and popular story teller. He weaves his stories from everyday encounters in his locality and the city. He is part of the team working on the tech-manual.

Rakesh Kumar has been with the lab for the last six months. An acute and sensitive observer of social relations, his writings are an attempt to think about the incongruities, ambiguities and brutalities of life.

Sudip Das has just finished his formal school education and is now working to support his family. He was at the lab for a brief period, during which he built long-term friendships with the other practitioners.

Daisy Hasan (Shillong) is currently pursuing a PhD on Television and Regional Identity at the University of Wales. daisyhasan@yahoo.co.uk

Daphne Meijer (Amsterdam) works as a novelist, reporter and documentary filmmaker for various Dutch media. She and her Afghan husband have spent 2003 living in Kabul and Delhi, where she is trying to finish two long overdue books. meije548@wxs.nl

Darshan Desai (Ahmedabad) has been covering Gujarat for the past 15 years, primarily with *The Indian Express*, but currently as a Special Correspondent with *Outlook*. He has covered all the major calamities that have struck Gujarat during this period, including the recent communal violence, the 2001 earthquake, the 1994 plague in Surat, and the post-Ayodhya violence of 1992. darshan104@rediffmail.com

David Garcia (Amsterdam) is a visual artist, conference organiser, critic, teacher, and co-founder and organizer of The Next 5 Minutes festival of Tactical Media. Currently he is a Professor of Design for Digital Cultures, University of Portsmouth/Hoogschool voor de Kunst Utrecht. davidg@xs4all.nl

Debjani Sengupta (Delhi) works as a translator and teacher of Literatures in English. Her edited and translated works include *Mapmaking: Partition Stories from Two Bengals* and *Selected Columns of Taslima Nasreen*. debjanisgupta@yahoo.com

Dr. Craig Etcheson (Takoma Park, Maryland) is an internationally recognized authority on Cambodian history and politics, and has been working for more than a decade to prepare a formal judicial accounting of crimes perpetrated during Cambodia's Khmer Rouge regime between 1975 and 1979. He is an independent consultant on the challenges of transitional justice and reconciliation. etcheson@ix.netcom.com

Geoff Cox (Plymouth) is an artist, teacher, projects organizer and Senior Lecturer in Computing, Communications & Electronics, at University of Plymouth, UK, where he is a member of the STAR (Science Technology Art Research) research group. He co-curated the touring exhibition 'Generator' (2002-3) with Spacex Gallery. www.generative.net/generator. He is now working on 'Vivaria', www.vivaria.net, engaging with ideas around artificial life. www.anti-thesis.net/, geoff@generative.net

Hansa Thapliyal (Bombay) is a filmmaker. She is currently working on a visual documentary archiving project with Majlis, Mumbai. She is interested in developing ways to look at story telling. hansatin@yahoo.com.in

Iftikhar Gilani (Delhi) is Bureau Chief (Delhi) of *Kashmir Times*, the largest circulated daily of Jammu & Kashmir headquartered at Jammu. He also works for *Radio Deutsche Welle* and is a regular contributer to *Daily Times* and *The Friday Times*, both highly acclaimed publications in Pakistan. iftikhar@vsnl.com

Infossil Corrective http://digital-log.hfg-karlsruhe.de/combinatoria/archives/cat_manifest.html

Ivo Skoric (Rutland, Vermont) is part of the Balkans Program and founding director of RACCOON, Inc. He is a widely published journalist (including BBC), web-master, and media activist. In New York he has produced dozens of cable programs including *Hrvatski Monitor*. He is the innovator of the Cyber-Yugo project and his hope is to serve as a vehicle for young Balkan exiles to set aside their grievances towards each other, begin to listen to their personal voices, and look at each other in a different light. ivo@balkansnet.org

Jamie Schulte (Palo Alto) is an engineer with an interest in designing systems that engage human aesthetics, culture, and politics. He received a Masters degrees in Electrical and Computer Engineering and in Knowledge Discovery and Data Mining (KDD) from Carnegie Mellon University. He is currently a robotics researcher at Stanford University. He has exhibited work throughout the US as well as internationally including Canada, Germany, Austria, England and Brazil. jscw+@andrew.cmu.edu

Janko Röttgers (Los Angeles) lives and works as a journalist and book author. In 2001, together with Armin Medosch, he co-edited *Netzpiraten*, a book about the culture of electronic crime. In 2003, his book *Mix Burn & R.I.P.* came out in Germany. www.lowpass.de, roettgers@lowpass.de

Joasia Krysa (Plymouth) is a curator at i-DAT (Institute of Digital Art and Technology) and Senior Lecturer in Interactive Media at the Computing, Communications & Electronics, University of Plymouth, UK. Currently she is researching in issues around digital curating at STAR (Science, Technology, Art Research). Most recently, she has co-curated conferences including 'Hybrid-Discourse' www.i-dat.org/projects/hybrid, 'anti-globalika: tensions in the new global disorder' (for WRO 03 Media Art Biennale, Poland) wrocenter.pl, and 'Artist as Engineer' (as part of 'Interrupt' symposia organised by Arts Council England) www.interrupt-symposia.org. http://x.i-dat.org/~jk/, joasia@CAIIA-STAR.NET

Gruppe Krisis Over and against the concepts of class and labour cultivated by labour movements as well as social-democratic parties, the work of the German Krisis Gruppe, a loose network of Marxist critics and theorists founded in 1986 to create "a theoretical forum for the rearticulation of radical social critique", retrieves a 'darker' and 'esoteric' Marx to offer a fundamental critique of labour and value. Authors associated with Krisis, including Robert Kurz, Ernst Lohoff, Franz Schandl, and Norbert Trenkle, draw on Marx's critique of commodity fetishism, situationism, and critical theory, as well as the writings of Alfred Sohn-Rethel and Moishe Postone. Krisis publishes a semi-annual magazine; see materials at www.krisis.org.

Kristian Lukic (Belgrade) is cultural worker and researcher and founder of Eastwood Real Time Strategy

Group. He is program developer in the new media centre kuda.org, Novi Sad, Serbia & Montenegro. www.eastwood-group.net, www.kuda.org, krist@neobee.net

Lawrence Liang (Bangalore) is a legal researcher with the Alternative Law Forum. He is currently working in collaboration with Sarai on a project that seeks to interrogate the politics of media and intellectual property laws. lawrenceliang99@yahoo.com

Lyn Graybill (Charlottesville) holds a PhD in Foreign Affairs from the University of Virginia and is a faculty member of UVA's Centre for the Study of Mind & Human Interaction (CSMHI). She is the author of *The South African Truth and Reconciliation Commission: Miracle or Model?, Religion and Resistance Politics in South Africa*, and editor (with Kenneth Thompson) of *Africa's Second Wave of Freedom: Development, Democracy and Rights*. graybill@peoplepc.com

Mahmoud Eid (Ottawa) is Doctoral Fellow and lecturer of International Communication at Carleton University. His publications and research interests include mass media and telecommunications, crisis management and conflict resolution, modernity, and the political economy of communication. mafeid@hotmail.com

Martin Hardie (Maputo/Durango) is a bit of a nomad. He has managed bands, worked in Aboriginal Art centres, been a solicitor, a barrister, an advisor to various members of the former East Timorese resistance, and a university lecturer. He currently spends his time as a moderator of the nettime list, undertaking his post-graduate research work and fulfilling his duties as a correspondent for www.cyclingnews.com. His ambition is to become the archetype of life within communism – at the break of dawn a cyclist, during the day a cook, cyber-conspiracist and correspondent, in the afternoons a student and philosopher and, at nights, simply pleasant company. auskadi@tvcabo.co.mz

Martin Shaw (Brighton) is Professor of International Relations and Politics at the University of Sussex, in Brighton, England. He is the author of many books on the sociology of war and global politics, mostly recently *War and Genocide* (Polity 2003), *Theory of the Global State* (Cambridge University Press 2000) and *Civil Society and Media in Global Crises* (Pinter 1996). m.shaw@sussex.ac.uk

Meena Nanji (Los Angeles/New Delhi) is an independent videomaker, freelance writer and curator currently based in Los Angeles and New Delhi. Her experimental video work deals with representations of race and culture. deluxo2000@yahoo.com

Muzamil Jaleel (Srinagar) is the Srinagar bureau chief of *The Indian Express*. He has written extensively on human rights issues related to Kashmir for *The Indian Express* and *The Guardian* (UK). He has been involved in training programmes for journalists on human rights issues. muzamiljaleel@hotmail.com

Nancy Adajania (Bombay) is a cultural theorist, art critic and independent curator. She has written and lectured on contemporary Indian art, especially new media art and its contexts. Venues include Documenta 11, Kassel; Zentrum für Kunst und Medien, Karlsruhe; the Transmediale, Berlin; the Danish Contemporary Art Foundation, Copenhagen; and Lottringer 13, Munich. She was Editor-in-Chief of *Art India*. Adajania is co-curator for the exhibition *Zoom! Art in Contemporary India* (Lisbon, April 2004). nancyadajania71@yahoo.co.uk

Nandita Haksar (Delhi) is a human rights activist and Supreme Court lawyer. She was a professor in law in the National Law School, Bangalore and the Law College, Cochin. She was in the legal defence team during the SAR Geelani trial and is a member of the All India Defence Committee for SAR Geelani. Nandita Haksar has documented human rights violations on the marginalized and oppressed by leading or being part of many fact-finding teams. Her consistent fight has brought the issue of gross human rights violations by the army on the people in the North-East to the centre of attention to democratic sections within India. hakhon239@yahoo.co.in

Nitin Govil (Charlottesville) is Assistant Professor of Media Studies and Sociology at the University of

Virginia. He is finishing his doctoral dissertation on Hollywood in India at New York University. npg1@nyu.edu

Oliver Ressler (Vienna) is an artist whose work includes exhibitions, site-specific projects and videos on issues such as racism, economic globalization, genetic engineering and forms of resistance. His recent ongoing exhibition project, "Alternative Economics, Alternative Societies", has been realized in Galerija Skuc in Ljubljana (SI) and Kunstraum Lueneburg (G). www.ressler.at, oliver.ressler@chello.at

Omar Kutty (Delhi/Chicago) is a Ph.D. candidate in Anthropology at the University of Chicago. He is currently conducting his fieldwork in Delhi on the Valmiki community and its relationship to the Indian welfare state. omarkutty7@yahoo.com

Paul Chan (New York) is an artist and a member of the Iraq Peace Team, a project of Voices in the Wilderness, a campaign to end the sanctions against Iraq. Chan's video work is distributed by Video Data Bank (www.vdb.org) and his new media work is at www.nationalphilistine.com. manwichartist@yahoo.com

Rachel Corrie (1979-2003) was a student at Evergreen State College in Olympia, Washington, USA. She joined the Palestinian-led organization 'The International Solidarity Movement' through the group 'Olympians for Peace and Solidarity'. The organization uses non-violent means to challenge Israeli army tactics in the West Bank and Gaza. Rachel was killed by an Israeli army bulldozer in the town of Rafah on March 16, 2003. Emails to her parents can be sent to rachelsmessage@the-corries.com. www.rachelcorrie.org

Ranjani Mazumdar (Delhi) is an independent filmmaker, film scholar and visiting faculty at the AJK Mass Communication Research Centre at Jamia Millia Islamia, Delhi. She is currently a fellow at the Shellby Cullom Davis Centre for Historical Studies at Princeton University (2003-04). Her publications and films focus on women's issues, popular cinema, politics, and everyday lives. Currently she is working on a historical study of the Bombay Film Poster funded by the India Foundation for the Arts, as well as a co-authored book on contemporary Indian film industry commissioned by the British Film Institute. rmazumdar2002@yahoo.com

Ranjit Hoskote (Bombay) is a cultural theorist and poet. He is the author of three collections of poetry, a biography of a distinguished Indian painter, a co-translation of the work of a regional poet, and an anthology of contemporary Indian poetry in English. His research interests include the relationship between globalization and the politics of neo-tribalism, and the development of urban cultural forms at the cusp between postcoloniality and globalization. Hoskote is also Assistant Editor at *The Hindu*. ranjithoskote@rediffmail.com

Raqs Media Collective (Delhi) is a group of media practitioners, filmmakers and writers. They are co-initiators of Sarai, with Ravi Vasudevan and Ravi Sundaram. Their work includes the installations *5 Pieces of Evidence, Architecture for Temporary Autonomous Sarai* (with Atelier Bow Wow), *A/S/L, Co-ordinates 28.28N/77.15E::2001/2002* and *Location*[n]; *OPUS*, an online application for collaborative creation; the CD-Rom *Global Village Health Manual v1.0* (with Mritunjay Chatterjee), and the films *In the Eye of the Fish* and *Present Imperfect, Future Tense*. www.raqsmediacollective.net, www.opuscommons.net. raqs@sarai.net

Rehan Ansari (Lahore/Mumbai) has been Editor, Independent Press Association-New York. He also wrote a weekly column for *Mid-day* (Mumbai) about life in Lahore in the late 90s and then about life in New York post 9/11. Currently in and out of Mumbai, he will return to Lahore in the fall to teach at Beaconhouse National University. ansarirehan@hotmail.com

Renu Iyer (Delhi) studied fine arts at the Faculty of Fine Arts, MS University, Baroda. She is an artist and works at the Sarai Media Lab as a designer and interface animator. renu@sarai.net

Ricardo Rosas (São Paulo) is a writer, net critic and senior editor of *Rizoma* (www.rizoma.net), an electronic magazine about activism and tactical media. He was a co-organizer of the Tactical Media Lab in São Paulo and is currently working on projects involving mediactivism and tactical art. ricardorosas@uol.com.br

Sanjay Kak (New Delhi) is a filmmaker whose most recent film, *Words on Water*, is about the struggle against large dams in the Narmada valley. After making his way through mainstream television (where he produced news, game-shows and travelogues!) he has worked in documentary film for the last 15 years. He is active in the documentary film movement and the Campaign against Censorship. octave@vsnl.com

Sanjay Sharma (Delhi) is a historian teaching at Delhi University and Zakir Husain College, New Delhi. He is the author of *Famine, Philanthropy and the Colonial State: North India in the Early Nineteenth Century* and *Capitalism and Imperialism*, and co-editor of *Deewan-e-Sarai*. He was an Asia Fellow in 2003 based in Beijing, and has worked as a freelance journalist and a broadcaster for the BBC. sanjaykusharma@yahoo.co.in

Sasja Barentsen (Amsterdam) is an accidental photographer. sasja@echomania.com

Shahid Amin (Delhi) is Professor of History and Dean of the Faculty of Social Sciences, University of Delhi. Among his publications are *Event, Metaphor, Memory: Chauri Chaura, 1992-1995 (1995)*, and, as co-editor, *"Peripheral'" Labour? Studies in the History of Partial Proletarianization* (1997). He is a founding editor of the journal *Subaltern Studies*, and is currently working on a Concise Encyclopedia of North Indian Peasant Life. shahid@csdsdelhi.org

Shakeb Ahmed (Delhi) works as a freelance television cameraman and has travelled to Iraq, Afghanistan, Pakistan, UAE and Jordan on news assignments. He has a post-graduate degree in Mass Communication from MCRC, Jamia Millia Islamia, New Delhi. Currently a Sarai Independent Fellowship holder (2003-04), he is studying "Locally Produced Media and Associated Practices in Jamia Nagar and Satellite Colonies, Delhi". ahmedshakeb@angelfire.com

Shohini Ghosh (Delhi) teaches video at the Mass Communication Research Centre, Jamia Millia Islamia, Delhi. She is an independent filmmaker and a co-founder of the Media Storm Collective. Her recent film, *Tales of the Night Fairies*, looks at the life and work of sex workers in Kolkata. shohini@nda.vsnl.net.in

Soenke Zehle (Saarbruecken) teaches in the Transcultural Anglophone Studies (TAS) program at Saarland University, Saarbruecken, Germany, focusing on media studies and political ecology. soenke.zehle@web.de

Stephen Marshall (New York) is the co-founder and creative director of Guerrilla News Network, a net-based alternative to the corporate-owned news media. A writer and Sundance-award winning documentary film-maker, Stephen's work has focused on challenging the conventional approach to story-telling. Over the past fifteen years, he has worked and traveled in over 50 countries. stephen@gnn.tv

Subarno Chatterji (Delhi) is a Reader in the Department of English, University of Delhi. He received his PhD from the University of Oxford in American poetry and the Vietnam War. Recent publications include *Memories of a Lost War: American Poetic Responses to the Vietnam War* (2001). He is the co-editor of *India in the Age of Globalization: Social Discourses and Cultural Texts* (2003). subarno@mantraonline.com

Sudhir Krishnaswamy (Oxford) is a College Teaching Fellow in Law at Pembroke College, Oxford. His teaching and research interests include Public Law, Jurisprudence and Property Law. He is an Independent Research Fellow as part of the Sarai-CSDS/ALF project on 'Intellectual Property and the Knowledge/Culture Commons'. sudhir.krishnaswamy@law.oxford.ac.uk

Taran Khan (Aligarh) is an independent filmmaker and writer. She is currently based in Aligarh. 133344@soas.ac.uk

Tarun Bhartiya-Maithil (Bihar/Shillong) is a Hindi poet, videomaker (all kinds of videos considered) and a member of the freedom project and splitENDS media group. tarunbhartiya@rediffmail.com

Taslima Nasrin (Boston) is a Bangladeshi writer, medical doctor, and spokesperson for human rights. She was exiled from Bangladesh by a fundamentalist *fatwa* calling for her death, following the publication of her novel *Lajja*. She is currently a fellow at the Carr Center for Human Rights Policy at the Kennedy School of Government at Harvard University. Nasrin has been awarded the *Ananda Purashkar*, and the Sakharov Prize for Freedom of Thought. Her recent book *Dwikhandita* has been banned in Bangladesh and in West Bengal, India. www.taslimanasrin.org. Taslima_Nasrin@ksg.harvard.edu

Toby Miller (New York/Riverside) is the editor of *Television & New Media* and the author of several books on citizenship, culture, the media, and sport. He is moving from New York University to start a new Department of Media and Performance at the University of California, Riverside, in 2004. toby.miller@nyu.edu

Zainab Bawa (Mumbai) is currently based in Mumbai City but travels across the world. She is passionately interested in the issues of human communication and conflict resolution. She is a creative writer and aspires to develop innovative systems of human, economic and community development. She is currently a Sarai Independent Fellowship holder (2003-04). zainabbawa@yahoo.com

EDITORS (in alphabetical order)

Awadhendra Sharan (Delhi) is a historian and a Visiting Fellow at the Centre for the Study of Developing Societies. He is also a Fellow of the Sarai programme. He is currently working on a research project that connects environment and urban space, with reference to the city of Delhi. He also coordinates the archival activities at Sarai. sharan@sarai.net

Geert Lovink (Amsterdam) is a Dutch-Australian media theorist, activist and internet critic. He is currently lecturer/researcher at Amsterdam Polytechnic/University of Amsterdam. He is the co-founder of mailinglists such as Nettime and Fibreculture, the Australian network for new media research and culture and author of *Dark Fiber*, *Uncanny Networks* and *My First Recession*. geert@xs4all.nl

Jeebesh Bagchi (Delhi) is a media practitioner, researcher, artist and filmmaker with the Raqs Media Collective, and one of the initiators of Sarai. He has been coordinating the Cybermohalla project (with Ankur, Delhi) and Knowledge/Culture Commons project (with ALF, Bangalore), and is currently working on a series of inter-media and digital projects at the Sarai Media Lab. jeebesh@sarai.net

Monica Narula (Delhi) is a media practitioner, artist, filmmaker cinematographer and photographer with the Raqs Media Collective, and one of the initiators of Sarai. She is currently working on a series of inter-media and digital culture projects at the Sarai Media Lab. monica@sarai.net

Ravi Sundaram (Delhi) is a fellow of the Centre for the Study of Developing Societies, Delhi, and one of the initiators of Sarai. He coordinates the Public and Practices in the History of the Present project at Sarai. ravis@sarai.net

Ravi S Vasudevan (Delhi) is with the faculty of the Centre for the Study of Developing Societies, and one of the initiators of Sarai. He coordinates Sarai's media city research project with Ravi Sundaram. He researches the history of film and has edited *Making Meaning in Indian Cinema* (2000). raviv@sarai.net

Shuddhabrata Sengupta (Delhi) is a media practitioner, artist, filmmaker and writer with the Raqs Media Collective, and one of the initiators of Sarai. He is currently working on a series of inter-media and digital culture projects at the Sarai Media Lab. shuddha@sarai.net

ACKNOWLEDGEMENTS

The *Sarai Reader 04* emerges from the Crisis/Media Workshop organized by Sarai-CSDS, Delhi and the Waag Society, Amsterdam, at Sarai in Delhi in March 2003. The editorial collective would like to acknowledge their gratitude to all the participants in this workshop, and especially to Rachel Magnusson, whose assistance was invaluable to the co-ordinators (Shuddhabrata Sengupta and Geert Lovink) of the workshop. We are also grateful to Ashish Mahajan and Ranita Chatterjee (at Sarai), and Paul Keller and Henk Buursen (at Waag Society) for their assistance in the logistical execution of the workshop.
http://www.sarai.net/events/crisis_media/crisis_media.htm

Image and Photo Credits
Inside cover and inside back cover : Signage from Coordinates <28^0 28" n/ 77^0 15"e>, an inter-media installation by Raqs Media Collective, 2002.
pg x, 19, 109, 118, 205, 210, 212, 214, 227, 256, 372, 486: Monica Narula
pg 52: Miguel Angel Cordera
pg 54: courtesy Kristian Lukic
pg 60: From Location[n], an inter-media installation by Raqs Media Collective, 2002.
pg 80, 82: courtesy Oliver Ressler
pg 92 - 97: courtesy Shahid Amin
pg 107: from a set of serigraphs titled "Labyrinths" by Renu Iyer
pg 158: courtesy All India Defence Committee for S A R Geelani
pg 200: courtesy Ivo Skoric
pg 258, 261, 262: Meena Nanji
pg 268, 273: Zabi Sangary
pg 276 - 289: drawings by Anna Faroqhi
pg 325: Sanjay Kak
pg 330, 331: Concept and photo, Ravi Aggarwal
pg 332, 337: Sanjay Sharma
pg 345: courtesy Hansa Thapliyal
pg 346, 349: courtesy Omar Kutty
pg 354: Batul Mukhtiar
pg 455: Graphic by Mrityunjay Chatterjee

SARAI READERS

The *Sarai Readers* are annual anthologies of essays, critical writing and image-text assemblages around a given theme. They have brought together perspectives on media, technology, culture, politics and city life. www.sarai.net/journal/journal.htm

01 THE PUBLIC DOMAIN (2001)

ENTERING THE PUBLIC DOMAIN - CLAIMING THE CITY - OLD MEDIA/NEW MEDIA: ONGOING HISTORIES - INTERNET INTERVENTIONS - WETWARE: BODIES IN THE DIGITAL DOMAIN - 'FREE AS IN FREEDOM': SOFTWARE AS CULTURE - <ALT/OPTION>

ISBN 1-57027-124-0 : INR 150 : US$ 12 : Euro 12

02 THE CITIES OF EVERYDAY LIFE (2002)

URBAN MORPHOLOGIES - THE CITY AS SPECTACLE AND PERFORMANCE - THE STREET IS THE CARRIER AND THE SIGN - FOR THOSE WHO LIVE IN CITIES - CYBERMOHALLA DIARIES - 9/11 - MEDIA CITY - VIRTUAL ARCHITECTURE + DIGITAL URBANISM - THE POLITICS OF INFORMATION - <ALT/OPTION>

ISBN 81-901429-0-9 : INR 250 : US$ 18 : Euro 18

03 SHAPING TECHNOLOGIES (2003)

LEVERAGES - EXCAVATIONS - SCANS - REGISTRATIONS - DEVICES: CYBERMOHALLA DIARIES - IMAGINATIONS + AESTHETICS - ENCODE + DECODE - PRACTICES + POLITICS - <ALT/OPTION>

ISBN 81-901429-3-3 : INR 295 : US$ 15 : Euro 15

SARAI HINDI READER DEEWAN-E-SARAI

The *Deewan-E-Sarai* brings together contemporary critical writing in Hindi on urban space, the politics of language, popular culture, media and the public domain.

01 MEDIA VIMARSH://HINDI JANPAD

VIRASAT: PRINT/RADIO/T.V - BHASHA KE BOL - SANCHAR KE NAVACHAR: SANDHARBH AUR VIKALP
ISBN 81-901429-2-5 : INR 175 : US$ 15 : Euro 15

02: SHAHARNAMA (forthcoming)

Focuses on cities past and present, especially Delhi, by enabling a dialogue between social science and literary imaginations in Hindi and Urdu. The collection brings together writings by young and emerging writers, revisits older histories and inscribes the contemproary in a fresh register.

MEDIA NAGAR 01 (Hindi)

Records contemporary transformations in the urban mediascape of Delhi. Emerging from a year's work of the Publics and Practices Project at Sarai, the document looks at labour, markets, distribution networks, intellectual property, copy cultures, cable, multiplexes, B-movies, posters and piracy. INR 25

THE CYBERMOHALLA PROJECT

The Cybermohalla Project's interpretative encounters with urban space in occasional publications www.sarai.net/community/saraincomm.htm

GALIYON SE/BY LANES

DIARIES FROM THE COMPUGHAR ISBN 81-901429-1-7 : INR 250 : US$ 15 : Euro 15

BOOK BOX

10 BOOKLETS, 5 POSTCARDS AND A CD ROM : INR 250 : US$ 12 : Euro 12

NOTICE

Journalists or any other Visa applicant of any occupation or profession, who intend to do media work in Myanmar must hold a certificate issued by the Embassy of the Union of Myanmar permitting the person concerned to do their media work while in the Union of Myanmar. The certificate authorising the person to do media work in Myanmar issued by the Embassy will be duly endorsed on arrival at any airport or sea-port by competent authorities responsible for this purpose.

Anyone found doing any work connected with the media without this duly endorsed certificate is liable to be fined and deported on immediate basis. *OR SHOT*

---

20   MONO

LIVE

"The thoughts and opinions expressed during the show are of the participating individuals alone. The channel and participating institutions may or may not subscribe to the same."